MW01629976

ספר פרפראות לחכמה

SACRED LETTERS, SACRED NUMBERS

SACRED LETTERS, SACRED NUMBERS

**Gematrioth for
Around the Year:
The Weekly Parshah, Shabbos,
Yamim Tovim and Tefillah**

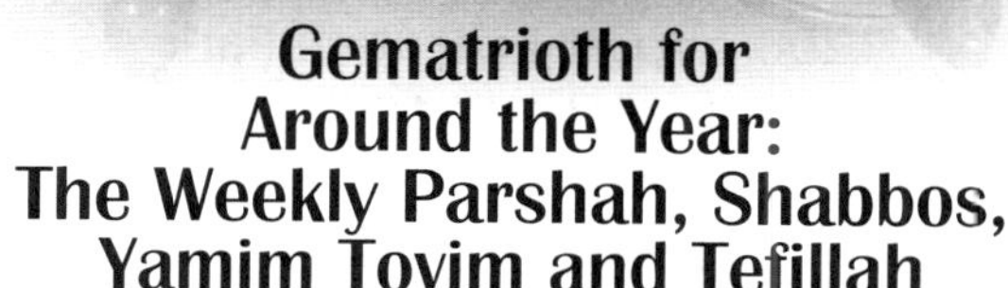

Distributed by
Feldheim Publishers
P.O.B. 43163
Jerusalem, Israel
208 Airport Executive Park
Nanuet, NY 10954

Printed in China

Approbations — הסכמות

RABBI YAAKOV E. FORCHHEIMER

604 6TH STREET

LAKEWOOD, N. J. 08701

בע"ה

הנה ראיתי הכתב יד של ידידי בעניני גימטריאות שרוצה להוציא
לאור ויקרא שמו בישראל "ספר פרפראות לחכמה," וגם מצאתי שכל חשבונותיו
נכונים הם. כבר ידעתי המחבר שליט"א מנעוריו ושמחה גדולה היא
אצלי לראות שקידתו בתורה שעושה תורתו קבע ומלאכתו עראי. גם
ניכר מאד מתוך הספר אהבת התורה וחיבוב המצוות של המחבר שליט"א,
וע"י חכמת הגימטריאות רוצה להמשיך לבב אחינו בית ישראל לתורה
ולמצוות כפרפרת הממשיך האכילה(עיין פי' תוס' יו"ט על מס' אבות
פ"ג משנה י"ח). אע"פ שכתב הרע"ב שם דחכמות הללו מכבדות את
בעליהם בעיני הבריות, מ"מ ענותנותו דהמחבר שליט"א גרם לו לאחוז
בפלך השתיקה להיות בורח מן הכבוד.

תקותי היא שיזכה המחבר שליט"א להמשיך עבודתו הנכבדת לשקוד
על דלתות בית המדרש ולהרביץ תורה ולעורר לבב אחינו בני ישראל
לעבודת ה'.

ע"ז בעה"ח לכבוד התורה ולכבוד המחבר שליט"א, ביום ב'
לסדר ובאו עליך כל הברכות האלה והשיגך. ט"ז אלול תשמ"ה,
לייקוואורד,נוא דזערסי.

יעקב אפרים הכהן פארכהיימער

ב״ה

באתי להמליץ ולהכיר תלמידנו הנכבד והמצוין החפץ
בעילם שמו שהרבה שנים למד בישיבתנו מתורתו של
מרן הגאון ראש הישיבה ר׳ משה פיינשטיין זצ״ל
שהוא מצוין ת״ח בתורה ויראת שמים ובמדות טובות
וחבר ספר על גימטריאות על כל פרשיות התורה וגם
על עיינים שונים שתכליתם להחזיק בתורה כפרפראות
הממשיכים לאכילה. אף שאיני בקי בשפה האנגלית
ואני סומך בזה על ידידי היקר הרה״ג ר׳ מרדכי
טנדלר שליט״א שקרא את הספר והסכים שכדאי
מאד להוציאם לדפוס לזכות הרבים
ויהנו מספרו וחזקה על חבר כמותו
שאינו מוציא מתחת ידו דבר שאינו מתוקן
וברכתי מעומק לבי לידידי היקר המחבר
שליט״א שיזכה ע״י זכות הרבים לברכת
התורה ברוך אשר יקים את התורה

ובאתי על החתום שנים ועשרים יום לחדש אדר ב׳
שנת תשנ״ב
בידידות
מיכל ברנבוים, משגיח רוחני של הישיבה

RABBI SIMON SCHWAB
736 WEST 186TH STREET
NEW YORK, N. Y. 10033
STUDY: 923-5936
RES: 927-0498

שמעון שוואב
רב דק"ק
קהל עדת ישרון
נוא־יארק, נ. י.

י' שבט תשנ"ב

הנה בא אלי האברך היקר החפץ
בעלום שמו, שאני הכרתי אותו מימי חורפו
והוא בן תורה, מוכתר במדות תרומיות, ונחבא אל
הכלים וירא שמים מרבים, צנוע ועוסק בתורה כעיקר
חייו ומלאכתו טפלה, ולומד ממה שלבו חפץ —
ובא אלי וספרו בידו. מלא וגדוש בגימטריאות
על כל פרשיות שבתורה, לבקש ממני לברכו
שחפץ ד' בידו יצליח, ויתקבלו דבריו
בעיני הבריות וימצא חן בעיני הקוראים
להגדיל תורה ולהאדירה. ויה"ר שיקוים בו
ההבטחה (תהלים פד) "חן וכבוד יתן
ד' לא ימנע טוב להולכים בתמים"

כעתירת ידידו מוקירו ודו"ש בלבו"נ
שמעון שוואב

MEYER GREENBERG
CHIEF ORTHODOX RABBI OF PATERSON

מאיר גרינבערג

ר׳מ ראשי בישיבה הגדולה דמאריסטאון

הרב הראשי לאגודת הקהילות דפעטערסאן יע״א

טעל. 2250 279 201   פעקס 2251 279 201

6 Manor Road

Paterson, New Jersey

07514

ב״ה כ״ה ניסן תשנ״ב לפ״ק

יען כי בא אלי אברך הרוצה בעילום שמו, שעומד כעת באמצע הדפסת ספרו ״ספר פרפראות לחכמה״, שהוא ספר של גימטריאות, וביקש ממני הסכמתי על הספר הלזה הכתוב בלשון אנגלי, וכולל גימטריאות בה׳ חומשי התורה הקדושה, הבנויות על מאמרי רז״ל, עיינתי בקונטרסי כת״י של החיבור הלזה, ומצאתי בו חידושים וביאורים יקרים, הראוים להתפרסם לכל יודעי לשון אנגלית, כי הספר כתוב בלשון צח, והרי הוא בנוי על יסוד של יראת שמים ואהבת התורה וקיום המצוות, על כן הריני מברכו שיצליח להוציא ספרו לאור הדפוס, ויתקבל בכל תפוצות ישראל, ויזכה המחבר שיזכה את הרבים מתוך הרחבת הדעת, ובזכות הפצת הפרפראות לחכמה, יזכה המחבר בתוך כלל בית ישראל לעידן כי מלאה הארץ דעה את ד׳ כמים לים מכסים.

הכו״ח ג׳ לסדר קדושים תהי׳ תשנ״ב לפ״ק,

ספר

פרפראות לחכמה

TABLE OF CONTENTS

DEDICATION

This sefer is dedicated to the memory of Rabbi Moshe Feinstein זצ״ל. I was contemplating how best to eulogize him, when the following tribute was published in *The Jewish Observer*, Agudath Israel of America's monthly journal of thought and opinion, April, 1986, XIX (4), p.4. It exemplifies my feelings.

[Published with permission from the publisher.]

WE GO TO PRESS NUMB AND GRIEF-STRICKEN AT THE SHOCKING NEWS THAT MARAN HAGAON RABBI MOSHE FEINSTEIN, זצ"יל, HAS BEEN CALLED TO THE YESHIVA SHEL MAALOH– THE CELESTIAL ACADEMY.

Up until his final years, Reb Moshe, as he was known, was an active presence in the leadership of *Klal Yisroel*—Rosh haYeshiva of Mesivta Tifereth Jerusalem, chairman of the *Moetzes Gedolei HaTorah* (Council of Torah Sages) of Agudath Israel of America, president of Agudath Horabonim, on the Board of Governors of Chinuch Atzmai and Torah Umesorah . . . but he was much more.

As a *poseik* (halachic decisor), he was without peer; there was no area of Torah law where he was not master. Even those who were of different traditions in *psak* were in awe of his command of the entire Talmud, the four sections of *Shulchan Aruch* and their classical commentaries—and his ability to draw on his vast knowledge and apply it to every conceivable situation . . . but he was much more than a great *poseik*.

Reb Moshe's fountain of wisdom flowed through his prolific pen, in the form of his seven volumes of definitive *halacha* in *Igros Moshe* and his Talmudic *shiurim* (lectures) contained in *Dibros Moshe* . . . but he was much more than an author.

Reb Moshe was both a caring father and a humble servant to his people—incredibly modest, unusually accessible. At the same time he was also very much a servant of his Creator, an *eved HaShem*. His *tefilla* was total concentration, consuming in its devotion. And he lost no opportunity to study and review and review once again—*Shas*, an astonishing 200-plus times—*Shulcan Aruch*, over countless times! An *eved Hashem* with no personal agenda, no private, self-centered interests. . . .

Rabbi Moshe Feinstein זצ"יל embodied a greatness that belonged to earlier, more pure, more pristine times—to an era that was clearer in Torah, closer to Sinai. In the words of the late Brisker Rav Maran Horav Yitzchak Zev Soloveitchik זצ"ל: "Had Reb Moshe lived 150 years ago, he would have been reckoned amongst the *Gedolei Hador,* the giants of that time." Thus, his passing leaves us bereft of a link to those earlier times. It is a loss without replacement. A shattering without repair.

In his infinite mercy, *Hashem Yisborach* permitted us to enjoy the richness of Torah, *Yiras Shamayim* and *Ahavas Yisroel* that Reb Moshe succeeded in embodying in one human being. In his absence we have but the legacy of his prolific writings and his towering example. May we be granted the wisdom to learn from both.

INTRODUCTION

ה' אלקי אתה ארוממך אודה שמך כי עשית פלא עצות
מרחק אמונה אמן (ישעי' כה,א).

Rabbi Julius Hirsch explains this pasuk to mean: *G-d* (regardless of whether my life was a happy one, or whether my fate was sad, at all times it was You who shaped it), *You are my G-d.* (You always considered what would be beneficial for my education so that I might accomplish the task You have set for me. Therefore,) *You, I will exalt and to Your Name I will render homage* (I will declare Your power and majesty, which surpasses all things and all people, and I will subordinate myself to You alone.), *for You have performed wonders.* (Your eternal all-surpassing power is evident in the way that everything which now takes place before our eyes and seems to us a miracle, a happening that runs counter to the natural course of the world, is actually nothing but the implementation of the decisions which You did frame at the beginning of Jewish history, indeed at the dawn of human history.) *The decisions of remote antiquity are faithful and trustworthy.* (The strength and lives of humans are not sufficient to turn their resolutions into reality. Your decisions alone are the quintessence of faithfulness and trustworthy support.) פירוש ספר ישעי', Commentary to Book of Isaiah, translation and commentary by Rabbi Julius Hirsch).

We must always acknowledge Hashem, regardless of whether He has shaped the fate of our lives as happy or sad. I feel particularly obligated to exalt and render homage to His great Name, for He has considered what would be beneficial for my education so that I could accomplish the writing of this sefer.

I hope that those who learn from this sefer will come to declare His power and majesty, which surpasses all things and all people, and will subordinate themselves to Hashem alone.

The wonders of the Torah are found in its every letter and word. Those who learn the Torah are privy to its wonders and are aware of its all-surpassing power. To Hashem, the Torah's eternal all-encompassing power is merely the implementation of His decisions which He framed in His Torah from before the dawn of human history (נדרים לט:, Nedarim 39b). The strength and lives of men are not sufficient to fully grasp the reality of the quintessence of faithfulness and trustworthy support of His Torah.

The Torah is written in לשון הקדש, the holy language, Hebrew. Every sentence, every word, and every letter is holy. The Torah is perfect, written by the perfect Hashem. Each and every time the Torah expresses a thought, every letter of every word that makes up that thought is highly significant. Every Hebrew letter has a numerical value, a gematria. The gematria of each letter together with its contextual placement in the Torah has special meaning.

The majority of the gematrioth in this sefer are based on the exact spelling of the words as they appear in the Torah, since the way they appear in the text is highly significant. Those occasional gematria calculations based on an altered spelling of the text, for example, the intentional omission of וו החבור, "the conjunction *vav*," have been listed in an appendix at the end of this sefer.

I hope that my brethren, Klal Israel, will read this sefer, and will gain some insight, however small, into how significant each and every letter of our holy Torah is, how privileged we are to be able to learn it, and how adamant we should be in our adherence to its every commandment. May it be G-d's will that this sefer achieves that goal!

To the best of my knowledge, this sefer is a rare one in its genre because it presents gematrioth with the Hebrew word or phrase followed by a translation and an explanation in English. All the gematrioth set forth in this sefer are the results of my efforts; none have been "borrowed." Many people have helped me with constructive comments and editorial changes, for which I am very grateful; however, should the reader find any mistakes, criticism should be directed to me alone, and not to those who have edited this work.

Numerous other works employ gematrioth; some of the better known ones are listed below for the reader's interest. To achieve the most accurate spelling of every author's name and to maintain consistency of nomenclature, I have recorded the spelling of each author's name from the title page of his published work.

The first twelve works listed below are organized according to the order of the sidroth of the Torah. I have listed them first, before the other works, because they are based solely on the meaning of the text of the Torah. They are followed by three works which, in contrast, are written about the Passover Haggadah. Next is a work written on the holidays in general, followed by eleven works which I have researched but which may not be as well known.

פירוש התורה לרבינו יעקב בעל הטורים מאת רבינו יעקב בן רבינו אשר
This commentary on the Torah is probably the commentary most famous for its frequent use of gematrioth. It is generally known as the Baal Haturim and in many Chumashim has been published alongside the text of the Torah, making it unique among this list of commentaries.

פירוש הרוקח על התורה מאת רבינו אלעזר מגרמייזא
This extensive commentary on the Torah is not published in conjunction with the text of the Torah, as is the commentary of the Baal Haturim. However, both of these commentaries are more prominent in Orthodox Jewish erudition than any others on this list.

ספר ילקוט משה מאת הרב משה בן הרב ישראל בנימין
This sefer has a page or two of discussion concerning the implied meaning of the text of each sidrah, including

gematrioth and abbreviations. The second section deals with various topics such as holidays.

ספר חדשים לקטרת מאת הרב אהרן טעננבויים
ספר קטרת סמים מאת הרב אהרן טעננבויים

These two sefarim follow the order of the sidroth, giving insights into various passages. The previous two listed works of this list, although they are commentaries on the Torah, they are published separately from the actual Torah text; this separation exists for the remainder of the works cited on this list.

ספר קול התור מאת הרב ישועה זרח

This sefer follows the order of the Sidroth and then comments on various books of the Bible. It delves extensively into gematrioth and abbreviations, similar to the style of the Baal Haturim; however, unlike the Baal Haturim, the author tends to expound in greater length on each topic.

ספר זבד בנימין מאת הרב בנימין וואלף בן הרב ראובן זעליגמן

The first forty pages of this work discuss the meaning of the letters of the Hebrew alphabet, and are organized according to the sidroth . They are followed by 28 pages dealing with other topics such as the Jewish holidays, Biblical and Talmu-dic expressions as they relate to the author's method of gematria calculation, and the meaning of the letters of the alphabet.

דרך אברהם מאת הרב רפאל לוי יצחק מגיד

This very extensive sefer is 1224 pages long. Following the order of the sidroth, it presents a myriad of gematrioth using different methods of calculation to arrive at an equiv-alence between the gematrioth of words, phrases, or ideas with the same value, but not necessarily the same method of calculation. For example, sometimes the letters which comprise a word or phrase are spelled out, and the gematria of those letters which spell that word or phrase is equated to a different gematria. Sometimes the את בש method is used. That is, where the value of a letter from the beginning of the alphabet is switched with a value of a letter occupying a similar position from the end of the alphabet, and vice versa. Other times ההפרש, the difference between two gematrioth, is calculated to show its significance. All the numbers and letters are clearly laid-out for the reader's benefit.

ספר גימטריאות על התורה מאת הרב שלמה בן הרב יהודה לייבוש מלובלין
This 124 page sefer has a brief thought on most, but not all the sidroth. It compares groups of letters to arrive at abbreviations which are compared to other sources. Only occasionally is a gematria introduced.

קול דודי
by Rabbi David Feinstein
This 255 page English work has several Torah thoughts on each and every sidrah. By changing the sequence of letters, or their vowels, greater meaning is revealed. Many times the gematria of a word or a group of words is given. What is particularity amazing is when the value of a gematria corresponds to the time of an historical event.

חשיבות גימטריאת הפסוק
This 185 page English sefer calculates the gematria of entire pesukim from either the Torah or Psalms, and demonstrates how significant that value is relative to a different pasuk with the same gematria, or a Torah concept with the same value. Besides the divrei Torah on every sidrah, there is also a section entitled "Chagim Uzemanim." The methodology is consistently applied. It is published anonymously.

ויספר משה מאת הרב משה בן הרב ישראל ווכסלער
ספר ברכת משה מאת הרב משה בן הרב ישראל ווכסלער
The former work is organized according to the order of the sidroth , but I have only located copies on Genesis. The author has substantiated Jewish laws and concepts by com-

paring groupings of words from pesukim with other words or phrases in rabbinical literature which have identical gematrioth. Many times one pasuk will have more than ten word groups equated to different concepts, all by means of their gematrioth. The latter work is only 38 pages, divided into two parts. The first 22 pages explain concepts in the Torah based on different gematrioth, while the last 16 pages, called רמזים בהגדה לליל שמורים, are not based on the Chumash, rather they deal with topics relating to the first night of Passover. The gematrioth of various phrases are equated, and substantiate concepts in rabbinical literature.

הגדה של פסח עם פירוש המיסתורין שבהגדה מאת הרב מתתיהו גלזרסון
This work includes a complete Passover Haggadah with a commentary. The commentary, which delves into the significance of the Hebrew letters, includes many gematrioth.

ספר מגיד מישרים מאת הרב משה בן הרב שמעון בלומענפעלד
This work is a commentary on part of the Passover Haggadah including gematrioth.

ספר משמיע שלום מאת הרב שמעון שלום בן מנחם מאמשינוב־אטוואצק
The first 65 pages of this sefer are thoughts about Jewish holidays, often with gematrioth to confirm the points. The last 28 pages are collected thoughts on various aspects of Jewish literature.

קונטרס מיני מתיקה מאת הרב רפאל משה בן הרב שמואל אלבאז
קונטרס עטרת פז מאת הרב רפאל משה בן הרב שמואל אלבאז
The former work, consisting of 34 pages, gives explanations, based on the Bible and rabbinical expressions, and is interspersed with gematrioth. The latter work, consisting of 30 pages, uses different combinations of letters and the significance of various numbers to explain one of the names of Hashem.

רמזים וגמטריאות מאת הרב מתתיה מנחם כהן
This short work of only 60 pages discusses thirteen topics

including Shabbath and prayer, sporadically employing gematrioth to illustrate a point.

אור התורה מאת משה צוריאל

This sefer is divided into two sections: The first has 137 pages, which are divided into 30 chapters, 26 of which examine how a particular author such as רבי מאיר שוורץ, מהרי״ם, רוטנברג, רבי יעקב האריז״ל, הרמ״ק צמח, uses gematrioth; the remaining four chapters of the first section focus on different applications of gematrioth and the shapes of Hebrew letters. The entire second section has 70 pages, which are divided into five chapters of anthology; the anthology is not necessarily related to gematrioth.

ספר גימטריאות על כל התורה מאת הרב שאול בן צבי הירש לנטשיץ
ספר תהלים עם לוח לחשבון גימריאות מאת הרב שאול בן צבי הירש לנטשיץ
The former work lists the gematrioth of every pasuk in the Torah, initially according to its numerical value, with the smallest value appearing first and the larger values appearing last, and subsequently, according to its order in the Torah. The latter work is a copy of the Book of Psalms, which also lists the gematrioth of every pasuk in the Book of Psalms according to its numerical value, with the smallest value appearing first and the larger value appearing last.

התורה בגימטריה מלה במלה מאת הרב אריה לייב סאלאנש
This work lists the words of the Torah grouped by their gematrioth in order of their increasing numerical magnitude.

תורה וגמטריא
by Gutman G. Locks

This work, succeeding התורה בגימטריה מלה במלה, is similar in that it lists all the words of the Torah grouped by their gematrioth in order of their increasing numerical value. For each word the source where it appears in the Torah is given, as well as the English translation, and its vowels. In addition, the sefer contains an introduction.

ספר גימטריקון
This work lists over 40,000 words and expressions, grouped

by their gematrioth in order of their increasing magnitude; values range from 1 to 1000. Under each gematria the entries are recorded according to their Hebrew alphabetical order. Although no author is given, the entries are from a more extensive list of מר שמעון נשר.

גימטריא ונוטריקון מאת צבי חיים בן הרב יצחק דוד זאלב

This work gives different methods of gematria calculation, such as אותיות מילואים, גימטריא עם הכולל, and so forth, to help explain various concepts such as those in the הלכה, Halakhah, "decided law," and מדרשי הגדה, the Great Midrashim.

צפונות במסורת ישראל מאת טוביה וכסלר

This work is a seven chapter book which uses gematrioth, their squares, and their square roots in topical discussions providing insights into the hidden meaning of certain texts.

  This list is intended only as a starting point for further research; there are multitudinous other sources which employ gematrioth. The Gemara itself uses gematrioth, one example is found on נדרים לב:, Gemara Nedarim 32b. Rashi also uses gematrioth to explain pesukim, (רש״י, בראשית כד,א, Rashi, Genesis 24,1). Although the use of gematrioth is an established method of Torah learning, a word of caution is necessary.

  The Mishnah Avoth wisely identifies gematrioth as פרפראות לחכמה, condiments to wisdom (אבות, פרק ג משנה יח, Avoth, Chapter 3, Mishnah 18). Numerical equivalents of Hebrew words alone have little value and can not be considered meaningful. However, a gematria applied within the framework of Torah ideology, as understood by a recognized authoritative rabbinical source, can assist in explaining authentic Torah concepts. One cannot take a random gematria and haphazardly use it to explain a pasuk because of a forced association with another gematria (אבן עזרא, בראשית יד,יד, Ibn Ezra, Genesis 14,14). The use of gematrioth are only condiments to wisdom, and their use must be within the bounds of recognized Torah scholarship. Bearing this caution in mind, the reader is encouraged to further study and employ gematrioth to develop the breadth and depth of his Torah pansophy.

ספר
פרפראות לחכמה

The title of this sefer comes from the Mishnah in Avoth, where gematrioth are described as פרפראות לחכמה, condiments to wisdom (אבות, פרק ג משנה יח, Avoth, Chapter 3, Mishnah 18).

The word or words whose gematria or gematrioth are vital for the comprehension of the דבר תורה, Torah thought, in which they are mentioned are allocated a separate line or lines with their numerical values. This allocation was done to assert the consequential nature of such crucial words, to make it easier for the reader to follow the cynosure which is under discussion, and to allow for easy confirmation of the legitimacy of such gematrioth.

Morning Prayers   תפלת שחרית

הבו לה׳ כבוד שמו שאו מנחה ובאו לפניו השתחוו לה׳
בהדרת־קדש (דברי הימים א טז,כט).
Give unto G-d the honor due His name; lift up
an offering and come before Him; quest for G-d
in the beauty of His holiness (I Chronicles 16,
29).

This pasuk from Chronicles is incorporated into the
morning services after ברוך שאמר in הודו. The gematria of
בהדרת, "in the beauty of," is 611.

בהדרת   611

In this pasuk, the word השתחוו, which normally is
translated as to prostrate oneself, can be defined as "quest,"
for Targum Onkelos defines the word והשתחוו as ויבעון, "quest"
(תרגום אונקלוס, שמות יא,ח, Targum Onkelos, Exodus 11,8). The
fact that the word ויבעון means quest is substantiated by the
Metsudath Zion, who defines the word תבעיון, "you will quest,"
as ענין שאלה ודרישה וגו׳, "a subject of asking and inquiring"
(מצודת ציון, ישעי׳ כא,יב, Metsudath Zion, Isaiah 21,12).
Various commentators have explained the meaning of
בהדרת, "in the beauty of," in different ways (מצודת דוד ורלב״ג,
Metsudath David and Ralbag); perhaps another explanation
can be added. The Gemara Derek Erez Zutra perceives a
person's beauty as his Torah, as stated, הדר בני אדם תורה, "the
beauty of a person is his Torah" (דרך ארץ זוטא, פרק י, לפי נוסחת
הגר״א, Derekh Eretz Zuta, Chapter 10, according to the version of Hagera). The gematria of תורה, "Torah," is 611.

תורה   611

Since the beauty of a person can be conceived of as his
Torah, when the pasuk declares, השתחוו לה׳ בהדרת קדש, "quest
for G-d in the beauty of his holiness," the meaning can be to
quest for Hashem in His Torah of holiness. This explanation is

further enhanced by the gematria of בהדרת,"in the beauty of," equal to the gematria of תורה, "Torah"; both are equal to 611.

ואנחנו נברך קה מעתה ועד עולם הללוקה (תהלים קטו,יח).
And we will bless G-d from now and forever, Halalukah (Psalms 115,18).

This pasuk from Psalm 115 is an appendage to the end of Psalm 145, אשרי, which is incorporated in the morning prayers between ברוך שאמר and ישתבח. The last word of this pasuk, הללוי־ה, "Halalukah," is a combination of two other words: הללו, "praise," and י־ה, "G-d." The gematria of הללוי־ה, "Halalukah," is 86.

הללוי־ה   86

Thus, the number 86 can represent the praising of Hashem Who is referred to as י־ה. When Hashem is referred to as י־ה, He is portrayed as G-d who is feared, as Rashi says, בשם י־ה שהוא ל' יראה כדמתרגמינן דחילא, "the name of י־ה is an expression of fear, as it is translated, awe-inspiring" (רש״י, תהלים סח,ה, Rashi, Psalms 68,5). Hashem is feared when He exacts judgment on man, as the Mesillath Yesharim states, אשר באמת ראוי להזדעזע ולהתחרד תמיד, כי מי יעמד ביום הדין ומי יצדק לפני בוראו באשר השקפתו מדקדקת על כל דבר קטן או גדול. וכן אמרו רבותינו ז״ל 'מגיד לאדם מה שחו,' (עמוס ד,יג) אפלו שיחה קלה שבין איש לאשתו, מגידים לו לאדם בשעת הדין (מסלת ישרים מאת הרב משה חיים לוצאטו פרק ד), "That in truth it is proper to shake and to shiver constantly, for who will be able to stand on the day of judgment, and who will be able to justify himself before his Creator, when He oversees and examines everything large or small. And so our Rabbis of blessed memory have said, 'And He tells a man his conversations,' (Amos 4,13) even the light conversation between a man and his wife are told to a man at the time of judgment" (Mesillath Yesharim by Rabbi Moshe Chaim Luzzatto, Chapter 4).

When Hashem's character of strict justice and judgment is alluded to, He is referred to as אלקים, as Rashi says, ויזכור אלקים. זה השם מדת הדין, "And G-d remembered. This name refers to His attribute of strict justice" (רש״י, בראשית א,ח, Rashi, Genesis 8,1). The gematria of אלקים, "G-d," is 86.

אלקים   86

Since the gematrioth of הללוקה, "Halalukah," and אלקים, "G-d," are identical, it can be understood that הללוי־ה, "Halalukah," is praising Hashem's attribute of fearsomeness, which alludes to אלקים, "G-d's attribute of judgment."

בונה ירושלם ה׳ נדחי ישראל יכנס (תהלים קמז,ב).
G-d builds up Jerusalem; He gathers together
the outcasts of Israel (Psalms 147,2).

Before the coming of משיח, Messiah, there will be tremulous times. The Gemara counsels that to survive such times one should learn Torah and perform acts of loving kindness, as it says, שאלו תלמידיו את רבי אלעזר מה יעשה אדם וינצל מחבלו של משיח יעסוק בתורה ובגמילות חסדים (סנהדרין צח:), "The students asked Rabbi Eleazar, 'What should a man do and be saved from the pre-Messianic tribulations?' He should busy himself with Torah and with acts of loving kindness" (Sanhdedrin 98b).

The coming of Messiah is depicted in Psalms as a time when Hashem will gather together the dispersed of Israel, as stated, בונה ירושלם ה׳ נדחי ישראל יכנס (תהלים קמז,ב), "G-d builds up Jerusalem; He gathers together the outcasts of Israel" (Psalms 147,2). The gematria of נדחי ישראל, "the outcasts of Israel," is 613.

נדחי   72
ישראל   541
613

This pasuk from Psalms is incorporated into תפלת שחרית, Morning Prayers; it is the second psalm after אשרי. The coming of Messiah is also depicted in Isaiah with the expression נדחי ישראל, "the outcasts of Israel," (ישעיי יא,יב, Issiah 11,12).

Who among the expelled of Israel will merit to be gathered by G-d? Since the counsel to be saved from the pre-Messianic tribulations is to learn Torah and perform acts of loving kindness, it can be concluded that those who follow such counsel can be construed as observing the mitzvoth. There is a total of 613 Mitzvoth. Therefore, it is befitting that the נדחי ישראל, "the outcasts of Israel," with a gematria of 613, can refer to those who observe the 613 Mitzvoth, and thus will survive the tribulations of the pre-Messianic times.

תקע בשופר גדול לחרותנו, ושא נס לקבץ גליותינו וקבצנו יחד מארבע כנפות הארץ (שמונה עשרה).
Sound the great horn for our freedom, and lift up the ensign to gather our exiles, and gather us from the four corners of the earth (Shemoneh Esreh).

One of the opinions in the Gemara is that משיח, Messiah, will come when the Bnei Yisroel will either be all righteous or all wicked (סנהדרין צח., Sanhedrin 98a). The אחרית לשלום, "Acharis Leshalom," explains that the blessing of תקע בשופר גדול לחרותנו, "Sound the great horn for our freedom," in שמונה עשרה, "Shemoneh Esreh," refers to a time when the Bnei Yisroel will be righteous, as stated, ברכת תקע בשופר גדול לחרותנו הוא בהיותנו מוכשרים. דאז הגאולה מתיחסת לנו לחרותנו החירות בזכותנו (סידור אוצר התפלות, ספרד, אחרית לשלום מאת הרב יצחק אליהו לנדא, דף קעא, ד"ה נדחי עמו ישראל) "The blessing, Sound the great horn for our freedom, refers to when we will be worthy. Then the redemption will be attributed to us as our freedom, the freedom on our merits" (Siddur Otzar Hatefiloth, Sefard,

Acharis Leshalom by Rabbi Yitzchak Eliyahu Landa, page 171, header words: The banished ones of Your people Israel). The sum of the gematrioth of תקע, "Sound," and גדול, "great," is 613.

תקע	570
גדול	43
	613

Since the blessing of תקע בשופר גדול לחרותנו, "Sound the great horn for our freedom," in שמונה עשרה, "Shemoneh Esreh," refers to a time when the Bnei Yisroel will be righteous, it is apt that the gematria of 613, which is equal to the number of commandments, should be found in this blessing.

ברוך אתה ה' הטוב שמך ולך נאה להודות (סידור בית יעקב מאת הרב יעקב מעמדין בן הרב צבי, אשכנזי, דף עג.).
Blessed are You G-d, the Good One is Your name, and to You it is becoming to give thanks (Siddur Beth Yaakov by Rabbi Yaakov from Emden ben Rabbi Zvi, Ashkenazi, page 73a).

The penultimate blessing in the Shemoneh Esreh asserts G-d as the Good One. The gematria of ה' הטוב ולך נאה להודות, "G-d, the Good One, and to You it is becoming to give thanks," is 611.

ה' הטוב ולך	104
נאה להודות	507
	611

What is the טוב, "good," to which this pasuk refers? The Gemara Berakoth states, ואין טוב אלא תורה (ברכות ה.), "And there is no good except Torah" (Berakoth 5a). The gematria of תורה, "Torah," is 611.

תורה	611

Since there is no good except Torah, therefore when the penultimate blessing in the Shemoneh Esreh asserts G-d is the Good One, it must have a meaning relating to Torah. It can be appreciated why the gematria of ה׳ הטוב ולך נאה להודות, "G-d, the Good One, and to You it is becoming to give thanks," is equal to the gematria of Torah.

The issue remaining is why the word שמך, "Your name," is excluded from the gematria calculation. The word שמך, "Your name," can remind one of תורה לשמה, "Torah for its own sake." One should always try to learn Torah for its own sake, for there are many wonderful outcomes for one who reaches that level of learning (אבות פרק ו, משנה א, Avoth Chapter 6, Mishnah 1).

When it comes to blessing G-d, a blessing not for its own sake can lead to a blessing for its own sake. The תוס׳ שאנץ, Tosafoth Sens, writes how Abraham persuaded his guests to bless G-d, as stated, וכי בתוס׳ שאנץ מהמדרש שלא רצו לברך עד שאמר אברהם שיפרעו בעד אכילתם שעולה ביוקר במדבר אז ברכו להקב״ה שלא ברצונם עי״מ שלא יפרעו עי״ש [וצי״ל בכוונת אברהם עי״ד שמתוך שלא לשמה בה לשמה] (ספר תורת הקנאות מאת משה בצלאל מסייני, פרק ראשון דף יא:, ד״ה וכי משלי אכלתם וכו׳), "And it is written in Tosafoth Sens from the Midrash, that they did not want to to bless, until Abraham said that they should pay for their food, which was expensive in the desert. Then they blessed the Holy One, Blessed be He, against their will, in order that they should not have to pay. Look it up there. [And it is necessary to say that the intention of Abraham was that he knew that which was not done for its own sake, will come to done for its own sake]" (Book of Torath Hakenaoth by Moshe Betsalel from Siani, First Chapter, page 11b, header words: And did you eat of mine). Since a blessing not for its own sake can lead to a blessing for its own sake, the word שמך, "Your name," which can indicate תורה לשמה, "Torah for its own sake," was excluded from the gematria calculation.

מי זה מלך הכבוד ה׳ עזוז וגבור ה׳ גבור מלחמה (תהלים
כד,ח).

Who is the King of honor? G-d strong and
mighty, G-d mighty in war (Psalms 24,8).

This pasuk from the שיר של יום, "Psalm of the Day," for
Sunday is from Psalm 24, and is always said near the end of
the morning prayers; it is also said when returning the Sefer
Torah to the ארון הקדש, Aron Hakodesh, the Holy Ark. Hashem
is described as a מלך, "King," who is עזוז, "strong." The
gematria of מלך, "King," is 90.

90   מלך

The gematria of עזוז, "strong," is also 90.

90   עזוז

Since this pasuk describes Hashem as a מלך, "King,"
Who is עזוז, "strong," it is fitting that both words should have
the same gematria.

ה׳ מלך גאות לבש לבש ה׳ עז התאזר אף־תכון תבל בל
תמוט (תהלים צג,א).
G-d reigns clothed with majesty; G-d is clothed; He has girded Himself with strength; He has also fixed the unalterable order of the universe (Psalms 93,1).

The last pasuk of Psalms immediately preceding לכה דודי, "Come my Friend," states, ה׳ עז לעמו יתן ה׳ יברך את עמו בשלום (תהלים כט,יא), "G-d will give strength to His people; G-d will bless His people with peace" (Psalms 29,11). Both the Gemara Zevachim and Rashi on this pasuk interpret עז, "strength," as referring to Torah. The Gemara says, כשניתנה תורה לישראל היה קולו הולך מסוף העולם ועד סופו וכל מלכי עובדי כוכבים אחזתן רעדה בהיכליהן ואמרו שירה שנאמר ובהיכלו כולו אומר כבוד נתקבצו כולם אצל בלעם הרשע ואמרו לו מה קול ההמון אשר שמענו... אמר להם חמדה טובה יש לו בבית גנזיו שהיתה גנוזה אצלו תתקע״ד דורות קודם שנברא העולם וביקש ליתנה לבניו שנאמר ה׳ עוז לעמו יתן וכו׳, (זבחים קטז.) "When the Torah was given to Israel, His voice went from one end of the world to the other end, and all the idolatrous kings were seized with trembling in their palaces. They said a song, as it says, And in his palace they all said, Honor. They all gathered next to the wicked Balaam and said, 'What is the voice of commotion which we heard?... He said, He has a good treasure in His storehouse which has been hidden with Him for 974 generations before the world was created, and He desires to give it to His children, as it says, G-d will give strength to His people, etc.'" (Zevachim 116a).

The first pasuk of the second chapter of Psalms said immediately following לכה דודי states, ה׳ מלך גאות לבש לבש ה׳ עז התאזר אף תכון תבל בל תמוט (תהלים צג,א), "G-d reigns, clothed with majesty; G-d is clothed; He has girded Himself with strength; He has also fixed the unalterable order of the universe" (Psalms 93,1). The gematria of התאזר, "He has girded Himself," is 613.

התאזר   613

This reference is the first time the word עז, "strength," is found in the Shabbath prayer after it was mentioned in Psalm 29,11, immediately preceding לכה דודי. Just as the first mention of עז, "strength," refers to Torah, so too the second mention of עז, "strength," can refer to Torah. Between these two citations of the word עז, "strength," comes לכה דודי which ushers in the Shabbath. In reference to the Shabbath, the Talmud Yerushalmi says, לא נתנו שבתות וימים טובים אלא לעסוק בהן בדברי תורה (תלמוד ירושלמי, שבת פרק טו, הלכה ג), "Shabbathoth and holidays were given only to be occupied with words of Torah on them" (Yerushalmi Gemara, Sabbath, Chapter 15, Halakhah 3). Thus, the purpose of Shabbath is for the learning of Torah.

The Gemara Kiddushin narrates the unanimity of opinion about the greatness of Torah study, as it says, נענו כולם ואמרו תלמוד גדול שהתלמוד מביא לידי מעשה (קדושין מ:), "They all answered and said, 'Study is greater, for it leads to deed'" (Kiddushin 29b). These deeds can be easily interpreted as mitzvoth. Since the purpose of Shabbath is for learning Torah, and learning leads to mitzvoth, Shabbath is a time to be concerned with mitzvoth. The Gemara Makkoth says that there is a total of 613 Mitzvoth given to Moses, as stated, דרש רבי שמלאי שש מאות ושלש עשרה מצות נאמרו לו למשה שלש מאות וששים וחמש לאוין כמנין ימות החמה ומאתים וארבעים ושמונה עשה כנגד איבריו של אדם (מכות כג:), "Rabbi Simlai expounded, Six hundred and thirteen Commandments were said to Moses. Three hundred and sixty-five negative Commandments corresponding to the number of days in a solar year, and two hundred and forty-eight positive Commandments corresponding to the number of limbs of a man" (Makkoth 23b).

It has already been stated that the gematria of התאזר,

"He has girded Himself," is 613. Since this gematria is equal to the number of the mitzvoth, and since the word התאזר, "He has girded Himself," follows the word עז, "strength," the expression עז התאזר, "He has girded Himself with strength," can be translated as, "By means of Torah," which is referred to as עז, "strength," Hashem התאזר, "He has girded Himself," with mitzvoth. This thought is a very appropriate way with which to greet the Shabbath, whose purpose is for learning Torah, and whose usherance lies between the two citations of the word עז, "strength."

והיו למשסה שאסיך ורחקו כל מבלעיך ישיש עליך אלקיך כמשוש חתן על כלה (סידור בית יעקב מאת הרב יעקב מעמדין בן הרב צבי, אשכנזי, דף קמו.).

And they who spoil you shall be a spoil, and all who would swallow you shall be far away; your G-d shall rejoice over you as a bridegroom re-joices over his bride (Siddur Beth Yaakov by Rabbi Yaakov from Emden ben Rabbi Zvi, Ash-kenazi, page 146a).

Toward the end of לכה דודי, the rejoicing of Hashem over His people is compared to the rejoicing of a bridegroom over his bride. The gematria of חתן על כלה, "as a bridegroom over his bride," is 613.

חתן	458
על	100
כלה	55
	613

The Talmud Yerushalmi says that observing the Shabbath is equated with all the other mitzvoth, as it states רבי אומר זו מצות שבת שהיא שקולה כנגד כל מצוותיה של תורה דכתיב ואת שבת קדשך הודעת להם ומצות וחוקים ותורה צוית וגו' להודיעך שהיא שקולה כנגד כל מצוותיה של תורה (תלמוד ירושלמי, ברכות, פרק א, הלכה ה) ,

"Rabbi said this refers to the mitzvah of Shabbath which is equated to all the mitzvoth of the Torah, as it is written, and Your holy Shabbath You made known to them, and You did command commandments, statutes, and a law, to teach you that it is equated to all the commandments of the Torah" (Yerushalmi Gemara, Berakoth, Chapter 1, Halakhah 5). Thus, the observing of Shabbath is equated with the number 613, the total number of mitzvoth.

The rejoicing of Hashem over His people can be explained with the aid of the previously mentioned gematria. Hashem rejoices over His people for observing Shabbath, which is equated to the 613 Mitzvoth. Thus, Hashem rejoices over His people as if they observed the 613 Mitzvoth, which could be the significance of the gematria of חתן על כלה, "a bridegroom over his bride," being equal to 613.

דרשתי את ה׳ וענני ומכל מגורותי הצילני (תהלים לד,ה).
I sought G-d and He answered me, from all my
fears He delivered me (Psalms 34,5).

The psalm containing the pasuk which says, "I sought Hashem and He answered me," is quoted in the Shabbath morning prayers after ברוך שאמר. The gematria of את ה׳ וענני, "G-d and He answered me," is 613.

את	401
ה׳	n26
וענני	186
	613

How can one be sure that Hashem will answer him? The Gemara Avodah Zarah designates a person whose wishes Hashem will fulfill, as it says, אמר ר׳ אבדימי בר חמא כל העוסק בתורה הקב״יה עושה לו חפציו שנאמר כי אם בתורת ה׳ חפצו (עבודה זרה יט.), "Rabbi Avdimi bar Hama said, everyone who occupies himself with the Torah, the Holy One, Blessed be He, will fulfill his wishes, as it says, But he who [is occupied] with the Torah of Hashem, his wishes [will be granted]" (Avodah Zarah 19a). The gematria of בתורה, "with the Torah," is 613.

613   בתורה

The Gemara mentioned above says that Hashem will fulfill the wishes of one who is occupied בתורה, "with the Torah." Since the pasuk from Psalms contains the gematria 613, and since בתורה, "with the Torah," has a gematria of 613, the two sources can be connected. The pasuk from Psalms is saying that Hashem answered me; the Gemara Avodah Zarah is saying that the reason Hashem answers may be because one is occupied with the Torah. Of course, the number 613, which connects these sources, is equal to the number of mitzvoth. This connection with the mitzvoth ties in nicely, for it is expected that one who is occupied with the Torah would also be an observer of mitzvoth.

ימי שנותינו בהם שבעים שנה, ואם בגבורת שמונים שנה,
ורהבם עמל ואון, כי גז חיש ונעפה (תהלים צ,י).

The days of our years are seventy years, and if with vigor they be eighty, and their pride is travail and nothingness; for it is soon cut off and we fly away (Psalms 90,10).

This pasuk from the ninetieth chapter of Psalms is incorporated into the Shabbath morning service between ברוך שאמר and אשרי. According to some commentators the phrase ואם בגבורת שמונים שנה, "and if with vigor they be eighty years," refers to the days of the man, and not to the man (רש"י, תהלים צ,י וסידור בית יעקב מאת הרב יעקב מעמדין בן הרב צבי, אשכנזי, דף מח: Rashi, Psalms 90,10 and Siddur Beth Yaakov by Rabbi Yaakov from Emden ben Rabbi Zvi, Ashkenazi, page 48b.). However, the Metsudath David explains this phrase as referring to the natural vigor which allows one to live until an age of eighty, as he states, ואם בהתגברות כח הטבע יהיו שמנים שנה, "and if invigorated with natural strength they will be eighty," (מצודת דוד תהלים צ,י, Metsudath David, Psalms 90,10).

There are a number of difficulties in explaining this pasuk in reference to natural vigor. First, if it refers to a man's natural strength, grammatically, the phrase is incorrect. The pasuk should have said ואם גבור הוא, "and if he is a vigorous man," instead of ואם בגבורת, "and if with vigor." Second, how does the number eighty relate to the number seventy mentioned earlier in the pasuk? Third, if the pasuk is expressing an extended life span due to natural vigor, why was the number eighty, as opposed to a much higher or a lower number, chosen? Fourth, the pasuk seems false; many vigorous individuals die young, and many weaklings live to an old age. Fifth, there is no mention of Shabbath in this entire chapter of Psalms; why was it chosen to be incorporated in the Shabbath morning service? Note, the Siddur Beth Yaakov does give a reason from a different phrase in this chapter, as stated, מזמור זה לפי שכתוב בו שבענו בבוקר חסדך שהוא בוקר של עולם הבא יום שכולו שבת, לכך אומרים אותו בשבת (סידור בית יעקב מאת הרב יעקב מעמדין בן הרב צבי, אשכנזי, דף מח:), "Since it is written in this Psalm, Satisfy us in the morning with Your loving kindness, which refers to the morning of the world to come, a day that is entirely Shabbath, therefore it is said on Shabbath" (Siddur Beth Yaakov by Rabbi Yaakov from Emden ben Rabbi Zvi, Ashkenazi, page 48b). But this reference to Shabbath is in relation to the world to come; there seems to be no mention of Shabbath in relation to this world. Although the שמונה עשרה of Shabbath afternoon also refers to the world to come (טור אורח חיים, סימן רצב, Tur, Orach Hayyim, Siman 292), could there be a better reason why the Bnei Yisroel incorporate this chapter of Psalms in the Shabbath morning prayers?

The previously mentioned pasuk from the ninetieth

chapter of Psalms can be explained based on two gemaroth, one Bavli and one Yerushalmi.

The Gemara Bezah says that on Shabbath a person is given an extra soul, as it states, דאמר ר׳ שמעון בן לקיש נשמה יתירה נותן הקב״ה באדם ערב שבת ולמוצאי שבת נוטלין אותה הימנו, שנאמר שבת ,וינפש כיון ששבת ווי אבדה נפש (ביצה טז. ותענית כז:) "Rabbi Simon ben Lakish said, on the eve of Shabbath the Holy One, Blessed be He, gives man an extra soul; at the conclusion of Shabbath He takes it from him, as it says, He rested and was refreshed [the word וינפש, may be divided so that it means:], once it ceased, woe that soul was lost" (Bezah 16a and Taanith 27b). Thus, a Shabbath observer lives one seventh more than one who is not a Shabbath observer, although both die at the same age. The Shabbath observer lives seven days with one soul and on Shabbath he gets an extra soul. One might have thought this gift is for the entire week, but the Gemara clearly says that it is only given for the duration of the Shabbath. Consequently, in a period of seven days, the Shabbath observer lives eight days; in a period of seven months, he lives eight months; in a period of seven years, he lives eight years; and in a period of seventy years, he lives eighty years.

Now examine the Yerushalmi Gemara. The Talmud Yerushalmi says that observing the Shabbath is equated with all the other mitzvoth, as it states, רבי אומר זו מצות שבת שהיא שקולה כנגד כל מצותיה של תורה דכתיב ואת שבת קדשך הודעת להם ומצות וחוקים ותורה צוית להודיעך שהיא שקולה כנגד כל מצותיו של תורה (תלמוד ירושלמי, ברכות, פרק א, הלכה ה), "Rabbi said this refers to the mitzvah of Shabbath which is equated to all the mitzvoth of the Torah, as it is written, 'And your holy Shabbath you shall make known to them, and You did command commandments, statutes, and a law,' to teach you that it is equated to all the commandments of the Torah" (Yerushalmi Gemara, Berakoth, Chapter 1, Halakhah 5). Thus, the observing of

Shabbath is equated with the number 613, the total number of mitzvoth; or all 613 Mitzvoth are equated to the observing of the Shabbath.

The pasuk from Psalms, which is incorporated into the Shabbath morning service, states, ימי שנותינו בהם שבעים שנה, ואם בגבורת שמונים שנה, ורהבם עמל ואון, כי גז חיש ונעפה (תהלים צ,י). "The days of our years are seventy years, and if with vigor they be eighty, and their pride is travail and nothingness, for it is soon cut off and we fly away" (Psalms 90,10). The gematria of בגבורת, "with vigor," is 613.

בגבורת   613

Since the gematria of בגבורת, "with vigor," is 613, and all 613 Mitzvoth are equated to Shabbath, בגבורת, "with vigor," can refer to Shabbath. From the Gemara Bezah it is known that one who is a Shabbath observer lives one seventh more, due to his extra soul, than one who is not a Shabbath observer. Accordingly, the pasuk from Psalms would be explained as follows: ימי שנותינו בהם שבעים שנה, "the days of our years are seventy years," the average life of a man lasts seventy years, ואם בגבורת, "and if with vigor," and if one is a Shabbath observer, שמונים שנה, "they be eighty," then those seventy years will be eighty years. With this explanation, the five difficulties mentioned in reference to this pasuk vanish. First, grammatically, the phrase is correct. The phrase ואם בגבורת, "and if with vigor," refers to the seventy years, and not the individual. Second, the number eighty is one seventh more than the number seventy, and therefore relates directly to it. Third, the number eighty specifically was chosen rather than a larger or smaller number. It refers to the extra soul which causes a Shabbath observer to live precisely one seventh longer than that of a non-Shabbath observer. Fourth, the pasuk is true: The additional one seventh more that a Shabbath observer lives applies to any Shabbath observer. The pasuk has nothing to do with natural strength. Fifth, it can easily be understood why this pasuk is incorporated into the Shabbath morning prayers. Thus, with this explanation, the five difficulties mentioned in reference to this pasuk vanish. Is it not a beautiful thought for Shabbath, to speak of the additional one seventh more that a Shabbath observer lives due to the extra soul which Hashem gives him?

באברתו יסך לך ותחת כנפיו תחסה צנה וסחרה אמתו (תהלים צא,ד).

He will cover you with His pinions and under His wings shall you trust; His truth shall be your shield and buckler (Psalms 91,4).

This pasuk from Psalms is incorporated into the Shabbath morning service after ברוך שאמר. The gematria of באברתו, "with His pinions," is 611.

באברתו   611

There is a pasuk in Deuteronomy which allegorizes G-d's care of the Bnei Yisroel to the eagle's treatment of its fledglings. It states, "As an eagle stirring its nest, fluttering over its young, spreading abroad its wings, it took them, it bore them upon its pinions" (דברים לב,יא, Deuteronomy 32,11). The Ibn Ezra explains באברתו, "upon its pinions," as quoted above from Psalms in the Shabbath morning service, as parallel to the expression of an eagle stirring its nest as mentioned in the pasuk from Deuteronomy. The Ibn Ezra states, והטעי כנשר יעיר קינו וכו׳ (אבן עזרא, תהלים צא,ד), "and the meaning of this expression is 'as an eagle stirring its nest,'" (Ibn Ezra, Psalms 91,4). The comparison to the pasuk in Deuteronomy is just to point out the idea of an eagle protecting its young with its pinions. Although the Ibn Ezra explains that here the reference is to faith and not Torah, still the pasuk he chose to quote refers to the Torah. Rashi explains this quoted pasuk as referring to how Hashem gave the Torah to the Bnei Yisroel, as he writes, כשבא לתן תורה לא נגלה עליהם מרוח אחת אלא מארבע רוחות, שנאמר ה׳ מסיני בא וזרח משעיר למו הופיע מהר פארן, אלוק מתימן יבא זו רוח רביעית (רש״יי, דברים לב,יא) "When He came to give Torah, He did not reveal Himself to them from one direction, but from four directions, as it says, and G-d came from Sinai, and He shone from Seir to them, He appeared from the mountain of Paran, G-d from Teman comes, this is the fourth direction" (Rashi, Deuteronomy 32,11). The gematria of תורה, "Torah," is 611.

תורה   611

Since באברתו, "with its pinions," can be explained by means of its usage in the pasuk of כנשר יעיר קנו וכו׳, "as the eagle stirring its nest, etc." and that pasuk is explained as metaphor to the way Hashem gave the Torah to the Bnei Yisroel, therefore באברתו, "with its pinions," can refer to giving of the תורה, "Torah." Thus, it is very fitting that באברתו, "with its pinions," should have the same gematria of תורה, "Torah".

מי שעשה נסים לאבותינו וגאל אותם מעבדות לחרות, הוא יגאל אותנו בקרוב ויקבץ נדחינו מארבע כנפות הארץ חברים כל ישראל ונאמר אמן (סידור בית יעקב מאת הרב יעקב מעמדין בן הרב צבי, אשכנזי, דף קעד.).
He who has wrought miracles for our fathers and redeemed them from slavery to freedom, may He redeem us soon, and gather our dispersed ones from the four corners of the earth, all Israel are united in friendship and let us say, Amen (Siddur Beth Yaakov by Rabbi Yaakov from Emden ben Rabbi Zvi, Ashkenazi, page 174a).

This prayer is part of the blessing of the new month which is said Shabbath morning before the Musaf Service.

Rabbi Samson Raphael Hirsch in his commentary on the siddur explains that while the Bnei Yisroel were still enslaved in Egypt, Hashem appointed the new moon for them. It serves as a symbol of His renewal to save the Bnei Yisroel; in every period of despair there is hope for Hashem's salvation (סידור תפילות ישראל מאת הרב שמשון רפאל הירש, תפילות לשבת אחר קריאת התורה, ד"ה מי שעשה, Siddur Tefiloth Yisroel by Rabbi Samson Raphael Hirsch, Shabbath service after the Torah reading, header words: Mi She-asah).

Rashi says that the mitzvah of the new moon was the first mitzvah given to the Bnei Yisroel, as he writes, מהחדש הזה לכם שהיא מצוה ראשונה שנצטוו בה ישראל, "from 'this month should be to you,' which is the first commandment that Israel was commanded" (רש"י, בראשית א,א ושפתי חכמים אות ב, Rashi, Genesis 1,1 and Sifthei Chachomim letter 2). Since this mitzvah serves as a symbol of G-d's renewed commitment to save the Bnei Yisroel, it follows that this mitzvah gave them hope for salvation. The words וגאל אותם מעבדות, "and redeemed them from slavery," in the siddur can refer to the Bnei Yisroel performing their first mitzvah, which gave them hope for salvation. This mitzvah which they received while still in Egypt, gave them hope to be redeemed מעבדות, "from slavery." This concept is connected with a gematria. The text from the siddur that says, וגאל אותם מעבדות לחרות, "and redeemed them from slavery to freedom," ends ונאמר אמן, "and let us say, Amen." The gematria of מעבדות, "from slavery," is 522.

מעבדות   522

The gematria of אמן, "Amen," is 91.

אמן   91

The sum of the two gematrioth is 613.

522
91
―――
613

The word before אמן, "Amen," is ונאמר, "and we will say." The message seems clear. The וגאל אותם מעבדות, "and redeemed them from slavery," can refer to the Bnei Yisroel performing the first mitzvah, which gave them hope for salvation. If the Bnei Yisroel of today follow that pattern of performing mitzvoth, as implied by the word ונאמר, "and we will say," then they too can hope for salvation.

The Gemara Makkoth says that there is a total of 613 Mitzvoth given to Moses, as stated, דרש רבי שמלאי שש מאות ושלש עשרה מצית נאמרו לו למשה שלש מאות וששים וחמש לאוין כמנין ימות החמה ומאתים וארבעים ושמונה עשה כנגד איבריו של אדם (מכות כג:), "Rabbi Simlai expounded, six hundred thirteen Commandments were said to Moses. Three hundred and sixty-five negative Commandments corresponding to the number of days in a solar year, and two hundred and forty-eight positive Commandments corresponding to the number of limbs of a man" (Makkoth 23b). When the Bnei Yisroel add their אמן, "Amen," to the מעבדות, "from slavery," of the Bnei Yisroel of Egypt, they are following the pattern of performing mitzvoth, as is indicated by the sum of their gematrioth being equal to 613, which is the number of mitzvoth.

טללי אורות ראשו נמלא, קווצותיו רסיסי לילה (סידור בית יעקב מאת הרב יעקב מעמדין בן הרב צבי , אשכנזי, דף קעו :).

His head is filled with dew of lights, and His locks with drops of the night (Siddur Beth Yaakov by Rabbi Yaakov from Emden ben Rabbi Zvi, Ashkenazi, page 176b).

This verse is the thirteenth in the אנעים זמירות hymn which is said on Shabbath and holidays. According to Rabbi Yaakov Emden the phrase טללי אורות, "dew of lights," refers to Torah, as he states, טללי אורות, על התורה שנקראת אור ולשון כתוב הוא ישעיי כ"ו (סידור בית יעקב מאת הרב יעקב מעמדין בן הרב צבי,

(אשכנזי, דף קעו:). "'Dew of lights,' refers to the Torah which is called light, and it is an expression of the scripture Isaiah 26" (Siddur Beth Yaakov by Rabbi Yaakov from Emden ben Rabbi Zvi, Ashkenazi, page 176b). Rashi comments on the pasuk to which Rabbi Emden refers, as he says, כי נאה לך לעשות כן שיהא טל תורתיך ומצותיך להם טל של אור (רש״יי, ישעיי כו,יט, דבור המתחיל: כי טל אורות טלך), "For it is pleasing to You to do so, that the dew of Your Torah and Your mitzvoth will be for them dew of lights" (Rashi, Isaiah 26,19, header words: For the dew of light is Your dew). From this Rashi it is apparent that "dew of lights" can refer to mitzvoth as well as the Torah. The gematria of אורות, "lights," is 613.

אורות   613

The referral of "dew of lights" to the mitzvoth is further indicated by the gematria of אורות, "lights," being equal to 613, the number of the mitzvoth.

The Night following the Shabbath   מוצאי שבת

> והשיב לב אבות על בנים ולב בנים על אבותם פן אבוא
> והכיתי את הארץ חרם (מלאכי ג,כד).
> And he shall turn the heart of the fathers to the children, and the heart of the children to their fathers; lest I come and smite the earth with a curse (Malachi 3,24).

It is customary to sing the first section of the last pasuk of The Twelve Prophets on the night following the Shabbath. That section of the pasuk says that אליהו הנביא, Elijah the prophet, will turn לב אבות על בנים ולב בנים על אבותם, "the heart of the fathers to the children, and the heart of the children to their fathers." There seems to be faulty parallelism in this pasuk. The pasuk says that Elijah the prophet will turn the hearts of אבות על בנים, "fathers to the children," then it says he will turn the hearts of בנים על אבותם, "children to their fathers." Either the pasuk should say אבות על בניהם, "the fathers to their children," or say בנים על אבות, "the children to the fathers." Why does the pasuk use the words בנים, "sons," and אבותם, "their children," which are not parallel?

The מלביי״ם, Malbim, gives an explanation which answers this question. He says that אבותם, "their fathers," is not referring to immediate fathers, but to the religion of the fathers, as he states, והוא ישיב את כל העולם בתשובה, עד שהבנים, שהודחו מתורת אבותיהם ישיב לב הבנים אל אבותיהם לחזור אל הדת ותורת אבותם, ועי״כ ישיב לב אבות על בנים (באר הענין, מאת הרב מאיר ליבוש מלביי״ם, מלאכי ג,כד), "And he will cause the entire world to turn back with repentance, until the children who have been led astray from the Torah of their fathers, those children he will cause their hearts to return to their fathers, to return to the religion and Torah of their fathers. And thereby, he will cause the hearts of the fathers to return to the children" (Be'ur Hainyan by Rabbi Meir Lebush Malbim, Malachi 3,24).

Thus, according to the Malbim, Elijah the prophet will cause the hearts of children to turn to the religion of their fathers, meaning the Torah of the fathers; that is why it says he will turn ולב בנים על אבותם, "and the heart of the children to their fathers."

There is a corroborating gematria to the Malbim's explanation. The pasuk says that Elijah the prophet will turn the hearts of אבות על בנים, "the heart of the fathers to the children," then it says he will turn ולב בנים על אבותם, "and the heart of the children to their fathers." The gematrioth of אבות, "fathers," בנים, "sons," and בנים, "sons," add up to 613.

אבות	409
בנים	102
בנים	102
	613

There is a total of 613 Commandments in the Torah. Since according to the Malbim's explanation, Elijah the prophet will cause the hearts of בנים, "children," to turn to the religion of their fathers, meaning the Torah of the fathers; and the hearts of אבות, "fathers," will turn to בנים, "children"; the fact that the gematria of those who will turn to the Torah is equal to the total number of commandments in the Torah, corroborates the Malbim's explanation.

Book of Genesis — ספר בראשית

Parashath Bereshith   פרשת בראשית

ויברא אלקים את האדם בצלמו בצלם אלקים ברא אתו
זכר ונקבה ברא אתם (בראשית א,כז).
And G-d created the man in His image, in the
image of G-d He created him, male and female
He created them (Genesis 1,27).

When the first person was created, he possessed both male and female characteristics, as Rashi says, שנבראו שני פרצופים בבריאה ראשונה ואחר כך חלקן, "They were originally created two-faced and afterwards He divided them" (רש"י, בראשית א,כז, Rashi, Genesis 1,27). Rashi elaborates on this facet of creation as a commentary on the words, זכר ונקבה, "male and female," from which it was derived, as stated, ויברא אלקים את האדם בצלמו בצלם אלקים ברא אתו זכר ונקבה ברא אתם (בראשית א,כז), "And G-d created the man in His image, in the image of G-d He created him, male and female He created them" (Genesis 1,27). The gematria of זכר, "male,"is 227.

227   זכר

The gematria of ונקבה, "and female," is 163.

163   ונקבה

After the first man was created possessing both male and female characteristics, Hashem removed the female characteristics from this first person (Genesis 2,22). This removal can be demonstrated by subtracting the gematria of ונקבה, "and female," from the gematria of זכר, "male," which leaves a remainder of 64.

227
-163
64

The Torah writes the following about Adam who was to

be divided, as stated, זה ספר תולדת אדם ביום ברא אלקים אדם בדמות אלקים עשה אתו (בראשית ה,א), "This is the book of the generations of Adam, in the day that G-d created Adam, in the likeness of G-d, He made him" (Genesis 5,1). The gematria of אדם, "Adam," is 45.

אדם   45

The Torah writes the following about Eve after the first person was divided, as stated, ויקרא האדם שם אשתו חוה כי הוא היתה אם כל חי (בראשות ג,כ), "And Adam called the name of his wife Eve, because she was the mother of all the living" (Genesis 3,20). The gematria of חוה, "Eve," is 19.

חוה   19

The combined gematria of אדם, "Adam," and חוה, "Eve," the names given to two separate people, is 64.

45
<u>19</u>
64

Since the subtraction of the gematria of ונקבה, "and female," from the gematria of זכר, "male," leaves a remainder equal to the combined gematria of אדם, "Adam," and חוה, "Eve," it alludes to Hashem's removing the female characteristics from the first person, resulting in אדם, "Adam," and חוה, "Eve."

ותפקחנה עיני שניהם וידעו כי עירמם הם ויתפרו עלה תאנה ויעשו להם חגרת (בראשית ג,ז).

And the eyes of both of them were opened and they knew that they were naked; and they sewed together fig leaves, and made themselves girdles (Genesis 3,7).

After Adam and Eve realized they were naked, they made for themselves חגרת, "girdles." The gematria of חגרת, "girdles," is 611.

חגרת   611

The Ramban explains this pasuk as referring to wisdom, and he quotes another pasuk (תהלים קיט,יח, Psalms 119,18) where a similar expression is used in reference to learning Torah (רמב״ן, בראשית ג,ז, Ramban, Genesis 3,7). Rashi too explains ותפקחנה עיני שניהם וידעו, "And the eyes of both of them were opened and they knew," as referring to wisdom, as he writes, (רש״י, בראשית ג,ז) לענין החכמה דבר הכתוב, "Regarding the subject of wisdom does the verse speak" (Rashi, Genesis 3,7).

It is essential to have people with some degree of wisdom, or wise people, in order to learn Torah. The Midrash says, אם אין חכמים אין תורה (מדרש רבה, סדר שמיני, פרשה י״א, אות ז), "If there are no wise people, there is no Torah" (Midrash Rabbah, Sidrah Shemini, Parashah 11, Letter 7). The gematria of תורה, "Torah," is 611.

תורה   611

Since חגרת, "girdles," and תורה, "Torah," have the same gematria, the pasuk could be interpreted as referring to Torah. Thus, ותפקחנה עיני שניהם, "And the eyes of both of them were opened," could mean that they acquired wisdom, as the Ramban and Rashi explain. Since some degree of wisdom is essential to learn Torah, hence ויעשו להם חגרת, "and made themselves girdles," could mean, and they acquired the wisdom needed to learn Torah, because the word חגרת, "girdles," can be replaced by the word Torah. This meaning is a דרש, "derash," on the pasuk, but it indicates the need for wisdom to learn Torah.

ויקרא הי אלקים אל האדם ויאמר לו איכה (בראשית ג,ט).
And the Lord G-d called to the man and He said
to him, "Where are you?" (Genesis 3,9).

When Hashem called to the first man He said לו, "to him," איכה, "Where are you?" The gematria of לו "to him," is 36.

לו   36

The gematria of איכה, "Where are you?" is 36.

איכה   36

One can reason as to why the gematria of לו, "to him," and איכה, "Where are you?" are equal. The pasuk did not have to include the word לו, "to him," since the thought of the pasuk seems complete without employing this word; there was no other man whom Hashem could have been addressing. Perhaps the word לו, "to him," was included in the pasuk to suggest that this first man was the person who hid from Hashem, causing Hashem to seek after him. It was specifically לו, "to him," specifically to this first man alone, that Hashem asked איכה, "Where are you ?" This reasoning could be why the gematria of לו, "to him," is equal to the gematria of איכה, "Where are you?"

Each and everyone can learn a lesson from this verse. Each of us has to be accountable for his actions before Hashem; there is no hiding from Him.

ויאמר מה עשית קול דמי אחיך צעקים אלי מן־האדמה
(בראשית ד,י).
And he said, "What have you done? The voice of
your brother's blood is crying to me from the
ground" (Genesis 4, 10).

Before Hashem punished Cain for killing Abel, Hashem spoke to Cain about the קול, "voice," of his brother's blood. The gematria of קול, "voice," is 136.

קול   136

Thus, 136 represents the reason Hashem gave for punishing Cain. When Cain was told of his punishment he responded, ‏ויאמר קין אל ה׳ גדול עוני מנשוא (בראשית ד,יג)‏, "And Cain said to G-d, 'My sin is greater than I can bear'" (Genesis 4,13). The gematria of עוני, "my sin," is 136.

עוני   136

Thus, 136 represents the punishment of Cain for his sinful act; punishing is one of Hashem's attributes. The Gemara Sanhedrin asserts, ‏שכל מדותיו של הקב״ה מדה כנגד מדה (שבת קה:, ונדרים לב., וסנהדרין צ.)‏, "All the attributes of the Holy One, Blessed be He, are meted out measure for measure" (Shabbath 105b, Nedarim 32a, and Sanhedrin 90a). Thus, it follows that when Hashem punished Cain, His punishment was measure for measure. Therefore, it is fitting that the gematria of the reason Hashem gave for punishing Cain, should be equal to the gematria of the punishment; the gematria of קול, "voice," equals the gematria of עוני, "my sin."

‏ויאמר ה׳ אמחה את־האדם אשר־בראתי מעל פני האדמה מאדם עד־בהמה עד־רמש ועד־עוף השמים כי נחמתי כי עשיתם (בראשית ו,ז).‏

And G-d said, "I will wipe from the face of the earth, the man whom I have created: from man unto beast, unto creeping things and unto fowl of the heaven; for I regret that I have made them" (Genesis 6,7).

The only time the Torah utilizes the word בראתי, "I have created," is when it recounts Hashem creating man. The gematria of בראתי, "I have created," is 613

בראתי   613

The purpose of man in this world is to do the Commandments of Hashem. This purpose is clearly stated at the end of Ecclesiastes, סוף דבר הכל נשמע את האלקים ירא ואת מצותיו שמור כי זה כל האדם (קהלת יב,יג), "The conclusion of the thing, all having been heard, fear G-d, and keep His commandments, for this is the whole of man" (Ecclesiastes 12,13). Thus, it follows that since the purpose of man in this world is to perform the commandments of Hashem, the reason Hashem created man was to do His commandments. There is a total of 613 Commandments. It is appropriate that the only time the Torah uses the word בראתי, "I have created," is in reference to Hashem's creating man; for the purpose of man's being created is to perform the 613 Commandments of Hashem, and the gematria of בראתי, "I have created," is 613.

It is interesting to note that the pasuk quoted from Genesis is the next to the last in Parashath Bereshith; the pasuk quoted from Ecclesiastes is the next to the last in the book of Ecclesiastes. Also note that these two pesukim are read within ten days of each other (the one from Ecclesiastes on the Sukkoth holiday, and the one from Genesis on Simhath Torah). Finally, Targum Jonathan ben Uzziel states, man was created with 248 limbs and 365 sinews, together totaling 613 body parts (תרגום יונתן בן עוזיאל בראשית א,כז, Targum Jonathan ben Uzziel, Genesis 1,27). It is fitting that the word בראתי, "I have created," should have a gematria of 613, since man was created with 613 parts. Every single body part was created to enable man to achieve his purpose of fulfilling the 613 Commandments.

ונח מצא חן בעיני ה' (בראשית ו,ח).

And Noach found grace in the eyes of G-d (Genesis 6,8).

The last pasuk in Parashath Bereshith says that Noach found חן, "grace," in Hashem's eyes. The gematria of חן, "grace," is 58.

חן 58

The first pasuk in Parashath Noach says that Noach was a righteous man, as stated, אלה תולדת נח נח איש צדיק תמים היה בדרתיו את האלקים התהלך נח (בראשית ו,ט), "These are the generations of Noach, Noach was a righteous man; he was perfect in his generations, Noach walked with G-d" (Genesis 6,9). The gematria of נח, Noach, is 58.

נח 58

Since Noach found grace in Hashem's eyes, נח, "Noach," can be equated with חן, "grace," both in conception, in letters, and in gematria.

Parashath Noach   פרשת נח

אלה תולדת נח נח איש צדיק תמים היה בדרתיו את
האלקים התהלך נח (בראשית ו,ט).

These are the generations of Noach, Noach was a righteous man; he was perfect in his generations, Noach walked with G-d (Genesis 6,9).

Rashi compares the righteousness of נח, "Noach," to the righteousness of אברהם, "Abraham," (רש"י, בראשית ו,ט, Rashi, Genesis 6,9). Gematrioth can shed some light on this comparison. The difference between נח, "Noach," and אברהם, "Abraham," in gematrioth is 190.

אברהם	248
נח	58
	190

Hashem told Noach of the upcoming destruction of the world, as stated, ויאמר אלקים לנח קץ כל בשר בא לפני כי מלאה הארץ חמס מפניהם והנני משחיתם את הארץ (בראשית ו,יג), "And G-d said to Noach, the end of all flesh has come before me, for the earth is filled with violence through them, and behold I will destroy them with the earth" (Genesis 6,13). The gematria of קץ, "the end," is 190.

קץ	190

Thus, it was in the lifetime of Noach that קץ, "the end," of all flesh occurred, that the 190 occurred. Noach did not try to prevent the destruction, i.e., to stop "the end" from occurring, in stark contrast to Abraham who pleaded for Sodom's end not to occur.

Hashem told Abraham that his seed would be enslaved in Egypt for four hundred years. But in reality the enslavement lasted only 210 years; the Bnei Yisroel were redeemed 190 years early. There are many reasons for the early redemption; a calculation is given by Rashi (רש״י, בראשית טו,יג, Rashi, Genesis 15,13). One explanation is that if the Bnei Yisroel had remained any longer in Egypt, they would have been unable to maintain their identity as Bnei Yisroel (הרחב דבר מאת הרב נפתלי צבי יהודה ברלין מוואלאזין, בראשית טו,יג, אות א, Harchev Davar by Rabbi Naphtali Zvi Judah Berlin from Volozhin, Genesis 15,13, Letter 1). The reason for the Children of Israel's existence is for the observance of the Torah, which would be given to them within weeks after the redemption from Egypt. Thus, the 190 years of early redemption were 190 years that prevented destruction.

Now the difference between Noach and Abraham can be understood. The difference between Noach and Abraham is 190; in the case of Noach, 190 represents destruction; in the case of Abraham, 190 represents early redemption that prevented destruction. This difference is indicated in the gematrioth of their names; the difference between נח, "Noach," and אברהם, "Abraham," in gematrioth is also 190.

ויהי המבול ארבעים יום על הארץ וירבו המים וישאו את התבה ותרם מעל הארץ. ויגברו המים וירבו מאד על־הארץ ותלך התבה על פני המים. והמים גברו מאד מאד על הארץ ויכסו כל ההרים הגבהים אשר תחת כל השמים. חמש עשרה אמה מלמעלה גברו המים ויכסו ההרים..... וימח את כל היקום אשר על פני האדמה מאדם עד בהמה עד רמש ועד עוף השמים וימחו מן הארץ וישאר אך נח ואשר אתו בתבה. ויגברו המים על־הארץ חמשים ומאת יום (בראשית ז,יז־כ, כג־כד).

And the flood was forty days upon the earth; and the waters increased and lifted the ark, and it rose from the earth. And the waters grew mighty and increased greatly upon the earth; and the ark went upon the face of the waters. And the waters grew exceedingly mighty on the earth; and all the high mountains that were under the whole heaven, were covered. Fifteen cubits upwards the waters grew mighty and the mountains were covered. And He blotted out every existing thing which was upon the face of the ground, from man unto cattle, unto creeping thing, and unto the fowl of the heaven; and they were blotted out from the earth; and only Noach remained and those who were with him in the ark. And the waters grew mighty upon the earth a hundred and fifty days (Genesis 7,17-20, 23-24).

The Torah uses four verbs to express what occurred to the ark, the instrument of saving; they are: וישאו, "and lifted," ותרם, "and it rose," ותלך, "and went," and וישאר, "and remained." The sum of the gematrioth of these four verbs is 1942.

וישאו	323
ותרם	646
ותלך	456
וישאר	517
	1942

Since these four verbs are associated with saving, the sum of their gematrioth is also associated with saving. The Torah uses אלקים, "G-d," to refer to Hashem remembering Noach and the animals that were with him in the ark to save them, as stated, ויזכר אלקים את נח ואת כל החיה ואת כל הבהמה אשר אתו בתבה ויעבר אלקים רוח על הארץ וישכו המים (בראשית ח,א), "And G-d remembered Noach, and all the beast, and all the cattle that was with him in the ark; and G-d made a wind to pass over the earth, and the waters assuaged" (Genesis 8,1). The gematria of אלקים, "G-d," is 86.

אלקים   86

When the gematria of אלקים, "G-d," is added to the gematrioth of the four verbs associated with saving, their total gematria is 2028.

1942
86
____
2028

Thus, the gematria of 2028 represents Hashem's acts of saving the ark in the flood. Hashem's saving can definitely be considered a manifestation of Hashem's attribute of goodness. The gematria of Hashem's name is added to the gematrioth of the verbs associated with saving but not to the gematrioth of the verbs associated with annihilation, in accordance with the Midrash that states, אין שמו של הקב״ה נזכר על הרעה, אלא על הטוב (מדרש תנחומא, פרשת תזריע, אות ט) "The name of G-d should not be mentioned in relationship to the evil, but in relationship to the good" (Midrash Tanhuma, Parashath Thazria, Letter 9).

Although some are repeated, the Torah uses eight variations of verb forms to express the surging water, the instrument of annihilation, in the flood; they are: וירבו, "and increased," ויגברו, "and grew mighty," וירבו, "and increased," גברו, "grew mighty," ויכסו, "and covered," גברו, "grew mighty," ויכסו, "and covered," and ויגברו, "and grew mighty." The sum of the gematrioth of these eight verbs is 1528.

וירבו	224
ויגברו	227
וירבו	224
גברו	211
ויכסו	102
גברו	211
ויכסו	102
ויגברו	227
	1528

Since these eight verbs are associated with annihilating, the sum of their gematrioth is also associated with annihilating. Thus, the gematria of 1528 represents the annihilation with the waters of the flood. Hashem's annihilation can definitely be considered a manifestation of Hashem's attribute of punishment. The difference between the gematrioth which represent Hashem saving and the gematrioth which represent punishment is 500.

$$
\begin{array}{r}
2028 \\
-1528 \\
\hline
500
\end{array}
$$

Rashi says that Hashem's attribute of goodness is 500 times greater than His attribute of punishment (רש"י, שמות כ,ו, Rashi, Exodus 20,6). Since the difference between the gematrioth which represent Hashem's acts of saving the ark in the flood, and the gematrioth which represent punishment with the waters of the flood, is 500, this difference can allude to the ratio between Hashem's attribute of goodness and His attribute of punishment, as established in Rashi.

חמש עשרה אמה מלמעלה גברו המים ויכסו ההרים
(בראשית ז,כ).

Fifteen cubits upwards the waters grew mighty and the mountains were covered (Genesis 7,20).

The Torah repeatedly uses the word המים, "the waters," in reference to the waters of the flood. The gematria of המים, "the waters," is 95.

המים   95

The waters of the flood caused all flesh that moved upon the earth to perish, as stated, ויגוע כל בשר הרמש על הארץ בעוף ובבהמה ובחיה ובכל השרץ השרץ על הארץ וכל האדם (בראשית ז,כא), "And all flesh perished, that moved upon the earth, in the fowl, and in the cattle, and in the beast, and in every creeping thing that creeps upon the earth, and every man" (Genesis 7,21). The gematria of ויגוע, "and perished," is 95.

ויגוע   95

Since המים, "the waters," caused ויגוע, "and perished," it is appropriate that both words should have the same gematria.

ובחדש השני בשבעה ועשרים יום לחדש יבשה הארץ
(בראשית ח,יד)

And in the second month on the twenty-seventh day of the month, the earth dried (Genesis 8,14).

After saying that the waters of the flood dried, the Torah says that the earth dried. Rashi comments, נעשה גריד כהלכתה (רש"י, בראשית ח,יד), "it became hard as it was customarily" (Rashi, Genesis 8,14). Why did Rashi choose to use the word כהלכתה, "as it was customarily"? This Rashi can be explained more fully with an understanding of the Midrash which says that Hashem looked into the Torah and then He created the world (בראשית רבה פרשה ב אות א, Genesis Rabbah Parashah 2, Letter 1). Hashem contemplated the mitzvoth which the Bnei Yisroel would be obligated to fulfill, and then He fashioned the world accordingly. Similarly, when Hashem dried the earth after the flood, He contemplated the mitzvoth which the Bnei Yisroel would be obligated to fulfill, and then He dried the earth accordingly. This explanation can be confirmed by a gematria. The Torah says that the earth dried. The gematria of יבשה הארץ, "the earth dried," is 613.

יבשה	317
הארץ	296
	613

Since the gematria of יבשה הארץ, "the earth dried," is equal to the total number of mitzvoth, this equality confirms that when Hashem dried the earth, He did so according to the requirements of the mitzoth. It can now be explained why Rashi chose to use the word כהלכתה, "as it was customarily." This word can also be translated as, "according to Jewish law." Perhaps the reason why Rashi chose this word is to bring to mind that when Hashem dried the earth after the flood, He contemplated the mitzvoth which the Bnei Yisroel would be obligated to fulfill, and then He dried the earth accordingly.

כל־רמש אשר הוא־חי לכם יהיה לאכלה כירק עשב נתתי
לכם את־כל (בראשית ט,ג).

Every moving thing which lives shall be food for you, as the green herb, I have given all to you (Genesis 9,3).

Hashem told Noach and his sons they could eat any moving thing, which will be to them as the green herb. The gematria of כירק עשב, "as the green herb," is 702.

כירק	330
עשב	372
	702

Rashi comments that Hashem was telling Noach and his sons that any moving thing will be to them as the green herb was to Adam, i.e., that any moving thing will be as ownerless property to Noach and his sons as the green herb was ownerless property to Adam (רש״י, בראשית ט,ג, Rashi, Genesis 9,3).

The Torah calls the Sabbatical year a Shabbath, as

ובשנה השביעת שבת שבתון יהיה לארץ שבת לה׳ שדך לא תזרע, stated,
וכרמך לא תזמר (ויקרא כה,ד), "And the seventh year shall be a
Shabbath of rest for the land, a Shabbath to G-d; your fields
you shall not sow, and your vineyards you shall not prune"
(Leviticus 25,4). The gematria of שבת, "Shabbath," is 702.

שבת   702

During the Sabbatical year one can gather only
ownerless crops from the field (רש״י, ויקרא כה,ה, Rashi, Leviticus 25,5).

When the Torah states כירק עשב, "as the green herb,"
in reference to Noach, and when the Torah states שבת,
"Shabbath," in reference to the Sabbatical year, both indicate
permission to partake of ownerless food. Thus, it is fitting
that כירק עשב, "as the green herb," and שבת, "Shabbath,"
should have the same gematria.

וירד ה׳ לראת את העיר ואת המגדל אשר בנו בני האדם.
ויאמר ה׳ הן עם אחד ושפה אחת לכלם וזה החלם לעשות
ועתה לא יבצר מהם כל אשר יזמו לעשות..... ויפץ ה׳ אתם
משם על פני כל הארץ ויחדלו לבנת העיר. על כן קרא שמה
בבל כי שם בלל ה׳ שפת כל הארץ ומשם הפיצם ה׳ על פני
כל־הארץ (בראשית יא, ה־ו, ח־ט).

And G-d came down to see the city and tower,
which the children of men had built. And G-d
said, "Behold they are one people, and they all
have one language, and this is what they begin
to do, and now nothing will be withholden from
them, which they purpose to do". . . . And G-d
scattered them from there upon the face of all
the earth, and they ceased to build the city.
Therefore was its name called Babel, because
G-d there confounded the language of all the
earth, and from there G-d scattered them upon
the face of all the earth (Genesis 11, 5-6, 8-9).

Five verbs are mentioned in relation to Hashem's actions taken in consequence of the evil of the men of the דור הפלגה, Dor Haflagah, "generation of division," also called, the generation of the tower of Babel; they are: וירד, "and came down," ויאמר, "and said," ויפץ, "and scattered," בלל, "confound," and הפיצם, "scattered." The sum of the gematrioth of these five verbs is 950.

וירד	220
ויאמר	257
ויפץ	186
בלל	62
הפיצם	225
	950

Thus, 950 represents the action taken by Hashem in consequence of the evil of the men of the generation of division.

Rashi in the Gemara Avodah Zarah demonstrates that Abraham lived at the time of the men of the generation of division (רש״י, עבודה זרה יט., ד״ה אברהם אבינו, Rashi, Avodah Zarah 19a, header words: Abram our father). The Gemara considers the counsel of the men of the generation of division to be the counsel of the wicked. Abraham did not join with this wicked counsel. The Gemara further identifies Abraham as the individual referred to in the first part of the first pasuk of Psalms, אשרי האיש אשר לא הלך בעצת רשעים ובדרך חטאים לא עמד ובמושב לצים לא ישב (תהלים א,א), "Praised is the man who does not walk in the counsel of the wicked, and does not stand in the path of sinners, and in the seat of the scornful does not sit" (Psalms 1,1). The gematria of אשרי האיש, "praised is the man," is 827.

אשרי	511
האיש	316
	827

The gematria of אשרי האיש, "praised is the man," can

be used in place of the gematria of אברהם, "Abraham," since the Gemara identifies Abraham as the individual to whom this phrase refers. This pasuk equates a praised man, Abraham, with someone who does not walk in the counsel of the wicked; the counsel of the wicked refers to the counsel of the men in Abraham's time, the men of the generation of division (Avodah Zarah 18b-19a). Since Abraham did not join with the wicked counsel of the men of his time, he avoided having Hashem take action against him. The men of the generation of division suffered the five actions which Hashem brought against them. The difference between the five actions taken by Hashem and a praised man, Abraham, who separated from those of wicked counsel, in gematrioth, is 123.

$$\begin{array}{r} 950 \\ -827 \\ \hline 123 \end{array}$$

Before the men of the generation of division sinned, they were עם אחד, "one people" (בראשית יא,ו, Genesis 11,6). This unity was taken away from the men of the generation of division and given to Abraham's children. The Bnei Yisroel are referred to as one people, ויאמר המן למלך אחשורוש ישנו עם אחד מפזר ומפרד בין העמים בכל מדינות מלכותך ודתיהם שנות מכל עם ואת דתי המלך אינם עשים ולמלך אין שוה להניחם (אסתר ג,ח), "And Haman said to king Ahasuerus, 'There is one people scattered and dispersed among the peoples in all the provinces of your kingdom; and their laws are different from every other people; and the laws of the king they do not do and for the king there is no value to tolerate them'" (Esther 3,8). The gematria of עם אחד, "one people," is 123.

$$\begin{array}{rr} עם & 110 \\ אחד & \underline{13} \\ & 123 \end{array}$$

The value of this gematria, representing the unity which was taken away from the men of the generation of division and given to Abraham's children, is equal to the value of the gematria which represents the difference between the five actions taken by Hashem and a praised man, Abraham, who separated himself from those of wicked counsel.

Parashath Lech Lecha   פרשת לך לך

ויאמר ה' אל אברם לך לך מארצך וממולדתך ומבית אביך
אל הארץ אשר אראך (בראשית יב,א).

And G-d said to Abram, "Go out for yourself from your country, from your birthplace, and from your father's house unto the land which I will show you" (Genesis 12,1).

At out the beginning of this sidrah, Hashem tells Abram, לך לך, "go out for yourself." The gematria of לך לך, "go out for yourself," is 100.

$$\begin{array}{rr} לך & 50 \\ לך & \underline{50} \\ & 100 \end{array}$$

Rashi comments that since travel usually diminishes propagation, wealth, and fame, hence Hashem promised to bestow these three blessings upon Abram (רש"י, בראשית יב,ב, Rashi, Genesis 12,2). Thus, Abram merited these three blessings because of a command whose gematria is 100. Toward the end of this sidrah, Hashem changes the name of Abram to Abraham (reflecting his future status as אב המון גוים, "father of a multitude of nations,") and then makes three promises to him, as stated, והפרתי אתך במאד מאד ונתתיך לגוים ומלכים ממך יצאו (בראשית יז,ו), "And I will make you exceedingly fruitful, and I will make nations of you, and kings shall come out of you" (Genesis 17,6). The gematria of ממך, "from you," is 100.

$$\begin{array}{rr} ממך & 100 \end{array}$$

Each of these promises can be considered to correspond to the blessings at the beginning of the sidrah. The first of these promises, "And I will make you exceedingly fruitful," can be considered to correspond to the blessing of propagation. The second of these promises, "and I will make nations of you," can be considered to correspond to the blessing of fame. The third of these promises, "and kings shall come out of you," can be considered to correspond to the blessing of wealth. All three promises are joined by the conjunction "and," implying that all the promises will be ממך, "from you." Since the gematria of לך לך, "go out for yourself," mentioned at the beginning of the sidrah, equals the gematria of ממך, "from you," mentioned at the end of the sidrah, it can be inferred that the reason Abraham merited Hashem's three promises, and the change of name which reflects these promises, was that Abraham had obeyed Hashem's original command of "go out for yourself."

אל מקום המזבח אשר עשה שם בראשנה ויקרא שם אברם בשם ה׳ (ברששית יג,ד).
To the place of the altar which he made there at first, and there Abram called in the name of G-d (Genesis 13,4).

The Torah says that Abram went to the place where he had previously made an altar, and there he called in the name of G-d. The gematria of אברם בשם ה׳, "Abram in the name of G-d," is 611.

אברם	243
בשם ה׳	368
	611

The pasuk before the pasuk just quoted, designates the place where Abram had previously made an altar, as the place where his tent had first been. The Torah uses the word tent to refer to a place of learning Torah. For example the Torah says, ויעקב איש תם ישב אהלים (בראשית כה,כז), "and Jacob was a simple man, dwelling in tents" (Genesis 25,27). The העמק דבר elucidates that the tents refer to אוהל תורה ותפלה, "tent of Torah and prayer." The gematria of תורה, "Torah," is 611.

תורה   611

Since Abram called in the name of G-d in the place where his tent had been at first, and the word tent can refer to a tent of learning Torah, it can be deduced that Abram's calling in the name of G-d, means Abram learned Torah there. This deduction is corroborated by the fact that the gematria of אברם בשם ה׳, "Abram in the name of G-d," is equal to the gematria of תורה, "Torah."

ויאמר ה׳ אלקים במה אדע כי אירשנה (בראשית טו,ח).
And he said, "Hashem, G-d, whereby shall I know that I shall inherit it?" (Genesis 15,8).

After G-d had told Abram that he would inherit the land, Abram questioned G-d, asking, "Whereby shall I know that I shall inherit it?" Inasmuch as G-d had just told Abram he would inherit the land, what was Abram's question? A possible answer can be derived from a Gemara, referring to Moses which says, א״ר יוחנן אר״יש בן יוחי מתשובתו של אותו צדיק (נדה סא.) אתה יודע מה היה בלבו, "Rabbi Johanan said Rabbi Simeon ben Yohai said, from the answer to that righteous man you can know what was in his heart" (Niddah 61a). The Gemara is saying from the answer G-d gave Moses, it can be inferred what was troubling Moses. Likewise, from the answer G-d gave Abram, it can be inferred what was troubling Abram.

The Gemara elucidates the answer G-d gave to Abram, as it says, אמר לפניו רבש״ע במה אדע אומר לו קחה לי עגלה משולשת וגו׳ אמר לפניו רבש״ע תינח בזמן שבית המקדש קיים בזמן שאין בית המקדש קיים מה תהא עליהם אמר לו כבר תקנתי להם סדר קרבנות כל זמן שקוראין בהן מעלה אני עליהן כאילו מקריבין לפני קרבן ומוחל אני על כל עונותיהם (מגילה לא:), "He said in front of Him, Master of the world, How will I know? He said to him, take for Me three calves, etc. He said in front of Him, Master of the world, that is good for the time when the Temple exists; for the time when the Temple does not exist, what will be, concerning them? He said to him, I have already instituted for them the order of the sacrifices. Any time they will read them, I will consider it as if they are offering a sacrifice in front of Me, and I will forgive all of their sins" (Megillah 31b). Note that the Gemara uses the word עונות, to designate sins. Also note that other commentators translate עגלה משלשת, as three calves (רמב״ן, בראשית טו,ט, Ramban, Genesis 15,9).

The Malbim clearly defines the meaning of עונות, "sins," as he says, המעוה הוא בעצת השכל שכופר במצוה או במצוה ע״י טענות השכל (התורה והמצוה, מאת הרב מאיר ליבוש מלביי״ם, ויקרא טז,כא), "The sinner is one, who under the influence of the intellect, denies a commandment, or the Commander, through the pleas of the intellect," (The Torah and the Mitzvah by Rabbi Meir Lebush Malbim, Leviticus 16,21). Note that the Malbim uses the word המעוה, to designate a sinner. It is clear that עונות can mean to deny a commandment, or G-d.

The words עונות and המעוה come from the same root. The Malbim definition of המעוה, "sinner," also applies to the עונות, "sins." The Gemara in Megillah says that when the Bnei Yisroel read about the sacrifices, G-d will forgive their עונות, "sins." Since the Malbim defines עונות, "sins," to include the denial of a commandment, and since from the answer G-d gave Abram, it can be inferred that Abram was troubled lest the Bnei Yisroel will deny a mitzvah, therefore such denial could cost them their inheritance in the land. There is a total of 613 Commandments which the Children of Israel are to observe (מכות כג:, Makkoth 23b). The denial of any one of these mitzvoth could cost the Children of Israel their inheritance in the land.

Returning to the pasuk first quoted, Abram questioned G-d saying, במה אדע כי אירשנה, "Whereby shall I know that I shall inherit it?" The gematria of במה, "whereby," and of אירשנה, "I shall inherit it," total 613.

במה	47
אירשנה	566
	613

This gematria of 613 gives credence to the inference that Abram was troubled lest the Bnei Yisroel will deny a commandment.

וגם את הגוי אשר יעבדו דן אנכי ואחרי כן יצאו ברכש גדול (בראשית טו,יד).

And also that nation, whom they shall serve, I will judge, and afterward they shall come out with great substance (Genesis 15,14).

The gematria of דן, "judge," is 54.

דן	54

The Ramban interprets the word דן, "judge," in this pasuk as "punishment" (רמב"ן, בראשית טו,יד, Ramban, Genesis 15,14). It can be deduced that the gematria of 54 is associated with the punishment of the Egyptians. One of the tools that Hashem instructed Moses to use was the מטה, "staff," as stated, ויאמר אליו ה' מזה בידך ויאמר מטה (שמות ד,ב), "And G-d said to him, 'What is in your hand?' And he said, 'a staff'" (Exodus 4,2). The gematria of מטה, "staff," is 54.

מטה	54

One of the purposes of Moses taking the מטה, "staff," was to afflict the Egyptians (מדרש רבה, סדר שמות, פרשה ג, אות כג, Midrash Rabbah, Sidrah Shemoth, Parashah 3, Letter 23). Part of the Egyptian punishment was the ten plagues. The abbreviations of the ten plagues, Detzach, Adash, and Beachav,were engraved on the staff which Hashem had instructed Moses to use (ילקוט שמעוני, שמות ד, אות קעג, Yalkut Shimoni, Exodus 4, Letter 173). Again it can be deduced that the gematria of 54 is associated with the punishment of the Egyptians. Perhaps the reason why the gematria of דן, "judge," is the same as the gematria of מטה, "staff," is to indicate that one of the instruments which Hashem used to punish the Egyptians was the staff.

ביום ההוא כרת ה' את אברם ברית לאמר לזרעך נתתי את
הארץ הזאת מנהר מצרים עד־הנהר הגדל נהר פרת
(בראשית טו,יח).

In that day G-d made a covenant with Abram saying, "To your seed I have given this land, from the river of Egypt unto the great river, the River Euphrates" (Genesis 15,18).

The solemn compact between G-d and Abram is referred to as a covenant; the gematria of ברית, "covenant," is 612.

ברית　　　　612

At the time that this covenant was made, Abram had fulfilled all 613 Commandments, minus the one commandment of circumcision (יומא כח:, וספר חדושי הגרי"ז על תנ"ך ואגדה, מפי השמועה, פרשת לך לך, ד"ה ידוע הקושיא, Yoma 28b, and Book of Chidushei Hagriz on the Tanach and Agadah from Oral Communication, Parashath Lech Lecha, header words: It is a Known Question). Thus, the gematria of ברית, "covenant," equals 612 because at the time this covenant was made, Abram had fulfilled 612 commandments.

ונמלתם את בשר ערלתכם והיה לאות ברית ביני וביניכם
(בראשית יז,יא)

And you shall circumcise the flesh of your foreskin, and it will be a sign of a covenant between Me and you (Genesis 17,11).

Circumcision is identified as the sign of a covenant; the gematria of ברית, "covenant," is 612.

ברית   612

The Gemara Nedarim lists one opinion that circumcision is equal to all the other commandments (נדרים לב., Nedarim 32a). Thus, if the commandment of circumcision were placed on one side of a scale, and the remaining 612 commandments were placed on the other side, the two sides would balance. This balance is based on the pasuk, as stated, ויאמר ה' אל משה כתב לך את הדברים האלה כי על פי הדברים האלה כרתי אתך ברית ואת ישראל (שמות לד,כז), "And G-d said to Moses: 'Write for yourself these words, for according to these words I have made a covenant with you and with Israel'" (Exodus 34,27). This Gemara derives that the ברית, "covenant," of this pasuk refers to circumcision, which is equated to all the other commandments. When people speak in their vernacular, a circumcision is often referred to as a "bris." The use of the word ברית, "covenant," to refer to circumcision in the two quoted pesukim, and in the vernacular, is very fitting; for circumcision is equated to the other 612 commandments, and the gematria of ברית, "covenant," is 612.

Parashath Vayyera   פרשת וירא

ותהר ותלד שרה לאברהם בן לזקניו למועד אשר דבר אתו אלקים (בראשית כא,ב).

And Sarah conceived, and bore Abraham a son in his old age at the set time of which G-d had spoken to him (Genesis 21,2).

The Torah says that Sarah gave birth to Isaac, למועד, "at the set time," of which Hashem had spoken to Abraham. The gematria of למועד, "at the set time," is 150.

150   למועד

Thus, 150 represents a specific time when Hashem acted with reference to a declaration He had made in the past.

Shortly after the birth of Isaac, the Torah records what Sarah said, as stated, ותאמר מי מלל לאברהם היניקה בנים שרה כי ילדתי בן לזקניו (בראשית כא,ז), "And she said, 'Who would have said to Abraham, that Sarah should give children suck? For I have borne a son in his old age'" (Genesis 21,7). The gematria of מי מלל, "Who would have said," is 150.

מי	50
מלל	<u>100</u>
	150

The expression מי מלל, "Who would have said," refers to Hashem, as Rashi comments, ראו מי הוא לשון שבח וחשיבות. "וכמה הוא שומר הבטחתו, הקב"ה מבטיח ועושה (רש"י, בראשית כא,ז), "It is a language of praise and importance. See Who He is and how He keeps His promise; The Holy One promises and does" (Rashi, Genesis 21,7). Thus, 150 represents a specific action of Hashem with reference to a declaration He made in the past.

It is very appropriate that למועד, "at the set time," and מי מלל, "Who would have said," have the same gematria. The former represents a specific time when Hashem acted, and the latter represents a specific action of Hashem; both were stated in reference to a declaration of Hashem made in the past.

ויקרא אברהם את שם בנו הנולד לו אשר ילדה לו שרה יצחק (בראשית כא,ג).

And Abraham called the name of his son that was born to him, whom Sarah bore to him, Isaac (Genesis 21,3).

It was destined that Isaac and Ishmael each would have children who would grow to be a nation. The Torah records Isaac's birth with the word ילדה, "bore." The gematria of ילדה, "bore," is 49.

ילדה   49

The Torah records Isaac's weaning with the word הילד, "the child," as stated, ויגדל הילד ויגמל ויעש אברהם משתה גדול ביום הגמל את יצחק (בראשית כא,ח), "And the child grew and was weaned; and Abraham made a great feast or the day that Isaac was weaned" (Genesis 21,8). The gematria of הילד, "the child," is 49.

הילד   49

Thus, the gematria of 49 is found twice in reference to the early years of Isaac's life. Similarly, the Torah records Ishmael's birth with the word ילדה, "bore," as stated, ותלד הגר לאברם בן ויקרא אברם שם בנו אשר ילדה הגר ישמעאל (בראשית טז,טו), "And Hagar bore Abram a son; and Abram called the name of his son whom Hagar bore, Ishmael" (Genesis 16,15). The gematria of ילדה, "bore," is 49.

ילדה   49

The Torah records Ishmael's being cast away, with the word הילד, "the child," as stated, ויכלו המים מן החמת ותשלך את

(בראשית כא,טו) הילד תחת אחת השיחים, "And the water was consumed from the bottle, and she cast the child under one of the shrubs" (Genesis 21,15). The gematria of הילד, "the child," is 49.

49   הילד

Thus, the gematria of 49 is found twice in reference to the early years of Ishmael's life. Ishmael is further compared to Isaac when G-d assures Abraham, as stated, ויאמר אלקים אל אברהם אל ירע בעיניך על הנער ועל אמתך כל אשר תאמר אליך שרה שמע בקלה כי ביצחק יקרא לך זרע. וגם את בן האמה לגוי אשימנו כי זרעך הוא (בראשית כא,יב-יג), "And G-d said to Abraham, 'Let it not be grievous in your eyes because of the lad and because of your bondwoman, all that Sarah says to you, hearken to her voice; for in Isaac shall your seed be called. And also the son of the bondwoman I will make to a nation, because he is your seed'" (Genesis 21,12-13). The gematria of וגם, "and also," is 49.

49   וגם

The gematria of לגוי, "to a nation," is also 49.

49   לגוי

Thus, the gematria of 49 is found twice when the Torah compares Ishmael to Isaac. The repeated recurrence of the gematria of 49 implies that each Isaac and Ishmael would grow לגוי, "to a nation."

ותאמר שרה צחק עשה לי אלקים כל השמע יצחק לי (בראשית כא,ו)

And Sarah said, "G-d has made laughter for me, anyone who hears will laugh for me" (Genesis 21,6).

When Sarah gave birth to Isaac, she said that others יצחק לי, "will laugh for me." The gematria of יצחק לי, "will laugh for me," is 248.

יצחק	208
לי	40
	248

Obviously, one of the persons who laughed for Sarah was Abraham. The happiness of Abraham is implied in the pasuk which follows the one quoted, "And she said, 'Who would have said to Abraham, that Sarah should give children suck? For I have borne a son in his old age'" (בראשית כא,ז, Genesis 21,7). This happiness is further attested to in the next pasuk, as stated, ויגדל הילד ויגמל ויעש אברהם משתה גדול ביום הגמל את יצחק (בראשית כא,ח), "And the child grew and was weaned, and Abraham made a large feast on the day that Isaac was weaned" (Genesis 21,8). The gematria of אברהם, Abraham is 248.

אברהם	248

The gematria of יצחק לי, "will laugh for me," is equal to the gematria of אברהם, "Abraham," for obviously the central person who laughed with Sarah was Abraham.

ותרא שרה את בן הגר המצרית אשר ילדה לאברהם מצחק.
(בראשית כא,ט)

And Sarah saw the son of Hagar the Egyptian, whom she had borne to Abraham, making sport (Genesis 21,9).

After Isaac was weaned, Sarah saw the son of הגר, "Hagar," making sport. The gematria of הגר, "Hagar," is 208.

הגר	208

Why did the Torah refer to Ishmael as the son of Hagar, instead of referring to him by name? The Sforno explains that Hagar was to blame for Ishmael's conduct, for he had heard of such conduct from his mother (ספורנו, בראשית

כא,ט, Sforno, Genesis 21,9). After Sarah had seen Ishmael's conduct, she gave instructions to Abraham, as stated, ותאמר לאברהם גרש האמה הזאת ואת בנה כי לא יירש בן האמה הזאת עם בני עם יצחק (בראשית כא,י) "And she said to Abraham, 'Drive away this bondwoman and her son, for the son of this bondwoman will not inherit with my son, with Isaac'" (Genesis 21,10). The gematria of יצחק, "Isaac," is 208.

יצחק   208

In this last pasuk, as in the previous one, Ishmael is not referred to by name. The Sforno's reason, that Hagar was the root cause of Ishmael's conduct, could easily be applied here. Therefore, Hagar was the cause of Ishmael's expulsion. When Sarah said, ". . . the son of this bondwoman will not inherit with my son, with Isaac," she was saying that one whose conduct is caused by Hagar, will not inherit with Isaac. It is interesting that הגר, "Hagar," has the same gematria as יצחק, "Isaac," that is, 208; for Sarah was saying that the two 208s should not be together; one was expelled to be separated from the other.

ותאמר לאברהם גרש האמה הזאת ואת בנה כי לא יירש בן האמה הזאת עם בני עם יצחק (בראשית כא,י).

And she said to Abraham, cast out this bondwoman and her son, for the son of this bondwoman shall not inherit with my son, with Isaac (Genesis 21,10).

Sarah said to Abraham to cast out Hagar and Ishmael, so that Ishmael will not inherit with Isaaac. What was the inheritance to which only Isaac was entitled?

The Torah seems to imply that Torah is an inheritance, as stated, תורה צוה לנו משה מורשה קהלת יעקב (דברים לג,ד) "Moses commanded us Torah, an inheritance of the congregation of Jacob" (Deuteronomy 33,4). However, the Mishnah in Avoth seems to imply that Torah is not an inheritance, as it says, רבי יוסי אומר... והתקן עצמך ללמוד תורה שאינה ירושה לך (אבות, פרק ב, משנה יב), "Rabbi Yose said . . . and prepare yourself to learn Torah, for it is not an inheritance for you" (Avoth, Chapter 2, Mishnah 12). Is the Torah an inheritance or not?

A possible answer can be proposed by examining how the Gemara comprehends the pasuk just quoted. The Gemara Makkoth says that this pasuk is proof that there are 613 Commandments given to Moses, as stated, דרש רבי שמלאי שש מאות ושלש עשרה מצות נאמרו לו למשה... אמר רב המנונא מאי קרא תורה צוה לנו משה מורשה (דברים לג,ד) תורה בגימטריא שית מאה וחד סרי הוי (מכות כג:-כד.), "Rabbi Simlai אנכי ולא יהיה לך מפי הגבורה שמענום expounded, Six hundred and thirteen Commandments were said to Moses. . . . Rav Hamnuna said, What is the verse? [It is,] 'Moses commanded us Torah, an inheritance' (Deuteronomy 33,4). The gematria of Torah is 611. 'I am,' and 'you shall not have,' were heard from the mouth of the Mighty One" (Makkoth 23b-24a). Thus, the Gemara comprehends that the commandments are an inheritance.

The learning of Torah is also an inheritance to the Children of Israel, as the Gemara states, אמר ר' יוחנן עובד כוכבים שעוסק בתורה מיתה חייב תורה צוה לנו משה מורשה לנו מורשה ולא להם (סנהדרין נט.) "Rabbi Johanan said, an idol worshiper who is engaged in the study of Torah is worthy of capital punishment, as it says, 'Moses commanded us Torah, an inheritance,' for us it is an inheritance, not for them" (Sanhedrin 59a). This Gemara refers to being engaged in Torah study, not in the performing of commandments.

The answer is that the Torah and the commandments were given to the nation of the Children of Israel as an inheritance in general, but specifically to any one person it is not an inheritance.

The Mishnah which seems to imply that Torah is not an inheritance, refers particularly to an individual learning Torah. This learning is a very individual experience. There are a multitude of different insights which can be learned from a pasuk, or a page of Gemara, as is evident by the various rabbinical commentators. The commandments are an inheritance, as is the learning of Torah, both of which are an inheritance for the nation.

The question, what was the inheritance to which only Isaac was entitled, can now be answered. The 613 Commandments are the inheritance to which he was entitled. An intimation of this inheritance can be seen in the words that Sarah used. Although the words לא יירש, "shall not inherit," refers to Ishmael, it can apply to Isaac in distinction to Ishmael. The gematria of לא יירש, "shall not inherit," plus the gematria of בני, "my son," is 613.

$$
\begin{array}{rr}
\text{לא יירש} & 551 \\
\text{בני} & \underline{62} \\
& 613
\end{array}
$$

This gematria could be an intimation that the 613 Commandments are the inheritance to which Isaac was entitled.

ועתה השבעה לי באלקים הנה אם תשקר לי ולניני ולנכדי כחסד אשר־עשיתי עמך תעשה עמדי ועם־הארץ אשר גרתה בה (בראשית כא,כג).

And now swear to me here by G-d that you will not deal falsely with me, nor with my son, nor with my grandson; but according to the kindness that I have done with you, you shall do with me, and with the land wherein you have sojourned (Genesis 21,23).

Abimelech wanted to make a covenant with Abraham which would extend to himself, his children, his grandchildren, and the land. The combined gematria of לי, "with me," ולניני, "with my son," ולנכדי, "with my grandson," and הארץ, "the land," is 612.

לי	40
ולניני	156
ולנכדי	120
הארץ	296
	612

Thus, 612 represents the extent of the proposed covenant. Abraham and Abimelech then made a covenant, as stated, ויקח אברהם צאן ובקר ויתן לאבימלך ויכרתו שניהם ברית (בראשית כא,כז), "And Abraham took sheep and oxen, and gave them to Abimelech; and both of them made a covenant" (Genesis 21,27). The gematria of ברית, "covenant," is 612.

ברית	612

Thus, 612 represents the covenant itself. Since 612 represents both the extent of the covenant and the covenant itself, it underscores the association between the two.

ויאמר אבימלך לא ידעתי מי עשה את הדבר הזה וגם אתה לא הגדת לי וגם אנכי לא שמעתי בלתי היום (בראשית כא,כו).

And Abimelech said, "I do not know who has done this thing, and also you did not tell me, and also I did not hear of it except today" (Genesis 21,26).

Before Abraham and Abimelech concluded the covenant, Abimelech responded to Abraham's rebuke concerning a well of water; he said that he did not know who had done the thing. The gematria of את הדבר, "the thing," is 612.

את	401
הדבר	211
	612

Thus, it was את הדבר, "the thing," with a gematria of 612, that had the potential to prevent the covenant. The next pasuk mentions the covenant, ויקח אברהם צאן ובקר ויתן לאבימלך ויכרתו שניהם ברית (בראשית כא,כז), "And Abraham took sheep and oxen, and gave them to Abimelech; and both of them made a covenant" (Genesis 21,27). The gematria of ברית, "covenant,"is 612.

ברית   612

It is noteworthy that the gematrioth of את הדבר, "the thing," and ברית, "covenant," are equal, for it was the thing that had the potential to prevent the covenant.

ויאמר כי את שבע כבשת תקח מידי בעבור תהיה לי לעדה
כי חפרתי את הבאר הזאת (בראשית כא,ל).

And he said, "For these seven ewe-lambs you shall take from my hand, that they should be for me a witness, that I dug this well" (Genesis 21,30).

As witness for the well, Abraham gave to Abimelech seven ewe-lambs. The gematria of כבשת, "ewe-lambs," is 722.

כבשת   722

Since there were seven כבשת, "ewe-lambs," as a derash on the pasuk, the gematria of 722 may be multiplied by seven; the product is equal to 5054.

722
x7
―――
5054

There was a covenant between Abraham and Abimelech, but before Abraham concluded the covenant, he rebuked Abimelech for a well stolen by Abimelech's servants

(בראשית כא,כב-לב,Genesis 21,22-32); therefore, the covenant and the well are connected. Thus, 5054 represents the seven ewe-lambs set aside as witness for the well and the covenant, since the two are connected. Abimelech had made claims about both subjects, the well and the covenant. Abimelech claimed that he did not know what had occurred with the well, nor had Abraham or anyone else told him, as stated, ויאמר אבימלך לא ידעתי מי עשה את הדבר הזה וגם אתה לא הגדת לי וגם אנכי לא שמעתי בלתי היום (בראשית כא,כו), "And Abimelech said, 'I do not know who has done this thing, and also you did not tell me, and also I did not hear of it except today'" (Genesis 21,26). The gematria of לא ידעתי, "I do not know"; לא הגדת לי, "you did not tell me"; and אנכי לא שמעתי, "I did not hear," is 1940.

לא	31
ידעתי	494
לא	31
הגדת	412
לי	40
אנכי	81
לא	31
שמעתי	820
	1940

Abimelech desired that his covenant with Abraham and with the land would be for three generations, as stated, ועתה השבעה לי באלקים הנה אם תשקר לי ולניני ולנכדי כחסד אשר עשיתי עמך תעשה עמדי ועם הארץ אשר גרתה בה (בראשית כא,כג), "And now swear to me here by G-d that you will not deal falsely with me, nor with my son, nor with my grandson; but according to the kindness that I have done with you, you shall do with me, and with the land wherein you have sojourned" (Genesis 21,23). The gematria of לי, "with me," ולניני, "with my son," ולנכדי, "with my grandson," and עמדי ועם הארץ, "with me and with the land," is 852.

לי	40
ולניני	156
ולנכדי	120
עמדי	124
ועם	116
הארץ	<u>296</u>
	852

The Torah uses specific expressions which can serve as headings for the subjects of the well and the covenant. The heading for the subject of the well can be the expression, "because of the well of water," as stated, והוכח אברהם את אבימלך על אדות באר המים אשר גזלו עבדי אבימלך (בראשית כא,כה), "And Abraham reproved Abimelech because of the well of water which Abimelech's servants had violently taken" (Genesis 21,25). The gematria of על אדות באר המים, "because of the well of water," is 809.

על	100
אדות	411
באר	203
המים	<u>95</u>
	809

The heading for the subject of the covenant can be the exprssion, "and they made a covenant," as stated ויכרתו ברית בבאר שבע ויקם אבימלך ופיכל שר צבאו וישבו אל ארץ פלישתים (בראשית כא,לב), "And they made a covenant in Beer-sheba; and Abimelech rose up, and Phichol the captain of the host, and they returned to the land of the Philistines" (Genesis 21,32). The gematria of ויכרתו ברית, "and they made a covenant," is 1254.

ויכרתו	642
ברית	<u>541</u>
	1254

The sum of the gematrioth for what Abimelech claimed about each subject, plus both subject headings, is 4855.

$$
\begin{array}{r}
1940 \\
852 \\
809 \\
\underline{1254} \\
4855
\end{array}
$$

The action which Abraham took to insure the claims of Abimelech about each subject was to set the ewe-lambs by themselves, as stated, ויצב אברהם את שבע כבשת הצאן לבדהן (בראשית כא,כח), "And Abraham set seven ewe-lambs of the flock by themselves" (Genesis 21,28). The gematria of ויצב, "and he set," plus the gematria of לבדהן, "by themselves," is 199.

$$
\begin{array}{rr}
\text{ויצב} & 108 \\
\text{לבדהן} & \underline{91} \\
& 199
\end{array}
$$

When 199 is added to 4855, the sum is 5054.

$$
\begin{array}{r}
4855 \\
\underline{199} \\
5054
\end{array}
$$

Thus, 5054 represents the action which Abraham did to insure the claims of Abimelech about each subject, plus the subject headings together with what Abimelech claimed about each subject. The subjects are the well and the covenant. Recall that 5054 also represents the seven ewe-lambs set aside as witness for the well and the covenant. Since there were seven כבשת, "ewe-lambs," the gematria of 722 was multiplied by seven; the product was equal to 5054. It is fitting that the two gematrioth are equal to 5054.

ויגר אברהם בארץ פלשתים ימים רבים. ויהי אחר הדברים
האלה והאלקים נסה את אברהם ויאמר אליו אברהם
ויאמר הנני (בראשית כא,לד-כב,א).

And Abraham sojourned in the land of the Philistines for many days. And it happened after these things that G-d tested Abraham; and He said to him, "Abraham," and he said, "Here I am" (Genesis 21,34-22,1).

The intention of the test of the עקידה, Akeidah, "binding," was to demonstrate that Abraham was G-d fearing, as the pasuk says, כי עתה ידעתי כי ירא אלקים אתה וגו' (בראשית כב,יב), "for now I know that you are G-d fearing, etc." (Genesis 22,12). The אבן עזרא, Ibn Ezra, clearly defines one who is ירא אלקים, "G-d fearing," as one who observes the commandments, as stated, ולא יסור ממנה ימין ושמאל וישמר המצות אשר יעשה אותם האדם וחי בהם בשני העולמות ובענין הזה חתם ספרו כי ירא אלקים יצא את כלם לאמת (אבן עזרא קהלת ז,יח), "And he will not turn from it right or left, and he will guard the commandments which a man shall do them and live in the both worlds; and on this subject he completed his book, for he who fears G-d will come out of all of them to reach the truth" (Ibn Ezra, Ecclesiastes 7,18).

Returning to Parashath Vayyera, what caused G-d to test Abraham? It was something which transpired when Abraham was living in the land of the Philistines for ימים רבים, "many days." The gematria of ימים רבים, "many days," is 352.

ימים	100
רבים	252
	352

The very next pasuk says that it was after הדברים, "these things," that G-d tested Abraham. The gematria of הדברים, "these things," is 261.

הדברים	261

One explanation given by Rashi of הדברים, "these things," which transpired in the ימים רבים, "many days," was that the Satan made an excuse to denounce Abraham, for he did not offer a single ox or ram to G-d at the feasts he made (רש״י, בראשית כב,א, Rashi, Genesis 22,1). The not offering an ox or a ram is not a violation of any commandment, but an excuse by the Satan to cause Abraham to be tested. Assuredly, Abraham observed all the commandments before being tested. Thus, it was הדברים, "these things" (דברים, means "words" as well as "things"), the words of the Satan which transpired in the ימים רבים, "many days," which caused G-d to test if Abraham was a ירא אלקים, "G-d fearing," which the אבן עזרא, Ibn Ezra, clearly defines as one who observes the Commandments.

The Gemara Makkoth says that there is a total of 613 Mitzvoth given to Moses, as stated, דרש רבי שמלאי שש מאות ושלש עשרה מצות נאמרו לו למשה שלש מאות וששים וחמש לאוין כמנין ימות החמה ומאתים וארבעים ושמונה עשה כנגד איבריו של אדם (מכות כג:), "Rabbi Simlai expounded, Six hundred and thirteen Commandments were said to Moses. Three hundred and sixty-five negative Commandments corresponding to the number of days in a solar year, and two hundred and forty-eight positive Commandments corresponding to the number of limbs of a man" (Makkoth 23b). When the gematria of ימים רבים, "many days," is added to the gematria of הדברים, "these things," the sum is 613.

ימים רבים	352
הדברים	261
	613

Thus, this gematria corroborates that it was הדברים, "these things," which transpired in the ימים רבים, "many days," which caused G-d to test if Abraham was a ירא אלקים, "G-d fearing," which the אבן עזרא, Ibn Ezra, clearly defines as one who observes the commandments, whose total is 613.

ויהי אחר הדברים האלה והאלקים נסה את־אברהם ויאמר
אליו אברהם ויאמר הנני (בראשית כב,א).

And it came to pass after these things, that G-d
tested Abraham, and said to him, "Abraham,"
and he said, "Here I am" (Genesis 22,1).

The Torah says that G-d tested Abraham, to which
Abraham responded, "Here I am." The gematria of נסה,
"tested," is 115.

נסה   115

The gematria of הנני, "here I am," is 115.

הנני   115

Rashi states that the expression "Here I am," is a term
of preparedness (רש״י, בראשית כב,א, Rashi, Genesis 22,1). The
response was matched to the challenge of G-d's test. Since,
הנני, "here I am," was Abraham's response of preparedness
which was adequate to when G-d נסה, "tested," it is very
fitting that both terms have the same gematria.

ויאמר קח נא את בנך את יחידך אשר אהבת את יצחק
ולך־לך אל־ארץ המריה והעלהו שם לעלה על אחד ההרים
אשר אמר אליך (בראשית כב,ב).

And He said, "Take now your son, your only
son, whom you love, Isaac, and go for yourself
to the land of the Moriah; and offer him there
for a burnt offering on one of the mountains
which I will tell you" (Genesis 22,2).

G-d told Abraham to take his son Isaac to the land of
המריה, "the Moriah," and to offer him as a burnt offering on
one of ההרים, "the mountains," which he would be told. The
gematria of המריה, "the Moriah," is 260.

המריה   260

The gematria of ההרים, "the mountains," is 260.

260   ההרים

According to the Ramban only the mountain on which the Temple stood is called Moriah, as he writes, וההר לבדו הוא נקרא מוריה ואברהם ידע את הארץ ולא ידע את ההר ולכן אמר לו שילך אל ארץ המוריה והוא יראנו אחד ההרים ששם שנקרא ככה (רמב"ן, בראשית כב,ב), "And only the mountain was called Moriah, and Abraham knew the land, but did not know the mountain. Therefore, He told him go to the land of Moriah, and He would designate which of the mountains which was so called" (Ramban, Genesis 2,22). Thus, when the Torah states the Moriah, it is referring to the one of the mountains mentioned later in the same pasuk. Since, המריה, "the Moriah," and ההרים, "the mountains," refer to the same place, it is appropriate that their gematrioth should be the same.

ויבאו אל המקום אשר אמר לו האלקים ויבן שם אברהם את המזבח ויערך את העצים ויעקד את יצחק בנו וישם אתו על המזבח ממעל לעצים (בראשית כב,ט).
And they came to the place of which G-d had told him; and Abraham built the altar there and he laid the wood in order, and bound Isaac his son and he placed him on the altar, upon the wood (Genesis 22,9).

Isaac, who is clearly designated as the son of Abraham, was the one who was bound upon the altar; the gematria of יצחק, "Isaac," is 208.

208   יצחק

The Torah narrates the blessing which Abraham received because of his obedience at the binding and intended sacrifice of Isaac, as stated, כי ברך אברכך והרבה ארבה את זרעך ככוכבי השמים וכחול אשר על שפת הים וירש זרעך את שער איביו (בראשית

(כב,יז), "For I will greatly bless you and I will exceedingly multiply your seed as the stars of the heaven and as the sand which is upon the seashore, and your seed shall possess the gate of his enemies" (Genesis 22,17). The gematria of ארבה, "will multiply," is 208.

ארבה   208

Rashi comments on the expression והרבה ארבה, "and I will exceedingly multiply," that one of the words is for the father and one of the words is for the son (רש״י, בראשית כב,יז, Rashi, Genesis 22,17). Thus, the first word refers to Abraham, and the second word, ארבה, "multiply," refers to יצחק, "Isaac." Since ארבה, "multiply," refers to יצחק, "Isaac," it is appropriate that the gematrioth of these words are identical.

ויאמר אל תשלח ידך אל הנער ואל תעש לו מאומה כי עתה ידעתי כי ירא אלקים אתה ולא חשכת את בנך את יחידך ממני (בראשית כב,יב).

And he said, "Stretch not your hand upon the lad, neither do anything to him, for now I know that you are G-d fearing, and you have not withheld your son, your only son, from Me" (Genesis 22, 12).

When the angel stopped Abraham from sacrificing his son, he called Abraham G-d-fearing. The gematria of ירא, "fearing," is 211.

ירא   211

Thus, it is through Abraham's obedience at the binding and intended sacrifice of Isaac that he proved that he was G-d fearing. When the angel called to Abraham a second time, he referred to the binding and intended sacrifice of Isaac as הדבר, "the thing," as stated, ויאמר בי נשבעתי נאם הי כי Isaac יען אשר עשית את הדבר הזה ולא חשכת את בנך את יחידך (בראשית

(כב,טז), "And he said, 'By myself I have sworn,' says G-d, 'that because you have done this thing, and have not withheld your son, your only son'" (Genesis 22,16). The gematria of הדבר, "the thing," is 211.

$$\text{הדבר} \qquad 211$$

It is quite suitable that ירא, "fearing," and הדבר, "the thing," have the same gematria, for the former refers to what the latter proved.

וישב אברהם אל נעריו ויקמו וילכו יחדו אל־באר שבע וישב אברהם בבאר שבע (בראשית כב,יט).

And Abraham returned to his young men, and they rose up and they went together to Beer-sheba; and Abraham dwelt in Beer-sheba (Genesis 22,19).

After the episode of the binding and intended sacrifice of Isaac, the Torah tells that Abraham lived in Beer-sheba. The gematria of בבאר שבע, "in Beer-sheba," is 577.

$$
\begin{array}{ll}
\text{בבאר} & 205 \\
\text{שבע} & \underline{372} \\
& 577
\end{array}
$$

Although Beer-sheba was associated with the Philistines in the time of Abraham, it was still part of the land of Israel and was later to be in the portion of the tribe of Simeon התורה והמצוה, מאת רבי מאיר ליבוש מלבי״ם, בראשית כב,יט) The, Torah and the Mitzvah by Rabbi Meir Lebush Malbim, Genesis 22,19). Even though the Gemara Yoma says that Abraham observed the entire Torah (יומא כח:, Yoma 28b), the Ramban limits this observance to the time that Abraham was in the land of Israel. The Ramban states, ונראה אלי מדעת רבותינו שלמד א״א התורה כלה ברוח הקודש ועסק בה ובטעמי מצוותיה וסודותיה ושמר אותה כלה כמי שאינו מצווה ועושה ושמירתו אותה היה בארץ בלבד וכו׳ (רמב״ן, בראשית כו,ה), "And it appears to me from the knowledge of our Rabbis, that Abraham, our father, learned the entire Torah by divine inspiration, and was busy with it and the reasons for its commandments and its secrets; and he observed it entirely as one who is not commanded and does, and his observance was in the land alone etc." (Ramban, Genesis 26,5).

It is simple to deduce that since Beer-sheba is part of the land of Israel, Abraham observed the 613 Commandments while living in Beer-sheba. This observance can be corroborated by a gematria. Immediately after saying that Abraham lived in Beer-sheba, the Torah lists the genealogies which include the eight persons whom Milcah bore, as stated, ובתואל ילד את רבקה שמנה אלה ילדה מלכה לנחור אחי אברהם (בראשית כב,כג), "And Bethuel begot Rebekah; these eight bore Milcah to Nahor, Abraham's brother" (Genesis 22,23). The gematria of אלה, "these," is 36.

אלה   36

Rashi says that all these genealogies were only recorded for the pasuk which culminates with the birth of Rebekah (רש"י, בראשית כב,כג, Rashi, Genesis 22,23). The word אלה, "these," is a demonstrative term specifying the eight to whom reference is being made. Since all the genealogies are only listed for the pasuk where אלה, "these," is the demonstrative term, the specification of what Abraham was told in Beer-sheba is captured by the word אלה, "these." Abraham was told with the word אלה, "these," about the birth of Rebekah who would continue in the observance of the commandments, and be a matriarch for the Children of Israel who are obligated to observe the 613 Commandments. When the gematria of בבאר שבע, "in Beer-sheba," is added to the gematria of אלה, "these," the total is 613.

577
36

613

Inasmuch as the gematria of בבאר שבע, "in Beer-sheba," plus the gematria of אלה, "these," [which delineates the specification of what Abraham was told in Beer-sheba] is equal to 613, the number of commandments which Abraham observed in the land of Israel, this gematria corroborates that Abraham observed the 613 Commandments while living in Beer-sheba.

Parashath Chayye Sarah   פרשת חיי שרה

ויהיו חיי שרה מאה שנה ועשרים שנה ושבע שנים שני חיי
שרה (בראשית כג,א)

And the life of Sarah was a hundred years and twenty years and seven years; these were the years of Sarah's life (Genesis 23,1).

The Torah refers to the life of Sarah with the expression, "and the life of Sarah was." The gematria of ויהיו חיי שרה, "and the life of Sarah was," is 570.

ויהיו	37
חיי	28
שרה	505
	570

The deaths of Abraham and Sarah are both recorded in Parashath Chayye Sarah. Notwithstanding, slightly different expressions are used with reference to these deaths. The Keli Yakar explains why this difference in expressions exists. One reason is that the life of Abraham was terminated early, which was not the case for Sarah. The Torah implies the early termination of Abraham's life by the expression אשר חי, "which he lived," (כלי יקר, בראשית כג,א, Keli Yakar, Genesis 23,1). The Torah says, ואלה ימי שני־חיי אברהם אשר חי מאת שנה ושבעים שנה וחמש שנים (בראשית כה,ז), "And these are the days of the years of Abraham's life which he lived, a hundred year, and seventy years, and five years" (Genesis 25,7). The gematria of אשר חי, "which he lived," is 519.

אשר	501
חי	18
	519

Rashi comments on this pasuk, that Abraham's life when was, "בן ק׳ כבן ע׳ ובן ע׳ כבן ה׳ בלא חטא (רש״י, בראשית כה,ז)

he was one hundred years old he was like seventy years old, and when he was seventy years old, he was like five years old, without sin" (Rashi, Genesis 25,7). The gematria of בלא חטא, "without sin," is 51.

בלא	33
חטא	18
	51

When the gematria of the expression which the Torah uses to refer to the life of Abraham is added to the gematria of the Rashi's comment about Abraham's life, the total is 570.

519
51
570

The expression with which the Torah refers to the life of Sarah has a gematria of 570; the expression with which the Torah refers to the life of Abraham plus Rashi's comment in reference to Abraham life also has a gematria of 570. This gematria gives substance to Rashi's comment at the beginning of the sidrah that Sarah was without sin, as well as Rashi's comment at the end of the sidrah that Abraham was without sin (רש״י, בראשית כג,א וכה,ז, Rashi, Genesis 23,1 and 25,7). The reason why the gematria of the expression which refers to Abraham's life is added to the gematria of Rashi's comment about Abraham's life, is that the expression which refers to Abraham's life indicates an incomplete life, one terminated prematurely, as the Keli Yakar states.

ויהיו חיי שרה מאה שנה ועשרים שנה ושבע שנים שני חיי
שרה (בראשית כג,א)

And the life of Sarah was a hundred years and twenty years and seven years; [these were] the years of Sarah's life (Genesis 23,1).

After saying how long Sarah lived, the Torah again refers to the years of Sarah's life. The gematria of שני חיי שרה, "the years of Sarah's life," is 893.

שני	360
חיי	28
שרה	505
	893

The significance of Sarah's life is indicated by the number 893. But after Hagar died the Torah does not mention how long she lived. Hagar is referred to as שפחת שרה, "Sarah's handmaid," as stated, ואלה תלדת ישמעאל בן אברהם, "And אשר ילדה הגר המצרית שפחת שרה לאברהם (בראשית כה,יב) these are the generations of Ishmael, Abraham's son, whom Hagar the Egyptian, Sarah's handmaid, bore to Abraham" (Genesis 25,12). The gematria of שפחת שרה, "Sarah's handmaid," is 1293.

שפחת	788
שרה	505
	1293

The significance of Hagar's life is indicated by the number 1293. Note that Hagar was also called Keturah (רש"י, בראשית כה,א, Rashi, Genesis 25,1), but that was only when she was no longer in the role of "Sarah's handmaid." The difference in gematrioth between the expressions שני חיי שרה, "these were the years of Sarah's life," and שפחת שרה, "Sarah's handmaid," is 400.

1293
-893
400

The difference between the significance of the lives of Sarah and Hagar is 400 in gematria. A major difference between Sarah and Hagar was that Sarah was considered among the matriarchs; Hagar was not. The Gemara Horayoth individualizes the matriarchs in the context of explaining a pasuk from שירת דבורה as the Gemara says, תבורך מנשים יעל אשת חבר הקיני מנשים באהל תבורך, מאן נינהו נשים באהל שרה רבקה רחל ולאה (הוריות י:), "'Blessed above women is Jael, wife of Heber the Kenite, above women in the tent she should be blessed.' Who are these women in the tent? Sarah, Rebekah, Rachel, and Leah" (Horayoth 10b). The gematria of נשים, "matriarchs," is 400.

נשים   400

Hagar had the status of a concubine, not a matriarch (רש״י, בראשית כה,ו, Rashi, Genesis 25,6). Accordingly, the gematria of a major difference between Sarah and Hagar is equal to the gematria of the difference between the significance of the lives of Sarah and Hagar.

ואברהם זקן בא בימים וה׳ ברך את אברהם בכל (בראשית כד,א).

And Abraham was old, advanced in age; and G-d had blessed Abraham with everything (Genesis 24,1).

When the Torah records that G-d had blessed Abraham with everything, Rashi comments that בכל עולה בגמטריא בן, "the sum of the numerical value of the word בכל, 'with everything,' equals the gematria of בן, 'son,'" (רש״י, בראשית כד,א, Rashi, Genesis 24,1). It can be reasoned that he who is blessed with a son is blessed with everything, or that he lacks nothing. The Gemara Niddah describes a phenomenon at the occurrence of the birth of a son, כיון שבא זכר בעולם בא שלום בעולם (נדה לא:), "When a male comes into the world peace comes into the world" (Niddah 31b). The gematria of זכר, "male," plus the gematria of שלום, "peace," is 603.

זכר   227

שלום   <u>376</u>

603

Based on this Rashi and Gemara, it can be deduced that he who is blessed with a son lacks nothing, and the birth of a son brings peace to the world. Thus, lacking nothing can be associated with the gematria of 603. The Torah refers to the land of Israel, ארץ אשר לא במסכנת תאכל־בה לחם לא־תחסר כל "A land בה ארץ אשר אבניה ברזל ומהרריה תחצב נחשת (דברים ח,ט) wherein you shall eat bread without scarceness, you shall not lack anything in it; a land whose stones are iron, and out of whose hills you may dig copper" (Deuteronomy 8,9). The gematria of לא במסכנת, "without scarceness," is 603.

לא   31

במסכנת   <u>572</u>

603

The Gemara Berakoth quotes the beginning of this pasuk as proof that the Land of Israel lacks nothing (ברכות לו:, Berakoth 36b). This lacking nothing is associated with the gematria of 603. Thus, the gematria of 603 implies here that he who is blessed with a son, and the land of Israel, are lacking nothing.

ויאמר ברוך ה׳ אלקי אדני אברהם אשר לא עזב חסדו

ואמתו מעם אדני אנכי בדרך נחני ה׳ בית אחי אדני

(בראשית כד,כז).

And he said, Blessed be G-d, the G-d of my master Abraham, Who did not forsake His kindness and truth from my master; I am on the way, G-d has led me to the house of the brother of my master (Genesis 24,27).

After Eliezer met Rebekah, he blessed G-d, initiating with the words, ברוך ה׳ אלקי אדני אברהם, "Blessed be G-d, the

G-d of my master Abraham." The gematria of ברוך ה׳ אלקי אדני, "Blessed be G-d, the G-d of my master," is 365.

ברוך ה׳	254
אלקי אדני	<u>111</u>
	365

The gematria of אברהם, "Abraham," is 248.

אברהם	248

The total of these two gematrioth is 613.

365
<u>248</u>
613

The Gemara Makkoth says that there is a total of 613 Mitzvoth given to Moses, as stated, דרש רבי שמלאי שש מאות ושלש עשרה מצות נאמרו לו למשה שלש מאות וששים וחמש לאוין כמנין ימות החמה ומאתים וארבעים ושמונה עשה כנגד איבריו של אדם (מכות כג:), "Rabbi Simlai expounded, six hundred thirteen Commandments were said to Moses. Three hundred and sixty-five negative Commandments corresponding to the number of days in a solar year, and two hundred and forty-eight positive Commandments corresponding to the number of limbs of a man" (Makkoth 23b). The association of the gematria of the number of positive commandments and the gematria of the number of the negative commandments to the blessing of Eliezer has a special message.

From the blessing of Eliezer it is learned that one should not begin a blessing without mentioning G-d's Kingship, as stated, שאין פותחין בברוך באזכרת השם בלא מלכות לפי שאין לשנות ממטבע הפסוק כלשון שהורה אליעזר עבד אברהם, ברוך ה׳ אלקי אדוני אברהם (רבינו יהודה ב״ר קלונימוס ב״ר מאיר בספר הרוקח הגדול חברו הרב אליעזר מגרמיזא, סימן שסג), "One should not begin with the word 'Blessed,' mentioning G-d's name, without His Kingship. For one should not change from the formula of the pasuk, as the language taught by Eliezer, the servant of Abraham, 'Blessed be the G-d of my master Abraham'" (Rabbeinu Yehudah ben Rav Kalonymos ben Rav Meir in Book of Harokeach Hagadol written by Rabbi Eliezer Migermaiza, Siman 363). The Gemara Berakoth has a somewhat similar assertion which is explained more fully by Tosafoth (תוספות, ברכות מ:, ד"ה אמר אביי כוותיה דרב מסתברא, Tosafoth, Berakoth 40b, header words: Abaye said, the opinion of Rav is more reasonable).

Mentioning G-d's Kingship is an indispensable part of a blessing. But there is no king without a nation, as stated, כי אין מלך בלא עם (כד הקמח מאת רבינו בחיי, דרשת ראש השנה (ב), ד"ה ועוד במצוה זו רמז למלכותו יתברך), "For there can be no king without a nation" (Kad Hakemach by Rabbeinu Bechaya, Derashah for Rosh Hashanah (2), header words: And more about this mitzvah which hints to His Blessed Kingdom). There is no nation except Israel, as stated, ואין עם אלא ישראל, "And שנא' עם זו יצרתי לי תהלתי יספרו (מדרש משלי, פרק יד, אות ב) there is no nation except Israel as it says 'This nation I have formed for Myself; My acclaim they should tell'" (Midrash Mishle, Chapter 14, Letter 2). But even Israel are only considered G-d's nation when they observed His 613 Commandments. The Metsudath David defines the designation of לא עמי, "not My nation," as when the Bnei Yisroel do not fear G-d's words to do them (מצודת דוד, הושע א,ט, Metsudath David, Hosea 1,9). Both the Ibn Ezra and the Radak define the designation of לא עמי, "not My nation," as when the Bnei Yisroel have done evil deeds (אבן עזרא ורד"ק, הושע ב,א, Ibn Ezra and Radak, Hosea 2,1). The Bnei Yisroel not fearing G-d's words to heed them, or the Bnei Yisroel doing evil deeds, can easily be understood as when they do not observe the 613 Commandments.

In summary, one should not begin a blessing without mentioning G-d's Kingship; there is no king without a nation;

there is no nation except Bnei Yisroel; and even the Bnei Yisroel are only considered G-d's nation when they observe His 613 Commandments. It follows that the special message is: when the Bnei Yisroel bless G-d, it is important that they refrain from violating the 365 negative Commandments and that they perform the 248 positive Commandments. The association of the gematria of the number of positive commandments and the gematria of the number of the negative commandments to the blessing of Eliezer indicates this special message.

Parashath Toledoth   פרשת תולדת

וישב יצחק בגרר (בראשית כו,ו)

And Isaac dwelt in Gerar (Genesis 26,6).

The Torah says that Isaac dwelt in Gerar. The gematria of יצחק בגרר, "Issac in Gerar," is 613.

יצחק	208
בגרר	405
	613

On the pasuk before this one, the Ramban says that the patriarchs observed the Torah only in the Land of Israel, as he writes about Abrham's observance of the Torah and Jacob's marring two sisters, ושמר אותה כלה כמי שאינו מצווה ועושה ושמירתו אותה היה בארץ לבד ויעקב בחוץ לארץ בלבד נשא שתי אחיות (רמב"ן, בראשית כו,ה), "And he [Abraham] kept it [the Torah] in its entirety as one who is not commanded, and does. And his keeping it was only in the land [of Israel]. And Jacob married two sisters only outside the land [of Israel]" (Ramban, Genesis 26,5). The dwelling of Isaac in Gerar was in response to G-d's command not to leave the Land of Israel (בראשית כו,ב-ג, Genesis 26,2-3). Therefore, even when Isaac was living in Gerar, he was dwelling where he observed the Torah, that is, the 613 Commandments. Thus, it is very fitting that יצחק בגרר, "Issac in Gerar," should have a gematria of 613, for Issac observed the 613 Commandments in Gerar.

ויריבו רעי גרר עם רעי יצחק לאמר לנו המים ויקר שם הבאר עשק כי התעשקו עמו (בראשית כו,כ).

And the herdsmen of Gerar strove with the herdsmen of Isaac, saying: "The water is ours." And he called the name of the well "Esek," because they contended with him (Genesis 26,20).

ויהי ביום ההוא ויבאו עבדי יצחק ויגדו לו על־אדות הבאר
אשר חפרו ויאמרו לו מצאנו מים (בראשית כו,לב).
And it came to pass on that same day, that Isaac's servants came and told him concerning the well that they had dug, and said to him: "We have found water" (Genesis 26,32).

The Torah does not write as extensively about Issac as it does about Abraham or Jacob. Although the wells which Isaac dug have deep spiritual meaning, the digging of some wells seems to be recorded as his primary accomplishment. Twice the word הבאר, "the well," is used in this recording. Note that according to the Ramban the digging of the wells alludes to the future conflict between the Bnei Yisroel and the Philistines, as he writes, והבאר הזאת להם תרמז על משכן שילה, ופלשתים סתמוהו בהלקח הארון וחזר וחפרו בו, כי כן השיבו הארון עם הדורון לאלקים (רמב״ן, בראשית כו,לג), "This well hints to the Tabernacle of Shiloh, and the Philistines stopped it up [hints to] with taking the Ark. And the re-digging it [by Isaac hints to], that the Ark was returned with a present to G-d" (Ramban, Genesis 26,33). The gematria of הבאר, "the well," is 208.

הבאר   208

The gematria of יצחק, "Isaac," is also 208.

יצחק   208

It seems fitting that Isaac's primary accomplishment should be described with the word הבאר, "the well," since its gematria is equal to the gematria of יצחק, "Isaac."

וירא אליו ה׳ בלילה ההוא ויאמר אנכי אלקי אברהם אביך
אל תירא כי אתך אנכי וברכתיך והרביתי את זרעך בעבור
אברהם עבדי (בראשית כו,כד).
And G-d appeared to him on that same night and said, "I am the G-d of Abraham your father. Fear not, for I am with with you, and will bless you and multiply your seed for the sake of Abraham, My servant" (Genesis 26,24).

Hashem appeared to Isaac, and said that He was with him, because of Abraham, עבדי, "my servant." The gematria of עבדי, "my servant," is 86.

עבדי   86

After Hashem appeared to Isaac, Abimelech with Ahuzzath and Phichol came to Isaac to make a covenant, because they saw that Hashem was with Isaac in the same way Hashem was with Abraham (רש״י, בראשית כו,כח, Rashi, Genesis 26,28). How did Abimelech envision Hashem? The Torah relates what Abimelech said when he approached Abraham to make a covenant, ויהי בעת ההוא ויאמר אבימלך ופיכל שר צבאו אל אברהם לאמר אלקים עמך בכל אשר אתה עשה (בראשית כא,כב) "And it came to pass at that time, that Abimelech and Phichol the captain of the host spoke to Abraham saying, G-d is with you in all that you do" (Genesis 21,22). The gematria of אלקים, "G-d," is 86.

אלקים   86

Thus, 86 represents the way Abimelech envisioned that Hashem was with Abraham, and the same number represents how Hashem described Abraham to Isaac. Therefore, the words אלקים, "G-d," and עבדי, "My servant," are connected contextually and numerically.

ויאמר הכי קרא שמו יעקב ויעקבני זה פעמים את־בכרתי לקח והנה עתה לקח ברכתי ויאמר הלא־אצלת לי ברכה (בראשית כז,לו).

And he said, "Is he not rightly called Jacob? For he has supplanted me these two times: He took away my birthright, and behold now he has taken away my blessing." And he said, "Have you not reserved a blessing for me?" (Genesis 27,36).

When Esau told Isaac that Jacob had outmaneuvered him twice, he used the word ויעקבני, "supplanted." The gematria of ויעקבני, "supplanted," is 248.

248   ויעקבני

Here the number 248 represents the two times that Jacob outmaneuvered Esau. When Isaac wanted to bless Esau, he intended to give him the blessings of Abraham. The Ramban says Isaac thought that Esau deserved these because he was the first-born, as he writes, היה בדעתו לברך אותו שיזכה הוא בברכת אברהם לנחול את הארץ ולהיות הוא בעל הברית לאלקים (רמב״ן, בראשית כז,ד) כי הוא הבכור, "It was his intent to bless him [Esau] that he should merit the blessing of Abraham, to inherit the land and to become the one with whom G-d would make the covenant, since he was the first-born" (Ramban, Genesis 27,4). The gematria of אברהם, "Abraham," is 248.

248   אברהם

Here the number 248 represents the blessings of Abraham which Isaac thought were to be transmitted by Isaac to Esau, since Isaac thought Esau was the first-born. Abraham was also the source of the priesthood. The priesthood was taken from Shem and given to Abraham forever (נדרים לב:, Nedarim 32b). Before the sin of the golden calf, the priesthood went to the first-born, and the reason Jacob bought the first-born right from Esau was in order to do the service of the priesthood (רש״י, בראשית כה,לא, Rashi, Genesis 25,31). Thus, the right of the first-born and the service of the priesthood were both from Abraham. The two times Jacob had outmaneuvered Esau were when Jacob bought the birthright from Esau, and when Isaac gave the blessings he meant for Esau to Jacob.

Since Jacob was the brother who deserved the blessings of Abraham, therefore he had to outmaneuver his brother Esau, and thus Jacob received the two factors entitling him to receive the blessings of Abraham. Hence, it is very appropriate that אברהם, "Abraham," and ויעקבני, "sup-planted," should have the identical gematria.

> ויֵרא עשו כי־ברך יצחק את־יעקב ושלח אתו פדנה ארם
> לקחת לו משם אשה בברכו אתו ויצו עליו לאמר לא תקח
> אשה מבנות כנען (בראשית כח,ו).

And Esau saw that Isaac had blessed Jacob, and sent him to Paddan-aram to take for himself a wife from there; as he blessed him he com-manded him saying, "Do not take a wife from the daughters of Canaan" (Genesis 28,6).

Esau saw that Isaac had sent Jacob פדנה ארם, "to Paddan-aram." The gematria of פדנה ארם, "to Paddan-aram," is 380.

פדנה	139
ארם	241
	380

Esau also saw that Isaac had sent Jacob to take a wife משם, "from there". The gematria of משם, "from there," is 380.

משם	380

Since פדנה ארם, "to Paddan-aram," and משם, "from there," refer to the same place, it is fitting that both words have the same gematria.

Parashath Vayyetze   פרשת ויצא

ויצא יעקב מבאר שבע וילך חרנה (בראשית כח,א).
And Jacob went out from Beer-sheba, and he
went to Haran (Genesis 28,10).

The Torah uses the word ויצא, "and he went out," to record Jacob's departure from Beer-sheba. The gematria of ויצא, "and he went out," is 107.

ויצא   107

The Keli Yakar offers various explanations as to why the word ויצא, "and he went out," is needed, but the last one is of particular interest. According to this last explanation, the word וילך, "and he went," implies leaving but intending to return or to maintain ties; the word ויצא, "and he went out," implies leaving with no intent to return or to maintain ties (כלי יקר, בראשית כח,י, Keli Yakar, Genesis 28,10). Thus, 107, the gematria of ויצא, "and he went out," implies leaving and breaking ties. Later in the sidrah, Laban pursues Jacob and overtakes with him at the mountain of Gilead (Genesis 31,25). Before Laban leaves Jacob, stones are gathered to form a pile, to which Jacob and Laban give different names, as stated, ויקרא לו לבן יגר שהדותא ויעקב קרא לו גלעד (בראשית לא,מז), "And Laban called it Jegar-sahadutha; and Jacob called it Galed" (Genesis 31,47). The gematria of גלעד, "Galed," is 107.

גלעד   107

Why did the Torah find it necessary to record what Jacob named the gathered stones, after it was recorded what Laban called them? It should be pointed out that in Hebrew Galed has the same letters as Gilead. Therefore, Jacob continued to call the place by the letters of the original name, despite the name Laban gave it. The gematria of גלעד, "Galed," is the same as the gematria as ויצא, "and he went out"; they both have a similar meaning. According to the Keli Yakar "and he went out," implies leaving and breaking ties. Jacob wanted to leave and break ties with Laban; thus, despite the name Laban gave it, he called the place "Galed," which has the same gematria as "and he went out."

ויאמר יעקב אל לבן את הבה כי אשתי כי מלאו ימי ואבואה אליה (בראשית כט,כא).

And Jacob said to Laban: "Give my wife for my days are fulfilled and I will go unto her" (Genesis 29,21).

After Jacob had worked seven years for Rachel, he asked Lavan, הבה, "give," my wife. The gematria of הבה, "give," is 12.

הבה 12

Rashi comments that Jacob spoke this way owing to his desire to establish twelve tribes (רש״י, בראשית כט,כא, Rashi, Genesis 29,31). Thus, it is fitting that the word הבה, "give," is used to depict the 12 tribes.

ותרא רחל כי לא ילדה ליעקב ותקנא רחל באחתה ותאמר אל־יעקב הבה לי בנים ואם אין מתה אנכי (בראשית ל,א).

And when Rachel saw that she did not bear children to Jacob, Rachel envied her sister; and she said to Jacob, "Give me children, and if not I am dead" (Genesis 30,1).

Rashi says that Rachel was envious of Leah's good deeds, as stated, קנאה במעשים הטובים אמרה אלולי שצדקה ממני לא זכתה לבנים (רש״י, בראשית ל,א), "She was envious of her good deeds. She said, 'If she were not more righteous than I, she would not have merited children'" (Rashi, Genesis 30,1). The gematria of קנאה, "she was envious," is 156.

קנאה 156

The envy that Rachel experienced, which she attributed to her lack of good deeds, can explain the disgrace she felt before she gave birth to Joseph. Once Joseph was born, this envy and disgrace ceased to exist, as stated, ותהר ותלד בן ותאמר אסף אלקים את חרפתי. ותקרא את־שמו יוסף לאמר יסף ה׳ לי בן אחר (בראשית ל,כג-כד), "And she conceived and bore a son, and she said, G-d has removed my reproach. And she called his name Joseph saying, 'May G-d add to me another son'" (Genesis 30,23-24). The gematria of יוסף, "Joseph," is 156.

יוסף 156

Since it was the birth of Joseph that removed Rachel's envy of of Leah, it is very fitting that קנאה, "she was envious," and יוסף, "Joseph," should have the same gematria.

ויעקב הלך לדרכו ויפגעו בו מלאכי אלקים (בראשית לב,ב)
And Jacob went on his way, and angels of G-d met him (Genesis 32,2).

After Jacob left Laban, he was met by angels. The gematria of ויעקב הלך ויפגעו בו מלאכי אלקים, "And Jacob went and angels of G-d met him," is 613.

ויעקב הלך	243
ויפגעו בו	183
מלאכי אלקים	187
	613

The word לדרכו, "on his way," has been omitted from the calculation; a plausible explanation for this omission can be based on the Ibn Ezra. The purpose of these angels was לעזרו בדרך, "to help him on the way" (אבן עזרא, בראשית לב,ב, Ibn Ezra, Genesis 32,2). Thus, the pasuk is proposing two thoughts; when Jacob went he met angels, and the purpose of these angels was to help him on his way. The latter of these two thoughts is associated with the word לדרכו "on his way." The former of these two thoughts can be associated with the rest of the pasuk. Since the word לדרכו, "on his way," conveys the purpose of the angels' help, it is excluded from the calculation. The Tifereth Zion says that Jacob merited to meet these angels because he observed the 613 Commandments in Laban's house, as stated, דכל הכבוד שהי׳ מגיע ליעקב הוא מחמת שכבש ליצרו גם בזמן היותו בבית לבן דשם מקום הטומאה שע״כ הי׳ מתפאר בזה עם לבן גרתי ותרי״ג מצות שמרתי. ולפי גודל הניצוח כן מגיע לו הכבוד (תפארת ציון, מאת רב יצחק זאב יאדלער, בראשית רבה, ויצא, פרשה ע״ד, אות טו), "All the honor that Jacob deserved was due to his overcoming temptation, even during the time of his stay in the house of Laban, which was the place of ritual defilement. Therefore, he was proud of this fact, that he dwelt with Laban and still observed the 613 Commandments. According to the greatness of one's victory he deserves honor" (Tifereth Zion by Rabbi Yitzchak Zev Yadler, Bereshith Rabbah, Vayyetze, Parasha 74, Letter 15).

It follows that when Jacob left he met angels, whom he merited to meet because he had observed the 613 Commandments in Laban's house. The connection of this merit to the 613 Commandments is reinforced by the fact that the gematria of the words which relate Jacob's meeting the angels is 613.

Parashath Vayyishlach · פרשת וישלח

ויאמר לו אלקים שמך יעקב לא יקרא שמך עוד יעקב כי
אם ישראל יהיה שמך ויקרא את שמו ישראל. ויאמר לו
אלקים אני אל שדי פרה ורבה גוי וקהל גוים יהיה ממך
ומלכים מחלציך יצאו (בראשית לה,י-יא)

And G-d said to him, "Your name is Jacob; your name should not be called Jacob any more, but Israel shall be your name"; and He cal ed his name Israel. And G-d said to him, "I am G-d All Sufficient, be fruitful and multiply; a nation and a company of nations shall be of you, and kings shall go forth from your loins" (Genesis 35, 10-11).

When G-d gave Jacob the name Israel, He also told him to be fruitful and multiply. The gematria of כי אם ישראל ישראל יהיה שמך, "but Israel shall be your name," is 1002.

כי	30
אם	41
ישראל	541
יהיה	30
שמך	360
	1002

The gematria of פרה ורבה, "be fruitful and multiply," is 498.

פרה	285
ורבה	213
	498

The sum of these two gematrioth is 1500.

1002
498
1500

Thus, 1500 represents Hashem's giving Jacob the name Israel, and Hashem's telling him to be fruitful and multiply.

Rashi explains the difference in the characteristics of the names Jacob and Israel, לא יקרא שמך עוד יעקב. לשון אדם הבא "Your name במארב ועקבה אלא לשון שר ונגיד (רש״י, בראשית לה,י) should not be called Jacob any more. That expresses a man who comes with ambuscade and supplanting, but your name should be an expression of a prince and a governor," (Rashi, Genesis 35,10). The gematria of במארב ועקבה, "with ambuscade and supplanting," is 428.

במארב	245
ועקבה	183
	428

The gematria of שר ונגיד, "a prince and a governor," is 573.

שר	500
ונגיד	73
	573

The Gemara Berakoth says that the name Jacob was not removed, but that it became טפל, "subsidiary," while the name Israel became עיקר, "principal," as stated, לא שיעקר יעקב "Not that the ממקומו אלא ישראל עיקר ויעקב טפל לו וכו׳ (ברכות יג.) name Jacob is uprooted from its place, but the name Israel is principal, and the name Jacob is subsidiary" (Berakoth 13a). The gematria of עיקר, "principal," is 380.

עיקר	380

The gematria of טפל, "subsidiary," is 119.

טפל	119

Hence Jacob retained both names, but one is principal and the other is subsidiary. When the gematrioth of the two characteristics are added to the respective gematrioth of עיקר, "principal," and טפל, "subsidiary," the sum is 1500.

במארב	245
ועקבה	183
טפל	119
	547

שר	500
ונגיד	73
עיקר	380
	953

	547
	953
	1500

Thus, 1500 represents the sum of the characteristics of each name plus its quality of being either principal or subsidiary.

Previously, it has been demonstrated that 1500 represents Hashem's giving Jacob the name Israel, plus Hashem telling him to be fruitful and multiply. Now it has been demonstrated that 1500 also represents the sum of the characteristics of each name plus its quality of being either principal or subsidiary. The equality of these gematrioth teaches a lesson. The Ibn Ezra says that to be fruitful and multiply is a blessing (אבן עזרא, בראשית לה,יא, Ibn Ezra, Genesis 35,11); therefore the name Israel was given with a blessing. But this blessing is realized when the characteristics of each name are correctly considered principal or subsidiary. This consideration of each name is represented by the gematria of 1500, the same gematria which also represents the realization of the blessing with the name of Israel.

ויקרא יעקב את שם המקום אשר דבר אתו שם אלקים בית
אל (בראשית לה,טו).

And Jacob called the name of the place where
G-d spoke with him Beth-el (Genesis 35,15).

Jacob gave a name to the place where G-d דבר אתו,
"spoke with him." The gematria of דבר אתו, "spoke with him"
is 613.

$$
\begin{array}{rr}
\text{דבר} & 206 \\
\text{אתו} & \underline{407} \\
& 613
\end{array}
$$

     The coupling of these two words is also found in the
two previous pesukim (בראשית לה, יג־יד, Genesis 35,13-14).
The gematria of these coupled words is significant, for the
Gemara Makkoth says that there is a total of 613 Mitzvoth
given to Moses, as stated, דרש רבי שמלאי שש מאות ושלש עשרה
מצות נאמרו לו למשה שלש מאות וששים וחמש לאוין כמנין ימות החמה
ומאתים וארבעים ושמונה עשה כנגד איבריו של אדם (מכות כג:), "Rabbi
Simlai expounded, six hundred thirteen Commandments
were said to Moses. Three hundred and sixty-five negative
Commandments corresponding to the number of days in a
solar year, and two hundred and forty-eight positive Commandments corresponding to the number of limbs of a man"
(Makkoth 23b).

     The pasuk immediately before the first mention of
these coupled words says that the Land of Israel will be given
to Jacob. The Ramban says that the primary observance of
the commandments is in the land of Israel as, stated, כי עיקר
כל המצות ליושבים בארץ ה' (רמב"ן ויקרא יח,כה), "For the primary
observance of all the commandments is for those who dwell
in the land of G-d" (Ramban, Leviticus 18,25).

     When G-d told Jacob that the land of Israel would be
given to him, it meant he would be given the place of the
primary observance of the commandments. Thus, the place

where G-d דבר אתו, "spoke with him" is the place of the primary observance of the commandments, which can hinted to by the gematria of these coupled words being 613.

Parashath Vayyeshev   פרשת וישב

וישב יעקב בארץ מגורי אביו בארץ כנען. (בראשית לז,א)
And Jacob dwelt in the land of his father's sojourning, in the land of Canaan (Genesis 37,1).

Jacob stayed in the land of Canaan until he went down to Egypt. The gematria of כנען, "Canaan," is 190.

כנען   190

The Ramban says that the intention of this pasuk, which says that Jacob dwelt in the land of Canaan, was that G-d's words to Abraham were being fulfilled with Jacob (רמב"ן, בראשית לז,א, Ramban, Genesis 37,1). The complete pasuk from which the Ramban quotes is, "And He said to Abram, know for sure that your seed will be a stranger in a land that is not theirs, and shall serve them, and they shall afflict them four hundred years" (בראשית טו,יג, Genesis 15,13).

Rashi counts the four hundred years that were foretold to Abram as starting from the birth of Isaac, the beginning of Abram's seed. Only 210 years were spent in Egypt; thus, 190 years were spent in the land of Canaan (רש"י, בראשית טו,יג, Rashi, Genesis 15,13). Isaac lived part of his life in Gerar (בראשית טו,ו), which is also considered part of the land of Canaan, as the Ramban writes, והכי שאמר בארץ פלשתים כי לך ולזרעך אתן את כל הארצות האל מן הטעם הזה היה כי הארץ ההיא היתה מתחלי לבני כנען ומפני זה הורישו ישראל בימי יהושע חמשת סרני פלשתים האשדודי האשקלוני הגתי והעקרוני והעוים שהיו כולם יושבי גבול הכנעני... מצידון בואכה גררה עד עזה וגו' (רמב"ן דברים ב,כג ורמב"ן בראשית כו,ב), "And the verse that says in the land of the Philistines, 'for to you and your seed I will give all these lands,' was stated because of this reason; for this land initially belonged to the sons of Canaan. And therefore in the days of Joshua, Israel dispossessed five Philistine princes, the Ashdodite, the

Ashkelonite, the Gittite, and the Ekronite, and the Avim, all of whom were living in the border of Canaan . . . from Zida as one comes to Gerar until Gaza, and so forth." (Ramban, Deuteronomy 2,23 and Ramban, Genesis 26,2).

Even when Jacob was with Laban, Isaac still lived in the land of Canaan, for Hashem had told him not to leave the land (בראשית לה,כז וספורנו, בראשית כו,ג, Genesis 35,27 and Sforno, Genesis 26,3). Thus, for all of the 190 years not spent in Egypt, some of Abraham's descendants dwelt in the land of Canaan. Since all 190 years not spent in Egypt can be counted as being spent in the land of Canaan, it is fitting that the gematria of כנען, Canaan, is 190.

וישב יעקב בארץ מגורי אביו בארץ כנען (בראשית לז,א).
And Jacob dwelt in the land of his father's sojourning, in the land of Canaan (Genesis 37,1).

It appears that Jacob was content to live in the land of Canaan, as he wanted to live there in tranquility (רש״י, בראשית לז,ב, Genesis 37,2). The gematria of כנען, "Canaan," is 190.

כנען   190

While Jacob was living in the land of Canaan he made a כתנת פסים, "coat of 'pasim,'" for Joseph (the word "pasim" is usually translated as many colors), as stated, וישראל אהב את יוסף מכל בניו כי בן זקנים הוא לו ועשה לו כתנת פסים (בראשית לז,ג), "And Israel loved Joseph more than all his sons, because he was the son of his old age, and he made him a coat of many colors" (Genesis 37,3). The gematria of פסים, "many colors," is 190.

פסים   190

What forced Jacob to leave the land of Canaan? The Gemara Shabbath focuses on the origin of his exile, ואמר רבא בר מחסיא אמר רב חמא בר גוריא אמר רב לעולם אל ישנה אדם בנו בין

הבנים שבשביל משקל שני סלעים מילת שנתן יעקב ליוסף יותר משאר בניו
נתקנאו בו אחיו ונתגלגל הדבר וירדו אבותינו למצרים (שבת י:) "And
Raba bar Mehasia said Rav Hama bar Goria said in Rav's
name, A man should never act differently with his son among
his other sons, for it was because of two sela's weight of silk
which Jacob gave to Joseph more than his other sons, that his
brothers became jealous of him and the issue evolved and
our forefathers descended to Egypt" (Shabbath 10b:). However, two sela's weight of silk was inadequate to make a
complete coat (מהרש״א שבת י: ד״ה משקל ב׳ סלעים כו׳, Maharsha,
Sabbath 10b, header words: The weight of two selas,etc.); so
Rashi quotes an explanation that the two sela's weigh of silk
were only for the hands, and so a coat of "pasim" refers to the
כתונת פסים סביב פס ידו נתן מילת ולא כל הכתונת (רש״י, שבת, palms,
י: ד״ה משקל ב׳ סלעים), "coat for the palms, around the palm of
his hand silk was put, and not the entire garment" (Rashi,
Shabbath 10b, header words: The weight of two selas). It
appears from the Gemara and Rashi that it was not the
making of the entire coat for Joseph that caused the jealousy,
but it was due to the "pasim."

What forced Jacob out of the land of Canaan? It was
the "pasim" that Jacob gave to Joseph. Since it was the
"pasim" that forced Jacob out of the land of Canaan, it is
appropriate the כנען, "Canaan," and פסים, "pasim," should
have the identical gematria.

ויאמר לו לך נא ראה את שלום אחיך ואת שלום הצאן
והשבני דבר וישלחהו מעמק חברון ויבא שכמה (בראשית
לז,יד)

And he [Jacob] said to him [Joseph], "Go now,
see the welfare of your brothers, and the welfare of the flock, and bring me back word." And
he sent him from the vale of Hebron, and he
came to Shechem (Genesis 37,14).

On this pasuk Rashi comments about Shechem, מקום מוכן לפורענות, שם קלקלו השבטים שם ענו את דינה, וכו' (רש״י, בראשית לז,יד), "It was a place prepared for punishment. There the tribes deteriorated; there Dinah was ravished, and so forth" (Rashi, Genesis 37,14). The gematria of קלקלו, "deteriorated," is 266.

קלקלו   266

Rashi seems to base himself on the Gemara Sanhedrin which says, תנא משום ר' יוסי מקום מזומן לפורענות בשכם עינו את דינה בשכם מכרו אחיו את יוסף, וכו' (סנהדרין קב.), "A tanna taught in the name of Rabbi Jose, It was a place ready for punishment. In Shechem Dinah was ravished; in Shechem the brothers sold Joseph, and so forth" (Sanhedrin 102a). The gematria of מכרו, "sold," is 266.

מכרו   266

If Rashi based himself on the Gemara, why did he change the language of the Gemara; why did he substitute קלקלו, "deteriorated," for מכרו, "sold"? An answer can perhaps be found in two pesukim from Psalms which state, בור כרה ויחפרהו ויפל בשחת יפעל. ישוב עמלו בראשו ועל קדקדו חמסו ירד (תהלים ז,טז-יז) "He who excavated a pit and dug it out, then he fell into the ditch which he made. His toil shall return upon his own head, and his violence shall come down upon his pate" (Psalms 7,16-17). He who undertakes to do harm to others will be victimized by his own evil actions. Thus, when the brothers sold Joseph, their deterioration was the consequence of their act of selling. Now it can be understood why Rashi substituted קלקלו, "deteriorated," for מכרו, "sold." The brothers' deterioration was determined by their act of selling, which is further indicated by the fact that the gematria of both words is 266.

וימצאהו איש והנה תעה בשדה וישאלהו האיש לאמר מה
תבקש (בראשית לז,טו).
And a man found him [Joseph] and behold he
was wandering in the field, and the man asked
him saying, "What do you seek?" (Genesis
37,15).

When Joseph went looking for his brothers he was
found by a man in a field. The gematria of איש, "a man," is
311.

איש   311

The gematria of בשדה, "in the field," is 311.

בשדה   311

There are various reasons given why the man found
Joseph when he was in the field (רמב״ן וכלי יקר, בראשית לז,טו,
Ramban and Keli Yakar, Genesis 37,15). Whatever the reason, the concept of איש, "a man," and the concept of בשדה, "in
the field," are connected. Since both words have the same
gematria, it is a further indication of this connection.

ועתה לכו ונהרגהו ונשלכהו באחד הברות ואמרנו חיה רעה
אכלתהו ונראה מה יהיו חלמתיו (בראשית לז,כ).
And now come let us kill him, and throw him
into one of the pits, and we will say an evil beast
has eaten him; and we shall see what will become of his dreams (Genesis 37,20).

Part of the plot which Joseph's brothers planned
against him was to throw him into one of the pits. The
gematria of הברות, "the pits," is 613.

הברות   613

Since there are 613 Commandments, the word הברות,
"the pits," with a gematria of 613, can be interpreted as

referring to the 613 Commandments. The Mishnah in Kiddu-shin describes the potent benefit that can be obtained by one who performs one single commandment; he will merit Hashem being good to him, as stated, כל העושה מצוה אחת מטיבין לו ומאריכין לו ימיו ונוחל את הארץ וכל שאינו עושה מצוה אחת אין מטיבין לו ואין מאריכין לו ימיו ואינו נוחל את הארץ (קדושין פרק א, משנה י), "Anyone who performs a commandment, good is done for him, and his days will be prolonged, and he will inherit the land; and anyone who does not perform a com-mandment, good is not done for him, and his days will not be prolonged, and he will not inherit the land" (Kiddushin, Chap-ter 1, Mishnah 10). This Mishnah can give insight to the pasuk mentioned previously. Joseph's brothers planned ונשלכהו באחד הברות, "and we will throw him on one of the 613 Com-mandments," since the word הברות, "the pits," with a gematria of 613, can be interpreted as referring to the 613 Commandments.

If Joseph had fulfilled one of the 613 Commandments, he would have the merit that Hashem would be good to him and save him; but if Joseph did not fulfill one of the 613 Commandments, he would not have the merit that Hashem would be good to him and save him. Then, the brothers reasoned, we will see what will become of his dreams.

וישבו לאכל־לחם וישאו עיניהם ויראו והנה ארחת ישמעאלים באה מגלעד וגמליהם נשאים נכאת וצרי ולט הולכים להוריד מצרימה (בראשית לז,כה).
And they sat down to eat bread; and they lifted up their eyes and they saw, and behold a cara-van of Ishmaelites came from Gilead, and their camels were bearing spicery, and balm, and ladanum, going to carry it down to Egypt (Gen-esis 37, 25).

After Joseph was thrown into a pit, his brothers saw a

caravan bearing spicery, balm, and ladanum. The gematria of נכאת וצרי ולט, "spicery, and balm, and ladanum," is 822.

נכאת	471
וצרי	306
ולט	45
	822

These spices were being carried for the sake of Joseph. Although normally Arabs carried unpleasant smelling petroleum and resin, for the benefit of Joseph G-d had this caravan carry pleasant spices (רש״י, בראשית לז,כה, Rashi, Genesis 37,25). Thus, the selling of Joseph can be associated with the number 822.

Later, a similar group of goods was carried for the sake of Joseph. Before their returning to Egypt, Jacob told his sons to take a little balm, a little honey, spicery, and ladanum, nuts, and almonds, as stated, ויאמר אלהם ישראל אביהם אם כן אפוא זאת עשו קחו מזמרת הארץ בכליכם והורידו לאיש מנחה מעט צרי ומעט דבש נכאת ולט בטנים ושקדים (בראשית מג,יא), "And Israel, their father, said to them, 'If so then do this, take of the choice fruits of the land in your vessels, and bring down a present to the man, a little balm, and a little honey, spicery, and ladanum, nuts, and almonds'" (Genesis 43,11). The gematria of מעט צרי ומעט דבש נכאת ולט בטנים ושקדים, "a little balm, and a little honey, spicery, and ladanum, nuts, and almonds," is 1937.

מעט	119
צרי	300
ומעט	125
דבש	306
נכאת	471
ולט	45
בטנים	111
ושקדים	460
	1937

These spices were being carried for the sake of Joseph. Thus, the going down to Egypt to see Joseph can be associated with the number 1937.

The two groups of goods mentioned are similar, first in their composition: Spicery, balm, and ladanum are included in each group. Second, they were similar in their purpose: Both were sent for the sake of Joseph. But the two groups of goods were also different. The second group of goods contained more types of spices than the first. The first group of goods was sent before Joseph matured, the second after he had matured. Therefore, the difference between the two groups can be seen as some indication of Joseph's maturity, development, or spiritual elevation. The difference in gematrioth between the two groups of goods is 1115.

$$
\begin{array}{r}
1937 \\
-822 \\
\hline
1115
\end{array}
$$

Thus, 1115 is some indication of the maturity, or spiritual elevation of Joseph between the times these two groups of goods were sent for his sake. The gematria of 1115 is also found in the Torah when discussing the offspring of Nahor, as stated, ופילגשו ושמה ראומה ותלד גם הוא את טבח ואת גחם ואת תחש ואת מעכה (בראשית כב,כד), "And his concubine, whose name was Reumah, she also bore Tebah, and Gaham, and Tachash, and Maacah" (Genesis 22,24). The gematria of ואת תחש, "and Tachash," is 1115.

$$
\begin{array}{lr}
\text{ואת} & 407 \\
\text{תחש} & 708 \\
\hline
& 1115
\end{array}
$$

Thus, 1115 can be associated with Tachash.

The name Tachash is related to the תחשים, "techashim," a covering of the Tabernacle (שמות כו,יד, Exodus

26,14). A tachash is a multicolored animal which only existed in the time of the building of the Tabernacle (רש"י שמות כה,ה, Rashi, Exodus 25,5). The word תחש, "tachash," means weakness; it represents a mixture of good and evil. This mixture is known as קליפת נוגה, "a shell concealing a shine," or concealing holiness. Different types of shells were elevated to holiness in the Tabernacle. The tachash represents a shell which was elevated to a level of holiness (אור התורה מאת צמח צדק, פרשת תרומה, עמוד אתקיג, וספר הזוהר מאת התנא רבי שמעון בן יוחאי, פרשת תרומה, דף קמז: , Or HaTorah by Tzemach Tzedek, Parashath Terumah, Page 1513, and The Book of the Zohar by the Tanna Rabbi Shimon ben Yochai, Parashath Terumah, Page 147b). The "techashim" covers were used only for the Tabernacle, which for the time it spent in Shiloh, was located in the portion of land allotted to Joseph (זבחים קיח:, Zevahim 118b). Thus, as was previously shown, the number 1115 is some indication of Joseph's maturity, or development. This same number is associated with the name Tachash, which relates to the techashim of the Tabernacle. Joseph's development corresponds to the techashim, which the Tabernacle, in Joseph's portion of the land, elevated.

It has been demonstrated that the difference in gematrioth between the two groups of goods sent for the sake of Joseph is 1115; this same gematria corresponds to the gematria of the name Tachash; both gematrioth represent elevated levels of holiness.

ויקחו את-כתנת יוסף וישחטו שעיר עזים ויטבלו את-הכתנת בדם (בראשית לז,לא).

And they took Joseph's coat and they slaughtered a he-goat and they dipped the coat in the blood Genesis 37,31).

Twice in Parashath Vayyeshev Joseph is treated wrongly, and the culprits report falsified information. The first time falsified information is reported is when the brothers took Joseph's coat and dipped it in the blood of a he-goat and then claimed that they found the coat. The gematria of שעיר עזים, "a he-goat," is 707.

$$
\begin{array}{rr}
שעיר & 580 \\
עזים & \underline{127} \\
& 707
\end{array}
$$

The taking of the he-goat was the initial step of reporting falsified information. The second time falsified information is reported is when the wife of Potiphar called the men of the house and then claimed that Joseph had tried to violate her, as stated, ותקרא לאנשי ביתה ותאמר להם לאמר ראו הביא לנו איש עברי לצחק בנו בא אלי לשכב עמי ואקרא בקול גדול (בראשית לט,יד), "And she called to the men of her house and she said to them saying, 'See he brought a Hebrew man to us to mock us, he came to me to lie with me and I called with a loud voice'" (Genesis 39,14). The gematria of ותקרא, "and she called," is 707.

$$
ותקרא \qquad 707
$$

The calling was the initial step of reporting falsified information. Since the initial step of reporting falsified information in both cases is characterized by terms with the same gematria, it is easy to see the parallel between the taking of the he-goat, and the wife of Potiphar calling out against Joseph.

ויאמר מה הערבון אשר אתן־לך ותאמר חתמך ופתילך ומטך אשר בידך ויתן־לה ויבא אליה ותהר לו (בראשית לח,יח).

And he [Judah] said, "What pledge shall I give you?" And she [Tamar] said, "Your signet and your cord, and your staff which is in your hand." And he gave them to her, and he came in unto her and she conceived by him (Genesis 38,18).

The earliest Shabbath on which Hanukkah can fall is Shabbath Parashath Vayyeshev, in which the staff of Judah is mentioned twice. The first time, the staff is written in its possessive form ומטך, "and your staff." The gematria of ומטך, "and your staff," is 75.

ומטך   75

The second time the staff is not written in the possessive form but as a simple nominative והמטה, "and the staff." At that time the staff was no longer serving Judah, but was sent to him from Tamar, as stated, הוא מוצאת והיא שלחה אל חמיה לאמר לאיש אשר אלה לו אנכי הרה ותאמר הכר נא למי החתמת והפתילים והמטה האלה (בראשית לח,כה), "When she was taken out, she sent to her father-in-law saying, 'I have conceived to the man to whom these belong.' And she said, 'Discern, please, to whom these belong, the signet, and the cords, and the staff'" (Genesis 38,25). The gematria of והמטה, "and the staff," is 65.

והמטה   65

Thus, 75 is the gematria of a staff in the possessive form, and 65 is the gematria of a staff in the nominative form.

The Maharal of Prague associates the words היכל, "palace," and כהן, "priest," and connects the significance of their gematrioth to Hanukkah: היכל עולה למספרו ס״ה אבל כהן במספר ע״ה (חבור נר מצוה מאת רבי יהודה ליוואי ברבי בצלאל הנקרא בפי כל מהר״יל מפראג, דף כב-כג), "the numerical value of palace adds up to 65, but the numerical value of priest is 75" (Chibbur Ner Mitzvah by Rabbi Yehudah Loew, the son of Rabbi Betzalel, who is known to all as the Maharal Mi Prague, pages 22-23). The gematria of היכל, "palace," is 65.

היכל   65

The gematria of כהן, "priest," is 75.

כהן   75

Both the palace, referring to the holy Temple, and the priest, were supports for the people of Israel; each served a role as a staff. But the difference between the holy Temple and the priest is that at the present time the holy Temple does not exist; however, many a priest does currently serve his people. Thus, the היכל, "palace," is a staff for the people of Israel, but since it is not at present in existence, it is not serving the people. The כהן, "priest," is still a staff for the people of Israel. Since many a priest does personally serve his people, he is to some extent, a personalized staff in the service of his people. The gematria of ומטה, "and the staff," is identical to the gematria of היכל, "palace," since both signify a staff that is not in the service of the people. The gematria of ומטך, "and your staff," is identical to the gematria of כהן, "priest," since both signify a personalized staff that is in the service of the people.

Amazingly, both words for staff are mentioned in Parashath Vayyeshev, the earliest Shabbath on which Hanukkah can fall.

ויאמר מה הערבון אשר אתן לך ותאמר חתמך ופתילך ומטך אשר בידך ויתן לה ויבא אליה ותהר לו (בראשית לח, יח).

And he [Judah] said, 'What pledge shall I give you?' And she [Tamar] said, 'Your signet and your cord, and your staff which is in your hand.' And he gave them to her, and he came in unto her and she conceived by him" (Genesis 38,18).

When Judah asked Tamar to specify a pledge, she said, "Your signet and your cord, and your staff." The gematria of חתמך, "your signet," ופתילך, "and your cord," and ומטך, "and your staff," total 1089.

חתמך	468
ופתילך	546
ומטך	75
	1089

Later Tamar asked Judah to identify these same objects, as stated, הוא מוצאת והיא שלחה אל חמיה לאמר לאיש אשר אלה לו אנכי הרה ותאמר הכר נא למי החתמת והפתילים והמטה האלה (בראשית לח,כה), "When she was taken out, she sent to her father-in-law saying, 'I have conceived to the man to whom these belong.' And she said, 'Discern, please, to whom these belong, the signet, and the cords, and the staff'" (Genesis 38,25). The gematria of החתמת, "the signet," והפתילים, "and the cords," and והמטה, "and the staff," total 1499.

החתמת	853
והפתילים	581
והמטה	65
	1499

The first time these three objects are mentioned in their possessive form; their form indicates they belonged to Judah; they were exclusively in his possession. The second time these three objects are not mentioned in their possessive form; their form does not indicate an owner or proprietor. The difference in gematrioth between the mentioning of these objects is 410.

$$\begin{array}{r} 1499 \\ -1089 \\ \hline 410 \end{array}$$

Thus, 410 represents Judah losing possession or ownership. Tamar asked for a pledge until Judah would send her a kid of the goats from the flock, as stated, ויאמר אנכי אשלח גדי עזים מן הצאן ותאמר אם תתן ערבון עד שלחך (בראשית לח,יז), "And he said, 'I will send a kid of the goats from the flock.' And she said, 'Will you give a pledge until you send it?'" (Genesis 38,17). The gematria of גדי עזים מן הצאן, "a kid of the goats from the flock," is 380.

גדי	17
עזים	127
מן	90
הצאן	146
	380

The gematria of שלחך, "you send it," is 358.

שלחך	358

When the gematria of גדי עזים מן הצאן, "a kid of the goats from the flock," is added to the gematria of שלחך, "you send it," the sum is 738.

380
358
738

Thus, 738 represents Judah sending what he was supposed to send, that is, doing what he was supposed to do. If Judah did as he was supposed to do, he was expecting to receive the pledge, which he never received. The gematria of ערבון, "pledge," is 328.

ערבון	328

When the gematria of ערבון "pledge," is subtracted from 738, the remainder is 410.

738
-328
410

Thus, 410 represents the difference between Judah doing what he was supposed to do and not obtaining what Judah expected to receive. Even when Judah did what he was supposed to do, Judah was disappointed and did not receive the possession he expected to receive. As was stated previously, 410 also represents Judah losing possession or ownership. Since the two ideas represented by 410 are analogous, it is appropriate that the same gematria should represent them.

ויאמרו אליו חלום חלמנו ופתר אין אתו ויאמר אלהם יוסף הלוא לאלקים פתרנים ספרו נא לי (בראשית מ,ח).

And they [the butler and baker] said to him, "We have dreamt a dream and there is none to interpret it," And Joseph said to them, "Do not interpretations belong to G-d? Please tell it to me" (Genesis 40,8).

Joseph used the term, נא לי, "please [tell it] to me," when he asked the chief of the butlers and the chief of the bakers each to tell their dream to him. The gematria of נא לי, "please [tell it] to me," is 91.

נא	51
לי	40
	91

Thus, 91 refers to Joseph when he asked to be told the dreams in prison. Later, Joseph used the term, לאדון, "to be a lord," when he asked his brothers to tell his father that G-d had made him a ruler in Egypt, as stated, מהרו ועלו אל אבי ואמרתם אליו כה אמר בנך יוסף שמני אלקים לאדון לכל מצרים רדה אלי אל תעמד (בראשית מה,ט), "Hasten and go up to my father, and you shall say to him, so said your son Joseph, G-d has made me to be a lord to all Egypt, come down to me, do not delay" (Genesis 45, 9). The gematria of לאדון, "to be a lord," is 91.

לאדון   91

Thus, 91 refers to Joseph when he was a ruler in Egypt. Since נא לי, "please [tell it] to me," and לאדון, "to be a lord," both refer to Joseph, it is very understandable that they have the same gematria. Another explanation can be given. Joseph became a ruler because he interpreted the dreams told to him in prison. Eventually, his prison interpretation led him to interpret the dreams of Pharaoh, who appointed him to be a ruler. Since what Joseph said נא לי, "please [tell it] to me," is what led him to be made לאדון, "to be a lord," it is very understandable that they have the same gematria.

Parashath Mikketz   פרשת מקץ

כלנו בני איש־אחד נחנו כנים אנחנו לא־היו עבדיך מרגלים
(בראשית מב,יא).

All of us are the sons of one man, we are honest men, your servants are not spies (Genesis 42,11).

The defense of Joseph's brothers to his accusation that they were spies, was twofold. The brothers claimed that they were the sons of one man, and that they were his servants. The gematria of כלנו, "all of us," is 106.

כלנו   106

The gematria of עבדיך, "your servants," is 106.

עבדיך   106

The Or Hachayyim and the Daat Zekenim Mibaale Hatosafoth explain that one defense of the brothers was that they were all the sons of one man. It would be illogical to send spies who were all brothers (דעת זקנים מבעלי התוספות, בראשית מב,יא, ד״ה כולנו בני איש, ואור החיים בראשית מב,יא, ד״ה כולנו בני איש וגו׳, Daat Zekenim Mibaale Hatosafoth, Genesis 42,11, header words: All of us are sons of, and the Or Hachayyim, Genesis 42, 11, header words: All of us are sons of). The Yalkut Me'am Loez explains that one defense of the brothers was that they said we are your servants, your subjects. Since the land of Canaan was under Egyptian dominion, it would be illogical that Egyptian subjects should spy on Egypt (ילקוט מעם לועז מאת הרב יעקב כולי, בראשית מב,יא, Yalkut Me'am Lo'ez by Rabbi Yaakov Culi, Genesis 42,11). Since the words כלנו, "all of us," and עבדיך, "your servants," crystallize the twofold defense of Joseph's brothers to his accusation that they were spies, it is very impressive that both words have the same gematria.

כלנו בני איש אחד נחנו כנים אנחנו לא היו עבדיך מרגלים
(בראשית מב,יא).

All of us are the sons of one man, we are honest men, your servants are not spies (Genesis 42,11).

The brothers of Joseph characterized themselves to Joseph as being כנים, "honest." The gematria of כנים, "honest," is 120.

כנים   120

Three pesukim before the end of the sidrah, Joseph characterized himself to his brothers, ויאמר להם יוסף מה המעשה הזה אשר עשיתם הלוא ידעתם כי נחש ינחש איש אשר כמני (בראשית מד,טו), "And Joseph said to them, 'What is this deed which you have done? Did you not know that a man such as I will surely divine'" (Genesis 44,15)? The gematria of כמני, "as I," is 120.

כמני   120

Not only are the gematrioth of כנים, "honest," and כמני, "as I," the same, but both words are composed of the same letters, just in different orders. Since the word used by the brothers to characterize themselves to Joseph has the same gematria as the word used by Joseph to characterize himself to his brothers, it indicates a relationship between the parties.

Note the ironic contrariety in roles at this point in time. The brothers accurately characterized themselves as honest, while Joseph inaccurately characterized himself as one who divines (although sadly necessary in order to achieve a reconciliation). When the brothers said כנים אנחנו, "we are honest men," the logical parallel response would have been for Joseph to say נחש אנחש אני, "I will surely divine." Perhaps the reason Joseph said כמני, "as I," and not just "I" may be to avoid being patently dishonest. Thus, the brothers of Joseph characterized themselves to Joseph with the word כנים, "honest"; while Joseph characterized himself to the brothers with the word כמני, "as I," to allow himself to be honest. The similarity in meaning and function of these words is enhanced by them having the same gematria.

בזאת תבחנו חי פרעה אם־תצאו מזה כי אם־בבוא אחיכם הקטן הנה (בראשית מב,טו).

With this you shall be tested, by the life of Pharaoh, you shall not go out hence, unless your younger brother comes hither (Genesis 42,15).

Joseph claimed he would test his brothers. The gematria of the word תבחנו, "you shall be tested," is 466.

תבחנו   466

This test led to Joseph's separating Simeon from the other brothers, as stated, ויסב מעליהם ויבך וישב אלהם וידבר אלהם ויקח מאתם את שמעון ויאסר אתו לעיניהם (בראשית מב,כד), "And he turned himself from them and cried; and he returned to them and spoke to them, and he took Simeon from them, and he bound him before their eyes" (Genesis 42,24). The gematria of שמעון, "Simeon," is 466.

שמעון   466

Since Joseph chose to test his brothers by specifically taking Simeon to be separated from the other brothers, it is very appropriate that the gematria of תבחנו, "you shall be tested," equals the gematria of שמעון, "Simeon."

ויאמר אלהם ישראל אביהם אם כן אפוא זאת עשו קחו מזמרת הארץ בכליכם והורידו לאיש מנחה מעט צרי ומעט דבש נכאת ולט בטנים ושקדים (בראשית מג,יא).

And Israel, their father, said to them, "If so, then do this, take of the choice fruits of the land in your vessels, and bring down a present to the man, a little balm, and a little honey, spicery, and ladanum, nuts, and almonds" (Genesis 43,11).

When Jacob agreed to let his sons take Benjamin down to Egypt, he used the word, אפוא, "then." Rashi comments on this word that, לשון יתר הוא, "the language is superfluous," (רש"י, בראשית מג,יא, Rashi, Genesis 43,11). The gematria of יתר הוא, "it is superfluous," is 622.

$$
\begin{array}{rr}
\text{יתר} & 610 \\
\text{הוא} & \underline{12} \\
& 622
\end{array}
$$

Previous to Jacob's using the word "then," Simeon had been separated from his brothers and held in Egypt, as stated, ויסב מעליהם ויבך וישב אלהם וידבר אלהם ויקח מאתם את שמעון ויאסר אתו לעיניהם (בראשית מב,כד), "And he turned himself from them and cried; and he returned to them and spoke to them, and he took Simeon from them, and he bound him before their eyes" (Genesis 42,24). The gematria of שמעון, "Simeon," is 466.

$$
\text{שמעון} \qquad 466
$$

Also previous to Jacob's using the word "then," he had said that he was bereaved of Joseph and Simeon, as stated, ויאמר אלהם יעקב אביהם אתי שכלתם יוסף איננו ושמעון איננו ואת בנימן תקחו עלי היו כלנה (בראשית מב,לו), "And Jacob their father said to them, 'You have bereaved me, Joseph is not, and Simeon is not, and Benjamin you will take away, upon me are all these things'" (Genesis 42,36). The gematria of יוסף, "Joseph," is 156.

$$
\text{יוסף} \qquad 156
$$

The combined gematria of שמעון, "Simeon," and יוסף, "Jo-seph," is 622.

$$
\begin{array}{rr}
\text{שמעון} & 466 \\
\text{יוסף} & \underline{156} \\
& 622
\end{array}
$$

Since the gematria of יתר הוא, "it is superfluous," is

equal to the combined gematrioth of שמעון, "Simeon," and יוסף, "Joseph," it could be that Rashi was indicating that when Jacob used the word "then," he was sighing concerning the loss of Simeon and Joseph.

וירחץ פניו ויצא ויתאפק ויאמר שימו לחם (בראשית מג,לא).

And he [Joseph] washed his face, and he went out and he refrained himself; and he said, "Set on bread" (Genesis 43,31).

Joseph used the expression ויאמר שימו "and he said, Set on," to represent the concept of serving food. The gematria of ויאמר שימו, "and he said, Set on," is 613.

ויאמר	257
שימו	356
	613

רב סעדיה גאון, Rav Saadia Gaon, translates the words שימו לחם, "Set on bread," as הגישו האוכל, "Serve the food," (רב סעדיה גאון בתורת חיים חמשה חומשי תורה, בעריכת הרב מרדכי ליב קצנלנבוגן, בראשית מג,לא, Rav Saadyah Goan in Torat Chaim Chamishah Chumshei Torah, edited by Rabbi Mordechai Leib Katzenellenbogen, Genesis 43,31). There are other incidents when the word לחם, "bread," is used to symbolize food in general (רש"י, בראשית לא,נד, Rashi, Genesis 31,54). But why did Joseph say "set on bread," rather than say, "serve the food?"

One possible answer could be deduced from the Shulhan Arukh. One should not eat just to enjoy his food, nor just to satisfy his appetite; quite conversely, one should eat to nourish himself to be able to serve his Creator. The Shulhan Arukh writes, אלא יתכוין שיאכל וישתה כפי חיותו לעבוד את בוראו (שלחן ערוך, אורח חיים, סימן רלא, סעיף א), "But one should intend that when he eats and drinks it should be adequate for his vitality in order to serve his Creator" (Shulhan Arukh, Orach Hayyim, Siman 231, Seif 1). Note that the Shulhan Arukh uses the word לעבוד, "to serve."

In פרשת משפטים, Parashath Mishpatim, the Torah uses a form of the word לעבוד, "to serve," as stated, ועבדתם את ה' אלהיכם וברך את לחמך ואת מימיך והסרתי מחלה מקרבך (שמות כג,כה) "And you shall serve Hashem, your G-d, and He will bless your bread and your water; and I will remove sickness from your midst" (Exodus 23,25). The ספר נתיבות שלום על התורה, Book of Netivot Shalom on the Torah, comments that in other incidences the Torah uses the word ועבדתם, "and you shall serve," to mean observing the commandments; however here the word refers to serving G-d beyond the realm of observing the commandments, as he states, במפרשים עמדו על מה קאי הקרא ועבדתם את ה' אלקיכם, שכל מקום בתורה נאמר זאת בקשר לקיום המצוות... ייל עוד דפיי ועבדתם את ה' אלקיכם בסתמא, היינו מחוץ לחלק של קיום התורה והמצוות, אלא איירי בכל עניני תענוגים והנאות ואפי המותרים, שתעבדו את השיית בזה (ספר נתיבות שלום של תורה, מאת הרב שלום נח ברזובסקי מסלונימא, משפטים, מאמר "ועבדתם את ה' אלקיכם"), "In the commentaries they confront, what is the concern of the verse, 'And you shall serve Hashem, your G-d.' In every place in the Torah where it uses this expression it is in connection with fulfilling the commandments. . . . An additional answer may be; that the explanation of 'And you shall serve Hashem, you G-d,' in general, is beyond the allotment of fulfilling the Torah and the commandments, but discusses all the subjects of pleasure and of enjoyment, and even of that which is allowed, to serve G-d with them" (Book of Netivot Shalom on the Torah by Rabbi Sholom Noach Berezovsky from Slonim, Mishpatim, Essay "And you shall serve G-d your G-d"). This serving Hashem beyond the realm of observing the commandments, includes eating to nourish oneself for the purpose of being to serve his Creator, just as the Shulhan Arukh writes.

Perhaps when Joseph said "Set on bread," he was saying to serve food, not just to enjoy the food, but to provide nourishment to serve the Creator. Serving Hashem can be equated to observing His 613 Commandments. It is possible that the reason why Joseph said "Set on bread," rather than saying "Serve the bread," is that the gematria of ויאמר שימו, "and he said, Set on," is 613, corresponding to the 613 Commandments, the purpose for which the food was being served.

Parashath Vayyiggash · פרשת ויגש

ויגש אליו יהודה ויאמר בי אדני ידבר נא עבדך דבר באזני אדני ואל יחר אפך בעבדך כי כמוך כפרעה (בראשית מד,יח).

And Judah came near to him, and he said, Oh my lord, please let your servant speak a word in the ears of my lord, and do not let your anger glow against your servant, for you are like Pharaoh (Genesis 44,18).

Rashi says that the word ויגש, "and he came near," can have three different meanings, as stated, מצינו הגשה למכחמה, ויגש יואב, והגשה לפיוס, ויגש אליו יהודה, והגשה לתפלה, ויגש אליהו הנביא (רש״י, בראשית יח,כג), "We find the word 'drawing near' in connection with war, And Joab drew near; and 'drawing near' in connection with conciliation, And Judah came near to him; and 'drawing near' in connection with prayer, And Elijah, the prophet came near" (Rashi, Genesis 18,23). As proof that the word 'drawing near' can refer to conciliation, Rashi quotes from the first pasuk of Parashath Vayyiggash. The Midrash Rabbah gives various definitions of the word ויגש, "and he came near," including conciliation, but it quotes a different pasuk (יהושע יד,ו, Joshua 14,6) as proof (מדרש רבה, סדר ויגש, פרשה צג, אות ו, Midrash Rabbah, Sidrah Vayyiggash, Parashah 93, Letter 6).

All three meanings stated by Rashi can be implied by the three words which begin with a ו, "vav," in the first pasuk of Parashath Vayyiggash; they are: ויגש, "and he came near," ויאמר, "and he said," and ואל, "and do not let." The word ויגש, "and he came near," can mean conciliation, as Rashi proved by quoting from the first pasuk of Parashath Vayyiggash, and the Midrash Rabbah proved by quoting from a different pasuk.

The word ויאמר, "and he said," can refer to prayer. The

ואין אמירה בכל מקום אלא תחנונים (ספרי, במדבר יב,א), "Sifre," says ספרי, "And in every place where the word אמירה, 'saying,' is used, it can refers to supplication" (Sifre, Numbers 12,1,). One is supposed to pray with תחנונים, "supplication," as the mishnah says, אל תעש תפלתך קבע, אלא רחמים ותחנונים לפני המקום ברוך הוא (אבות, פרק ב, משנה יג), "Do not make your prayer a fixed mechanical routine, but an appeal for mercy and supplication before the Omnipresent, Blessed be He" (Avoth, Chapter 2 Mishnah 13). Since in every place where the word אמירה, 'saying,' is, it can refer to supplication," and since one is supposed to pray with supplication, therefore the word ויאמר, "and he said," in the first pasuk of Parashath Vayyiggash can mean prayer.

The word ואל, "and do not let," can hint to war, When the Torah says (דברים כא,י) כי תצא למלחמה, "When you go out to war" (Deuteronomy 21,10), the Keli Yakar says explicitly that the pasuk can also refers to the war against the יצר הרע, "evil inclination," as stated, אין זה כי אם צר ואויב פנימי והוא שטן הוא יצר הרע (כלי יקר דברים כא,י), "This is none other than the inner foe and enemy, and it is the Satan, it is the evil inclination" (Keli Yakar, Deuteronomy 21,10). So when the Torah talks about going out to war, it can refer to a person's war against the evil inclination. The exact same expression, the יצר הרע, "evil inclination," used by the Keli Yakar, is also used by Rashi to explain a pasuk in Ecclesiastes. When Ecclesiastes it states, והסר כעס מלבך והעבר רעה מבשרך כי הילדות והשחרות הבל (קהלת יא,י), "And remove anger from your heart, and cause evil to pass away from your flesh, for childhood and youth are vanity" (Ecclesiastes 11,10), Rashi says explicitly that the evil refers to the evil inclination (רש"י, קהלת יא,י, Rashi, Ecclesiastes 11,10). So when Ecclesiastes talks about removing anger, it can refer to the evil inclination. It follows that by combining the Keli Yakar on the Torah, with the Rashi on Ecclesiastes, that one way of winning the war against the evil inclination is to remove anger from oneself. Therefore, when Judah approached Joseph and said ואל יחר אפך, "and do not let your anger glow," it could be understood that Judah told Joseph not to get angry, for then Joseph would lose the war against his evil inclination. This understanding of the pasuk is very different from the first blush interpretation of war. In any case, the word ואל, "and do not let," in the first pasuk of Parashath Vayyiggash can mean war against the evil inclination.

The three words which begin with a ו, "vav," in the first pasuk of Parashath Vayyiggash are: ויגש, "and he came near," ויאמר, "and he said," and ואל, "and do not let." The gematria of ויגש, "and he came near," is 319.

ויגש   319

The gematria of ויאמר, "and he said," is 257.

ויאמר   257

The gematria of ואל, "and do not let," is 37.

ואל   37

The sum of the gematrioth of the three words which begin with a ו, "vav," in the first pasuk of Parashath Vayyiggash is 613.

319
257
 37
―――
613

Each of the meanings which was ascribed to the three words which begin with a vav can fall under the rubric of mitzvoth. Seeking conciliation to bring peace between members of the Children of Israel, praying to G-d, and having someone control his anger, can all can fall under the rubric of mitzvoth. The Gemara Makkoth states that there is a total of

613 Mitzvoth, Commandments (מכות כג:, Makkoth 23b). The fact that the sum of the gematrioth of the three words which begin with a ו, "vav," in the first pasuk of Parashath Vayyiggash is equal to the total number of commandments can indicate that when Judah approached Joseph, he was desiring to be performing a mitzvah. This desire can be justified in light of the Gemara Sotah, as stated, מצוה בין בעידנא דעסיק בה בין בעידנא דלא עסיק בה אגוני מגנא אצולי לא מצלא (סוטה כא.), "A commandment both during the time when one is busy with it, or during the time when one is not busy with it, it protects, but does not save" (Sotah 21a). Thus, Judah wanted to be performing a commandment when he approached Joseph, so it would protect him, even after he had performed it. This desire of Judah could explain why the sum of the gematrioth of the three words which begin with a ו, "vav," in the first pasuk of Parashath Vayyiggash is 613.

ולקחתם גם את זה מעם פני וקרהו אסון והורדתם את שיבתי ברעה שאלה (בראשית מד,כט).
And if you take also this one from me, and harm befalls him, then you will bring down my gray hairs with evil to the grave (Genesis 44,29).

The purpose of man's life in this world is the performance of mitzvoth. The Mesillath Yesharim unequivocally asserts this purpose, as it says, והנה מה שהורונו חכמינו ז"ל הוא, שהאדם לא נברא אלא להתענג על ה' ולהנות מזיו שכינתו... והאמצעים המגיעים את האדם לתכלית הזה, הם המצות אשר צונו עליהן הקל יתברך שמו. ומקום עשית המצות הוא רק העולם הזה (מסלת ישרים מאת הרב משה חיים לוצאטו פרק א), "And behold that which our sages of blessed memory have instructed us, that man was only created to delight with G-d, and benefit from the splendor of His divine Presence. . . . And the means which allow man to achieve this aim are the mitzvoth which G-d blessed be His Name, commanded us about them. And the place for the performance of mitzvoth is only in this world" (Mesillath Yesharim by Rabbi Moshe Chaim Luzzatto, Chapter 1).

In Parashath Vayyiggash there is an unconventional expression to describe premature death. When Judah spoke to Joseph, he said if something were to happen to Benjamin, it would bring down Jacob's gray hairs ברעה שאלה, "with evil to the grave." Rashi says that Benjamin provided Jacob comfort for the loss of Benjamin's mother and brother, but if he were to die, it would seem as if all three of them died in one day (רש״י, בראשית מד,כט, Rashi, Genesis 44,29). Why did Judah use the expression ברעה שאלה, "with evil to the grave," rather than simply saying death? The question becomes more poignant because Jacob in fact referred to his own death with the words (והורדתם את שיבתי ביגון שאולה (בראשית מב,לח, "you will bring down my gray hairs with sorrow to the grave" (Genesis 42,38). Also note that the word שאלה, "to the grave," which Judah used has no vav, but the word שאולה, "to the grave," which Jacob used has a vav. An answer can be given via a gematria.

The Gemara Makkoth says that there is a total of 613 Mitzvoth given to Moses, as stated, דרש רבי שמלאי שש מאות ושלש עשרה מצות נאמרו לו למשה שלש מאות וששים וחמש לאוין כמנין ימות החמה ומאתים וארבעים ושמונה עשה כנגד איבריו של אדם (מכות כג:), "Rabbi Simlai expounded, six hundred thirteen Commandments were said to Moses. Three hundred and sixty-five negative Commandments corresponding to the number of days in a solar year, and two hundred and forty-eight positive Commandments corresponding to the number of limbs of a man" (Makkoth 23b). When a person is alive he can observe the 613 Mitzvoth, but not when he is dead. The gematria of ברעה שאלה, "with evil to the grave," is 613.

ברעה	277
שאלה	336
	613

Since there is a total of 613 Mitzvoth, and since the purpose of man's life in this world is the performance of mitzvoth, therefore premature death would mean the termination of the opportunity to perform mitzvoth. The version of the word שאלה, "to the grave," which Judah used, lacks a vav, which is called in Hebrew חסר, "lacking"; emphasizing that death would cause Jacob to be lacking the ability to observe commandments. Thus, Judah's use of the expression ברעה שאלה, "with evil to the grave," whose gematria is 613, underscores, that that in death Jacob would no longer be able to observe the mitzvoth.

ועתה כבאי אל עבדך אבי והנער איננו אתנו ונפשו קשורה בנפשו (בראשית מד,ל).

And now when I come to your servant, my father, and the lad is not with us, and his soul is tied with his soul (Genesis 44,30).

Judah said to Joseph that the soul of Jacob was קשורה, "tied," to the soul of Benjamin. The gematria of קשורה, "tied," is 611.

קשורה   611

Thus, 611 represents the link between Jacob and Benjamin. The Gemara Eruvin says that one should not depart from his friend without mentioning an halakhah, "decided law," (עירובין סד. וברכות לא.‏), Eruvin 64a and Berakoth 31a). Thus, Torah becomes a bond, a tie, between departing people. The gematria of תורה, "Torah," is 611.

תורה   611

When Benjamin departed from Jacob, words of Torah were certainly spoken, words that would serve as a tie between them, similar to words of Torah that were spoken when Joseph left Jacob (רש״י בראשית מה,כז‏, Rashi Genesis 45,27).

Since the gematria of קשורה, "tied," is equal to the gematria of תורה, "Torah," it can be explained that the tie which Judah said to Joseph refers to the Torah spoken between Jacob and Benjamin when they separated.

ולא יכל יוסף להתאפק לכל הנצבים עליו ויקרא הוציאו כל איש מעלי ולא עמד איש אתו בהתודע יוסף אל אחיו (בראשית מה,א).

And Joseph was not able to restrain himself before all those standing by him, and he called, "Cause every man to go out from me." And no man stood with him when Joseph made himself known to his brothers (Genesis 45,1).

Just before Joseph revealed himself to his brothers, the Torah records that he was not able to restrain himself. The gematria of להתאפק, "to restrain himself," is 616.

להתאפק   616

Thus, the gematria of 616 is associated with the concept to restrain, to repress, or to hold back from action. When Joseph sent his brothers back to Jacob, after he had revealed himself to them, he told them not to quarrel on the way, as stated, וישלח את אחיו וילכו ויאמר אלהם אל תרגזו בדרך (בראשית מה,כד), "And he sent his brothers, and they left, and he said to them, 'Do not quarrel on the way'" (Genesis 45,24). The gematria of תרגזו, "quarrel," is 616.

תרגזו   616

Joseph told his brothers to refrain from quarrelling, or feuding (רש״י, בראשית מה,כד, Rashi, Genesis 45,24). Although the word תרגזו, "quarrel," is the object of what to refrain from, and the word להתאפק, "to restrain himself," is the infinitive, to restrain, still there is a connection between the words. Perhaps Joseph was indicating to his brothers that an alternative to quarrel is to restrain oneself. Thus, the gematria of 616 is again associated with the concept to restrain, to repress, or to hold back from action.

וכלכלתי אתך שם כי עוד חמש שנים רעב פן־תורש אתה וביתך וכל אשר לך (בראשית מה,יא).
And I will sustain you there, for there are still five years of famine; lest you come to poverty, you and your household, and all that you have (Genesis 45,11).

Joseph said that he would support his father and brothers for five years. The gematria of וכלכלתי, "and I will sustain," is 516.

וכלכלתי   516

The gematria of שנים, "years," is 400.

שנים   400

Joseph did as he said; he supported his father and brothers, as stated, ויכלכל יוסף את אביו ואת אחיו ואת כל בית אביו לחם לפי הטף (בראשית מז,יב), "And Joseph sustained his father, and his brothers, and all his father's household, with bread according to the wants of the little ones," (Genesis 47,12). The gematria of ויכלכל, "and he sustained," is 116.

ויכלכל   116

The difference in gematria between what Joseph said he would do, and what he did, is 400.

516
-116
400

As was just shown, the gematria of שנים, "years," the time for which Joseph said he would support his father and brothers, is 400. Thus, according to the simple meaning of what the Torah records, the difference in gematrioth between what Joseph said he would do and what he did is equal to the time for which he said he would do it. Joseph did what he said he would, for the time he said he would do it. In reality, Joseph supported Jacob for the entire seventeen years his father was in Egypt (דעת זקנים מבעלי התוספות בראשית מז,כח, ד״ה ויחי יעקב, Daat Zekenim Mibaale Hatosafoth, Genesis 47,28, header words: And Jacob lived). Joseph also offered to support his brothers after Jacob's death (בראשית נ,כא, Genesis 50,21), even though the famine had ended when Jacob came to Egypt (רש״י, בראשית מז,יט, Rashi, Genesis 47,19).

וישלח את אחיו וילכו ויאמר אלהם אל תרגזו בדרך (בראשית מה,כד).
And he sent his brothers, and they left, and he said to them, "Do not quarrel on the way" (Genesis 45,24).

When Joseph sent his brothers back to Jacob, after he had revealed himself to them, he told them not to quarrel on the way. The gematria of תרגזו, "quarrel," is 616.

תרגזו   616

The Sifthei Chachomim translates the word תרגזו, "quarrel," as to err or stray from the path (שפתי חכמים, בראשית מה,כד, Sifthei Chachomim, Genesis 45,24). It has been further explained, somewhat differently, that Joseph instructed his brothers not to cease from learning Torah, ומה שאמר כאן אל תעמידו עצמכם מד״ית הכונה אל תפסיקו למיגרס (עץ יוסף, מדרש רבה, סדר ויגש, פרשה צד, אות ב), "And that which it says here, do not hold yourselves back from words of Torah, the intention is, do not cease to study" (Eitz Yosef, Midrash Rabbah, Sidra Vayyiggash, Parashah 94, Letter 2). Thus, the gematria of 616 is associated with Joseph instructing his brothers not to stray from the path, as well as not to cease from learning

Torah. To stray from the path would mean to turn from the correct path to the right or left. The Torah directs that if there is a concealed issue, go to the priests, the Levites, and to the judge, and do as they instruct, as stated, על פי התורה אשר יורוך ועל המשפט אשר יאמרו לך תעשה לא תסור מן הדבר אשר יגידו לך ימין ושמאל (דברים יז,יא), "According to the law which they shall teach you, and according to the judgment which they shall say to you, you shall do; you shall not turn aside from the sentence which they will tell you to the right nor to the left" (Deuteronomy 17,11). The gematria of התורה, "the law," is 616.

616   התורה

There is a double significance to the gematria of תרגזו, "to stray from the path," being equal to the gematria of התורה, "the Torah." First, when Joseph instructed his brothers not to stray from the path, he was instructing them not to cease from learning the Torah. Note that the Gemara Taanith says that when traveling, certain learning is allowed, such as reviewing and reciting, but other learning, such as cognition and analyzing, are forbidden (תענית י:, Taanith 10b). Thus, the specific type of Torah learning which is allowable to learn when traveling, is what Joseph warned his brothers not to cease from learning. Since Joseph warned the brothers to engage in a specific type of learning, it follows that the gematria of התורה, the Torah, with the ה' הידיעה, the definite article, is employed. Second, if the brothers of Joseph violated his instructions and did cease from learning the Torah, they would be turning to the right or to the left, just as violators of the instructions of the priests and judges, would be turning to the right or left. The pasuk which mentions this latter turning to the right or left is the same one which contains the word, התורה, "the Torah." Hence, there is a double significance to the gematria of תרגזו, "to stray from the path," being equal to the gematria of התורה, the "Torah."

ויגדו לו לאמר עוד יוסף חי וכי הוא משל בכל ארץ מצרים
ויפג לבו כי לא האמין להם (בראשית מה,כו).

And they told him saying, "Joseph is still alive, and he is a ruler over all the land of Egypt," and his heart fainted because he did not believe them (Genesis 45,26).

When Jacob was told that Joseph was alive, his heart fainted because he did not believe his sons. The gematria of ויפג לבו, "and his heart fainted," is 137.

$$\begin{array}{lr} \text{ויפג} & 99 \\ \text{לבו} & \underline{38} \\ & 137 \end{array}$$

The gematria of לא האמין, "he did not believe," is 137.

$$\begin{array}{lr} \text{לא} & 31 \\ \text{האמין} & \underline{106} \\ & 137 \end{array}$$

The effect of Jacob's heart fainting was caused by his not believing. This cause and and effect relationship is further emphasized by the gematria of ויפג לבו, "and his heart fainted," being equal to the gematria of לא האמין, "he did not believe."

ויסע ישראל וכל אשר לו ויבא בארה שבע ויזבח זבחים
לאלהי אביו יצחק (בראשית מו,א).

And Israel journeyed and all that he had, and he came to Beer-sheba; and he sacrificed sacrifices to the G-d of his father Isaac (Genesis 46,1).

The Torah records the traveling of Jacob, including his coming to Beer-sheba and sacrificing to the G-d of Isaac. The gematria of בארה, "to Beer," is 208.

באֵרה   208

The gematria of יצחק, "Isaac," is 208.

יצחק   208

      On this pasuk Rashi felt compelled to comment on two problems: 1. What does בארה, "to Beer," mean? 2. Why is G-d designated as the G-d of יצחק, "Issac," here? It is obvious that Rashi felt these words are difficulties or oddities which he needed to explain to understand the pasuk (רש״י, בראשית מו,א, Rashi, Genesis 46,1). It is possible that the Torah chose to write the word בארה, "to Beer," instead of the word לבאר, "to Beer," since the gematria of the former is equal to the gematria of Isaac. This equality would tend to emphasize that Issac is designated in the pasuk. This equality also connects the two problems upon Rashi felt compelled to comment in order to explain this pasuk.

      Also note, that when Issac gave the name Beer-sheba, the name was given forever, as the Torah writes, until this day, as stated ויקרא אתה שבעה על כן שם העיר באר שבע עד היום הזה (בראשית כו,לג) "And he called its name Shibah, therefore the name of the city is Beer-sheba, until this day" (Genesis 26,33), in contradistinction to the name given by Abraham, which was temporary, since when he gave the name it never says until this day. Rashi says, כל מקום שנאמר עד היום הזה לעולם ולעולמי עולמים הוא (רש״י, סוטה מו: ד״ה ויקרא שמה לוז), "Every place where it says until this day, it means forevermore" (Rashi, Sotah 46b, header words: And he called its name Luz). Note, the Gemara in Yoma (יומא נד., Yoma 54a) has a different perspective. Still, it is further possible that the Torah chose to write the word בארה, "to Beer," instead of the word לבאר, "to Beer," since the gematria of the former is equal to the gematria of Isaac, who gave the place its permanent name.

ויכלכל יוסף את אביו ואת אחיו ואת כל־בית אביו לחם לפי
הטף (בראשית מז,יב).

And Joseph sustained his father, and his brothers, and all his father's household, with bread
according to the wants of the little ones (Genesis 47,12).

All of Joseph's father's household came to Egypt,
where they were sustained by Joseph. The gematria of ואת כל
בית אביו, "and all his father's household," is 888.

ואת	407
כל	50
בית	412
אביו	19
	888

Joseph told his brothers that he would sustain them
since there would be five more years of famine, as stated,
וכלכלתי אתך שם כי עוד חמש שנים רעב פן תורש אתה וביתך וכל אשר לך
(בראשית מה,יא), "And I will sustain you there, for there are still
five years of famine; lest you come to poverty, you and your
household, and all that you have" (Genesis 45,11). The
gematria of רעב, "famine," is 272.

רעב   272

During a time of famine it is forbidden to cohabit with
one's wife (רש״י, בראשית מא,נ, Rashi, Genesis 41,50). Ergo, in
the time of famine, all of Joseph's father's household could
not reproduce. If the gematria of רעב, "famine," is subtracted
from the gematria of ואת כל בית אביו, "and all his father's
household," the remainder is 616.

888
-272
616

Thus, 616 represents what happened to Joseph's father's household after the restriction of the time of famine was removed, taken away, or subtracted. What did happen to Joseph's father's household after the restriction on reproduction was removed? The last pasuk of the sidrah provides an answer, as stated, וישב ישראל בארץ מצרים בארץ גשן ויאחזו בה ויפרו וירבו מאד (בראשית מז,כז), "And Israel dwelt in the land of Egypt, in the land of Goshen; and they had possession therein, and they were fruitful, and multiplied exceedingly" (Genesis 47,27). The gematria of ויאחזו בה ויפרו וירבו מאד, "and they had possession therein, and they were fruitful, and multiplied exceedingly," is 616.

ויאחזו	38
בה	7
ויפרו	302
וירבו מאד	269
	616

Thus, 616 represents the time when the people of Israel, the household of Jacob, were fruitful and reproducing. Since there are two gematrioth equal to 616, it can be concluded that their equality implies that after the time of famine, Jacob's household was fruitful and reproductive.

Parashath Vayyechi פרשת ויחי

ושכבתי עם־אבתי ונשאתני ממצרים וקברתני בקברתם
ויאמר אנכי אעשה כדברך (בראשית מז,ל).
And I will lie with my fathers, and you shall carry me out of Egypt, and bury me in their burial place. And he said, "I will do according to your word"(Genesis 47,30).

Joseph agreed to fulfill the request of Jacob to bury him in the land of Israel, with the words אעשה כדברך, "I will do according to your word." The gematria of אעשה כדברך, "I will do according to your word," is 622.

אעשה	376
כדברך	246
	622

After this agreement, Jacob recounted to Joseph about Rachel's death and burial, as stated, ואני בבאי מפדן מתה עלי רחל בארץ כנען בדרך בעוד כברת ארץ לבא אפרתה ואקברה שם בדרך אפרת הוא בית לחם (בראשית מח,ז), "And as for me, when I came from Padan, Rachel died by me in the land of Canaan on the way, when there was still a tract of land to come to Ephrath; and I buried her there on the way of Ephrath, which is Beth-lehem" (Genesis 48,7). The gematria of כברת, "a tract," is 622.

כברת	622

Jacob was concerned that since he had buried Rachel on the road to Ephrath, in the purlieus of Beth-lehem, and not carried her to the nearby Beth-lehem, that Joseph would harbor ill will toward him (רש"י, בראשית מח,ז, Rashi, Genesis 48,7). Thus, the tract of land to which Jacob did not carry Rachel could have been the cause of ill will, especially since Joseph had agreed to bury Jacob in the distant land of Israel. Therefore, Joseph agreeing to bury Jacob in the land of Israel when he said, אעשה כדברך, "I will do according to your word," and Jacob mentioning כברת, "a tract," of land are connected. This connection can also be observed from the fact that both expressions have the same gematria.

וירא ישראל את־בני יוסף ויאמר מי־אלה (בראשית מח,ח).

And Israel saw the sons of Joseph and he said, "Who are these?" (Genesis 48,8).

When Jacob saw the sons of Joseph, he asked מי אלה, "Who are these?" The gematria of מי אלה, "Who are these?" is 86.

מי	50
אלה	36
	86

Rashi explains that when Jacob said, "Who are these?" he was asking prophetically about future descendents of these sons; from where did these emerge who are not worthy of a blessing (רש״י, בראשית מח,ח, Rashi, Genesis 48,8)? This question is obviously a question of judgment. When Hashem's attribute of judgment is alluded to, He is referred to as אלקים, "G-d" (א,א רש״י, בראשית, Rashi, Genesis 8,1). The gematria of אלקים, "G-d," is 86.

אלקים	86

Inasmuch as מי אלה, "Who are these?" is a question of judgment, it is fitting that its gematria equals that of אלקים, "G-d," which refers to His attribute of judgment. Not only are the gematrioth equal, but the letters of מי אלה, "Who are these?" are the same as those of אלקים, "G-d." Note that Joseph referred to אלקים, "G-d," when he answered his father, ויאמר יוסף אל אביו בני הם אשר נתן לי אלקים בזה ויאמר קחם נא אלי ואברכם (בראשית מח,ט), "And Joseph said to his father, 'They are my sons whom G-d has given me with this.' And he said, 'Please bring them to me, and I will bless them'" (Genesis 48,9). The referral to Hashem as אלקים, "G-d," when Joseph answered his father, further substantiates the judgmental nature of the conversation between Joseph and his father, and adds significance to the fact of the equality of the gematrioth.

וימאן אביו ויאמר ידעתי בני ידעתי גם הוא יהיה לעם וגם הוא יגדל ואולם אחיו הקטן יגדל ממנו וזרעו יהיה מלא הגוים (בראשית מח,יט).

And his father refused and said, "I know, my son, I know; he shall also become a people and he shall also be great, however his younger brother shall be greater than he, and his seed will be a multitude of nations" (Genesis 48,19).

When Jacob placed his right hand on Ephraim and his left hand on Manasseh to bless Joseph's sons, Joseph tried to reverse their positions; Jacob refused. Several questions can be asked about Jacob's response. Why did Jacob say ידעתי, "I know," twice? Why did he say בני, "my son," it was already known that Joseph was Jacob's son? Why did Jacob say גם הוא, "he shall also," twice? Various commentaries have given different answers, but the seemingly extra words have an interesting gematria.

The Gemara queries if Rabbi Judah expressed דעת תורה, "knowledge of the Torah," inasmuch as his opinion could be based on a pasuk (חולין צ:-צא., Hullin 90b-91a). Thus, it can be deduced that if one knows Torah, he has דעת, "knowledge." Since Yaakov knew Torah he had דעת, "knowledge." The gematria of בני ידעתי גם הוא, "my son I know; he shall also be," is 611.

בני ידעתי	556
גם הוא	55
	611

The gematria of תורה, "Torah," is also 611.

תורה	611

Perhaps the reason why Jacob said twice ידעתי, "I know," why he said בני, "my son," and why he said twice גם הוא, "he shall also," is that the gematria of these seeming extra words is equal to the gematria of תורה, "Torah." Jacob may have been implying that he knew what he was doing when he placed his right hand on Ephraim and his left hand on Manasseh, since he knew Torah, he had דעת, "knowledge."

שמעון ולוי אחים כלי חמס מכרתיהם (בראשית מט,ה).

Simeon and Levi are brothers; instruments of violence are their weapons (Genesis 49,5).

When Jacob blessed his sons, he referred to Simeon and Levi as brothers, שמעון ולוי אחים, "Simeon and Levi are brothers." The gematria of שמעון ולוי אחים, "Simeon and Levi are brothers," is 577.

שמעון	466
ולוי	52
אחים	59
	577

In the next pasuk Jacob separates his honor from these brothers, as stated, בסדם אל תבא נפשי בקהלם אל תחד כבדי כי באפם הרגו איש וברצנם עקרו שור (בראשית מט,ו), "Let my soul not come into their council, let my honor not be united in their assembly; for in their anger they killed a man, and in their self-will they hamstrung an ox" (Genesis 49,6). The gematria of כבדי, "my honor," is 36.

כבדי	36

Jacob said that he did not want his honor to be joined with Simeon and Levi. When the gematria of כבדי, "my honor," is added to the gematria of שמעון ולוי אחים, "Simon and Levi are brothers," the total is 613.

$$577$$
$$\underline{36}$$
$$613$$

Perhaps Jacob did not want his honor to be united with the brothers Simeon and Levi, because the total gematria of this union is 613, the number of the mitzvoth. Being surrounded with mitzvoth is a sign of endearment. The Gemara Menahoth states that since Israel is beloved by Hashem, He surrounds them with mitzvoth (מנחות מג:, Menahoth 43b). At the time when Jacob was speaking to Simeon and Levi he expressed detachment, not endearment, towards these brothers. It could be that Jacob was saying that he did not want to join כבדי, "my honor," with שמעון ולוי אחים, "Simeon and Levi are brothers," in order to withhold a sign of endearment from them. Linking their names to the sum of the mitzvoth, would be such a sign.

בסדם אל־תבא נפשי בקהלם אל־תחד כבדי כי באפם הרגו
איש וברצנם עקרו־שור (בראשית מט,ו).
Let my soul not come into their council, let my honor not be united in their assembly; for in their anger they killed a man, and in their self-will they hamstrung an ox (Genesis 49,6).

When referring to the anger of Simeon and Levi, Jacob said that in their anger they killed a man. Why was the singular word "man" used by Jacob? Rashi comments on this pasuk, ופשוטו אנשים הרבה קורא איש (רש״י בראשית מט,ו), "And its simple meaning is, that many men are called man" (Rashi, Genesis 49,6). The gematria of אנשים הרבה, "many men," is 613.

אנשים	401
הרבה	212
	613

The Gemara Makkoth states that there is a total of 613 Mitzvoth (מכות כג:, Makkoth 23b). It is conceivable to explain that since the expression אנשים הרבה, "many men," has a gematria equal to the total number of mitzvoth, that Jacob used the word איש, "man," in place of אנשים הרבה, "many men," when referring to the anger of Simeon and Levi, so he would not imply that they were not observing the 613 Mitzvoth.

בסדם אל תבא נפשי בקהלם אל־תחד כבדי כי באפם הרגו איש וברצנם עקרו־שור. ארור אפם כי עז ועברתם כי קשתה אחלקם ביעקב ואפיצם בישראל (בראשית מט, ו־ז).
Let my soul not come into their council, let my honor not be united in their assembly; for in their anger they killed a man, and in their self-will they hamstrung an ox. Cursed be their anger for it was fierce, and their wrath for it was cruel; I will divide them in Jacob, and scatter them in Israel (Genesis 49,6-7).

Jacob cursed the anger and the wrath of Simeon and Levi because they were fierce and cruel. The combined gematrioth of עז, "fierce," and קשתה, "cruel," is 882.

עז	77
קשתה	805
	882

Thus, 882 represents why Jacob cursed the anger and wrath of Simeon and Levi. The last words in the pasuk preceding the one describing the anger and wrath of Simeon and Levi, depict their behavior by saying, "in their self-will they hamstrung an ox." The gematria of עקרו שור, "they hamstrung an ox," is 882.

עקרו	376
שור	506
	882

Thus, 882 represents the depiction of the behavior of Simeon and Levi. Since 882 represents why Jacob cursed the anger and wrath of Simeon and Levi, and 882 also represents the depiction of the behavior of Simeon and Levi, it can be concluded that one of the reasons Jacob cursed their anger and wrath was their behavior.

זבולן לחוף ימים ישכן והוא לחוף אניות וירכתו על־צידן (בראשית מט,יג).

Zebulun shall dwell at the shore of the sea; and he shall be a shore for ships, and his flank shall be upon Zidon (Genesis 49,13).

When Jacob blessed Zebulun he used the word sea. The gematria of ימים, "sea," is 100.

ימים	100

Rashi comments that this pasuk telling of Zebulun trading on the sea, is the counterpart to the blessing of Moses (רש״י, בראשית מט,יג, Rashi, Genesis 49,13). When Moses blessed Zebulun he used the word בצאתך, "in your going out," as stated, ולזבולן אמר שמח זבולן בצאתך ויששכר באהליך (דברים לג,יח), "And to Zebulun he said, rejoice Zebulun in your going out; and Isaachar in your tents" (Deuteronomy 33,18). The gematria of בצאתך, "in your going out," is 513.

בצאתך	513

Rashi comments on this pasuk that Zebulun dwelt at the seashore and would go out in ships to trade (רש״י, דברים לג,יח, Rashi, Deuteronomy 33,18). Thus, the same thought is found both when Jacob and when Moses blessed Zebulun. In the blessing of Jacob, the word ימים, "sea," is used; in the blessing of Moses, the word בצאתך, "in your going out," is used. In the blessing of Jacob, Rashi quotes the word בצאתך, "in your going out," from Moses' blessing; in the blessing of Moses, Rashi quotes the word ימים, "sea," from Jacob's blessing. The combined gematrioth of ימים, "sea,"and בצאתך, "in your going out," is 613.

$$
\begin{array}{r}
100 \\
513 \\
\hline
613
\end{array}
$$

On both pesukim Rashi comments that the trade of Zebulun was to enable Isaachar to engage in Torah study. Thus, Zebulun's going out on the sea was for the sake of Torah, for the sake of the 613 Mitzvoth. Since the בצאתך, "in your going out" to the ימים, "sea," of Zebulun was for the sake of the 613 Mitzvoth, it is very appropriate that the gematrioth of these words should total 613.

ויהי בשכן ישראל בארץ ההוא וילך ראובן וישכב את־בלהה פילגש אביו וישמע ישראל ויהיו בני־יעקב שנים עשר (בראשית לה,כב).

And it came to pass, when Israel dwelt in that land, that Reuben went and [it was as if] he lay with Bilhah his father's concubine; and Israel heard of it. And the sons of Jacob were twelve (Genesis 35,22).

ויאמרו שנים עשר עבדיך אחים אנחנו בני איש אחד בארץ כנען והנה הקטן את־אבינו היום והאחד איננו (בראשית מב,יג).

And they said, 'Your servants are twelve brothers, the sons of one man in the land of Canaan, and behold the youngest is with our father today, and one is not' (Genesis 42,13).

שנים עשר אנחנו אחים בני אבינו האחד איננו והקטן היום
את אבינו בארץ כנען (בראשית מב,לב).
We are twelve brothers, sons of our father; one
is not and the youngest is today with our father
in the land of Canaan (Genesis 42,32).

כל אלה שבטי ישראל שנים עשר וזאת אשר דבר להם
אביהם ויברך אותם איש אשר כברכתו ברך אתם (בראשית
מט,כח).
All of these are the twelve tribes of Israel, and
this is what their father spoke to them; and he
blessed them, every one according to his
blessing he blessed them (Genesis 49,28).

The term שנים עשר, "twelve," is used four times in the
Torah in reference to the sons of Jacob. The first and last
mentions of the number twelve are third person references,
the second and third mentions of the number twelve are first
person references by the sons of Jacob to themselves. Each
reference attributes a better characteristic to the sons of
Jacob than its predecessor. The first reference just identifies
the sons of Jacob as the sons of Jacob; the second identifies
the sons of Jacob as brothers, the sons of one man, although
the term, "your servants," is used; the third reference identifies the sons of Jacob as the sons of our father, not merely
the sons of one man, and the term "your servants," is
dropped; the fourth reference identifies the sons of Jacob as
"tribes of Israel," the highest level of character of the four
references. Since the first and the last references to the sons
of Jacob are in the third person, these references identify the
extent of their development as viewed by the Torah; since
the second and the third reference are in the first person,
these references identify how the sons of Jacob viewed
themselves. The first and last references represent how far

advanced their character development extended; the second and third references represent how, through what transformation process, the sons of Jacob advanced their character development.

In the second reference the key word is עבדיך, "your servants." Note how similar the second and third references are, with the exclusion of the word עבדיך, "your servants." Although there are differences between the second and third references, the use of the term "your servants," gives the most insight into how the sons of Jacob developed. They had to call themselves "your servants," in order to make the transition from reference one to reference four, to develop from being the sons of Jacob to being the tribes of Israel. Initially they they had to call themselves "your servants," it displays that they had humbled themselves to another person. Thus, the word, עבדיך, "your servants," represents how the sons of Jacob developed. The gematria of עבדיך, "your servants," is 106.

עבדיך   106

The first and last references to the twelve sons of Jacob represent how far their character developed. The Torah seems to set apart these two references, perhaps to show that these two references are terminal points marking the start and finish of their development; their gematrioth are 1251 and 1918 respectively. The gematria of ויהיו בני יעקב שנים עשר, "And the sons of Jacob were twelve," is 1251.

ויהיו	37
בני	62
יעקב	182
שנים	400
עשר	570
	1251

The gematria of כל אלה שבטי ישראל שנים עשר, "All of these are the twelve tribes of Israel," is 1918.

כל	50
אלה	36
שבטי	321
ישראל	541
שנים	400
עשר	570
	1918

The combined gematria of the first and fourth references is 3169.

$$1251$$
$$1918$$
$$3169$$

The number 106 represents the means by which the sons of Jacob developed, and the number 3169 represents the extent of their development. The sum of these two gematrioth is 3275.

$$106$$
$$3169$$
$$3275$$

Thus, the number 3275 represents the complete development process. The Torah records the names given to the twelve sons of Jacob at their births. The gematria of ראובן, "Reuben," (Genesis 29,32), שמעון, "Simeon," (Genesis 29,33), לוי, "Levi," (Genesis 29,34), יהודה, "Judah," (Genesis 29,35), דן, "Dan," (Genesis 30,6), נפתלי, "Naphtali," (Genesis 30,8), גד, "Gad," (Genesis 30,11), אשר, "Asher," (Genesis 30,13), יששכר, "Issachar," (Genesis 30,18), זבלון, "Zebulun," (Genesis 30,20), יוסף, "Joseph," (Genesis 30,24), and בנימין, "Benjamin," (Genesis 35,18) is 3176.

ראובן	259
שמעון	466
לוי	46
יהודה	30
דן	54
נפתלי	570
גד	7
אשר	501
יששכר	830
זבלון	95
יוסף	156
בנימין	162
	3176

The number 3176 represents the twelve sons of Jacob as they were called at birth. When Jacob called his sons together before he blessed them, he called to his twelve sons who had risen in character development from birth to be fit to be "his sons." This development meant that they had risen in character development from being just the sons of Jacob to the level of being called "his sons." When they were on the level of being called "his sons," they were called the tribes of Israel. This rise in character development can be seen in the the use of the words "the sons of Jacob," in the first reference and "the tribes of Israel," in the fourth reference. When Jacob called his sons together, prior to the fourth reference, to bless them, the Torah uses the words "to his sons," as stated, ויקרא יעקב אל בניו ויאמר האספו ואגידה לכם את אשר יקרא אתכם באחרית הימים (בראשית מט,א), "And Jacob called to his sons and said, 'Gather yourselves together, and I will tell you that which will befall you in the end of days'" (Genesis 49,1). The gematria of אל בניו, "to his sons," is 99.

אל	31
בניו	68
	99

The number 3176 represents what the sons of Jacob were called prior to the first reference, and the number 99 represents what they were called prior to the fourth reference. The sum of these two gematrioth is 3275.

$$3176$$
$$99$$
$$\overline{3275}$$

Thus, 3275 represents the development of the sons of Jacob from birth until their father called them to bless them, that is, from prior to the first reference to prior to the fourth reference. The gematria representing the complete development process of the sons of Jacob, 3275; it also equals the gematria representing the development of the sons of Jacob, 3275. The message is that the level to which a person rises depends on his developmental process.

ויכל יעקב לצות את־בניו ויאסף רגליו אל־המטה ויגוע
ויאסף אל־עמיו (בראשית מט,לג).

And when Jacob finished to command his sons, he gathered his feet into the bed, and he expired, and was gathered unto his people (Genesis 49,33).

The Torah describes the cessation of Jacob's life, as, "and he expired, and was gathered unto his people." The gematria of ויגוע ויאסף אל עמיו, "and he expired, and was gathered unto his people," is 409.

ויגוע	95
ויאסף	157
אל	31
עמיו	126
	409

Since the word death is not mentioned in this pasuk, Rashi, quoting a Gemara Taanith (תענית ה:, Taanith 5b), says,

רש"י, בראשית), "Jacob our father did not die," יעקב אבינו לא מת
מט,לג, Rashi, Genesis 49,33). The gematria of לא מת, "he did not die," is 471.

$$\begin{array}{rr} \text{לא} & 31 \\ \text{מת} & \underline{440} \\ & 471 \end{array}$$

The gematria of מת,"he died," is 440.

$$\text{מת} \qquad 440$$

The difference between these gematrioth is 31.

$$\begin{array}{r} 471 \\ \underline{-440} \\ 31 \end{array}$$

The difference between the gematria of ויגוע ויאסף אל
עמיו, "and he expired, and was gathered unto his people," and
the gematria of מת, "he died," is also 31.

$$\begin{array}{r} 440 \\ \underline{-409} \\ 31 \end{array}$$

Since the difference between לא מת, "he did not die,"
and מת, "he died," in gematrioth is equal to the difference
between ויגוע ויאסף אל עמיו, "and he expired, and was gathered unto his people," and מת, "he died," in gematrioth, this
difference in gematria corroborates that which Rashi says,
יעקב אבינו לא מת, "Jacob our father did not die."

Book of Exodus — ספר שמות

Parashath Shemoth   פרשת שמות

וַיַּעֲבִדוּ מִצְרַיִם אֶת בְּנֵי יִשְׂרָאֵל בְּפָרֶךְ (שמות א,יג).
And the Egyptians made the Children of Israel
serve with rigor (Exodus 1,13).

The Children of Israel were in Egypt for only 210 years,
although G-d had said that they would be afflicted in a
strange land for 400 years (רש״י, בראשית טו,יג, Rashi, Genesis
15,13). One of the reasons for this shortened time was the
severity of the labor, which equated the time the Children of
Israel were afflicted in Egypt to 400 years (ספר קול אליהו מאת
הרב אליהו מווילנא, פרשה שמות, אות מח, ד״ה בפסוק וימררו את חייהם
בעבודה קשה, Book of Kol Eliyahu by Rabbi Eliyahu from Vilna,
Parashath Shemoth, Letter 48, header words: With the
pasuk, And they made their lives bitter with hard service).

The first and last words of the pasuk "And the Egyptians made the Children of Israel serve with rigor" (Exodus
1,13), depicts the severity of the servitude. Those words,
ויעבדו, "and they made serve," and בפרך, "with rigor," have a
combined gematria of 400.

ויעבדו	98
בפרך	302
	400

Interestingly, the severity of the servitude, which
equated the time the Children of Israel were afflicted in Egypt
to 400 years, is depicted by two words whose combined
gematria is 400.

וַתֹּאמַרְןָ אִישׁ מִצְרִי הִצִּילָנוּ מִיַּד הָרֹעִים וְגַם דָּלֹה דָלָה לָנוּ
וַיַּשְׁקְ אֶת הַצֹּאן (שמות ב,יט).
And they said: "An Egyptian man saved us from
the hand of the shepherds, and he also rigorously drew water for us and watered the flock"
(Exodus 2,19).

After Moses rescued the daughters of Yithro from the shepherds, the daughters related to their father the incident, and also that Moses drew water for them. The gematria of דלה דלה, "he rigorously drew water," is 78.

דלה	39
דלה	39
	78

Yithro's response to his daughter's narrative was, "Why did you leave him? Call him and he may eat bread." Rashi elucidates that Yithro recognized that Moses was from the seed of Jacob, since the water rose to him, and that when Yithro said bread he referring to matrimony (רש״י, שמות ב,כ, Rashi, Exodus 2,20).

Three questions are apparent. First, why did the daughters of Yithro use a double expression, דלה דלה, "he rigorously drew water," which implies emphasis? It seems that the word דלה, "he drew water," would have been adequate. Second, how did Yithro know that Moses was from the seed of Jacob? After all, the daughters of Yithro described Moses as an Egyptian man, and Jacob had blessed Pharaoh that the Nile's water should rise to his feet (רש״י, בראשית מז,י, Rashi, Genesis 47,10), so the water could rise for an Egyptian man too. Third, why did Yithro use the word bread to refer to matrimony? Rashi quotes from a pasuk which uses the word bread to refer to the wife of Potiphar (רש״י, שמות ב,כ, Rashi, Exodus 2,20). It compels notice that in two incidents the word bread refers to matters of a wife. But the quoted situation was different, for Joseph resisted seduction by the wife of Potiphar, the metaphor was suitable; it shows contrast. Yithro, however, was acting naturally as a father, seeking a husband for one of his daughters. The metaphor was unnecessary.

These three questions perhaps can be answered with an understanding of what may have occurred. Moses was the humblest of men (במדבר יב,ג, Numbers 12,3). He was aware that the water rose to him, but he tried to hide this fact from the daughters of Yithro. He pretended, feigned, that it was a strenuous, vigorous, task to draw the water. Therefore, when the daughters of Yithro told of his drawing water, they said, דלה דלה, "he rigorously drew water," using a double expression to emphasize the feigned strenuous efforts of Moses. Thus, the first question is answered.

In truth, the daughters of Yithro realized that the water rose to Moses, and his strenuous efforts were a pretense. When they told Yithro their realization, he knew that Moses was from the seed of Jacob, for only one of such lineage would try to hide a miracle which occurred for his benefit. Thus, the second question is answered.

When Yithro suggested a possible matrimonial relationship between Moses and one of his daughters, as stated, ויאמר אל בנתיו ואיו למה זה עזבתן את האיש קראן לו ויאכל לחם (שמות ב,כ), "And he said to his daughters, And where is he? Why is it that have you deserted the man? Call him and he may eat bread" (Exodus 2,20). The gematria of לחם, "bread," is 78.

לחם   78

The gematria of לחם, "bread," is equal to the gematria of דלה דלה, "he rigorously drew water." Perhaps Yithro used the word לחם, "bread," to indicate that because his daughters used the expression דלה דלה, "he rigorously drew water," to emphasize that the feigned strenuous efforts of Moses were to hide a miracle which had occurred for his benefit, therefore Yithro was interested in having Moses marry one of them. Thus, the third question has been answered.

According to this explanation, Yithro was interested in Moses as a son-in-law, not because the water rose to Moses, but because Moses tried to hide the miracle. This explanation has obvious implications of the importance of modesty for those seeking a matrimonial relationship.

ויען משה ויאמר והן לא יאמינו לי ולא ישמעו בקולי כי
יאמרו לא נראה אליך ה׳ (שמות ד,א).
And Moses answered and said, "But behold, they will not believe me, nor hearken to my voice, for they will say, 'G-d did not appear to you'" (Exodus 4,1).

When Hashem told Moses to go to Egypt, he answered by saying that the Bnei Yisroel would neither believe him nor hearken to his voice. The gematria of לא יאמינו ולא ישמעו, "will not believe nor hearken," is 611.

לא	31
יאמינו	117
ולא	37
ישמעו	426
	611

Thus, 611 represents what Moses thought the Bnei Yisroel would not do, that is, they would not believe him nor listen to what Moses would say. In reality, the Bnei Yisroel did believe and did listen that Hashem had remembered them, as stated, ויאמן העם וישמעו כי פקד ה׳ את בני ישראל וכי ראה את ענים ויקדו וישתחוו (שמות ד,לא) "And the people believed, and when they heard that G-d had remembered the Children of Israel, and seen their affliction, then they bowed their heads and prostrated themselves" (Exodus 4,31). The gematria of פקד ה׳ את, "that G-d remembered," is 611.

פקד	184
ה׳	26
את	401
	611

Thus, 611 represents what the Bnei Yisroel did believe and they did listen, that is, that Hashem had remembered them. Why is the gematria of what Moses thought the Bnei

Yisroel would not do equal to the gematria of what the Bnei Yisroel actually did?

Moses' doubting the faith of the Bnei Yisroel was not considered virtuous. The Gemara Shabbath quotes the pasuk which narrates Moses' doubting, אמר ריש לקיש החושד בכשרים לוקה בגופו דכתיב והן לא יאמינו לי וגו'... ממאי דלקה דכתיב ויאמר ה' לו עוד, הבא נא ידך בחיקך וגו' (שבת צז.), "Resh Lakish said, He who suspects an innocent person is bodily smitten, as it says, 'But behold, they will not believe me, etc.,' ... from what source do we know that he (Moses) was smitten? As it is written, 'and G-d said further to him, Bring your hand into your bosom, etc.'" (Shabbath 97a). The Mishnah Sotah states the principle that, במדה שאדם מודד בה מודדין לו (סוטה פרק א משנה ז), "In the measure with which a man measures, it is meted out to him" (Sotah Chapter 1 Mishnah 7). This principle can be applied to Moses doubting the faith of the Bnei Yisroel. The extent of the doubt of what Moses thought the Bnei Yisroel would not believe him nor listen to what he would say, is equal to the extent of what the Bnei Yisroel did believe and did listen. To the extent that Moses suspected the innocent, to that same extent he observed that the people believed and listened that Hashem had remembered the Bnei Yisroel. The application of this principle could be the reason why the gematria of what Moses thought the Bnei Yisroel would not do is equal to the gematria of what they did believe and they did listen.

והיה אם לא יאמינו לך ולא ישמעו לקל האת הראשון
והאמינו לקל האת האחרון (שמות ד,ח).

And it shall come to pass, if they will not believe you, and they will not hearken to the voice of the first sign, that they will believe the voice of the last sign (Exodus 4,8).

After Hashem gave Moses two signs, He told him that if the Bnei Yisroel will not listen to the voice of the first sign, they will believe the voice of the second sign. The gematria of האת, "the sign," is 406.

האת　　　406

Since the word האת, "the sign," is mentioned twice in the pasuk its gematria can be doubled, equaling 812.

406
× 2

812

Thus, 812 represents the repetition of the word האת, "the sign." The next pasuk uses the word האתות, "these signs," as stated, והיה אם לא יאמינו גם לשני האתות האלה ולא ישמעון לקלך ולקחת ממימי היאר ושפכת היבשה והיו המים אשר תקח מן היאר והיו לדם ביבשת (שמות ד,ט), "And it shall come to pass, if they will also not believe to these two signs, and they will not hearken to your voice, that you shall take from the water of the river, and pour it upon the dry land, and the water which you shall take out of the river shall be blood upon the dry land" (Exodus 4,9). The gematria of האתות, "these signs," is 812.

האתות　　　812

Since האתות, "these signs," mentioned in this pasuk refers to האת, "the sign," mentioned twice in the previous pasuk, it is fitting that the gematria of the former is double the gematria of the latter.

ודבר הוא לך אל העם והיה הוא יהיה לך לפה ואתה תהיה
לו לאלהים (שמות ד,טז).

And he will speak for you to the people, and it shall come pass, he will be for you as a mouth, and you will be for him as a leader (Exodus 4,16).

When G-d told Moses to return to Egypt, He also told him that Aaron would speak for him, and Moses would be for him as a leader. Rashi comments that the word לאלהים, "as a leader," means לרב ולשר, "for a master and for a commander," (רש"י, שמות ד,טז, Rashi, Exodus 4,16). The gematria of לרב ולשר, "for a master and for a commander," is 768.

לרב	232
ולשר	536
	768

On that very word לאלהים, "as a leader," the שערי אהרן, Shaarei Aaron, comments, נראה לי שפירש, דמש"כ ואתה תהיה לו לאלהים מתפרש בשני אנפין, א' ואתה תהיה לו לרב, ב' ואתה תהיה לו מול אלקים, כעין מש"כ לקמן יח-יט, היה אתה לעם מול האלקים (ספר שערי אהרן על התורה מאת אהרן ישעי' רוטר, פרשת שמות, פרק ד, פסוק טז, ד"ה ואתה תהיה לו לאלקים), "It appears to me that he [referring to Targum ascribed to Jonathan] explains that, that which is written, and you will be in G-d's stead, can be explained in two modes. One you will be a master to him. Two, you will be facing G-d, as it is written later, 18-19, you will be for the people facing G-d" (Book of Shaarei Aaron on the Torah by Aaron Yeshayah Roter, Parashath Shemoth, Chapter 4, pasuk 16, header words: And you will be for him as a G-d). Although the Shaarei Aaron says both modes of his explanation on the word לאלהים, "as a leader," these concepts parallel two expressions in the pasuk.

The expression תהיה לו לרב, "will be a master to him," in the Shaarei Aaron, corresponds to the words in the pasuk, תהיה לו לאלהים, "be for him as a leader." The expression היה אתה לעם, "you will be for the people," in the Shaarei Aaron, corresponds to the words in the pasuk, לך אל העם, "for you to the people"; although they refer to Aaron, they were for Moses' benefit. The gematria of תהיה לו לרב, "will be a master to him," plus the gematria of לך אל העם, "for you to the people," is 768.

תהיה לו לאלהים	572
לך אל העם	196
	768

Since the gematria of the words which Rashi used to explain the word לאלהים, "as a leader," equals the words in the pasuk which corresponds to the two modes the Shaarei Aaron used to explain the word לאלהים, "as a leader," credence is added to the explanations of both.

ואת המטה הזה תקח בידך אשר תעשה בו את האתת
(שמות ד,יז).

And take this staff in your hand, wherewith you
shall do the signs, (Exodus 4,17).

Hashem told Moses to take the staff in his hand. The gematria of המטה הזה בידך אשר, "this staff in your hand, wherewith," is 613.

המטה	59
הזה	17
בידך	36
אשר	501
	613

Two questions can be raised. One, what is the significance of the gematria of 613, the number which is equal to the sum of the commandments, in relation to the staff? Two, if Moses was to perform signs with the staff, of course he would have to take it. Why did Hashem have to tell Moses to take the staff?

Hashem had told Moses that due to the merit of the forefathers, Abraham, Isaac, and Jacob, He would treat the Bnei Yisroel with mercy (מדרש רבה, סדר שמות, פרשה ג, אות ז, Midrash Rabbah, Sidrah Shemoth, Parashah 3, Letter 7). Each of the forefathers observed what is written in the Torah. The Midrash says, "Abraham observed the entire Torah ... Isaac observed what is written in the Torah ... Yaakov observed what is written in the Torah,"(מדרש רבה, סדר ויקרא, פרשה ב, אות י, Midrash Rabbah, Sidrah Vayyikra, Parashah 2,

Letter 10). Since a total of 613 Mitzvoth are written in the Torah (מכות כג:, Makkoth 23b), it can be deduced that each of the forefathers observed 613 Mitzvoth. Perhaps, due to the merit of the forefathers' observance of the 613 Mitzvoth, Hashem said He would treat the Bnei Yisroel with mercy.

The Yalkut Me'am Lo'ez says that the names of each of the forefathers were engraved on the staff of Moses (ילקוט מעם לועז, מאת הרב יעקב כולי שמות ד,יז, Yalkut Me'am Lo'ez by Rabbi Yaakov Culi, Exodus 4,17). It is conceivable that the names of each of the forefathers served as a reminder of 613 Mitzvoth they observed, and due to their merit Hashem would treat the Bnei Yisroel with mercy; so the staff represented this merit. Question number one has been answered.

The second question that was raised can now be answered. The significance of the gematria of 613 in relation to the staff is apparent. Since the names of the forefathers were engraved on the the staff, it could serve as a reminder of the merit of the forefathers' observance of the 613 Mitzvoth. When Hashem told Moses to take the staff, it could have a deeper meaning than the simple physical act. Moses was reluctant to lead the Bnei Yisroel out of Egypt. When Hashem told Moses to take the staff, He was saying to Moses that with the staff he would be symbolically taking the merit of the forefathers' observance of the 613 Mitzvoth with him, which would help insure Moses' success in leading the Bnei Yisroel out of Egypt. Question number two has been answered.

ויאמן העם וישמעו כי פקד ה׳ את בני ישראל וכי ראה את עניים ויקדו וישתחוו (שמות ד,לא).

And the people believed, and when they heard that G-d had remembered the Children of Israel, and seen their affliction, then they bowed their heads and prostrated themselves (Exodus 4,31).

The people believed when they heard the words which Hashem had told Moses, and saw Hashem's signs. The gematria of ויאמן, "and they believed," is 107.

ויאמן   107

Thus, 107 represents the Bnei Yisroel believing that Hashem had remembered them. The Gemara Shabbath derives from this pasuk that the Bnei Yisroel are believers, הן מאמינים דכתיב ויאמן העם (שבת צז). "They are believers, as it is written, 'And the people believed,'" (Shabbath 97a).

When the Bnei Yisroel went out of Egypt, only one fifth of the people were redeemed (רש״י, שמות יג,יח, Rashi, Exodus 13,18). The Keli Yakar says that those who were redeemed were the believers (כלי יקר, שמות יג,יז, Keli Yakar, Exodus 13,17). Note that the Keli Yakar learns that the believers were redeemed, from the same word that Rashi learns that only one fifth of the people were redeemed. Probably, the four fifths who died were in some way lacking faith.

In describing the exodus from Egypt the Torah used the word יצאו, "went out," as stated, ויהי מקץ שלשים שנה וארבע מאות שנה ויהי בעצם היום הזה יצאו כל צבאות ה' מארץ מצרים (שמות יב,מא) "And it came to pass at the end of four hundred and thirty years, on the self-same day, it came to pass that all the hosts of G-d went out of the land of Egypt" (Exodus 12,41). The gematria of יצאו, "went out," is 107.

יצאו   107

Thus, 107 represents the exodus from Egypt. Since the gematria of יצאו, "went out," equals the gematria of ויאמן, "and they believed," there is further evidence to the explanation of the Keli Yakar, that those who were redeemed were the believers. Note that this evidence does not mean that all those who believed when they heard the words which Hashem had told Moses exited Egypt; but it does mean that all those who exited Egypt were at that time believers.

ואת מתכנת הלבנים אשר הם עשים תמול שלשם תשימו
עליהם לא תגרעו ממנו כי נרפים הם על כן הם צעקים
לאמר נלכה נזבחה לאלקינו (שמות ה,ח).

And the full number of the bricks which they
were making yesterday and heretofore you
shall impose upon them, you shall not diminish
aught, for they are lazy, therefore they cry saying: Let us go sacrifice to our G-d (Exodus 5,8).

Pharaoh instructed the taskmasters to increase the
work load of the Bnei Yisroel, claiming that the Bnei Yisroel
were lazy. The gematria of נרפים, "lazy," is 380.

נרפים   380

The irony of the situation is titanic. The Bnei Yisroel
were working for the Egyptians as slaves, they were forced to
work with rigor, and the Egyptians drowned the male Jewish
newborns (שמות א,יג-טז, Exodus 1, 13-16). Under such circumstances the Bnei Yisroel surely were not lazy; the people
who were lazy were the Egyptians, who forced the Bnei
Yisroel to build up their country. It is bitterly ironic that the
Bnei Yisroel should be called lazy by Pharaoh.

When Pharaoh had justified enslaving the Bnei Yisroel,
he had said, "Come, let us deal wisely with them, lest they
multiply, and it come to pass if there happens to be a war,
that they also join with our enemies and fight against us and
go up from the land" (שמות א,י, Exodus 1,10). Rashi comments, that when Pharaoh said that in the event of war the
Bnei Yisroel will leave the land; what Pharaoh actually meant
was that the Egyptians would be forced leave the land (רש"י,
שמות א,י, Rashi Exodus 1,10). From this Rashi it is apparent
that Pharaoh would use a negative feature of his own nation,
Egypt, to describe the Bnei Yisroel. When Pharaoh called the
Bnei Yisroel נרפים, "lazy," he was again using a vice of his own
nation, Egypt, to describe the Bnei Yisroel. Although it is true

that the Egyptians were lazy, the pasuk first quoted refers to the Bnei Yisroel, as it concludes, "therefore they cry saying: Let us go sacrifice to our G-d." This use of a negative feature of his own nation to describe others is similar to the expression in the Gemara Kiddushin, כל הפוסל... במומו פוסל (קדושין ע:), "Everyone who disqualifies others ... with his own defect he disqualifies" (Kiddushin 70b). One would expect that Pharaoh should lie.

The Torah records that when Moses was disheartened, Hashem reassured him, as stated, וגם אני שמעתי את נאקת בני ישראל אשר מצרים מעבדים אתם ואזכר את בריתי (שמות ו,ה), "And also I have heard the groaning of the Children of Israel whom Egypt compels to labor; and I have remembered my covenant" (Exodus 6,5). The gematria of מצרים, "Egypt," is 380.

מצרים   380

Since the gematrioth of נרפים, "lazy," and מצרים, "Egypt," are equal, it corroborates that when Pharaoh called the Bnei Yisroel נרפים, "lazy," he was again using a vice of his own nation, Egypt, to describe the Bnei Yisroel.

והנגשים אצים לאמר כלו מעשיכם דבר יום ביומו כאשר בהיות התבן (שמות ה,יג).

And the taskmasters urged, saying, Complete your work, the daily portion in its day, as when there was straw (Exodus 5,13).

The taskmasters urged the Bnei Yisroel to כלו, "complete," the work of a יום, "day," in its day (רש"י, שמות ה,יג, Rashi, Exodus 5,13). The gematria of כלו, "complete," is 56.

כלו   56

The gematria of יום, "day," is also 56.

יום   56

Since these two words are interrelated, it is fitting that they should have the same gematria.

Parashath Vaayra   פרשת וארא

וארא אל אברהם אל יצחק ואל יעקב בקל שקי ושמי הי לא
נודעתי להם (שמות ו,ג).
And I appeared to Abraham, unto Isaac, and
unto Jacob, as Kel Shakkai, but by My name
Hashem I was not known to them (Exodus 6,3).

The second pasuk in this sidrah tells of Hashem appearing to the patriarchs. The gematria of וארא, "And I appeared," is 208.

וארא   208

The gematria of יצחק, "Isaac," is 208.

יצחק   208

What is the connection between these two words which have the same gematria? Although Hashem appeared to all the patriarchs as the quoted pasuk affirms, nevertheless it could be suggested that Isaac saw more of Hashem's presence than any of the other patriarchs. Being more exposed to Hashem's revelation was one reason for his blindness. The Midrash Rabbah says, בשעה שעקד אברהם אבינו את בנו על גבי המזבח תלה עיניו והביט בשכינה, אמר הקדוש ברוך הוא אם הורגו אני, עכשו אני מבריע את אברהם אוהבי אלא גוזר אני שיכהו עיניו. וכיון שהזקין כהו עיניו (מדרש רבה, סדר תולדות, פרשה סה, אות י), "At the time when our forefather Abraham bound his son on the altar, his (Isaac's) eyes gazed and saw the Divine Presence. Said the Holy One, Blessed be He: 'If I slay him, now I will oppress Abraham, My friend; rather I decree that his eyes should be dimmed' and since he grew old, his eyes were dimmed" (Midrash Rabbah, Sidrah Toledoth, Parashah 65, Letter 10). The Yalkut Me' am Loez also attributes Isaac's blindness to his gazing heavenward when he was bound on the altar (ילקוט מעם לועז מאת רבי יעקב כולי, בראשית כז,א, Yalkut Me'am Lo'ez by Rabbi Yaakov Culi, Genesis 27,1).

Since Isaac saw more of G-d's appearance than any of the other patriarchs, therefore when Hashem said וארא, "And I appeared," perhaps an emphasis is placed on Isaac. This emphasis could be indicated by the gematria of וארא, "And I appeared," being equal to the gematria of יצחק, "Isaac."

However, there is also a different answer to the question of what the connection is between these two words which have the same gematria. The answer comes from a pasuk in Micah and a Gemara in Sabbath.

The future redemption of the Children of Israel will be in some way similar to the redemption from Egypt, as stated, כימי צאתך מארץ מצרים אראנו נפלאות (מיכה ז,טו), "Like the days that you went out of the land of Egypt, I will show him marvelous things" (Micah 7,15). The future redemption of the Children of Israel will be to some extent specifically on the merit of Isaac, but not on the merit of Abraham nor on the merit of Jacob. Referring to the sins of the Children of Israel, Isaac will say to G-d, אם אתה סובל את כולם מוטב ואם לאו פלגא עלי ופלגא עליך ואתי"ל כולם עלי הא קריבית נפשי קמך פתחו ואמרו אתה אבינו אמר להם יצחק עד שאתם מקלסין לי קלסו להקב"ה (שבת פט:), "If You will bear all of them, it is good. And if not, let half be on me, and half will be on You. And if You were to say all should be on me, I offered myself before You. They [the Children of Israel] opened up and said, 'You are our father.' Isaac said to them, 'Rather then laud me, laud the Holy One, Blessed be He'" (Shabbath 89b).

Since the future redemption of the Children of Israel will be in some way similar to the redemption from Egypt, and that future redemption will be to some extent on the merit of Isaac, therefore the Midrash Rabbah implies that the redemption of the Children of Israel was to some extent specifically on the merit of Isaac. To that extent, when G-d said He appeared to the forefathers, it is only His appearance to Isaac which is similar to the future redemption. This similarity is indicated by the gematria of וארא, "And I appeared," being equal to the gematria of יצחק, "Isaac."

וגם אני שמעתי את נאקת בני ישראל אשר מצרים מעבדים אתם ואזכר את בריתי (שמות ו,ה).
And I have also heard the groaning of the Children of Israel, whom the Egyptians compel to serve them, and I have remembered My covenant (Exodus 6,5).

In contrast to the Midrash Rabbah which implied that the redemption of the Children of Israel was to some extent specifically on the merit of Isaac, the Midrash Tanhuma says that it was in the merit of Jacob that the Bnei Yisroel were redeemed from Egypt, as it states, ובזכות יעקב נגאלו ממצרים שנאמר ויעמידה ליעקב לחק (תהלים קה,י) (מדרש תנחומא, פרשת שמות, אות ד,) "And in the merit of Jacob they were redeemed from Egypt, as it says, 'and He upheld it for Jacob as a statute'" (Psalms 105,10) (Midrash Tanhuma, Parashath Exodus, Letter 4). The statute quoted by the Midrash Tanhuma is from a pasuk in Psalms (תהלים קה,י, Psalms 105,10), and refers to its antecedent, "the word which He commanded to a thousand generations," mentioned two pesukim earlier. The word which Hashem will keep for a thousand generations is the covenant which He will keep with those who love Him and keep His mitzvoth. Both Rashi and the Metsudath David (רש״י, ומצודת דוד, תהלים קה,ח, Rashi, and Metsudath David, Psalms 105,8) base their explanation on a pasuk from the Torah, "And know that Hashem is your G-d, He is the G-d, the faithful G-d, Who keeps the covenant and the kindness with those who love Him and with those who keep His mitzvoth for a thousand generations" (דברים ז,ט, Deuteronomy 7,9). Thus, if one loves Hashem and keeps His mitzvoth, Hashem will keep His covenant with that person for a thousand generations. The Midrash Rabbah says, יעקב קיים מה שכתוב בתורה,

"Jacob observed what is written in the Torah," (מדרש רבה, סדר ויקרא, פרשה ב, אות י, Midrash Rabbah, Sidrah Leviticus, Parashah 2, Letter 10). Since Jacob observed what is written in the Torah, that is, he observed all 613 Mitzvoth, he merited having Hashem keep His covenant with him for a thousand generations. Therefore, the statute quoted by the Midrash Tanhuma, whose antecedent is דבר צוה לאלף דור, "the word which He commanded to a thousand generations," is based on the fact that Jacob observed all of the 613 Mitzvoth. Since the Midrash Tanhuma says that in the merit of Jacob the Bnei Yisroel were redeemed from Egypt, therefore it can be deduced that in the merit of Jacob observing the 613 Mitzvoth the Bnei Yisroel were redeemed from Egypt. In short, since Jacob observed the 613 Mitzvoth, the Bnei Yisroel were redeemed. By the employment of a gematria, this explanation can be discerned in the pasuk first quoted from the Torah, as stated, וגם אני שמעתי את נאקת בני ישראל אשר מצרים מעבדים אתם ואזכר את בריתי (שמות ו,ה), "And I have also heard the groaning of the Children of Israel, whom the Egyptians compel to serve them, and I have remembered my covenant" (Exodus 6,5). The gematria of נאקת בני, "the groaning of the Children," is 613.

$$
\begin{array}{rr}
\text{נאקת} & 551 \\
\text{בני} & \underline{62} \\
& 613
\end{array}
$$

Jacob was also called Yisroel (בראשית לה,י, Genesis 35,10); so נאקת בני, "the groaning of the Children," can denote the 613 Mitzvoth which Jacob observed. Thus, the entire pasuk would be explained as follows: וגם אני שמעתי, And I still recall, את נאקת בני, the 613 Mitzvoth, ישראל, of Jacob, אשר מצרים מעבדים אתם, in relation to the bondage of Egypt, ואזכר את בריתי, I will remember My covenant. Note that both this pasuk from Exodus and the pasuk from Psalms refer to Hashem's covenant, which adds credence to this explanation.

כי ידבר אלכם פרעה לאמר תנו לכם מופת ואמרת אל אהרן
קח את מטך והשלך לפני פרעה יהי לתנין (שמות ז,ט).
When Pharaoh shall speak to you, saying, "Give for yourself a wonder," then you shall say to Aaron, "Take your staff and cast it down before Pharaoh." It shall be a serpent (Exodus 7,9).

Hashem had instructed Moses that when Pharaoh would demand a sign, Moses should tell Aaron to throw down his staff. The Torah uses the word אלכם, "to you," to designate the second person regarding Moses and Aaron. The gematria of אלכם, "to you," is 91.

אלכם   91

Pharaoh's asking for a sign was only an excuse; he refused to let the Bnei Yisroel leave even after he saw the sign which he had demanded. That which Pharaoh was to ask of Moses and Aaron, which the Torah records he would would say, אלכם, "to you," was only a refusal to let the Bnei Yisroel leave cloaked in a request. Note, the Sforno comments later that Pharaoh's heart remained hard despite his recognizing the difference between the wonders which Moses and Aaron had performed and the deeds of the Egyptian magicians (ספורנו, שמות ז,יד, Sforno, Exodus 7,14). The Sforno's comment would lead one to believe that Pharaoh's request was only an excuse.

The Sforno's comment is on the pasuk in which Hashem tells Moses that Pharaoh's heart is hard, refusing to let the Bnei Yisroel leave, as stated, ויאמר ה' אל משה כבד לב פרעה מאן לשלח העם (שמות ז,יד), "And G-d said to Moses, Pharaoh's heard is hardened, he refuses to send away the people" (Exodus 7,14). The gematria of מאן, "refuses," is 91.

מאן   91

The fact that the gematria of אלכם, "to you," is equal

to the gematria of מאן, "refuses," could be an indication that Hashem had instructed Moses that what Pharaoh will demand אלכם, "to you," is only that Pharaoh מאן, "refuses," to let the Bnei Yisroel leave. His refusal was cloaked in a request.

כי אם אינך משלח את עמי הנני משליח בך ובעבדיך ובעמך ובבתיך את הערב ומלאו בתי מצרים את הערב וגם האדמה אשר הם עליה (שמות ח,יז).

For if you will not send away My people, behold I will send a mixture of noxious beasts upon you, and upon your servants, and upon your people, and into your houses; and the houses of the Egyptians shall be full of a mixture of noxious beasts, and also the ground whereon they are (Exodus 8,17).

The word הנני, "behold I," is not mentioned in regard to any of the ten plagues until after the plague of כנים, "lice," at which point it is used in connection with the plague of ערב, "a mixture of noxious beasts." The gematria of הנני, "behold I," is 115.

הנני   115

Why is the word הנני, "Behold I," not mentioned until after the plague of כנים, "lice"? Perhaps the answer lies in what the Torah says about the plague of lice. Namely, that it was only after the magicians of Pharaoh could not reproduce the lice, that they acknowledged the plague to be an act of G-d (Exodus 8,14-15). Two pesukim before this acknowledgment of the magicians, the Torah says how the plague of lice occurred, as stated, ויעשו כן ויט אהרן את ידו במטהו ויך את עפר הארץ ותהי הכנם באדם ובבהמה כל עפר הארץ היה כנים בכל ארץ מצרים (שמות ח,יג), "And they did so, Aaron stretched out his hand with his staff and he smote the dust of the earth, and the lice were upon the man and the beasts, all the dust of the land became lice throughout all the land of Egypt" (Exodus 8,13). The gematria of הכנם, "the lice," is 115.

הכנם   115

It is appropriate that the gematria of הנני, "Behold I," is equal to the gematria of הכנם, "the lice," for it was only after the plague of הכנם, "the lice," that Hashem used the word הנני, "Behold I," in reference to the ten plagues. The plague of lice was like a prerequisite for the use of the word "Behold I," by Hashem. Only after the plague of lice was there recognition of Hashem by the Egyptians; only after Hashem was recognized by the Egyptians did He state "Behold I." Conceivably, Hashem held back until after the plague of lice, when His presence was sufficiently felt by the Egyptians to warrant the use of the word הנני, "Behold I."

ויאמר פרעה אנכי אשלח אתכם וזבחתם לה׳ אלקיכם במדבר רק הרחק לא תרחיקו ללכת העתירו בעדי (שמות ח,כד).

And Pharaoh said, "I will send you out and you may sacrifice to the Lord your G-d in the desert; only do not go very far away, and pray for me" (Exodus 8,24).

When Pharaoh asked that Moses pray for him, he used the work בעדי, "for me." The gematria of בעדי, "for me," is 86.

בעדי   86

Pharaoh's request was that Moses pray for the plague of a ערב, "a mixture of noxious beasts," to cease; for he realized that the plague had come because the Children of Israel had not been able to sacrifice to G-d (אבן עזרא, שמות ח,כא, Ibn Ezra, Exodus 8,21). Pharaoh wanted Hashem to deal with him in a merciful manner, not with strict judgment. When Hashem's attribute of judgment is alluded to, He is referred to as אלקים, "G-d" (רש״י, בראשית ח,א, Rashi, Genesis 8,1). The gematria of אלקים, "G-d," is 86.

אלקים   86

Since the gematria of בעדי, "for me," equals the gematria of אלקים "G-d," one can comprehend that Pharaoh's request of Moses was that he wanted Hashem to deal with him in a merciful manner, not with strict judgment.

ויכבד פרעה את לבו גם בפעם הזאת ולא שלח את העם (שמות ח,כח).

And Pharaoh hardened his heart also this time, and he did not send out the people (Exodus 8,28).

After the plague of a mixture of noxious beasts, Pharaoh would not let the Bnei Yisroel leave since ויכבד, "and he hardened," his heart. The gematria of ויכבד, "and he hardened," is 42.

ויכבד   42

Immediately after the Torah tells of this hardening of the heart, it is reported that Hashem told Moses to warn Pharaoh, that if he should refuse to send out the Bnei Yisroel, the plague of דבר, "murrain," will occur. In the warning the pronoun used to refer to the Bnei Yisroel is בם, "them," as stated, כי אם מאן אתה לשלח ועודך מחזיק בם (שמות ט,ב), "For if you refuse to send [them] out, and you still hold them" (Exodus 9,2). The gematria of בם, "them," is 42.

בם   42

Since the gematria of ויכבד, "and he hardened," and the gematria of בם, "them," are identical, that is, the gematria of why Pharaoh did not let the Bnei Yisroel leave, and the gematria of the pronoun used to refer to the Bnei

Yisroel, are identical, there is an insight into Hashem's warning before the plague of murrain. The warning may have been that Pharaoh should not refuse to send out the Bnei Yisroel by hardening his heart as he had done following the plague of a mixture of noxious beasts.

ויאמר ה' אל משה השכם בבקר והתיצב לפני פרעה ואמרת אליו כה אמר ה' אלקי העברים שלח את עמי ויעבדני (שמות ט',יג).

And G-d said to Moses, "Rise up early in the morning and stand before Pharaoh, and you shall say to him, Thus says G-d, the G-d of the Hebrews: Send out My people and they will serve Me" (Exodus 9,13).

Before the plague of ברד, "hail," Moses was commanded to tell Pharaoh that Hashem wants His people freed. Hashem refers to the Bnei Yisroel as עמי, "My people." The gematria of עמי, "my people," is 120.

עמי   120

In Parashath Ekev the Torah tells us that the Bnei Yisroel are to walk in G-d's ways (Deuteronomy 11,22). On this pasuk Rashi says, He is merciful, you should be merciful. He performs acts of kindness, you should perform acts of kindness (רש"י, דברים יא,כב, Rashi, Deuteronomy 11,22). This pasuk means that we are to act in the same manner as G-d acts, we are to emulate His ways. Before the plague of ברד, "hail," Moses was further commanded to tell Pharaoh that the purpose the plague of ברד, "hail," is that Pharaoh should know that there is none like G-d, as stated, כי בפעם הזאת אני שלח את כל מגפתי אל לבך ובעבדיך ובעמך בעבור תדע כי אין כמני בכל הארץ (שמות ט,יד), "For this time I will send all of My plagues upon your heart, and upon your servants, and upon your people; in order that you may know that there is none like Me in all the earth" (Exodus 9,14). The gematria of כמני, "like Me," is 120.

כמני   120

Since the gematria of עמי, "my people," and כמני, "like me," are the same, it can be explained that the time Hashem says the Bnei Yisroel are considered עמי, "my people," is when they are כמני, "like Me"; that is, when they fulfill the pasuk in Parashath Ekev where the Torah tells them that they are to act in the same manner as G-d acts.

The above mentioned concept can be enhanced by the following observation. The plague before the plague of דבר, "pestilence," was the plague of ערב, "a mixture of noxious beasts". The plague before the plague of a mixture of noxious beasts was the plague of כנים, "lice" (שמות ח,יב־טו, Exodus 8,12-15). The Torah says how the plague of lice occurred, as stated, ויעשו כן ויט אהרן את ידו במטהו ויך את עפר הארץ ותהי הכנם באדם ובבהמה כל עפר הארץ היה כנים בכל ארץ מצרים (שמות ח,יג), "And they did so, Aaron stretched out his hand with his staff and he smote the dust of the earth, and the lice were upon the man and the beasts, all the dust of the land became lice through-out all the land of Egypt" (Exodus 8,13). The gematria of כנים, "lice," is 120.

כנים   120

The gematria of כמני, "like me," and the gematria of כנים, "lice," are the same, as are their letters. A parallel may be drawn. Hashem gave something to the Bnei Yisroel and something to the Egyptians, each represented by the same gematria. To the Bnei Yisroel He gave the opportunity of being כמני, "like Me"; to the Egyptians He gave the כנים, "lice." Although this last observation is a דרשה, "homiletical inter-pretation," and not the פשט, "plain meaning," peshat, another point can be added. The word כמני, "like me," is stated in reference to the plague of hail; the word כנים, "lice," is stated in reference to the plague of lice; thus the plague of a mixture of noxious beasts is between the plague where כמני, "like me," is mentioned and the plague where כנים, "lice," is mentioned. Since it was said that כמני, "like me," and כנים, "lice," represent different things given to the Bnei Yisroel and to the Egyptians respectively, the plague of a mixture of noxious beasts separates between that which was given to the Bnei Yisroel and that which was given to the Egyptians.

In reference to the plague of a mixture of noxious beasts the Torah states, ושמתי פדת בין עמי ובין עמך למחר יהיה האת הזה (שמות ח,יט), "And I will put a deliverance between my people and your people; tomorrow shall be this sign" (Exodus 8,19). Although the word פדת is often translated as "division," Onkelos more accurately translates the word פדת as "deliverance." Onkelos gives a similar translation to the word תפדה, "you shall redeem," where redemption is surely meant (Exodus 13,13). On this pasuk in reference to the plague of a mixture of noxious beasts Rashi says, that the deliverance will separate between my people and your people (רש"י, שמות ח,יט, Rashi, Exodus 8,19). Continuing along the path of the derash, it can be said that the division stated in reference to the plague of a mixture of noxious beasts refers to the fact that the plague of a mixture of noxious beasts separates between that which was given to the Bnei Yisroel and that which was given to the Egyptians in the plagues of hail and lice respectively. Note that Hashem gave all the plagues to the Egyptians, but a reason for singling out the plague of lice is that it was the first plague that the Egyptians acknowledged as being from G-d (שמות ח,טו, Exodus 8,15).

Parashath Bo   פרשת בא

ויאמר ה' אל משה ואל אהרן בארץ מצרים לאמר
(שמות יב,א).
And G-d said to Moses and to Aaron in the land
of Egypt, saying (Exodus 12,1).

When Hashem commanded the mitzvah of the new
month, He addressed both Moses and Aaron. The combined
gematria of משה, "Moses," and אהרן, "Aaron," is 601.

$$\begin{array}{lr} \text{משה} & 345 \\ \text{אהרן} & \underline{256} \\ & 601 \end{array}$$

The mitzvah of the new month was the first which
Hashem commanded the Bnei Yisroel, and it was through
Moses and Aaron, (רש״י, שמות יב,א, Rashi, Exodus 12,1).
When Hashem spoke to Moses and Aaron, he said,
החדש הזה לכם ראש חדשים ראשון הוא לכם לחדשי השנה (שמות יב,ב),
"This month shall be to you the beginning of months; it shall
be to you the first of the months of the year" (Exodus 12,2).
The gematria of הוא, "it," is 12.

$$\text{הוא} \qquad 12$$

When the gematria of משה, "Moses," and אהרן, "Aaron," is
added to the gematria of הוא, "it," the total is equal to 613.

$$\begin{array}{r} 601 \\ \underline{12} \\ 613 \end{array}$$

There is a total of 613 Mitzvoth which Hashem commanded the Bnei Yisroel. Thus, the phrase, ראשון הוא לכם, "it
is the first to you," can be read: ראשון, this mitzvah which is
the first of the 613 so commanded, הוא, is the mitzvah of the
new month, לכם, was commanded to the Bnei Yisroel through

you, Moses and Aaron. Since the total gematria of משה, "Moses," and אהרן, "Aaron," when added to the gematria of הוא, "it," is equal is 613, the rereading of the phrase in relationship to the 613 Mitzvoth ties the gematria and the phrase together.

החדש הזה לכם ראש חדשים ראשון הוא לכם לחדשי
השנה (שמות יב,ב).

This month shall be to you the beginning of months; it shall be to you the first of the months of the year (Exodus 12,2).

When the mitzvah of the new month was stated, the year was referred to as לחדשי השנה, "of the months of the year." The gematria of לחדשי השנה, "of the months of the year," is 712.

לחדשי	352
השנה	360
	712

The expression לחדשי השנה, "of the months of the year," seems superfluous, for the meaning of the pasuk is clear without these words. Why was this expression written in the Torah?

The Jewish lunar calendar which is based on a twelve lunar month year, falls short of the civil solar calendar by approximately ten, eleven, or twelve days annually. In any given year, this difference depends on both the months of Heshvan and Kislev being maleh (full, consisting of 30 days) or haser (defective, consisting of 29 days), or one is maleh and the other is haser (משנה תורה, ספר זמנים הלכות קדוש החדש, פרק ח הלכה ה, Mishnah Torah, Book of Zeraim, Laws of Sanctification of the New Moon, Chapter 8, Law 5). To account for this difference, in every nineteen years the Jewish lunar calendar has seven leap years, in which a month is added to the year. But even after nineteen years, the Jewish lunar calendar is still 1 hour and 485 חלקים, hallakim, short of nineteen solar years.

There is a total of 1080 hallakim in one hour. Thus, every nineteen Jewish lunar years differ from nineteen solar years by 1 hour and 485 hallakim, or 1565 hallakim.

$$\begin{array}{r} 1080 \\ \underline{485} \\ 1565 \end{array}$$

This difference is accounted for by Heshvan and Kislev being 30 as opposed to 29 days (שבילי דרקיע מאת הרב ישראל, Shevilei Derakia by ליפשיץ הקדמה למשניות, סדר מועד אות יז־מ, Rabbi Yisroel Lipschitz, Introduction to the Mishnayoth, Seder Moed, Letter 17-40). The 1565 hallakim are significant, since they represent the difference between the Jewish lunar and the civil solar calendars. Most of the discrepancy is accounted for regularly by the seven leap years every nineteen years. But the 1565 hallakim are a difference which is not accounted for by the regular constant cycle. Thus, 1565 is the difference between the Jewish lunar and the civil solar calendars.

Originally, the months in the Jewish calendar were named in Hebrew as first, second, etc., starting from Nisan. The first month means the first month after the Egyptian Galuth, the same for the second, third, etc. After the Babylonian Galuth the months assumed Persian names, which they still have. The reason is that the months now commemorate the exodus from the Egyptian Galuth and the Babylonian Galuth (רמב״ין שמות יב,ב, Ramban, Exodus 12,2). The gematria of גלות, "exile," plus the gematria of מצרים, "Egyptian," and בבל, "Babylonian," is 853.

$$\begin{array}{rr} \text{גלות} & 439 \\ \text{מצרים} & 380 \\ \text{בבל} & \underline{34} \\ & 853 \end{array}$$

When 853 is added to 712, which, as was shown, is the gematria of לחדשי השנה, "of the months of the year," the total is 1565.

$$712$$
$$853$$
$$\overline{1565}$$

Since 1565 is the number of hallakim that the Jewish lunar calendar differs from the civil solar calendar, the pasuk which mentions לחדשי השנה, "of the months of the year," can be interpreted as follows: החדש הזה לכם ראש חדשים, the lunar month of Nisan is your first month, ראשון הוא לכם, it is first in importance to you, לחדשי השנה, to count the months of the year in relation to the Egyptian and Babylonian Galuth. Note that "first," is used to mean first in importance, not just first as opposed to second.

Why is it most important to count the months of the year in relation to the Egyptian and Babylonian Galuth? Since the gematria of לחדשי השנה, "of the months of the year," when added to the gematria of גלות, "exile," plus the gematria of מצרים, "Egyptian," and בבל, "Babylonian," total 1565, which is the number of hallakim that the Jewish lunar calendar differs from the civil solar calendar, the pasuk is instructing that for a Jew, Jewish issues should be first in importance, rather than civil issues.

These thoughts can help explain the Gemara which says that one should be able to rejoice with his suffering (שבת פח:, Shabbath 88b). How can one rejoice with his suffering? If Jewish issues are prominent in a Jew's life, if time centers around Jewish issues and not secular ones, then life has more meaning. Life is devoted to a heritage, a people, a religion. When life is devoted to such ideals, then the troubles of life are easier to bear. The troubles are part of the purpose of life; under these circumstance one can rejoice with his suffering.

והיה היום הזה לכם לזכרון וחגתם אתו חג לה׳ לדרתיכם
חקת עולם תחגהו (שמות יב,יד).

And this day shall be to you for a memorial and you shall celebrate it as a holiday to G-d, throughout your generations, an ordinance forever, you shall celebrate it (Exodus 12,14).

The Torah tells that the day of the going forth from Egypt is to be לזכרון, "for a memorial." The gematria of לזכרון, "for a memorial," is 313.

לזכרון   313

Rashi derives the date of the day of the going forth from Egypt, which is to be a memorial, from the Torah's reference to this day as the "morrow after the Passover" (רש״י שמות יב,יד, Rashi, Exodus 12,14). Thus, the Passover sacrifice is associated with making this day לזכרון, "for a memorial." It also seems obvious that part of making this day for a memorial is for one to have brought the Passover sacrifice the previous day. If one has not brought a Passover sacrifice, he has not done all he could do to fulfill making this day for a memorial. One of the references the Torah uses to designate one who has not brought a Passover sacrifice, is he who is on a journey רחקה, "afar off," as stated, דבר אל בני ישראל לאמר איש איש כי יהיה טמא לנפש או בדרך רחקה לכם או לדרתיכם ועשה פסח לה׳ (במדבר ט,י), "Speak to the Children of Israel saying, 'If any man of you or of your generations shall be ritually defiled due to a dead body, or be on a journey afar off, he shall make the Passover to G-d,'" (Numbers 9,10). The gematria of רחקה, "afar off," is 313.

רחקה   313

The gematria of לזכרון, "for a memorial," and רחקה, "afar off," are the same. The reason could be that one who is רחקה, "afar off," has not done all one could do to fulfill making the day of the going forth from Egypt לזכרון, "for a memorial."

וביום הראשון מקרא קדש וביום השביעי מקרא קדש יהיה לכם כל מלאכה לא יעשה בהם אך אשר יאכל לכל נפש הוא לבדו יעשה לכם (שמות יב,טז).

And on the first day there should be a holy convocation, and on the seventh day a holy convocation to you, all manner of work should not be done on them, however, that which every man must eat, that alone may be done by you (Exodus 12,16).

Although doing work is forbidden on the first day of Yom Tov, the preparation of food is allowed. The gematria of אכל לכל נפש לבדו, "that which every man must eat, alone," is 613.

יאכל	61
לכל נפש	510
לבדו	42
	613

The next pasuk begins (שמות יב,יז) ושמרתם את המצות, "And you shall observe the unleavened bread" (Exodus 12,17). Rashi quotes a Rabbi Josiah who said, אל תהי קורא אֶת הַמַצוֹת אלא את הַמִצְווֹת (רש״י, שמות יב,יז), "Do not read 'the unleavened bread,' but rather 'the commandments'" (Rashi, Exodus 12,17).

Note that the first word of this pasuk begins with a ו, "vav," which joins it to the previous pasuk which allows the preparation of food on Yom Tov. The message could be, that one should eat only to be able to observe G-d's commandments, which corresponds to gematria of אכל לכל נפש לבדו, "that which every man must eat, alone," being 613. This same idea is expressed by the שלחן ערוך, Shulhan Arukh, who writes, אלא יתכוין שיאכל וישתה כפי חיותו לעבוד את בוראו (שלחן ערוך, אורח חיים, סימן רלא, סעיף א), "But one should intend when he eats and drinks that it should be adequate for his vitality in order to serve his Creator" (Shulhan Arukh, Orach Hayyim,

Siman 231, Seif 1). Serving G-d can easily be explained to mean observing G-d's commandments; the message of joining of these two pesukim could be the same idea expressed by the שלחן ערוך, Shulhan Arukh.

והיה כי תבאו אל הארץ אשר יתן ה' לכם כאשר דבר ושמרתם את־העבדה הזאת (שמות יב,כה).

And it shall be, when you come to the land which G-d will give to you, as He has spoken, that you shall observe this service (Exodus 12,25).

The Torah connects the service of the Passover sacrifice with והיה כי, "it shall be when," the Bnei Yisroel come to the land of Israel. The gematria of והיה כי, "it shall be when," is 56.

$$\begin{array}{rr} \text{והיה} & 26 \\ \text{כי} & \underline{30} \\ & 56 \end{array}$$

Rashi says that this mitzvah depends on the time of והיה כי, "it shall be when," the land is entered (רש״י, שמות יב,כה, Rashi, Exodus 12,25). The Torah describes the purpose of the service of the Passover as being לה', "to G-d," as stated, ואמרתם זבח פסח הוא לה' אשר פסח על בתי בני ישראל במצרים בנגפו את מצרים ואת בתינו הציל ויקד העם וישתחוו (שמות יב,כז), "And you shall say, 'It is a Passover sacrifice to G-d Who passed over the houses of the Children of Israel in Egypt when He smote the Egyptians and our houses he delivered'; and the people bowed their heads and they prostrated themselves" (Exodus 12,27). The gematria of לה', "to G-d," is 56.

$$\text{לה'} \quad\quad 56$$

Since the Torah makes this mitzvah dependent on the time of והיה כי, "it shall be when," and the Torah describes the purpose of this mitzvah as being לה׳, "to G-d," these attributes of the Passover sacrifice are related. This relationship is further strengthened by the fact that their gematrioth are identical.

וילכו ויעשו בני ישראל כאשר צוה ה׳ את משה ואהרן כן עשו (שמות יב,כח).

And the Children of Israel went and did as G-d commanded Moses and Aaron, so they did (Exodus 12,28).

After being told about the commandment of קרבן פסח, "Passover sacrifice," the Torah says the Children of Israel went and did as G-d had commanded. The gematria of וילכו... ישראל, "and Israel ... went," is 613.

וילכו	72
ישראל	541
	613

Why does the Torah say וילכו ויעשו, "and they went and did"; it would seem sufficient just to say ויעשו, "and they did"? One answer given in the Torah Sheleimah is that the word וילכו, "and they went," is written to teach that the reward for the preparation of performing a commandment is on par with the reward for performing the commandment. It is written, היינו ששכר הכנת המצוה הוא כמו שכר מצוה (חומש תורה שלמה עם באור "תורה שבעל פה" מאת מנחם מ. בן הרב יצחק פרץ כשר, שמות יב,כח, אות תפז), "That is, that the reward for preparing for a commandment is like the reward for the commandment" (Chumash Torah Sheleimah im Be'ur Torah Shebeal Peh by Menachem M. ben Harov Yitzchak Peretz Kasher, Exodus 12,28 Letter 487).

Since There is a total of 613 Commandments in the Torah (מכות כג:, Makkoth 23b), there are 613 opportunities to gain reward for the preparation of performing these Commandments. The gematria of וילכו ישראל, "and Israel went," being equal to 613 is an allusion to these opportunities.

ויקם פרעה לילה הוא וכל עבדיו וכל מצרים ותהי צעקה גדלה במצרים כי אין בית אשר אין שם מת (שמות יב,ל).
And Pharaoh rose up at night, he and all his servants and all the Egyptians; and there was a great cry in Egypt, for there was not a house where there was not one dead (Exodus 12,30).

The Torah records Pharaoh rising in the לילה, "night." The gematria of לילה, "night," is 75.

לילה   75

The Or Hachayyim explains that the Torah uses the word לילה, "night," because that particular night was bright as day. Although for Pharaoh the night was dark, at the exact same time it was bright for the Bnei Yisroel (אור החיים, שמות יב,ל, Or Hachayyim, Exodus 12,30). A similar thought is found in other commentaries (ספר הזוהר מאת התנא רבי שמעון בן יוחai, פרשת בא, דף לח., וחומש תורה שלמה עם באור "תורה שבעל פה" מאת מנחם מ. בן הרב יצחק פרץ כשר, שמות יב,מב, אות תרטז, The Book of the Zohar by the Tanna Rabbi Shimon ben Yochai, Parashath Bo, Page 38a, and Chumash Torah Sheleimah im Be'ur Torah Shebeal Peh by Menachem M. ben Harov Yitzchak Peretz Kasher, Exodus 12,42, Letter 616). The Or Hachayyim supports this explanation with a רמז, "hint," from another pasuk where ביום ההוא, "on that day," refers to the miracle of that night which was bright as day (אור החיים שמות יב,ל, Or Hachayyim, Exodus 12,30). The pasuk which the Or Hachayyim quoted states, והגדת לבנך ביום ההוא לאמר בעבור זה עשה ה' לי בצאתי ממצרים (שמות יג,ח), "And you shall tell your son on that day saying; 'It is because of that which G-d did for me when I went forth from Egypt'" (Exodus 13,8). The gematria of ביום ההוא, "on that day," is 75.

ביום	58
ההוא	17
	75

The gematria of לילה, "night," equals the gematria of ביום ההוא, "on that day." Since both לילה, "night," and ביום ההוא, "on that day," refer to the miracle of that night which was bright as day, it is extremely appropriate that their gematrioth are identical.

בבית אחד יאכל לא תוציא מן הבית מן הבשר חוצה ועצם
לא תשברו בו (שמות יב,מו).

In one house it shall be eaten; you shall not take out from the house from the meat outside, and you shall not break a bone of it (Exodus 12,46).

When Hashem gave the laws of the Passover sacrifice in Egypt, one of the stipulations was that the meat of the sacrifice should not be taken out of the house where it was eaten. Rashi explains that the word house in this pasuk means group (רש"י שמות יב,מו, Rashi Exodus 12,46). Since Rashi defines מן הבית, "from the house," as מן החבורה, "from the group," it is understood from the pasuk that there is an association between the group and the meat. The gematria of מן הבית, "from the house," is 507.

מן	90
הבית	417
	507

The gematria of הבשר. "the meat," is 507.

הבשר	507

The Gemara Pesahim focuses on the unique stipulation of a Passover sacrifice, when it discusses if one can leave his group when eating הבשר, "the meat," of the Passover sacrifice (:פסחים פה.-פו, Pesahim 85a-86b). This Gemara further confirms the association between מן הבית, "from the house," and הבשר, "the meat." Furthermore, the gematria of מן הבית, "from the house," and the gematria of הבשר, "the meat," being equal, ratifies the association between them.

והיה לך לאות על ידך ולזכרון בין עיניך למען תהיה תורת ה' בפיך כי ביד חזקה הוצאך ה' ממצרים (שמות יג,ט).

And it should be for you a sign on your hand, and a memorial between your eyes, in order that G-d's Torah shall be in your mouth, for with a strong hand G-d took you out of Egypt (Exodus 13,9).

Toward the end of the sidrah there is a pasuk telling the Children of Israel to wear תפלין, "phylacteries," tefillin. From the words of this pasuk the Gemara derives that one should first put the tefillin on one's arm, and afterwards put tefillin on one's head (.מנחות לו, Menahoth 36a). The נתיבי חיים, Netivei Hayim, gives a reason for this principle. The tefillin on one's arm symbolize observing the commandments; the tefillin on one's head symbolize contemplation about the commandments. It is essential that one first observe the commandments; afterwards he may contemplate about them, as stated, אבל להיפך של ראש בלי הנחת תפילין של יד לא תתכן. לפי שזקוקים אנו למעשה וקיום המצוות אפילו אם לא מבינים את טעמי המצוות (נתיבי חיים מאת הרב חיים משה ראובן אלעזרי, ספר שמות, פרשת בא, דף קעד), "But to reverse the order, placing the tefillin for one's head without placing the tefillin for one's arm, is not proper. Since we are obligated to the practice and maintenance of the commandments, even if we do not understand the reason for the commandments" (Netivei Hayim by Rabbi Chaim Moshe Reuven Elazary, Book of Exodus, Parashath Bo, page 174).

There is an astounding gematria which supports the reason of the Netivei Hayim. The first four words of the pasuk towards the end of the sidrah telling the Children of Israel to wear תפלין, "phylacteries," tefillin, enounce the tefillin for one's arm first. The gematria of והיה לך לאות על, "And it should be for you a sign on," is 613.

והיה לך	76
לאות על	537
	613

Since there is a total of 613 Commandments in the Torah (מכות כג:, Makkoth 23b), the first four words of the pasuk telling the Children of Israel to wear tefillin can indicate the obligation for the practice and observance of the commandments. The next word in the pasuk designates the tefillin for the arm. Thus, the first five words of the pasuk are saying the tefillin for one's arm symbolize observing the commandments, which supports the reason of the נתיבי חיים, Netivei Hayim.

והיה לך לאות על ידך ולזכרון בין עיניך למען תהיה תורת ה' בפיך כי ביד חזקה הוצאך ה' ממצרים (שמות יג,ט).
And it shall be a sign for you on your hand and a memorial between your eyes, in order that the Torah of G-d should be in your mouth; for with a strong hand G-d took you out of Egypt (Exodus 13,9).

To determine the construction of the tefillin Rashi says the word טט, "tat," in Coptic language means two, and פת, "pas," in African language means two. Although these meanings are based on a Gemara (סנהדרין ד:, Sandehrin 4b) it is a difficult explanation, for why did the Torah have to resort to two foreign languages so that the number of compartments in the head tefillin could be derived? Also according to Rashi the Torah does not say where the head tefillin should be worn. Even when the pasuk says "between the eyes," it means the position opposite between the eyes. The Ramban has a different perspective.

The Ramban says clearly that the purpose of the tefillin is a reminder to observe the commandments, as he writes, למען שתהיה תורת ה׳ בפיך לשמור מצותיו ותורותיו (רמב״ן שמות יג,ט), "In order that the Torah of G-d should be in your mouth to observe His commandments and His Torahs" (Ramban, Exodus 13,9). Seven pesukim later the Ramban, differing from Rashi, defines the word ולטוטפת, "and for frontlets," as an ornament placed on the head, as he writes, אבל רבותינו יקראו הדבר המנח בראש טוטפת (רמב״ן שמות יג,טז), "But our Rabbis called the thing which rests on the head, frontlets" (Ramban, Exodus 13,16). The Ramban justifies his definition by quoting from the Gemara which says, אמר רבי אבהו טוטפת המוקפת לה מאזן לאזן (שבת נז:), "Rabbi Abbahu said, A frontlet is that which wraps around her from ear to ear" (Shabbath 57b). Thus, the definition of the Ramban is very appealing, for now the word ולטוטפת, "and for frontlets," is designating where the head tefillin are worn.

There are two additional words which designate where the tefillin are worn. One is ידכה, "your arm," in a feminine form (שמות יג,טז, Exodus 13,16), which the Gemara defines as the weaker arm, that is, the left arm for most people (מנחות לז., Menahoth 37a). The other is ידך, "your arm," in a masculine form (שמות יג,ט, Exodus 13,9), which on that same page of the Gemara, R. Jose Hahorem says that the word can also refer to the right arm. The Malbim, based on that Gemara, defines this form of the word as referring to either arm, as he writes, ולמה בפי כי יביאך ובפי שמע אמר ידך שכולל גם ימין, ומשיב שמלמד שאם הוא גידם שנקטעה יד שמאלו יתן בימין (התורה והמצוה, מאת הרב מאיר ליבוש מלביי״ם, שמות יג, ט), "And why in the portion of 'When He will bring you,' and in the portion of 'Hear,' does it say ידך, 'your arm,' which also includes the right? And he [R. Jose Hahorem] answers that it teaches that if it is lopped off, that is, his left arm is truncated, he should place [the tefillin] on his right arm" (The Torah and the Mitzvah by Rabbi Meir Lebush Malbim Exodus 13,9).

Thus, there are three words which designate where the tefillin are worn. The gematria of ולטוטפת, "and for frontlets," ידכה, "your arm," and ידך, "your arm," is 613.

ולטוטפת	540
ידכה	39
ידך	34
	613

Since the gematria of the three words which designate where the tefillin are worn is equal to the total number of commandments, there is substantiation to the Ramban's saying that the purpose of the tefillin is a reminder to observe the commandments.

Parashath Beshallach   פרשת בשלח

וה' הלך לפניהם יומם בעמוד ענן לנחתם הדרך ולילה
בעמוד אש להאיר להם ללכת יומם ולילה (שמות יג,כא).

And G-d was going before them by day in a
pillar of loud, to lead them the way; and by
night in a pillar of fire, to give light to them, to
go by day and by night (Exodus 13,21).

The respective purposes of the pillar of cloud and of
the pillar of fire were לנחתם הדרך, "to lead them the way," and
to provide light. The gematria of לנחתם הדרך, "to lead them
the way," is 757.

528	לנחתם
<u>229</u>	הדרך
757	

The Gemara Baba Mezia seeks to pinpoint the exact
reason why the Bnei Yisroel merited the pillar of cloud and the
pillar of fire in the desert. According to both Rav Judah in
Rav's name and R. Hama son of R. Hanina, the reason was
the merit of Abraham. The Gemara says, אמר רב יהודה אמר רב
כל מה שעשה אברהם למלאכי השרת בעצמו עשה הקב"ה לבניו בעצמו וכל
מה שעשה אברהם ע"יי שליח עשה הקב"ה לבניו ע"יי שליח... ואברהם הולך
עמם לשלחם והי הולך לפניהם יומם... ופליג דר' חמא בר' חנינא דאמר ר'
חמא בר' חנינה וכן תנא דבי רבי ישמעאל... בשכר והוא עומד עליהם זכו
לעמוד הענן (בבא מציעא פו:), "Rav Judah said in Rav's name,
Everything which Abraham did by himself for the ministering
angels, the Holy One, Blessed be He, did by himself for his
descendants. And everything which Abraham did through a
emissary, the Holy One, Blessed be He, did through an emissary for his descendants ... And Abraham went with them to
escort them; and G-d went before them by day [in a pillar of
cloud] ... And he argues with R. Hama the son of R. Hanina.
R. Hama the son of R. Hanina said, and also it was taught in

School of Rabbi Ishmael, that ... and [because] he stood over them, they merited the pillar of cloud" (Baba Mezia 86b). The gematria of אברהם, "Abraham," is 248.

אברהם   248

The sum of the gematrioth of לנחתם הדרך, "to lead them the way," and אברהם, "Abraham," is 1005.

248
757
1005

Thus, 1005 represents why the Bnei Yisroel had the pillars which led them on the way.

The Torah tells that the time when the Bnei Yisroel had the pillars accompanying them was ללכת יומם ולילה, "to go by day and by night." The gematria of ללכת יומם ולילה, "to go by day and by night," is 657.

ללכת   480
יומם   96
ולילה   81
657

Rashi on this pasuk says that the Bnei Yisroel were guided by a שליח, "emissary," which was the pillar of cloud. Rashi states, אף כאן להנחותם על ידי שליח ומי הוא השליח עמוד הענן והקב״ה בכבודו מוליכו לפניהם (רש״י, שמות יג,כא) "Also here they were led by an emissary. And what was the emissary? The pillar of cloud, which G-d Himself would cause to go in front of them" (רש״י שמות יג,כא, Rashi, Exodus 13,21). The gematria of שליח, "emissary," is 348.

שליח   348

The sum of the gematrioth of ללכת יומם ולילה, "to go by day and by night," and שליח, "emissary," is 1005.

$$657$$
$$348$$
$$\overline{}$$
$$1005$$

Thus, 1005 represents the time when the Bnei Yisroel were guided by an emissary in the form of a pillar.

The gematrioth given show that 1005 represents why the Bnei Yisroel had the pillars which led them on the way, and it also represents the time when the Bnei Yisroel were led by an emissary in the form of a pillar. This equality has a logical explanation. It was in the merit of Abraham that the Bnei Yisroel were led on the way by the pillars which acted as emissaries both by day and by night.

וה׳ הלך לפניהם יומם בעמוד ענן לנחתם הדרך ולילה
בעמוד אש להאיר להם ללכת יומם ולילה (שמות יג,כא).
And G-d was going before them by day in a
pillar of cloud, to lead them the way; and by
night in a pillar of fire, to give light to them, to
go by day and by night (Exodus 13,21).

Hashem led the Bnei Yisroel with pillars. During the day there was one pillar; during the night another, but for both pillars the Torah uses the word בעמוד, "in a pillar." The gematria of בעמוד, "in a pillar," is 122.

בעמוד   122

The purpose of each pillar was to lead the Bnei Yisroel, as the pasuk says. To lead someone or some group is to ensure that they do not become lost. Pharaoh concluded that the Bnei Yisroel were נבכים, "lost," as stated, ואמר פרעה לבני ישראל נבכים הם בארץ סגר עליהם המדבר (שמות יד,ג), "And Pharaoh will say of the Children of Israel, they are lost in the land, the wilderness has shut them in" (Exodus 14,3). The gematria of נבכים, "lost," is 122.

נבכים   122

The gematria of בעמוד, "in a pillar," equals the gematria of נבכים, "lost." This parity might well be to convey that if Hashem did not lead the Bnei Yisroel בעמוד, "in a pillar," they might well have been נבכים, "lost."

וה' הלך לפניהם יומם בעמוד ענן לנחתם הדרך ולילה בעמוד אש להאיר להם ללכת יומם ולילה (שמות יג,כא).

And G-d was going before them by day in a pillar of cloud, to lead them the way; and by night in a pillar of fire, to give light to them, to go by day and by night (Exodus 13,21).

Hashem led the Bnei Yisroel with pillars. During the day was one pillar; during the night another pillar. The purpose of the pillar during the day was לנחתם, "to lead them." The gematria of לנחתם, "to lead them," is 528.

לנחתם   528

The purpose of the pillar during the night was להאיר, "to give light." The gematria of להאיר, "to give light," is 246.

להאיר   246

The combined gematria of לנחתם, "to lead them," and להאיר, "to give light," is 774.

$$528$$
$$\underline{246}$$
$$774$$

The Torah further tells that the pillars were with the Bnei Yisroel day and night, as stated, לא ימיש עמוד הענן יומם ועמוד האש לילה לפני העם (שמות יג,כב), "He did not remove the pillar of cloud by day, nor the pillar of fire by night from before the people" (Exodus 13,22). The gematria of יומם, "by day," is 96.

יומם   96

The gematria of לילה, "by night," is 75.

לילה   75

The combined gematria of יומם, "by day," and לילה, "by night," is 171.

96
75
___
171

Thus, 774 represents the purpose of the pillars, to lead them and to give light; 171 represents the time the pillars functioned, by day and by night. The time the pillars functioned, fulfilling their purpose, would be represented by the sum of 774 plus 171, which is 945.

774
171
___
945

The Torah tells that Hashem was going before the Bnei Yisroel in the pillars יומם ולילה, "by day and by night," as stated, וה׳ הלך לפניהם יומם בעמוד ענן לנחתם הדרך ולילה בעמוד אש להאיר להם ללכת יומם ולילה (שמות יג,כא), "And G-d was going before them by day in a pillar of cloud, to lead them the way; and by night in a pillar of fire, to give light to them, to go by day and by night" (Exodus 13,21). The gematria of יומם ולילה, "by day and by night," is 177.

יומם   96
ולילה   81
___
177

Rashi informs that the pillars themselves functioned in two ways: One can be considered a denotation and the other, a connotation; first, the pillar of cloud was a שליח, "emissary"; second, the two pillars were משלים, "complements," to each other. The pillar of cloud was an emissary, as stated, להנחותם ע״י שליח (רש״י, שמות יג,כא), "to lead them by means of an emissary," (רש״י, שמות יג,כא, Rashi, Exodus 13,21). The gematria of שליח, "an emissary," is 348.

שליח   348

Rashi also informs that the two pillars ccmplemented each other, as stated, מגיד שעמוד הענן משלים לעמוד האש ועמוד האש משלים לעמוד הענן (רש״י, שמות יג,כב), "it teaches that the pillar of cloud complemented the pillar of fire, and the pillar of fire complemented the pillar of cloud" (Rashi, Exodus 13,22). The gematria of משלים, "complemented," is 420.

משלים   420

The combined gematria of שליח, "an emissary," and משלים, "complemented," is 768.

348
420
———
768

Thus, 768 represents the denotation and the connotation of the pillars. First, the pillar of cloud was a שליח, "emissary,"; second, the two pillars were משלים, "complements," to each other. Hashem went before the Bnei Yisroel in the pillars יומם ולילה, "by day and by night." Thus, 177, represents the time when this denotation and this connotation occurred. The time when the pillars fulfilled their denotation and their connotation would be represented by the sum of 768 plus 177, which is 945.

768
177
———
945

Now there are two gematrioth equal to 945. The gematria representing the time the pillars functioned fulfilling their purpose is equal to the gematria representing the time the pillars fulfilled their denotation and their connotation. A moral lesson can be learned from the joining the gematrioth which represent their denotation and their connotation. A person has a purpose and also a denotation and a connotation to fulfill in life. These should be akin. A Jew who fulfills his purpose leading a Torah true life should also extend himself to observe mitzvoth beyond the letter of the law, that is, he should fulfill the denotation (the commandments themselves) and the connotation (extending himself beyond the letter of the law) of a Torah true life. The equality of this gematria teaches this moral lesson.

ויהי הלך לפניהם יומם בעמוד ענן לנחתם הדרך ולילה בעמוד אש להאיר להם ללכת יומם ולילה (שמות יג,כא).
And G-d was going went before them by day in
a pillar of cloud, to lead them the way; and by
night in a pillar of fire, to give light to them, to
go by day and by night (Exodus 13,21).

The pasuk begins saying, And Hashem led the Bnei Yisroel. The gematria of ויה׳, "And G-d," is 32.

ויה׳   32

Since the letter ו, "vav" is added to G-d's name, making its gematria 32, an interesting interpretation can be given. In the first paragraph of Shema it says, ואהבת את ה׳ אלקיך בכל לבבך ובכל נפשך ובכל מאדך (דברים ו,ה), "And you shall love G-d, your G-d, with all your heart, with all your soul, and with all your might" (Deuteronomy 6,5). However, in the second paragraph of Shema, the Torah only says to love G-d with all your heart and with all your soul (דברים יא,יג, Deuteronomy 11,13). A question can be asked; why does the first paragraph of Shema command to love Hashem with all your might, but the second paragraph does not? A standard answer is that all your soul means that one is required to give up his life for Hashem; with all of your might means one is required to give up all of his wealth for Hashem. It would seem obvious that if one has to give up his life for Hashem, he would be willing to give up his wealth for Hashem. The mentioning of wealth seems unnecessary. However, there are some individuals who would prefer to lose their life, rather than their wealth. On account of these individuals the Torah writes, with all your might, requiring one to love Hashem with all his wealth, even if his wealth is more dear to him than his life. In general, most people love their life more than their wealth. So, since the Torah requires them to give up their life for Hashem, it includes the giving up of one's wealth for Hashem. The first paragraph of Shema is written in the singular; it includes every type of individual, and says, "with all of your might," meaning wealth. The second paragraph of Shema is written in the plural; it excludes the individuals who would prefer to lose their life rather than wealth, and does not say, "with all of your might." From the above question and answer it is clear that most people, who love their life more than their wealth, are required to love Hashem with their heart and soul. People are required to place these two before their own desires, even at the expense of one's life Or Hachayyim, אור החיים, דברים יא,יג, ד״ה, בכל לבבכם ובכל נפשכם) Deuteronomy 11,13, header words: With all your heart and with all your soul). The gematria of לב, "heart," is 32.

לב   32

The Ibn Ezra in Parashath Vayyechi comments that the word honor can refer to the soul (אבן עזרא, בראשית מט,ו, Ibn Ezra, Genesis 49,6). As an example, he also quotes the pasuk, למען יזמרך כבוד ולא ידם ה׳ אלקי לעולם אודך (תהלים ל,יג)" "In order that honor may sing praise to You, and not be silent, O G-d, my G-d, I will give thanks to you forever" (Psalms 30,13). The gematria of כבוד, "honor," is 32.

כבוד   32

Thus, the word honor can refer to the soul (אבן עזרא בראשית מט,ו, Ibn Ezra, Genesis 49,6).

The gematria of וה', "And G-d," in the pasuk that began by saying, "And Hashem led the Bnei Yisroel," is 32, as was shown. Since the gematria of וה', "And G-d," equals the gematria of כבוד, "honor," and also equals the gematria of לב, "heart," the pasuk can be read as follows. People should place their heart and soul for Hashem, that is, before their own desires. Note that honor is being used as a substitute for soul. Also note that the pasuk is in the plural, using the word לפניהם, "in front of them," the plural form, corresponding to the second paragraph of Shema, which is also in the plural. For, according to this interpretation, the pasuk refers to most people who love their life more than their wealth.

Additional significance to the gematrioth of לב, "heart," and כבוד, "honor," can be found in the פרקי אבות, Ethics of the Fathers, section in the the end of the נספח, Appendix, of this sefer.

ויסר את אפן מרכבתיו וינהגהו בכבדת ויאמר מצרים אנוסה מפני ישראל כי ה' נלחם להם במצרים (שמות יד,כה).

And He took off their chariot wheels, and made them drive heavily; the Egyptians said, "Let us flee from the face of Israel, for G-d is fighting for them against the Egyptians" (Exodus 14,25).

The Egyptians recognized that Hashem was fighting against them, for the Bnei Yisroel; the gematria of ה' נלחם להם במצרים, "G-d is fighting for them against the Egyptians," is 611.

ה'	26
נלחם	128
להם	75
במצרים	382
	611

G-d told Moses the reason the Bnei Yisroel were privileged to be redeemed from Egypt, including Hashem's fighting for them against the Egyptians, was the Torah which they would receive at Mt. Sinai, as stated, ויאמר כי אהיה עמך וזה לך האות כי אנכי שלחתיך בהוציאך את העם ממצרים תעבדון את האלקים על ההר הזה (שמות ג,יב ורש״י על הפסוק), "And He said, 'Because I will be with you, and this shall be a token for you that I have sent you, when you have brought the people out of Egypt you shall serve G-d on this mountain'" (Exodus 3,12 and Rashi on this pasuk). The token refers to the giving of the Torah when Moses became known to all as Hashem's messenger, as stated, ואז אודיע לכל שאני שלחתיך כדכ׳ במתן תורה ואמר ה׳ וכו׳ (דעת זקנים מבעלי התוספות, שמות ג,יב), "And then I will make known to all that I sent you, as it is written at the giving of the Torah, and G-d said, etc." (Daat Zekenim Mibaale Hatosafoth, Exodus 3,12). The gematria of תורה, "Torah," is 611.

תורה   611

Thus, the reason that the Bnei Yisroel were privileged to Hashem's fighting for them against the Egyptians was their acceptance of the תורה, "Torah," which has a gematria of 611. As was demonstrated, the gematria of ה׳ נלחם להם במצרים, "G-d is fighting for them against the Egyptians," is 611. Since the reason the Bnei Yisroel were privileged to Hashem's fighting for them against the Egyptians was because of their acceptance of the Torah, it is very appropriate that this expression should have a gematria equal to the gematria of Torah.

ויצעק אל ה׳ ויורהו ה׳ עץ וישלך אל המים וימתקו המים שם שם לו חק ומשפט ושם נסהו (שמות טו,כה).

And he cried out to G-d; and G-d showed him a tree, and he cast it into the waters and the waters became sweet; there He put for them a statute and an ordinance, and there He tested them (Exodus 15,25).

There are a number of difficulties in understanding this pasuk which mentions שם שם, "there He put." The gematria of שם שם, "there He put," is 680.

$$\begin{array}{rr} \text{שם} & 340 \\ \text{שם} & \underline{340} \\ & 680 \end{array}$$

The first question that arises is: The beginning of the pasuk speaks of Moses casting a tree (לפי תרגום יונתן בן עוזיאל, according to Targum Jonathan ben Uzziel) into water to sweeten the water; the end of the pasuk speaks of a statute and an ordinance. Why were these ideas brought together in one pasuk?

The Gemara Berakoth says, ואי״ר חלבו אמר רב הונא כל הנהנה מסעודת חתן ואינו משמחו עובר בחמשה קולות שנא׳ קול ששון וקול שמחה קול חתן וקול כלה קול אומרים הודו את ה׳ צבקות (ירמי׳ לג,יא). ואם משמחו מה שכרו אמר רבי יהושע בן לוי זוכה לתורה שנתנה בחמשה קולות שנא׳ ויהי ביום השלישי בהיות הבקר ויהי קולות וברקים וענן כבד על ההר וקול שופר וגו׳, ויהי קול השופר וגו׳ והאלקים יעננו בקול (שמות יט,טז) (ברכות ו:), "And Rabbi Helbo said in the name of Rav Huna. Anyone who enjoys the meal of a bridegroom and does not felicitate him violates five voices, as is stated, 'The voice of joy and the voice of gladness, the voice of the bridegroom, and the voice of the bride, the voice of those who give thanks to the G-d of Hosts' (Jeremiah 33,11). And if he does felicitate him what is his reward? Rabbi Joshua ben Levi said, he merits Torah which was given with five voices, as is stated, 'And it was on the third day, when it was morning and there was thunder and lighting, and a heavy cloud upon the mountain, and the voice of the shofar, etc. And it was the voice of the shofar, etc. And G-d answered him with a voice'" (Exodus 19,16) (Berakoth 6b).

The second question that arises is: Why does the Gemara choose to use the expression, "violate five voices," and "which was given with five voices?" The Gemara was not lacking punishments nor rewards, expressed in derogatory or complimentary terms, so why was this novel concept of five voices introduced here? The gematria of קול, "voice," is 136.

$$\text{קול} \qquad 136$$

When the gematria of קול, "voice," is multiplied by five, since the Gemara refers to five voices, the product is 680.

$$\begin{array}{r} 136 \\ \times\,5 \\ \hline 680 \end{array}$$

The gematria of שם שם, "there He put," is also 680 (שמות טו,כה, Exodus 15,25), as was shown. The third question that arises is: What connection is there between the five voices with a gematria of 680 and the gematria of שם שם, "there He put," which is also 680?

Thus, there are three questions. One, why was the casting of a tree into water to sweeten the water, and the statute and ordinance brought together in one pasuk? Two, why did the Gemara introduce the concept of the five voices where it did? Three, what connection is there between the five voices with a gematria of 680, and the gematria of שם שם, "there He put," which is also 680?

Perhaps all three questions posed above can be resolved on the basis of a Gemara in Baba Kamma which states, אין מים אלא תורה (בבא קמא פב.), "there is no mention of water which can not be explained to be Torah" (Baba Kamma 82a). Thus, wherever water is mentioned in the Torah, it can allude to, or infer, Torah. When the pasuk says that the waters became sweet, it can indicate that the Torah became sweet. Immediately after the pasuk says that the waters became sweet, are the words שם שם "there He put." On these words Rashi comments that some of the sections of the Torah were taught here in Marah (רש״י, שמות טו,כה, Rashi, Exodus 15,25). Thus it can be comprehended, that when Moses cast a tree, he made the Torah taught in Marah sweet, as the pasuk says, "the waters became sweet." The waters refer to Torah, since wherever water is mentioned it can imply Torah. The שם שם, "there he put," refers to the Torah of Marah, the Torah which was made sweet. The sound of Torah, the voice of Torah, is a sweet sound, a happy sound. This explanation resolves question number one; why the beginning of the pasuk speaks of casting a tree into water to sweeten the water, and the end of the pasuk speaks of a statute and an ordinance. The beginning and the end of the pasuk are referring to the same concept, the sweet sound of Torah. This explanation can resolve question number two, why the Gemara chooses to use the expressions "violates five voices" and "which was given with five voices." If one goes to a wedding meal, a mitzvah meal, he goes to a place of joy, a place where the sweet happy voice of Torah should be heard. If one goes to such a place of Torah joy, and does not add to the joy, does not partake in the happiness, and does not felicitate the bridegroom, then he violates five voices. He does not incur a specific punishment, as the violator of a specific law; but he has violated the spirit of the Torah. The reason being that he had a chance to strengthen, to add, to the sweet voice of the Torah and he did not. The wedding meal is considered one of the happiest times of a man's life, and this happiness should be associated with Torah. This association is why the Gemara chose to introduce the concept of the five voices here, which answers question number two.

This explanation can resolve question number three; what connection is there between the five voices with a gematria of 680, and the gematria of שם שם, "there He put," which is also 680? The שם שם, "there He put," refers to the Torah of Marah, the Torah which was made sweet. The five voices refer to the Torah of Mount Sinai, which should also be sweet. Just as the Torah of Marah was made sweet, so too the

Torah of Mount Sinai should also be sweet. Both have an association to the gematria of 680 number since both should be sweet. Question number three has been answered.

What is the antipode of a proper Jewish wedding meal? The antipode of such a wedding meal is when one, G-d forbid, marries out of the faith; then the happiness is turned into sadness. According to Maimonides, if one does marry out of the faith he violates, "And you shall not marry them, your daughter you should not give to his son, and his daughter you shall not take for your son" (Deuteronomy 7,3). Maimonides also tells of the violator's punishment, לא פגעו בו קנאים ולא הלקוהו ב״ד, הרי עונשו מפורש בדברי קבלה שהוא בכרת שנאמר כי חלל משנה תורה, הלכות איסורי ביאה, פרק שנים) ,יהודה קדש ה׳ (מלאכי ב,יא) ו ,עשר, הלכה א) "If zealots did not kill him, and the court did not flagellate him, behold his punishment is explained in the words of the Prophets, that it is excision, as is stated, 'for Judah profaned the holiness of G-d'"(Malachi 2,11), (Mishnah Torah, Book of Kedushah, Laws of Forbidden Relations, Chapter 12, Law 1 and 6). The gematria of הלקהו, "flagellate him," is 152.

הלקוהו   152

The gematria of חלל יהודה קדש ה׳, "Judah profaned the holiness of G-d," is 528.

חלל	68
יהודה	30
קדש	404
ה׳	26
	528

The combination of these two gematrioth is 680.

152
528
680

Thus, according to Maimonides, one who marries out of the faith, if he is not killed by a zealot, should suffer הלקוהו, "flagellate him," or if not, be excised since he is reckoned under חלל יהודה קדש ה׳, "Judah profaned the holiness of G-d." There is a connection between one who marries out of his faith to the gematria of 680. Since 680 is associated with the sweet voice of Torah, the joy of Torah, and one who felicitates a bridegroom, one who marries out of the faith destroys this joy. He faces a punishment associated with 680, a punishment for destroying the sweet voice of Torah.

ויאמר ה׳ אל משה הנני ממטיר לכם לחם מן השמים ויצא העם ולקטו דבר יום ביומו למען אנסנו הילך בתורתי אם לא (שמות טז,ד).

And G-d said to Moses, Behold I will cause to rain to you bread from heaven and the people will go out and gather a daily portion, daily, in order to test them, if they will go in my Torah, or not (Exodus 16,4).

In reference to the bread which rained from heaven, the Torah uses the word לכם, "to you." The gematria of לכם, "to you," is 90.

לכם   90

It is from the word לכם, "to you," which is written in reference to the manna, that the Gemara learns that sustenance is granted for the sake of the many (תענית ט., Taanith 9a). Thus, the word לכם, "to you," has a distinct association to the manna; it says something distinctive about the manna.

In reference to the bread which rained from heaven, the Torah also uses the word ידעו, "know," as the pasuk says ויראו בני ישראל ויאמרו איש אל אחיו מן הוא כי לא ידעו מה הוא ויאמר משה אלהם הוא הלחם אשר נתן ה׳ לכם לאכלה (שמות טז,טו), "And the Children of Israel saw it and one man said to his brother,

'What is that?' for they did not know what it was; and Moses said to them, 'It is the bread which G-d has given you for food'" (Exodus 16,15). The gematria of מן, "What is?" is 90.

מן   90

The gematria of ידעו, "know," is 90.

ידעו   90

The reason the Bnei Yisroel employed the word מן, "What is?" is that they did not ידעו, "know," what it was. Thus, the word מן, "What is?" comes because of a deficiency of ידעו, "know." It is therefore appropriate that both words have the same gematria. Also, since the word לכם, "to you," tells something distinctive about the manna, so it is appropriate that all three words have the same gematria.

Additional significance to the gematria of מן, "manna," can be found in the פרשת עקב, Parashath Ekev, section of this sefer.

ויאמר משה אלהם איש אל יותר ממנו עד בקר (שמות טז,יט).

And Moses said to them let no man leave over until morning (Exodus 16,19).

At the time when the manna was first given, a pasuk in Parashath Beshallach uses the word איש, "a man," to instruct the Children of Israel not to leave any until בקר, "morning." The gematria of איש, "a man,"is 311.

איש   311

The gematria of בקר, "morning,"is 302.

בקר   302

Two difficulties are apparent in this pasuk. One, although the pasuk is not to exclude woman, why does this pasuk specify a man, as opposed to a woman? Two, why does this pasuk specify not to leave until the morning, as opposed to the מחר, "the next day"? These questions can be answered with a דרשה, "homiletical interpretation," derashah, based on a gematria.

The main reward for fulfilling the commandments is life in the world to come. This reward is indicated by Rashi on the Hummash (רש״י, דברים ז,יא, Rashi, Deuteronomy 7,11), and expressed in a more pellucid style by the Rambam, as he writes, מאחר שנודע שמתן שכרן של מצות והטובה שנזכה לה אם שמרנו דרך ה׳ הכתוב בתורה היא חיי העולם הבא וכו׳ (משנה תורה, ספר המדע, הלכות תשובה, פרק תשיעי, הלכה א), "Whereas it is known that the reward given for commandments, and the good that we shall merit if we observe the way of G-d written in the Torah, is life in the world to come, etc." (Mishnah Torah, Book of Hamadda, Laws of Repentance, Chapter 9, Law 1).

Three additional sources are needed to construct the derashah. The first is from Rashi on the Hummash, where a form of the word יותר, "leave over," is defined as residue (רש״י, בראית ל,לו, Rashi, Genesis 30,36). The second is from the Gemara where it says a derash that the word איש, "man," can refer to G-d, as stated, ואין איש אלא הקב״יה שנא׳ ה׳ איש מלחמה (סוטה מב:), "And the word man refers to no one but the Holy One, Blessed be He, as it says, G-d is a man of war" (Sotah 42b). The third is a Gemara where the world to come is referred to as day, in contrast to this world which is referred to as night, as stated, הכי קאמר דוד אני אמרתי אך חשך ישופני לעוה״יב שהוא דומה ליום עכשיו העולם הזה שהוא דומה ללילה אור בעדי (פסחים ב:), "In this manner David said, I said that also darkness will envelope me in the world to come, which is similar to day; now this world which is similar to night, is light for me" (Pesahim 2b). Since בקר, "morning," is part of the day, it can refer to the world to come.

Combining all three sources perhaps a new meaning can be given to the pasuk in Parashath Beshallach which instructed the Children of Israel at the time when the manna was first given. Moses told the Children of Israel that he prayed to G-d. He prayed, איש, "man," meaning G-d, since אין איש אלא הקב"ה, "And the word man refers to no one but the Holy One, Blessed be He"; do not leave over manna in the world to come, for the word יותר, "leave over," is defined as residue; and בקר, "morning," can refer to the world to come.

The derashah is, Moses was telling the Children of Israel, as stated, ויאמר משה אלהם, "And Moses said to them," that the manna was in answer to his prayer that G-d should give the Children of Israel some manna in this world too, and not have it all left over as their reward in the world to come.

The two difficulties in this pasuk are now answerable. One, why does this pasuk specify a man as opposed to a woman? The answer is that איש, "man," is specified because it can refer to G-d. Two, why does this pasuk specify not to leave until the morning? The answer is that בקר, "morning," can refer to the world to come.

From Rashi on the Hummash and from the Rambam it was shown that the reward for fulfilling the commandments is life in the world to come. Previously, it was demonstrated that the gematria of איש, "a man,"is 311; and the gematria of בקר, "morning,"is 302. Their combined gematria is 613.

$$311$$
$$\underline{302}$$
$$613$$

There is a total of 613 Commandments in the Torah (מכות כג:, Makkoth 23b). Since the pasuk can be understood as referring to the world to come, and since the reward for fulfilling the commandments, which total 613, is life in the world to come, the gematria of 613 in the pasuk accentuates this understanding of the pasuk. Although this is a derashah for this pasuk, the next pasuk returns to the פשט, "plain meaning," peshat, that Moses told the Children of Israel not to leave over manna until morning, and they did not listen to Moses.

ודבורה אשה נביאה אשת לפידות היא שפטה את ישראל בעת ההיא (שופטים ד,ד).

And Deborah was a prophetess, the wife of Lapidoth; she judged Israel at that time (Judges 4,4).

There is a difference of opinions as to where to begin the Haftarah of Parashath Beshallach; according to one opinion the first pasuk to be read is the one quoted. It says that Deborah was a prophetess. It is the responsibility of a prophet to exhort the Bnei Yisroel to observe the 613 Mitzvoth of the Torah (רשב״ם, דברים יח,טו, Rashbam, Deuteronomy 18,15). The gematria of ודבורה אשה נביאה and היא, "And Deborah, a prophetess," and "she," is 613.

ודבורה	223
אשה	306
נביאה	68
היא	16
	613

It is very appropriate that this pasuk, which says that Deborah was a prophetess, should contain the gematria of 613, for a true prophet, or prophetess, has a responsibility to exhort the Bnei Yisroel to observe the 613 Mitzvoth.

כן יאבדו כל אויביך ה' ואהביו כצאת השמש בגברתו ותשקט הארץ ארבעים שנה (שופטים ה,לא).

So let perish all of Your enemies, G-d; but they who love Him are as the sun when it goes forth in its might. And the land rested for forty years (Judges 5,31).

The last pasuk in the Haftarah says that they who love Hashem are as the sun going forth בגברתו, "in its might." The gematria of בגברתו, "in its might," is 613.

בגברתו   613

There is a total of 613 Mitzvoth in the Torah, thus בגברתו, "in its might," can refer to the 613 Mitzvoth observed by them who love Him.

Parashath Yithro   פרשת יתרו

וייחד יתרו על כל הטובה אשר עשה ה׳ לישראל אשר הצילו
מיד מצרים (שמות יח,ט).

And Yithro rejoiced for all the goodness that
G-d had done for Israel; that He had saved him
from the hand of Egyptians (Exodus 18,9).

When Moses left for Egypt, Yithro told him, לך לשלום,
"Go for peace," as stated, וילך משה וישב אל יתר חתנו ויאמר לו אלכה
נא ואשובה אל אחי אשר במצרים ואראה העודם חיים ויאמר יתרו למשה
(שמות ד,יח) לך לשלום, "And Moses went and returned to Yithro,
his father-in-law, and said to him, 'Please let me and I will
return to my brethren who are in Egypt, and I will see whether
they are still alive,' and Yithro said to Moses: Go for peace"
(Exodus 4,18). The gematria of לשלום, "for peace," is 406.

לשלום   406

Quoting from this pasuk the Gemara says, ואמר רבי אבין
הלוי הנפטר מחברו אל יאמר לו לך בשלום אלא לך לשלום שהרי יתרו
שאמר לו למשה לך לשלום עלה והצליח דוד שאמר לו לאבשלום לך בשלום
(ברכות סד.) הלך ונתלה, "And Rabbi Abin Halevi said, When one
departs from his friend, do not say to him, 'Go in peace,' but,
'Go for peace.' For behold, [in the case of] Yithro who said to
Moses, Go for peace, he [Moses] went and was successful.
[In the case of] David [who] said to Absalom, Go in peace,
[Absalom] went and was hanged" (Berakoth 64a). A similar
Gemara is found at the end of Moed Katon (מועד קטן כט., Moed
Katon 29a). The מגן אברהם, Magen Avraham, who is a source
of the decided law, quotes this distinction between לשלום, "for
peace," and בשלום, "in peace," (מגן אברהם, אורח חיים, סימן קי,
סעיף קטן ט, Magen Avraham, Orach Hayyim, Siman 101, Seif
Katon 9). The gematria of בשלום, "in peace," is 378.

בשלום   378

The difference in gematrioth between לשלום, "for peace," and
בשלום, "in peace," 28.

$$406$$
$$-378$$
$$28$$

Later when Yithro comes to Moses the Torah describes his delight with the word ויחד, "and he rejoiced." The gematria of ויחד, "and he rejoiced," is 28.

ויחד   28

Perhaps the reason the Torah chose to use the word ויחד, "and he rejoiced," rather than another more frequently used word, was that Yithro had said to Moses to go לשלום, "for peace," rather than to go בשלום, "in peace." The difference in gematrioth between the two expressions is equal to the gematria of ויחד, "and he rejoiced."

This rendering of the pasuk is reinforced by Rashi's comment that above all, Yithro rejoiced that Hashem took the Children of Israel out of Egypt (רש״י, שמות יח,ט, Rashi, Exodus 18,9). The taking the Children of Israel out of Egypt was achieved with the כח, "strength," of G-d, as stated, ותחת כי אהב את אבתיך ויבחר בזרעו אחריו ויוצאך בפניו בכחו הגדל ממצרים (דברים ד,לז), "And because He loved your fathers and chose their seed after them, and took you out from Egypt with His presence, with His great strength" (Deuteronomy 4,37). The gematria of כח, "strength," is 28,

כח   28

Thus, there is a further connection between ויחד, "and he rejoiced," and the gematria of 28.

ואתם תהיו לי ממלכת כהנים וגוי קדוש אלה הדברים אשר תדבר אל בני ישראל (שמות יט,ו).

And you will be to Me a kingdom of priests and a holy nation; these are the words that you shall speak to the Children of Israel (Exodus 19,6).

In Parashath Yithro there is an occasion when G-d uses the verb תדבר, "you shall speak"; it is when He tells Moses this message to transfer to the Children of Israel. The gematria of תדבר, "you shall speak," is 606.

$$\text{תדבר} \qquad 606$$

Rashi comments that the words Moses was told to speak are to be (רש"י, שמות יט,ו) לא פחות ולא יותר, "not less and not more" (Rashi, Exodus 19,6). Yet when Moses went to tell the elders of the people, the Torah does not use the verb דבר, "speak"; but the Torah uses the words ויבא, "and he came," ויקרא, "and he called," and וישם, "and he set," as stated, ויבא משה ויקרא לזקני העם וישם לפניהם את כל הדברים האלה אשר צוהו ה' (שמות יט,ז), "And Moses came and he called for the elders of the people, and he set before them all these words which G-d had commanded him" (Exodus 19,7). The combined gematria of ויבא, "and he came," ויקרא, "and he called," and וישם, "and he set," is 692.

ויבא	19
ויקרא	317
וישם	356
	692

Why is the gematria of what Moses did not equal to the gematria of what Moses was told to do?

A possible answer can be found in the כתב סופר על חמשה חמשי תורה, Ksav Sofer al Chamishah Chumshei Torah. There it is explained that G-d told Moses to speak "not less and not more" so that Moses would not try to persuade or convince the Children of Israel to accept the Torah. But Moses was worried lest the Children of Israel infer from his lack of persuasion that Moses was opposed to them accepting the Torah. What did Moses do? He told the Children of Israel what G-d had instructed him, but added that G-d had limited his speech, as stated, לכן הוצרך משה לומר להם כי ה' אמר שלא יוסף

דברים יותר ממה ששם בפיו (כתב סופר על חמשה חומשי תורה, מאת רבי אברהם שמואל בנימין סופר, פרשת יתרו, ד"ה אלה הדברים), "Therefore it was necessary for Moses to say to them that G-d had said not to add any words more than what was placed in his mouth" (Ksav Sofer al Chamishah Chumshei Torah by Avraham Shmuel Binyamin Sofer, Parashath Yithro, header words: These are the words). With this thought it is possible to explain why the gematria of what Moses did is not equal to the gematria of what Moses was told. Moses was told תדבר, "you shall speak," which has a gematria of 606; what Moses did was ויבא, "and he came," ויקרא, "and he called," and וישם, "and he set," which have a combined gematria of 692. The difference between these two gematrioth is 86.

$$
\begin{array}{r}
692 \\
-606 \\
\hline
86
\end{array}
$$

When G-d's character of strict justice is alluded to, He is referred to as אלקים, "G-d"; when G-d's character of mercy is alluded to, He is referred to as ה׳, "G-d," (רש"י, בראשית א,א וח,א, Rashi, Genesis 1,1 and 8,1). The gematria of אלקים, "G-d," is 86.

אלקים   86

Moses added that G-d had limited his speech; fittingly, there is the added gematria of 86, which alludes to this name of G-d.

One might ask why G-d's name of אלקים, "G-d," was alluded to as opposed to ה׳, "G-d," which was used to describe this message of G-d (שמות יט,ג וז-יא, Exodus 19, 3 and 7-11). A basic answer is that G-d told Moses two instructions: One was the message to tell the Children of Israel; two was the instruction to Moses to limit the message to what G-d had said, and "not less and not more." The first instruction was directed to the Children of Israel, and G-d is characterized as

ה׳, "G-d"; the second instruction was directed to Moses, to be precise, and G-d was accordingly characterized as אלקים, "G-d." Thus, when recording what Moses did, the verbs have an added gematria of 86, to allude to G-d's character of strict justice, which was how G-d was characterized to him when he was told to limit his speech.

This interpretation helps to elucidate another problem. The Torah says, ומשה עלה אל האלקים ויקרא אליו ה׳ מן ההר לאמר "And Moses went, כה תאמר לבית יעקב ותגיד לבני ישראל (שמות יט,ג) up to G-d, and G-d called to him from the mountain saying, so you shall say to the house of Jacob and tell the Children of Israel" (Exodus 19,3). The problem is, why does the Torah say Moses went up to האלקים, "G-d," and then say ה׳, "G-d," called him? Either G-d's name as אלקים, "G-d," should be used in both places, or G-d's name as ה׳, "G-d," should be used in both places. The Or Hachayyim gives one answer. He says that when the pasuk says אל האלקים, "to G-d," it is referring to a previous pasuk where Moses was told to serve האלקים, "G-d." But when the pasuk writes that ה׳, "G-d," called to Moses, it is a expression of inviting, showing endearment to Moses (אור החיים, שמות יט,ג, Or Hachayyim, Exodus 19,3).

The interpretation previously given can elucidate the problem differently than the answer of the Or Hachayyim. When the Torah says "And Moses went up to האלקים, 'G-d'" it is referring to G-d who would give Moses a message to tell the Children of Israel. When the Torah says "and ה׳, 'G-d' called to him," it is referring to G-d who would say something directly to Moses. When G-d told Moses to transfer His message, it was to be what G-d said and "not less and not more"; G-d was personified as אלקים, "G-d." This calling is in contrast to when G-d called Moses giving him a message to tell the Children of Israel where G-d is personified as ה׳, "G-d." Thus, it is understandable why two different names of G-d are used in the same pasuk.

ויהי ביום השלישי בהית הבקר ויהי קלת וברקים וענן כבד
על ההר וקל שפר חזק מאד ויחרד כל העם אשר במחנה
(שמות יט,טז).

And it was on the third day, when it was morning that there was thunder and lighting, and a
heavy cloud upon the mountain, and the voice
of the shofar was very strong, and all the people
who were in the camp trembled (Exodus
19,16).

The word שפר, "shofar," in all its different forms appears only five times in the Torah. The first three times, שפר,
"shofar," is mentioned in reference to the giving of the Ten
Commandments; the last two times שפר, "shofar," is mentioned in reference to the jubilee year. The first time shofar is
mentioned is in Parashath Yithro, as stated, וקל שפר חזק מאד,
"and the voice of the shofar was very strong." The gematria
of שפר, "shofar," is 580.

שפר   580

The second and third time shofar is mentioned, the
form used is השפר, "the shofar" (שמות יט,יט וכ,טו, Exodus 19,19
and 20,15). Notice that all three times refer to G-d's blowing
the shofar, and all three times שפר, "shofar," is spelled חסר,
"deficient orthographically," without the letter ו, "vav."
The last two times shofar is mentioned, the form used
is שופר, "shofar," (ויקרא כה,ט, Leviticus 25,9). Notice that both
times refer to a human blowing the shofar; and both times
שופר, "shofar," is spelled מלא, "complete orthographically,"
with the letter ו, "vav"; and both times are in one pasuk.
The fact that shofar is spelled deficient orthographically when referring to G-d's blowing, but shofar is spelled
complete orthographically when referring to man's blowing,
shows that the meaning of shofar is different when mentioned in different contexts. By examining both contexts

where shofar is mentioned, its full meaning can be perceived. It stands to reason that G-d's blowing the shofar, as opposed to man's blowing the shofar, encompasses the fuller meaning, since it is based on divine intelligence. Therefore, 580, the gematria of shofar without the vav, is used to represent the fuller meaning of the shofar.

After the first three times shofar is mentioned, the first message G-d tells Moses is to remind the the Children of Israel what they have seen, as stated, ויאמר ה׳ אל משה כה תאמר אל בני ישראל אתם ראיתם כי מן השמים דברתי עמכם (שמות כ,יט) "And G-d said to Moses, so you shall say to the Children of Israel, you have seen that I have talked with you from the heavens" (Exodus 20,19). The gematria of עמכם, "with you," is 170.

עמכם   170

The word עמכם, "with you," is obviously the key word in the pasuk; it tells that G-d has communicated with the Children of Israel. The other words in the pasuk do not have the same role; it is already known that G-d is in the heavens, and that He can speak.

G-d told Moses to tell the Children of Israel that G-d has communicated with them. The communication was the giving of the Ten Commandments. Thus, G-d's direct communication with the Children of Israel follows the mention of the shofar. This direct communication with the Children of Israel is embodied in the word עמכם, "with you," which has a gematria of 170.

After the last two times shofar is mentioned, which is in reference the jubilee year, in the very next pasuk the message G-d tells Moses is to tell the the Children of Israel to proclaim דרור, "freedom," as stated, וקדשתם את שנת החמשים שנה וקראתם דרור בארץ לכל ישביה יובל הוא תהיה לכם ושבתם איש אל אחזתו ואיש אל משפחתו תשבו (ויקרא כה,י), "And you shall hallow the fiftieth year, and proclaim freedom throughout the land, for all it inhabitants, it shall be a jubilee year for you, and every man shall return to his inheritance, and every man shall return to his family" (Leviticus 25,10). The gematria of דרור, "freedom," is 410.

דרור   410

The word דרור, "freedom," is obviously the key word in the pasuk; the freedom of the jubilee year is embodied in it; its gematria is 410.

Thus, the two key words which embody G-d's communication to the Children of Israel after the mentioning of the shofar in reference to the giving of the Ten Commandments and the jubilee year, are עמכם, "with you," and דרור, "freedom." The combination of their gematrioth is 580.

170
410
———
580

Thus, 580 represents the combination of עמכם, "with you," and דרור, "freedom." The gematria of שפר, "shofar," is also 580; it represents the same combination. Why is G-d's communication to the Children of Israel with the giving of the Ten Commandments combined with freedom?

One obvious answer is that there is no freedom, unless one learns Torah, as the Mishnah states, שאין לך בן חורין אלא מי שעוסק בתלמוד תורה (אבות, פרק ו, משנה ב), "There is no one who is free except one who occupies himself with Torah study" (Avoth, Chapter 6, Mishnah 2). Since shofar is stated in reference to G-d's communication to the Children of Israel with the giving of the Ten Commandments, which is a prerequisite for freedom, and shofar is stated in reference to the jubilee year, which is also a prerequisite for freedom, it is appropriate that the gematria of שפר, "shofar," is equal to the combined gematria of עמכם, "with you," and דרור, "freedom."

There is a second reason why G-d's communication to the Children of Israel with the giving of the Ten Commandments is combined with freedom. The giving of the Ten Commandments and the jubilee year both represent התחדשות, "renewal," rejuvenation, and starting anew. After the Children of Israel received the Ten Commandments, they began new lives of studying the Torah. After the jubilee year, slaves stopped working, land returned to its owners, and economic life began anew. The two key words which embody G-d's communication to the Children of Israel after the mentioning of the shofar in reference to the giving of the Ten Commandments and the jubilee year, are עמכם, "with you," and דרור, "freedom." Both of these words are associated with rejuvenation and starting anew. The Midrash Rabba also associates the shofar of Rosh Hashanah with התחדשות, "renewal," as stated, איזהו חדש שנכסה ויש לו חג וחגו בן יומו אי אתה מוצא אלא בחדש תשרי בחדש זה יתחדשו מעשיכם בשופר (מדרש רבה, סדר אמר, פרשה כט, אות ו), "Which month is it that (the moon) is covered, and has a holiday, and its holiday is one day? You will only find the month of Tishrei. In this month there is renewal of your deeds with the shofar" (Midrash Rabba, Sidrah Emor, Parashah 29, Letter 6).

The gematria of שפר, "shofar," which represents renewal, is equal to the combined gematrioth of עמכם, "with you," and דרור, "freedom," for they also represent renewal.

ויאמר משה אל ה' לא יוכל העם לעלת אל הר סיני כי אתה העדתה בנו לאמר הגבל את ההר וקדשתו (שמות יט,כג).
And Moses said to G-d, "The people cannot come up to Mount Sinai for You have warned us, saying, Set bounds around the mountain and sanctify it" (Exodus 19,23).

Hashem had warned Moses הגבל את ההר, "set bounds around the mountain." The gematria of את ההר, "the mountain," is 611.

את	401
ההר	201
	611

The gematria of תורה, "Torah," is also 611.

תורה   611

Since תורה "Torah," has the same gematria as את ההר, "the mountain," one can read the pasuk as if it said הגבל תורה "set bounds around the Torah." The need to set bounds around the Torah has been expressed by a Mishnah in Avoth, עשו סיג תורה (אבות, פרק א, משנה א), "Make a fence around the Torah" (Avoth, Chapter 1, Mishnah 1). Thus, this pasuk expresses the same idea as the Mishnah.

Parashath Mishpatim   פרשת משפטים

אם אדניו יתן לו אשה וילדה לו בנים או בנות האשה
וילדיה תהיה לאדניה והוא יצא בגפו (שמות כא,ד).

If the master should give him a wife and she has borne him sons or daughters, the wife and her children shall belong to her master and he shall go out by himself (Exodus 21,4).

In discussing how an עבד עברי, "a Jewish servant," goes free after six years, the Torah uses the words לאדניה, "to her master," and יצא, "he shall go out." The gematria of לאדניה, "to her master," is 100.

            לאדניה   100

The gematria of יצא, "he shall go out," is 101.

            יצא   101

An association can be made with "belonging to her master" and the number 100, and with "he shall go out" and the number 101.

Two pesukim after the previously mentioned pasuk, regarding the ear piercing of a Jewish servant who does not wish to go free, Rashi writes that Hashem says, כי לי בני ישראל עבדים עבדי הם ולא עבדים לעבדים (רש"י, שמות כא,ו), "'For unto me the Bnei Yisroel are servants,' they are My servants, and not servants to servants" (Rashi, Exodus 21,6). From this Rashi it is clear that a person is either a servant to Hashem, or a servant to servants. Even a wicked person who claims to be independent is in fact a servant to servants, for a person who is not a servant to Hashem is a servant to himself or to his own desires; thereby he is a servant to servants. This idea of freedom is substantiated by the Tifereth Yisroel, who writes that only one who is committed to learning Torah is not a servant to his bodily desires. He defines such a person with the phrase, וזאת, שרק הוא אינו משתעבד וגם אינו משועבד להגופניות,

החירות, שנפשו אינה משועבדת לתאות הגופני וכו' (תפארת ישראל, אבות
מג אות יכין, ב, משנה ו, (פרק, "Only he is not enslaved, nor is he
enslaved to his bodily needs; this is the freedom, that his soul
is not enslaved to his bodily desires" (Tifereth Yisroel, Avoth,
Chapter 6, Mishnah 2, Yachin, Letter 43).

The Gemara Hagigah contrasts one who serves
Hashem to one who does not serve Hashem with the following phraseology, עבדו ולא עבדו תרוייהו צדיקי גמורי ניניהו ואינו דומה
(חגיגה ט:) שונה פרקו מאה פעמים לשונה פרקו מאה ואחד, "The one
who serves Him and the one who does not serve Him are both
completely righteous; rather, the one who repeats his chapter of study a hundred times and the one who repeats his
chapter of study a hundred and one times are not comparable" (Hagigah 9b).

Thus, one who serves Hashem repeats his studies 101
times; one who does not serve Hashem, although he is still
righteous, but to some degree he is not considered fully
serving Hashem, repeats his studies 100 times. One who
serves Hashem fully is associated with the number 101; one
who does not serve Hashem fully is associated with the
number 100. Since the previously mentioned Rashi implies
that a person is either a servant to Hashem or a servant to
servants, therefore one who repeats his learning 100 times is
not a servant to Hashem fully, but rather a servant to servants. But he who repeats his learning 101 times is a servant
to Hashem.

These ideas can explain the gematrioth in the pasuk
initially quoted. The term תהיה לאדנייה, "shall belong to her
master," contains the gematria 100; it signifies one who is
not fully a servant to Hashem, but a servant to servants, i.e.,
one who repeats his studies 100 times. The gematria contained in the term corresponds to the number of times one
repeats his studies if he is a servant to servants, which is
what the meaning of the term can signify. The other term יצא

והוא בגפו, "and he shall go out," contains the gematria of 101; it signifies one who is not a servant to servants, but is a servant to Hashem, i.e., he repeats his studies 101 times. The gematria contained in the term corresponds to the number of times one repeats his studies if he is a servant to Hashem, which is what the meaning of the term can signify.

Thus, the gematria of לאדניה, "to her master," and יצא, "he shall go out," 100 and 101 respectively, can be combined with the Gemara in Hagigah to explain this pasuk.

וכי יכה איש את עבדו או את אמתו בשבט ומת תחת ידו נקם ינקם (שמות כא,כ).

And when a man shall smite his bondman or his bondwoman with a rod, and he die under his hand, he shall surely be avenged (Exodus 21,20).

The first pasuk in שני, the second portion of Parashath Mishpatim, talks of when a man יכה, "will smite," his bondman or his bondwoman. The gematria of יכה, "will smite," is 35.

יכה   35

But just five pesukim preceding this pasuk the Torah says, ומכה אביו ואמו מות יומת (שמות כא,טו), "And he who smites his father or his mother shall surely be put to death" (Exodus 21,15). Why does the language of the pesukim change? Either say יכה, "will smite," in both pesukim or say ומכה, "And he who smites," in both pesukim. A credible answer can be given with the use of a gematria.

Immediately prior to the words וכי יכה, "And when a man shall smite," is the pasuk which ends with words ורפא ירפא, "and he shall cause him to be thoroughly healed." The Gemara learns from these words that authorization is given to the doctor to heal (בבא קמא פד:, Baba Kamma 84b). The חפץ חיים, Hafetz Hayyim, explicates these words in greater detail.

The words ורפא ירפא, "and he shall cause him to be thoroughly healed," can refer to a mortal doctor applying his limited abilities, who might exert force or strike a patient in order to try to heal that person. When G-d cures directly the process is different. Although all curing, whether directly from G-d or mortal doctor, is ultimately from G-d, still there is a difference. When G-d cures directly there is no need for operations nor for strong medicines, as written, בוא וראה, מה בין רפואה הבאה מידי רופא כל בשר לבין אדם המתרפא ע״י רופא בו״ד. אצל הקב״ה כתיב ״ירפאך״ ב״פא״ רפה, מרפא כהרף עין בלי יגיעה ועמל וסמים חריפים, שולח דברו וירפאהו. לא כן בבו״ד כתיב ״ורפא ירפא״ (שמות כא יט) בשתי ״פאין״ ושניהם בדגש חזק, כלומר שצריך להתאמץ ולהתעסק ברפואות ולפעמים גם בנתוחים ולזמן ממושך (ספר חפץ חיים על התורה, שנאמרו מפי הרב ישראל מאיר הכהן, נארך ונסדר ע״י הרב שמואל גריינימן, פרשת משפטים, ד״ה ורפא ירפא, פירוש מעשי למלך), "Come and see, how different a cure which comes from the Physician of all flesh [G-d] is from a person who receives a cure through a physician of flesh and blood. Regarding the Holy One, Blessed be He, it is written, He will cure you, with a "פ," pay [fay] He heals as quickly as the blink of an eye, without toil and labor or strong drugs. He sends His word and the person is cured. It is not so with a healer of flesh and blood. It is written, "and he shall cause him to be thoroughly healed," (Exodus 21,19) with two hard "פים," pays, and both with a strong dot (דגש) dagesh. It means to say, he may need to exert himself and to work with medicines and occasionally also operations and long-term treatments," (Book of Hafetz Hayyim on the Torah, which was said from the mouth of Rabbi Israel Meir Hakohen, arranged and ordered by Rabbi Shmuel Greiniman, Parashath Mishpatim header words: And he shall cause him to be thoroughly healed, Commentary Maasai Lamelech). Thus, when a mortal doctor treats a patient, it could be that he יכה, "will smite," his patient in the process. The pasuk referring to a mortal doctor uses the words ורפא ירפא, "and he shall cause him to be thoroughly healed," as stated, אם יקום והתהלך בחוץ על משענתו ונקה המכה רק שבתו יתן ורפא ירפא (שמות כא,יט), "If he shall rise and go outside on his staff, and the smiter shall be quit, only he shall pay for his lost time, and he shall cause him to be thoroughly healed" (Exodus 21,19). The gematria of ורפא ירפא, "and he shall cause him to be thoroughly healed," is 578.

ורפא	287
ירפא	<u>291</u>
	578

This curing by a mortal doctor may cause that he will יכה, "will smite," his patient in the process. As was shown, the gematria of יכה, "will smite," is 35. When the gematria of ורפא ירפא, "and he shall cause him to be thoroughly healed," is added to the gematria of יכה, "will smite," the sum is 613.

578
<u>35</u>
613

Man was created with 248 limbs and 365 sinews, together totaling 613 body parts, (תרגום יונתן בן עוזיאל בראשית א,כז, Targum Jonathan ben Uzziel, Genesis 1,27). These are the 613 body parts a mortal doctor tries to heal. Therefore, a credible answer to why the language of the pesukim changes from ומכה, "And he who smites," to יכה, "will smite," is to link the words ורפא ירפא, "and he shall cause him to be thoroughly healed," to the word יכה, "will smite," so the sum of their gematrioth would be 613.

וישלח את נערי בני ישראל ויעלו עלת ויזבחו זבחים שלמים לה' פרים (שמות כד,ה).

And he sent the young men of the Bnei Yisroel and they offered burnt offerings and they sacrificed peace offerings of oxen to G-d (Exodus 24,5).

The Torah records that Moses sent נערי בני ישראל, "young men of the Bnei Yisroel," who offered פרים, "oxen," to Hashem. The gematria of נערי, "young men of," is 330.

נערי   330

The gematria of פרים, oxen, is 330.

פרים   330

Since the נערי, "young men of," were sent, and they offered פרים, "oxen," it is fitting that these two words should have the same gematria.

ויקח ספר הברית ויקרא באזני העם ויאמרו כל אשר דבר
ה׳ נעשה ונשמע (שמות כד,ז).

And he took the book of the covenant, and he read it in the ears of the people; and they said, "All that G-d has spoken we will do and we will obey" (Exodus 24,7).

The Torah tells us that the Bnei Yisroel said נעשה ונשמע, "we will do and we will obey." The gematria of נעשה, "we will do," is 425.

נעשה   425

The gematria of ונשמע, "and we will obey," is 466.

ונשמע   466

The difference between the gematrioth of these two words is 41.

466
-425
41

Thus, 41 represents the difference between נעשה, "we will do," and ונשמע, "and we will obey."

The fact that the Bnei Yisroel said נעשה, "we will do," before saying ונשמע, "and we will obey," is of major importance. It is not just the random verbalization of two words; the order was not chosen arbitrarily; but it is an indication of an attitude toward Hashem's Torah. The fact that the Bnei Yisroel realized this attitude is shown by their trenchant response.

The Gemara Shabbath comments, אמר רבי אלעזר בשעה שהקדימו ישראל נעשה לנשמע יצאה בת קול ואמרה להן מי גילה לבני רז זה שמלאכי השרת משתמשין בו (שבת פח.), "Rabbi Eleazar said, 'At the time when Israel said we will do before we will obey, a heavenly voice went out and said to them: Who revealed this secret to My children that ministering angels use?'" (Shabbath 88a).

Thus, the saying of "we will do" before "we will obey" represents a special attitude toward Hashem's Torah. The pasuk following the one where נעשה, "we will do," precedes ונשמע, "and we will obey," states, ויקח משה את הדם ויזרק על העם ויאמר הנה דם הברית אשר כרת ה׳ עמכם על כל הדברים האלה (שמות כד,ח). "And Moses took the blood and he sprinkled it on the people and he said, 'Behold the blood of the covenant which Hashem made with you concerning all of these words'" (Exodus 24,8). The gematria of האלה, "these," is 41.

האלה   41

Perhaps the word האלה, "these," signifies the saying of נעשה, "we will do," before ונשמע, "and we will obey," which represents the special attitude toward Hashem's Torah. Therefore, the pasuk says that Hashem made a covenant based on the Bnei Yisroel saying "we will do" before "and we will obey." This location would be a fitting place for such a pasuk, since it follows the pasuk where "we will do and we will obey" are mentioned. This explanation is further strengthened owing to the fact that the difference between the gematrioth of נעשה, "we will do," and ונשמע, "and we will obey," is 41, which is also the gematria of האלה, "these," which refers to the words on which the covenant was made.

ויקח משה את הדם ויזרק על העם ויאמר הנה דם הברית
אשר כרת ה׳ עמכם על כל הדברים האלה (שמות כד,ח).
And Moses took the blood and he sprinkled it on
the people and he said, "Behold the blood of the
covenant which G-d made with you concerning
all of these words"(Exodus 24,8).

The Torah reports that Moses took הדם, "the blood," and sprinkled it on the people. The gematria of הדם, "the blood", is 49.

הדם   49

It is from the sprinkling of הדם, "the blood," that the Gemara Kerithoth learns that immersion in a mikveh is necessary for somebody to convert to Judaism. (The law of immersion is still practiced today, although sprinkling of the blood is not). The Gemara Kerithoth says, רבי אומר ככב כאבותיכם מה אבותיכם לא נכנסו לברית אלא במילה וטבילה והרצאת דם אף הם לא יכנסי לברית אלא במילה וטבילה והרצאת דמים... אלא טבילה מנין דכתיב ויקח משה את הדם ויזרק על העם ואין הזאה בלא טבילה (כריתות ט., ויבמות מו:, ורש״י, ברכות מז: ד״ה עד שימול ויטבול), "Rabbi says, 'You, just as your forefathers only entered into the covenant through circumcision, immersion, and the sprinkling of the blood, so too they may only enter into the covenant through circumcision, immersion, and the sprinkling of the blood ... but from where do we know immersion, as it is written, And Moses took the blood and he sprinkled it on the people. And there can be no sprinkling without immersion'" (Kerithoth 9a, and Yebamoth 46b, and Rashi, Berakoth 47b header words: Until he has done circumcision and ablution).

Thus, it is from the pasuk where הדם, "the blood," is a key word that one of the requirements of becoming Jewish is derived. This same requirement was fulfilled by Abraham, the first patriarch of the Children of Israel, whom Hashem said will grow לגוי, "into a nation," as stated, ואברהם היו יהיה לגוי גדול ועצום ונברכו בו כל גויי הארץ (בראשית יח,יח)" "And Abraham will surely become a great and mighty nation, and all the nations of the earth shall be blessed through him" (Genesis 18,18). The gematria of לגוי, "into a nation," is 49.

49   לגוי

The gematria of הדם, "the blood," and לגוי, "into a nation," are both 49. It is from the pasuk where הדם, "the blood," is a key word that one of the requirements for becoming Jewish is learned. This requirement was fulfilled by Abraham before he begot Isaac, from whom a nation was born. Thus, it is very fitting that הדם, "the blood," and לגוי, "to a nation," have the same gematria, since they are associated; from הדם, "the blood," a requirement is derived that was fulfilled by Abraham before he begot Isaac, who grew לגוי, "into a nation."

Parashath Terumah   פרשת תרומה

דבר אל בני ישראל ויקחו לי תרומה מאת כל איש אשר
ידבנו לבו תקחו את תרומתי (שמות כה,ב).
Speak to the Bnei Yisroel, and they should take for Me an offering; from every man whose heart makes him willing, you shall take My offering (Exodus 25,2).

This pasuk, which discusses the giving of an offering (donations for the mishkan, tabernacle) to Hashem, uses the verb "take" twice. The two words immediately following the verb "take" are, לי תרומה, "for Me an offering," and את תרומתי, "My offering." The gematria of לי תרומה, "for Me an offering," and את תרומתי, "My offering," are 40, 651, 401, and 1056 respectively.

לי	40
תרומה	651
את	401
תרומתי	1056

Both uses of the verb "take" in this pasuk can denote subtraction. In the first instance the phrase ויקחו לי תרומה, "and they shall take for Me an offering," can be interpreted as, and they shall subtract the gematria of לי, "to Me," from the gematria of תרומה, "an offering." When such a subtraction is performed, the remainder is 611.

תרומה	651
לי	-40
	611

In the second instance תקחו את תרומתי, "you shall take My offering," can be interpreted as, you shall subtract the gematria of את, (this word is placed before the definite direct object of a verb in the Hebrew language and has no English equivalent) from the gematria of תרומתי, "My offering." When such a subtraction is performed, the remainder is 655.

$$
\begin{array}{rr}
תרומתי & 1056 \\
את & -401 \\
\hline
 & 655
\end{array}
$$

The gematrioth of 611 and 655 are very meaningful. The fourth pasuk of Parashath Vezoth HaBerachah contains the gematria of 611, as stated, תורה צוה לנו משה מורשה קהלת יעקב (דברים לג,ד), "Moses commanded us Torah, an inheritance of the congregation of Jacob," (Deuteronomy 33,4). The gematria of תורה, "Torah," is 611

$$
תורה \quad\quad 611
$$

The fourth pasuk from the end of Parashath Tetzaveh contains the gematria of 655, as stated, והקטיר עליו אהרן קטרת סמים בבקר בבקר בהיטיבו את הנרת יקטירנה (שמות ל,ז), "And Aaron shall burn incense of sweet spices on it; every morning when he dresses the lamps he shall burn it" (Exodus 30,7). The gematria of הנרת, "the lamps," is 655.

$$
הנרת \quad\quad 655
$$

Thus, the gematrioth of 611 and 655 are very meaningful; the former is the gematria of תורה, "Torah," the latter is the gematria of הנרת, "the lamps." The rationale for the linkage of these two words and their gematrioth can be found in a pasuk from Proverbs which states, כי נר מצוה ותורה אור וגו' (משלי ו,כג), "For the commandment is a lamp and the Torah is light, etc." (Proverbs 6,23). The Ibn Ezra comments on this pasuk כי המצוה כנר להאיר לפניך בענין מצות ה' ברה מאירת עינים והתורה כאור ללומדיה והכסיל בחשך הולך (אבן עזרא, משלי ו,כג), "For the mitzvah is as a lamp to give light in front of you, as is evident by the pasuk, 'The commandment of Hashem is clear, enlightening the eyes,' and the Torah is as light to those who learn it, and the fool walks in darkness" (Ibn Ezra, Proverbs

6,23). Thus, the mitzvoth, which are compared to the lamps, enlighten the eyes. The light of the eyes is a source of joy for the heart, as stated, מאור עינים ישמח לב שמועה טובה תדשן עצם (משלי טו,ל), "The light of the eyes rejoices the heart, and a good report fattens the bones" (Proverbs 15, 30). Since הנרת, "the lamps," with a gematria of 655, are compared to the mitzvoth, which are light to the eyes, and the light of the eyes makes the heart happy, the gematria of 655 can be associated with a happy heart.

Now the first half of the pasuk from Parashath Terumah can be explained accordingly. The second half of the pasuk quoted from Proverbs, which says that the Torah is light, can help explain the first half of the pasuk from Parashath Terumah. The Ibn Ezra comments that the Torah is light to those who learn it. It is characteristic of the Bnei Yisroel to bring light to the world, as the Midrash states, מה יונה זו הביאה אירה לעולם כן ישראל מביאין אורה לעולם שנא׳ והלכו גוים לאורך (שיר השירים רבה ד,ה), "Just as this dove brought light to the world also Israel brings light to the world, as is stated, and the nations shall come to your light" (Song of Songs Rabbah 4,5). Whenever אור, "light," is mentioned, it can refer to Torah as the Gemara Ta'anith says, ואין אור אלא תורה שנאמר כי נר מצוה ותורה אור (תענית ז:), "There is no light other than Torah, as is stated, 'For the commandment is a lamp and the Torah is light'" (Ta'anith 7b). Since Torah, with a gematria of 611, can be referred to as light, and it is characteristic of Bnei Yisroel to bring light to the world, thus the gematria of 611 can be associated with this characteristic of the Bnei Yisroel.

Now the first half of the pasuk from Parashath Terumah can be explained in this vein. It states, דבר אל בני ישראל ויקחו לי תרומה (שמות כה,ב), "Speak to the Bnei Yisroel, and they should take for Me an offering" (Exodus 25,2). The explanation is: דבר אל בני ישראל, speak to the Bnei Yisroel, i.e., speak to those who care to have this characteristic Bnei

Yisroel, ויקחו לי תרומה, subtract the gematria of לי, "to Me," from the gematria of תרומה, "an offering," which leaves a remainder of 611. The gematria of תורה, "Torah," is 611; Torah can be referred to as light, and it is characteristic of Bnei Yisroel to bring light to the world.

The association between Bnei Yisroel and Torah has been stated more succinctly, namely, שאומתינו בני ישראל אינה אומה אלא בתורותיה (ספר הנבחר האמונות ודעות מאת הגאון רבינו סעדיה בן יוסף, מאמר שלישי פרק ז), "Our nation, the Children of Israel, is a nation only by virtue of her Torah." (Book of Hanivchar He-emunoth Vadeoth by The Goan Rabbeinu Saaadia ben Yosef, Article Three Chapter 7). After the subtraction is performed in the first half of the pasuk from Parashath Terumah, it leaves a remainder of 611. It can be explained that since the gematria of תורה, "Torah," is 611, and since the very existence of Bnei Yisroel depends on Torah, therefore those who wish to be part of Bnei Yisroel should heed the message of the subtraction of the gematria of לי, "to me," from the gematria of תרומה, "an offering."

Now the second half of the pasuk from Parashath Terumah can be explained accordingly. It states, מאת כל איש אשר ידבנו לבו תקחו את תרומתי (שמות כה,ב), "from every man whose heart makes him willing, you should take my offering" (Exodus 25,2). The explanation is: מאת כל איש, from every man, אשר ידבנו לבו, whose heart compels him to give, i.e., he cares to give, תקחו את תרומתי, subtract the gematria of את from the gematria of תרומתי, "my offering," which leaves a remainder of 655. The gematria of הנרת, "the lamps," is 655; the lamps are compared to the mitzvoth which are light to the eyes, and light of the eyes makes the heart happy. Note that Rashi explains נדיב לבו, "a willing heart," as whose heart makes him willing to give (רש"י, שמות לה,ה, Rashi, Exodus 35,5). So he who gives, whose heart makes him willing to give, does that which will make his heart happy.

The parallel of the second pasuk of Parashath Terumah, with its implied gematrioth of תורה, "Torah," and הנרת, "the lamps," to the pasuk from Proverbs can be further clarified. The pasuk in Proverbs parallels a lamp and Torah to a mitzvah and light respectively. Since a mitzvah and Torah are affiliated with the spiritual world, and a lamp and a light are affiliated with the physical world, would it not have been more appropriate for the subjects of the pasuk to be a mitzvah and Torah to which a lamp and light are compared, or vice versa?

A possible solution could be that the pasuk in Proverbs has נר, "lamp," and תורה, "Torah," as subjects since they are both tangible and substantial. This tangibility is evident in the prayer recited before returning the Torah to its ark. This prayer is וזאת התורה, "and this is the Torah"; the word זאת, "this," is used when there is a tangible object that can be pointed to by a person. Thus, the Torah can be referred to as something tangible; נר, "lamp," is obviously tangible. A commandment is often an action, thus it is intangible, not physically substantial; אור, "light," is obviously intangible. The pasuk from Proverbs may have used נר, "lamp," and תורה, "Torah," as subjects since they are both tangible and substantial. Likewise, the pasuk in Parashath Terumah may have implied Torah and lamps since they are tangible and substantial.

Note that the pasuk in Parashath Terumah implies תורה, "Torah," first and and then הנרת, "the lamps." Why does the pasuk in Proverbs reverse the order? Why is נר, "lamp," implied first and then תורה, "Torah"? It could be that the pasuk in Proverbs is referring to the general relationship between Torah and commandments, i.e., first one does the commandment and then he learns the Torah relating to that commandment. This idea is similar to what the Gemara Shabbath says, דרש רבי סימאי בשעה שהקדימו ישראל נעשה לנשמע

באו ששים ריבוא של מלאכי השרת לכל אחד ואחד מישראל קשרו לו שני "Rabbi Simai כתרים אחד כנגד נעשה ואחד כנגד נשמע (שבת פח.) expounded, at the time that Israel preceded 'we will do' to 'we will obey,' six hundred thousand ministering angels came to each one of Israel and placed on him two crowns, one corresponding to 'we will do' and one corresponding to 'we will obey'" (Shabbath 88a).

The pasuk in Parashath Terumah is not referring to the general relationship between Torah and the commandments, but to the specific commandments to build a tabernacle, a mishkan. In the case of the mishkan, the commandments were given first in Parashath Terumah and Parashath Tetzaveh; the actual building is described in Parashath Vayakhel and Parashath Pekudey. Thus, the Torah first gives the commands and then describes how the mitzvoth of the mishkan were done. The pasuk in the beginning of Parashath Terumah also first implies the Torah and then the lamps, i.e., the mitzvoth, since the Torah itself in the specific case of the mishkan, first gives the commands and then describes how the mitzvoth were executed.

Explaining the second pasuk in Parashath Terumah by means of its implied gematria has an additional benefit; it resolves the question: Why state the pasuk? The third pasuk begins, "And this is the offering, and so forth," thus, it is clear that an offering was required. Why not eliminate the second pasuk? However, now that this pasuk has been explained as implying the Torah and mitzvoth in the specific case of the mishkan, the understanding of the pasuk is enhanced. This pasuk also serves as a warning to the Bnei Yisroel that the mishkan should be built exactly as the Torah commanded. A person's best efforts must be spent to ensure that all mitzvoth will be observed exactly as commanded; however, in the case of the mishkan there is an additional warning. This warning could be because the mishkan intimated the creation of heaven and earth, as the Ramban states, יודע היה בצלאל לצרף אותיות שנבראו בהן שמים וארץ, והעניין כי המשכן ירמוז באלו, והוא היודע ומבין סודו (רמב"ן, שמות לא,ב), "Bezalel knew to combine the letters with which heaven and earth were created. The intention is that the Tabernacle alludes to these, and he knew and understood its secrets" (Ramban, Exodus 31,2).

In light of this warning, it is understandable that the Torah found it necessary to repeat in Parashath Vayakhel and Parashath Pekudey the exact way the mitzvoth relating to the mishkan were accomplished, after having commanded the way to do the mitzvoth in Parashath Terumah and Parashath Tetzaveh. The Torah repeats the way the mitzvoth were accomplished to show that the Bnei Yisroel heeded the warning implied by the second pasuk of Parashath Terumah, and built the mishkan exactly as they were commanded. Lastly, one can take note of the importance of doing Hashem's mitzvoth exactly as commanded, which applies not only to the mishkan, but to all facets of Torah life at all times.

Parashath Terumah   פרשת תרומה
or a Siyyum on Moed   או סיום מועד

ונתת על השלחן לחם פנים לפני תמיד (שמות כה,ל).
And you shall place showbread on the table in
front of Me always (Exodus 25,30).

The last Mishnah in Seder Moed and Tractate Hagigah
says that the kohanim were warned to be careful with the
table, as stated, כיצד מעבירים על טהרת העזרה. מטבילין את הכלים
שהיו במקדש, ואומרין להם הזהרו שלא תגעו בשלחן ותטמאוהו (חגיגה פרק
ג, משנה ח), "How did they transfer items for the purpose of
cleaning the courtyard? They immersed the vessels that were
in the Temple and they said to them, 'Be careful not to touch
the table and make it ritually defiled'" (Hagigah Chapter 3,
Mishnah 8). The extra warning regarding the table was due to
the fact that all the vessels could be transferred and immersed in a mikvah, except the table. This restriction is
based on the pasuk ונתת על השלחן לחם פנים לפני תמיד (שמות כה,ל),
"And you shall place showbread on the table in front of Me
always" (Exodus 25,30). In order that the showbread would
remain on the table uninterruptedly, it could not be removed
even to be immersed in a mikvah. The warning not to touch
the table in the היכל, hekhal, "palace," was given to the
kohanim during the holidays, lest the table should be ritually
defiled. This restriction may also be viewed as a distinction.
The table was distinct for it was a source of blessing for food
for the entire world, as it says, ומניה נפיק מזונא לכל עלמא (ספר
"and הזוהר מאת התנא רבי שמעון בן יוחאי, פרשת תרומה, דף קנג:),
from it issues forth food for the entire world" (Book of the
Zohar by the Tanna Rabbi Shimon ben Yochai, Parashath
Terumah, Page 153b). Now that the the Children of Israel do
not have the Temple, nor the table, each individual's tables in
the homes of Children of Israel serve as a source of atonement (מנחות צז., Menahoth 97a).

There are two primary mitzvoth which may enhance the sanctity of an individual's table. The first mitzvah is to learn תורה, "Torah," at one's table; the second mitzvah is to do הכנסת אורחים, "hospitality," to invite guests who are poor to one's table, as it says, זכאה איהו מאן דאלין תרין קיימין על פתיריה, מלי דאורייתא וחולקא למסכנין (ספר הזוהר מאת התנא רבי שמעון בן יוחאי, פרשת תרומה, דף קנד.), "Worthy is he who has these two prevailing at his table: words of Torah, and a portion to feed the poor" (The Book of the Zohar by the Tanna Rabbi Shimon ben Yochai, Parashath Terumah, Page 154a). The Talmudic Encyclopedia based on the Rambam (משנה תורה, ספר שופטים, הלכות אבל, פרק יד, הלכה ב, Mishnah Torah, Book of Shofetim, Laws of a Mourner, Chapter 14, Law 2), defines the critical aspects of the latter mitzvah. Two critical aspects of the mitzvah of הכנסת אורחים, "hospitality," are: the inviting of the guests and the escorting of the guests. The latter aspect is the more important one, as it says, גדולה מצות ליווי האורחים יותר מהכנסתם, שבהכנסת אורחים הוצרך אברהם לומר אל נא תעבור מעל עבדך. ואילו בלויה כתוב: ואברהם הלך עמם לשלחם, וה׳ אמר המכסה אני מאברהם וגו׳ ונתעכבה לו שכינה עד בואו (אנציקלופדיה תלמודית, חלק ט, בעניין הכנסת אורחים, אות ג, דף קלא), "The mitzvah of escorting the guests is greater than inviting them, for when inviting the guests Abraham needed to say to Hashem, 'Please do not pass over your servant.' And whereas when escorting it is written, 'And Abraham went with them to send them on their way. And Hashem said, Shall I hide from Abraham, etc.' The divine Presence delayed for him until he came" (Talmudic Encyclopedia, Part 9, in the subject of hospitality, letter 3, page 131).

As was mentioned, there are two primary mitzvoth which may enhance the sanctity of an individual's table. The first mitzvah is to learn תורה, "Torah," at one's table. The gematria of תורה, "Torah," is 611.

תורה   611

The second mitzvah is to do הכנסת אורחים, "hospitality," to invite guests who are poor to one's table. Two critical aspects to being hospitable are: the inviting of guests and the escorting of the guests. When the number two, for these critical aspects, is added to the gematria of Torah, the sum is 613.

$$611$$
$$\underline{2}$$
$$613$$

The last Mishnah in Seder Moed says the kohanim were warned הזהרו שלא תגעו בשלחן, "Be careful not to touch the table." The gematria of הזהרו בשלחן, "Be careful with the table," is 613.

הזהרו	223
בשלחן	390
	613

The message is distinctly perceptible. One should be careful to perform the two mitzvoth which enhance the sanctity of an individual's table, for the individual tables of the Children of Israel serve as a source of blessing, and are associated with the gematria of 613, the gematria of הזהרו בשלחן, "Be careful with the table."

Parashath Tetzaveh פרשת תצוה

ושמת את שתי האבנים על כתפת האפד אבני זכרן לבני
ישראל ונשא אהרן את שמותם לפני ה׳ על שתי כתפיו לזכרן
(שמות כח,יב).

And you shall put the two stones on the shoulder pieces of the ephod, stones of memorial for
the Children of Israel; and Aaron shall bear
their names before G-d on his two shoulders for
a memorial (Exodus 28,12).

The pasuk before שני, the second portion of Parashath
Tetzaveh, says that ונשא אהרן, "and Aaron shall bear," the
names of the Children of Israel on the onyx stones. Why is the
word "bear," used, would not the word "wore," be more
appropriate, since the stones were part of his garment?

An answer can be found in אזנים לתורה, Oznaim
Latorah, which says that these stones were an allegory to the
Ten Commandments which were also written in stone. The
Ten Commandments intimate the 613 Commandments, as
stated, הנה "אבני זכרון לבני ישראל", שהם נושאים על כתפיהם את שני
לחות הברית, לחות אבן, ומקיימים את התרי"ג מצות הרמוזים בהם (אזנים
לתורה מאת הרב זלמן סורוצקין, שמות כח,יב ד"ה ושמת את בי האבנים
על כתפת האפד אבני זכרן לב"י), "Behold 'the stones of memorial
for the Children of Israel' [meaning that]: They bear on their
shoulders the Tablets of the Covenant, tablets of stone, and
fulfill the 613 Commandments which are hinted in them"
(Oznaim Latorah by Rabbi Zalman Sorotzkin, Exodus 28,12,
header words: And you shall put the two stones on the
shoulder pieces of the ephod, stones of memorial for the
Children of Israel).

Thus, the Children of Israel bear the responsibility, the
obligation, of the 613 Commandments, and therefore, when
the Torah says that Aaron bears their names, this bearing
could allegorically be representing their bearing the responsibility of the 613 Commandments. It is possible that the

pasuk before שני, the second portion of Parashath Tetzaveh, says that ונשא אהרן "and Aaron shall bear," because its gematria also alludes to the idea that the Children of Israel bear the responsibility, the obligation, of the 613 Commandments. The gematria of ונשא אהרן, "and Aaron shall bear," is 613.

ונשא	357
אהרן	<u>256</u>
	613

This gematria strengthens the explanation of the אזנים לתורה, Oznaim Latorah, that Aaron bears their names, allegorically representing the Children of Israel bearing the responsibility of fulfilling the 613 Commandments. The question of why the word "bear," was used, and not the word "wore," has been answered.

רבוע יהיה כפול זרת ארכו וזרת רחבו (שמות כח,טז).
It shall be square, double; a span in length, and
a span in breadth (Exodus 28,16).

The Torah uses the word וזרת, "and a span," when recording the measurements of the breastplate. The gematria of the וזרת, "and a span," is 613.

וזרת	613

Both Rashi and the Keli Yakar state that the breastplate was to atone for the sin of perverse judgment (רש״י, וכלי יקר, שמות כח,טו, Rashi, and Keli Yakar, Exodus 28,15). The Keli Yakar just mentioned also equates perverse justice with the sin of idol worship. The Gemara Horayoth says that idol worship is equated to the violation of all the commandments, as stated, אמר רבא ואי תימא ר׳ יהושע בן לוי ואמרי לה כדי אמר קרא וכי תשגו ולא תעשו את כל המצות האלה איזו היא מצוה שהיא שקולה ככל המצות הוי אומר זו עבודת כוכבים (הוריות ח.), "Raba said, others say Rabbi Joshua ben Levi, and others say Kadi, the pasuk says,

'When you shall blunder, and do not observe all of these mitzvoth.' Which mitzvah is equated as all the other mitzvoth? Say it is idol worship" (Horayoth 8a). The Gemara equates all the mitzvoth with idol worship. Since there is a total of 613 Mitzvoth, idol worship may then be associated with the number 613 as well. The Keli Yakar equates perverse justice to idol worship, which the Gemara equates with all the mitzvoth; thus it can be deduced that perverse justice is associated with the number 613.

The breastplate was to atone for the sin of perverse judgment. Therefore, it is very appropriate that the number 613, the gematria of וזרת, should be found in the description of the breastplate; the breastplate was to atone for that which was equated to idol worship, which is equated to the 613 Mitzvoth.

It is interesting to note the language of the Keli Yakar, as stated, וחשן הבא לכפר על קלקול הדינים כי הדיניין הם דברים מסורים אל לב הדיין כי אין לדיין כי אם מה שעיניו רואות וכו' (כלי יקר, שמות כח,טו), "And the breastplate was to atone for the sin of perverse judgments, for the judgments are matters bestowed to the heart of the judge; for a judge is limited to what his eyes see" (Keli Yakar, Exodus 28,15). The gematria of רואות, "see," is 613.

רואות   613

It is because of what the eyes רואות, "see," that perverse judgments could result. Since perverse judgments are associated with the gematria 613, it is interesting that רואות, "see," also has a gematria of 613.

ועשית שתי טבעות זהב ושמת אתם על שני קצות החשן על שפתו אשר אל עבר האפוד ביתה (שמות כח,כו).
And you should make two rings of gold, and you shall place them on the two edges of the choshen, upon its border which is toward the side of the ephod, inward (Exodus 28,26).

This sidrah tells how the holy garments were made and worn. The first two garments described are the ephod, "apron," and the choshen, "breastplate" (שמות כח,א-ל, Exodus 28,1-30). The choshen was worn on top of the ephod attached to its rings, as stated, אל עבר האפוד ביתה, "toward the side of the ephod, inward." The gematria of האפוד, "the ephod," is 96.

האפוד   96

The Gemara Zevachim says אפוד מכפר על עבודת כוכבים (זבחים פח:), "The ephod atoned for idolatry" (Zevachim 88b). Thus, 96 may be seen to represent atonement for the sin of idolatry. Idolatry stems from lack of knowledge of G-d; for if one was truly aware of G-d, he would not turn to idols. It follows that the true full atonement results in being more fully aware of G-d. Since the ephod provides atonement, it brings a greater awareness of G-d. Therefore, 96 may also represent a higher degree of knowledge, and a greater awareness of G-d.

The latter part of the sidrah discusses more about the holy garments, as well as how to sanctify the priests (Exodus 29, 1-44). The closing pasuk of the sixth section summarizes the purpose of the preceding subjects, as stated, וידעו כי אני ה', אלקיהם אשר הוצאתי אתם מארץ מצרים לשכני בתוכם אני ה' אלקיהם (שמות כט,מו) "And they shall known that I am G-d, their G-d, who took them out of the land of Egypt, that I might dwell among them, I am G-d their G-d" (Exodus 29,46). The gematria of וידעו, "and they shall know," is 96.

וידעו   96

The number 96 in this pasuk represents a higher degree of knowledge of G-d, and a greater awareness of Him. The gematrioth of האפוד, "the ephod," and וידעו, "and they shall know," are similar, and the ideas which they represent are also similar.

ונתת אל חשן המשפט את האורים ואת התמים והיו על לב
אהרן בבאו לפני ה׳ ונשא אהרן את משפט בני ישראל על
לבו לפני ה׳ תמיד (שמות כח,ל).

And you shall put into the breastplate of judgment the Urim and Thummim; and they shall be
upon the heart of Aaron when he comes before
G-d, and Aaron shall carry the judgment of the
Children of Israel upon his heart before G-d
continually (Exodus 28,30).

Regarding the Urim and Thummim being placed into
the breastplate of judgment, the pasuk says that ונשא אהרן,
"and Aaron shall carry," the judgment of the Children of
Israel. The gematria of ונשא אהרן, "and Aaron shall carry," is
613.

$$
\begin{array}{rr}
\text{ונשא} & 357 \\
\text{אהרן} & \underline{256} \\
& 613
\end{array}
$$

The exact same expression is found earlier (שמות כח,יב,
Exodus 28,12), where a different explanation is given for the
same gematria. The commentary תורה שבעל פה, Torah
Shebeal Peh, explains that the the judgment mentioned in
this pasuk includes all the sins of the Children of Israel, as he
writes, ונשא אהרן את שמות בני ישראל בחשן המשפט על לבו בענין
שיתבררו כל הדברים במשפט לרחם על ישראל מכל חטאתם ומכל משפטם
(חומש תורה שלמה עם באור "תורה שבעל פה" מאת מנחם מ. בן הרב יצחק
פרץ כשר, שמות כח,ל, אות צ), "And Aaron shall carry the names
of the Children of Israel on the breastplate of judgment upon
his heart; so that all matters shall be clarified in judgment to
have mercy on Israel from all their sins and from all judgment" (Chumash Torah Sheleimah im Be'ur Torah Shebeal
Peh by Menachem M. ben Harov Yitzchak Peretz Kasher,
Exodus 28,30, Letter 90).

All the sins of the Children of Israel can include a

potential violation of any mitzvah. There is a total of 613 Commandments, as the Gemara says, דרש רבי שמלאי שש מאות ושלש עשרה מצות נאמרו לו למשה שלש מאות וששים וחמש לאוין כמנין ימות החמה ומאתים וארבעים ושמונה עשה כנגד איבריו של אדם (מכות כג:), "Rabbi Simlai expounded, Six hundred and thirteen Commandments were said to Moses. Three hundred and sixty-five negative Commandments corresponding to the number of days in a solar year, and two hundred and forty-eight positive Commandments corresponding to the number of limbs of a man" (Makkoth 23b). Since the gematria of ונשא אהרן, "and Aaron shall carry," is equal to the total number of commandments, it is a support to the explanation of the commentary תורה שבעל פה, Torah Shebeal Peh, that the judgment of this pasuk included all the potential sins of the Children of Israel.

וידעו כי אני ה' אלקיהם אשר הוצאתי אתם מארץ מצרים
לשכני בתוכם אני ה' אלקיהם (שמות כט,מו).
And they shall know that I am G-d, their G-d,
Who took them out of the land of Egypt, that I
might dwell among them, I am G-d their G-d
(Exodus 29,46).

Toward the end of the sidrah the Torah states, וידעו כי אני ה' אלקיהם, "And they shall known that I am G-d, their G-d." This phrase could be translated as, וידעו כי אני, "And they shall know that I," ה', "G-d," אלקיהם, "am their G-d." Thus, "that I," who took you out of Egypt is equated to "their G-d"; the latter quote could be considered a predicate nominative referring to the former quote.

This explanation is made more plausible when considering the following gematria. The gematria of כי אני, "that I," is 91.

כי	30
אני	61
	91

The gematria of אלקיהם, "their G-d," is 91.

אלקיהם   91

Since the gematrioth of כי אני, "that I," and אלקיהם, "their G-d," are equal, the explanation that "that I," is equated to "their G-d," is more plausible.

Parashath Ki Thissa   פרשת כי תשא

כי תשא את ראש בני־ישראל לפקדיהם ונתנו איש כפר נפשו
להי בפקד אתם ולא יהיה בהם נגף בפקד אתם (שמות ל,יב).
When you take the sum of the Children of Israel, according to their numbers, and they shall give every man an atonement for his soul to G-d, when you number them; so that there should not be a plague among them when you number them (Exodus 30,12).

The second pasuk in this sidrah refers to the giving of איש כפר, "every man an atonement," to Hashem. The gematria of איש כפר, "every man an atonement," is 611.

איש	311
כפר	300
	611

The gematria of Torah is also 611.

תורה	611

The connection between these two gematrioth is clear; תורה, "Torah," is כפר, "atonement" for the soul of an איש, "man." This connection can be validated by a Gemara Rosh Hashanah which states, אמר רבא בזבח ובמנחה אינו מתכפר אבל מתכפר בתורה (ראש השנה יח.), "Raba said, '[This sin] can not be atoned for by a sacrifice, nor by a meal offering, but it can be atoned for with Torah'" (Rosh Hashanah 18a).

העשיר לא ירבה והדל לא ימעיט ממחצית השקל לתת את
תרומת הי לכפר על נפשתיכם (שמות ל,טו).
The rich shall not give more, and the poor shall not give less, than the half a shekel, when they give an offering to G-d, to atone for your souls (Exodus 30,15).

The Torah says that there are twenty gerahs to a shekel (Exodus 30,13). Therefore, half of a shekel was ten gerahs. There is an opinion of Rabban Johanan ben Zakkai in the Talmud Yerushalmi, that the half shekel was a requirement for the Bnei Yisroel to be forgiven for not observing the Ten Commandments; ר׳ יהושע ב׳ ר׳ נחמיה בשם ר׳ יוחנן בן זכאי לפי שעברו על עשרת הדברות יהיה נותן כל אחד ואחד עשרה גרה (תלמוד ירושלמי, שקלים, פרק ב, הלכה ג), "Rabbi Joshua the son of Rabbi Nechemich in the name of Rabban Yochanan ben Zakai since they violated the Ten Commandments, every single one of them should give ten gerahs" (Yerushalmi Gemara, Shekalim, Chapter 2, Halakhah 3). This opinion explains why the Torah defines the shekel as twenty gerahs: so that it should be a realization that the half shekel was ten gerahs, corresponding to the Ten Commandments.

There is a total of 613 Commandments; why did G-d choose to give just these ten, as the Ten Commandments? Rashi, quoting Rabbi Saadia Gaon, says that all 613 Commandments are able to be found in the Ten Commandments (רש״י, שמות כד,יב, Rashi, Exodus 24,12). Thus, this Rashi tells why G-d chose to give these mitzvoth as the Ten Commandments: because they contain the 613 Mitzvoth in concentrated form, which means that each command of the Ten Commandments is a concentrated form of part of the Torah. A סם, "potion," is generally a small quantity which has power concentrated in it (The Pentateuch translated and explained by Rabbi Samson Hirsch, Genesis 11,6). Therefore, it can be said that each command of the Ten Commandments is like a potion.

This argument is enhanced by the fact that the Gemara refers to the Torah as a סם, "potion," as the Gemara Yoma says, אמר רבי יהושע בן לוי... זכה נעשית לו סם חיים לא זכה נעשית לו סם מיתה (יומא עב:), "Rabbi Joshua ben Levi says ... 'If he is meritorious, it (the Torah) is for him a potion of life, if he is not meritorious, it is for him a potion of death'" (Yoma 72b). To further enhance this argument, note that the letters of the word סם, "potion," are implied in the Ten Commandments. The tablets were engraved from one side through to the other side. If so, how could the ס, "samech," and ם, "mem," have hung in mid-air? The Gemara Megillah explains "Rav, אמר רב חסדא מ״ם וסמ״ך שבלוחות בנס היו עומדין (מגילה ב:-ג.) Hisda said, the mem and samech in the tablets stood miraculously" (Megillah 2b-3a). Thus, the two letters which spell סם, "potion," existed with the power of a miracle.

The Gemara which states, מ״ם וסמך שבלוחות בנס היו עומדין, "the mem and the samech in the tablets miraculously stood," could be interpreted as: the power of the Torah to be either סם חיים, "a potion of life," or סם מיתה, "a potion of death," as the Gemara Yoma states, is by means of a miracle. This power of the Torah is miraculous, since G-d lets it exist, בנס היו עומדין, "stood miraculously." This power is especially true for the Ten Commandments, since each command is like a סם, "potion." The gematria of סם, "potion," is 100.

סם   100

Since each command of the Ten Commandments is a concentrated form of part of the Torah, each command is akin to a potion. Ergo being that there are Ten Commandments, each of which is like a סם, "potion," its gematria is multiplied by ten, which then equals 1,000.

100
x 10
———
1000

Thus, 1,000 may represent the miraculous power of the Ten Commandments.

The pasuk first quoted from Ki Thissa says that the half shekel was לכפר על נפשתיכם, "to atone for your souls." The gematria of על נפשתיכם, "for your souls," is 1000.

על	100
נפשתיכם	900
	1000

Therefore, it can be said that the the half shekel was to atone for the 1000, which represents the miraculous power of the Ten Commandments. This exposition fits in beautifully with the opinion of Rabban Johanan ben Zakkai in the Yerushalmi Gemara, that the half shekel was for the Bnei Yisroel to be forgiven for not observing the Ten Commandments.

Parashath Shekalim is read on the Shabbath before Rosh Chodesh Adar. The reason for this reading is discussed in a Mishnah which says that on the first of Adar announcements were made about the collection of the shekelim. The Penei Moshe says that this date was designated so that the newly offered money could be expended to purchase sacrifices in Nisan, as stated, כדי שיהא להם פנאי שלשים יום ושיביאו את שקליהן בזמנן ותיתרום תרומת הלשכה בזמנה להביא קרבנות הצבור מתרומת חדשה באחד בניסן (פני משה מאת הרב משה מרגלית בן הרב שמעון, תלמוד ירושלמי, שקלים, פרק א, הלכה א) "In order that they should have leisure of thirty days, and they should bring their shekalim in the right time, and separate a treasury portion in time to bring public sacrifices from the new portion on the first of Nisan" (Penei Moshe by Rabbi Moshe Margoliot son of Rabbi Shimon, Yerushalmi Gemara, Shekalim, Chapter 1, Halakhah 1). Perhaps an additional reason can be given as to why the first of Adar was chosen as the time to announce the collection of the shekalim. The announcement was made on the first of Adar, and the money was collected during the rest of the month, the completion of which would be near the beginning of the month of Nisan. Passover comes on the 15th of Nisan, shortly after the completion of the collection. Passover and Shavuoth are connected by the omer counting, and can therefore be considered as a joint holiday season.

On Passover, everyone is to see himself as if he went out of Egypt, as the Passover Haggadah states in the paragraph, after בכל דור ודור חיב אדם, מרור זה, "this bitter herb"; (הגדה של פסח) לראות את עצמו כאלו הוא יצא ממצרים, "In every generation one is obligated to view himself as if he went forth from Egypt," (Haggadah for Passover). The aim of the exodus from Egypt was to receive the Torah (שמות, ג,כד ותרגום יונתן בן עוזיאל על הפסוק, Exodus 3,12 and Targum Yonathan ben Uzziel on this pasuk). Both Rabbi Naftoli Tzvi Yehuda Berlin and Rabbi Yeruchem HaLevi Levovitz expound upon this aim. Rabbi Naftoli Tzvi Yehuda Berlin writes about the direct link between the exodus from Egypt and the receiving of the Ten Commandments, as he says, והתועלת מזו המחשבה מובנת, כי היא באה להגביה את לב האדם בדרך ה', אחרי אשר כל בריאת השמים והארץ היתה בשבילו — אם כן עליו להכשיר את עצמו שיהא ראוי לקיום ה׳עשרה מאמרות׳ של הקב״ה. וכן במה שיחשוב, שבשבילו לבדו היה כל העסק הגדול של יציאת מצרים יהא בזה למדי להגביה את נפשו בדרך התורה שבשביל זו התכלית היתה יציאת מצרים (סדר הגדה של פסח עם פירוש אמרי שפר מאת הרב נפתלי צבי יהודה ברלין מוואלאזין, ד״ה בכל דור ודור חייב אדם לראות את עצמו כאלו הוא יצא ממצרים). "The outcome from this thought is understood, that it comes to raise man's spirit in the service of G-d, since all the creation of heaven and earth was for his benefit - If so it is incumbent upon him to prepare himself so that he should be fit to fulfill the 'ten statements' of the Holy One, Blessed be He. Similarly, one should think that for him alone was all the great enterprise of the exodus from Egypt. As a result of this one should learn to lift up his soul in the ways of the Torah since because of this goal there was the exodus from Egypt," (Seder Passover Haggadah with the explanation Imrei Shefer by Rabbi Naphtali Zvi Judah Berlin from Volozhin, header words: In every generation and generation a person is obligated to see himself as if he went out of Egypt).

This idea is further explained by Rabbi Yeruchem Halevi Levovitz, as he says, ״להיות לכם לאלקים״ הוא עניין יצ״מ ו״להיות לו לעם נחלה,״ (דברים כ,ב) שיצאו מרשותו של פרעה ונכנסו לרשותו של הקב״ה, שזהו תכלית יצ״מ. ״אנכי ה׳ אלי אשר הוצאתיך, מארץ מצרים״ — כי רש״י (שמות כ,ב): כדאי היא ההוצאה שתהיו משועבדים לי (ספר חבר מאמרים דעת חכמה ומוסר מאת הרב ירוחם הלוי ליוואוויץ, מאמר מא, ״אתה בסממניך ואני בכבודי״ — סוד המעשים "The idea of the exodus from Egypt is 'that He should be to you as a G-d,' and 'to be to Him a people of inheritance' (Deuteronomy 20,2). That they went out of the domain of Pharaoh and entered the domain of the Holy One, Blessed Be He; this is the purpose of the exodus from Egypt. 'I am G-d, your G-d, Who took you out from the Land of Egypt' — Rashi writes (Exodus 20,2): The Exodus was sufficient, that you shall be servile to Me," (Book of Chever Maamarim Daas Chochmah Umusur by Rabbi Yeruchem Halevi Levovitz, Maamar 41, "You with your spices and I in My glory"—Secret of Deeds).

In order to really feel the receiving of the Ten Commandments anew, it is important to be forgiven for not observing these commandments in the past. The purpose of the half shekel, according to Rabban Johanan ben Zakkai in the Talmud Yerushalmi, was for the Bnei Yisroel to be forgiven for not observing the Ten Commandments. Thus, it is very fitting that the Mishnah says that on the first of Adar announcements were made about the collection of the shekalim; the collection should be completed before Passover and of course before Pentecost, thereby ensuring that the Bnei Yisroel would be forgiven for not observing the Ten Commandments before these holidays.

The timing of the half shekel collection ties in with a gematria. The Torah says when matzah shall be eaten, as stated, ששת ימים תאכל מצות וביום השביעי עצרת לה׳ אלקיך לא תעשה מלאכה (דברים טז,ח), "Six days you shall eat unleavened bread, and on the seventh day shall be a solemn assembly for Hashem your G-d, you shall not do work," (Deuteronomy 16,8). The gematria of ששת, "six," is 1000.

1000 ששת

Since the gematria of על נפשתיכם, "for your souls," is also 1000, the pasuk just quoted can be explained to mean that by the time these six days come, one should have faith that he has been forgiven על נפשתיכם, "for your souls," for not having properly observed the Ten Commandments, the miraculousness of which is associated with the gematria of 1000. Also this forgiveness is על נפשתיכם, "for your souls," which also has a gematria of 1000.

The pasuk ששת ימים תאכל מצות וביום השביעי עצרת לה' אלקיך לא תעשה מלאכה, "Six days you shall eat unleavened bread, and on the seventh day shall be a solemn assembly for Hashem your G-d, you shall not do work," (דברים טז,ח), can be explained as pertaining to faith. The appertaining of this pasuk to faith could be a derash in what the לקוטי תורה means when it refers to matzah as מיכלא דמהימנותא, "food of faith," (לקוטי תורה מאת בעל התניא, פרשת צו דף יב:). A similar thought is also presented in the Zohar, as it says, לאכול מצה בפסח, בגין דאיהו דוכרנא לדרי דרין על רזא דמהימנותא (ספר הזוהר מאת התנא רבי שמעון בן יוחאי, פרשת בא, דף מא.), "To eat unleavened bread on Passover, since it is a remembrance for generations and generations of the secret of faith" (The Book of the Zohar by the Tanna Rabbi Shimon ben Yochai, Parashath Bo, Page 41a). The meaning would then be that a person should have faith that G-d has forgiven him for not keeping the Ten Commandments, so that he can feel on Passover as if he went out of Egypt, and then he can feel on Shavuoth as if he himself were receiving the Ten Commandants anew.

The idea of 1000 representing faith in receiving forgiveness might shed some light on a pasuk in Parashath Vayyelech. When Moses talked to Joshua before his death, he reassured him that G-d would not forsake him, and that Joshua should not be afraid, וה' הוא ההלך לפניך הוא יהיה עמך לא ירפך ולא יעזבך לא תירא ולא תחת (דברים לא,ח), "And Hashem, it is He that goes before you, He will be with you, He will not fail you, nor will He forsake you; do not fear, and do not be dismayed" (Deuteronomy 31,8). The difference between Joshua's fear and G-d's forsaking him could well be the doubt, or lack of faith, that G-d had forgiven the Bnei Yisroel for not having observed the Ten Commandments, or the mitzvoth which they represent. The difference between Joshua's fear and G-d's forsaking him is the difference between ירפך, "He will fail you," plus יעזבך, "He will forsake you," and between תירא, "fear," plus תחת, "dismayed."

The Torah writes that Moses told Joshua, והי הוא ההלך לפניך הוא יהיה עמך לא ירפך ולא יעזבך לא תירא ולא תחת (דברים לא,ח), "And Hashem, it is He that goes before you, He will be with you, He will not fail you, nor will He forsake you; do not fear, and do not be dismayed" (Deuteronomy 31,8). The gematria of ירפך, "He will fail you," plus יעזבך, "He will forsake you," is 419.

<pre>
ירפך   310
יעזבך   109
          419
</pre>

The gematria of תירא, "fear," plus תחת, "dismayed," is 1419.

<pre>
תירא   611
תחת   808
          1419
</pre>

The difference between the gematria of ירפך, "He will fail you," plus יעזבך, "He will forsake you," and the gematria of תירא, "fear," plus תחת, "dismayed," is 1000.

<pre>
          1419
          -419
          1000
</pre>

The gematria of 1000 can represent faith that Hashem will forgive or has forgiven. This gematria ties in well with what was said, that the miraculous powers of the Ten Commandments are also associated with the gematria of 1000. Thus, the doubt that Joshua could have had was if Hashem had totally forgiven the Bnei Yisroel for not having observed the Ten Commandments, or the mitzvoth which they represent.

והלחת מעשה אלקים המה והמכתב מכתב אלקים הוא
חרות על־הלחת (שמות לב,טז).

And the tablets were the work of G-d and the writing was the writing of G-d, graven upon the tablets (Exodus 32,16).

The Torah describes the tablets as being graved with the writing of G-d, חרות על הלחת, "graven upon the tablets." The gematria of חרות, "graven," is 614.

חרות   614

In relationship to the word חרות, "graven," our Rabbis have said, אל תקרא חרות אלא חירות, "Do not read, charuth, 'graven,' but rather cheiruth, 'freedom'" (אבות, פרק ו, משנה ב, Avoth, Chapter 6, Mishnah 2). The כלי יקר, Keli Yakar, quotes a Midrash which gives three applications of of the meaning of freedom; the second one of which is חירות מן מלאך המות, "freedom from the angel of death," (כלי יקר, שמות לב,טז, Keli Yakar, Exodus 32,16). The Keli Yakar enhances this second application by employing the following pesukim from Psalms: אני אמרתי אלהים אתם ובני עליון כלכם. אכן כאדם תמותון וכאחד השרים תפלו (תהלים פב, ו־ז), "I said, you are gods, and all of you are children of the Most High. But you will die as men, and fall as one of the princes" (Psalms 82,6-7). This explanation of the Keli Yakar is similar to how Rashi understands these pesukim from Psalms. These pesukim from Psalms tell us that the Bnei Yisroel could be כבני אלקים, "as the sons of G-d," that is free from death, but the deeds of the Bnei Yisroel spoiled their situation and caused them to die (כלי יקר, שמות לב,טז, Keli

Yakar, Exodus 32,16). Thus, according to this explanation, חרות, "freedom," can be explained as freedom from death.

When Moses came down from Mount Sinai and saw the golden calf, he told the sons of Levi that each man should go through the camp and kill his [half] brother, his companion, and his relative, as stated, ויאמר להם כה אמר ה' אלקי ישראל שימו איש חרבו על ירכי עברו ושובו משער לשער במחנה והרגו איש את אחיו ואיש את רעהו, ואיש, את קרבו (שמות לב,כז), "And he said to them, 'Thus G-d, the G-d of Israel said, Put every man his sword upon his thigh, go to and fro from gate to gate in the camp, and kill every man his brother, and every man his companion, and every man his relative'" (Exodus 32,27). The combined gematria of אחיו, "his brother," רעהו, "his companion," and קרבו, "his relative," is 614.

אחיו	25
רעהו	281
קרבו	308
	614

The brothers, companions, and relatives were the people designated to be killed because they did not heed the freedom message of the tablets; the deeds of these members of the Bnei Yisroel spoiled their situation which caused death to return. This association is further strengthened by virtue of the fact that חרות, "freedom," has the same gematria as the combined gematria of אחיו, "his brother," רעהו, "his compan-ion," and קרבו, "his relative."

 וידבר ה' אל משה פנים אל פנים כאשר ידבר איש אל רעהו ושב אל המחנה ומשרתו יהושע בן נון נער לא ימיש מתוך האהל (שמות לג,יא).

And G-d spoke to Moses face to face, as a man speaks to his friend, and he would return to the camp; and his minister Joshua the son of Nun did not depart out of the tent (Exodus 33,11).

After the Torah describes how G-d spoke to Moses, the Torah describes Joshua's devotion; both topics are mentioned in the same pasuk. The gematria of פנים אל פנים, "face to face," is 391.

פנים	180
אל	31
פנים	180
	391

The gematria of לא ימיש, "did not depart," is also 391.

לא	31
ימיש	360
	391

The expression פנים אל פנים, "face to face," is the key phrase in describing how G-d spoke to Moses. The expression לא ימיש, "did not depart," is the key phrase in describing Joshua's devotion. The Gemara comments about both of these expressions.

In relationship to the expression פנים אל פנים, "face to face," the Gemara says, א״ר יצחק אמר לו הקב״ה למשה משה אני ואתה נסביר פנים בהלכה איכא דאמרי כך אמר לו הקב״ה למשה כשם שאני הסברתי, לך פנים כך אתה הסביר פנים לישראל והחזר האהל למקומו (ברכות סג:) "Rabbi Isaac said, 'The Holy One, Blessed be He, said to Moses, Moses, I and you will clarify aspects in Jewish law. Others say, in this manner The Holy One, Blessed be He, said to Moses, Just as I have shown you a pleasant face, likewise you should show Israel a pleasant face and return the Tent to its place'" (Berakoth 63b). According to the first opinion, the expression פנים אל פנים, "face to face," is associated with Moses learning Torah from G-d. Thus, the expression פנים אל פנים, "face to face," relates to a way of learning Torah, which is from a teacher. Just as Moses learned Torah from G-d, so too the Children of Israel will in every generation learn Torah from their teachers.

In relationship to the expression לא ימיש, "did not depart," the Gemara says ...דאמר ר' ישמואל בר נחמני א"ר יונתן ראה הקב"ה את יהושע שדברי תורה חביבים עליו ביותר שנאמר ומשרתו יהושע בן נון נער לא ימיש מתוך האהל אמר לו הקדוש ברוך הוא יהושע כל כך חביבין עליך דברי תורה לא ימוש ספר התורה הזה מפיך (מנחות צט:), "that Rabbi Samuel bar Nahmani said that Rabbi Jonthan said ... The Holy One saw that to Joshua, words of Torah were especially beloved by him, as it says, 'and his minister Joshua did not depart from the tent,' The Holy One said to him, 'Joshua, so much are words of Torah beloved by you, this book of Torah will not depart from your mouth'" (Menahoth 99b). According to this opinion in the Gemara, the expression לא ימיש, "did not depart," is associated with Joshua learning with constant involvement. Just as Joshua learned Torah with constant involvement, so too the Bnei Yisroel for generations have learned Torah with constant involvement.

The consequences of neglecting either of these two features of Torah learning is discussed in the Gemara Taanith. This Gemara pinpoints two, and only two, situations of a student who was having difficulty learning, identified as תלמיד שתלמודו קשה עליו כברזל, "a student whose studies are as difficult as iron to him." This Gemara says, ריש לקיש אמר אם ראית תלמיד שלמודו קשה עליו כברזל בשביל משנתו שאינו סדורה עליו.... מאי תקנתיה ירבה בישיבה.... רבא אמר אם ראית תלמיד שלמודו קשה עליו כברזל בשביל רבו שאינו מסביר לו פנים.... מאי תקנתיה ירבה עליו רעים (תענית ז:-ח.), "Resh Lakish said, 'If you see a student whose studies are as difficult as iron to him, it can be attributed to his studies which are disorganized for him.... What is his remedy? He should increase time studying.' ... Raba said, 'If you see a student whose studies are as difficult as iron to him, it can be attributed to his teacher who did not show his pleasant countenance... What is his remedy? He should increase his circle of friends.'" (Taanith 7b-8a) For one situation the remedy is to ירבה בישיבה, "increase time studying," which corresponds to how the words לא ימיש, "did not depart," were explained. For the other situation, the remedy is to increase his circle of friends, who can intercede for him, and improve the rapport between the teacher and the student, for in this circumstance the Gemara blames the teacher, identified as בשביל רבו שאינו מסביר לו פנים, "because of his teacher who has not adequately explained to him." This second remedy corresponds to how the words פנים אל פנים, "face to face," were explained. Thus, the two crucial features of Torah learning derived from the words פנים אל פנים, "face to face," and the words לא ימיש, "did not depart," are pinpointed by the Gemara Taanith for situations of תלמיד שתלמודו קשה עליו כברזל, "a student whose studies were as difficult as iron to him."

The cardinal significance of these two features of Torah learning has been stressed by the rabbis. Learning from a rav is viewed as the perfection of Torah learning, as stated, יהושע בן פרחיה כו' עשה לך רב כו' אמר שתועלת הלמוד הוא בלומד מזולתו כי הידיעה המקבלת עם בחינת הלמוד ופלפול בהם הוא השלמות... הלומד מפי אחרים תלמודו עומד, כלו' שלימודו הוא בדרך קיום והעמדה וכו' (ספר בית הבחירה על מסכת אבות מאת רבינו מנחם המאירי, פרק א, משנה ו), "Joshua, the son of Perachyah, etc. Make for yourself a teacher, etc. He said that the benefit of the learning is in learning from others. For the transmitted knowledge with the examination of one's learning and the discussion in them, that is the perfection... Someone who learns from others his learning remains, that is to say, that his learning is in a way that remains and lasts, etc." (Book of Beit Habechirah on Tractate Avoth by Rabbeinu Menachem Hameiri, Chapter 1, Mishnah 6).

Constant involvement in Torah learning is based on a pasuk from the Torah, as stated, ואמר יהגה ולא אמר יעסוק או יקרא כי מלאכתו אימתי נעשית אבל יאמר שתהיי מחשבתו דבוקה בקל יתי אפילו בהתעסקו בדברי הרשות כאו' (דברים יי) ובו תדבק וכו' (פירוש לספר

(תהלִים מאת הרב יוסף יעבץ הדורש, תהלים פרק א, פסוק ב), "And it says he meditates (day and night), and it does not say he is busy, or he reads, for when will his work be done? But it means to say that his thoughts should be clinging to the blessed G-d, even when he is busy with permissible matters, etc., as it says,(Deuteronomy 10) 'to Him you shall cleave, etc.'" (Commentary to the Book of Psalms by Rabbi Joseph Yavetz Hadoresh, Chapter 1, verse 2).

Is it more crucial to learn from a teacher or is it more crucial to learn with constant involvement? The answer is that both features are indispensable. One must learn Torah from a teacher and one must learn Torah with constant involvement. At times these need to be combined, so there will be constant involvement in learning from a teacher. Since both of these aspects of learning Torah are equally valid, it is appropriate that פנים אל פנים, "face to face," and לא ימיש, "did not depart," should have the same gematria, for these two expressions correspond to two indispensable methods of learning Torah.

ויאמר הראני נא את כבדך (שמות לג,יח).
And he said, please show me Your honor (Exodus 33,18).

והסרתי את כפי וראית את אחרי ופני לא יראו (שמות לג,כג).
And I will remove my palm, and you shall see My back, but My countenance shall not be seen (Exodus 33,23).

After Moses had asked G-d to show him His honor, G-d answered, וראית את אחרי ופני לא יראו, "and you shall see My back, but My countenance shall not be seen." How does this statement of G-d relate to the honor Moses sought to perceive, that is, how did G-d answer Moses? Rashi comments that G-d's answer was that He would show Moses the knot of His tefillin (רש״י, שמות לג,כג, Rashi, Exodus 33,23). What does the knot of the tefillin have to do with G-d's honor? Perhaps these two questions can be answered.

I do not pretend to understand this perplexing subject, but only hope to open a possible avenue which may help one gain an insight into what G-d answered Moses.

To begin one should try to understand the Torah's concept of honor. The Torah commands that one should honor his parents (שמות כ,יב, Exodus 20,12). The תלמוד ירושלמי, "Talmud Yerushalmi," relates the honor of parents to the honor of G-d, as stated. נאמר כבד את אביך ואת אמך ונאמר כבד את ה׳ מהונך, הקיש כיבוד אב ואם לכיבוד המקום (תלמוד ירושלמי פאה, פרק א, הלכה א). "It says, 'Honor your father and your mother'; and it says, 'Honor G-d with your prosperity.' It compares honoring one's father and one's mother to honoring G-d" (Yerushalmi Gemara, Pe'ah, Chapter 1, Halakhah 1). Thus, it is valid to compare the honor mentioned in reference to parents to the honor mentioned in reference to G-d. The Gemara includes in its definition of the honor mentioned in reference to parents as fulfilling the wishes of the parents. Rabbi Ishmael was told to honor his mother by fulfilling her wishes, as stated, אמרו לו הואיל והוא רצונה הוא כבודה (תלמוד ירושלמי, פאה, פרק א, הלכה א) "They said to him, since it is her desire, it is her honor" (Yerushalmi Gemara, Pe'ah, Chapter 1, Halakhah 1).

Jewish law stipulates that in order to properly fulfill the mitzvah of honoring one's parents, one should not only do that which the parents desire, but he should do it בסבר פנים יפות (שלחן ערוך, יורה דעה סימן רמ, סעיף ד), "with a pleasant disposition" (Shulhan Arukh, Yoreh De'ah, Siman 240, Seif 4). Thus, one should do that which his parents want him to do, as if he perceives that it is virtuous to do so; and he should not do that which his parents do not want him to do, as if he perceives it is virtuous not to do so. Since honor mentioned in reference to parents may be defined as fulfilling the desires of the parents with a pleasant disposition, so too honor mentioned in reference to G-d can then be defined as fulfilling the desires of G-d with a pleasant disposition.

What is the desire of G-d; what does G-d want from us? Obviously, G-d wants us to do what he commanded us to do. G-d has commanded the Children of Israel to observe 613 Mitzvoth, divided between 248 positive Mitzvoth and 365 negative Mitzvoth, as stated, דרש רבי שמלאי שש מאות ושלש עשרה מצות נאמרו לו למשה שלש מאות וששים וחמש לאוין כמנין ימות החמה ומאתים וארבעים ושמונה עשה כנגד איבריו של אדם (מכות כג:), "Rabbi Simlai expounded, 613 Commandments were said to Moses, three hundred and sixty-five negative Commandments corresponding to the number of days in a solar year, and two hundred and forty-eight positive Commandments corresponding to the limbs of a person" (Makkoth 23b). Thus, it follows that if one observes the 248 positive Commandments, and does not transgress the 365 negative Commandments, he is doing what G-d wants him to do. Further, to show honor to G-d, one should observe the 248 positive Commandments as if he perceives that it is virtuous to observe them, and one should not transgress the 365 negative Commandments as if he perceives that it is virtuous not to transgress them.

When G-d answered Moses, He used the word וראית (שמות לג,כג), "And you shall see" (Exodus 33,23). The word וראית, "and you shall see," is not limited to the literal sense of sight, as it is commonly translated. For example, when Yaakov came to his father, Yitzchok, to receive the blessings, Yitzchok smelled the clothes of Yaakov and said ראה ריח בני כריח שדה אשר ברכו ה' (בראשית כז,כז), "Perceive, the fragrance of my son is like the fragrance of the field which G-d has blessed" (Genesis 27,27). In this instance the word ראה can not mean see, inasmuch as Yitzchok being blind could not see, and inasmuch as smell is invisible. The word ראה has the broader meaning of to sense, grasp, comprehend, or perceive something which is liked or disliked. The negative connotation of something disliked expresses a feeling of displeasure, irritation, or resentment with that which is comprehended, as the word ראית (בראשית כ,י), "Did you see," (Genesis 20,10). Note that this form of the word is the same form as the one previously quoted in the pasuk from Parashath Ki Thissa (Exodus 33,23). The negative connotation of what follows the word ראה, in different forms is found in numerous other pesukim, for example, בראשית (לא,נ), בראשית (לט,יד), שמות (ג,ז), שמות (ג,ט), שמות (ה,כא), דברים (ט,יג), וקהלת (ו,א), Genesis (31,50), Genesis (39,14), Exodus (3,7), Exodus (3,9), Exodus (5,21), Deuteronomy (9,13), and Ecclesiastes (6,1). This negative connotation can likewise be applied to the pasuk from Exodus (33,23).

The first question was that after Moses had asked G-d to see His honor, G-d answered, וראית את אחרי ופני לא יראו, "and you shall see My back, but My countenance shall not be seen." How does this statement of G-d relate to His honor, that is, how did G-d answer Moses? The gematria of אחרי ופני, "My back but My countenance," is 365.

אחרי	219
ופני	146
	365

The gematria of לא יראה is 248.

לא	31
יראו	217
	248

Since the gematria of אחרי ופני, corresponds to the number of negative mitzvoth, and the gematria of לא יראו, corresponds to number of positive mitzvoth, G-d's answer to Moses can be interpreted related to the mitzvoth. To show honor to G-d, one should observe the 248 positive Commandments as if he perceives that it is virtuous to observe them, and one should not transgress the 365 negative Commandments as if he perceives that it is virtuous not to transgress them. The 365 negative Commandments should be viewed as abominable actions to commit; the 248 positive Commandments should be viewed as melioristic to perform. Moses asked to be shown G-d's honor. G-d answered that if one observes that which I want you to observe as if you perceive it to be virtuous to do so, and if you do not transgress that which I told you not to transgress as if you perceive it to be virtuous not to do so, then you will be giv ng Me honor. When G-d answered by saying וראית את אחרי ופני, "and you shall see My back but My countenance," meaning you shall view the 365 negative Mitzvoth as being abominable; לא יראו, "shall not be seen," meaning you shall not view the 248 positive Mitzvoth similarly.

The first question was that how did G-d answer Moses? Moses had asked to see G-d's honor. G-d answered that His honor is determined by how the mitzvoth are perceived. Also note that the words אחרי ופני, "My back and My countenance," can mean the back and front, or from beginning to end; that is, the 365 negative Mitzvoth should be seen completely, that is, perceived of in their entirely. The first question has been answered.

The second question was that Rashi comments that G-d answered Moses by showing him the knot of His tefillin (רש״י, שמות לג,כג, Rashi, Exodus 33,23). What does the knot of the tefillin have to do with G-d's honor? The word קשר, can mean knot, but it can also mean connection. If the latter meaning is adopted, it can be understood that G-d showed Moses the connection, or link, of the tefillin. What is the significance of the tefillin? The Gemara Kiddushin says הוקשה כל התורה כולה לתפלין (קדושין לה.), "All of the Torah in its entirety can be compared to the tefillin" (Kiddushun 35a). There is a

Midrash which says, כל התורה כלה תרי״ג מצות (שיר השירים רבה א,יג), "All of the Torah in its entirety is 613 Commandments" (Song of Songs Rabbah 1,13). Since all the Torah in its entirety is compared to the tefillin, and all of the Torah in its entirety is 613 Commandments, then it follows that the 613 Mitzvoth are connected to the tefillin. Thus, when G-d showed Moses the knot of the tefillin, He showed him the connection to the 613 Mitzvoth. Moses asked to see G-d's honor; G-d answered that His honor is determined by how the 613 Mitzvoth are perceived.

The significance of the tefillin is that they are compared to the 613 Mitzvoth, which when correctly perceived are an honor to G-d. It is now understood what the knot of the tefillin has to do with G-d's honor; the first and second questions have both been answered.

ויאמר הנה אנכי כרת ברית נגד כל עמך אעשה נפלאת אשר לא נבראו בכל הארץ ובכל הגוים וראה כל העם אשר אתה בקרבו את מעשה ה' כי נורא הוא אשר אני עשה עמך (שמות לד,י).

And He said, 'Behold I make a covenant, opposite all your people I will do wonders which have not been wrought in all the earth, and in all the nations, and all the people whom you are in the midst of shall see the work of G-d, for it is fearful that which I am about to do with you' (Exodus 34,10).

G-d said He would make a covenant, and all העם, "the people," will see. The gematria of העם, "the people," is 115.

העם   115

The next two pesukim begin שמר לך, "Observe for yourself," and השמר לך, "Take heed for yourself"; their antecedent is העם, "the people." In the second of these pesukim the Torah warns not to make a covenant with the inhabitants of the land upon which you go up, as stated, השמר לך פן תכרת ברית ליושב הארץ אשר אתה בא עליה פן יהיה למוקש בקרבך (שמות לד,יב), "Take heed for yourself lest you make a covenant with the inhabitants of the land upon which you come, lest they be a snare in your midst" (Exodus 34,12). The gematria of עליה, "upon," is 115.

עליה   115

Since the gematria of העם, "the people," and עליה, "upon which," are equal, it is a reflection of the fact that the people will come upon the land. Recall that the antecedent of "Take heed," is העם, "the people"; therefore the antecedent of אתה, "you," in the same pasuk is also, "the people." Consequently, the pasuk is saying you, העם, "the people," will come upon the land of Israel.

The concept of the people coming upon the land of Israel can be coupled with the Tosafoth which states דאין לך אדם שאין לו ארבע אמות בארץ ישראל (תוספות, בבא בתרא מד:, ד"יה דלא הוה ליה), "That there is no one who does not have four cubits in the land of Israel," (Tosafoth, Baba Bathra 44b, header words: That does not have). Thus, since every Jew is a part of the העם, "the people," every Jew can feel that he can come to the Land of Israel and be עליה, "upon it."

ויכל משה מדבר אתם ויתן על פניו מסוה (שמות לד,לג).
And when Moses had finished speaking with them he put a veil over his face (Exodus 34,33).

At the end of this sidrah the Torah tells that Moses put on a veil when among the Children of Israel. The gematria of מסוה, "veil," is 111.

מסוה   111

When Moses spoke with G-d, or when he told the Bnei

Yisroel that which he had been commanded, he removed the veil, as stated, ובבא משה לפני ה׳ לדבר אתו יסיר את המסוה עד צאתו ויצא ודבר אל בני ישראל את אשר יצוה (שמות לד,לד), "And when Moses came before G-d to speak with Him, he removed the veil, until he came out; and he came out and spoke to the Children of Israel that which he was commanded" (Exodus 34,34). The gematria of יצוה, "he was commanded," is 111.

יצוה   111

When Moses was with the Children of Israel there was an either/or situation. Either Moses was telling the Children of Israel that which he was commanded, or he was wearing a veil. This either/or description is enhanced by virtue of the fact that the gematrioth of מסוה, "veil," and the gematria of יצוה, "he was commanded," are equal.

Parashath Vayyakhel   פרשת ויקהל

ויאמרו אל משה לאמר מרבים העם להביא מדי העבדה
למלאכה אשר צוה ה׳ לעשת אתה (שמות לו,ה).
And they said to Moses saying, "The people are bringing more than enough for the service of the work, which G-d commanded to make" (Exodus 36,5).

The Torah says that the people were bringing more מדי, "than enough," for the work. The gematria of מדי, "than enough," is 54.

מדי   54

Two pesukim later the Torah says that the material brought was sufficient for all the work, as stated, והמלאכה היתה דים לכל המלאכה לעשות אתה והותר (שמות לו,ז), "And the material was sufficient for all the work to make it and much more" (Exodus 36,7). The gematria of דים, "sufficient," is 54.

דים   54

Since the gematria of מדי, "than enough," and דים, "sufficient," are the same (also their letters are the same), it can be understood that when the Torah relates that the Children of Israel brought more מדי, "than enough," for the work, the meaning is, it was more than דים, "sufficient."

ויאמרו אל משה לאמר מרבים העם להביא מדי העבדה
למלאכה אשר צוה ה׳ לעשת אתה (שמות לו,ה).
And they said to Moses saying, "The people are bringing more than enough for the service of the work, which G-d commanded to make" (Exodus 36,5).

The Torah says that the Children of Israel brought more than enough for העבדה, "the work." The gematria of העבודה, "the work," is 86.

העבודה 86

When G-d's character of strict justice is alluded to, He is referred to as אלקים, "G-d," (רש"י, בראשית א,א וח,א, Rashi, Genesis 1,1 and 8,1). The gematria of אלקים, "G-d," is 86.

אלקים 86

Since העבודה, "the work," and אלקים, "G-d," have the same gematria, it can indicate that Moses was told that the material brought was in excess of the requirements not only if one were were to measure generously, but even if one were to measure with strict justice. Also implied is the fact that the work was done for the sake of G-d.

ויצו משה ויעבירו קול במחנה לאמר איש ואשה אל יעשו עוד מלאכה לתרומת הקדש ויכלא העם מהביא (שמות לו,ו).

And Moses commanded and they caused an announcement to be transmitted throughout the camp saying, Neither man nor woman should not do any more work for the offerings of the sanctuary. And the people ceased from bringing (Exodus 36,6).

When Moses told the Children of Israel not to bring any more materials, he used the word עוד, "any more." The gematria of עוד, "any more," is 80.

עוד 80

When Moses told the Children of Israel not to do any more work, the question could be asked, any more than what work? Does it mean more work than they wished to do? Does it mean more work than they had started? Does it mean for all the work of the Sanctuary? The answer could be in the very next pasuk which states, והמלאכה היתה דים לכל המלאכה לעשות אתה והותר (שמות לו,ז), "And the material was enough for all the work to do it and extra" (Exodus 36,7). The gematria of לכל, "for all," is 80.

80   לכל

Since the gematria of עוד, "any more," and לכל, "for all," are the same, it could denote that when Moses told the Children of Israel not to bring עוד, "any more," he meant not to bring any more than לכל, "for all," of the work of the sanctuary.

Parashath Pekudey פרשת פקודי

ושמת שם את ארון העדות וסכת על הארן את הפרכת
(שמות מ,ג).

And you shall put there the ark of testimony and you shall overspread upon the ark with the dividing curtain. (Exodus 40,3).

The Torah refers to the ark, as the ark העדות, "of testimony." The gematria of העדות, "of testimony," is 485.

485 העדות

Earlier in the Book of Exodus, the Gur Aryeh explains that the deficiency of the testimony precludes the ark's existence, as stated, ועל זה אמר עוד ונתת אל הארון את העדות שנה עליו "And more לעכב שלא יהיה ארון אם אין עדות (גור אריה, שמות כה,כא), about this was said, 'and you shall put into the ark the testimony,' it repeats to make it essential, that there is no ark if there is no testimony" (Gur Aryeh, Exodus 25,21). The existence of the ark was for the testimony.

To what does העדות, "the testimony," refer? Rashi clearly illuminates that the testimony refers to the commandments, as he states, התורה שהיא העדות ביני וביניכם העדות. שציויתי אתכם מצות הכתובות בה (רש"י, שמות כה,טז) "The testimony. The Torah which is testimony between Me and you, that I commanded you the commandments which are written therein" (Rashi, Exodus 25,16). G-d has commanded us to observe 613 Mitzvoth, divided between 248 positive Mitzvoth and 365 negative Mitzvoth, as stated, דרש רבי שמלאי שש מאות ושלש עשרה מצות נאמרו לו למשה שלש מאות וששים וחמש לאוין כמנין ימות החמה ומאתים וארבעים ושמונה עשה כנגד איבריו של אדם (מכות כג:), "Rabbi Simlai expounded, 613 Commandments were said to Moses, three hundred and sixty-five negative Commandments corresponding to the number of days in a solar year, and two hundred and forty-eight positive Commandments corresponding to the limbs of a person" (Makkoth 23b). Thus, there is a total of 613 Commandments.

From שמות מ,ג, Exodus 40,3, the pasuk which was first quoted, the Gemara ascertains that the word על, "al," can mean next to, as stated, רבי אומר על בסמוך אתה אומר על בסמוך או אינו אלא על ממש כשהוא אומר וסכות על הארון את הפרוכת היו אומר על בסמוך (מנחות סב.), "Rabbi said the word על, 'al,' can mean next to. You say 'al,' means next to, or perhaps it is not so, rather 'al,' actually means upon. When it says and you shall overspread upon the ark with the dividing curtain, you must say that al means next to" (Menahoth 62a). The gematria of בסמוך, "next to," is 128.

בסמוך   128

Since the Gemara ascertains that על, "on," can mean בסמוך, "next to," from a pasuk which mentions הארון, "the ark," whose existence was for העדות, "the testimony," then the expression על הארון, "on the ark," can be expounded to mean בסמוך, "next to," העדות, "the testimony." The gematria of בסמוך "next to," plus the gematria of העדות "the testimony," is 613.

בסמוך	128
העדות	485
	613

Thus, when the Torah writes על הארון, "on the ark," it can be explained to mean בסמוך, "next to," העדות, "the testimony," the sum of whose gematria is 613. This gematria is highly significant, for העדות, "the testimony," refers to the commandments and there are a total of 613 Commandments.

Book of Leviticus — ספר ויקרא

Parashath Vayyikra פרשת ויקרא
or Parashath Korach או פרשת קרח

ויקרא אל משה וידבר ה' אליו מאהל מועד לאמר (ויקרא
א,א).

"And He called to Moses, and G-d spoke to him from the tent of the meeting, saying" (Leviticus 1.1).

In the beginning of Book of Vayyikra, the first "א," of the first word is diminutive, as stated, "And ויקרא אל משה וידבר, He called to Moses, and He spoke." The gematria of ויקרא, "and He called," excluding the א, "aleph," since it is written smaller than the other letters, is 316.

ויקר 316

On this pasuk, רש"י, Rashi, says that הקול הולך ומגיע "The voice would go לאזניו וכל ישראל לא שומעין (רש"י, ויקרא א,א) and would reach his ears, and all of Israel did not hear" (רש"י, ויקרא א,א, Rashi, Leviticus 1,1) Thus, the gematria 316 relates to an action not known to others, hidden from the knowledge of others. Also, the word ויקרא, "and He called," introduces the topic of sacrifices, which brings about atonement.

In Parashath Korach the Torah states, ויקח אהרן כאשר דבר משה וירץ אל תוך הקהל והנה החל הנגף בעם ויתן את הקטרת ויכפר על העם (במדבר יז,יב), "And Aaron took, as Moses had spoken, and he ran into the midst of the assembly, and behold the plague had began with the people, and he placed the incense, and he atoned for the people" (Numbers 17,12). The gematria of ויכפר, "and he atoned," is 316.

ויכפר 316

On this pasuk the Gemara Zevachim says, ותני דבי רבי ישמעאל על מה קטורת מכפרת על לשון הרע יבא דבר שבחשאי ויכפר על

(זבחים פח:) מעשה חשאי, "It was taught in the yeshiva of Rabbi Ishmael, for what does the incense atone? For malignant speech, let come that which is secretive, and make atonement for a deed done in secret" (Zevachim 88b). Thus, the gematria of 316 relates to an action not known to others, that is hidden from the knowledge of others. Since the word ויקרא, "And He called," in the beginning of Book of Vayyikra, and and the word ויכפר, "and he atoned," in Parashath Korach, both relate to an action not known to others, and to atonement, it is very appropriate that both words should have the identical gematria.

Parashath Vayyikra   פרשת ויקרא

ויקרא אל משה וידבר ה׳ אליו מאהל מועד לאמר (ויקרא
א,א).

"And He called to Moses, and G-d spoke to him from the tent of the meeting, saying" (Leviticus 1.1).

As noted above, in the beginning of Sefer Vayyikra, the first א, "aleph," of the first word is diminutive, as stated, ויקרא אל משה וידבר ה׳ אליו מאהל מועד לאמר (ויקרא א,א), "And He called to Moses, and G-d spoke to him from the tent of the meeting, saying" (Leviticus 1,1). The gematria of ויקרא, "and He called," excluding the א, "aleph," since it is written smaller than the other letters, is 316.

ויקר   316

The Baal Haturim gives one reason for the א, "aleph," being diminutive; Moses did not want to write the aleph, but since Hashem told him to write it, he wrote it small. What would Moses have gained by writing the aleph small? Why did he want to exclude that letter? The Baal Haturim explains that Moses wished the word to be read as ויקר, "and he chanced upon," since Moses did not want the honor, the fame, of G-d calling him personally. The Baal Haturim says, כדרך שנאמר בבלעם כאלו לא נראה לו השם אלא במקרה (בעל הטורים, ויקרא א,א), "Similar to the manner which was written with Balaam, as if G-d did not appear to him except by chance" (Baal Haturim, Leviticus 1,1). As was shown, the gematria of ויקרא, "and He called," excluding the א, "aleph," since it is written smaller than the other letters, is 316.

When Moses fled from Egypt to Midian he saved the daughters of Yithro from some shepherds. Apparently, he did not make himself known as Moses, for when Yithro wanted to call him, Moses is only referred to him as האיש, "the man," as

ויאמר אל בנתיו ואיו למה זה עזבתן את האיש קראן לו ויאכל לחם, stated,
(שמות ב,כ), "And he said to his daughters: 'And where is he?
Why did you leave the man? Call him and he may eat bread'"
(Exodus 2,20). The gematria of האיש, "the man'" is 316.

האיש   316

Thus, 316 represents Moses being called without a
name, that is, without fame or honor. Also note that the
Torah uses the word והאיש, "and the man," to distinguish
Moses as the most modest of all men (במדבר יב,ג, Numbers
12,3). When Moses was called האיש, "the man," his name was
unknown to the caller. Therefore, it is precisely fitting that
Moses wanted to write the ויקרא, "and he called," without the
aleph, for the gematria and the meaning of ויקר, "and he
called," and האיש, "the man," concord with each other, each
an expression of Moses' humility.

ואם מן־העוף עלה קרבנו לה' והקריב מן־התרים או מן־בני
היונה את־קרבנו (ויקרא א,יד).
And if his burnt offering to G-d is from the fowl,
then he shall offer his sacrifice from the turtle
doves or from the young pigeons (Leviticus
1,14).

The Torah says that a person can bring a burnt offering
from turtle doves or from young pigeons. Two questions can
be asked about the Torah's language. Many times the Torah
gives the option for a person to bring turtle doves or young
pigeons as a sacrifice (ויקרא ה,ז; יב,ח; יד,כב; טו,יד, Leviticus
5,7; 12,8; 14,22; 15,14). These pesukim refer to two turtle
doves or two young pigeons. But only in two places does the
Torah use the expression מן התורים או מן בני היונה, "from the
turtle doves or from the young pigeons" (ויקרא א,יד; יד,ל,
Leviticus 1,14; 14,30). These pesukim refer to only one turtle
dove or one young pigeon. The Gemara Zevachim says, תי"ר
והקריבו מה תי"ל לפי שנאמר והקריב מן התורים או מן בני היונה יכול

המתנדב עוף לא יפחות משני פרידין תי״ל והקריבו אפילו פרידה אחת יביא (זבחים סה.), אל המזבח, "Our Rabbis have taught, 'And he shall offer it,' why is it stated? Since it says, 'and he shall offer from the turtle doves or from the young pigeons,' one may have thought that he who vows a bird, should not bring less than two birds, therefore it states, 'and he shall offer it,' even a single bird can be brought to the altar" (Zevachim 65a).

As was mentioned, only in two places does the Torah use the expression מן התורים או מן בני היונה, "from the turtle doves or from the young pigeons" (ויקרא א,יד ; יד,ל), Leviticus 1,14; 14,30). A first question is, why is this particular expression used in these two places? A second question is, why is there a repetition of the word מן, "from?" The same thought that this expression conveys, could have been written without the second mention of the word מן, "from."

To answer these two questions, examine the locations where the expression מן התורים או מן בני היונה, "from the turtle doves or from the young pigeons," is used. The first location where the expression is used refers to the קרבן עילה, "burnt offering." The Midrash says that the קרבן עולה, "burnt offering," might be brought because one had an improper thought, as stated, העולה באה על הרהור הלב, "the burnt offering was brought because of thoughts of the heart," (מדרש תנחומא, פרשת ואתה תצוה, אות טו, Midrash Tanhuma, Parashath Tetzaveh, Letter 15). An improper thought could be defined as contemplating the violation of any of the 613 Mitzvoth. The second location where the expression is used refers to the קרבן עולה וקרבן חטאת של המצרע, "the burnt offering and the sin offering of the metzora." Rashi says that a person might be stricken with tzoraas because he spoke לשון הרע, "evil talk," (רש״י, ויקרא יד,ד, Rashi, Leviticus 14,4). The Gemara Arakin says that he who speaks evil talk is equated with one who worships idols, as stated, תנא דבי רבי שמעאל כל המספר לשון הרע מגדיל עונות כנגד שלש עבירות עבודת כוכבים וכו״ (ערכין טו:), "It was taught in the Yeshiva of Rabbi Ishmael, anyone who speaks evil talk, magnifies his sins until they are equated with the three (cardinal) sins, idol worship, etc." (Arakin 15b). The Gemara Horayoth further says that worshiping idols is equated to violating all the commandments, as stated, איזו היא מצוה שהיא שקולה ככל המצות, הוי אומר זו עבודת כוכבים (הוריות ח.) "Which commandment is equivalent to all the commandments? Say it is idol worship" (Horayoth 8a). Since one who speaks evil talk is equated with one who worships idols, and since worshiping idols is equated to violating all the mitzvoth, thus speaking evil talk is equated to violating all the mitzvoth. There is a total of 613 Mitzvoth.

Now it can be explained why there is repetition of the word מן, "from," in the expression מן התורים או מן בני היונה, "from the turtle doves or from the young pigeons." The gematria of מן, "from," is 90.

מן   90

The gematria of התרים, "the turtle doves," plus the gematria of בני היונה, "the young pigeons," is 793.

התרים	655
בני	62
היונה	76
	793

Since the word מן, "from," is repeated, its gematria is doubled, which equals 180. The word מן, "from," can be seen to indicate subtraction; when 180 is subtracted from 793 the remainder is 613.

$$793$$
$$-180$$
$$613$$

Perhaps the reason the Torah repeated the word מן, "from," was to double its gematria, to arrive at the remainder of 613, which emphasizes the significance of these sacrifices; each of which has an association to the 613 Mitzvoth.

The two questions asked earlier can now be answered. The particular expression, מן התורים או מן בני היונה, "from the turtle doves or from the young pigeons," is used in the two places associated with the 613 Mitzvoth. The word מן, "from," is repeated in this expression to double its gematria, to arrive at the remainder 613.

Finally, although everyone could bring a קרבן עולה, "burnt offering," because of an improper thought, why was the implication of the 613 Mitzvoth found specifically in reference to a poor man's sacrifice? The answer may come from Rashi on the Gemara, where it is explained that the חטאת, "sin offering," and the עולה, "burnt offering," were slaughtered in the same place, in order not to embarrass those people who brought the sin offering (רש"י, סוטה לב:, ד"ה שהרי לא חלק הכתוב וכו', Rashi, Sotah 32b, header words: The verse made no distinction, etc.). Thus, there was a concern not to embarrass those who brought a sin offering, albeit the cause of the poor man's mortification is different, for he had no alternative other than to bring a bird, and suffer embarrassment; when he brought turtle doves or young pigeons, other people saw that he could not afford a large animal. Therefore, the implication of the 613 Mitzvoth is found specifically in reference to a poor man's sacrifice, for the poor man, who, in spite of such embarrassment, brought his sacrifice. Although everyone entertaining an improper thought could bring a קרבן עולה, "burnt offering," which atones for sins associated with the 613 Mitzvoth, nonetheless this implication is found specifically in reference to a poor man's sacrifice. The Torah takes into account his mortification.

או מצא אבדה וכחש בה ונשבע על שקר על אחת מכל אשר יעשה האדם לחטא בהנה (ויקרא ה,כב).

Or if one found a lost object, and denied it and swore falsely, from any of all which a man may do to sin therein (Leviticus 5, 22).

After one and a half pesukim of listing sins, the Torah has a concluding comment, as stated, מכל אשר יעשה האדם לחטא בהנה, "from any of all which a man do may to sin therein," The gematria of יעשה, "does," is 385.

יעשה   385

Thus, 385 represents the committing of any of those listed sins (ויקרא ה,כא-כב, Leviticus 5,21-22). In order to repent, the Torah tells that one should try to undo what he did and then bring a sacrifice, as stated, ואת אשמו יביא לה׳ איל תמים מן הצאן בערכך לאשם אל הכהן (ויקרא ה,כה), "And his trespass offering, he should bring to G-d, an unblemished ram, from the sheep, according to your evaluation for a trespass offering, to the priest" (Leviticus 5,25). The gematria of איל תמים, "an unblemished ram," is 531.

איל   41
תמים   <u>490</u>
          531

The gematria of הצאן, "the sheep," is 146.

הצאן   146

The word מן, "from," which separates the words איל תמים, "an unblemished ram," from the word הצאן, "the sheep," can be interpreted as subtraction. Thus, with the application of this interpretation, the pasuk would be saying to subtract the gematria of איל תמים, "an unblemished ram," from the gematria of הצאן, "the sheep," which leaves a remainder of -385.

146
<u>-531</u>
-385

Previously it was shown that 385 represents the committing of any any of those listed sins (ויקרא ה,כא-כב, Leviticus

5,21-22). If one had committed one of these sins, and tried to undo what he had done, as the Torah instructs, afterwards he brings an איל תמים "an unblemished ram," from הצאן, "the sheep." This undoing, represented by the gematria of -385, will cancel out what he has done. This successful repentance is indicated by the equating of the negative value of the remainder of the gematria of איל תמים "an unblemished ram" (after the gematria of from הצאן, "the sheep," has been subtracted from it), to the positive value of the gematria of יעשה "does," that is, committing any of those listed sins (ויקרא ה,כא-כב, Leviticus 5,21-22). This explanation is also corroborated by the last pasuk in the parashah, which again uses the word יעשה, "can do," as stated, וכפר עליו הכהן לפני ה׳ ונסלח לו על אחת מכל אשר יעשה לאשמה בה (ויקרא ה,כו) "And the priest shall atone for him before Hashem, and it shall be forgiven to him, for any of all which a man may do to trespass therewith" (Leviticus 5,26).

Parashath Tzav פרשת צו

צו את אהרן ואת בניו לאמר זאת תורת העלה הוא העלה
על מוקדה על המזבח כל הלילה עד הבקר ואש המזבח
תוקד בו (ויקרא ו,ב).

Command Aaron and his sons saying, This is the law of the burnt offering. It is the burnt offering which shall be upon the hearth upon altar the entire night until the morning, and the fire of the altar shall burn on it (Leviticus 6,2).

It is from this second pasuk of this parashah that the sidrah derives it name, as stated, צו את אהרן ואת בניו לאמר זאת תורת העלה הוא העלה על המזבח כל הלילה עד הבקר ואש (ויקרא ו,ב) המזבח תוקד בו, "Command Aaron and his sons saying, This is the law of the burnt offering. It is the burnt offering which shall be burnt upon the altar the entire night until the morning, and the fire of the altar shall burn on it" (Leviticus 6,2). The gematria of צו, "command," is 96.

צו   96

The Or Hachaim, based on statements of our Rabbis of blessed memory, explains that the word צו, "command," is used in a situation of a possible monetary loss. He calls this loss, a loss to the pocket, as stated, אמרו ז"ל בת"כ אין צו אלא זירוז מיד ולדורות אמר רבי שמעון ביותר צריך הכתוב לזרז כל מקום שיש חסרון כיס ע"כ (אור החיים, ויקרא ו,ב) "Our Rabbis of blessed memory have said in Torath Kohanim, Tzav, command, can only mean urging, immediately and for future generations. Rabbi Simon says, the pasuk has to use extra urging in every instance where there is loss to the pocket" (Or Hachayyim, Leviticus 6,2). The gematria of מקום, "instance," is 186.

מקום   186

The gematria of כיס, "pocket," is 90.

כיס   90

The phrase כל מקום שיש חסרון כיס, "in every instance where there is loss to the pocket," could be interpreted as, in every instance of 186, which is lacking 90. When 90 is subtracted from 186 the remainder is 96.

$$186$$
$$-90$$
$$96$$

As was shown earlier, the gematria of צו, "command," is 96. It is very appropriate that the gematria of צו, "command," is 96, since the remainder from the phrase כל מקום שיש חסרון כיס, "in every instance where there is loss to the pocket," is also 96; it is from this phrase that the Or Hachaim explains the use of the word צו, "command."

Please note that Rashi gives a similar explanation to the pasuk, but seems to quote a slightly different version of the Torath Kohanim; he quotes במקום, "in an instance," but the Or Hachaim quotes מקום, "instance." This gematria communicates an important message. Every instance when one is faced with a monetary loss in the performance of a mitzvah, he may have to apply the word צו, "command," to himself. Although it is difficult to be zealous and enthusiastic when bearing a monetary loss, one must try to do G-d's will and overcome the hardship.

ופתח אהל מועד תשבו יומם ולילה שבעת ימים ושמרתם את משמרת ה' ולא תמותו כי כן צויתי (ויקרא ח,לה).
And at the entrance of the tent of meeting you shall abide day and night, for seven days, and you shall keep G-d's charge, and not die, for so I have been commanded (Leviticus 8,35).

Aaron and his sons were commanded to be sequestered for seven days until "the days of your consecration are completed," (ויקרא ח,לג, Leviticus 8,33). There was a similar period of sequestration for the kohen gadol prior to the Day of Atonement, as well as for the kohen who burnt the פרה אדומה, "red heifer" (רש״י, ויקרא ח,לד, Rashi, Leviticus 8, 34).

The Mishnah Yoma explains that part of the purpose of the period of sequestration for the kohen gadol was for him to learn the laws of the sacrifices (משנה יומא, פרק א, משנה ב-ג, Mishnah Yoma, Chapter 1, Mishnah 2-3). Based on that Mishnah Yoma, the פיוטים מוסף ליום כפור, "Poetry for the Additional Service for the Day of Atonement," after the paragraph beginning אמיץ כח, "Mighty in Strength," clearly depicts this process, as it says, מחזיקי אמנה שבוע קדם לעשור מפרישים כהן הראש כדת המלאים. מזים עליו מי חטאת לטהרו, זורק מקטיר ומטיב להתרגל בעבודה, "Those who uphold the faith sequestered the High Priest a week prior to the tenth day, as ordained by the law of consecration. The waters of the sin offering were sprinkled on him to purify him; and he sprinkled the sacrificial blood, burnt the incense, and dressed the lamps, to be acquainted with the service."

With regard to the kohen who burnt the פרה אדומה, "red heifer," the Rambam writes, הלשכה שהיה יושב בה כל שבעה צפונית מזרחית היתה, כדי להזכירו שזו כחטאת הנשחטת בצפון אע״פ שהיא נשחטת בחוץ (משנה תורה, ספר טהרה, הלכות פרה אדומה, פרק ב, הלכה ג), "The chamber where he dwelt all seven days was in the northeast, in order to remind him that this is like the sin offering which is sacrificed in the north, even though this one is slaughtered outside" (Mishnah Torah, Book of Tohorah, Laws of the Red Heifer, Chapter 2, Law 3). A similar thought is found in the Mishnah (תפארת ישראל, פרה, פרק ג, משנה א, אות ג, Tifereth Yisroel, Parah, Chapter 3, Mishnah 1, Letter 3).

Thus, for both the seven days of sequestration preceding the Day of Atonement, and the seven days of sequestration preceding the burning the red heifer, various laws were instructed. The Torah refers to these days of sequestration as what G-d had commanded, as stated, ופתח אהל מועד תשבו

יומם ולילה שבעת ימים ושמרתם את משמרת ה׳ ולא תמותו כי כן צויתי
(ויקרא ח,לה), "And at the entrance of the tent of the meeting
you shall abide day and night, for seven days, and you shall
keep G-d's charge, and not die, for so I have been commanded" (Leviticus 8, 35). The gematria of כי כן צויתי, "for so
I have been commanded," is 616.

כי	30
כן	70
צויתי	<u>516</u>
	616

Thus, the gematria of 616 is associated with a time
when various laws of the sacrifices were instructed.

The Torah concludes its discussion of the laws of a
number of the sacrifices with the expression, זאת התורה, "this
is the law," as stated, זאת התורה לעלה למנחה ולחטאת ולאשם
ולמלואים ולזבח השלמים (ויקרא ז,לז), "This is the law for the burnt
offering, for the meal offering, and for the sin offering, and for
the guilt offering, and for the consecration offering, and for
the sacrifice of the peace offering" (Leviticus 7,37). The
gematria of התורה, "the law," is 616.

התורה   616

Thus, the gematria of 616 is associated with various
laws of the sacrifices. Since כי כן צויתי, "for so I have been
commanded," is associated with a time when various laws of
the sacrifices were instructed, and since התורה, "the law," is
associated with various laws of the sacrifices, it is appropriate
that both texts have the same gematria.

Parashath Shemini   פרשת שמיני

ויקחו בני אהרן נדב ואביהוא איש מחתתו ויתנו בהן אש
וישימו עליה קטרת ויקריבו לפני ה׳ אש זרה אשר לא צוה
אתם (ויקרא י,א).

And the sons of Aaron, Nadav and Avihu, took each man his firepan, and they put in them fire, and placed on it incense, and they brought near before G-d, a strange fire which He had not commanded them (Leviticus 10,1).

The Torah records that the sons of Aaron, Nadav and Avihu, took each man his firepan, and brought an אש זרה, "strange fire," before G-d. The gematria of זרה, "strange," is 212.

זרה   212

Their death was, according to one opinion, due to the fact that they had decided a law in front of their teacher, Moses (רש״י, ויקרא י,ב, Rashi, Leviticus 10,12); thus the strange act was a consequence of an act of negation: the negation of Moses' authority.

There are at least two incidents recorded in the Torah where quarrel denotes an act of negation. In Parashath Lech Lecha the Torah records that there was a ריב, quarrel, between the shepherds of Abram and the shepherds of Lot, as stated, ויהי ריב בין רעי מקנה אברם ובין רעי מקנה לוט והכנעני והפרזי אז ישב בארץ (בראשית יג,ז), "And there was a quarrel between the herdsmen of Abram's cattle, and the headmen of Lot's cattle; and the Canaanite and the Perizzite dwelt then in the land" (Genesis 13,7). The gematria of ריב, "quarrel," is 212.

ריב   212

The reason that they quarreled was that the shepherds of Lot claimed land that was not rightfully theirs (רש״י, בראשית יג,ז, Rashi, Genesis 13,7); thus the quarrel was a consequence of an act of negation: the negation of the land owner's legitimate claim to his land.

In Parashath Beshallach it is recorded that there was a quarrel between the Children of Israel and G-d, as stated, ויקרא שם המקום מסה ומריבה על ריב בני ישראל ועל נסתם את ה׳ לאמר היש ה׳ בקרבנו אם אין (שמות יז,ז), "And he called the name of the place Massah and Meribah, because of the quarrel of the Children of Israel and their trying G-d, saying, 'Is G-d in our midst or not?'" (Exodus 17,7). As was shown, the gematria of ריב, "quarrel," is 212.

ריב   212

The reason for the quarrel was that the Children of Israel questioned if the presence of G-d was with them; thus, the quarrel was a consequence of an act of negation: the negation of G-d's presence.

In both sources quoted, the quarrel was a consequence of an act of negation. Since the strange fire which Nadav and Avihu brought was also a consequence of an act of negation, it is fitting that זרה, "strange," and ריב, "quarrel," should have the same gematria.

ויאמר משה אל אהרן הוא אשר דבר ה׳ לאמר בקרבי אקדש ועל פני כל העם אכבד וידם אהרן (ויקרא י,ג).
And Moses said to Aaron, "It is what G-d spoke, saying, with those who are close to Me I will be sanctified, and before all the people I will be glorified," and Aaron was silent (Leviticus 10,3).

After Nadav and Avihu were killed, Moses tried to comfort Aaron by identifying Aaron's sons as the ones about whom G-d said, בקרבי, "with those who are close to Me," I will be sanctified. The gematria of בקרבי, "with those who are close to Me," is 314.

בקרבי   314

Rashi explains, Moses told Aaron that Nadav and Avihu were greater than we are (רש״י, ויקרא י,ג, Rashi, Leviticus 10,13). The Yalkut Me'am Lo'ez comments on this pasuk that Nadav and Avihu died so that the Children of Israel will learn rebuke from the following קל וחומר, "inference drawn from a minor premise to a major one," as stated, שבשעה שהקב״ה עושה דין בצדיקים מתיירא מתעלה ומתקלס, שמזה לומדים הבריות לקח שאם הקב״ה עושה דין עם בני אדם גדולים כאלו ואינו נוהג עמם במשוא פנים בגלל המעשים הטובים שעשו, עאכו״כ בשאר האנשים שעוברים על מצותיו (ילקוט מעם לועז מאת רבי יעקב כולי, ויקרא י,ג), "At the time that the Holy One, Blessed be He, does justice with the righteous, He becomes feared, exalted, and praised, from this his creatures learn rebuke. That if the the Holy One, Blessed be He, does strict justice with such great people as these and does not treat them with preferential treatment because of their good deeds which they did, how much more so with other people who violate His commandments" (Yalkut Me'am Lo'ez by Rabbi Yaakov Culi, Leviticus 10,3). Thus, the Yalkut Me'am Lo'ez demonstrates that the word בקרבי, "with those who are close to Me," is associated with G-d's attribute of strict justice. This idea is related to the word בקרבי, "with those who are close to me," and its gematria of 314.

When Abram was ninety-nine years old, G-d appeared to him, as stated, ויהי אברם בן תשעים שנה ותשע שנים וירא ה׳ אל אברם ויאמר אליו אני קל שקי התהלך לפני והיה תמים (בראשית יז,א), "And Abram was ninety-nine years old, and G-d appeared to Abram and He said to him, I am G-d All Sufficient ; walk before Me and be perfect" (Genesis 17,1). The gematria of שקי, "All Sufficient," is 314.

שקי   314

After exploring other definitions of שקי, "All Sufficient," on this pasuk, the Ramban says, וזהו הנכון כי היא מדת הגבורה מנהגת העולם שיאמרו בה החכמים מדת הדין של מטה (רמב״ן בראשית יז,א), "And this [definition of שקי] is correct, for it is the characteristic of strength with which He treats the world, that our [Torah-oriented] wise men have said about it, His attribute of strict justice below" (Ramban, Genesis 17,1). Thus, the Ramban demonstrates that the word שקי, "All Sufficient," is associated with G-d's attribute of strict justice. This idea is related to the word, שקי, "All Sufficient," and its gematria of 314.

Since the idea associated with the word בקרבי, "with those those who are close to me," and the idea associated to the word שקי, "All Sufficient," are the same, it is appropriate that these words should have the identical gematria.

ויאמר משה אל אהרן הוא אשר דבר ה' לאמר בקרבי אקדש ועל פני כל העם אכבד וידם אהרן (ויקרא י,ג).
And Moses said to Aaron, "It is what G-d spoke, saying, with those who are close to Me I will be sanctified, and before all the people I will be glorified," and Aaron was silent (Leviticus 10,3).

After the death of Nadav and Avihu, the Torah quotes Moses comforting Aaron, telling him, "It is what G-d spoke, saying, with those that are close to Me, I will be sanctified." The gematria of the expression ה' לאמר בקרבי, "G-d saying, with those that are close to Me," is 611.

ה'	26
לאמר	271
בקרבי	314
	611

How did what Moses said to Aaron comfort him? There are different answers to this question, but another avenue of thought can be explored.

רש"י, Rashi, in פרשת עקב, Parashath Ekev, states, שקשה מיתתן של צדיקים לפני הקב"ה כיום שנשתברו בו הלוחות (רש"י, דברים

ז,י), "The death of the righteous is as difficult before the Holy One, Blessed be He, as the day when the tablets were broken" (Rashi, Deuteronomy 10,7). The אור החיים, Or Hachayyim, in פרשת יתרו, Parashath Yithro, states, אוי ז״ל שכל התורה כולה רמוזה בעשרת הדברות (אור החיים, שמות כ,א), "It has been said by the Rabbis of blessed memory, that all of the entire Torah is hinted to in the Ten Commandments" (Or Hachayyim, Exodus 20,1). The quote from רש״י, Rashi, in פרשת עקב, Parashath Ekev, can easily be combined with the quote from the אור החיים, Or Hachayyim, in פרשת יתרו, Parashath Yithro. Since all of the Torah is hinted to in the Ten Commandments, which were engraved in the tablets, the word Torah can be substituted for the words Ten Commandments. Thus, it follows, that the death of the righteous is as difficult before the Holy One, as the day when the Torah was broken.

An analogous result can be derived from a pasuk in פרשת משפטים, Parashath Mishpatim. רש״י, Rashi, in פרשת משפטים, Parashath Mishpatim, states, כל שש מאות ושלש עשרה מצות בכלל עשרת הדברות הן (רש״י, שמות כד, יב), "All six hundred and thirteen Commandments are included in the Ten Commandments" (Rashi, Exodus 24,12). The תלמוד ירושלמי, "Talmud Yerushalmi," comments on that same pasuk, as stated, ואתנה לך את הלוחות האבן והתורה והמצוה הקיש תורה למצות (ירושלמי, ברכות, פרק ששי, הלכה א) "'And I will give you tablets of stone, and the Torah, and the commandments'; the Torah is compared to the commandments." (Yerushalmi Gemara, Berakoth, Chapter six, Halakhah 1). The gematria of תורה, "Torah," is 611.

תורה   611

Since all six hundred and thirteen Commandments are included in the Ten Commandments, which were engraved in the tablets, and the Torah is compared to the commandments, the word Torah can be substituted for the words Ten Commandments. Thus, it follows, that the death of the righteous is as difficult before the Holy One, as the day when the Torah was broken.

However, for the Holy One to be said to have such feelings, there must have been the death of a genuinely righteous person or persons. Now it can be understood what Moses said to Aaron to comfort him. Moses said, both of your sons were genuinely righteous, therefore their death was as difficult before the Holy One as the day when the תורה, "Torah," was broken.

When Moses said to Aaron הי לאמר בקרבי, "G-d saying, with those that are close to me," I will be sanctified, Moses was saying that the sons of Aaron were genuinely righteous persons. That is why their death was as difficult before the Holy One as the day when the Torah was broken. Now the perspicacity of Moses' comfort is clear, as is the reason why what he said is enhanced by an expression which has a gematria equal to the gematria of תורה, "Torah," when he comforted Aaron.

הן לא הובא את דמה אל הקדש פנימה אכול תאכלו אתה בקדש כאשר צויתי (ויקרא י,יח).

Behold, its blood was not brought within the holy place, you should certainly have eaten it in the holy place, as I commanded (Leviticus 10,18).

In פרשת שמיני, Parashath Shemini, when Moses asked Eleazar and Ithamar why they had not eaten the sin offering as commanded, he began his inquiry with the word הן, "Behold." The gematria of הן, "behold," is 55.

הן   55

When Aaron answered Moses' inquiry, he began his answer with the word הן, "behold," as stated, וידבר אהרן אל משה הן היום הקריבו את חטאתם ואת עלתם לפני ה' ותקראנה אתי כאלה

(ויקרא י,יט) ואכלתי חטאת היום הייטב בעיני ה', "And Aaron spoke to Moses, Behold, today they have offered their sin offering and their burnt offering before G-d, and there happened to me like these things, and if I had eaten the sin offering today, would it be good in the eyes of G-d?" (Leviticus 10,19). As was mentioned, the gematria of הן, "behold," is 55.

הן   55

It is evident that both Moses and Aaron mentioned the word הן, "behold," whose gematria is 55.

The sidrah terminates with the topic of what is and what is not ritually defiled, as well as the topic of what may and what may not be eaten, as stated, להבדיל בין הטמא ובין הטהר ובין החיה הנאכלת ובין החיה אשר לא תאכל (ויקרא יא,מז), "To distinguish between the ritually defiled and the ritually not defiled, and the beast that may be eaten and the beast that can not be eaten," (Leviticus 11,47). The gematria of הנאכלת, "that may be eaten," associated with the permission to eat, is 506.

הנאכלת   506

The gematria of (לא) תאכל, "that can (not) be eaten," associated with the prohibition against eating, is 451.

תאכל   451

The difference between הנאכלת, "that may be eaten," and (לא) תאכל, "that can (not) be eaten," in gematrioth is 55.

506
−451
―――
55

The difference between הנאכלת, "that may be eaten," and (לא) תאכל, "that can (not) be eaten," used with the prohibition against eating, are the letters ה, "hey," and נ, "nun," which spell הן, "behold." The addition of these two letters is associated with that which may be eaten; the deletion of these two letters is associated with that which can not be eaten. As was mentioned, the gematria of these two letters is 55.

With this insight into the significance of the addition and the deletion of these two letters, a דרש, derash, "by the route of a homily," can be read into Moses' question and Aaron's answer. Moses asked why the sin offering had not been eaten — the letters ה, "hey," and נ, "nun," which spell הן, "behold," were not to be removed: הן לא הובא, "behold they did not bring," would be translated as, the הן was not to be removed. When the הן, "behold," is not removed, the remaining word is הנאכלת, "that may be eaten," which is associated with the additional gematria of 55, and eating. Aaron's answer that the הן was removed, הן היום הקריבו וגו', "Behold, today they have offered, etc." would be translated as, the הן was sacrificed, therefore it is no longer here, it was removed. When the הן is removed, the word הנאכלת, "that may be eaten," becomes תאכל, "that can be eaten," of the phrase לא תאכל, "that can not be eaten," associated with the prohibition to eat. Thus Aaron said that Eleazar and Ithamar were correct that they did not eat their sin offering.

מבשרם לא תאכלו ובנבלתם לא תגעו טמאים הם לכם
(ויקרא יא,ח).

From their flesh you shall not eat and their carcasses you shall not touch; they are ritually defiled to you (Leviticus 11,8).

After listing the animals that are not kosher (lawfully permissible to eat), the Torah prohibits eating their flesh. The gematria of מבשרם לא, "From their flesh you shall not," is 613.

$$
\begin{array}{rr}
\text{מבשרם} & 582 \\
\text{לא} & \underline{31} \\
& 613
\end{array}
$$

A possible reason why the Torah prohibits eating the meat of these animals which are ritually defiled is given in ספר החנוך, Book of Hachinuch, as it says, כי יודע אלקים כי כל המאכלות שהרחיק מעמו אשר בחר, יש בהם נזקים מצויים לגופים (ספר החנוך מאת הרב אהרן הלוי, פרשת שמיני, מצוה קנד), "For G-d knows that all the foods which He distanced from His people, which He has chosen, contain damaging components to the body," (Book of Hachinuch by Rabbi Aaron Halevi, Parashath Shemini, Mitzvah 154). The רמב"ן, Ramban, expresses a similar idea (אגרת הקודש מאת רבינו משה בן נחמן ד"יה ועתה נאמר לך הקדמה זו פרק הרביעי), Iggereth Hakodesh by Rabbeinu Moshe ben Nachman, header words: And now I will tell you this introduction, the Fourth Chapter).

Targum Jonathan ben Uzziel states, man is created with 248 limbs and 365 sinews, together totaling 613 body parts, (תרגום יונתן בן עוזיאל, בראשית א,כז), Targum Jonathan ben Uzziel, Genesis 1,27). Thus there is a total of 613 body parts. When the Torah prohibits eating meat that is ritually defiled, it is for the benefit of these 613 body parts. This benefit could be why the gematria of מבשרם לא, "From their flesh you shall not," is 613.

מכל האכל אשר יאכל אשר יבוא עליו מים יטמא וכל משקה אשר ישתה בכל כלי יטמא (ויקרא יא, לד).
From all the food which may be eaten, upon which water shall come shall be ritually defiled; and all drinks which can be drunk in every vessel, shall be ritually defiled (Leviticus 11,34).

The Torah tells that certain qualifying liquids, which can be drunk in a vessel, are subject to ritual defilement. The gematria of כלי, "vessel," is 60.

כלי   60

The gematria of יטמא, "shall be ritually defiled," is 60.

יטמא   60

Since the concepts learned from these words are related, it is appropriate that these words have the same gematria.

כי אני ה' המעלה אתכם מארץ מצרים להית לכם לאלקים
והייתם קדשים כי קדוש אני (ויקרא יא,מה).

For I am G-d Who raised you up out from the land of Egypt to be your G-d, and you shall be holy, for I am holy (Leviticus 11,45).

In the first pasuk of the Maftir for פרשת שמיני, Parashath Shemini, Hashem identifies Himself as the One Who raised the Children of Israel up out of the land of Egypt. The gematria of המעלה אתכם, "who raised you up," is 611.

המעלה	150
אתכם	461
	611

Usually Hashem identifies Himself as the One Who took the Children of Israel out of Egypt; why here does Hashem identify Himself as the One Who raised the Children of Israel up out of the land of Egypt? Although Rashi cites one answer to this question from the Gemara Baba Mezia 61a (רש"י, ויקרא יא,מה Rashi, Leviticus 11,48), a different response might be given with the application of a gematria.

The Mishnah says that anyone who is involved in learning Torah is elevated, as stated, כל מי שעוסק בתלמוד תורה הרי זה מתעלה (אבות, פרק ו, משנה ב), "Everyone who engages himself with study of the Torah is to be raised up" (Avoth, Chapter 6, Mishnah 2). The gematria of תורה, "Torah," is 611.

תורה   611

Note that the word המעלה, "Who raised you up," used by the Torah, and the word מתעלה, "is to be raised up," used by the Mishnah, both have the same root. The word המעלה,

"Who raised you up" is the causative mode of the verb; the word מתעלה, "is to be raised up," is the reflexive mode of the verb.

The period from Pesach to Shavuoth is an especially appropriate period when a Jew should try to raise himself up spiritually (קדושת ציון מאת הרב בן ציון הלבערשטאם, חלק ב, דף סז, Kedushath Zion by Rabbi Ben Zion Halbershtam, Part 2, page 67). Since Shavuoth commemorates Hashem giving the Torah to the Children of Israel, and everyone who learns Torah is elevated, it stands to reason that in the period from Pesach to Shavuoth a Jew should try to raise himself up spiritually by learning Torah.

פרשת שמיני, "Parashath Shemini," is always read on the first Shabbath after Pesach, in a non-leap year, (שלחן ערוך, אורח חיים, סימן תכח, סעיף ד, ושבילי דרקיע מאת הרב ישראל ליפשיץ, הקדמה למשניות, סדר מועד אות טז, Shulhan Arukh, Orach Hayyim, Siman 428, Seif 4, and Shevilei Derakia by Rabbi Yisroel Lipschitz, Introduction to the Mishnayoth, Seder Moed, Letter 16). Thus, usually פרשת שמיני, "Parashath Shemini," is the first full sidrah read in the period from Pesach to Shavuoth. Of course, what is written in the Torah is what G-d wished to write for His reasons. However, this particular wording, with its gematria, here, does seem especially apt. Now, with the application of a gematria, a different response might be given to why G-d identified Himself as the One Who brought the Children of Israel up out of the land of Egypt. The reason for this identification might be that the gematria of המעלה אתכם, "Who raised you up," is 611, which is equal to the gematria of Torah, and this expression is written in the first full sidrah read in the period when a Jew should try to raise himself up spiritually by learning Torah. Certainly, a Jew should always try to raise himself spiritually by learning Torah, but in the period from Pesach to Shavuoth it is particularly so designated.

Parashath Thazria   פרשת תזריע

דבר אל בני ישראל לאמר אשה כי תזריע וילדה זכר וטמאה
שבעת ימים כימי נדת דותה תטמא (ויקרא יב,ב).
Speak to the Children of Israel saying, when a woman will cause fructification of seed and will bear a male child, then she shall be ritually defiled for seven days, as in the days of the impurity of her sickness, she shall be ritually defiled (Leviticus 12,2).

The second pasuk in Parashath Thazria refers to the birth of a son. The gematria of אשה כי תזריע, "when a woman will cause fructification of seed," is 1023.

אשה	306
כי	30
תזריע	687
	1023

The Gemara expounds on this verse, as it says, אמר רבי יצחק אמר רבי אמי אשה מזרעת תחילה יולדת זכר איש מזריע תחילה יולדת נקבה שנאמר אשה כי תזריע וילדה זכר (נדה לא.), "Rabbi Isaac said that Rabbi Ammi said, If a woman causes fructification of seed first, then she bears a male child; if a man causes fructification of seed first, then she bears a female child, as it says, 'When a woman will cause fructification of seed and will bear a male child'" (Nidda 31a). From this Gemara it is unequivocal that the determining factor of a baby's sex is who has caused fructification of seed first. The gematria of אשה כי תזריע, "when a woman will cause fructification of seed," 1023, refers to the reason why a male child is born.

The beginning of Parashath Thazria presents various laws for when a male or female child is born. The laws and the time periods designated are solely Torah guidelines, the practice of the הלכה, Halakhah, "decided law," today is different (שלחן ערוך, יורה דעה, סימן קצד, סעיף א, Shulhan Arukh, Yoreh Deah, Siman 194, Seif 1).

In reference to the birth of a male child, the Torah says, the period of טומאה, "ritual defilement," of the mother, until she obtains complete purification, is seven days. The gematria of וילדה זכר וטמאה שבעת ימים כימי נדת דותה תטמא, "and will bear a male child, then she shall be ritually defiled for seven days, as in the days of the impurity of her sickness, she shall be ritually defiled," is 2614.

וילדה	55
זכר	227
וטמאה	61
שבעת ימים	872
כימי נדת	534
דותה תטמא	865
	2614

When the seven days of ritual defilement pass, the mother enters a period of thirty-three days of purity. The Torah says, ושלשים יום ושלשת ימים תשב בדמי טהרה בכל קדש לא תגע ואל המקדש לא תבא עד מלאת ימי טהרה (ויקרא יב,ד), "And for thirty-three days she shall remain in the blood of her purification; she shall not touch any hallowed thing, and she shall not come into the sanctuary, until the days of her purification are fulfilled" (Leviticus 12,4). The gematria of ושלשים יום ושלשת ימים תשב בדמי טהרה, "And for thirty-three days she shall remain in the blood of her purification," is 2855.

ושלשים יום	742
ושלשת ימים	1136
תשב	702
בדמי	56
טהרה	219
	2855

The sum of the gematrioth which correspond to the

birth of a male child, the ritual defilement which follows, and the duration of the pure state, is 5469.

$$2614$$
$$\underline{2855}$$
$$5469$$

In reference to the birth of a female child, the Torah says the period of טומאה, "ritual defilement," of the mother, until she obtains complete purification, is fourteen days. When the fourteen days of ritual defilement pass, the mother enters a period of sixty-six days of purity. The Torah says, ואם נקבה תלד וטמאה שבעים ושש ימים תשב על דמי טהרה (ויקרא יב,ה), "And if she bear a female child, then she shall be ritually defiled for two weeks, as in her impurity, and for sixty-six days she shall remain in the blood of her purification," (Leviticus 12,5). The gematria of נקבה תלד וטמאה שבעים כנדתה וששים יום וששת ימים תשב על דמי טהרה (ויקרא יב,ה), "She bear a female child, then she shall be ritually defiled for two weeks, as in her impurity, and for sixty-six days she shall remain in the blood of her purification," is 4446.

נקבה תלד	591
וטמאה שבעים כנדתה	962
וששים יום	712
וששת ימים	1106
תשב על	802
דמי טהרה	273
	4446

The gematria which corresponds to the birth of a female child, the ritual defilement which follows, and the duration of the pure state is 4446.

The difference in gematrioth between the birth of a male child and a female child, the טומאה, "ritual defilement," which follows each birth, and the duration of each pure state is equal to 1023.

$$5469$$
$$-4446$$
$$\overline{1023}$$

Thus, the difference between the birth of a son and the birth of a daughter, the ensuing ritual defilement, and the duration of each pure state, in gematrioth is that the gematrioth associated with a son are 1023 greater than the gematrioth associated with a daughter. The explanation for this difference seems clear. Since the gematria of אשה כי תזריע, "when a woman will cause fructification of seed," 1023, refers to the reason why a son was born, it is fitting that the difference in gematrioth between the birth of a male child and a female child, the טמאה, "ritual defilement," which follows each birth, and the duration of each pure state, is that the gematria for a male child is 1023 greater that the gematria for a female child.

דבר אל בני ישראל לאמר אשה כי תזריע וילדה זכר וטמאה
שבעת ימים כימי נדת דותה תטמא (ויקרא יב,ב).

Speak to the Children of Israel saying, when a woman will cause fructification of seed and will bear a male child, then she shall be ritually defiled for seven days, as in the days of the impurity of her sickness, she shall be ritually defiled (Leviticus 12,2).

The Torah says תטמא, "she shall be ritually defiled," in reference to the birth of a son, but does not use the identical language in reference to the birth of a daughter. The gematria of תטמא, "she shall be ritually defiled," is 450.

תטמא   450

The same pasuk also says that the duration of the ritual defilement which the birth of a male child causes, is for one week. The gematria of וטמאה שבעת ימים, "then she shall be ritually defiled for seven days," is 933.

וטמאה	61
שבעת	772
ימים	100
	933

Thus, 933 represents the duration of the ritual defilement which the birth of a male child causes.

When referring to the טומאה, "ritual defilement," which follows the birth of a daughter the Torah states, ואם נקבה תלד וטמאה שבעים כנדתה וששים יום וששת ימים תשב על דמי טהרה (ויקרא יב,ה), "And if she bear a female child, then she shall be ritually defiled for two weeks, as in her impurity, and for sixty-six days she shall remain in the blood of her purification," (Leviticus 12,5). The gematria of וטמאה שבעים, "then she shall be ritually defiled for two weeks," is 483.

וטמאה	61
שבעים	422
	483

Thus, 483 represents the duration of the ritual defilement which the birth of a female child causes.
The difference in gematrioth between the duration of the ritual defilement which the birth of a male as opposed to a female child causes is 450.

933
-483
450

As has been said previously, the gematria of תטמא, "she shall be ritually defiled," is 450. This gematria is very appropriate, for תטמא, "she shall be ritually defiled," is only stated in reference to the birth of a son. Thus, it is תטמא, "she shall be ritually defiled," that is equal to the difference between the duration of the ritual defilement which the birth of a male as opposed to a female child causes. This difference is seen clearly in their respective gematrioth.

Parashath Metzora   פרשת מצורע

ואיש כי תצא ממנו שכבת זרע ורחץ במים את כל בשרו
וטמא עד הערב (ויקרא טו,טז).

And when a man will emit flow of seed, then he shall wash all his flesh in water, and he will be ritually defiled until the evening (Leviticus 15,16).

Although the Torah uses the word הערב, "the evening," which can mean the evening, it can also mean the night. For example, there is a pasuk which refers to vessels which became ritually defiled from a dead creeping creature, as stated, וכל אשר יפל עליו מהם במתם יטמא מכל כלי עץ או בגד או עור או שק כל כלי אשר יעשה מלאכה בהם יובא במים וטמא עד הערב וטהר (ויקרא יא,לב), "And whatever any of them fall when they are dead, shall be ritually defiled, whether it be any wooden vessel, or a raiment, or a hide, or a sack, any vessel with which work is done, shall be brought into water, shall be ritually defiled until the evening, and then it shall be ritually not defiled" (Leviticus 11,32). Although the pasuk uses the word הערב, "the evening," the Gemara derives from this pasuk that vessels which became ritually defiled from a dead creeping creature, after immersion in a mikvah, still require nightfall (יבמות עה:, Yebamoth 75a). Also the Rambam recognizes the necessity of nightfall, as he writes, אין הטמאים אוכלין בתרומה עד שיעריבו שמשן ויצאו שלשה כוכבים בינונים וזהו עת כמו שליש שעה אחר שקיעת החמה (משנה תורה, ספר זרעים, הלכות תרומות, פרק ז הלכה ב). "Those who were ritually defiled could not eat of Terumah until the sun had set and three median size stars had appeared, and this time is approximately one third of an hour after sunset" (Mishnah Torah, Book of Zeraim, Laws of Terumah, Chapter 7, Law 2).

Returning to the pasuk from Parashath Metzora, the Torah says that the emission of seed from a man makes him ritually defiled until the evening. The gematria of זרע, "seed," is 277.

זרע   277

The gematria of הערב, "the evening," is 277.

הערב   277

Since זרע, "seed," makes a man ritually defiled until הערב, "the evening," therefore, it is notable that the gematrioth of the two words are equal. It can be added that the proper time for the emission of זרע, "seed," is in הערב, meaning night, as stated, אסור לשמש ביום אלא אם כן הוא בית אפל (שלחן ערוך, אורח חיים, סימן רמ, סי׳ יא), "It is forbidden to have sexual relations in the day, unless it is in a dark house" (Shulhan Arukh, Orach Hayyim, Siman 240, Seif 11). Since the proper time for the emission of זרע, "seed," is in הערב, "the evening," therefore, it is notable that the gematrioth of the two words are equal.

Parashath Acharey Moth   פרשת אחרי מות

למען אשר יביאו בני ישראל את זבחיהם אשר הם זבחים
על פני השדה והביאם לה׳ אל פתח אהל מועד אל הכהן
וזבחו זבחי שלמים לה׳ אותם (ויקרא יז,ה).

In order that the Children of Israel will bring
their sacrifices which they sacrifice upon the
open field, and they may bring them to G-d, to
the entrance of the tend of the meeting to the
kohen and they will sacrifice them as peace
offerings to G-d (Leviticus 17,5).

The sacrifices which the Children of Israel were accustomed to bring on a במה, "private altar," (which was illegitimate after a central altar was established) were required to
be brought to the עזרה, "Inner Court of Temple." The במה,
"private altar," on which they had sacrificed was referred to
as אשר הם זבחים על פני השדה, "which they sacrifice on the face
of the field," (התורה והמצוה, מאת הרב מאיר ליבוש מלביי״ם, ויקרא,
יז,ה, The Torah and the Mitzvah by Rabbi Meir Lebush Malbim,
Leviticus 17,5). The gematria of אשר הם זבחים, "which they
sacrifice," is 613.

אשר	501
הם	45
זבחים	67
	613

The Gemara Zevahim enumerates when the sacrificing on a במה, "private altar," was allowed and when it was
forbidden, as stated, ... עד שלא הוקם המשכן היו הבמות מותרות
ומשהוקם המשכן נאסרו הבמות ... באו לגלגל הותרו הבמות ... באו לשילה
נאסרו הבמות ... באו לנוב וגבעון הותרו הבמות ... באו לירושלים נאסרו
הבמות ולא היה להן היתר (זבחים קיב:), "Before the mishkan was
erected, the private altars were allowed ... once the mishkan
was erected the private altars were forbidden ... when they

came to Gilgal the private altars were allowed ... when they came to Shiloh the private altars were forbidden ... when they came to Nob and Givon the private altars were allowed ... when they came to Jerusalem the private altars were forbidden, and they were no longer allowed" (Zevahim 112b).

When the Children of Israel first came to the land of Israel, they erected the mishkan which stood for fourteen years in Gilgal, three hundred and sixty-nine years in Shiloh, and then fifty-seven years in Nob and Givon. The רמב״ם, Rambam, writes, כיון שנכנסו לארץ העמידו המשכן בגלגל ארבע עשרה שנה ... ושס״ט שנה עמד משכן שילה. וכשמת עלי חרב. ובאו לנב ובנו שם מקדש. וכמת שמואל חרב. ובאו לגבעון ובנו שם מקדש. ומגבעון באו לבית העולמים. וימי נב וגבעון שבע וחמשים שנה. (משנה תורה, ספר עבודה, הלכות בית הבחירה, פרק א, הלכה ב). "When they entered the Land, they set up the mishkan in Gilgal for fourteen years ... The mishkan in Shiloh stood for three hundred and sixty-nine years. When Eli died, it was destroyed. And they came to Nob and they built there a mikdash. And when Samuel died it was destroyed. And they came to Givon and they built there a mikdash. And from Givon they came to the everlasting House. And the days of Nob and Givon were fifty-seven years," (Mishnah Torah, Book of Avodah, Laws of the Temple, Chapter 1, Law 2). During the times the mishkan stood in Shiloh and when the Temple stood, it was forbidden to offer sacrifices on a במה, "private altar."

Rashi in the Gemara says that forbidden sacrificing on a במה, "a private altar," is tantamount to sacrificing to idols, as he writes, בשעת איסור הבמות כזובח על פני השדה לעבודת כוכבים (רש״י, עבודה זרה נא : ד״ה בשעת היתר), "At the time when the private altars were forbidden, it is as if one sacrificed on the face of the field to idol worship" (Rashi, Avodah Zarah 51b, header words: At the time it was allowed).

There is a total of 613 Mitzvoth (מכות כג:, Makkoth 23b).

The Gemara Horayoth says that worshiping idols is equated to violating all the commandments, as stated, איזו היא מצוה שהיא שקולה ככל המצות, הוי אומר זו עבודת כוכבים (הוריות ח.), "Which commandment is equivalent to all the commandments? Say it is idol worship" (Horayoth 8a). The Rambam also sets forth in words and explains this equality (משנה תורה, ספר המדע, הלכות עבודה כוכבים, פרק ב, הלכה ד, Mishnah Torah, Book of Hamadda, Laws of Idol Worship, Chapter 2, Law 4). Since illegitimate sacrificing on a במה, "private altar," is tantamount to worshiping idols, since worshiping idols is equated to violating all the mitzvoth, and since there is a total of 613 Mitzvoth, therefore when the Torah says אשר הם זבחים, "which they sacrifice," in reference to sacrificing on a במה, "private altar," it is distinctive that these three words have a gematria of 613.

ערות אשה ובתה לא תגלה את בת בנה ואת בת בתה לא תקח לגלות ערותה שארה הנה זמה הוא (ויקרא יח,יז). A woman's and her daughter's nakedness you shall not uncover; her son's daughter or her daughter's daughter you shall not take to uncover her nakedness, they are near kinswomen; it is lewdness (Leviticus 18,17).

The Torah describes certain acts as זמה הוא, "it is lewdness." The gematria of זמה הוא, "it is lewdness," is 64.

זמה	52
הוא	12
	64

Note that the word הוא, "it is," is spelled with a ו, "vav," and not with a י, "yud." Closer to the conclusion of the parashah the Torah warns, אל תטמאו בכל אלה כי בכל אלה נטמאו הגוים אשר אני משלח מפניכם (ויקרא יח,כד), "Do not defile yourself with all of these, because with all of these the nations which I cast out before you have become defiled" (Leviticus 18,24). The gematria of הגוים, "the nations," is 64.

הגוים   64

The Torah says that the nations who were in the land of Israel did that which the Torah describes as lewdness (among their various other acts of immorality). Since the gematrioth of זמה הוא, "it is lewdness," and הגוים, "the nations," are equal, it adds to the reality that the nations who were in the land of Israel did that which the Torah describes as lewdness.

Parashath Kedoshim   פרשת קדושים

לא תקם ולא תטר את בני עמך ואהבת לרעך כמוך אני ה׳
(ויקרא יט,יח).

Do not take vengeance and do not bear a grudge against the children of your people, but you shall love your neighbor as yourself; I am G-d (Leviticus 19,18).

The Torah commands to love your neighbor כמוך, "as yourself." The gematria of כמוך, "as yourself," is 86.

86   כמוך

Sometimes people feel that when they empathize with their fellow man, they are doing something wonderful which is לפנים משורת הדין, "beyond the strict letter of the law"; that is, they are doing more that what Jewish law requires of them. In truth they are doing something wonderful, but it is what the הלכה, Halakhah, "decided law," requires. The Torah requires one to empathize with our fellow man and his burdens.

When G-d's character of strict justice is alluded to, He is referred to as אלקים, "G-d," (רש״י, בראשית א,א וח,א), Rashi, Genesis 1,1 and 8,1). The gematria of אלקים, "G-d," is 86.

אלקים   86

Since the gematrioth of כמוך, "as yourself," and אלקים, "G-d," are identical, it could be understood that when one empathizes with his fellow man, that is, when he fulfills the command to love your neighbor כמוך, "as yourself," he is doing what the Halakhah requires.

A different explanation can be given as to why the gematrioth of כמוך, "as yourself," and אלקים, "G-d," are identical. The שפתי חכמים, "Sifthei Chachomim," מזרחי, "Mizrachi," and the תורה תמימה, "Torah Temimah," all mention a similar concept in reference to this pasuk. This concept is found in the Gemara Shabbath which says that Hillel responded to a heathen, דעלך סני לחברך לא תעביד זו היא כל התורה כולה ואידך

(שבת לא.) פירושה הוא, "That which is hateful to you, do not do to your friend; this is all the Torah in its entirety, the rest is its explanation" (Shabbath 31a). Note that on this phrase of the Gemara, the "Chidushei Halakhoth and Aggadoth from the Maharsha," says, (חדושי) והיינו דכתיב ואהבת לרעך כמוך וגו' הלכות ואגדות מהרש"א), "And this is what is written in the Torah, 'but you shall love your neighbor as yourself,' etc." (Chidushei Halakhoth and Aggadoth from the Maharsha). Thus, this concept of Hillel is an explanation of "you shall love your neighbor as yourself."

When G-d judges the world with מדת הדין, "strict justice," He is very exacting, as the Mesillath Yesharim says, מי יעמד ביום הדין ומי יצדק לפני בוראו באשר השקפתו מדקדקת על כל דבר קטן או גדול (מסלת ישרים מאת הרב משה חיים לוצאטו, פרק ד), "Who will be able to stand on the judgment Day; who will be deemed righteous before his Creator in His meticulous view of everything small or large" (Mesillath Yesharim by Rabbi Moshe Chaim Luzzatto, Chapter 4). Ergo, when G-d judges with strict justice He is very exacting. When one fulfills the command to "love your neighbor as yourself," he should also examine himself very exactly. Everything, large or small, which falls into the category of "That which is hateful to you," one should try to avoid doing to his friend. When one fulfills the command to love your neighbor, כמוך, "as yourself," he should try to do it with the exactness of אלקים, "G-d"; this explanation could be why these words have the identical gematria.

וכי תבאו אל הארץ ונטעתם כל עץ מאכל וערלתם ערלתו את פריו שלש שנים יהיה לכם ערלים לא יאכל (ויקרא יט,כג).

And when you shall come into the land, and you shall have planted any food tree, then you shall surely close off its fruit; for three years it shall be closed off to you, it shall not be eaten (Leviticus 19,23).

The Torah forbids eating the fruit of tree for the first three years after its planting; such fruit is called ערלים, "closed off," Orlah. The gematria of ערלים, "closed off," is 350.

350   ערלים

Why did the Torah repeat itself, saying יהיה לכם ערלים, "it shall be closed-off to you," in the latter half of the pasuk, after already saying וערלתם ערלתו את פריו, "then you shall surely close off its fruit," in the first part of the pasuk? The Gemara learns certain laws from the repetition (פסחים כד:, Pesahim 24b); perhaps the repetition can also be expounded upon בדרך דרוש, "by route of a homily."

Another question can be asked in relation to this pasuk. On this pasuk the מדרש רבה, Midrash Rabbah, states, ההי"ד עץ חיים היא למחזיקים בה (מדרש רבה, סדר קדשים, פרשה כה, אות א), "This is what is written, 'It is a tree of life to those who grasp it'" (Midrash Rabbah, Sidrah Kedoshim, Parashah 25, Letter 1). What possible connection can there be between Orlah and the Torah being compared to a tree of life?

One possible explanation to answer these questions is based on a Mishnah in Avoth which states, רבי מאיר אומר הוי ממעט בעסק ועסוק בתורה (אבות, פרק ד, משנה י), "Rabbi Meir said, 'Limit your business activity and busy yourself in Torah'" (Avoth, Chapter 4, Mishnah 10). The importance of limiting business activities and engaging in Torah has been stressed by our Rabbis in other sources. Later in Avoth, the Mishnah lists במיעוט סחורה, "With limitedness in trade," as one of the 48 ways one can acquire Torah (אבות, פרק ו, משנה ה, Avoth, Chapter 6, Mishnah 5). Another source is the Gemara which comments on the pasuk, ולא מעבר לים הוא לאמר מי יעבר לנו אל עבר הים ויקחה לנו וישמענו אתה ונעשנה (דברים ל,יג), "And neither is it beyond the sea, that you should say, 'Who will pass over to the other side of the sea for us and and take it for us and cause us to hear it that we may do it?'" (Deuteronomy 30,13). The Gemara says, רבי יוחנן אמר... ולא מעבר לים היא לא

(עירובין נה.) תמצא לא בסחרנים ולא בתגרים, "Rabbi Johanan said, ... And neither is it beyond the sea; you will not find it, not with the merchants nor with the traders" (Eruvin 55a).

If one limits his business activity and engages in Torah, he will know better how to comply with the Torah, and thereby reinforce G-d's Kingdom in this world. Of course, G-d is always the King over the world, but one must heed the Torah if he wants to be considered part of the nation which recognizes this Kingship, rather than rebelling against it, as stated, "For it כי עם מרי הוא בנים כחשים בנים לא אבו שמוע תורת ה׳ (ישעי׳ ל,ט) is a rebellious nation, deceiving children, children who refuse to heed G-d's Torah" (Isaiah 30,9). Stated positively, one who heeds the Torah reinforces that G-d is King over the world, for by heeding the Torah he is part of G-d's nation. It is essential in human perception that there be a nation in order to have a king, as stated, כי אין מלך בלא עם (כד הקמח מאת רבינו בחיי, דרשת ראש השנה (ב), ד״ה ועוד במצוה זו רמז למלכותו יתברך), "For there can be no king without a nation" (Kad Hakemach by Rabbeinu Bechaya, Derashah for Rosh Hashanah (2), header words: And more about this mitzvah which hints to His Blessed Kingdom). A similar thought is found in the Ramban (רמב״ן, דברים לג,ה ד״ה ויהי בישורון מלך, Ramban, Deuteronomy 33,5 header words: And there was a King in Jeshurun). Thus, If one limits his business activity and engages in Torah, he reinforces G-d's Kingdom in this world.

The Kingship of G-d in this world relates to His possessing the world and all that is in it, as can be observed from Rabbi Samson Raphael Hirsch's connecting the first and the seventh pesukim of תהלים פרק כד, "Psalms Chapter 24." The first pasuk proclaims G-d's ownership of the world, as stated, "A Psalm לדוד מזמור לה׳ הארץ ומלואה תבל וישבי בה (תהלים כד,א) to David. To G-d is the earth and its fullness, the world and those who dwell in it" (Psalms 24,1). The seventh pasuk refers to G-d as a King, as stated, שאו שערים ראשיכם והנשאו

(תהלים כד,ז) פתחי עולם ויבא מלך הכבוד, "Gates, lift up your heads, and be lifted up, everlasting doors, and the King of honor will enter" (Psalms 24,7). Thus, by connecting the concepts of these pesukim, it is observed that G-d who possesses the whole world, is the King of the world (ספר תהלים, מתורגם ומבואר מאת הרב שמשון בן הר״יר רפאל הירש, פרק כד, Book of Psalms, translation and commentary by Rabbi Samson Raphael Hirsch, Chapter 24).

The thoughts just presented can be joined. If one decreases his business activity and engages in Torah, he will better know how to comply to the Torah. By heeding the Torah one confirms G-d's Kingship in the world, meaning that G-d possesses all that is in the world. Therefore, one who decreases his business activity and engages in Torah, affirms that G-d is King who possesses all that is in the world.

The אם יקרא, ילקוט שמעוני, "Yalkut Shimoni," states, וישנה וישמש ת״ח וימעט בסחורה וירבה בישיבה באותה שעה הקב״ה אומר לו העולם הזה שלי ושלך (ילקוט שמעוני, פרשת נצבים ל, אות תתקי״א), "If one studies and reviews (Torah), and serves talmidei hakhamim, and decreases trade, and increases Torah sessions, at that time G-d says to him, 'This world is Mine and yours'" (Yalkut Shimoni, Parashath Nitzavim 30, letter 901). The affirmation of G-d as King Who possesses all that is in the world, by one who decrease his business activity and engages in Torah, could be the reason G-d would say to that person העולם הזה שלי ושלך, "This world is Mine and yours."

Limiting the extent of one's business activities could be a possible theme of Orlah. Rashi defines the word ערלים, literally, "uncircumcised," Orlah, as closed and shut (רש״י, ויקרא יט,כג, Rashi, Leviticus 19,23). The pasuk about Orlah could perhaps be interpreted as follows: ונטעתם כל עץ מאכל, "When you plant a fruit tree," וערלתם ערלתו את פריו, "then you shall surely close off its fruit," שלש שנים יהי לכם ערלים, "When you undertake any business activity for three years, it should be limited or closed for you," so you can learn Torah, which confirms G-d as King, Who possesses the whole world.

The rationale why decreasing business activity to learn Torah is placed with the pasuk about Orlah, could be that people's business perspective is for three years. That is, one must always decrease his business activity and engage in Torah, not just for three years, but the Torah understands that people's occupational perspective is for three-year intervals.

The source for the three-year perspective is a Tosafoth in the Gemara Kiddushin which cites a verse in Isaiah 16,14 as confirmation that the years of a hireling are three. It states, (תוס', קידושין יז., ד"ה אם כן מצינו דשנים דשכיר הן שלש שנים), "If so we find that the years of hiring are three years" (Tosafoth, Kiddushin 17a, header words: If he was sick three years and worked three years, he is not obligated to complete). The three-year interval is also indicated by an account in Gemara Shabbath which states, ומעשה באדם אחד שירד מגליל העליון ונשכר אצל בעל הבית אחד בדרום שלש שנים (שבת קכז:), "And there was an incident with one man who came down from the Upper Galilee, and was hired by a homeowner in the South for three years" (Shabbath 127b). The דרכי משה, Darkhe Mosheh, also recognizes the three-year interval (דרכי משה, טור חושן משפט, סימן שלא, ס"ק א), Darkhe Mosheh, Tur Hoshen Mishpat, Siman 331, Small Seif 1). Further note that the רמ"א, "Rema," says, אסור לפועל אפי' מלמד או סופר להשכיר עצמו להיות בבית בעל הבית בקבע שלשה שנים (רמ"א, שלחן ערוך, חושן משפט, סימן שלג, סעיף ג), "It is forbidden for a worker, even a teacher or a scribe to hire himself out to be permanently in the house of a homeowner owner for three years" (Rema, Shulhan Arukh, Hoshen Mishpat, Siman 333, Seif 3). The ש"ך, "Shakh," bases this rule on pesukim from Parashath Reeh and from Isaiah, as stated, והיינו דכתי' כי משנה שכר שכיר עבדך דהיינו שש כדכתי' בישעי' שלש שנים כימי שכיר א"כ ע"ע

ו' שנים היינו משנה שכר שכיר (שפתי כהן, חושן משפט, סימן שלג, סעיף ג, ס״ק יז), "And this is what is written, 'for double the wage of a hireling he has served,' which is six, as it is written in Isaiah 'within three years, as the years of hireling.' If so, the six years of a Hebrew servant that is double the wage of a hireling" (Sifthe Kohen, Hoshen Mishpat, Siman 333, Seif 3, Small Seif 17).

Since the human inclination is to be concerned to the extent of a three-year interval for business activity, it can be said to correspond to the pasuk about Orlah which exhorts for a three-year interval. One of the tribes most famous for limiting business activities in order to learn Torah was יששכר, "Issachar"; the members of that tribe devoted themselves to learning Torah, and left business activities to the tribe of זבולן, "Zebulun," who supported them (רש״י, דברים לג,יח, Rashi, Deuteronomy 33,18).

There are different opinions as to which stones of the חשן, "breastplate," Hoshen, correspond to which tribe of the Children of Israel (התורה והמצוה, שמות כח,יז, מאת הרב מאיר ליבוש מלביי״ם, The Torah and the Mitzvah by Rabbi Meir Lebush Malbim, Exodus 28,17), but according to the שפתי חכמים, "Sifthei Chachomim," the ספיר, "sapphire," corresponds to the tribe of Issachar (רש״י ושפתי חכמים, שמות כח, כא, Rashi and Sifthei Chachomim, Exodus 28,21). The sapphire was one of the stones listed on the Hoshen, as stated, והטור השני נפך ספיר ויהלם (שמות כח,יח), "And the second row a carbuncle, a sapphire, and a diamond" (Exodus 28,18). The gematria of ספיר, "sapphire," is 350.

350   ספיר

The ספיר, "sapphire," corresponds to the tribe of יששכר, "Issachar," who devoted itself to learning Torah, which confirms G-d as King, possessing all that is in the world.

The punishment for not acknowledging that the earth belongs to G-d is being sent into exile. The Torah refers to the years that the land rests as השמה, "it lies desolate," as stated, אז תרצה הארץ את שבתתיה כל ימי השמה ואתם בארץ איביכם אז תשבת הארץ והרצת את שבתתיה (ויקרא כו,לד), "Then the land shall satisfy its Shabbathoth, all the days it lies desolate, and you are in your enemies' land, then the land shall rest, and satisfy its Shabbathoth" (Leviticus 26,34). The gematria of השמה, "it lies desolate," is 350.

השמה   350

The ספרא, Sifra, explains that the reason for the time of השמה, "it lies desolate," is (ספרא, שלי היא שהארץ שתדעו בשביל, "in order that you know that the land is Mine" (ויקרא כו,לד), (Sifra, Leviticus 26,34). This reason parallels the themes associated with the words Orlah and sapphire.

By decreasing business activity and engaging in To-rah, the Children of Israel acknowledge G-d as King Who possesses all that is in the world, consubstantially when the land lies desolate it is an acknowledgment that G-d possesses it. Since the words ערלים, "it should be limited," השמה, "it lies desolate," and ספיר, "sapphire," are all associated, it is appro-priate that all three words have the identical gematria of 350.

With this interpretation, the two questions initially asked about the pasuk stated in reference to Orlah can be answered. One, the Torah repeated itself, saying יהיה לכם ערלים, "it shall be closed off to you," in the latter half of the pasuk after saying וערלתם ערלתו את פריו, "then you shall surely close off its fruit," in the first part of the pasuk, because the first part of the pasuk refers to limiting the extent of the benefits of a newly planted tree; the latter half of the pasuk refers to limiting business activities which are seen as having a three-year perspective. One should limit his business activ-ity so that he can learn Torah, similar to that which was done by the tribe of Issachar, whose stone in the Hoshen was a ספיר, "sapphire." Two, the מדרש רבה, Midrash Rabbah, con-nects Orlah and the Torah being compared to a tree of life because from Orlah one can learn how to hold on to the tree of life. That is, the theme of the pasuk about Orlah is to limit other activities and learn Torah. Surely an ideal parallel pasuk is the one that says "It is a tree of life to those who grasp it"; by limiting other activities and learning Torah, one is grasping the Torah. Thus, with this interpretation the two questions initially asked about the pasuk stated in reference to Orlah have been answered.

Another interpretation can be given which will also answers the two questions initially asked about the pasuk related to Orlah. When is the Torah a tree of life to those who cling to it? When they realize it has קדושה, "sanctity." One should cling to the Torah, for it is a tree of life, but one should also realize that it has קדושה, "sanctity." Just as the fruits of the first three years of a tree's life should not be used for personal benefit, so too the Torah should not be used for personal benefit. This concept is based in a Mishnah in Avoth, as stated, רבי צדוק אומר אל תעשה עטרה להתגדל בהם ולא קרדום לחפור בהם וכן היה הלל אומר ודשתמש בתגא חלף הא למדת, כל הנהנה מדברי תורה נוטל חייו מן העולם (אבות, פרק ד, משנה ה ונדרים לז.), "Rabbi Zadok said, 'Do not make words of Torah a crown to aggrandize yourself, nor a spade with which to dig.' And also Hillel said, 'He who uses the crown of Torah improperly, passes away: So you learn, anyone who derives improper benefit from words of Torah, takes his life from the world'" (Avoth, Chapter 4, Mishnah 5 and Nedarim 37a.)

The pasuk stated in reference to Orlah represents holiness, the abstention from eating the fruit of tree for the first three years after its planting. The pasuk the Midrash quotes represents clinging to the Torah, but one should also realize that it has קדושה, "sanctity"; the Torah should not be used for personal benefit. When one recognizes the similarity of these two concepts, a comparison can be drawn between the Torah being a tree of life, and Orlah. This interpretation answers the two questions initially asked about the pasuk stated in reference to Orlah, and bonds with the gematria, similar to the first interpretation.

ולא תלכו בחקת הגוי אשר אני משלח מפניכם כי את כל אלה עשו ואקץ בם (ויקרא כ,כג).

And you shall not walk in the statutes of the nations which I am casting out before you; for they did all these things and I abhorred them (Leviticus 20,23).

The two pesukim between שביעי ומפטיר, "the seventh portion of the sidrah and the Maftir," seems to be an entity which tells an important message. The first pasuk informs that G-d is casting out the nations who were in the land of Israel before the Children of Israel, and why those nations are being expelled. The gematria of משלח מפניכם, "casting out before you," is 618.

משלח	378
מפניכם	240
	618

The gematria of ואקץ בם, "and I abhorred them," is 239.

ואקץ	197
בם	42
	239

The combined gematrioth of משלח מפניכם, "casting out before you," and ואקץ בם, "and I abhorred them," is 857.

$$618$$
$$239$$
$$857$$

The reason that G-d gives for His saying, "I am casting out before you," is His saying, "and I abhorred them."

The second pasuk of the entity between שביעי ומפטיר, "the seventh portion of the sidrah and the Maftir," informs that G-d will give, and the Children of Israel will acquire, the land of Israel, as stated, ואמר לכם אתם תירשו את אדמתם ואני אתננה לכם לרשת אתה ארץ זבת חלב ודבש אני ה׳ אלקיכם אשר הבדלתי אתכם מן העמים (ויקרא כ,כד), "And I have said to you, you shall inherit their land, and I will give it to you to possess it, a land flowing with milk and honey; I am Hashem, your G-d, Who separated you from the nations" (Leviticus 20,24). The gematria of ואני אתננה, "and I will give it," is 573.

ואני	67
אתננה	506
	573

The gematria of לרשת אתה, "to possess it," is 1336.

לרשת	930
אתה	406
	1336

The combined gematrioth of ואני אתננה, "and I will give it," and לרשת אתה, "to possess it," is 1909.

573
1336
1909

The reason that G-d gives for His saying, "to possess it," is His saying "I will give it." G-d is telling that He will give the land, and the Children of Israel will possess it; His giving is the reason why the Children of Israel will acquire the land of Israel.

The cause of the expulsion of the nations who were in the land of Israel before the Children of Israel, and the cause of the inheritance of the Children of Israel of the land of Israel, which the Torah stated palpably, can also be found in the gematrioth of how the Torah expresses these ideas. The difference between the reason for the expulsion of the nations who were in the land of Israel before the Children of Israel, and why the Children of Israel will possess the land of Israel, is a calculable gematria. This difference is equal to the difference between משלח מפניכם, "casting out before you," plus ואקץ בם, "and I abhorred them," and ואני אתננה, "and I will give it," plus לרשת אתה, "to possess it"; which is 1052 in gematrioth.

$$1909$$
$$-857$$
$$1052$$

The Torah, in the pasuk quoted above, describes the land of Israel as being ארץ זבת חלב ודבש, "a land flowing with milk and honey." The gematria of ארץ זבת חלב ודבש, "a land flowing with milk and honey," is 1052.

ארץ	291
זבת	409
חלב	40
ודבש	312
	1052

There is a profound meaning to the Torah describing the land of Israel as a land flowing with milk and honey. In פרשת שלח לך, Parashath Shelach Lecha, the Chatham Sofer quotes the Ramban to explain such a meaning, as he states, כי מה שאמר הקב"ה ארץ טובה ורחבה ארץ זבת חלב ודבש לא בשבח עצים ואבנים דיבר כי אם ארץ טובה לתורה למצות רחבה מצותך מאד חלב ודבש סתרי תורה וכו' (ספר תורת משה מאת הרב משה סופר, פרשת שלח לך ד"יה טובה הארץ מאד מאד), "For that which the Holy One, Blessed Be He, said, 'A good and broad land, a land flowing with milk and honey,' was not said for the praise of wood and stones. Rather, a good land suitable for Torah, and broad for mitzvoth; Your mitzvoth are very broad, the secrets of Torah are milk and honey, etc." (Book of Torath Moshe by Rabbi Moses Sofer, Parashath Shelach Lecha, header words: The land is exceedingly good). Thus, when the Torah describes the land of Israel as flowing with milk and honey, it is referring to knowledge of the secrets of the Torah.

According to one opinion in the Gemara, the pasuk in Isaiah 23,18 which mentions dignified clothing, unequivocally refers to one who conceals the secrets of the Torah, as stated, מאי למכסה עתיק זה המכסה דברים שכיסה עתיק יומין ומאי נינהו סתרי תורה (פסחים קיט.), "What does 'for dignified clothing,' mean? It means one who conceals things which He of antiquity concealed. And what are these? The secrets of the Torah" (Pesahim 119a). Although the pesukim in the Torah refer to possessing of the land of Israel affiliated with the exodus from Egypt, and this pasuk from Isaiah refers to the time of משיח, "Messiah"; they can be commensurable, as stated, כימי צאתך מארץ מצרים אראנו נפלאות (מיכה ז,טו ורדק, שם), "Just like the days when you went out of the land of Egypt, I will show him wondrous things" (Micah 7,15, and Radak, there). Since one must have knowledge of the secrets of the Torah in order to conceal them, therefore ארץ זבת חלב ודבש, "a land flowing with milk and honey," which may be said to refer to knowledge of the secrets of the Torah, can be applied to the pasuk in Isaiah which can be explained to unequivocally refer to one who conceals the secrets of the Torah.

The Radak explains that this pasuk in Isaiah as well as the following section, is a prophecy for the time of Messiah (רד"יק ישעי' כג,יח, Radak, Isaiah 23,18). The Radak explains that the following section to include G-d fighting against the nations who will encamp around Jerusalem, and the honor which will come to the elders of His people, the Children of Israel. This prophecy is associated with an earlier prophecy in Isaiah 4,2, as stated, שם יחנו על ירושלים גם יכבשו חצי העיר ויצא השם ונלחם בגוים ההם ואז יכירו כל הנשארים מכל הגוים כי לה' המלוכה

ויהיה נגד זקני עמו לכבוד ולתפארת כמו שאמר בראש הספר (פרק ד, פסוק ב), יהיה צמח לה' לצבי ולכבוד וגו' (רד"ק, ישעי' כד,כג) "There they will encamp upon Jerusalem, also they will capture half of the city. And G-d will go out and fight with those nations. Then all those who remain from all those nations will recognize that the Kingship belongs to G-d, and the honor and the splendor will be in front of the elders of His people, as it says towards the beginning of the book, (Chapter 4, pasuk 2) the growth will be for G-d comely and honorable, etc." (Radak, Isaiah 24,23).

Since the nations who encamped around Jerusalem at that time were surely in the land of Israel, the prophecy for the time of Messiah from Isaiah 23,18 (which is associated with fighting in an earlier prophecy) must refer to G-d fighting against nations in the land of Israel, and honoring the elders of His people, the Children of Israel. The fighting against the nations in the land of Israel, and the establishment of G-d's power in the land of Israel, is the reason why the Children of Israel will keep the land of Israel in the days of Messiah, and is also the topic of the prophecy in Isaiah 4,2. The prophet clearly says that the sins of the nations is the reason why G-d will take action against them, as stated, וכבד עליה פשעה (ישעי' כד,כ), "her transgressions shall be heavy upon her" (Isaiah 24,20).

These thoughts can be joined. When the Torah describes the land of Israel as a land flowing with milk and honey, it can be referring to knowledge of the secrets of Torah. According to one opinion in the Gemara, there is a pasuk in Isaiah which refers to one who conceals the secret of Torah. The Radak says that the prophecy of this pasuk is for the time of Messiah, as is also the prophecy of the following section. That section tells why G-d will take action against the nations, and why the Children of Israel will keep the land of Israel. Thus, when the Torah describes the land of Israel as a land flowing with milk and honey, it is telling that in the time of Messiah G-d will take action against other nations and why the Children of Israel will keep the land of Israel.

It is significant that the gematria of ארץ זבת חלב ודבש, "a land flowing with milk and honey," is 1052, for the difference between the reason for the expulsion of the nations who were in the land of Israel before the Children of Israel, and why the Children of Israel will possess the land of Israel, is also equal to 1052. This difference is encompassed in the concept that the land is ארץ זבת חלב ודבש, "a land flowing with milk and honey." For the time when the nations will be expelled, and the Children of Israel will possess the land of Israel, can be found be found in the difference in the gematrioth of how the Torah expresses these ideas.

Parashath Emor

פרשת אמר

כל איש אשר בו מום מזרע אהרן הכהן לא יגש להקריב את
אשי ה' מום בו את לחם אלקיו לא יגש להקריב (ויקרא
כא,כא).

Any man who has a blemish, from the seed of
Aaron the priest, shall not approach to offer
G-d's fire offerings; he has a blemish; he should
not approach to offer the bread of his G-d (Leviticus 21,21).

The Torah forbids those priests who have a blemish
from offering sacrifices, which are designated as לחם,
"bread," of G-d. The gematria of לחם, "bread," is 78.

לחם   78

The תרגום אונקלוס, Targum Onkelos, renders word לחם,
"bread," in this pasuk as קורבניא, "sacrifice." In the next
pasuk Targum Onkelos also has a similar rendition of this
bread of G-d. The following pasuk warns, אך אל הפרכת לא יבא
ואל המזבח לא יגש כי מום בו ולא יחלל את מקדשי כי אני ה' מקדשם
(ויקרא כא,כג), "Only unto the dividing curtain he should not go,
and unto the altar he shall not approach, because he has a
blemish, and he shall not profane My sanctuaries, for I am
G-d who sanctifies them" (Leviticus 21,23). The gematria of
יחלל, "he shall profane," is 78.

יחלל   78

Although the warning of "he shall not profane" refers
to the first part of the pasuk which states, "unto the dividing
curtain he should not go, and unto the altar he shall not
approach," still the connection between "he shall not profane" and the aforementioned "bread" seems clear. A priest
who has a blemish should not enter unto the altar where
sacrifices were offered.

These sacrifices were referred to as לחם, "bread." A priest who has a blemish who enters to bring a sacrifice into this area designated for the לחם, "bread," violates the avoiding associated with יחלל, "he shall profane." Thus, it is fitting that לחם, "bread," and יחלל, "he shall profane," have the same gematria.

וכהן כי יקנה נפש קנין כספו הוא יאכל בו ויליד ביתו הם יאכלו בלחמו (ויקרא כב,יא).

And when a priest acquires someone, the purchase of his money, that person may eat of it, and those born in his house, may eat of his bread (Leviticus 22,11).

In the Torah it is written that someone who is an acquisition of the priest's money, which includes the priest's wife, can eat of his Terumah, which is called בלחמו, "of his bread," (רש"י, ויקרא כב,יא, Rashi, Leviticus 22,11). The gematria of בלחמו, "of his bread," is 86.

בלחמו   86

In general, a man has a legal obligation to feed his wife, as the Gemara says, אמר רבא האי תנא סבר מזונות מדאורייתא דתניא שארה אלו מזונות וכו' (כתובות מז:), "Raba says, This Tanna holds that providing food is a Pentateuchal obligation, as was learned, sheerah, refers to food, etc." (Kethuboth 47b). There is a Mishnah which phrases the same idea negatively, as stated, ושלא לזון את אשתו אינו רשאי (גיטין, פרק א, משנה ו), "And not to provide food for his wife, is not allowed," (Gittin, Chapter 1, Mishnah 6).

A priest can fulfill his legal obligation to feed his wife by giving her Terumah; therefore, it is a legal right that the wife of a priest can eat Terumah. G-d's attribute of justice is identified with His name of אלקים, "G-d," as stated, ויזכר אלקים. זה השם מדת הדין הוא (רשי, בראשית ח,א), "And G-d Remembered. This name is identified with His attribute of strict justice," (רש״י, בראשית ח,א, Rashi, Genesis 8,1). The gematria of אלקים, "G-d," is 86.

אלקים   86

Since it is from the pasuk where Terumah is called בלחמו, "of his bread," that it is learned that there is a legal right that the wife of a priest can eat Terumah, and G-d's attribute of justice is identified with His name of אלקים, "G-d," it is proper that בלחמו, "of his bread," and אלקים, "G-d," have the same gematria. Both terms are associated with His attribute of strict justice.

ולקחתם לכם ביום הראשון פרי עץ הדר כפת תמרים וענף עץ עבת וערבי נחל ושמחתם לפני ה׳ אלקיכם שבעת ימים (ויקרא כג,מ).

And you shall take for yourselves on the first day the fruit of a majestic tree, branches of date palm trees, and the boughs of a thick tree, and willows of the brook; and you shall rejoice before Hashem, your G-d, for seven days (Leviticus 23,40).

The Torah gives the designation כפת תמרים, "branches of date palm trees," to what is commonly referred to as a לולב, "lulav." The gematria of כפת תמרים, "branches of date palm trees," is 1190.

כפת	500
תמרים	690
	1190

On the חג הסכות, "Sukkoth holiday," the ארבעה מינים, "Four Varieties," namely, the ethrog, lulav, hadas, and arava, (which are the citron, branches of date palm trees, myrtle, and willow) are taken together. But the blessing said on all four only mentions the lulav, that is, על נטילת לולב, "concerning taking the lulav." The Gemara says that since it is higher than the others, therefore the blessing is made upon it (סוכה לז:, Sukkah 37b). Appropriately, this higher lulav also has a gematria higher than the other three varieties.

A מצוה דרבנן, "a commandment prescribed by the Rabbis," is fulfilled when the "Four Varieties" are taken together for all the seven days that people sit in a סוכה, sukkah, "a booth." Only on the first day of the holiday is it a מצוה דאורייתא, "a commandment prescribed by the Torah," to take the "Four Varieties"; the other days it is a מצוה דרבנן, "a commandment prescribed by the Rabbis" (סוכה מא., Sukkah 41a). The Torah commands to dwell in a sukkah, a booth, for seven days, as stated, בסכת תשבו שבעת ימים כל האזרח בישראל ישבו בסכת (ויקרא כג,מב), "You shall dwell in booths for seven days; every citizen in Israel shall dwell in booths" (Leviticus 23,42). The gematria of בסכת תשבו, "You shall dwell in booths," is 1190.

$$
\begin{array}{rr}
\text{בסכת} & 482 \\
\text{תשבו} & \underline{708} \\
& 1190
\end{array}
$$

Since the gematria of כפת תמרים, "branches of date palm trees," is equal to the gematria of בסכת תשבו, "You shall dwell in booths," it is felicitous that the blessing said over the "Four Varieties" should designate the lulav; for the time the command to dwell in a sukkah applies is the exact time the Rabbis command that the "Four Varieties" be taken together.

This gematria corresponds to the Gemara quoted previously, which said that since the lulav is higher than the others, therefore a blessing is made upon it (סוכה לז:, Sukkah 37b). This correspondence is that the expression the Torah uses for a lulav, כפת תמרים, "branches of date palm trees," has a gematria higher, meaning, more significant, than that of the expressions the Torah uses for any of the other "Four

Varieties." In addition to the כפת תמרים, "branches of date palm trees," relating to the time when the "Four Varieties" are taken, the gematria of כפת תמרים, "branches of date palm trees," is equal to the gematria of בסכת תשבו, "You shall dwell in booths."

ולקחתם לכם ביום הראשון פרי עץ הדר כפת תמרים וענף עץ עבת וערבי נחל ושמחתם לפני ה׳ אלקיכם שבעת ימים (ויקרא כג,מ).

And you shall take for yourselves on the first day the fruit of a majestic tree, branches of date palm trees, and the boughs of a thick tree, and willows of the brook; and you shall rejoice before Hashem, your G-d, for seven days (Leviticus 23,40).

The Torah calls כפת תמרים, "branches of date palm trees," to what is commonly referred as a לולב, "lulav." The gematria of כפת תמרים, "branches of date palm trees," is 1190.

כפת	500
תמרים	690
	1190

The gematria of וערבי נחל, "and willows of the brook," is 376.

וערבי	288
נחל	88
	376

The Midrash says that since the branches of the palm tree have taste but no smell, they are comparable to a Jew who has Torah, but lacks good deeds. Since the willows of a brook have neither taste nor smell, they are comparable to a Jew who has neither Torah nor good deeds (ילקוט שמעוני, פרשת אמר כג, אות תרנא, Yalkut Shimoni, Parashath Emor, 23, Letter 551).

If a Jew who has Torah, but not good deeds, separates himself from those Jews who have neither Torah nor good deeds—if part of his not having good deeds manifests itself in his feeling superior to those who have neither Torah nor good deeds—then he is no better than just being a citizen of the Children of Israel: His only credential is that he is a citizen of the Children of Israel. This lack of credentials can be substantiated from a Gemara in Tractate Pesahim and an assertion from the Midrash Tanhuma. The Gemara states, אמר רב יהודה אמר רב כל המתייהר אם חכם הוא חכמתו מסתלקת ממנו (פסחים סו:), "Rav Judah said that Rav said, Anyone who is a braggart, if he is wise, his wisdom will be removed from him" (Pesahim 66b). The Midrash says, אין חכמה אלא תורה (מדרש תנחומא, פרשת וילך, אות ב), "There is no wisdom, except Torah" (Midrash Tanhuma, Parashath Vayyelech, Letter 2). Since there is no wisdom except Torah, the word Torah can replace the word חכמה, "wisdom," in the Gemara; the Gemara would now read, כל המתייהר אם חכם הוא תורתו מסתלקת ממנו "Anyone who is braggart, if he is Torah scholar, his Torah will be removed from him."

If a Jew who has Torah, but not good deeds, feels superior to those who have neither Torah nor good deeds, then his Torah will depart from him, for he is in the category of כל המתייהר, "Anyone who is a braggart." Such a person is no better than just being a citizen of the Children of Israel. This reduction is reflected with gematrioth.

If a Jew who has Torah, but not good deeds, separates himself from those who have neither Torah nor good deeds, it is comparable to separating the וערבי נחל, "and willows of a brook," from כפת תמרים, "branches of date palm trees"; the difference between these terms in gematrioth is 814.

1190
-376
———
814

The second pasuk after the pasuk where the ארבעה מינים, "Four Varieties," (namely, the ethrog, lulav, hadas, and arava) are mentioned, states, בסכת תשבו שבעת ימים כל האזרח בישראל ישבו בסכת (ויקרא כג,מב), "You shall dwell in booths for seven days; every citizen in Israel shall dwell in booths" (Leviticus 23,42). The gematria of כל האזרח בישראל, "every citizen in Israel," 814.

כל	50
האזרח	221
בישראל	<u>543</u>
	814

The difference between the וערבי נחל, "and willows of a brook," and כפת תמרים, "branches of date palm trees," in gematrioth, is equal to the gematria of כל האזרח בישראל, "every citizens in Israel." Thus, the gematrioth underscore that a Jew who has Torah, but not good deeds, and who separates himself from those who have neither Torah nor good deeds, is no better than one whose only credential is being a citizen of the Children of Israel.

צו את בני ישראל ויקחו אליך שמן זית זך כתית למאור להעלת נר תמיד (ויקרא כד,ב).

Command the Children of Israel, that they shall bring to you pure olive oil beaten for the light, to cause the lamps to burn continually (Leviticus 24,2).

Before the incident of the מקלל, "blasphemer," Moses is commanded to tell the Children of Israel to take שמן, "oil," beaten from olives for the candelabrum (the Menorah), and סלת, "fine flour," baked into cakes for the table (the Shulhan). The gematria of שמן, "oil," is 390.

שמן	390

In reference to the סלת, "fine flour," the Torah states, ולקחת סלת ואפית אתה שתים עשרה חלות שני עשרנים יהיה החלה האחת (ויקרא כד,ה), "And you shall take fine flour and bake it into twelve cakes, two tenth parts of an ephah for one cake" (Leviticus 24,5). The gematria of סלת, "fine flour," is 490.

סלת   490

The difference between the gematria of שמן, "oil," and the gematria of סלת, "fine flour," is 100.

490
-390
100

In reference to the oil for the candelabrum (the Menorah), the word על, "upon," is written once, as stated, על המנרה הטהרה יערך את הנרות לפני ה׳ תמיד (ויקרא כד,ד), "Upon the pure candelabrum, he shall arrange the lamps before G-d, continually" (Leviticus 24,4). The gematria of על, "upon," is 100.

על   100

In reference to the fine flour which was baked into cakes for the table (Shulhan), the word על, "upon," is written twice, as stated, ושמת אותם שתים מערכות שש המערכת על השלחן הטהר לפני ה׳. ונתת על המערכת לבנה זכה והיתה ללחם לאזכרה אשה לה׳ (ויקרא כד,ו-ז), "And you shall set them in two columns, six in a column, upon the pure table before G-d. And you shall put pure frankincense upon each column and it shall be a memorial for the bread, a fire offering to G-d" (Leviticus 24, 6-7). The gematria of על, "upon," twice, is 200.

על   100
על   100
200

The oil was placed in the cups upon the top of the Menorah; the flour was baked into cakes, ten of which were placed on rods above the דף השולחן, "the tabletop"; two of the cakes rested on the tabletop itself.

Note that the בזיכי לבונה, "dishes of frankincense," had flat bottoms, as the Gemara states, תנו רבנן כל הבזיכין שבמקדש לא היו להן שוליים חוץ מבזיכי לבונה של לחם הפנים שמא יניחום ויפרוס הלחם (פסחים סד:), "Our Rabbis taught, all the dishes in the Temple did not have flat bottoms, except for the dishes of frankincense of the showbread, lest they be placed down and break the bread" (Pesahim 64b). There is a difference of opinions as to where the two בזיכי לבונה, "dishes of frankincense," were placed. In the Mishnah, Abba Saul says they rested on the tabletop between the columns of the showbread, as stated, שם היו נותנים שני בזיכי לבונה של לחם הפנים (מנחות, פרק יא, משנה ה), "There they used to place the two dishes of frankincense pertaining to the showbread" (Menachoth, Chapter 11, Mishnah 5). Rabbi Meir says the showbread did not cover the entire tabletop. The Torah says that the Shulhan was two by one amoth (Exodus 25,23); Rabbi Meir holds that the amoth were six tefachim, so that the tabletop was twelve-by-six tefachim. The two showbreads, with five tefachim width and ten tefachim length, did not cover the length of the tabletop. Therefore, there was space for the dishes of frankincense between the loaves of showbread. The הלכה, halakhah, "decided law," is like Rabbi Meir about the length of the table.

In contrast, Rabbi Judah says the showbread did cover the entire tabletop. The Torah says that the Shulhan was two by one amoth (Exodus 25,23); Rabbi Judah holds that the amoth were five tefachim, so that the tabletop was only ten-by-five tefachim. The two showbreads, with five tefachim width and ten tefachim length, did cover the length of the tabletop. Therefore, there was no space for the dishes of frankincense between the loaves of showbread; rather, the dishes were placed on top of the uppermost loaves.

The two gematrioth of 100 associated with the fine flour which was baked into cakes, can be applied according to either opinion. According to Rabbi Meir, since the frankincense was placed in dishes on the דף השולחן, "the tabletop," it was above the bottom two loaves, which were directly on the table—not in dishes. These two loaves were the bottom-most loaves of each column. In reference to the fine flour which was baked into cakes for the table (Shulhan), the word על, "upon," is written twice. One time על, "upon," is written in reference to the fine flour baked into cakes, to indicate that they were placed upon the tabletop. One time על, "upon," is written in reference to the fine flour baked into cakes, to indicate that frankincense was placed in dishes which also rested on the tabletop, above where the bottom two loaves were placed. Since the frankincense was in dishes that rested on the tabletop, that frankincence was slightly above where the first two loaves of the columns of showbread were placed. According to Rabbi Judah, the frankincense was placed on top of the uppermost loaf. One time על, "upon," is written in reference to the fine flour baked into cakes to indicate that they were there placed upon the tabletop. One time על, "upon," is written in reference to the fine flour baked into cakes, to indicate that frankincense was placed above all of the cakes.

In contrast to the two gematrioth of 100 associated with the fine flour, the one time that על, "upon," is written in reference to the oil, indicates that it was put on the top of the Menorah. The difference between the gematria of שמן, "oil," and the gematria of סלת, "fine flour," is 100. The fact that the word על, "upon," with a gematria of 100, is written twice in reference to the fine flour, but only once in reference to the oil, is indicated by the gematria of סלת, "fine flour," being 100 more than the gematria of שמן, "oil."

ואיש כי יתן מום בעמיתו כאשר עשה כן יעשה לו (ויקרא
כד,יט).

And if a man maims his neighbor, as he has
done, so shall be done to him (Leviticus 24,19).

The Torah says what should be done to one who inflicts
a מום, "blemish," on his neighbor. The gematria of מום,
"blemish," is 86.

מום   86

Our Rabbis unequivocally teach that this verse refers
to monetary restitution. In truth, someone who damages
another person deserves to suffer that same damage, as a
cursory reading of the pasuk would indicate (רמב״ן ואבן עזרא,
שמות כא,כד, Ramban and Ibn Ezra, Exodus 21,24). In particular, the ספורנו, Sforno, says, (ספורנו, כך היה ראוי כפי הדין הגמור
שמות כא,כד), "So it would be deserving according to the strict
law" (Sforno, Exodus 21,24). Thus, the strict letter of the law
would indeed require the inflictor to suffer the same blemish
he has inflicted. This same thought is found in reference to
the pasuk from Parashath Emor (אבן עזרא, ויקרא כד,יט, Ibn
Ezra, Leviticus 24,19). However, Torah law only demands
monetary indemnity (רש״י, ויקרא כד,כ, Rashi, Leviticus 24,20),
but if the strict law were to prevail, the inflictor would deserve
to suffer the same damage he has inflicted.

When G-d's character of strict justice is alluded to, He
is referred to as אלקים, "G-d," (רש״י, בראשית א,א וח,א, Rashi,
Genesis 1,1 and 8,1). The gematria of אלקים, "G-d," is 86.

אלקים   86

Since the gematria of מום, "blemish," and אלקים, "G-d,"
are the same, it can be understood that the strict letter of the
law requires the inflictor to suffer the same damage he inflicts. This thought is analogous to what the end of the pasuk
in Parashath Emor says, "as he has done so shall be done to
him."

Parashath Behar פרשת בהר

ואיש כי לא יהיה לו גאל והשיגה ידו ומצא כדי גאלתו (ויקרא כה,כו).

And if a man has no redeemer, and he achieved sufficient means and found according to the measure for its redemption (Leviticus 25,26).

This pasuk talks about one who has gained sufficient means to redeem a field which he had sold (רש״י, ויקרא כה,כה, Rashi, Leviticus 25,25). The gematria of ומצא כדי גאלתו, "and found according to the measure for its redemption," is 611.

ומצא	137
כדי	34
גאלתו	440
	611

An apparent problem with the pasuk is that the two expressions והשיגה ידו, "and he achieved sufficient means," and ומצא כדי גאלתו, "and found according to the measure for its redemption," both seem to express the same idea. Both seem to say: one who has sufficient means to redeem. Why does the Torah seem to repeat the same idea twice?

With the aid of the אזנים לתורה, Oznaim Latorah, a different meaning can be given to the latter expression. In this commentary on the latter expression, it is demonstrated that the word גאל, "redeems," as opposed to other expressions of redemption, refers to G-d redeeming the Children of Israel, as he states, כי בלשון ״גאל״ אנו מדגישים שהי׳ מכרנו והוא ית׳ גאל אותנו (אזנים לתורה מאת הרב זלמן סורוצקין, ויקרא כה,כו, ד״ה ומצא כדי גאלתו), "For with the language of 'redeem' we are emphasizing that G-d sold us, and He, Blessed be He, redeems us" (Oznaim Latorah by Rabbi Zalman Sorotzkin, Leviticus 25,26, header words: And found according to the measure for its redemption). So when the pasuk says ומצא כדי

גאלתו, "and found according to the measure for its redemption," it can mean that G-d grants him his freedom. The word גאלתו, "for its redemption," as opposed to meaning that he has sufficient funds to redeem what he has sold, now means that G-d grants him his freedom.

To take this idea further, how does one receive the grant of freedom from G-d? It is only received when one learns Torah, as stated, שאין לך בן חורין אלא מי שעוסק בתלמוד תורה (אבות, פרק ו, משנה ב), "For no man is free unless he is busy learning Torah" (Avoth, Chapter 6, Mishnah 2). The gematria of תורה, "Torah," is 611.

תורה   611

The gematria of ומצא כדי גאלתו, "and found according to the measure for its redemption," is equal to the gematria of תורה, "Torah." Thus, when the pasuk says ומצא כדי גאלתו, "and found according to the measure for its redemption," it can mean that G-d grants him his freedom if he learns Torah. This meaning is supported by the fact that the gematria of ומצא כדי גאלתו, "and found according to the measure for its redemption," is equal to the gematria of תורה, "Torah."

את כספך לא תתן לו בנשך ובמרבית לא תתן אכלך (ויקרא כה,לז).

Your money you shall not give to him with interest, and for an increase you shall not give your victuals (Leviticus 25,37).

The commandment not to take interest is mentioned three times in the Torah (שמות כד,כב; ויקרא כה,לז; ודברים כג,כ, Exodus 22,24; Leviticus 25,37; and Deuteronomy 23,20). (Also compare to תהלים טו,ה, Psalms 15,5). After the second mention, the Torah immediately mentions the giving of the land of Israel. The key word that specifies the giving of the land of Israel, after the commandment not to take interest, is

את כספך לא תתן לו בנשך ובמרבית לא תתן, "to give," as stated, לתת אכלך. אני ה' אלקיכם אשר הוצאתי אתכם מארץ מצרים לתת לכם את ארץ כנען, להיות לכם לאלקים (ויקרא כה,לז-לח). "Your money you shall not give to him with interest, and for an increase you shall not give your victuals. I am the Hashem, your G-d, who brought you out of the land of Egypt to give you the land of Canaan, to be to you for a G-d" (Leviticus 25,37-38). The gematria of לתת, "to give," is 830.

לתת   830

Why did the Torah combine the mitzvah of not taking interest with the giving of the land of Israel by placing these two pesukim together? What association is there between these two pesukim?

As was mentioned, the key word that specifies the giving of the land of Israel is לתת, "to give," which has a gematria of 830. Rashi on the header words that begin with the word לתת, "to give," states, בשכר שתקבלו מצותי, "As reward that you shall accept My commandments" (רש"י, ויקרא כה,לח, ד"ה לתת לכם את ארץ כנען, Rashi, Leviticus 25,38, header words: To give you the land of Canaan). Thus, the key word that specifies the giving of the land of Israel, לתת, "to give," which has a gematria of 830, is identified with the reward of accepting G-d's commandments.

The מדרש רבה, Midrash Rabbah, comments on the first time the Torah mentions taking interest, as stated, אבל מי שהוא מלוה בלא רבית מעלה עליו הקב"ה כאילו עשה כל המצות שנא' כספו לא נתן בנשך וגו' (מדרש רבה, סדר משפטים, פרשה לא, אות יג) "But, he who lends without interest, G-d considers it as if he per-formed all the commandments, as it says, 'his money he did not lend with interest, etc.'" (Midrash Rabbah, Sidrah Mishpatim, Parashah 31, Letter 13). Thus, if one does lend without taking interest, it is as if he had performed all the commandments.

Since the giving of the land of Israel is reward for

accepting the commandments, and if one lends without taking interest, it is as if he had performed all the commandments, therefore if one does not accept interest it is as if he merited receiving his part in the land of Israel. This reward could be why the Torah placed the commandment of not taking interest next to the giving of the land of Israel.

The third time the Torah mentions not taking interest is in the book of Deuteronomy, as stated, לא תשיך לאחיך נשך (דברים כג,כ) כסף נשך אכל נשך כל דבר אשר ישך, "You shall not charge interest to your brother, interest for money, interest for victuals, interest for anything which is lent upon interest" (Deuteronomy 23,20). The gematria of לא תשיך לאחיך, "You shall not charge interest to your brother," is 830.

לא	31
תשיך	730
לאחיך	69
	830

Thus, the third time the Torah commands not to take interest has a gematria of 830.

Since the key word that specifies the giving of the land of Israel, לתת, "to give," has a gematria of 830, which is identified with the reward of accepting the commandments, and if one observed the commandment not to take interest, which has a gematria of 830, it is as if he fulfilled all the commandments, therefore there is a strong association between the observance of the command not to take interest and the giving of the land of Israel. This association is affirmed by the two identically valued gematrioth of 830. Please note that all three mentions of the commandment not to take interest in the Torah have been employed to present this gematria.

Parashath Bechukosai

פרשת בחקתי

אף אני אעשה זאת לכם והפקדתי עליכם בהלה את השחפת
ואת הקדחת מכלות עינים ומדיבת נפש וזרעתם לריק
זרעכם ואכלהו איביכם (ויקרא כו, טז).

Also I will do this to you: And I will appoint over
you terror, consumption, and the burning ague,
that make the eyes fail, and the soul languish;
and you shall sow in vain your seed, and your
enemies shall eat it (Leviticus 26,16).

The first curse listed in Parashath Bechukosai mentions בהלה, "terror," as stated, ואם בחקתי תמאסו ואם את משפטי
תגעל נפשכם לבלתי עשות את כל מצותי להפרכם את בריתי. אף אני אעשה
זאת לכם והפקדתי עליכם בהלה את השחפת ואת הקדחת מכלות עינים
ומדיבת נפש וזרעתם לריק זרעכם ואכלהו איביכם (ויקרא כו,טו־טז), "And
if My statutes you will despise, and if My ordinances your soul
will abhor, so that you will not do all of My commandments,
to break My covenant. Also I will do this to you: And I will
appoint over you terror, consumption, the burning ague, that
makes the eyes fail, and the soul languish; and you shall sow
in vain your seed, and your enemies shall eat it" (Leviticus
26, 15-16). The gematria of עליכם בהלה את, "over you terror,"
is 613.

עליכם	170
בהלה	42
את	401
	613

These three words come together in the Torah; the
word את, is included for the gematria calculation, although it
relates to the next phrase. The appropriateness of the
gematria of 613 here is obvious. There is a total of 613
Commandments. The Gemara Makkoth says that there is a
total of 613 Mitzvoth given to Moses, as stated, דרש רבי שמלאי

שש מאות ושלש עשרה מצות נאמרו לו למשה שלש מאות וששים וחמש לאוין כמנין ימות החמה ומאתים וארבעים ושמונה עשה כנגד איבריו של אדם (מכות כג:), "Rabbi Simlai expounded, Six hundred and thirteen Commandments were said to Moses. Three hundred and sixty-five negative Commandments corresponding to the number of days in a solar year, and two hundred and forty-eight positive Commandments corresponding to the number of limbs of a man" (Makkoth 23b).

The Torah introduces the curses with a portrayal of the Children of Israel not adhering to all the commandments, as was quoted, "And if My statutes you will despise, and if My ordinances your soul will abhor, so that you will not do all of My commandments," then as a denouement, the next pasuk says, "Also I will do this to you; And I will appoint over you terror." It is stressed that G-d will punish for not observing the 613 Mitzvoth; therefore it is fitting that the text of the punishment should contain the gematria of 613.

ואם משדה אחזתו יקדיש איש לה' והיה ערכך לפי זרעו זרע חמר שערים בחמשים שקל כסף (ויקרא כז,טז).
"And if from a field of his inheritance, a man will sanctify to G-d, then your evaluation shall be in proportion to its sowing, the sowing of a homer of barley, for fifty shekels of silver (Leviticus 27,16).

The Torah says that when an איש, "man," sanctifies his possessed field (ancestral inheritance), that is, donates it to the Temple treasury, whether it is considered good or bad, it is to be valued בחמשים שקל כסף, "for fifty shekels of silver," (רש"י, ויקרא כז,טז, Rashi, Leviticus 27,16). For each homer of barley seed used in sowing, the evaluation was fifty shekel for forty-nine years until the jubilee year. The gematria of איש, "man," is 311.

איש   311

The gematria of בחמשים שקל כסף, "at fifty shekels of silver" is 990.

בחמשים	400
שקל	430
כסף	160
	990

If a איש, "man," comes to redeem the field, its value is calculated by decreasing from the field's value according to the remaining years until the jubilee year, as stated, ואם אחר היבל יקדיש שדהו וחשב לו הכהן את הכסף על פי השנים הנותרת עד שנת (ויקרא כז,יח) היבל ונגרע, מערכך, "And if after the jubilee year he shall sanctify his field, then the priest shall reckon to him the money according to the years that remain until the year of the jubilee year, and an abatement shall be made from your evaluation" (Leviticus 27,18). The gematria of ונגרע מערכך, "and a reduction shall be made from your evaluation," is 697.

ונגרע	329
מערכך	350
	679

Keeping in mind that sela equals a sacred shekel, Rashi says, והבא לגאול יתן סלע ופונדיון לכל שנה לשנים הנותרות עד שנת היובל (רש״י ויקרא כז,יח), "And one who comes to redeem, shall give a sela and a dupondium for every year for the remaining years, until the jubilee year" (Rashi, Leviticus 27, 18). The process of evaluating a field of one's inheritance, when an איש, "man," comes to redeem the field, is explained fully by Rashi (רש״י, ויקרא כז,טז-כא, Rashi, Leviticus 27, 16-21). This process is also indicated by a gematria. When the gematria of ונגרע מערכך, "and a reduction shall be made from your evaluation," is subtracted from the gematria of בחמשים שקל כסף, "at fifty shekels of silver" the remainder is equal to the gematria of איש, "a man."

$$990$$
$$-679$$
$$\overline{311}$$

The process is connoted by subtracting the value of ונגרע מערכך, "and a reduction shall be made from your evaluation," from the value of בחמשים שקל כסף, "at fifty shekels of silver," to determine what remains for the איש, "man." Thus, this process is indicated by the above computed gematria.

ואם משדה אחזתו יקדיש איש לה' והיה ערכך לפי זרעו זרע
חמר שערים בחמשים שקל כסף (ויקרא כז,טז).

And if from a field of his inheritance, a man will sanctify to G-d, then your evaluation shall be in proportion to its sowing, the sowing of a homer of barley, for fifty shekels of silver (Leviticus 27,16).

The Torah says that if there is a sanctified field of someone's inheritance (ancestral inheritance), and another person wishes to redeem that field, for each זרע חמר שערים, "the sowing of a homer of barley," he must pay בחמשים שקל כסף, "at fifty shekels of silver." The gematria of זרע חמר שערים, "the sowing of a homer of barley," is 1145.

זרע	277
חמר	248
שערים	620
	1145

The gematria of בחמשים שקל כסף, "at fifty shekels of silver" is 990.

בחמשים	400
שקל	430
כסף	160
	990

The difference in gematrioth between זרע חמר שערים, "the sowing of a homer of barley," and בחמשים שקל כסף, "at fifty shekels of silver" is 155.

$$1145$$
$$-990$$
$$155$$

The remainder of 155 can be associated with a situation where one sanctified from a field of his inheritance, but for each of the זרע חמר שערים, "the sowing of a homer of barley," he did not pay בחמשים שקל כסף, "at fifty shekels of silver." The difference between the expressions is calculated, since for each זרע חמר שערים, "the sowing of a homer of barley," there was lacking payment בחמשים שקל כסף, "at fifty shekels of silver."

The Torah tells that if after one sanctified from a field of his inheritance, he did not redeem it, or if the treasurer of the Holy Temple sold it (i.e., for each זרע חמר שערים, "the sowing of a homer of barley," he did not pay בחמשים שקל כסף, "at fifty shekels of silver") then the one who sanctified the field can no longer redeem it; it does not go back to him in the jubilee year, as stated, ואם לא יגאל את השדה ואם מכר את השדה לאיש אחר לא יגאל עוד (ויקרא כז,כ), "And if he will not redeem the field, or if he [the treasurer] had sold the field to a different man, it shall no longer be redeemed" (Leviticus 27,20). The gematria of לא יגאל עוד, "it shall no longer be redeemed," is 155.

לא	31
יגאל	44
עוד	80
	155

Previously it was demonstrated that the remainder 155 can be associated with a situation when one sanctified from a שדה אחזה, "a field of his inheritance," but for each of the sowing of a homer of barley, he did not pay fifty shekels of silver. Now it has been demonstrated that the consequences which will result form such a situation has a gematria of 155. Thus, the two instances of a gematria 155 relate to the same situation.

ואם משדה אחזתו יקדיש איש לה׳ והיה ערכך לפי זרעו זרע חמר שערים בחמשים שקל כסף (ויקרא כז,טז).

And if from a field of his inheritance, a man will sanctify to G-d, then your evaluation shall be in proportion to its sowing, the sowing of a homer of barley, for fifty shekels of silver (Leviticus 27,16).

The Torah says the valuation for שדה אחזתו, "a field of inheritance," (ancestral inheritance) is according to the sowing of חמר שערים בחמשים, "a homer of barley at fifty," silver shekels. The gematria of חמר שערים בחמשים, "a homer of barley at fifty," is 1268.

חמר	248
שערים	620
בחמשים	400
	1268

Thus, the evaluation of a field of inheritance is according to a homer of barley at fifty silver shekels, which is associated with the number 1268.

The Torah also gives the evaluation for שדה מקנתו, "a bought field" (not an ancestral inheritance), as stated, וחשב לו הכהן את מכסת הערכך עד שנת היבל ונתן את הערכך ביום ההוא קדש לה׳ (ויקרא כז,כג), "And the priest shall reckon to him the worth of your evaluation until the jubilee year, and he shall give your evaluation on that day as a holy thing to G-d" (Leviticus 27,23). The gematria of וחשב לו הכהן את מכסת הערכך, "And the priest shall reckon to him the worth of your evaluation," is 1668.

וחשב	316
לו הכהן	116
את	401
מכסת הערכך	835
	1668

Thus, the valuation of a bought field is according to how, "and the priest shall reckon to him the worth of your evaluation until the jubilee year," which is associated with the number 1668. According to the תנא קמא, "the first quoted opinion in a mishnah," the difference between a field of inheritance and a bought field is the method of their evaluation (ערכין, פרק ג משנה ב, ותורה תמימה, ויקרא כז,כב, אות קלד, Arakin, Chapter 3, Mishanh 2, and Torah Teminah, Leviticus 27,22, Letter 134). If two fields, both being the sowing of a homer of barley, are worthless, the field of inheritance will be valued בחמשים, "at fifty," shekels of silver more than the worthless "bought field," as stated, זרע חמר שערים בחמשים שקל כסף (ויקרא כז,טז), the sowing of a homer of barley, for fifty shekels of silver (Leviticus 27,16). The gematria of בחמשים, "at fifty," is 400.

בחמשים	400

The difference between the method of evaluating a field of inheritance and a bought field is the difference between חמר שערים בחמשים, "a homer of barley at fifty," and וחשב לו הכהן את מכסת הערכך, "And the priest shall reckon to him the worth of your evaluation," which have gematrioth of 1268 and 1668 respectively. The difference between their gematrioth is 400.

$$1668 - 1268 = 400$$

Therefore, the difference between the value of a

worthless field of inheritance, and a worthless bought field is בחמשים, "at fifty," shekels of silver, which is equal to the difference in gematria between the methods of evaluating a worthless field of inheritance and a bought field.

Note that Rashi explains the redemption of a bought field somewhat differently (רש״י ויקרא כז, כב, Rashi, Leviticus 27,22). Elsewhere that explanation has been queried and elucidated (משנה למלך, משנה תורה, ספר הפלאה, הלכות ערכין וחרמין, פרק ד, הלכה כו, Mishneh Lemelech, Mishnah Torah, Book of Haflaah, Laws of Valuation of a Person and Consecration of an Object, Chapter 4, Law 26).

Book of Numbers — ספר במדבר

Parashath Bemidbar   פרשת במדבר

 וידבר ה' אל משה במדבר סיני באהל מועד באחד לחדש
השני בשנה השנית לצאתם מארץ מצרים לאמר (במדבר
א,א).

And G-d spoke to Moses in the wilderness of
Sinai, in the tent of the meeting, on the first day
of the second month, in the second year after
their going out of the land of Egypt, saying
(Numbers 1,1).

There is a midrash in reference to this first pasuk of
Parashath Bemidbar which states, וידבר ה' אל משה במדבר סיני.
למה במדבר סיני מכאן שנו חכמים בג' דברים ניתנה התורה. באש ובמים
ובמדבר (מדרש רבה, סדר במדבר, פרשה א, אות ז) "And G-d spoke to
Moses in the wilderness of Sinai.' Why does it say in the
wilderness of Sinai? From here our sages have taught,
through three things the Torah was given, through fire,
through water, and through wilderness" (Midrash Rabba, Sidrah Bemidbar, Parashah 1, Letter 7).

There are various explanations why the Torah was
given through fire, through water, and through wilderness,
but the following one is based on the מעיינה של תורה, "Wellsprings of Torah." The Torah was given through fire, through
water, and through wilderness because these three things
each represent the devotion, which an individual or the
masses of the Children of Israel displayed.

Fire, the first example of devotion, dedication, and
sacrifice, is represented by the fiery furnace into which
אברהם, "Abraham," allowed himself to be thrown (רש"י,
בראשית יא,כח, Rashi, Genesis 11,28). Yet, one might doubt the
significance of this event, since it only involved one individual.

Water, the second example of devotion, dedication,
and sacrifice, is represented by the large mass of people, all

of the Children of Israel, who crossed the Sea of Reeds. Although the ultimate devotion was shown by נחשון בן עמינדב, "Nachshon ben Aminadav," for he jumped into the sea first (רש״י, תהלים קיד,ב, Rashi, Psalms 114,2), the masses of people who followed him also showed devotion, even if not to the same degree. These masses were כבן עמינדב, "like ben Aminadav." Yet, one might doubt the significance of even this event, for although it involved a large mass of people, it lasted only a short span of time.

Wilderness, the third and last example of devotion, dedication, and sacrifice, is represented by the large mass of people, all the Children of Israel, for a long period of time when they entered במדבר, "in the wilderness," willingly, trusting in Hashem, (מעינה של תורה מאת הרב אלכסנדר זושא פרידמן, במדבר א,א, Wellsprings of Torah by Rabbi Alexander Zusia Friedman, Bemidbar 1,1). The faith in Hashem as exhibited by their entering the desert, is the theme of a famous pasuk in Jeremiah, as הלך וקראת באזני ירושלם לאמר כה אמר ה' זכרתי לך חסד נעוריך אהבת כלולתיך לכתך אחרי במדבר בארץ לא זרועה (ירמיה ב,ב ורש״י על הפסוק), "Go and call in the ears of Jerusalem saying, So G-d says, I remember the loving kindness of your youth, the love of your espousals, when you went after Me in the wilderness in a land that was not sown" (Jeremiah 2,2 and Rashi on the pasuk).

According to the explanation presented, through fire refers to אברהם, "Abraham"; through water refers to the masses who were כבן עמינדב, "like ben Aminadav"; and through wilderness refers to במדבר, "in the wilderness," the desert which the Children of Israel entered willingly, trusting in Hashem, where they remained for a long period of time. These three concepts can be connected by a gematria of 248; which is also the number of positive mitzvoth in the Torah. The gematria of אברהם, "Abraham," is 248.

אברהם   248

The gematria of כבן עמינדב, "like ben Aminadav," is 248.

כבן	72
עמינדב	<u>176</u>
	248

The gematria of במדבר, "in the wilderness," is 248.

במדבר	248

Since אברהם, "Abraham," כבן עמינדב, "like ben Aminadav," and במדבר, "in the wilderness," all refer to the same concept, an extremely high level of performing and devotion to G-d, it is appropriate that their gematrioth are equal to 248, the number of the Torah's positive mitzvoth.

ובא אהרן ובניו בנסע המחנה והורדו את פרכת המסך וכסו
בה את ארן העדת (במדבר ד,ה).

And Aaron and his sons shall go in when the
camp shall travel, and they shall take down the
veil of the screen, and cover with it the ark of
the testimony (Numbers 4,5).

The Torah tells that Aaron and his sons were to cover the objects which were holy, and then the sons of Kohath were to carry them (במדבר ד,ה-טו, Numbers 4, 5-15). After a break of one pasuk, which tells the responsibility of Eleazar the son of Aaron, the last four pesukim of the sidrah again tell that Aaron and his sons were to envelop the holy objects and afterwards the tribe of the families of the Kohathites were to carry them (במדבר ד,יז-כ, Numbers 4,17-20).

Interestingly, the Torah does not use the same word for cover in the first set of pesukim (במדבר ד,ה-טו, Numbers 4, 5-15), as in the last set of pesukim (במדבר ד,יז-כ, Numbers 4, 17-20). In the first set of pesukim the word מכסה, "covering," is used; in the last set of pesukim the word כבלע, "as they are being enveloped," is used. However, Rashi comments that the last set of pesukim is indeed referring back to the subject of the first set of pesukim; the last four words in Rashi on the sidrah are (רש״י, במדבר ד,כ) ובלוע שלו הוא כסויו, "and its envelopment, it is its covering" (Rashi, Numbers 4,20).

The question to be addressed is Rashi's choice of words; he writes (רש״י במדבר ד,כ) ובלוע שלו הוא כסויו, "and the envelopment of it, is its covering" (Rashi, Numbers 4,20). He could have written either, ובלועו הוא כסויו, "and its envelopment, is its covering," or ובלוע שלו הוא כסוי שלו, "and the envelopment of it, is the covering of it," both of which have the same meaning, but either of the latter two expressions is more parallel than the mixed expression Rashi in fact uses. It would seem to be to Rashi's advantage to use expressions portraying the greatest degree of parallelism, since he is trying to show that the two expressions have the same meaning, i.e., they represent parallel concepts.

A possible answer can be given with the adoption of a gematria. The last Rashi of Parashath Bemidbar states, ובלוע שלו הוא כסויו, "and its envelopment, it is its covering" (רש״י, במדבר ד,כ, Rashi, Numbers 4,20). The gematria of ובלוע, "and the envelopment," is 114.

ובלוע   114

The gematria of הוא כסויו, "it is its covering," is 114.

הוא	12
כסויו	102
	$\overline{}$
	114

It is conceivable that Rashi used the expression ובלוע שלו הוא כסויו, "and its envelopment, it is its covering", so that he could incorporate the words ובלוע, "and the envelopment," and הוא כסויו, "it is its covering," in a form that their gematrioth would be equal. The fact that these gematrioth are equal is a further indication that these words represent parallel concepts.

Parashath Naso   פרשת נשא

דבר אל אהרן ואל־בניו לאמר כה תברכו את בני ישראל
אמור להם (במדבר ו,כג).
Speak to Aaron and his sons saying, on this wise shall you bless the Children of Israel, saying to them (Numbers 6,23).

Before the priests, the kohanim, may bless the Children of Israel, they must meet specific criteria. One criterion is that there should not be hatred between the priests and the people. A second criterion is that none of the priests should be a מומר לעבודת אלילים, "an apostate for spite, deliberately worshiping idols." Both of these criteria are recorded in Jewish law.

The first criterion is alluded to in the blessing that the priests say before blessing the people, which is recorded in the שלחן ערוך, Shulhan Arukh, as stated, מברכין אשר קדשנו בקדושתו של אהרן וצונו לברך את עמו ישראל באהבה (שלחן ערוך, אורח חיים, סימן קכח, סעיף יא), "They bless, 'Who has hallowed us with the sanctity of Aaron and commanded us to bless His people Israel with love'" (Shulhan Arukh, Orach Hayyim, Siman 128, Seif 11). The gematria of באהבה, "with love," is 15.

באהבה   15

On this word באהבה, "with love," the באר היטב, Bear Haitaiv, says, הטעם שאומריכ באהבה משום דאיתא בזוהר כל כהן דלא רחים לעמא או עמא לא רחמין ליה לא ישא כפיו (באר היטב, שלחן ערוך, אורח חיים, סימן קכח, סעיף יא, סעיף קטן כ), "The reason that they say 'with love,' is that it says in the Zohar, 'any priest who does not feel positive affection for the people, or the people do not feel positive affection for him, should not raise his hands to bless them'" (Bear Haitaiv, Shulhan Arukh, Orach Hayyim, Siman 128, Seif 11, Small Seif 20). Thus, the word

באהבה, "with love," with a gematria of 15, can represent the criterion that there must be love between the priest and the people he blesses.

The second criterion, that none of the priests should be a מומר לעבודת אלילים, "an apostate for spite, deliberately worshiping idols," is also recorded in the שלחן ערוך, Shulhan Arukh, as stated, מומר לעבודת אלילים לא ישא את כפיו (שלחן ערוך, אורח חיים, סימן קכח, סעיף לז), "An apostate for spite, deliberately worshiping idols, should not raise his hands to bless them" (Shulhan Arukh, Orach Hayyim, Siman 128, Seif 37). The first Rashi on עירובין סט:, "Eruvin 69b," explains the significance of a מומר לעבודת אלילים, "an apostate for spite, deliberately worshiping idols," as stated דההוא ודאי חשוד לכל מילי דאמר מר חמורה ע״ג שכל המודה בה ככופר בכל התורה כולה דכתיב וכי תשגו ולא תעשו את כל המצוה האלה (ויקרא כו,יד) ובע״ג משתעי קרא (רש״י, עירובין סה:, ד״ה עד דהוי מומר לע״ג) ,בהוריות, "That such a person is certainly suspected for everything, for it has been said, idol worship is so severe, that all who agree to it are compared to one who denies all the Torah in its entirety, as it is written, 'and if you err and do not observe these commandments' (Leviticus 26,14); and the verse is referring to idol worship, as expressed in Horayoth" (Rashi, Eruvin 69b, header words: Until he was an apostate for spite, deliberately worshiping idols).

Since Rashi refers to a person, and quotes the expression, כל המודה וכו׳, "all who agree to it," this Rashi is quoted here as it seems a clearer source than the Gemara in Horayoth, to which Rashi refers. Although that Gemara quotes the pasuk, it refers to the service and not to a person. Rashi in his commentary on the Chumash, also quotes the expression שכל המודה בע״ז ככפר בכל התורה כלה (רש״י, במדבר טו,כג), "that all who agree to idol worship are compared to one who denies all the Torah in its entirety" (Rashi, Numbers 15,23). This expression is based on the ספרי, "Sifre," on the pasuk.

From these sources it is apparent that a מומר לעבודת

אלילים, "an apostate for spite, deliberately worshiping idols," is considered as if he denied all 613 Mitzvoth. Thus, the number 613, the sum of the mitzvoth, can represent the criterion that none of the priests should be מומר לעבודת אלילים, "an apostate for spite, deliberately worshiping idols."

It has been demonstrated that the word באהבה, "with love," with a gematria of 15, can represent the criterion that there must be positive affection between the priest and the people; it has also been demonstrated that the number 613, the sum of the mitzvoth, can represent the criterion that none of the priests should be מומר לעבודת אלילים, "an apostate for spite, deliberately worshiping idols." The sum of these two numbers is 628.

$$\begin{array}{r} 15 \\ \underline{613} \\ 628 \end{array}$$

Thus, 628 can represent the two specific criteria that the priests must satisfy before they can bless.

In the Torah it is written that Hashem told Moses to tell Aaron and his children how to bless the Bnei Yisroel, as stated, דבר אל אהרן ואל בניו לאמר כה תברכו את בני ישראל אמור להם (במדבר ו,כג), "Speak to Aaron and his sons saying, on this wise shall you bless the Children of Israel, say to them" (Numbers 6,23). The gematria of תברכו, "shall you bless," is 628.

תברכו   628

Since 628 can represent two of the specific criteria which the priests must satisfy before they can bless the Children of Israel, the pasuk can be interpreted as referring to these criteria. The pasuk could mean, כה, "in this manner," תברכו, when these two criteria are met, "shall you bless," the Children of Israel. Let us hope that the Children of Israel will always have priests who meet the criteria, and that their blessing will have the desired results.

ושמו את שמי על בני ישראל ואני אברכם (במדבר ו,כז).
And they shall put My name upon the Children
of Israel, and I will bless them (Numbers 6,27).

In this week's sidrah G-d tells Moses to tell the priests to put שמי, "My name," upon the Children of Israel, and then אברכם, "I will bless them." The ספרי, "Sifre," on the word אברכם, "I will bless them," says that one of the pesukim which is an example the fruition of this blessing is the pasuk from Parashath Ki Thavo, which states, יפתח ה׳ לך את אוצרו הטוב את השמים, "G-d will open to you His good treasure, the heaven" (ספרי, במדבר ו,כז, Sifre, Numbers 6,27). Three pesukim before this quoted one, the Torah makes G-d's blessing dependent upon keeping His commandments; two pesukim before this quoted one, the Torah also says that G-d's name will be called upon you (דברים כח,ט-י, Deuteronomy 28,9-10). Having G-d's name called upon one, is reminiscent of the priests putting G-d's name on the Children of Israel.

It could be that the ratiocination of the Sifre saying that the fruition of the word אברכם, "I will bless them," is a pasuk which makes G-d's blessing dependent upon keeping the commandments, so too the fruition of אברכם, "I will bless them," is also dependent upon observing the commandments.

An integral part of the blessing could be that G-d will help His people to observe His commandments. Similar to what the Gemara Shabbath says, בא ליטהר מסייעים אותו (שבת קד.), "If one comes to purify himself, he is helped" (Shabbath 104a). The Rambam says, והוא מה שאמרו רז״ל בא לטהר מסייעין אותו כלומר ימצא עצמו נעזר על הדבר (משנה תורה, ספר המדע, הלכות תשובה, פרק ו, הלכה ה), "And it is what our Rabbis, who should be remembered for a blessing, have said, if one comes to purify himself, he receives divine help. That means to say, he finds himself aided in the matter" (Mishnah Torah, Book of Hamadda, Laws of Repentance, Chapter 6, Law 5).

G-d told Moses to tell the priests to put שמי, "My name," upon the Children of Israel, and then אברכם, "I will bless them." The gematria of שמי, "My name," is 350.

שמי 350

The gematria of אברכם, "I will bless them," is 263.

אברכם 263

The sum of the gematrioth of שמי, "My name," and אברכם, "I will bless them," is 613.

$$
\begin{array}{r}
350 \\
263 \\
\hline
613
\end{array}
$$

Since there is a total of 613 Mitzvoth (מכות כג:, Makkoth 23b), the sum of the gematrioth of these two words being equal to 613 may indicate that an integral part of the blessing could be that G-d will help the Children of Israel to observe His commandments.

ושמו את שמי על בני ישראל ואני אברכם (במדבר ו,כז).

And they shall put My name upon the Children of Israel and I will bless them (Numbers 6,27).

If the priests, the kohanim, bless the Children of Israel as commanded, then G-d will give them His blessings. The gematria of ואני אברכם, "and I will bless them," is 330.

$$
\begin{array}{r}
\text{ואני} \quad 67 \\
\text{אברכם} \quad 263 \\
\hline
330
\end{array}
$$

Although it is a mitzvah to have the priests bless the people also outside the Beth Hamikdash, the ideal realization of the mitzvah is in the Beth Hamikdash. The Gemara Sotah says, ושמו את שמי שמי המיוחד לי יכול אף בגבולין כן נאמר כאן ושמו

את שמי (במדבר ו,כז) ונאמר להלן לשום את שמו שם (דברים יב,ה) מה ,להלן בית הבחירה אף כאן בבית הבחירה (סוטה לח.) "'And you shall put My name', My name which is unique for Me. One might think, that also outside the Temple, it should be so. It is stated here, 'And you shall put My name' (Numbers 6,27), and it is stated afterwards, 'To put His name there' (Deuteronomy 12,5). Just as afterwards it indicates the Temple, also here it indicates the Temple" (Sotah 38a). Thus, the ideal realization of ואני אברכם, "and I will bless them," with a gematria of 330, can only occur when Hashem returns to Zion, and the Beth Hamikdash is rebuilt.

Just prior to the Priests' blessing in the Musaf service there is a prayer which begins with the words ותערב עליך עתירתנו, "And may our entreaty be pleasant to You." In that prayer it is written, ותחזינה עינינו בשובך לציון ברחמים, "And let our eyes behold when You return to Zion with mercy." The gematria of בשובך, "when You return," is 330.

בשובך   330

The word בשובך, "when you return," has a gematria of 330, just as the expression ואני אברכם, "and I will bless them," has a gematria of 330. The fact that these gematrioth are identical, and the prayer which begins with ותערב עליך עתירתנו, "And may our entreaty be pleasant to You," is said just prior to the priest's blessing, could well be to stress that we pray to be able to behold בשובך, "when you return," to Zion, when the ideal realization of ואני אברכם, "and I will bless them," will occur.

כף אחת עשרה זהב מלאה קטרת (במדבר ז,יד).
One spoon ten (shekels its weight) of gold full
of incense (Numbers 7,14).

The incense offerings of the princes were presented by them on golden spoons. On this pasuk Rashi says that the incense offered by the princes is the only instance of an individual offering incense on the outer altar (רש״י, במדבר ז,יד, Rashi, Numbers 7,14). The Gemara says, בנשיאים הוראת שעה היתה (מנחות נ:), "With the princes, it was a one time dispensation" (Menahoth 50b). The gematria of הוראת, "dispensation," is 612.

הוראת   612

In a different tractate, the Gemara says that the idea of a one-time dispensation can apply to all the commandments except that of idol worship (סנהדרין צ., Sanhedrin 90a). Since there is a total of 613 Commandments, and one-time dispensations can apply to all the commandments except idol worship, that is, it can be applied to 612 Commandments, therefore this application to 612 Commandments could be hinted to by the gematria of הוראת, "dispensation," which is equal to 612.

ויהי איש אחד מצרעה ממשפחת הדני ושמו מנוח ואשתו עקרה ולא ילדה (שופטים יג,ב).

And there was a certain man from Tzorah, from the family of the Danites, and his name was Manoah; and his wife was barren, and bore not (Judges 13,2).

Manoah had a barren wife who is described as ולא ילדה, "and bore not." The gematria of ולא ילדה, "and bore not," is 86.

ולא	37
ילדה	49
	86

The Gemara Nedarim says, ארבעה חשובין כמת עני ומצורע וסומא ומי שאין לו בנים (נדרים סד:), "Four are considered as if they were dead: A poor man, a metzora, a blind person, and one who has no children" (Nedarim 64b). In the Torah there is an instance of a woman who did not have children and considered herself as dead (א,ל בראשית ,רש״י, Rashi, Genesis 30,1); it is a punishment or a misfortune when a woman is barren. Punishment and misfortune are associated with G-d's attribute of strict justice, which is identified with His name of אלקים, "G-d," as stated, זה השם מדת הדין הוא (רש״י, בראשית א,ח), "And G-d remembered. This name is identified with His attribute of strict justice," (Rashi, Genesis 8,1). The gematria of אלקים, "G-d," is 86.

אלקים   86

Since ולא ילדה, "and bore not," is a punishment or a misfortune, which is associated with אלקים, "G-d," it is appropriate that both terms should have the same gematria.

Parashath Behaalosecha   פרשת בהעלתך
or Hanukkah   או חנוכה

וידבר ה׳ אל משה לאמר. דבר אל אהרן ואמרת אליו
בהעלתך את הנרת אל מול פני המנורה יאירו שבעת הנרות.
ויעש כן אהרן אל מול פני המנורה העלה נרתיה כאשר צוה
ה׳ את משה (במדבר ח,א־ג).

And G-d spoke to Moses saying. Speak tc Aaron
and say to him: When you light the lamps,
opposite the face of the candlestick shall the
seven lamps give light. And Aaron did so, opposite the face of the candlestick he lit the seven
lamps, as G-d had commanded Moses (Numbers 8, 1-3).

In the first three pesukim of Parashath Behaalosecha
G-d tells Moses to tell Aaron to light the menorah. There are
two striking questions. One, after the Torah says that Aaron
did as he was commanded, why does the Torah repeat אל מול
פני המנורה העלה נרתיה כאשר צוה ה׳ את משה, "opposite the face of
the candlestick he lit the seven lamps, as G-d had commanded Moses"? Why say, he lit the the menorah as he was
commanded; is it not obvious that Aaron did as he was
commanded? Two, Rashi comments on the words ויעש כן
אהרן, "And Aaron did so," that these words are to tell the the
praise of Aaron, that he did not veer (רש״י, במדבר ח,ג, Rashi,
Numbers 8,3). Why was the fact that Aaron, the Kohen
Gadol, did as G-d commanded him considered a praise for
him?

To answer these two striking questions, a probe into
the deeper meaning of these pesukim could be helpful. The
word בהעלתך, "when you light," can be translated to mean,
"when you raise yourself up," an indication that there were
were steps in front of the menorah (רש״י, במדבר ח,ב, Rashi,
Numbers 8,2). The word נר, "lamp," in an allegorical sense,

can refer to a commandment, as stated, כי נר מצוה ותורה אור וגו׳ (משלי ו,כג), "For the commandment is a lamp, and the Torah is light, etc.," (Proverbs 6,23). Since a commandment can be referred to as a lamp, then commandments can be refered to as lamps; therefore the first part of the pasuk from Parashath Behaalosecha can mean, when you raise yourself up to perform the commandments.

In order to perform the commandments, a knowledge of Torah is necessary, as can be demonstrated from two separate sources. The first source is from a Rashi on the Torah, which says that anyone who is not be included among those who have learned, can also can not be included among those who perform (the commandments properly) (רש״י, דברים יב,כח, Rashi, Deuteronomy 12,28). The second source is from a Rashi on the Gemara, which says that the reason one should not live with a neighbor who is an ignoramus is that he does not know the fine points of the commandments (רש״י, שבת סג. ד״ה אל תדור בשכונתו, Rashi, Sabbath 63a, header words: Do not live in his neighborhood).

Since in order to perform the commandments a knowledge of Torah is necessary, how can one acquire such knowledge? The Mishnah says one method of acquiring knowledge of Torah is through יראה, "reverence of G-d," (אבות, פרק ו, משנה ד, Avoth, Chapter 6, Mishnah 4). But reverence and wisdom are indispensable for each other, as the Mishnah states, אם אין חכמה אין יראה. אם אין יראה אין חכמה (אבות, פרק ג, משנה יז), "If there is no wisdom, there is no reverence. If there is no reverence, there is no wisdom" (Avoth, Chapter 3, Mishnah 17). Thus, one of the ways of acquiring knowledge of Torah is via wisdom, for which reverence is indispensable. So raising oneself up to perform the commandments could include reaching a level of reverence of G-d, and a level of wisdom.

The next issue is how may one acquire חכמה, "wisdom." When one prays, the Gemara says, אמר רבי יצחק הרוצה שיחכים ידרים ושיעשיר יצפין (בבא בתרא כה:), "Rabbi Isaac said, One who wants to become wise should face to the south; and one who wants to become rich should face to the north" (Baba Bathra 25b).

He who wishes to gain חכמה, "wisdom," should pray facing toward the south since the candlestick was on the southern side of the בית המקדש, "Temple." Further note, that he who gains חכמה, "wisdom," can gain knowledge of Torah, as the Midrash says, ואין חכמה אלא תורה (מדרש תנחומא, פרשת וילך, אות ב), "And there is no knowledge except Torah" (Midrash Tanhuma, Parashath Vayyelech, Letter 2).

To summarize, it is necessary for one to raise himself up to perform the commandments; in order to perform the commandments, a knowledge of Torah is necessary. This knowledge of Torah can be acquired via חכמה, "wisdom," which may be gained by praying facing toward the south. Now the two striking questions can be answered. The first part of the pasuk from Parashath Behaalosecha can mean, when you raise yourself up to perform the commandments. The second part of the pasuk can mean, it is necessary to have knowledge of the Torah, which can be acquired via חכמה, "wisdom," which may be gained by praying facing toward the south. The next pasuk can mean, and Aaron did so, he prayed facing toward the menorah when he raised himself up to perform commandments as G-d had commanded Moses. The first question was, why the repetition? The answer, according to this proposed explanation, is that when the Torah added אל מול פני המנורה העלה נרתיה כאשר צוה ה׳ את משה, "opposite the face of the candlestick he lit the seven lamps, as G-d had commanded Moses," it is not a repetition; it is imparting that Aaron always prayed toward toward the south. The second question was, why was Aaron, the Kohen Gadol, doing as G-d commanded him considered a praise for him? The answer is that Aaron did not veer; he never once prayed toward the north, which could have resulted in his becoming rich. He always prayed toward the south, for he always valued חכמה, "wisdom," more than riches. This continuity is a praise of Aaron.

This explanation of the pesukim also gives meaning to a gematria. The Midrash says, גדולה התורה שבה הבדיל הקב"ה את ישראל עמו מאומות העולם (אוצר מדרשים, נאסף ונערך ע"יי יהודה דוד תורה תלמוד בעניין חמישי פרק ד"ה עט עמוד (אייזענשטיין,), "Great is the Torah; for with it the Holy One has separated Israel, His people, from the nations of the world" (Otsar Hamidrashim, compiled and edited by Judah David Eisenstein, page 79, header words: Chapter five on the subject of Torah Study). The pesukim at the beginning of פרשת בהעלתך, Parashath Behaalosecha, could mean, when you raise yourself up to perform the commandments, you should pray מול, "toward," the south, to gain חכמה, "wisdom," which is one of the methods of acquiring knowledge of Torah. It is through knowledge of Torah that G-d distinguishes the Children of Israel from the other nations. The combined gematria of בהעלתך, Behaalosecha, and מול, "toward," is 603.

בהעלתך	527
מול	76
	603

Just before the end of Parashath Behar, the Torah states, כי לי בני ישראל עבדים עבדי הם אשר הוצאתי אותם מארץ מצרים אני ה' אלקיכם (ויקרא כה,נה), "For to Me are the Children of Israel are servants; they are My servants, whom I brought out of the land of Egypt; I am Hashem, your G-d," (Leviticus 25,55). The gematria of בני ישראל, "the Children of Israel, is 603.

בני	62
ישראל	541
	603

On this pasuk the Haamek Davar says, שנשתעבדו לי בקבלת התורה (העמק דבר מאת הרב נפתלי צבי יהודה ברלין מוואלאזין, ויקרא כה,נה), "In order that you shall serve Me, with the acceptance of the Torah" (Haamek Davar by Rabbi Naphtali Zevi Judah Berlin from Volozhin, Leviticus 25,55). Thus, this gematria can show that through knowledge of Torah G-d distinguishes the Children of Israel from the other nations.

This explanation of the pesukim and the gematria can give added significance to Hanukkah. The concluding pesukim read in the Torah portion of the last day of Hanukkah in most congregations are the first four pesukim of Parashath Beha-alosecha. On the second pasuk of Parashath Behaalosecha Rashi says that when Aaron saw the dedication offerings of the princes he was discouraged. G-d reassured Aaron that his lighting of the lamps is greater than their dedication offerings (רש"י, במדבר ח,ב, Rashi, Numbers 8,2). The Ramban says that the lamps refer to of of Hanukkah (רמב"ן במדבר ח,ב, Ramban, Numbers 8,2). The Ramban quotes from מגלת סתרים לרבנו נסים, Megillath Sesarim of Rabbeinu Nissim, saying, ראיתי במדרש כיון שהקריבו שנים עשר שבטים ולא הקריב שבט לוי וכו' אמר לו הקב"ה למשה, דבר אל אהרן ואמרת אליו יש חנכה אחרת שיש בה הדלקת הנרות ואני עושה בה לישראל על ידי בניך נסים ותשועה וחנכה שקרויה על שמם, והיא חנוכת בני חשמונאי (רמב"ן, במדבר ח,ב), "And I saw in the Midrash, since the twelve tribes brought their offerings and the tribe of Levi did not offer, etc., the Holy One, blessed be He, said to Moses. Speak to Aaron and say to him, There will be another inauguration ("Hanukkah") that has lamp kindling, and I will make it by means of miracles and salvation for Israel through your sons and an inauguration which will be called with their name. It is the inauguration of the House of Hasmoneans" (Ramban, Numbers 8,2).

Why are the lamps of Hanukkah considered so great? According to the explanation presented, the lighting of the lamps refers to the raising of oneself up to perform Commandments by acquiring knowledge of Torah. It is through knowledge of Torah that G-d distinguishes the Children of Israel from the other nations. Thus, the Hanukkah lamps represent following the Torah dictates to perform the Commandments. This message of the hanukkah lamps can be the key to how the Children of Israel were able to survive so many years of exile. This message of the Hanukkah lamps could be the reason why G-d reassured Aaron that their lighting is greater than the dedication offerings of the princes.

אלה מסעי בני ישראל לצבאתם ויסעו (במדבר י,כח).

These were the journeys of the Children of Israel, according their hosts; and they set forward (Numbers 10,28).

In this sidrah, the Torah finishes its discussion of the travels of Bnei Yisroel with the word ויסעו, "and they set forward." The gematria of ויסעו, "and they set forward," is 152.

ויסעו   152

The word ויסעו, "and they set forward," is used throughout the preceding pesukim, (במדבר י,יב-כח, Numbers 10,12-28). There is a controversy if the Beth Hamikdash stood in both the portion of Benjamin and Judah, or if the Beth Hamikdash stood in an area which was not the portion of any particular tribe. The Gemara Zevachim assumes that Jerusalem was divided between the tribes, but the Gemara Yoma presents a controversy if Jerusalem was so divided (תוספות, יומא יד., ד"ה ירושלים לא נתחלקה לשבטים, וגם זבחים נג:-נד.,) וגם ר"ע מברטנורה, זבחים, פרק ה, משנה ד, וגם ספרי ומלבים דברים לג,יב, Tosafoth, Yoma 14a, header words: Jerusalem was not divided by tribes, and also Zevahim 53b-54a, and also Rabbi Ovadiah Bertinoro, Zevahim, Chapter 5, Mishnah 4, and also

Sifrei and Malbim Deuteronomy 33,12). The Torah records that Joseph cried on the neck of Benjamin, as stated, ויפל על צוארי בנימן אחיו ויבך ובנימן בכה על צואריו (בראשית מה,יד), "And he fell on the neck of Benjamin, his brother, and cried; and Benjamin cried on his neck" (Genesis 45,14). The gematria of בנימן, "Benjamin," is 152.

בנימן   152

On this verse, Rashi simply decided and states that both the first and the second Temples were in the portion of Benjamin (רש"י, בראשית מה,יד, Rashi, Genesis 45,14). Thus, 152 represents the tribe in whose portion the Temple was to be built. Consequently, 152 represents the area to which the Children of Israel would be traveling after they settled in the Land of Israel. It is appropriate that ויסעו, "and they set forward," and בנימן, "Benjamin," should have the same gematria; for the Children of Israel "set forward," three times a year, to travel to the Beth Hamikdash which was in the portion of Benjamin.

The Children of Israel setting forth three times a year to go to the Beth Hamikdash, which was in the portion of Benjamin, was a unifying factor. The traveling from all over the Land of Israel to one place, brought the Children of Israel together. This unifying of the Children of Israel could be what Jacob alluded to when he said האספו, "gather yourselves together," as stated, ויקרא יעקב אל בניו ויאמר האספו ואגידה לכם את אשר יקרא אתכם באחרית הימים (בראשית מט,א), "And Jacob called to his sons and said, 'Gather yourselves together and I will tell you what will befall you in the end of days'" (Genesis 49,1). The gematria of האספו, "Gather yourselves together," is 152.

האספו   152

Thus, 152 represents a unifying factor which brought the Children of Israel together. At a time of gathering, all the

men of the Children of Israel are considered companions, as
the Rabbi Ovadiah Bertinoro states, דאמר קרא ויאסף כל איש
ישראל אל העיר כאיש אחד חברים קראם הכתוב בשעת אסיפה כולם
חברים, ורגל שעת אסיפה היא (ר״ע מברטנורה, חגיגה, פרק ג, משנה ו, ד״ה
התרומה על אף הרגל ובשעת), "That the verse says, 'And he
gathered together every man of Israel to the city like one
man, companions.' The verse calls them at the time of their
gathering, all of them are companions, and a holiday is a time
of gathering," (Rabbi Ovadiah Bertinoro, Hagigah, Chapter 3,
Mishnah 6, header words: And at the time of the holiday also
for the Terumah). This universal law of companionship would
further unify the Children of Israel.

It is appropriate that ויסעו, "and they set forward,"
בנימן, "Benjamin," and האספו, "gather yourselves together,"
have the same gematria; for the setting forward of the Children of Israel to the Beth Hamikdash in the portion of Benjamin, was a unifying factor that caused them to gather themselves together.

ויהי בנסע הארן ויאמר משה קומה ה' ויפצו איביך וינסו
משנאיך מפניך. ובנחה יאמר שובה ה' רבבות אלפי ישראל
(במדבר י,לה-לו).

And it was when the ark would travel, that
Moses said, 'Rise up G-d, and let Your enemies
be scattered, and let those that hate You flee
before You.' And when it would rest, he said,
'Return G-d to the myriads of thousands of
Israel' (Numbers 10, 35-36).

In Parashath Behaalosecha the two pesukim quoted
above are set apart from the others by an upside down,
backward נ, "nun," preceding and following the verses (במדבר
י,לה-לו, Numbers 10, 35-36). The gematria of נ, nun, is 50.

נ   50

What is the significance of these nuns? The Gemara Shabbath says that these two verses between the nuns are, "considered a book by itself" (Shabbath 116a). There is a different Gemara which says that the purpose of a book is (גיטין כא.), "to narrate something," (Gittin 21b). Since the purpose of a book is to narrate something, and these two pesukim which were previously quoted are considered a book by themselves, therefore these two pesukim tell a ספירת דברים בפני עצמו, "a unique story," a novel message.

The story of the exile of the Children of Israel first began with Abram, as stated, ויאמר ה' אל אברם לך לך מארצך וממולדתך ומבית אביך אל הארץ אשר אראך. ואעשך לגוי גדול ואברכך ואגדלה שמך והיה ברכה (בראשית יב,א־ב), "And G-d said to Abram, 'Go out for yourself, from your land, from your kindred, and from your father's house, to the land which I will show you. And I will make you into a great nation, and I will bless you, and I will make your name great, and you shall be a blessing" (Genesis 12,1-2). The gematria of לך, "go out," is 50.

לך   50

The gematria of לך, "for yourself," is 50.

לך   50

On the second pasuk just quoted Rashi says, לפי שהדרך גורמת לשלשה דברים, ממעטת פריה ורביה וממעטת את הממון וממעטת את השם לכך הוזקק לשלש ברכות הללו שהבטיחו על הבנים ועל הממון ועל השם (רש"י, בראשית יב,ב), "Since traveling causes three things: It diminishes being fruitful and multiplying (propagation), it diminishes money, and it diminishes reputation, therefore he was bound to these three blessings. He was promised about sons, about money and about reputation" (Rashi, Genesis 12,2). Thus, לך לך, "Go out for yourself," with a gematria of 50 and 50, denotes the three blessings that Hashem blessed Abraham.

The Midrash Tanhuma states, סימן נתן לו הקדוש ברוך הוא

לאברהם, שכל מה שארע לו ארע לבניו (מדרש תנחומא, פרשת לך לך, אות ט), "G-d gave a sign to Abraham, that all which happened to him, will happen to his descendants" (Midrash Tanhuma, Parashath Lech Lecha, Letter 9). Just as Abraham received these three blessings because he was to be uprooted, and thus forced to travel, so too the Bnei Yisroel can receive these three blessings because they will be forced to travel in exile. No people could have withstood so many long, harsh exiles, with so much torture, and with so many evil decrees through which the Bnei Yisroel suffered, and emerged as successfully as the Bnei Yisroel, without these blessings from Hashem. The exiles of the people of Israel are a unique story. The blessings with which G-d blessed Abraham, and with which G-d has and will also bless his descendants, the people of Israel, are what make this story unique.

One reason for the upside down, backward nun נ, "nun," preceding and following the two verses (Numbers 10, 35-36) in Parashath Behaalosecha, could be to allude to לך לך, "Go out for yourself," since the gematria of נ, "nun," and נ, "nun," is 50 and 50; and the gematria of לך לך, "Go out for yourself," is likewise 50 and 50. Just as G-d had blessed Abraham in his travels with three blessings, so too He has and will bless the people of Israel with these same blessings. These blessings may well be the unique story of the two pesukim which are set apart from the others by an upside down, backward נ, "nun," preceding and following the verses (במדבר י,לה-לו, Numbers 10, 35-36) in Parashath Beha-alosecha. The reason these verses are considered a book by themselves, could be that these two pesukim tell a ספירת דברים בפני עצמו, "a unique story," a novel message.

One can easily read this novel message in these two verses, in the form of a דרוש, "homily." The verses would be explained as follows: ויהי בנסע הארן, And it will be that when the nation of Israel is forced to travel, that is, to go into exile, that they will take the ark with them. They will go into exile with the Torah and the observance of its mitzvoth. Although the word ויהי, "And it was," usually refers to the past (בראשית א,ג, Genesis 1,3), בדרך דרוש, "by the route of a homily," it can be applied to the future. The Mekhilta says, דבר אחר ויהי לי לישועה, היה לי לא נאמר אלא ויהי לי, היה לי לשעבר ויהי לי לעתיד לבא (מכלתא, שמות טו,ב, פרשת בשלח, ג), "Another explanation for, And it will be for me a salvation: It does not say, 'and it was for me,' but 'and it will be for me'; 'and it was for me,' indicates the past, 'and it will be for me,' indicates the future to come," (Mekhilta, Exodus 15,2, Parashath Beshallach, 3). ויאמר משה, And Moses said, that is, And Moses prayed to G-d: קומה ה', G-d, arise and be with them; fulfill the three blessings that were promised to Abraham. ויפצו איביך וינסו משנאיך מפניך, and let Your enemies be scattered, and let those that hate You flee before You. These enemies are the enemies of the people of Israel, enemies who would like to destroy the people of Israel and prevent the fulfillment of these three blessings. ובנחה יאמר, And when it is left in its place, that is, when the people go into exile, and leave behind the ark, i.e., they desert the ark: When they go into exile and abandon the Torah and forsake the mitzvoth, Moses prayed to G-d: שובה ה' רבבות אלפי ישראל, G-d, return to the myriads of thousands of Israel. Even when the Children of Israel are not worthy to have You with them, please return to them to fulfill the three blessings that were promised to Abraham.

May Hashem bless the Jews in exile with the three blessings which He promised to Abraham; and may He bring an end to this exile soon, במהרה בימינו אמן!

ויען יהושע בן נון משרת משה מבחריו ויאמר אדני משה כלאם (במדבר יא,כח).

And Joshua the son of Nun, the minister of Moses from his boyhood, answered and said, 'My master Moses, cause them to cease' (Numbers 11,28).

When Eldad and Medad prophesied in the camp, and Joshua the son of Nun requested that Moses stop them, he used the word כלאם, "cause them to cease." The gematria of כלאם, "cause them to cease," is 91.

כלאם   91

How did Joshua the son of Nun know that Moses could stop Eldad and Medad from prophesying?

Moses' power and ability as a prophet came from Hashem. In reference to Hashem sending Moses, the Torah calls Moses an angel, as stated, ונצעק אל ה׳ וישמע קלנו וישלח מלאך ויצאנו ממצרים והנה אנחנו בקדש עיר קצה גבולך (במדבר כ,טז), "And we cried to G-d, and He heard our voice, and He sent an angel, and he took us out from Egypt, and behold we are in Kadesh, a city in the uttermost of your border" (Numbers 20,16). The gematria of מלאך, "angel," is 91.

מלאך   91

Rashi says that the angel of this verse is Moses, as stated, זה משה מכאן שהנביאים קרואים מלאכים (רש״י, במדבר כ,טז, ד״ה מלאך), "This is Moses; from here it is learned that prophets are called angels" (Rashi, Numbers, 20,16, header word: Angel). It is apparent that while Moses, a prophet sent by Hashem, was called an angel, of course he was not an actual angel. Moses was a mortal human being who ate food and was later to die; however he had some powers and qualities of an angel. Perhaps one of these could be the ability to control another person's faculty to prophesy.

The Malbim says that Moses could stop Eldad and Medad from prophesying because it was Moses himself who empowered them to prophecy, as he states, מצד זה בעצמו אמר שראוי שמשה יכלא וימנע שפע הנבואיית מהם, אחר שכל כח נבואתם הוא מצנורו של משה ומאצילות רוחו, הלא יש בכחו למנוע מהם שפע ההוא, כי זה תלוי ברצונו להשפיע או לכלוא את הרוח וכו׳ (התורה והמצוה, מאת הרב מאיר ליבוש מלבי״ם, במדבר יא,כח), "From this angle itself he said, it is suitable that Moses could and should restrain the flow of prophecy from them, since all the strength of their prophecy was from the channel of Moses, and from the emanation of his spirit. Behold it is in his strength to restrain from them that flow; for this is dependent on his will to cause the spirit to flow or to cease, etc." (The Torah and the Mitzvah by Rabbi Meir Lebush Malbim, Numbers 11,28).

Now, the question of how did Joshua the son of Nun know that Moses could stop Eldad and Medad from prophesying, can be answered. Since Moses, when being sent by Hashem as a prophet, is called an angel, and a prophet who empowered another person to prophecy, can control that person's faculty to prophesy, so Moses could stop Eldad and Medad from prophesying. The word that Joshua the son of Nun used when he requested Moses to stop Eldad and Medad from prophesying was כלאם, "cause them to cease." The word the Torah uses, which indicates that prophets are called angels is מלאך, "angel." This ability of a prophet who empowered another person to prophecy, to control that person's faculty to prophecy, could be why כלאם, "cause them to cease," and מלאך, "angel," have the exact same gematria; they also are spelled with the exact same letters. Since כלאם, "cause them to cease," and מלאך, "angel," have the exact same gematria, it can be implied that Joshua the son of Nun requested Moses use his power as a מלאך, "angel," to stop Eldad and Medad from prophesying.

לא כן עבדי משה בכל ביתי נאמן הוא (במדבר יב,ז).

Not so with My servant Moses; in all My house
he is trusted (Numbers 12,7).

Hashem referred to Moses as עבדי, "My servant." The gematria of עבדי, "My servant," is 86.

עבדי   86

When Moses prayed to G-d to heal Miriam, he employed the expression heal נא לה, "her please," as stated, "ויצעק משה אל ה׳ לאמר קל נא רפא נא לה (במדבר יב,יג), "And Moses cried out to G-d, saying, G-d, please heal her, please" (Numbers 12,13). The gematria of נא לה, "her, please," is 86.

נא	51
לה	35
	86

When G-d's character of strict justice is alluded to, He is referred to as אלקים, "G-d," (רש״יי, בראשית א,א וח,א, Rashi, Genesis 1,1 and 8,1). The gematria of אלקים, "G-d," is 86.

אלקים   86

The reason why G-d referred to Moses as עבדי, "My servant," which has a gematria of 86, could be because 86 is also the gematria of אלקים, "G-d." Thus, Hashem was saying that Moses is considered My servant, even if I were to judge him with strict justice.

The reason why Moses, when he prayed that G-d should heal Miriam, employed the expression נא לה, "her, please," which has a gematria of 86, could be because 86 is also the gematria of אלקים, "G-d." Thus, Moses was praying that G-d should overrule His character of strict justice and heal Miriam.

Since עבדי, "My servant," and נא לה, "her please," have the identical gematria, they can be connected to each other without an affiliation to the gematria of אלקים, "G-d." When Moses prayed that Hashem should heal Miriam, he prayed using his power as G-d's servant. Moses was saying that since G-d has called him His servant, therefore He should please heed his prayer and heal Miriam. Thus, עבדי, "My servant," and נא לה, "her, please," can be connected to each other directly.

Parashath Shelach Lecha   פרשת שלח לך

ויציאו דבת הארץ אשר תרו אתה אל בני ישראל לאמר
הארץ אשר עברנו בה לתור אתה ארץ אכלת יושביה הוא
וכל העם אשר ראינו בתוכה אנשי מדות (במדבר יג,לב).
And they put forth an evil report of the land
which they had spied out to the Children of
Israel, saying: The land which we passed
through to spy it out, is a land which consumes
its inhabitants, and all the people whom we saw
in it were men of stature (Numbers 13,32).

When describing the denigrating report of the land
that most of spies put forth, the Torah uses the expression
דבת הארץ, "evil report of the land." Targum Onkelos defines
the word דבת, "evil report," as שום ביש, "a bad valuation,"
(תרגום אונקלוס, במדבר יג,לב, Targum Onkelos, Number 13,32).
The gematria of דבת הארץ, "evil report of the land," is 702.

דבת	406
הארץ	296
	702

Thus, the number 702 can be associated with the
pernicious report which some of the spies gave. This pernicious report caused distress to the Children of Israel, which
led to their sinning, and G-d's punishment.

After this series of events, the Children of Israel felt
themselves no longer obligated toward the mitzvoth. To combat this mistaken notion, one man, Zelophehad, deliberately
violated the mitzvah of Shabbath; he was the one who gathered wood on Shabbath, precisely so as to incur the death
penalty. Tosafoth states, (שבת דף צו:) נראה לרשב״א דסבר לה כמ״ד
צלפחד היינו מקושש ומעשה המקושש היה בתחלת ארבעים מיד אחר מעשה
מרגלים דאמר במדרש דלשם שמים נתכוין שהיו אומרים ישראל כיון שנגזר

עליהן שלא ליכנס לארץ ממעשה מרגלים שוב אין מחויבין במצות עמד וחילל שבת כדי שיהרג ויראו אחרים (תוספות, בבא בתרא קיט:, ד״ה אפילו קטנה שבהן לא נשאת פחות מארבעים שנה; וגם סוף דברי דוד מאת הרב דוד בן שמואל הלוי, פרשת שלח לך, ד״ה ויהיו בני ישראל וגו׳ בגנותן של ישראל), "It appears that Rabbi Shimon ben Elazar is of the same opinion as the one who says, (Shabbath page 96b) Zelophehad was the wood gatherer. And the event of the wood gatherer was at the beginning of the forty (years), immediately after the event of the spies, as it says in the midrash. He had intended for the sake of Heaven. For Israel were saying, since it has been decreed upon them that they can not enter the land, because of the event of the spies, they are no longer obligated with the commandments. He stood up and profaned the Shabbath in order that he should be killed, and others will see" (Tosafoth, Baba Bathra 119b, header words: Even the youngest of them would not get married at less than forty years old; and also the last comments of Divrei David by Rabbi David ben Samuel Halevi, Parashath Shelach Lecha, header words: And while the Children of Israel etc. about the defamation of Israel). The gematria of שבת, "Shabbath," is 702.

שבת 702

Therefore, the violation of the mitzvah of Shabbath by the wood gatherer, was an attempt to combat the mistaken assumption that the obligation of the commandments no longer applies. The gematria of שבת, "Shabbath," is equivalent to the gematria of דבת הארץ, "evil report of the land." The reason for this equivalence can be readily comprehended; the דבת הארץ, "evil report of the land," by some of the spies, caused the Children of Israel to feel no longer obligated toward the mitzvoth, which the wood gatherer sought to combat with violation of the mitzvah of שבת, "Shabbath."

אני ה׳ דברתי אם לא זאת אעשה לכל העדה הרעה הזאת
הנועדים עלי במדבר הזה יתמו ושם ימתו (במדבר יד,לה).
I, G-d have spoken; surely I will do this to all
this evil congregation, who are gathered together against Me; in this desert they will be
consumed and there they will die (Numbers
14,35).

The pasuk says that the congregation who gathered
together against G-d would be forced to die in the desert.
There are seemingly three difficulties with this pasuk. First,
why is it necessary to mention the desert; is it not already
known that the Children of Israel were in the desert? Second,
why is it necessary to say הזה, "this," when there was no
other desert where the Children of Israel were located? Third,
why is it necessary to use the word ושם, "and there"? Simply
say here they will be consumed, or here they will die. Perhaps
these three difficulties can be resolved by means of a
gematria.

The Torah is compared to a desert; just as a desert is
limitless, so too the Torah is limitless. A פסיקתא, "Pesikta,"
quoted by the חומש תורה שלמה, Chumash Torah Sheleimah,
says, מה המדבר הזה אין לו סוף, כך דברי תורה אין להם סוף שנאמר
ארכה מארץ מדה ורחבה מני ים (איוב יא,ט) (חומש תורה שלמה עם באור
"תורה שבעל פה" מאת מנחם מ. בן הרב יצחק פרץ כשר, במדבר א,א, אות
ט), "Just like this desert has no limit, so too words of Torah
have no limit, as it says, 'Its measure is longer than the earth,
and broader than the sea'" (Job 11,9) (Chumash Torah
Sheleimah im Be'ur Torah Shebeal Peh by Menachem M. ben
Harov Yitzchak Peretz Kasher, Numbers 1,1, Letter 9). The
gematria of תורה, Torah," is 611.

תורה   611

There is also a Midrash which says that to maintain the
Torah, one should make himself like a desert, as stated, דבר

אחר, במדבר מי מקים את התורה מי שמשים עצמו כמדבר ומפליג עצמו מן הכל (מדרש רבה, סדר חקת, פרשה יט, אות כו) "Another interpretation for 'In the desert' is: Who maintains the Torah? He who make himself like a desert, and separates himself from everything" (Midrash Rabbah, Sidrah Chakkuth, Parashath 19, Letter 26).

The pasuk initially quoted from Parashath Shelach Lecha includes the words במדבר, "in the desert"; הזה, "this"; and ושם, "and there": The sum of their gematrioth is 611.

במדבר	248
הזה	17
ושם	346
	611

Since this pasuk mentions the desert, and since the Midrash says that to maintain the Torah one should make himself like a desert, it is meaningful that the pasuk includes three words whose gematria sum is equal to the gematria of Torah. The three words במדבר, "in the desert"; הזה, "this"; and ושם, "and there" may have been included in the pasuk to stress the importance that to maintain the Torah one should make himself like a desert. Thus, each of these three words could have been embedded in the pasuk for the sum of their gematrioth, which resolves the three difficulties with this pasuk.

וישכמו בבקר ויעלו אל ראש ההר לאמר הננו ועלינו אל המקום אשר אמר ה' כי חטאנו (במדבר יד,מ).

And they arose early in the morning, and they went up to the top of the mountain, saying, 'Here we are and we shall go up to the place which G-d has said, for we have sinned' (Numbers 14,40).

After the episode of the spies, some of the Children of

Israel tried to rectify the situation by trying to go up to the land of Israel and conquer it. After their defeat, the Torah does not record any conversation that Moses had with them, but proceeds to discuss some of the sacrifices (Numbers 15, 1-31). What is the connection between their defeat and the sacrifices? One answer is given by Rashi: בשר להם שיכנסו לארץ (רש״י, במדבר טו,ב), "He announced to them that they will enter the land" (Rashi, Numbers 15,2); an additional possible answer will be suggested.

What some of the Children of Israel said prior to their going to fight for the land of Israel, might have sounded proper and right, but it was not what Hashem wanted at that time; what they said was, הננו ועלינו אל המקום אשר אמר ה' כי חטאנו, "Here we are and we shall go up to the place which G-d has said, for we have sinned." Surely Hashem would want that the Children of Israel should be ready to go to fight for the land of Israel, and that the Children of Israel should admit their sins. The gematria of הננו ועלינו אל המקום אשר אמר ה' כי חטאנו, "Here we are and we shall go up to the place which G-d has said, for we have sinned," is 1377.

הננו	111
ועלינו	172
אל המקום	222
אשר אמר	742
ה' כי חטאנו	130
	1377

Thus, 1377 represents the seemingly proper expression said by some of the Children of Israel, but it was not what Hashem wanted at that time. Even though what they said might have seemed proper and right, it was not what Hashem wanted at that time, since they had turned from Him. Moses had told them that this turning from G-d was the reason why they would not succeed, as stated, כי העמלקי והכנעני שם לפניכם ונפלתם בחרב כי על כן שבתם מאחרי ה' ולא יהיה ה' עמכם (במדבר יד,מג),

"For the Amalekite and the Canaanite are there in front of you, and you will fall by the sword, inasmuch as you have turned back from G-d, and G-d will not be with you" (Numbers 14,43). The gematria of שבתם מאחרי ה׳, "you have turned back from G-d," is 1027.

שבתם	742
מאחרי	259
ה׳	26
	1027

Thus, 1027 represents violating what Hashem wanted for that time.

The difference in gematrioth between the expression which sounded proper and right but which was not what Hashem wanted at that time, and the expression which tells of violating what Hashem wants for that time, is 350.

$$1377$$
$$-1027$$
$$350$$

The number, 350, represents that which sounds proper and right but which was not what Hashem wanted at that time, and removing that which violates what Hashem wants for that time. Thus, this remainder, 350, can represent doing that which sounds proper and right at a time when Hashem wants it to be done.

At the outset of the discussion of the sacrifices after recording the defeat of some of the Children of Israel, the Torah uses the expression ריח ניחח לה׳, "a sweet savor to G-d," as stated, ועשיתם אשה לה׳ עלה או זבח לפלא נדר או בנדבה או במעדיכם לעשות ריח ניחח לה׳ מן הבקר או מן הצאן (במדבר טו,ג), "And when [it occurs that] you will make an offering by fire to G-d, a burnt offering or a sacrifice for an uttered vow, or a freewill offering, or in your appointed seasons, to make a sweet savor to G-d, from the cattle or from the sheep," (Numbers 15,3). The gematria of ריח ניחח לה׳, "a sweet savor to G-d," is 350.

ריח	218
ניחח	76
לה׳	56
	350

The expression ריח ניחח לה׳, "a sweet savor to G-d," is used frequently in discussions of the sacrifices, as exhibited in this parashah (במדבר טו,ג; טו,ז; טו,י; טו,יג; טו,יד, Numbers 15,3; 15,7; 15,10; 15,13; 15,14).

The gematria of ריח ניחח לה׳, "a sweet savor to G-d," is equal to 350, which also equals the gematria which represents doing that which sounds proper and right at a time when Hashem wants it to be done. When one does what Hashem wants when Hashem wants it to be done, it is a ריח ניחח לה׳, "a sweet savor to G-d." Perhaps this equipoise is the reason for the connection between the defeat of those who tried to capture the land of Israel, and the sacrifices. When some of the Children of Israel, the מעפילים, "Mapilim," who tried to go up to the land of Israel returned defeated, they may have been told that, "What you said seemed proper and right, but it was not what Hashem wanted at that time; but when the Children of Israel come to the land of Israel and bring sacrifices, it will be what Hashem wants when He wants it." Those sacrifices at that time will be a ריח ניחח לה׳, "a sweet savor to G-d."

This concept is also applicable to the bringing of a sacrifice on the במות, bamoth, "private altars." When Noach brought a burnt offering on his private altar the Torah says, וירח ה׳ את ריח הניחח (בראשית ח,כא), "And G-d smelled the sweet savor" (Genesis 8,21). During the time that the private altars were permitted, it was pleasing to G-d (though not required) to bring a sacrifice on a bamah (זבחים קיט:, Zevachim 119b). Although it was not required at that time (רבינו עובדיה מברטנורא, זבחים פרק יד, משנה י, ד״ה וריח ניחוח, Rabbeinu Ovadiah Bertinoro, Zevachim, Chapter 14, Mishnah 10, header words:

And a pleasing savor), it could be considered what Hashem wanted when He wanted it; (as can be inferred from the words of the Rabbi Ovadiah Bertinoro) that then it could be a ריח ניחח לה׳, "a pleasing savor to G-d." However, one who perpetrates the same deed when it is forbidden to sacrifice on the bamoth, is subject to the punishment of כרת, kareth, "premature death," (ויקרא יז,ד; וזבחים פרק יד, משנה ד-ט), Leviticus 17,4; and Zevachim, Chapter 14, Mishnah 4-9); it is not what Hashem wanted for that time.

כי העמלקי והכנעני שם לפניכם ונפלתם בחרב כי על כן שבתם מאחרי ה׳ ולא יהיה ה׳ עמכם (במדבר יד,מג).

For the Amalekite and the Canaanite are there in front of you, and you will fall by the sword, inasmuch as you have turned back from G-d, and G-d will not be with you (Numbers 14,43).

והקריב המקריב קרבנו לה׳ מנחה סלת עשרון בלול ברבעית ההין שמן. ויין לנסך רביעית ההין תעשה על העלה או לזבח לכבש האחד (במדבר טו,ד-ה).

And the one who brings his offering shall present to G-d a meal offering a tenth part (of an ephah) of fine flour mingled with a fourth part of a hin of oil. And wine for a libation offering, a fourth part of a hin, you shall make with the burnt offering, or for the sacrifice, for a sheep (Numbers 15, 4-5).

Why are the fine flour for a meal offering, and the wine for a libation offering, discussed immediately after the unsuccessful attempt of some of the Children of Israel, the מעפילים, "Mapilim," to capture the land of Israel? Various commentators have answered this question. Essentially they say that fine flour for a meal offering, and wine for a libation offering, are mitzvoth associated with the land of Israel; they are mentioned here to assure the Children of Israel that eventually they would enter the land (רש״י, רמב״ן, אבן עזרא, ואור החיים, במדבר טו,ב, Rashi, Ramban, Ibn Ezra, and Or Hachayyim, Numbers 15,2); please G-d, another thought will be advanced here.

Moses had said that the attempt to capture the land of Israel would not succeed because Hashem was not with the fighters. The gematria of ולא יהיה ה׳ עמכם, "and G-d will not be with you," is 263.

ולא	37
יהיה	30
ה׳	26
עמכם	170
	263

Thus, 263 represents the absence of G-d's spiritual underpinning; that is, Hashem was not with the fighters. The spiritual part of the the fine flour for a meal offering, was using the fine flour, a physical object, toward a spiritual end, as stated, והקריב המקריב קרבנו לה׳ מנחה סלת עשרון בלול ברביעית ההין שמן (במדבר טו,ד), "And the one who brings his offering shall present to G-d a meal offering a tenth part (of an ephah) of fine flour mingled with a fourth part of a hin of oil" (Numbers 15,4). The gematria of מנחה, "meal offering," is 103.

מנחה   103

The next verse says the spiritual part of using wine for a libation offering, was using the wine, a physical object, toward a spiritual end, as stated, ויין לנסך רביעית ההין תעשה על העלה או לזבח לכבש האחד (במדבר טו,ה), "And wine for a libation offering, a fourth part of a hin, you shall make with the burnt offering, or for the sacrifice, for a sheep" (Numbers 15,5). The gematria of לנסך, "for a libation offering," is 160.

לנסך   160

The sum of the gematria of מנחה, "meal offering," plus the gematria of לנסך, "for a libation offering," is 263.

מנחה	103
לנסך	<u>160</u>
	263

The gematria of ולא יהיה ה׳ עמכם, "and G-d will not be with you," is equal to the sum of the gematria of מנחה, "meal offering," plus the gematria of לנסך, "for a libation offering." This equality might well be the reason that fine flour for a meal offering, and the wine for a libation offering, are discussed immediately after the unsuccessful attempt of some of the Children of Israel, the מעפילים, "Mapilim," to capture the land of Israel. The gematria of 263 represents the absence of G-d's spiritual underpinning; that is, Hashem was not with the fighters. The gematria of 263 also represents the spiritual part of the fine flour for a meal offering, and the wine for a libation offering, the spiritual part Hashem wants and commands. The two gematrioth are equal, for ולא יהיה ה׳ עמכם, "and G-d will not be with you," is the antithesis of the מנחה, "meal offering," and the לנסך, "for a libation offering."

ויעפלו לעלות אל ראש ההר וארון ברית ה׳ ומשה לא משו מקרב המחנה (במדבר יד,מד).

And they insisted to go up to the top of the mountain, but the ark of the covenant of G-d and Moses did not depart from the midst of the camp (Numbers 14,44).

After the unsuccessful attempt of some of the Children of Israel, the מעפילים, "Mapilim," to conquer the land of Israel by force, against Hashem's wishes, the Torah discusses sacrifices (במדבר יד,מ־טו,לא, Numbers 14,40-15,31). Both the subject of the unsuccessful attempt to conquer the land of Israel, and the first part of the subject of the sacrifices, are included in the fourth section of this sidrah; the fifth section does not start until the middle of the discussion of the sacrifices (במדבר טו,ח, Numbers 15,8). Why are these two subjects included together?

When some of the Children of Israel went to fight, the ark of the covenant of G-d did not go with them (במדבר יד,מד, Numbers 14,44). Although this group of the Children of Israel was armed and full of fight, there was a lack of spiritual backing, for they were transgressing the dictate of Hashem's prophet. Moses referred to this brazen defiance, as the Torah quotes him saying, כי אין ה' בקרבכם (במדבר יד,מב), "for G-d is not among you," (Numbers 14,42). Those who went up to conquer the land of Israel had the stubborn insistence to conquer the land when they were explicitly prohibited from so doing. They lacked spiritual backing; in spite of this deficiency they insisted and went to the top of the mountain. The gematria of ויעפלו לעלות אל ראש ההר, "And they insisted to go up to the top of the mountain," is 1480.

ויעפלו	202
לעלות	536
אל ראש	532
ההר	210
	1480

This attempt to conquer the land of Israel failed, but Hashem will give this land to the Children of Israel when He chooses. The assurance to give the land of Israel to the Children of Israel is written directly after the unsuccessful attempt to conquer the land, as stated, דבר אל בני ישראל ואמרת אלהם כי תבאו אל ארץ מושבתיכם אשר אני נתן לכם (במדבר טו,ב), "Speak to the Children of Israel, and say to them, When you come into the land of your habitations, which I give to you" (Numbers 15,2). The gematria of אני נתן לכם, "I give to you," 651.

אני	61
נתן	500
לכם	90
	651

What is the difference between the stubborn insistence to conquer the land when they were explicitly prohibited from so doing, and Hashem's assurance that He will give the land to the Children of Israel when He chooses? The difference in gematria is 829.

$$1480$$
$$-651$$
$$829$$

After the unsuccessful attempt of some of the Children of Israel, the מעפילים, "Mapilim," to conquer the land of Israel by force, the Torah in its discussion of the sacrifices orders that fine flour be brought for a meal offering, and wine for a libation offering (במדבר טו,ד-ה, Numbers 15, 4-5). The fine flour and wine are physical objects; the meal offering and the libation offering represent spiritual concepts. The Torah has the Children of Israel sanctify the fine flour and the wine, by hallowing them as an offering. The fine flour which was to be brought for a meal offering, and the wine which was to be for a libation offering, are joined by a ו, "vav," thereby coupling the two sanctities, as stated, והקריב המקריב קרבנו לה׳ מנחה סלת עשרון בלול ברביעית ההין שמן. ויין לנסך רביעית ההין תעשה על העלה או לזבח לכבש האחד (במדבר טו,ד-ה), "And the one who brings his offering shall present to G-d a meal offering a tenth part [of an ephah] of fine flour mingled with a fourth part of a hin of oil. And wine for a libation offering, a fourth part of a hin, you shall make with the burnt offering, or for the sacrifice, for a sheep" (Numbers 15,4-5). The gematria of מנחה סלת, "a meal offering of fine flour," is 593.

מנחה	103
סלת	490
	593

The gematria of ויין לנסך, "and wine for a libation offering," is 236.

וייּן	76
לנסך	<u>160</u>
	236

The combined gematrioth of מנחה סלת, "a meal offering of fine flour," and ויין לנסך, "and wine for a libation offering," is 829.

$$593$$
$$\underline{236}$$
$$829$$

    Recall that 829 is the difference in gematrioth between the stubborn insistence to conquer the land when the Children of Israel were explicitly prohibited from so doing, and Hashem's assurance that He will give the land to the Children of Israel when He chooses. This difference in gematrioth could be telling that the reason why their attempt failed was a lack of spiritual backing; their attempt was not hallowed. The Children of Israel should sanctify their motivation to be in the land of Israel; they should proceed only at the time indicated by G-d, and they will then be privileged to conquer the land of Israel. This reproof could be the reason why both the subject of the attempt to conquer the land of Israel, and the subject of the sacrifices, are included together in the fourth section of this sidrah.

והקריב המקריב קרבנו לה׳ מנחה סלת עשרון בלול ברביעית ההין שמן. ויין לנסך רביעית ההין תעשה על העלה או לזבח לכבש האחד (במדבר טו,ד-ה).

And the one who brings his offering shall present to G-d a meal offering a tenth part [of an ephah] of fine flour mingled with a fourth part of a hin of oil. And wine for a libation offering, a fourth part of a hin, you shall make with the burnt offering, or for the sacrifice, for the one sheep (Numbers 15,4-5).

Immediately after the unsuccessful attempt by some of the Children of Israel, the מעפילים, "Mapilim," to conquer the land of Israel by force, the Torah discusses sacrifices (במדבר יד,מ-טו,לא, Numbers 14,40-15,31). The Torah, in its discussion of the sacrifices, orders that fine flour be brought for a meal offering, and wine be brought for a libation offering, with every sacrifice that was an עולת ראיה, "burnt offering of appearing," שלמי חגיגה, "peace offering of celebration," נדר, "vow offering," or נדבה, "gift offering"; but it does not order these with a sacrifice that was a חטאת, "sin offering," אשם, "guilt offering," פסח, "Passover offering," מעשר, "tithe offering," or בכור, "first born offering," (במדבר טו,א-טז, Numbers 15,1-16; מנחות צ:-צא:, Menahoth 90b-91b; and The Pentateuch translated and explained by Rabbi Samson Hirsch, Numbers 15, 3-4). To simplify, the Torah's differentiation can be expressed succinctly: Only those sacrifices which were not an obligation, such as an עולה, "burnt offering," or שלמים, "peace offering," were included; but those sacrifices which were an obligation, such as a חטאת "sin offering," or אשם, "guilt offering," were excluded from the orders that fine flour for a meal offering, and wine for a libation offering, be brought with them (תורה תמימה, במדבר טו,ג, אות ו, Torah Teminah, Numbers 15,3, Letter 6). The חטאת, "sin offering," and אשם, "guilt offering," of the metzora were exceptions; they required the fine flour be brought for a meal offering, and wine for a libation offering (רש״י ויקרא יד,י, Rashi, Leviticus 14,10).

It should be noted that the עולת צבור, "burnt offering of the community," was included (במדבר כח,ז-ח ויד-טו Numbers 28, 7-8 and 14-15); the שלמי צבור, "peace offerings of the community," were also included (משנה תורה, ספר עבודה, הלכות מעשה הקרבנות, פרק ב, הלכה ב, Mishnah Torah, Book of Avodah, Laws of Doing the Sacrifices, Chapter 2, Law 2). The individual's עולת ראיה, "burnt offerings of appearance," and the שלמי חגיגה, "peace offerings of celebration," were included although they were obligatory, as the Gemara learns from the words או במעדיכם, "or in your appointed seasons," (במדבר טו,ג, Numbers 15,3 and Menahoth 90b). It seems apparent that although these sacrifices were obligatory, they were included, inasmuch as the Torah did not want to distinguish between the different types of עולות "burnt offerings," or שלמים "peace offerings," be they for the community or for the individual; they all had the same requirement. But the basic differentiation remains: Only those sacrifices which were not an obligation were included; but those sacrifices which were an obligation, were excluded from the orders that fine flour for a meal offering, and wine for a libation offering, be brought with them.

Two questions come to the fore immediately. One, why did the Torah differentiate those sacrifices which were an obligation, from the orders that fine flour for a meal offering, and wine for a libation offering, be brought with these sacrifices? Two, why immediately after the unsuccessful attempt of some of the Children of Israel, the מעפילים, "Mapilim," to conquer the land of Israel by force, does the Torah discuss the fine flour for a meal offering, and wine for a libation offering?

It should be observed that several commentators have given answers to the second question. All basically contend that since the the fine flour for a meal offering, and wine for a libation offering, are mitzvoth associated with the land of Israel, they were mentioned here to assure the Children of Israel that eventually they would enter the land (רש"י, רמב"ן, אבן עזרא, ואור החיים, במדבר טו,ב, Rashi, Ramban, Ibn Ezra, and Or Hachayyim, Numbers 15,2). However, this answer is only a partial answer, for it explains why these mitzvoth associated with the land of Israel are mentioned, but it does not explain why these mitzvoth in particular, the mitzvoth of fine flour for a meal offering, and wine for a libation offering, are the ones mentioned. Note that the ספורנו, Sforno, does give a different answer to the second question. He explains that the addition of the fine flour for a meal offering, and wine for a libation offering, were required for sacrifices of the community after the sin of the golden calf, and were required for the individual sacrifices after the sin of the spies. These additions were now required in order to compensate for those sins, so that subsequent sacrifices will be sweet savor to G-d (ספורנו, במדבר טו, ג, Sforno, Numbers 15,3).

A different possible key to resolving both of these questions can be found in Gemara Berakoth which states, דרש בר קפרא איזוהי פרשה קטנה שכל גופי תורה תלויין בה בכל דרכיך דעהו והוא יישר ארחותיך (ברכות סג.), "Bar Kappara expounded: Which is the small section, upon which the entire body of the Torah depends? In all your ways know Him, and He will straighten out your paths'" (Berakoth 63a). This Gemara is the basis of a law in the שלחן ערוך, Shulhan Arukh, as stated, וכן בכל מה שיהנה בעוה"ז לא יכוין להנאתו אלא לעבודת הבורא יתברך כדכתיב בכל דרכיך דעהו, ואמרו חכמים כל מעשיך יהיו לש"ש שאפילו דברים של רשות כגון האכילה והשתיה וההליכה וכו' (שלחן ערוך, אורח חיים, סימן רלא, סעיף א), "And so whatever one enjoys from this world, he should not intend for his own pleasure, [but] rather to serve his blessed Creator, as it is written, 'In all your ways know Him.' And our sages have said, all your deeds should be for the sake of Heaven, even those things which are permitted, such as eating drinking, walking, etc." (Shulhan Arukh, Orach Hayyim, Siman 231, Seif 1). From this law it is clear that there are two distinct levels of serving Hashem. The first level is doing what is obligatory, such as eating kosher food, and not wearing shatnez. The second level is that all our deeds should be done for the sake of Heaven, such as eating to get energy to learn Torah, and wearing clothes fitting for one who learns Torah.

How does one fulfill the mitzvah of "In all your ways know Him?" The source of knowledge is the heart, as stated, ולא נתן ה' לכם לב לדעת ועינים לראות ואזנים לשמע עד היום הזה (דברים כט,ג), "And G-d has not given you a heart to know, and eyes to see, and ears to hear, until this day," (Deuteronomy 29,3). The divine service of the heart is supposed to be with joy, as stated, תחת אשר לא עבדת את ה' אלהיך בשמחה ובטוב לבב מרב כל (דברים כח,מז), "Because you did not serve G-d, your G-d, with joyfulness, and with gladness of heart, out of the abundance of all," (Deuteronomy 28,47).

How does one cause the heart to be joyful? The answer is found in Psalms, as stated, ויין ישמח לבב אנוש להצהיל פנים משמן ולחם לבב אנוש יסעד (תהלים קד,טו), "And wine makes joyful the heart of man, and oil to make his face shine; and bread stayeth a man's heart" (Psalms 104,15). The Malbim on this pasuk explains that having bread is a requisite qualification for wine to cause the heart to be joyful, as he says, כי בלעדי הלחם ימר שכר לשותיו וכו' (באור הענין, מאת הרב מאיר ליבוש מלבי"ם, תהלים קד,טו), "For without bread, the intoxicating liquor will be bitter to the one imbibing, etc." (Be'ur Ha'inyan by Rabbi Meir Lebush Malbim, Psalms 104,15). Thus, this pasuk shows that wine and bread are two essential ingredients that cause the heart to be joyful. There is also a pasuk in Ecclesiastes which emphasizes that bread is essential for joy, as stated, לשחוק עשים לחם ויין ישמח חיים והכסף יענה את־הכל (קהלת י,יט), "For laughter they make bread, and wine makes life joyful, and money answers everything," (Ecclesiastes 10,19). On this pasuk the Ibn Ezra comments, והלא יראו כי כל שמחה שבעולם ושחוק עיקרם בכחם שעושים היין המשמח חיי אדם וכו' (אבן עזרא, קהלת י,יט), "And will they not see that all joy in the world and laughter are primarily with bread made by its makers, and wine makes joyful the life of man, etc." (Ibn Ezra, Ecclesiastes 10,19). The Rosh also mentions that bread is essential for joyfulness, as he states, דחייב אדם לאכול פת ביו"ט משום שמחה

"A משום חלקהו חציו לאכילה (רבינו אשר, ברכות, פרק שביעי, סימן כג) person is obligated to eat bread on the holidays, in order to be in a joyous state because of the admonition to 'split' [the holiday], half for eating [enjoyment]" (Rabbeinu Asher, Berakoth, Chapter 7, Siman 23).

But obviously these sources do not mean one should be a glutton and a drunkard, since the Torah speaks disparagingly of a stubborn and rebellious son, who is described as a glutton and a drunkard (Deuteronomy 21,20). So how does one use wine and bread to cause the heart to be joyful in order to fulfill the small section, upon which the entire body of the Torah depends, "In all your ways know Him?" The source of bread is flour, thus the bread mentioned in Psalms and Ecclesiastes can be equated to fine flour. The way one fulfills the mitzvah of "In all your ways know Him," is by dedicating wine and fine flour for a sacrifice, one of the highest levels of holiness.

The bringing of a sacrifice is itself bound with the concept of joyfulness; for on the day one brings a sacrifice, he is forbidden to do work as on a holiday (תוספות, פסחים נ.,) ד"ה מקום שנהגו, Tosafoth, Pesahim 50a, header words: In a place where they are accustomed). This concept is still in force today on the eve of Passover, albeit there is no Beit Hamikdash in existence, as the Mishnah Berurah says, ויום שמביאין קרבן הוא כיו"ט ולכן אסור מד"ס במלאכה ואפילו בזה"ז דליכא קרבן עדיין האיסור במקומו עומד (משנה ברורה, סימן תסח, ס"ק א), "And the day on which one brings a sacrifice is like a holiday, and therefore the sages have made it forbidden to do work. Even in our times when there is no sacrifice, the prohibition from the sages still stands in force" (Mishnah Berurah, Siman 468, Small Seif 1). The dedicating of fine flour and wine is what the Torah prescribes when it requires fine flour for a meal offering, and wine for a libation offering, to be offered with those sacrifices which were not obligatory.

Rabbi Simeon, in the Gemara, believes it is inappropriate for a sacrifice which evolved from sin to have oil and frankincense. The joy to the heart which the dedicating of wine for libation could do to the חטאת, "sin offering," and dedicating oil and frakincense could do to the sinner's מנחה, "meal offering," could be the intention of the Gemara Menahoth which describes such sacrifices if they had these additions, as מהודר, "resplendent," (מנחות ו.־ו:, Menahoth 6a-6b). The ideas of הדר, "resplendent," and שמחה, "joy," can be connected (תהלים כא,ו-ז, Psalms 21,6-7). This connection can be augmented by a further association in Gemara Menahoth; the Gemara establishes a link between the libations (showing joy) and the gaining of atonement, after it refutes a different link, as it says, מאי טעמא אכילה ושתיה אדרבה כפרה ושמחה (מנחות כ.), "What is the reason [for the link between the libations and the burning the portions of sacrifices]? [Seemingly] It is because eating and drinking go together; [but in fact] just the opposite, it is atonement and joy that go together" (Menahoth 20a). Thus, the libation is associated with the joy of obtaining atonement. It is known that the land of Israel is a place of joy, as the Or Hachayyim asserts שאין לשמוח אלא בישיבת הארץ (אור החיים, דברים כו,א), "One should not be joyful, unless he is living in the Land," (Or Hachayyim, Deuteronomy 26,1). Also the commandments of Hashem in general, including those that apply to the land of Israel, bring joy to the heart, as stated, פקודי ה' ישרים משמחי לב מצות ה' ברה מאירת עינים (תהלים יט,ט), "The precepts of G-d are upright, rejoicing the heart; the commandment of G-d is crystalline, enlightening the eyes" (Psalms 19,9). Therefore, the rejection of the land of Israel by some of the spies was a rejection of the joyfulness of the mitzvah to be in the land of Israel.

Now the original two questions can be answered. One, why does the Torah differentiate those sacrifices which were an obligation, from the requirement of fine flour for a meal offering, and wine for a libation offering? The answer seems pellucid. The fine flour for a meal offering, and wine for a libation offering, can be equated with the wine and bread mentioned in Psalms 104,15 and in Ecclesiastes 10,19, as causing the heart to be joyful, so one can fulfill the mitzvah of "In all your ways know Him."

As was previously remarked, there are two distinct levels of serving Hashem. The first level is doing what is required, obligatory; the second level is that all of one's deeds should be done for the sake of Heaven; that is, "In all your ways know Him." A person who offers one of the sacrifices which is an obligation is on the first level of doing what is required. But, the fine flour for a meal offering, and wine for a libation offering, were to enable one to fulfill the mitzvah of "In all your ways know Him"; that is, to reach the second level. Thus, they were only offered with those sacrifices which were not obligatory. The two levels of serving Hashem correspond to the Torah's differentiation of those sacrifices which were obligatory from those which were not obligatory. Only a person on the second level needed fine flour for a meal offering, and wine for a libation offering, to fulfill the mitzvah of "In all your ways know Him." The first question has been answered.

Two, why immediately after the unsuccessful attempt of some of the Children of Israel to conquer the land of Israel by force, does the Torah discuss the fine flour for a meal offering, and wine for a libation offering? The answer is somewhat complicated. According to the Keli Yakar, the spies said they would rather spend forty years in an Egyptian famine, than the forty days they spent in the land of Israel. The spies did not regard the joy of the mitzvah of being in the land of Israel; they said that they would prefer the misery of being outside the land of Israel, in Egypt, as stated, ‫נשובה מצרימה כי‬ ‫יותר טוב לנו להיות בשממת מצרים מ׳ שנה מאותן מ׳ יום אשר בהם היינו‬ ‫בסכנת מות‬, "Let us return to Egypt. For it is better for us to be in the Egyptian desolation for forty years, than the forty days which we were in fear of death." The misery of the famine in Egypt was real; note that the Keli Yakar refers to a source from Ezekiel. In contrast, the fear of the land of Israel was false, and the crying that ensued was for naught, as stated by the Keli Yakar, ורז״ל אמרו כי יום זה היינו ט׳ באב כי בו בכו בכיה לחנם וקבעו בכיה לדורות (כלי יקר, במדבר יד,לד), "And our Rabbis of blessed memory have said that this day was the Ninth of Av. Since they cried on it [that day] for nothing, they established it for crying for generations" (Keli Yakar, Numbers 14,34). Thus, the Children of Israel created a mournful day, the Ninth of Av, since their crying was for naught, and the fear of the land of Israel was false. Some of the spies and some of the Children of Israel seemingly preferred the predicted misery of the famine in Egypt rather than the joy of the mitzvah of being in the land of Israel.

Now it can be explained why immediately after the unsuccessful attempt of some of the Children of Israel to conquer the land of Israel by force, does the Torah discuss the fine flour for a meal offering, and wine for a libation offering. The unsuccessful attempt of some of the Children of Israel to conquer the land of Israel by force, terminated the episode of the spies, which produced the sad day of the Ninth of Av. As was said previously, since the fine flour for a meal offering, and wine for a libation offering, can be equated with the wine and bread mentioned in Psalms 104,15 and in Ecclesiastes 10,19, for they cause the heart to be joyful, so one can fulfill the mitzvah of "In all your ways know Him." The fine flour for a meal offering, and wine for a libation offering, are the antithesis of the episode of the spies. The former causes the heart to be joyful; the latter produced the sad day of the Ninth of Av, and rejected the joy of the mitzvah of being in the land of Israel. Thus, by discussing the fine flour for a meal offering, and wine for a libation offering, after the episode of the spies, Hashem was saying to the Children of Israel, "You have created a Ninth of Av, and rejected the joy of the mitzvah of living in the land of Israel, but know that the land of Israel is a place of joyfulness. One of the mitzvoth associated with the land of Israel which causes the heart to be joyful is the requirement of fine flour for a meal offering, and wine for a libation offering." The second question has been answered.

The answers to the two questions are the foundation for a gematria. As was mentioned, one way by which one can fulfill the mitzvah of "In all your ways know Him," is by dedicating wine and fine flour for a sacrifice, one of the highest levels of holiness. The dedicating of fine flour for a meal offering, and wine for a libation offering, is what the Torah prescribed only for those sacrifices which were not an obligation. The fine flour and wine are physical objects; the meal offering and the libation offering represent spiritual goals. The Torah has the Children of Israel sanctify fine flour and wine by hallowing them. The fine flour was to be brought for a מנחה, "meal offering," and wine which was to be for a נסך, "libation offering." The Torah repeatedly uses the expression מנחה סלת ויין לנסך (במדבר טו, ד-ה, ו-ז, ט-י), "a meal offering of fine flour, and wine for a libation offering," (Numbers 15, 4-5, 6-7, 9-10). The gematria of מנחה, "a meal offering," plus the gematria of לנסך, "for a libation offering," is 263.

מנחה	103
לנסך	160
	263

The gematria of סלת, "fine flour," plus the gematria of ויין, "and wine," is 566.

סלת	490
ויין	76
	566

Thus, 566 represents physical objects; 263 represents

spiritual goals. The difference in gematrioth between the physical objects and the spiritual goals is equal to 303.

$$566$$
$$-263$$
$$303$$

The Torah begins its discussion of the fine flour for a meal offering, and wine for a libation offering, by first affirming that the Children of Israel would come to the land of Israel, as stated, דבר אל בני ישראל ואמרת אלהם כי תבאו אל ארץ מושבתיכם אשר אני נתן לכם (במדבר טו,ב), "Speak to the Children of Israel and say to them, when you come to the land of your habitations, which I give to you" (Numbers 15,2). The gematria of כי תבאו, "when you come," is 439.

כי	30
תבאו	409
	439

Why was the attempt of some of the Children of Israel to conquer the land of Israel unsuccessful? Moses told them that it was because they turned away from Hashem, as stated, כי העמלקי והכנעני שם לפניכם ונפלתם בחרב כי על כן שבתם מאחרי ה' ולא יהיה ה' עמכם (במדבר יד,מג), "For the Amalekite and the Canaanite are there before you, and you will fall by the sword, because you have turned away from G-d, and G-d will not be with you" (Numbers 14,43). The gematria of שבתם, "you have turned away," is 742.

שבתם 742

If the turning away from Hashem (represented by 742) is taken, and one then removes from it the difference between the physical objects and the dedicating them to spiritual goals, then the remainder would be the privilege to merit to enter the land of Israel. This difference can be expressed as follows: Serving spiritual goals with physical material is the difference between turning from Hashem, as the Children of Israel did after the episode of the spies, and being privileged to enter the land of Israel.

As has been shown above, difference between the physical objects and dedicating them to spiritual goals is 303 in gematrioth; turning from Hashem as the Children of Israel did after the episode of the spies, is 742 in gematrioth; and being privileged to merit entering to the land of Israel is 439 in gematrioth. If the gematria of the difference between the physical objects and dedicating them to spiritual goals is removed from the gematria of turning from Hashem as the Children of Israel did after the episode of the spies, the remainder is equal to the gematria of being privileged to merit coming to the land of Israel.

$$742 - 303 = 439$$

The gematria of שבתם, "you have turned away," minus 303 equals the gematria of כי תבאו, "when you come." Hence, the gematria calculation reaffirms the explanation of the fine flour for a meal offering, and wine for a libation offering, as it is connected to the episode of the spies.

The explanation given helps to resolve another question. The Torah refers to joy when speaking about the holiday of Tabernacles (ויקרא כג־מ ודברים טז,יג־טו, Leviticus 23,40 and Deuteronomy 16,13-15). Also in its שמונה עשרה, Shemoneh Esreh, and in its קדוש, Kiddush, the holiday of Tabernacles is identified as the time of our joy. Why is joy explicitly associated with the holiday of Tabernacles?

A possible answer to this question can be found by examining the purpose of sitting in a sukkah, a booth. The purpose is for generations to know that Hashem made the Children of Israel dwell in booths, as stated, בסכת תשבו שבעת ימים כל האזרח בישראל ישבו בסכת. למען ידעו דרתיכם כי בסכות הושבתי את בני ישראל בהוציאי אותם מארץ מצרים אני ה' אלקיכם (ויקרא כג,

מב-מג), "In booths you shall dwell for seven days; every citizen of Israel shall dwell in booths. In order that your generations may know that I made the Children of Israel dwell in booths when I brought them out of the land of Egypt; I am G-d your G-d" (ויקרא כג,מב-מג, Leviticus 23,42-43). From these verses it is apparent that there is a special feature of knowing, on the holiday of Tabernacles. As was said previously, the source of knowledge is the heart, as stated, ולא נתן ה׳ לכם לב לדעת ועיניים לראות ואזנים לשמע עד היום הזה (דברים כט,ג), "And G-d has not given you a heart to know, and eyes to see, and ears to hear, until this day," (Deuteronomy 29,3). The divine service of the heart is supposed to be with joy, as stated, תחת אשר לא עבדת את ה׳ אלהיך בשמחה ובטוב לבב מרב כל (דברים כח,מז), "Because you did not serve G-d, your G-d, with joyfulness, and with gladness of heart, out of the abundance of all," (Deuteronomy 28,47). Since the source of knowledge is the heart, and the divine service of the heart is supposed to be with joyfulness, therefore on the holiday of Tabernacles, when there is a special mitzvah of knowing, those who fulfill the mitzvah should be joyful. The question of why joy is explicitly associated with the holiday of Tabernacles has been answered.

Lastly, observe that the holiday of Tabernacles comes at the beginning of the year, signifying the start of a new year on a positive note, on a note of joy.

דבר אל בני ישראל ואמרת אלהם ועשו להם ציצת על כנפי בגדיהם לדרתם ונתנו על ציצת הכנף פתיל תכלת (במדבר טו,לח).

Speak to the Children of Israel, and say to them, and they shall make for themselves a fringe, on the corners of their garments, throughout their generations. And they shall put on the fringe of the corner a blue thread (Numbers 15, 38).

When Hashem began to tell Moses about the mitzvah of ציצת, tsitsith, He referred to the Children of Israel in the third person; the words, אלהם, "to them," ועשו, "and they shall make," להם, "for themselves, "בגדיהם, "of their garments," לדרתם, "throughout their generations," and ונתנו, "and they shall put," are all in the third person. But then the wording switches to second person, as stated, והיה לכם לציצת וראיתם אתו וזכרתם את כל מצות ה' ועשיתם אתם ולא תתורו אחרי לבבכם ואחרי עיניכם אשר אתם זנים אחריהם (במדבר טו,לט), "And it shall be for you for a fringe and you shall see it, and you shall remember all the commandments of G-d, and you shall do them, and you shall not turn after your heart, and after your eyes, which you go astray after them" (Numbers 15,39). The words לכם, "for you," וראיתם, "and you shall see," וזכרתם, "and you shall remember," ועשיתם, "and you shall do," תתורו, "you shall turn," לבבכם, "your heart," עיניכם, "your eyes," and אתם, "you," are all in the second person. Why does the Torah here, when recording the word of Hashem, switch from the third to the second person? This question can be answered by examining how the Or Hachayyim answers another question.

Why does the Torah introduce the mitzvah of ציצת, tsitsith, with the word ויאמר, "And He said," as opposed to the more frequently employed word וידבר, "and He spoke," which is used numerous times in the Torah? The Or Hachayyim explains, כשראה משה מעשה המקושש אמר לפני ה' בימי החול לובשין ישראל תפלין וזוכרין המצות, ביום השבת במה יזכרו. והשיב הקדוש ברוך הוא הריני נותן להם מצות ציצית שבה יזכרו וכו' (אור החיים, במדבר טו, לז, ד"ה ויאמר ה' אל משה), "When Moses saw the deed of the [wood] gatherer [who defied the laws of Shabbath], he said before G-d, 'During the days of the week Israel wears tefillin and remembers the commandments. On the Shabbath day, with what will they remember?' And the Holy One, Blessed be He, answered, 'Behold I will give them the commandment of tsitsith, through which they will remember, etc.'" (Or

Hachayyim, Numbers 15,37, header words: And G-d said to Moses). Thus, for the benefit of the Children of Israel, Moses had asked for a reminder of the mitzvoth. Therefore, the word ויאמר, "And He said," is used, to indicate an answer to a question. Note that this usage of the word also explains why the mitzvah of tsitsith follows the episode of the wood gatherer. The wood gatherer, who had violated the mitzvah of Shabbath, prompted Moses to ask for a Shabbath day reminder of the mitzvoth, which led to Hashem's responding with the mitzvah of tsitsith; hence, it is natural for the mitzvah of tsitsith to follow the story of the wood gatherer.

But the ציצת, tsitsith, are more than just a reminder of the mitzvoth. The Or Hachayyim explains that besides being a a reminder of the mitzvoth, the color and the number of the strings of the tsitsith hint to two distinct characteristics of G-d, as stated, וצוה שיהיו החוטין לבן לרשם סימניו יתברך כי מדותיו הם מדות הרחמים והטוב הרמוז במין הלבן. גם התכלת לרמז על שליטתו בשמים, כי התכלת דומה לרקיע. גם מספר החוטין ארבעה שהם שמונה ירמיז לשמו יתברך שהוא שם בן ארבע ויחודו בהיכלו הוא בן שמונה (אור החיים, במדבר טו,לט, ד״ה ומעתה באנו להשכיל), "And He commanded that the strings are white, to denote a sign of the Blessed be He, for His characteristics are merciful and good, which are hinted to with the white type. And also the blue is to hint to His rulership over the Heaven, for the blue is comparable to the firmament. Also the number of the strings, four, which are [doubled to] eight, hints to His blessed Name which is four [letters], and His Oneness in His palace, which is eight [letters]" (Or Hachayyim, Numbers 15,39, header words: And now we have come to the understanding). Thus, there are in the commandment of tsitsith, two aspects. One is to be a reminder to observe the mitzvoth; two is denotation of G-d's characteristics and His Oneness.

The initial question can now be resolved. The question was, why does the Torah, when recording the word of

Hashem, switch from the third person to the second person? The Torah repeats the word tsitsith three times in this section. The first two times correspond to the role of the tsitsith as a reminder to observe the mitzvoth. This reminder was only necessary for the Children of Israel, but not for Moses. Therefore, when Hashem articulated the word tsitsith the first two times, Hashem said them in the third person, for Moses to relay them to the Children of Israel, but these did not apply to Moses. However, the third time the word tsitsith is mentioned corresponds to the denotation of G-d's characteristics and His oneness, with which even Moses had to be concerned. Therefore, when Hashem articulated the word tsitsith the third time, Hashem said it in the second person, for Moses as well. Thus, the third time tsitsith is mentioned, the Torah switches to the second person to include Moses. The initial question, why does the Torah, when recording the word of Hashem, switch from the third to the second person has been resolved.

From what has been written it is understood that tsitsith besides being a reminder of the mitzvoth, also is a denotation of G-d's characteristics and His oneness.

The three repetitions of the word ציצת, tsitsith, relate to a fascinating gematria. The gematrioth of the key words preceding each mention of the word ציצת, tsitsith, add up to 613. The key words are: להם, "for themselves," ונתנו, "and they shall put," and והיה, "and it shall be." The words להם, "for themselves," and ונתנו, "and they shall put," are in the third person, for they refer to the need that the Children of Israel have to be reminded that they are to observe the mitzvoth. The word והיה, "and it shall be," refers to the Oneness of G-d. Note that the word לכם, "to you," (before the third mention of the word ציצת, tsitsith) was skipped, for although it immediately precedes the word לציצת, "for a fringe," the significant key word is והיה, "and it shall be," which indicates the Oneness of G-d. It also consists of the same letters as the name of G-d — Who is always One. The oneness of the mitzvah is that the white and the blue fringes combine, coalesce, unite, to be one mitzvah. Even according to the one opinion which says that the four fringes are four separate mitzvoth, the word והיה, "and it shall be," indicates the unity of each corner, which would have to mean that the white and blue fringes do combine. Although every word in the Torah is significant, the significance of the word והיה, "and it shall be," is clearly given by the Malbim, as stated, כבר בארתי באילת השחר שכשמזכיר דין אחד על כמה דברים יבא הפעל בלשן רבים, ואם בא בלשון יחיד מורה שהם מצטרפין זב"ז וכן ממה שלא אמר והיו לכם לציצית למדו שארבעתן מצוה אחת, ור' ישמעאל ס"ל שבא פעל והיה בלשון יחיד להורות שכל כנף מצוה בפ"ע וגם כנף ארד מובן למצוה ומובא במנחות (התורה והמצוה, מאת הרב מאיר ליבוש מלביי"ם, במדבר טו,לח), "I have already explained in Ayeleth HaShachar that when it mentions one law applying to several things, the verb comes in plural. And if it comes in singular it teaches that they are joined one to the other. And since it does not say, 'and they shall be for them fringes,' we learn that the four of them are one mitzvah. And Rabbi Ishmael held that the verb 'and it shall be,' is in the singular to teach that every corner is a mitzvah by itself. And also one corner is understood to be a mitzvah, and it is cited in Menahoth" (The Torah and the Mitzvah by Rabbi Meir Lebush Malbim, Numbers 15,38).

Referring back to the parashah (section) of the tsitsith, the gematrioth of key words preceding each mention of the word tsitsith can be examined. The Torah mentions the word ציצת, tsitsith, three times, as stated, דבר אל בני ישראל ואמרת אלהם ועשו להם ציצת על כנפי בגדיהם לדרתם ונתנו על ציצת הכנף פתיל תכלת. והיה לכם לציצת וראיתם אתו וזכרתם את כל מצות ה' ועשיתם אתם ולא תתורו אחרי לבבכם ואחרי עיניכם אשר אתם זנים אחריהם (במדבר טו,לח-לט), "Speak to the Children of Israel, and say to them, and they shall make for themselves a fringe, on the corners of their garments, throughout their generations. And they shall put on the fringe of the corner a blue thread. And it shall be for you for a fringe and you shall see it, and you shall remember all the commandments of G-d, and you shall do them, and you shall not turn after your heart, and after your eyes, which you go astray after them" (Numbers 15,38-39). The gematria of להם, "for themselves," is 75.

להם   75

The gematria of ונתנו, "and they shall put," is 512.

ונתנו   512

The gematria of והיה, "and it shall be," is 26.

והיה   26

The sum of these gematrioth is 613.

75
512
26
___
613

This gematria indicates that the tsitsith are a reminder of the 613 Mitzvoth, and also a denotation of G-d's characteristics and His oneness. It reinforces what the Torah says, "and you shall see it, and you shall remember all the commandments of G-d, and you shall do them." May Hashem help that the mitzvah of tsitsith shall be fulfilled in the fullest way possible.

Parashath Korach

פרשת קרח

ויקח קרח בן יצהר בן קהת בן לוי ודתן ואבירם בני אליאב
ואון בן פלת בני ראובן (במדבר טז,א).

And Korach the son of Izhar, the son of Kehath, the son of Levi, took himself, and Dathan and Abiram, the sons of Eliab, and On, the son of Peleth, the sons of Reuben (Numbers 16,1).

The first pasuk of this week's sidrah lists Korach's genealogy. Why was this genealogy written in a shorted form, going back several generations, but stopping short of listing Yaakov, Korach's great-great grandfather? Rashi clarifies, that Yaakov wished to be excluded from having his name enumerated with Korach's genealogy (רש״י, במדבר טז,א, וסנהדרין קט:, Rashi, Numbers 16,1, and Sanhedrun 109b); perhaps an additional meaning can be observed.

Moses constantly prayed on behalf of the Children of Israel, even when they sinned, but here he beseeched Hashem to ignore the incense offering of Korach and his cohorts. This beseeching can be understood by what the Malbim says: כי היסוד העקר שבו תלוי התאמתות התורה וקיומה לדור דורים הוא מה שירד ה׳ לעיני כל ישראל על הר סיני באותות ובמופתים וכולם שמעו מפי הקדש פנים בפנים שהוא ממנה את משה שיהיה שלוחו לתת להם תורה ומצות קיימים לעולמים וצוה שיאמינו לכל המצות שיצוה להם משה מפי ה׳ (התורה והמצוה מאת הרב מאיר ליבוש מלבי״ס, במדבר טז,כח), "For the quintessential foundation on which the essence of the Torah and its endurance throughout the generations depends, is that G-d came down in sight of all Israel on Mount Sinai with signs and wonders. And they all heard from His holy mouth, face to face, that He appointed Moses to be His messenger to give them Torah and mitzvoth to endure forever. And he commanded that they should believe that all the mitzvoth which Moses commanded them were from the mouth of G-d" (The Torah and the Mitzvah by Rabbi Meir

Lebush Malbim, Numbers 16,28,). Thus, Korach challenged not only Moses, rather he challenged the quintessential foundation of all the mitzvoth. This challenge could be alluded to in the listing of Korach's genealogy. The gematria of קרח, "Korach," plus the gematria of יצהר, "Izhar," is 613.

$$
\begin{array}{rr}
\text{קרח} & 308 \\
\text{יצהר} & \underline{305} \\
& 613
\end{array}
$$

Since there is a total of 613 Mitzvoth (מכות כג:, Makkoth 23b), the gematria of 613 in Korach's genealogy could allude to his challenge of the quintessential foundation of all the mitzvoth.

It is worth calling attention to the lengths to which Yaakov had gone so as not to imply that any of his children, including Shimon and Levi, were in violation of the 613 Commandments. As was pointed out in the פרשת ויחי, Parashath Vayyechi, (בראשית מט,ו, Genesis 49,6) section of this sefer, it is conceivable to explain that when Jacob denounced Simeon and Levi, he used the word איש, "man," in place of אנשים הרבה, "many men" (in referring to the anger of Simeon and Levi), so that he would not imply that they were not observing the 613 Mitzvoth. Korach, in contrast, challenged the quintessential foundation of all the mitzvoth, the very foundation which Yaakov had tried to instill. This contrast, then, gives a deeper meaning as to why Yaakov wished to be excluded from the genealogy of Korach.

מכל מתנתיכם תרימו את כל תרומת ה' מכל חלבו את מקדשו ממנו (במדבר יח,כט).

From all your gifts you shall set apart all that is to be set apart for G-d, from all the best thereof, that which is to be consecrated from it (Numbers 18,29).

At the end of Parashath Korach, the Torah instructs the Levites concerning the setting aside terumath maaser, terumah of tithes, מכל חלבו, "from all the best." The gematria of מכל חלבו, "from all the best," is 136.

מכל	90
חלבו	46
	136

The gematria of ממנו, "from it," is 136.

ממנו	136

Since מכל חלבו, "from all the best," and ממנו, "from it," refer to the same thing, it is befitting that their gematrioth are the same.

ואמרת אלהם בהרימכם את חלבו ממנו ונחשב ללוים
כתבואת גרן וכתבואת יקב (במדבר יח,ל).

And you shall say to them, when you set apart the best from it, it shall be counted for the Levites as the produce of the threshing floor, and as the produce of the winepress (Numbers 18,30).

In reference to the תרומת מעשר, "terumah of tithes," the Torah says that after the Levites will have given a tenth to the priests from the best part which they had received from the laity of the Children of Israel, then the remainder shall be considered theirs, as חולין, "unsanctified." The gematria of ללוים, "for the Levites," is 116.

ללוים	116

Thus, 116 represents the status of the produce "for the Levites," after the תרומת מעשר, "terumah of tithes," had been separated. Two verses later, again in reference to the תרומת מעשר, "terumah of tithes," the Torah states, ולא תשאו

עליו חטא בהרימכם את חלבו ממנו ואת קדשי בני ישראל לא תחללו ולא תמותו (במדבר יח,לב), "And you shall bear no sin because of it, when you set apart the best from it; and the holy things of the Children of Israel you shall not profane, and you shall not die" (Numbers 18,32). The gematria of עליו, "because of it," is 116.

עליו   116

Thus, 116 represents the status of the produce wherewith the Levites will be free from sin after the תרומת מעשר, "terumah of tithes," had been separated. Since both the words ללוים, "for the Levites," and עליו, "because of it," relate to the status of produce after the תרומת מעשר, "terumah of tithes," had been separated, it is appropriate that both words should have the same gematria.

Parashath Chukkath   פרשת חקת

וידבר ה׳ אל משה ואל אהרן לאמר. זאת חקת התורה אשר
צוה ה׳ לאמר דבר אל בני ישראל ויקחו אליך פרה אדמה
תמימה אשר אין בה מום אשר לא עלה עליה על (במדבר
יט,א־ב).

And G-d spoke to Moses and Aaron saying. This
is the statute of the Torah, which G-d commanded saying: Speak to the Children of Israel
and they shall take for you a perfectly red
heifer, which has no blemish, upon which has
never came a yoke (Numbers 19,1-2).

In the beginning of Parashath Chukkath there is a
pasuk with a seeming inverted word order. The העמק דבר,
"Haamek Davar," based on the רמב״ן, "Ramban," points out
that the word order of the second pasuk seems to be inverted. The words of the pasuk should have been transposed
to read, דבר אל בני ישראל זאת חקת התורה אשר צוה ה׳ לאמר ויקחו
וגו׳, "Speak to the Children of Israel, this is the statute of the
Torah, which G-d commanded saying: And they shall take,
etc." The reason why the Torah inverted the words of this
pasuk, is to teach that the פרה אדמה, "red heifer," of Moses
was different from the red heifer of other generations. The
pasuk should be interpreted as follows: זאת חקת התורה אשר
צוה ה׳ לאמר ויקחו וגו׳, "This is the statute of the Torah, which
G-d commanded saying: And they shall take, etc.," this
phrase refers to the red heifer of future generations; דבר אל
בני ישראל ויקחו אליך וגו׳, "Speak to the Children of Israel and
they shall take for you, etc.," this phrase refers to the red
heifer of Moses (העמק דבר מאת רבי נפתלי צבי יהודה ברלין
מוואלאזין, במדבר יט,ב, Haamek Davar by Rabbi Naphtali Zevi
Judah Berlin from Volozhin, Numbers 19,2).

Two questions need to be answered: One, in what way
was the red heifer of Moses different from other red heifers?

Two, why did the Torah tell this difference? A possible answer to these questions can be found by examining what the רמב״ן "Ramban," says about the word חרש, "deaf." The word חרש, "deaf," appears twice in the Torah, and the Ramban explains different meanings for this word.

The first time the word חרש, "deaf," appears in the Torah is in פרשת שמות, "Parashath Shemoth," as stated, ויאמר ה׳ אליו מי שם פה לאדם או מי ישום אלם או חרש או פקח או עור הלא אנכי ה׳ (שמות ד,יא), "And G-d said to him: Who has made a mouth for man, or Who made him dumb, or deaf, or seeing or blind? Is it not I G-d?" (Exodus 4,11). On this pasuk the Ramban says, או מי ישום אלם, פירש בו שהוא נמשך לאדם או מי ישום אלם, כלומר מי ברא אדם שהוא אלם והשימה לאדם כי האלמות לא יושם כי איננו דבר אבל הוא העדר הדבור (רמב״ן שמות ד,יא), "Or who made him dumb. They explain that it extends to man, 'or who makes a man dumb?' That is to say, 'who creates a man who is dumb?' and the making refers to man, for dumbness can not be produced, for it is not a thing, but it is the absence of speech" (Ramban, Exodus 4,11). Although the Ramban refers to an אלם, one who is dumb, the exact same concept can be applied to a חרש, one who is deaf. The concept is that deafness is a nonentity, a nonexistence of hearing. Just as a vacuum is not an entity, but an area void of matter, so too, deafness is not an entity, but a person lacking the ability to hear. It is this line of reasoning which led the Ramban in his commentary to amend the words of the pasuk from או מי ישום אלם או חרש, "Or who made him dumb, or deaf," to או מי ישום אדם אלם או אדם חרש, "Or who made man dumb or a man deaf?" What is a חרש, "deaf person?" According to this Ramban in פרשת שמות, "Parashath Shemoth," a חרש, "deaf person," is one from whom G-d has withheld the ability to hear. The Ramban also gives another explanation (רמב״ן, שמות ד,יא, Ramban, Exodus 4,11).

The second time the word חרש, "deaf," appears in the

Torah is in פרשת קדושים, "Parashath Kedoshim," as stated, לא תקלל חרש ולפני עור לא תתן מכשל ויראת מאלהיך אני ה' (ויקרא יט,יד), "Do not curse the deaf, nor put a stumbling block before the blind, and you shall fear your G-d, I am G-d" (Leviticus 19,14). On this pasuk the Ramban says, וחזר והזהיר באומללים שבעם והוא החרש, ומהם ילמדו בנין אב אל כל שאר העם, כי מן הראש ועד הסוף הכל בכלל האזהרה (רמב"ן ויקרא יט,יד), "And then [the Torah] returned and warned [against cursing] the lowest of the people, and he is one who is deaf. And from them, they learn a standard rule to include all the rest of the people, for from the foremost to the end, all are included in the warning," (Ramban, Leviticus 19,14). According to the Ramban, the warning לא תקלל, "Do not curse," is only half of the mitzvah; the other half of the mitzvah is found in פרשת משפטים, "Parashath Mishpatim," as stated, אלקים לא תקלל ונשיא בעמך לא תאר (שמות כב,כז), "You shall not revile G-d, and a ruler among your people you shall not curse" (Exodus 22,27). Note that Rashi encompasses in the first words of the pasuk a warning not to curse a judge, for the word אלקים, can translated as "judges," (רש"י, שמות כב,כז, Rashi, Exodus 22,27).

The warning against cursing is given by these two verses conjointly. The pasuk in פרשת קדשים, "Parashath Kedoshim," uses the word חרש, "deaf," to refer to the lowest stratum of the Children of Israel; the pasuk in פרשת משפטים, "Parashath Mishpatim," uses the word אלקים, "judges," to refer to the highest stratum of the Children of Israel. Thus, the entire gamut of the Children of Israel is included in this commandment, as stated in the previously quoted Ramban, מן הראש ועד הסוף, "from the foremost to the end."

According to the Ramban in פרשת קדשים, "Parashath Kedoshim," a חרש, "deaf," is an individual with status, one who sets the limit, establishes the criterion, determines the standard of judgment of the lowest level or grade of the Children of Israel. The Ramban also gives another explanation (רמב"ן, ויקרא יט,יד, Ramban, Leviticus 19,14).

The two different meanings which the Ramban ascribes to the word חרש, "deaf," or "one with deafness," can now be comprehended. In פרשת שמות, "Parashath Shemoth," the Ramban can be said to define a חרש, "deaf person," as one from whom G-d has withheld the ability to hear: deafness as a nonentity, a nonexistence. In פרשת קדשים, "Parashath Kedoshim," the Ramban can be said to define a חרש, "deaf person," as an individual with status, one who sets the limit, establishes the criterion.

Returning to the the פרה אדמה, "red heifer," in Parashath Chukkath, the אור החיים, "Or Hachayyim," says that Moses alone comprehended the reason for the red heifer, but he did not tell the Children of Israel, as stated, ומתוך הדברים אתה למד שנאמר למשה דברים מוטעמים במצוה זו אלא שמה שצוה עליו לאמר הוא חקה ובזה לא יתבעוהו ישראל לומר להם טעם הדבר וכו' (אור החיים במדבר יט,ב ד"ה אשר צוה ה' לאמר), "And from these words you learn that reasons concerning this commandment were said to Moses, but that he was commanded to say that it is a statute, and because of this Israel will not demand of him to say to them the reason of the thing, etc." (Or Hachayyim Numbers 19,2, header words: Which G-d commanded saying).

Rashi explains that the Torah calls the mitzvah of פרה אדמה, "red heifer," a statute, because of a lack of a perceived rationale, the Children of Israel will be taunted about it, as stated, לפי שהשטן ואמות העולם מונים את ישראל לומר מה המצוה הזאת ומה טעם יש בה לפיכך כתב חקה גזרה היא מלפני אין לך רשות להרהר אחריה (רש"י, במדבר יט,ב), "Since the Satan and the nations of the world taunt Israel saying, 'What is this commandment and what is the reason for it?' Therefore, it is written as a statute; It is a decree before Me, and you have no permission to speculate about it," (Rashi, Numbers 19,2). What, then, can the Children of Israel answer when they are taunted about this commandment? Nothing! What can the

Children of Israel do when they are taunted about this commandment? They can make themselves like one who is חרש, "deaf," not to hear the taunts, i.e., the taunts should fall on deaf ears. Thus, the concept of חקת, "statute," is linked to the concept of חרש, "deaf."

This link is reinforced by the following gematria. The word חקת, "statute," is found in the second verse of Parashath Chukkath, as stated, זאת חקת התורה אשר צוה ה' לאמר דבר אל בני ישראל ויקחו אליך פרה אדמה תמימה אשר אין בה מום אשר לא עלה עליה על (במדבר יט,ב), "This is the statute of the Torah, which G-d commanded saying: Speak to the Children of Israel and they shall take for you a perfectly red heifer, which has no blemish, upon which has never come a yoke" (Numbers 19,1-2). The gematria of חקת, "statute," is 508.

חקת   508

The word חרש, "deaf," is found in Parashath Shemoth, as stated, ויאמר ה' אליו מי שם פה לאדם או מי ישום אלם או חרש או פקח או עור הלא אנכי ה' (שמות ד,יא), "And G-d said to him: Who has made a mouth for man, or Who made him dumb, or deaf, or seeing or blind? Is it not I, G-d?" (Exodus 4,11). The gematria of חרש, "deaf," is 508.

חרש   508

The word חרש, "deaf," is also found in Parashath Kedoshim, as stated, לא תקלל חרש ולפני עור לא תתן מכשל ויראת מאלקיך אני ה' (ויקרא יט,יד), "Do not curse the deaf, nor put a stumbling block before the blind, and you shall fear your G-d, I am G-d" (Leviticus 19,14). As mentioned, the gematria of חרש, "deaf," is 508.

The gematria of חקת, "statute," is equal to the gematria of חרש, "deaf." This matching gematria reinforces the link between a חקת, "statute," and a חרש, "deaf": namely, that when the Children of Israel are taunted about the statute of the Torah, they should make themselves deaf. There are two ways one can behave as deaf when being taunted. Either one can know the reason for the commandment about which he is being taunted, and remain silent, or one can be ignorant of the reason of the commandment about which he is being taunted, and remain silent. Obviously, to set a precedent to remain silent when being taunted, one would have to know the reason for the commandment about which he was being taunted; in spite of the fact that he knew the reason, he still remained quiet. Since Moses alone knew the reason for the פרה אדמה, "red heifer," but did not tell the Children of Israel, the red heifer of Moses was different from those of other generations, and his red heifer set a precedent to remain silent when taunted about this commandment.

The difference between the פרה אדמה, "red heifer," of Moses and those of other generations parallels the two different meanings the Ramban explained for the word חרש, "deaf." In פרשת שמות, "Parashath Shemoth," the Ramban explained a חרש, "deafness" as a nonentity, a person from whom G-d has withheld the ability to hear. This explanation parallels the red heifer of the generations after Moses, since no one of those generations knew the reason for the commandment. They were like a nonentity concerning the statute of the Torah; they were like a person from whom G-d had withheld the ability to know. In פרשת קדשים, "Parashath Kedoshim," the Ramban explained a חרש, "deaf" as an individual with status, one who establishes a criterion. This explanation parallels the red heifer of Moses, since he knew the reason for the commandment but did not reveal it. He set a precedent to remain silent when taunted about this commandment.

The parallel between the פרה אדמה, "red heifer," and חרש, "deaf," helps answer the two questions on the interpretation of the העמק דבר, "Haamek Davar": One, in what way was the red heifer of Moses different from other red heifers? Two, why did the Torah tell this difference? The answers seem apparent. The red heifer of Moses is the case where an individual knew the reason for the commandment but did not reveal it. The Torah tells this difference to make aware that Moses set a precedent in remaining silent when taunted about this commandment, likewise when the Children of Israel are taunted, they should make themselves deaf. Thus, both questions asked on the interpretation of the העמק דבר, "Haamek Davar," have been answered.

Now, according to the Haamek Davar, which was quoted previously, the verse should be interpreted as follows: זאת חקת התורה אשר צוה ה׳ לאמר, "This is the statute of the Torah, which G-d commanded saying." This phrase refers to the red heifer of future generations who will not know the reason for this commandment, but will follow the example of Moses. דבר אל בני ישראל ויקחו אליך וגו׳, "Speak to the Children of Israel and they shall take for you, etc." This phrase refers to the red heifer of Moses, who knew the reason for this commandment, but did not reveal it, and set an example of remaining silent when taunted.

Note that the word צוה, "commanded," is used to refer to future generations. This application of the word צוה, "commanded," to future generations can be substantiated by the first Rashi in פרשת צו, "Parashath Tzav," as stated, אין צו אלא לשון זרוז מיד ולדורות וכו׳ (רש״י, ויקרא ו,ב). "The word tzav (command) is only an expression of spurring on, immediately, and for the future generations," (Rashi, Leviticus 6,2).

The application of the word צוה, "commanded," to future generations can explain the difference between the questions of the wise son and the wicked son in the Hagadah of Passover. At first glance these two sons seem to be asking the same question. The מחזה אברהם, "Machazeh Avraham," points out that the wise son uses the word צוה, "commanded," מחזה אברהם על הגדה של פסח, מאת אברהם אביש מן (פראנקפורט, ד״ה חכם מה אומר, Mahazeh Avraham on the Haggadah shel Pesah by Avraham Abusch from Frankfurt, header words: The wise son, what does he say). Since the word צוה, "commanded," applies to future generations, the wise son is asking: What is this service that you have been commanded for generations? The wicked son does not use the word צוה, "commanded," because he feels that the service which he is questioning is something created recently, and not a command to be kept for generations.

These thoughts are applicable in today's troubled times. Religious Jews are chided. There are people who criticize those who keep the dietary laws; who disapprove of those who observe the Shabbath and Jewish holidays; who take affront at those who comply by the rules of family purity; who constantly find fault with those who establish time for prayer and learning Torah; and who scorn those who live a Torah life. Some people have gained sadistic pleasure from ruthlessly criticizing Torah Judaism. Some of these have the audacity to parade their bogus authority under the banner of a leader. The Gemara Gittin says כל המיצר לישראל נעשה ראש (גיטין נו:), "All who torment Israel become leaders." (Gittin 56b). How are Torah-true Jews to respond to such a barrage of criticism? A Torah Jew should make himself like a חרש, "deaf person"; such foolish talk should fall on deaf ears. The message of the פרה אדמה, "red heifer," is extraordinarily relevant to our generation.

The Gemara Pesahim says that Rav Joseph the son of Rabbi Joshua ben Levi saw the world to come, and reported, עולם הפוך ראיתי עליונים למטה ותחתונים למעלה, אמר לו בני עולם ברור ראית (פסחים נ.), "An upside-down world I saw; the exalted ones were low and the lowly were exalted. (His father) said to him: My son, you saw a clear world" (Pesahim 50a). Thus, this world is the true upside-down world. The red heifer caused a reversal of circumstances, as stated, לטהר טמאים לטמא טהורים (יוצר לפרשת פרה) "It would purify the ritually defiled, and make defiled the ritually pure" (Liturgical hymns for Shabbath Porah). If the message of the פרה אדמה, "red heifer," is heeded in our time, אי״ה, "G-d willing," it will cause a reversal of circumstances and set upright our upside-down world. Please G-d, the Jewish people should be worthy to be purified by the red heifer in Jerusalem, may it be speedily rebuilt in our days.

ויאמר ה׳ אל משה ואל אהרן יען לא האמנתם בי להקדישני לעיני בני ישראל לכן לא תביאו את הקהל הזה אל הארץ אשר נתתי להם (במדבר כ,יב).

And G-d said to Moses and to Aaron, since you did not believe in Me to sanctify Me in the eyes of the Children of Israel, therefore you shall not bring this congregation into the land which I have given to them (Numbers 20,12).

In פרשת חקת, Parashath Chukkath, it is recorded that Moses sinned. Although it is difficult to imagine what slight sin he did, perhaps via a gematria some light can be shed on this subject.

There are five questions which can be addressed. One, the Gemara Sanhedrin asserts, שכל מדותיו של הקב״ה מדר כנגד מדה (שבת קה. ;ונדרים לב. ;וסנהדרין צ.), "All the attributes of the Holy One, Blessed be He, are meted out measure for measure" (Shabbath 105b; Nedarim 32a; and Sanhedrin 90a). How was denying Moses entrance into the land of Israel a measure for an equal measure? Two, if Moses' sin was hitting the rock as opposed to speaking to it, as Rashi (רש״י, במדבר כ,יב, Rashi, Numbers 20,12) says, why did the Torah say, לא האמנתם בי, "you did not believe in Me," it should have said, לא שמעתם לי, "you did not listen to Me"? Three, If Moses sinned by hitting the rock, why was Aaron punished? Four, the pasuk quoted above says ויאמר ה׳ אל משה ואל אהרן, "And G-d said to Moses and to Aaron." Simply say, ויאמר ה׳ אל משה ואהרן, "And G-d said to Moses and Aaron." Why is there a seemingly extra word אל, "to"? Five, the pasuk says, לא האמנתם בי, "you did not believe in Me." Of course, lack of belief refers to belief in G-d. The word בי, "in Me," could have been eliminated without loss of meaning; why was it written?

By examining four sources a possible answer to each of the five questions can be ascertained. The first source is the Gemara Horayoth which individualizes idolatry as the commandment which is equated to all 613 Commandments, as stated, איזו היא מצוה שהיא שקולה ככל המצות הוי אומר זו עבודת כוכבים (הוריות ח.), "Which commandment is equivalent to all the commandments? Say it is idol worship" (Horayoth 8a). The second source is the Rambam which says, אמרו חכמים הראשונים כל הכועס כאילו עובד עבודה זרה (משנה תורה, ספר המדע, הלכות דעות, פרק ב, הלכה ג) "Our early [Torah oriented] wise men have said, All those who get angry is as if they worshiped idols" (Mishnah Torah, Book of Hamadda, Laws of Knowledge, Chapter 2, Law 3). The Zohar also says, כל הכועס כאלו עובד ע״ז (ספר הזוהר מאת התנא רבי שמעון בן יוחאי, פרשת בראשית, דף כז:), "All those who get angry is as if they worshiped idols" (The Book of the Zohar by the Tanna Rabbi Shimon ben Yochai, Parashath Bereshith, Page 27b). Things equal to the same thing are equal to each other. Since one who get angry is as if he worshiped idols, and since idol worship is equated to all 613 Commandments, therefore one who gets angry is as if he violated all the commandments. The third source is the Ramban, who based on a Sifrei, states, ישיבת ארץ ישראל שקולה כנגד כל המצות שבתורה (רמב״ן, ויקרא יח,כה), "Dwelling in the land of Israel is counterbalanced to all the commandments of the Torah" (Ramban, Leviticus 18,25). The fourth and final source is the Abarbanel who writes, והדעת הגי הוא לרב הגדול המימוני שכתב שהיה חטאו של משה במה שכעס בחנם על ישראל והכעס בחק כסילים ינוח (קהלת ז,ט)…. ודעתי בזה שמשה ואהרן שניהם נענשו בעבור עונות שעשו, אם אהרן בעון העגל (פירוש על התורה מאת הרב יצחק אברבנאל, פרשת חקת, במדבר כ,א־יג, ד״ה והדעת הגי ודעתי בזה),

"And the third reason is according to great Rabbi Hamaimoni who wrote that the sin of Moses was that he got angry with Israel for nothing, and the anger rests in the bosom of fools (Ecclesiastes 7,9)... And my opinion of this matter is that both Moses and Aaron were punished because of sins that they had committed. In the case of Aaron, it was the sin of the [golden] calf" (Commentary on the Torah by Rabbi Yitzchak Abarbanel, Parashath Chukkath, Numbers 20,1-13, header words: And the third reason, and header words: And in my opinion of this matter).

Keeping these four sources in mind, the five original questions can now be answered. One, how was denying Moses entrance into the land of Israel a measure for an equal measure? When Moses said (במדבר כ,י) שמעו נא המרים, "Listen, you rebels" (Numbers 20,10), he showed some degree of anger. Since one who gets angry is as if he violated all the commandments, so G-d punished him by denying him entrance to the land of Israel, the place in which residency is considered equated to all the commandments. Two, why did the Torah say, לא האמנתם בי, "you did not believe in Me," it should have said, לא שמעתם לי, "you did not listen to Me"? When someone gets angry it is due to a lack of total faith in G-d. One who has total belief in G-d, trusts that He will do whatever is necessary to rectify every situation. So when Moses got angry, it showed, to some degree, a lack of total belief in G-d; that is why the Torah says, לא האמנתם בי, "you did not believe in Me." Three, if Moses sinned by hitting the rock, why was Aaron punished? When G-d punished Moses, he gave the same punishment to Aaron, but for a different reason. Aaron was punished for his role in making the golden calf; that role connected him to idol worship. Since idol worship is equated to all 613 Commandments, so G-d punished him, like Moses, by denying him entrance to the land of Israel, the place in which residency is considered equated to all the commandments. Four, why didn't the pasuk simply say, ויאמר ה' אל משה ואהרן, "And G-d said to Moses and Aaron"? The complete pasuk records G-d's reaction, as stated, ויאמר ה' אל משה ואל אהרן יען לא האמנתם בי להקדישני לעיני בני ישראל לכן לא תביאו את הקהל הזה אל הארץ אשר נתתי להם (במדבר כ,יב). "And G-d said to Moses and to Aaron, since you did not believe in Me to sanctify Me in the eyes of the Children of Israel, therefore you shall not bring this congregation into the land which I have given to them" (Numbers 20,12). The gematria of משה, אהרן, and בי, "Moses, Aaron" and "in Me," is 613.

משה	345
אהרן	256
בי	12
	613

It is plausible that the Torah writes each name without a ו, "vav," so the gematria of those three words would equal 613, the number of the commandments. Five, and lastly, the word בי, "in Me," could have been eliminated without loss of meaning; why was it written? It is also plausible that the Torah writes the word בי, "in Me," so that there would be a gematria of 613 in this pasuk. From this gematria the Children of Israel can fathom how important it is not to get angry, and to avoid any association with idol worship.

וידר ישראל נדר לה' ויאמר אם נתן תתן את העם הזה בידי
והחרמתי את עריהם (במדבר כא,ב).
And Israel vowed a vow to G-d, and said, If You
indeed give this people into my hand, then I will
utterly destroy their cities (Numbers 21,2).

The Torah records that the Children of Israel made a vow requesting G-d to deliver this people into בידי, "my hand," (Numbers 21,2). The gematria of בידי, "my hand," is 26.

בידי   26

Rashi explains that the vow actually was, that if G-d will deliver the people (who were really Amalek, but had changed their language to that of Canaan) into the hand of Israel, then Israel will consecrate the enemy's cities to G-d (רש״י, במדבר כא,א-ג, Rashi, Numbers 21, 1-3). When the Children of Israel made this vow, the name of G-d which they used was ה׳, and G-d heeded the request of the Children of Israel, as stated, וידר ישראל נדר לה׳ ויאמר אם נתן תתן את העם הזה בידי והחרמתי את עריהם. וישמע ה׳ בקול ישראל ויתן את הכנעני ויחרם אתהם ואת עריהם ויקרא שם המקום חרמה (במדבר כא,ב-ג), "And Israel vowed a vow to G-d, and said, If you indeed give this people into my hand, then I will utterly destroy their cities. And G-d hearkened to the voice of Israel, and delivered the Canaanites, and he destroyed them and their cities; and the name of the place was called Hormah" (Numbers 21,2-3). The gematria of ה׳, "G-d," is 26.

ה׳   26

When the Torah refers to G-d's attribute of mercy, the name ה׳, "G-d," is used (א,א וח,א בראשית, רש״י, Rashi, Genesis 1,1 and 8,1). It is possible that the Children of Israel made the vow to ה׳, "G-d," for they were requesting success in battle, that is, that G-d should show mercy to them.

It is appropriate that בידי, "my hand," should have the same gematria as ה׳, "G-d," since Israel had said: That which G-d in His mercy puts in my hand, will be consecrated to Him.

Parashath Balak   פרשת בלק

וישלח מלאכים אל בלעם בן בעור פתורה אשר על הנהר
ארץ בני עמו לקרא לו לאמר הנה עם יצא ממצרים הנה
כסה את עין הארץ והוא ישב ממלי (במדבר כב,ה).
And he sent messengers to Balaam the son of
Beor to Pethor, which is by the river, the land of
the children of his people, to call him, saying,
"Behold a people went out of Egypt, and behold
they cover the face of the land, and they dwell
opposite me" (Numbers 22,5).

Balak sent messengers to Balaam who was in a place
which the Torah describes as "by the river, the land of the
children of his people." Three questions can be asked. One,
why does the Torah mention that this place was "by the river?"
Was the Torah trying to give a geography lesson? Two, why
does the Torah mention that that this land was "of the children
of his people?" Commentaries differ as to whether this land
was native to Balaam or Balak (רש״י, רמב״ן, במדבר כב,ה, Rashi,
Ramban, Numbers 22,5). Why does the Torah have this vague
reference, rather than identifying the land as either native to
Balaam or Balak? Three, why does the Torah mention these
two facts together? What possible connection could there be
between the fact that the place was "by the river," and the fact
that this land was "of the children of his people?"

These three questions can be answered with the aid of
a gematria. Targum Onkelos on this verse identifies the river
which flowed by the place of Balaam as the Euphrates River
(תרגום אונקלוס, במדבר כב,ה). The Torah uses this selfsame
Euphrates River to contour the border of the land of Israel, as
stated, כל המקום אשר תדרך כף רגלכם בו לכם יהיה מן המדבר והלבנון
Every" ,מן הנהר נהר פרת ועד הים האחרון יהיה גבלכם (דברים יא,כד)
place where the sole of your foot will tread upon, shall be
yours; from the desert and the Lebanon, from the river, the

Euphrates River, until the hinder sea, shall be your border" (Deuteronomy 11,24). If Balaam lived on one side of the river, he would be in the land of Israel; if Balaam lived on the other side of the river, he would be outside the land of Israel.

The Torah uses the word עמו, "His people," to refer to G-d's people, the Children of Israel, as stated, וישמע יתרו כהן מדין חתן משה את כל אשר עשה אלקים למשה ולישראל עמו כי הוציא ה׳ את ישראל ממצרים (שמות יח,א), "And Yithro, the priest of Midian, Moses' father-in-law, heard all that G-d did for for Moses and Israel, His people, for G-d had taken Israel out of Egypt" (Exodus 18,1). Consequently, when the verse in Parashath Balak says, "the land of the children of His people," the word "His people" might possibly refer to G-d's people, the Children of Israel. The verse is designating this land as part of the land of Israel.

When the Torah says that Balaam lived by the river, it is unclear if he lived inside or outside the land of Israel, owing to the fact that the Euphrates River was the border of the land of Israel. When the Torah added that Balaam lived in "the land of the children of His people," designating this land as part of the land of Israel, it is clear that he lived in the land of Israel.

The Ramban, quoting a Sifre, says that living in the land of Israel is equated to all the commandments in the Torah (רמב״ן ויקרא יח,כה, Ramban, Leviticus 18,25). The Gemara Makkoth says that There is a total of 613 Commandments in the Torah (מכות כג:, Makkoth 23b). Therefore, living in the land of Israel is equated to 613 Commandments. The Torah describes this part of the land of Israel as על הנהר ארץ בני עמו, "by the river, the land of the children of his people," The gematria of הנהר ארץ בני, "the river, the land of the children," is 613.

הנהר	260
ארץ	291
בני	62
	613

Since living in the land of Israel is equated to the 613 Commandments, it is very appropriate that the expression that the Torah uses to describe this part of the land of Israel contains the gematria of 613.

Now the three questions asked can be answered. One, why does the Torah mention that this place was "by the river?" The answer is that this river is the Euphrates River, which contours the border of the land of Israel. Two, why does the Torah mention that this land was "of the children of his people?" The answer is that the word עמו, "His people," can refer to G-d's people, the Children of Israel, and the verse is designating this land as part of the land of Israel. Three, why does the Torah mention these two facts together? What possible connection could there be between the fact that the place was "by the river," and the fact that this land was "of the children of His people?" The answer is that from the first fact, that this river is the Euphrates River which contours the border of the land of Israel, it is not clear if Balaam lived inside or outside the land of Israel, owing to the fact that the Euphrates River was the border of the land of Israel. From the second fact that he lived in "the land of the children of His people," designating this land as part of the land of Israel, it is clear that he lived in the land of Israel.

Since living in the land of Israel is equated to the 613 Commandments, the gematria of 613 contained in the expression to describe this part of the land of Israel enhances this interpretation.

ויאמר אלקים אל בלעם לא תלך עמהם לא תאר את העם
כי ברוך הוא (במדבר כב,יב).

And G-d said to Balaam do not go with them, do not curse the people, for they are blessed (Numbers 22,12).

When Balaam wanted to go and curse the Children of

Israel, G-d originally told him not to go because they are blessed. The gematria of ברוך הוא, "they are blessed," is 240.

ברוך	228
הוא	12
	240

The question is, why did the Torah need to say that the Children of Israel are blessed? It would have been sufficient to say, do not curse the people. Rashi gives one explanation (רש"י, במדבר כב,יב, Rashi, Numbers 22,12), but a different one can be given with the aid of a משל, "parable."

There once was a king who was fond of hunting. Frequently, he would remove his crown and royal garments to don a hunting outfit.

Late one afternoon while the king was hunting, his horse galloped too close to a tree, in pursuit of a fox. The king was thrust against the tree's trunk and his head collided against one of the tree's branches. He was knocked from his horse and lay unconscious on the forest floor with a concussion, several broken ribs, a broken leg, and several minor cuts. The king's horse ran away, and as darkness descended, none of the royal hunting party could find the king.

Meanwhile, a poor Jewish woodworker heading home stumbled on the body of an injured hunter. The Jew, not realizing that the hunter was the king, carried the injured hunter to his very simple dirt floor hut in the forest. There he set the king's broken bones, dressed his wounds, and lay the king down in a very plain bed of straw.

The Jewish woodworker had really saved the king from the jaws of death. When the king regained consciousness, he told the the woodworker and his family that he was no ordinary hunter, but a rich and powerful king. Neither the woodworker nor his family took the the hunter's claim to royalty very seriously. The woodworker invited the injured hunter to stay with him, and instructed his wife to feed the guest until he regained his health. The poor woodworker only ate with austere wooden plates and spoons for himself and his family. As the king's health improved he told the woodworker, "I am the king. It is not proper for you to serve me with these austere wooden spoons and plates; please buy some proper china and silverware for me." The poor Jewish woodworker purchased some china and silverware for his guest, although he still did not take the hunter's claim to royalty very seriously.

The poor woodworker lived in an unadorned one room, dirt floor hut. As the king's health improved further, he told the woodworker, "I am the king. It is not proper for me to eat and sleep in the same room with common folks; please move yourself, your wife, and your children outside while I stay in your home." The poor Jewish woodworker and his entire family moved outside to an unprotected shed, open to the sky, leaving his home for his guest to occupy, although he still did not take the hunter's claim to royalty very seriously.

The poor woodworker only provided coarse black bread and water for himself and his family. As the king's health improved further, he told the woodworker, "I am the king. It is not proper for me to eat and drink this primitive food; please buy some lean meat, white bread, vegetables, and wine for me." The poor Jewish woodworker bought lean meat, white bread, vegetables, and wine for his guest, although he still did not take the hunter's claim to royalty very seriously.

While the woodworker was in the process of providing his guest with all that he requested, the other forest inhabitants constantly derided, ridiculed, and mocked the Jewish woodworker and his family for allowing a stranger to disrupt their lives. Eventually, the king recuperated completely, thanked his host, and bade farewell to the woodworker and his family.

Approximately one year later, the poor Jewish wood-worker traveled to the capital city to seek a suitable young man to marry his daughter. Being that he lived in abject poverty, and could not provide his daughter with a dowry, he felt his choice of bridegrooms would be extremely limited. As the woodworker was walking through the streets of the capital city, he noticed a large crowd had gathered around the royal coach to get a glimpse of the king. The poor wood-worker also moved forward into the crowd as he attempted to see the king.

When the king descended from his coach, the poor woodworker received the shock of his life. The injured hunter whom he had saved from the jaws of death really was the king. It was true! The injured hunter was a powerful king who reigned over many lands, and a rich monarch who had su-preme ownership of unimaginable wealth. The woodworker screamed loudly until he gained the king's attention; the king, in turn, invited him into his royal carriage, again thanked him for saving his life, and acknowledged that he had nursed him back to health. The king then inquired why the woodworker had traveled to the capital city.

As the poor Jewish woodworker told of his plight, and how bleak the prospects for his daughter seemed, the king's face broke into a wide smile. "Have no fear," he assured the woodworker, "my chief financial advisor is a fine Jewish man of knowledge, wisdom and wealth. His son, a handsome scholar with an exceptionally sincere character, is looking to marry a woman your daughter's age. I can arrange all the details for the match. I will provide your daughter with a dowry fit for a princess; you may use my castle's largest hall for the ceremony, invite as many guests as you like for the celebration, order any food or drink you wish from the royal kitchen, and select any home site where you desire me to build a luxurious house to your specifications for the newly wedded couple. All of these provisions will be at my expense."

The king did everything he said he would. The poor Jewish woodworker never envisioned he would receive such a marvelous reward for saving the hunter's life. When members of the royal family or advisors to the king criticized the king for being so lavish with a poor woodworker, he simply answered that since the woodworker had given him special attention, he would give the woodworker special attention.

That is the משל, "parable." This story has a נמשל, "moral." The king represents G-d, Who is the most powerful King reigning over all the lands, and a rich monarch Who has supreme ownership of unimaginable wealth; the poor Jewish woodworker represents the Children of Israel. Just as the woodworker and his family did not take the hunter's claim to royalty very seriously, so too, many individuals and families of the Children of Israel do not really feel that all they are doing in this world is examined very closely by G-d. So many commandments are performed mechanically, without any feeling that their fulfillment is for the King of Kings. Just as the king in the parable asked the poor woodworker to buy some proper china and silverware for him, so too G-d requires the Jewish people to purchase new dishes and silverware for the Passover holiday. Just as the king in the parable asked the poor woodworker to please move himself, his wife, and his children outside to an unprotected shed, open to the sky, while he stayed in the woodworker's home, so too G-d requires the Jewish people to move from their warm homes to roofless huts for the Sukkoth holiday. Just as the king in the parable asked the poor woodworker to please buy some lean meat, white bread, vegetables, and wine for him, so too G-d requires the Jewish people to purchase kosher food the entire year, as well as superior food for Shabbath and Yom Tov.

Just as the other forest inhabitants constantly derided,

ridiculed, and mocked the Jewish woodworker and his family for allowing a stranger to disrupt their lives, so too the nations of the world persecute, torture, and kill the members of the Jewish faith for living according to the laws of G-d's Torah. When the king descended from his coach, the poor woodworker received the shock of his life when he realized that the injured hunter whom he had saved from the jaws of death was a powerful king who reigned over many lands, a rich monarch who had supreme ownership of unimaginable wealth. So too members of the Jewish faith will be shocked when they arrive at the next world and realize what they had done was for G-d, Who is the most powerful King, reigning over all the lands, a rich Monarch Who has supreme ownership of unimaginable wealth.

Just as the king in the parable gave special attention to the woodworker because of the special attention the woodworker had given the king, so too G-d will give the Children of Israel special attention in the next world because of the unique treatment the Children of Israel gave to G-d in this world. An analogous thought is also found in the Gemara Berakoth, as stated, אמר להם הקב"ה לישראל אתם עשיתוני חטיבה אחת בעולם ואני אעשה אתכם חטיבה אחת בעולם (ברכות ו.), "The Holy One, Blessed be He, said to Israel, You have made Me singularly the object of love in the world, and I shall make you singularly the object of love in the world," (Berakoth 6a).

Now that the משל, "parable," and the נמשל, "moral," have been presented, the gematria can be elucidated. As was set forth, the gematria of ברוך הוא, "they are blessed," is 240. The simplest way to represent 240 with Hebrew letters is with the letters ר, "resh," and ם, "mem." The word רם, "high," is found in the עזרת אבותינו תפלה, "Help of our Fathers prayer" of תפלת שחרית, "Morning Service," as stated, רם ונשא גדול ונורא משפיל גאים ומגביה שפלים מוציא אסירים ופודה ענוים ועוזר דלים ועונה לעמו בעת שועם אליו (סידור בית יעקב מאת הרב יעקב מעמדין בן הרב צבי,

(אשכנזי, דף, סה), "He Who is high and exalted, great and re-vered; Who lowers the haughty, and raises the lowly, takes out the prisoners, delivers the meek, helps the poor, and answer His people when they cry out to Him" (Siddur Beth Yaakov by Rabbi Yaakov from Emden ben Rabbi Zvi, Ashke-nazi, page 65a). The word רם, "high," is also found in ספר תהלים, "the Book of Psalms," as stated, רם על כל גוים ה׳ על השמים כבודו. מי כה׳ אלקינו המגביהי לשבת. המשפילי לראות בשמים ובארץ (תהלים קיג,ד-ו), "G-d is high above all nations, above the heavens is His glory. Who is like G-d, our G-d, Who dwells exalted? Who humbles himself to look upon the heaven and earth?" (Psalms 113,4-6). There is also a second source in ספר תהלים, "the Book of Psalms," as stated, כי רם ה׳ ושפל יראה וגבה ממרחק יידע (תהלים קלח,ו), "For G-d is high, and yet He sees the humble, and the haughty He knows from afar" (Psalms 138,6). The gematria of רם, "high," is 240.

רם   240

The gematria of רם, "high," is equal to the gematria of ברוך הוא "they are blessed"; both are 240. To understand the connection, note that in each of the three sources quoted, where the word רם, "high," is used to refer to Hashem, He is depicted as concerned with man's lowly life. Perhaps the explanation is that since the Children of Israel "make" Him King, רם, "high," therefore He takes an interest in the Chil-dren of Israel. As the Gemara Berakoth, previously quoted, stated, אמר להם הקב״ה לישראל אתם עשיתוני חטיבה אחת בעולם ואני אעשה אתכם חטיבה אחת בעולם (ברכות ו.), "The Holy One, Blessed be He, said to Israel, You have made Me singularly the object of love in the world, and I shall make you singularly the object of love in the world," (Berakoth 6a).

What empowers the commandments the Jews perform to exalt G-d, that is, "make" Him רם, "high"? Many of the commandments are preceded by blessings. The Gemara Berakoth designates a fundamental aspect of a blessing, as stated, לרבי יוחנן דאמר כל ברכה שאין בה מלכות אינה ברכה (ברכות יב.) "According to Rabbi Johanan, who said, every blessing which does not contain mention of kingship is not a blessing" (Berakoth 12a). Thus, blessings are linked to kingship. Almost all the major mitzvoth, such as those associated with the Passover holiday, the Sukkoth holiday, and eating kosher food, are done in conjunction with a blessing.

It could be that those mitzvoth performed in connection with blessings, which acknowledge G-d as King, that is, רם, "high," have the power to enthrone G-d. It could also be because the Children of Israel make G-d רם, "high," that He will make them singularly the object of love in the next world.

Now the original question (from במדבר כב,יב, Numbers 22,12) can be answered. The question is why did the Torah say that the Children of Israel are blessed? It would have been sufficient to say, do not curse the people. G-d told Balaam that the Children of Israel are blessed because they bless G-d. The blessings of the Children of Israel are linked to kingship; their blessings empower the mitzvoth which "make" G-d רם, "high"; therefore He takes an interest in the Children of Israel. This link is more apparent from the reality that the gematria of רם, "high," is equal to the gematria of ברוך הוא, "they are blessed"; both are 240. Since the Children of Israel make G-d רם, "high," He will make them singularly the object of love in the world. Thus, G-d told Balaam do not curse the people, for they are blessed.

Parashath Pinchas   פרשת פינחס

פינחס בן אלעזר בן אהרן הכהן השיב את חמתי מעל בני ישראל בקנאו את קנאתי בתוכם ולא כליתי את בני ישראל בקנאתי (במדבר כה,יא).

Pinchas the son of Eleazar, the son of Aaron the priest, has turned My wrath away from the Children of Israel, in that he was jealous for My jealousy among them. And I did not consume them in My jealousy (Numbers 25,11).

The second verse of this sidrah relates the result of what פינחס, "Pinchas," did. The gematria of פינחס, "Pinchas," is 208.

פינחס   208

The Gemara Sanhedrin says that although Pinchas had a right to kill Zimri, if Zimri had killed Pinchas in self-defense, Zimri would have been free from capital punishment, as stated, נהפך זמרי והרגו לפנחס אין נהרג עליו שהרי רודף הוא (סנהדין פב.), "If Zimri had turned about and killed Pinchas, he would not have been killed, for he [Pinchas] was a pursuer" (Sanhedrin 82a). Thus, Pinchas put his life on the line for the sake of Heaven. In ספר תהלים, the Book of Psalms, there is reference to Pinchas, as stated, ויעמד פינחס ויפלל ותעצר המגפה (תהלים קו,ל), "And Pinchas stood up and executed judgment; and the plague was halted" (Psalms 106,30). The אבן עזרא, "Ibn Ezra," and מצודת דוד, "Metsudath David," both explain this pasuk as referring to Pinchas executing דין, "judgment," when he killed Zimri. Thus, Pinchas is associated with the מדת הדין, "attribute of justice." The two salient characteristics mentioned about Pinchas are that he put his life on the line for the sake of Heaven, and that he is associated with the attribute of justice.

These two salient characteristics mentioned about Pinchas are also found in יצחק, "Isaac." Isaac was willing to let himself be slaughtered as a sacrifice, as Rashi says, אף על פי שהבין יצחק שהוא הולך להשחט ׳וילכו שניהם יחדיו,׳ בלב שוה (רש״י, בראשית כב,ח), "And even though Isaac comprehended that he was going to be slaughtered, 'both of them went together,' with equivalent hearts," (Rashi, Genesis 22,8). Thus, Isaac put his life on the line for the sake of Heaven. The Ramban explains that when Jacob swore by the fear of his father Isaac, he was referring to the מדת הדין, "attribute of justice," as stated, ועל דרך האמת יבא הלשון כפשוטו ומשמעו והוא מדת הדין של מעלה (רמב״ן בראשית לא,נג), "And according to the way of truth, the language comes in accordance with its simple meaning and understanding, and that is His attribute of strict justice of high" (Ramban, Genesis 31,53). Thus, Isaac is associated with the מדת הדין, "attribute of justice." The two salient characteristics mentioned about Isaac are that he put his life on the line for the sake of Heaven, and that he is associated with the attribute of justice.

At the beginning of עקידת יצחק, "the Binding of Isaac," G-d tells Abraham to take Isaac, as stated, ויאמר קח נא את בנך את יחידך אשר אהבת את יצחק ולך לך אל ארץ המריה והעלהו שם לעלה על אחד ההרים אשר אמר אליך (בראשית כב,ב), "And He said, please take your son, your only one, whom you love, Isaac, and go for yourself to the land of Moriah, and offer him there as a burnt sacrifice on one of the mountains which I will tell you," (Genesis 22,2). The gematria of יצחק, "Isaac," is 208.

יצחק   208

Since both Pinchas and Isaac had the same salient characteristics, it is fitting that their names should have the same gematria.

ויאמר ה׳ אל משה עלה אל הר העברים הזה וראה את הארץ אשר נתתי לבני ישראל (במדבר כז,יב).

And G-d said to Moses, Go up to this mountain Abarim, and see the land which I have given to the Children of Israel (Numbers 27,12).

Before Moses died, G-d told him to see the land that He had given to the Children of Israel. The gematria of וראה את, "and see," is 613.

וראה	212
את	401
	613

The Gemara Makkoth says that when Moses received the Torah he was told of the 613 Mitzvoth, as stated, דרש רבי שמלאי שש מאות ושלש עשרה מצות נאמרו לו למשה שלש מאות וששים וחמש לאוין כמנין ימות החמה ומאתים וארבעים ושמונה עשה כנגד איבריו של אדם (מכות כג:), "Rabbi Simlai expounded, 613 Commandments were said to Moses, three hundred and sixty-five negative Commandments corresponding to the number of days in a solar year, and two hundred and forty-eight positive Commandments corresponding to the limbs of a person" (Makkoth 23b). In ספר תהלים, Book of Psalms, it says that G-d's commandments enlighten the eyes, as stated, פקודי ה׳ ישרים משמחי לב מצות ה׳ ברה מאירת עינים (תהלים יט,ט), "The precepts of G-d are upright, rejoicing the heart; the commandment of G-d is crystalline, enlightening the eyes" (Psalms 19,9). Since a total of 613 Commandments were told to Moses, and since the commandments enlighten the eyes, therefore it is very meaningful that G-d used the words וראה את, "and see," whose gematria equals 613, when He told Moses to see the land that He had given to the Children of Israel. A slightly different interpretation of these words is given in the פרשת האזינו, Parashath Haazinu, section of this sefer.

מלבד עלת הבקר אשר לעלת התמיד תעשו את אלה (במדבר כח,כג).

Besides the burnt offering of the morning, which is for the continual burnt offering, you should do these (Numbers 28,23).

In reference to the sacrifices of Passover, the Torah uses the word, מלבד, "besides." The gematria of מלבד, "besides," 76.

מלבד   76

Thus, 76 represents that which is sacrificed especially for Passover, that is, that which is sacrificed besides the burnt offering of the morning. The next pasuk in the Torah says that these Passover sacrifices are a pleasant savor to G-d, as stated, כאלה תעשו ליום שבעת ימים לחם אשה ריח ניחח לה׳ על עולת התמיד יעשה ונסכו (במדבר כח,כד), "Like these you shall do daily, for seven days, the bread of the fire offering, which is a pleasant savor to G-d; it shall be done besides the continual burnt offering, and its drink offering" (Numbers 28,24). The gematria of ניחח, "pleasant," is 76.

ניחח   76

Thus, 76 represents what is pleasant to G-d. These two pesukim tell that which is sacrificed especially for Passover, is pleasant to G-d. This idea is further reinforced by virtue of the fact that the gematrioth of מלבד, "besides," and the gematria of ניחח, "pleasant," are equal.

ויאמר משה אל בני ישראל ככל אשר צוה ה׳ את משה (במדבר ל,א).
And Moses said to the Children of Israel like all which G-d had commanded Moses (Numbers 30,1).

The very last pasuk in Parashath Pinchas says that Moses told the Children of Israel a facsimile of all that G-d had commanded him. The gematria of ישראל, "Israel," is 541.

ישראל   541

The gematria of ככל, "like all," is 70.

ככל   70

The query of the pasuk is why does it say that Moses told a facsimile of all that G-d had commanded him. Why not say without qualification that Moses told the Children of Israel all that G-d had commanded him?

The בעל הטורים, Baal Haturim, in this sidrah, Parashath Pinchas, writes, סײת תורה לומר שהעוסק בתורה כאילו הקריב קרבן (בעל הטורים, במדבר כח,א, דײה משה לאמר צו את), "The end letters spell Torah; to tell you that he who learns Torah, is as if he offered a sacrifice" (Baal Haturim, Numbers 28,1, header words: Moses saying command). The gematria of תורה, "To-rah," is 611.

תורה   611

This same basic idea is also found in the Gemara (מנחות קי., Menakoth 110a) and in the currently much referred-to Mishnah Berurah (משנה ברורה, סימן נ סעיף קטן ב, Mishnah Berurah, Siman 50, Seif Katon 2). Ideally קרבנות, "sacrifices," are actually offered on the altar, but if that is not possible, one should at least learn the Torah sections pertaining to sacrifices. Throughout much of Jewish history there has been no בית המקדש, "Temple," so the alternative was to learn the Torah pertaining to sacrifices. This alternative could be what the very last pasuk in Parashath Pinchas refers to when it says Moses told the Children of Israel a facsimile of all that G-d had commanded him.

As was demonstrated the gematria of ישראל, "Israel," is 541, and the gematria of ככל, "like all," is 70. Their combined gematria is 611.

540
  70
——
611

As was also demonstrated, the gematria of תורה, "Torah," is 611. The equivalency of these gematrioth gives credence to the explanation that when Moses told the Children of Israel a facsimile of all that G-d had commanded him, he may well have been referring to learning Torah as an alternative to offering sacrifices.

Parashath Mattoth   פרשת מטות

> ושמע אישה והחרש לה לא הניא אתה וקמו כל נדריה וכל
> אסר אשר אסרה על נפשה יקום (במדבר ל,יב).
> And her husband heard and was silent to her,
> he did not disallow for her, and all her vows
> shall stand, and every bond which she bound on
> her soul shall stand (Numbers 30,12).

The Sidroth of Parashath Mattos and Parashath Massey often come together as a double sidrah. It is not merely by coincidence that these two parashiyyoth come together; there is more than one reason that can be given for their union. A possible thought in this arena will be presented. In Parashath Mattos it states וקמו כל נדריה וכל אסר, "and all her vows shall stand, and every bond." The gematria of וקמו, "and they shall stand," is 152.

וקמו   152

The Torah says that under certain conditions a נדר, "vow," will "stand," that is, have status, exist, and be maintained. The שפתי חכמים, "Sifthei Chachomim," says that a vow has the status of קדש, "a consecrated item," as stated, ופי' לא יזלזל דבריו כזלזול החולין שאינו חושש בשמירתן מטומאה רק כקדש (שפתי חכמים, במדבר ל,ג, אות מ), "And the explanation is, he should not make petty his words, as one makes petty things which are unconsecrated, about which one is not apprehensive in guarding them from becoming ritually defiled; rather it should be as a sanctified item," (Sifthei Chachomim, Numbers 30,3, Letter mem). This same idea is expressed by the ספר החינוך, Book of Hachinuch, as stated, וענין זה הוא דומה להקדש שמצאנו בתורה שיש כח באדם להקדיש את שלו בדברי פיו ויהיה אסור מיד לו ולכל העולם כדכתיב "ואיש כי יקדש ביתו" (ספר החינוך מאת הרב אהרן הלוי, מצוה ל), "And this subject is similar to consecration in that we find in the Torah that there is the ability within man to consecrate what is his, with the words of his mouth, and it will be forbidden immediately to him and to the entire world, as it is written, 'And when a man will consecrate his house, etc.'" (Book of Hachinuch by Rabbi Aaron Halevi, Mitzvah 30). Thus, נדר, "a vow," resembles consecrated things, in that it has been declared with G-d's name (במדבר ל,ג, Numbers 30,3).

A שבועה, "oath," also involves G-d, for an oath is made in G-d's name (רמב"ן, במדבר ל,ג, ור"ן נדרים ב:, ד"ה ושבועות כשבועות, Ramban, Numbers 30,3, and Ran Nedarim 2b, header words: And oaths like oaths). Since both vows and oaths involve G-d, they can stand independently, since each has status and importance. This underlying thought may be associated with the word וקמו, "and they shall stand," and its gematria of 152.

In Parashath Massey all the travels of the Children of Israel are read together without an interruption. This uninterrupted reading is owing to a law, as stated, מ"ב מסעות שבפרשת ואלה מסעי אין להפסיק בהם שהוא נגד שם מ"ב (מגן אברהם, אורח חיים, סימן תכח, סעיף קטן ח), "The forty-two journeys in Parashath Massey, no interruption should be made while reading them, for they parallel G-d's mystical name of forty-two letters (מגן אברהם, אורח חיים סימן תכח, סעיף קטן ח, Magen Avraham, Orach Hayyim, Siman 428, Seif Katon 8). Thus, the travels of the Children of Israel involve G-d and therefore have status and importance. When the Torah records these travels, it repetitiously uses the word ויסעו (במדבר לג, ג-מח), "And they journeyed," (Numbers 33,3-48). The gematria of ויסעו, "And they journeyed," is 152.

ויסעו   152

Since the journeys involve G-d, they have status and importance. This thought is associated with the word ויסעו, "and they journeyed," and its gematria of 152.

The involvement of G-d with vows and oaths, as well

as with the journeys of the Children of Israel, gave status and importance to each; each was also associated with the same gematria of 152. Since the Sidroth of Parashath Mattos and Parashath Massey both begin with a similar underlying thought, it is very appropriate that they should come together as a double sidrah.

בלתי כלב בן יפנה הקנזי ויהושע בן נון כי מלאו אחרי ה' (במדבר לב,יב).

Except for Caleb the son of Jephunneh the Kenizzite, and Joshua the son of Nun, because they wholly followed G-d (Numbers 32,12).

When Moses responded to the children of Reuben and the children of Gad, he recounted the incident of the spies, G-d's anger with the men, and the exclusion of Caleb and Joshua from that anger. The pasuk which tells of that exclusion identifies Caleb as הקנזי, "the Kenizzite." On this pasuk Rashi says that Caleb was the step-son of Kenaz and the half brother of Othniel, as stated, חורגו של קנז היה וילדה לו אמו של כלב את עתניאל (רש"י, במדבר לב,יב), "He was the step-son of Kenaz, and the mother of Caleb bore to him Othniel" (Rashi, Numbers 32,12). The combined gematrioth of כלב, "Caleb," and עתניאל, "Othniel," is 613.

כלב	52
עתניאל	561
	613

Each of these half brothers did something which is equal to fulfilling all 613 Commandments. The Midrash says א"ר אחא כל הנושא אשה כשרה כאלו קיים כל התורה מראש ועד סוף (ילקוט שמעוני, רות פרק ד רמז תרו, ד"ה יתן ה' את האשה), "Rabbi Aha says, Anyone who marries a proper woman, it is as he fulfilled the entire Torah from its beginning and until its end" (Yalkut Shimoni, Ruth Chapter 4, Section 606, header words: G-d should give the woman). The Gemara cites Caleb's marrying Miriam as an example of marrying לשם שמים, "for the sake of Heaven," (סוטה יב., Sotah 12a). Further, Miriam is identified by a different Midrash as a צדקת, "righteous woman, (מדרש רבה, סדר כי תצא, פרשה ו, אות ט, Midrash Rabbah, Sidrah Ki Thetsa, Parashah 6, Letter 9). Also, independent of Moses, she was a prophetess, as the Gemara states, אמר רב עמרם אמר רב ואמרי לה אמר רב נחמן אמר רב מלמד שהיתה מתנבאה כשהיא אחות אהרן ואומרת עתידה אמי שתלד בן שמושיע את ישראל (סוטה יב:-יג.), "Rav Amram said that Rab said, and others say, Rav Nahman said that Rab said, It instructs that she prophesied when she was the sister of Aaron. And she said in the future my mother will give birth to a son who will save Israel" (Sotah 12b-13a). So surely when Caleb married Miriam, it was the very epitome of marrying "a proper woman," "for the sake of Heaven." Consequently, when Caleb married Miriam, it was as if he fulfilled all 613 Commandments.

Othniel was the first judge of Israel (שופטים ג,ט, Judges 3,9). The Gemara says that Othniel prayed and G-d granted his request (תמורה טז., Temurah 16a). Rashi explains that he prayed not to be idle from Torah study, as stated, שלא ישגבני יצר הרע לבטל מתלמוד תורה (רש"י, תמורה טז., ד"ה ועשית לי מרעה לבלתי), "That the evil inclination will not overcome me to idle me from studying Torah" (Rashi, Temurah 16a, header words: And You shall keep me from evil that it may not). The first Mishnah in Tractate Peah says, ותלמוד תורה כנגד כולם (פאה, פרק א משנה א), "And Torah study is equated to all of them" (Peah, Chapter 1 Mishnah 1). The Ramban elaborates this concept, as he states, אין לך מצוה בכל המצות כולן שהיא שקולה כנגד תלמוד תורה, אלא תלמוד תורה כנגד כל המצות כולן (משנה תורה, ספר המדע, הלכות תלמוד תורה, פרק ג הלכה ז), "You will not find a commandment among all the commandments in their entirety which is equated to Torah study; but Torah study is equated to all the commandments in their entirety" (Mishnah

Torah, Book of Hamadda, Laws of Torah Study, Chapter 3, Law 7). So surely when G-d granted Othniel's request not to be idle from Torah study, it was as if he had fulfilled all 613 Commandments.

Thus, it can be concluded that each of these half brothers, כלב, "Caleb," and עתניאל, "Othniel," did something which is equal to fulfilling all 613 Commandments. Being that they were half brothers, how felicitous that the sum of the gematrioth of their names equals 613.

בנו לכם ערים לטפכם וגדרת לצנאכם והיצא מפיכם תעשו
(במדבר לב,כד).

Build for yourselves cities for your young children and folds for your sheep; and that which proceeds from your mouth do (Numbers 32, 24).

The tribes of Gad and Reuben had asked Moses for their portion to be of the land of Israel on the east side of the Jordan River. In response to Moses' rebuke, they said first they would build the folds and then the cities (במדבר לב,טז Numbers 32,16); Moses complied with their request on certain conditions. Moses rebuked them for their prioritizing, as Rashi says, חסים היו על ממונם יותר מבניהם ובנותיהם, שהקדימו מקנייהם לטפם. אמר להם משה לא כן, עשו העקר עקר והטפל טפל. בנו לכם "They, תחלה ערים לטפכם ואחר כן גדרות לצאנכם (רש"י, במדבר לב,טז) had greater consideration for their money than for their sons and their daughters, for they preceded [mention of] their cattle to their young children. Moses said to them, it is not right, make the major major and the minor minor. First build for yourself cities for your young children, and afterwards folds for your sheep" (Rashi, Numbers 32,16).

The Keli Yakar explains that the tribes of Gad and Reuben wanted to build folds for their cattle first, which would provide protection from enemies, and then cities for their young children in the protected areas. Moses rebuked them for their lack of trust בתשועת ה', "in G-d's salvation" (כלי יקר, במדבר לב,א, Keli Yakar, Numbers 32,1). Perhaps G-d's salvation can be interpreted as referring to the mitzvoth. The Gemara Shabbath says, מה יונה זו כנפיה מגינות עליה אף ישראל מצות מגינות עליהן (שבת קל.), "Just like this dove, her wings protect her, also Israel, mitzvoth protect them" (Shabbath 130a). Thus, when Moses said to build cities for the young children first, and not to rely on the folds for protection, it is reasonable to assume that he was telling them to rely on the protection that the 613 Mitzvoth provide. He told them to build ערים לטפכם וגדרת לצנאכם, "cities for your young children and folds for your sheep." The gematria of וגדרת, "and folds," is 613.

וגדרת 613

Thus, Moses could have told the tribes of Gad and Reuben not to rely on the folds for protection; rather they should rely on the 613 Mitzvoth for protection, as implied by the word וגדרת, "and folds," which has a gematria of 613. Note that when the tribes of Gad and Reuben made their request of Moses, the Torah uses the word גדרת, "folds,"(במדבר לב,טז, Numbers 32,16), which does not have a gematria of 613.

Parashath Massey   פרשת מסעי

ויסעו בני ישראל מרעמסס ויחנו בסכת. ויסעו מסכת ויחנו באתם אשר בקצה המדבר (במדבר לג,ה־ו).

And the Children of Israel journeyed from Rameses, and they encamped in Succoth. And they journeyed from Succoth, and they encamped in Etham which is on the edge of the desert (Numbers 33, 5-6).

In Parashath Massey the Torah uses the words ויסעו, "and they journeyed," and ויחנו, "they encamped," repeatedly. The gematria of ויסעו, "and they journeyed," is 152.

ויסעו   152

The gematria of ויחנו, "and they encamped," is 80.

ויחנו   80

The difference between the words ויסעו, "and they journeyed," and ויחנו, "they encamped," in gematrioth is 72.

ויסעו   152
ויחנו   -80
          72

Each instance of ויסעו, "and they journeyed," and each instance of ויחנו, "and they encamped," refers to the travels of the Children of Israel, as stated, אלה מסעי בני ישראל אשר יצאו מארץ מצרים לצבאתם ביד משה ואהרן (במדבר לג,א), "These are the journeys of the Children of Israel who went forth out of the land of Egypt by their hosts under the hand of Moses and Aaron" (Numbers 33,1). The gematria of ישראל, "Israel," is 541.

ישראל   541

When the difference between the words ויסעו, ויחנו, "and

they journeyed, and they encamped," in gematrioth is added to the gematria of ישראל, "Israel," the sum is 613.

$$72$$
$$\underline{541}$$
$$613$$

G-d has commanded the Children of Israel to observe 613 Mitzvoth, divided between 248 positive Mitzvoth and 365 negative Mitzvoth, as stated, דרש רבי שמלאי שש מאות ושלש עשרה מצות נאמרו לו למשה שלש מאות וששים וחמש לאוין כמנין ימות החמה ומאתים וארבעים ושמונה עשה כנגד איבריו של אדם (מכות כג:), "Rabbi Simlai expounded, 613 Commandments were said to Moses, three hundred and sixty-five negative Commandments corresponding to the number of days in a solar year, and two hundred and forty-eight positive Commandments corresponding to the limbs of a person" (Makkoth 23b). The connection between the travels of the Children of Israel and the 613 Mitzvoth is easy to justify. The Mishnah in Avoth says, רבי יוסי אומר... וכל מעשיך יהיו לשם שמים (אבות, פרק ב, משנה יב), "Rabbi Yose says ... and all your deeds should be for the sake of Heaven" (Avoth, Chapter 2, Mishnah 12). Thus, the purpose, intention, of all the travels of the Children of Israel were, or should have been, for the sake of heaven, for the sake of G-d's mitzvoth. The difference between the words ויסעו, "and they journeyed," and ויחנו, "they encamped," represents the travels of the Children of Israel; that is, ויסעו, "and they journeyed," until ויחנו, "and they encamped." Astoundingly, when the difference between the words ויסעו, ויחנו, "and they journeyed, and they encamped," in gematrioth is added to the gematria of ישראל, "Israel," the sum is 613, which equals the total number of mitzvoth.

או בכל אבן אשר ימות בה בלא ראות ויפל עליו וימת והוא
לא אויב לו ולא מבקש רעתו (במדבר לה,כג).
Or with any stone wherewith he may die, without seeing him, and cast it on him and he died,
and he was not his enemy, nor sought his harm
(Numbers 35,23).

When describing one who is obliged to flee to a city of
refuge because he killed another person by accident, there is
a pasuk which begins by listing an example of such an acci-
dental killing, the smiting with a stone. Since the previous
pasuk ends with או השליך עליו כל כלי בלא צדיה (במדבר לה,כב), "or
hurled on him any object, without lying in wait" (Numbers
35,22), it would have been adequate just to write, שימות,
"that he may die," and omit the words או בכל אבן אשר, "Or with
any stone wherewith." If the killing with any object whatso-
ever obligates one to flee to a city of refuge, certainly smiting
with a stone obligates one to flee to a city of refuge. Why did
the Torah write the words או בכל אבן אשר, "Or with any stone
wherewith"? These four words could have been omitted, and
replaced by merely adding the letter "ש," "that," to the next
word ימות, "he may die."

Perhaps a deeper meaning is implied with the words או
בכל אבן אשר, "Or with any stone wherewith." The Midrash
refers to the outer altar as being made of stones which create
peace between Israel and their Father in heaven (מדרש
תנחומא, פרשת יתרו, אות יז, Midrash Tanhuma, Parashath Yisro,
Letter 17). The Gemara Kethuboth says that the altar atoned
for sins (כתובות י:, Kthuboth 10b), for violations of the 613
Commandments which G-d has commanded.

Killing a person does not have to be the literal physical
act. Leading one astray or tricking one into violating one of
the 613 Commandments, which is synonymous with causing
one to commit a sin, can at times be considered destroying a
life. Since the altar is referred to as being made of stones, and

these stones atone for violation of the 613 Commandments, perhaps the words או בכל אבן אשר, "Or with any stone where-with," are written to include one who tricks another intoviolating one of the 613 Commandments. The gematria of או בכל אבן אשר, "Or with any stone wherewith," is 613.

או בכל	59
אבן אשר	554
	613

The inclusion of one who tricks another into violation one of the 613 Commandments is reinforced by the first four words of the pasuk having a gematria equal to 613. Of course, the law of cities of refuge does not apply to everyone who tricks another into sinning; but as a דרשה, derashah, "homiletical interpretation," on the pasuk, perhaps it can help to remind one of the gravity of tricking one to sin.

Book of Deuteronomy — ספר דברים

Parashath Devarim   פרשת דברים

בעבר הַיַרדן בארץ מואב הואיל משה באר את התורה
הזאת לאמר (דברים א,ה).

On the other side of the Jordan in the land of Moab, Moses began to elucidate this Torah, saying (Deuteronomy 1,5).

The fifth pasuk of this sidrah says that Moses began to elucidate this Torah. Two questions are apparent. One, the Torah usually records Moses as saying or commanding the Children of Israel; why does this pasuk use the verb באר, "elucidate," to record Moses's action? Two, there is only one Torah; why does this pasuk use the adjective הזאת, "this," to modify the Torah?

Different answers are found in the commentaries (רש״י, והעמק דבר, דברים א,ה, Rashi, and Haamek Davar, Deuteronomy 1,5), but perhaps one of the most satisfying is that of the אבן עזרא, Ibn Ezra. He says the pasuk records that Moses explained to the sons born in the desert all the mitzvoth, including the Ten Commandments, which their fathers had heard from G-d, so that the sons also heard them from a reliable envoy, as stated, והנה משה החל לפרש לבנים שנולדו במדבר מה שאירע לאבותיהם ואמר להם כל המצות גם עשרת הדברים ששמעו אבותיהם מפי השם ישמעום גם הם מפי ציר נאמן (אבן עזרא, דברים א,ה), "And behold Moses began to explain to the sons born in the desert what occurred to their fathers. And he said to them all the commandments, also the Ten Commandments, that their fathers heard from G-d, that they should also hear it from the mouth of a reliable envoy" (Ibn Ezra, Deuteronomy 1,5). Keep in mind that not all of the Ten Commandments were heard by the fathers. Rashi, based on a Gemara Makkoth says, כשהיה משה מְדבר ומשמיע הדברות לישראל, שהרי לא שמעו מפי הגבורה אלא אנכי ולא יהיה לך והקדוש ברוך הוא מסיעו לתת בו כח להיות קולו מגביר ונשמע (רש״י, שמות יט,יט, ד״ה

(משה ידבר), "When Moses would speak and cause the commandments to be heard to Israel, after all, they heard from G-d's mouth only, 'I am,' and 'There shall not be.' The Holy One, Blessed be He, helped him, to give to him strength, so his voice would be powerful and heard" (Rashi, Exodus 19,19).

Now the two apparent questions can be answered. One, the pasuk uses the verb באר, "elucidate," because here Moses was elucidating to the sons that which had already been said, or commanded, to the fathers. Two, the pasuk uses the adjective הזאת, "this," because here the reference is to the Torah which Moses had begun to elucidate to the sons. It is notable that according to Iba Ezra the pasuk does not record that Moses elucidated Torah to the members of his generation, but to their children. The Gemara Sanhedrin focuses on the significance of one who teaches Torah to the son of his friend, as it states, ר' אלעזר אומר כאילו עשאן לדברי תורה שנאמר ושמרתם את דברי הברית הזאת ועשיתם אותם (דברים כט,ח) (סנהדרין צט:), "Rabbi Eleazar says, it is as if he made the words of Torah, as it says, And you shall keep the words of this covenant and make them" (Deuteronomy 29,8), (Sanhedrin 99b). The Maharsha explains this passage. If you teach Torah to the son of your friend, then since you cause him to expand the Torah by discussion in learning, it is as if you made those words of Torah (מהרש"א, סנהדרין דף צט:, ד"ה כאלו עשה לדברי תורה וכו', Maharsha, Sanhedrin 99b, header words: As if he made those words of Torah, etc.).

The teaching of Torah to the son of one's friend is exactly what Moses did, according to the way the אבן עזרא, Ibn Ezra, explains the words באר, "elucidate," and הזאת, "this." It follows that according to the way the Maharsha explains this passage in the Gemara Sanhedrin, that it is considered as if Moses made the words of Torah when he elucidated all the mitzvoth to the sons born in the desert.

The explanation of the Ibn Ezra can be supported with a gematria of three of the words found in this pasuk. The fifth pasuk of this sidrah says that Moses began to elucidate this Torah. The gematria of באר, "elucidate," is 203.

באר   203

The gematria of הזאת, "this," is 413.

הזאת   413

The combined gematria of באר, "elucidate," and הזאת, "this," is 616.

203
413

616

The gematria of התורה, "the Torah," is 616.

התורה   616

Since the words באר, "elucidate," and הזאת, "this," according to the Ibn Ezra, refer to Moses elucidating all the mitzvoth, including the Ten Commandments, to the sons of his friends, and since such elucidation can be considered as if Moses had made those words of Torah, the combined gematria of באר, "elucidate," and הזאת, "this," being equal to the gematria of התורה, "the Torah," fits in meticulously with the explanation of the אבן עזרא, Ibn Ezra, of the pasuk.

והימים אשר הלכנו מקדש ברנע עד אשר עברנו את נחל זרד שלשים ושמנה שנה עד תם כל הדור אנשי המלחמה מקרב המחנה כאשר נשבע ה' להם (דברים ב,יד).

And the days in which we came from Kadesh-barnea, until we passed over the brook Zered, were thirty-eight years; until all the generation of the men of war were consumed from the midst of the camp, as G-d swore to them (Deuteronomy 2,14).

The Torah describes a period of thirty-eight years, as the time until all of the men of war died. The אוצר חיים, Otzar Hayyim, explains that the expression אנשי המלחמה, "men of war," בלשון סגי נהור, is used euphemistically, not referring to actual warriors, but rather to those who speak לשון הרע, "malignant speech," slanderers, calumniators, against the land. He says, כי כך דרכה של בעלי לשוה"ר שמדברים כל דבר אסור כנגד מי שחלש מהם, אבל כלפי מי שתקיף מהם ידמו כאבן בפניו (ספר אוצר חיים, מאת הרב חיים יעקב צוקרמן, דברים, פרשת דברים, ד"ה ויהי כאשר תמנו כל אנשי המלחמה למות), "For so is the way of those who speak slander, that they say anything which is forbidden about someone who is weaker than they are, but about someone who is who stronger than they are, they are silent as a stone in front of him" (Book of Otzar Hayyim by Rabbi Chayim Jacob Zuckerman, Deuteronomy, Parashath Devarim, header words: And it was when all the men of war finished dying).

The Gemara Arakin states that one who speaks לשון הרע, "malignant speech," enlarges his sin until the level of idolatry, immorality, and murder, as stated, תנא דבי רבי ישמעאל כל המספר לשון הרע מגדיל עונות כנגד שלש עבירות עבודת כוכבים וגילוי עריות ושפיכות דמים (ערכין טו:), "It was taught in the school of Rabbi Ishmael, Anyone who speaks malignant speech, enlarges his sins until the level of three sins: idol worship, immorality, and murder" (Arakin 15b). The Gemara Horayoth individualizes idolatry as a commandment which is equated to all 613 Commandments, as stated, איזו היא מצוה שהיא שקולה ככל המצות הוי אומר זו עבודת כוכבים (הוריות ח.), "Which commandment is equivalent as all the commandments? Say it is idol worship" (Horayoth 8a).

Things equal to the same thing are equal to each other. Since one who speaks malignant speech is equated with one who worships idols, and since worshipping idols is equated to violating all the mitzvoth, thus speaking evil talk may be equated to violating all the mitzvoth. There is a total of 613 Mitzvoth.

As was mentioned, the אוצר חיים, Otzar Hayyim, explains that the expression בלשון "men of war," אנשי המלחמה, סגי נהור, euphemistically, not referring to actual warriors, but rather to those who spoke לשון הרע, slanders, calumniators, against the land. Hence their sin, speaking evil talk, can be equated to violating all 613 Commandments. This equality can be verified with a gematria. The gematria of עד כל אנשי המלחמה, "until all the men of war," is 613.

$$
\begin{array}{rr}
\text{עד כל אנשי} & 485 \\
\text{המלחמה} & \underline{128} \\
& 613
\end{array}
$$

In addition to the fact that speaking evil talk is equated to violating all 613 Commandments, there is another ominous quality to this sin. The תלמוד ירושלמי, "Talmud Yerushalmi," states, שלא חרב הבית בראשונה אלא שהיו עובדים כו"ם ומגלים עריות ושופכי דמים וכן בשני (תלמוד ירושלמי, יומא, פרק א, הלכה א), "The first Temple was only destroyed because they worshiped idols, were immoral, and committed murder, and so too for the second Temple" (Yerushalmi Gemara, Yoma, Chapter 1, Halakhah 1). As was quoted, the Gemara Arakin states that one who speaks לשון הרע, "malignant speech," enlarges his sin until the level of idolatry, immorality, and murder. The Talmud Yeru-shalmi says that it was these three sins which caused the destruction of both the first and the second Temples. It follows that by speaking לשון הרע, "malignant speech," one's sins are enlarged until a level which could cause the destruction of the Temple. Parashath Devarim is always read before the observance of ט' באב, "the Ninth of Av," the anniversary of the destruction of both the first and the second Temples. This gematria and the ominous quality of speaking לשון הרע, "malignant speech," are opportune messages for the Children of Israel to receive before ט' באב, "the Ninth of Av."

וגם יד ה׳ היתה בם להמם מקרב המחנה עד תמם (דברים ב,טו).

And also the hand of G-d was against them to destroy them from the midst of the camp, until they were consumed (Deuteronomy 2,15).

The sidrah of Devarim has at least two associations with the Ninth of Av, Tisha B'Av. Firstly, the Mishnah Taanith informs that it was on the Ninth of Av that the pronouncement was made upon our forefathers in the desert, as stated, "On בתשעה באב נגזר על אבותינו שלא יכנסו לארץ (תענית פרק ד משנה ו) the Ninth of Av it was decreed upon our forefathers that they should not enter the land," (Taanith Chapter 4, Mishnah 6); משנה ברורה, סימן תקמט, סעיף קטן ב Mishnah Berurah, (see also Siman 549, Seif Katon 2). It is recorded in Parashath Devarim that this pronouncement which occurred on the Ninth of Av, was made upon our forefathers. Secondly, Parashath Devarim is read on the Shabbath immediately preceding the Ninth of Av. This Shabbath is known as Shabbath Hazon since the Haftarah begins with the words חזון ישעי׳ (ישעי׳ א,א־כז), "The vision of Isaiah" (Isaiah 1, 1-27).

These two associations with the Ninth of Av can be linked to a gematria. The word יד, "hand," recorded in Parashath Devarim, is used in connection with G-d inflicting punishment upon the Children of Israel, which was the execution of the pronouncement made to our forefathers on the Ninth of Av, as stated, וגם יד ה׳ היתה בם להמם מקרב המחנה עד תמם (דברים ב,טו), "And also the hand of G-d was against them, to destroy them from the midst of the camp, until they were consumed," (Deuteronomy 2,15). The gematria of יד, "hand," is 14.

יד   14

Parashath Devarim is read on the Shabbath immediately

preceding the Ninth of Av. The gematria of ט' באב, "the Ninth of Av," is 14.

ט'	9
באב	5
	14

Thus, 14 represents G-d inflicting punishment against the Children of Israel which was the execution of the pronouncement made upon our forefathers on the Ninth of Av, as recorded in Parashath Devarim; and it also represents the time when G-d afflicted punishment on the Children of Israel, that is the Ninth of Av. These two associations with the Ninth of Av are linked with a gematria.

אעברה בארצך בדרך בדרך אלך לא אסור ימין ושמאול (דברים ב,כז).

Let me pass through your land, on the way, on the way, I will go; I will not turn toward the right nor the left (Deuteronomy 2,27).

When Moses recounted his request of Sihon king of Heshbon to allow the Children of Israel to pass through his land, he repeated בדרך, "on the way," twice. When the actual request was previously recorded, the Torah uses the phrase בדרך המלך נלך, "on the king's way we will go," (במדבר כא,כב, Numbers 21,22), but the word בדרך, "on the way," was not repeated there. Why is the word בדרך, "on the way," repeated here? Also, why did the Torah use the word נלך, "we will go," when the actual event was recorded, but when Moses recounted his request the word אלך, "I will go," was used?

The repeating of the word בדרך, "on the way," can be explained, and the changing of the word נלך, "we will go," to אלך, "I will go," can be explained, with the application of a gematria. The Gemara Zebahim says that all turns made on the altar should be made toward the right, as stated, כל פינות

(זבחים סב:) שאתה פונה לא יהו אלא דרך ימין, "All turns which you make should only be towards the right" (Zebahim 62b). Note that the Gemara uses the word to דרך, "way," to describe the right turns. There is a synonymic Gemara in Yoma (יומא נח:, Yoma 58b). It should be noted that although the Gemara Zebahim uses the word "all," there were three exceptions. The Gemara Sukkah states, כל העולין למזבח עולין דרך ימין ומקיפין ויורדין דרך שמאל חוץ מן העולה לשלשה דברים הללו שעולין דרך שמאל וחוזרין על העקב ואלו הן ניסוך המים וניסך היין ועולת העוף כשרבתה במזרח (סוכה מח:) (זבחים סג.-סג:), "All those who ascend the altar went up on the right side, encompass [it], and descend on the left side, except for he who ascend for these three things. They ascend on the left side, returning on their heel [the way they came]. And these are they: the water libation, and the wine libation, and the burnt sacrifice of the bird, when the altar [the southeastern corner] was replete" (Sukkah 48b). The Gemara Zebahim gives smoke pollution as the reason for the exceptions (זבחים סד., Zebahim 64a). With the exclusion of these three exceptions, all turns made on the altar should be made toward the right.

Another Gemara says that the altar atoned for sins, as stated, אמר רבי אלעזר מזבח מזיח ומזין מחבב מכפר היינו מכפר היינו מזיח מזיח גזירות ומכפר עונות (כתובות י:), "Rabbi Eleazar said, The altar removes, and sustains, creates love, atones. Are not atones and removes the same thing? It removes decrees and atones for sins" (Kethuboth 10b). Sins can be considered any violation of the 613 Mitzvoth which G-d has commanded. Thus, the altar is associated with the 613 Mitzvoth, and all turns made on the altar had to be to the right. These two aspects of the altar can perhaps be inferred from the pasuk first quoted.

In Hebrew a word can be repeated to show emphasis (מצודת דוד, ישעיי מ,א, Metsudath David, Isaiah 40,1). When the word בדרך, "on the way," is repeated, it could be to show emphasis. When Moses recounted to the Children of Israel his request of Sihon king of Heshbon to be allowed to pass through his land, Moses was emphasizing that although all turns on the altar had to be toward the right, he had assured Sihon that the Children of Israel would not turn off the road, neither toward to the right nor the left. Even though these uses of the word דרך, "way," are very different (one was the request of Sihon, the other the turns made on the altar), still they can be contrasted. The Gemara often says, מלתא אגב אורחיא קא משמע לן (בבא מציעא נב.), "It comes to teach something circumstantially" (Baba Mezia 52a). So too here, the Torah records that when Moses recounted his request of Sihon, he also included circumstantially inside information. The gematria of בדרך בדרך אלך ימין, "on the way, on the way, I will go; I will turn toward the right," is 613.

בדרך	226
בדרך	226
אלך ימין	161
	613

The meaning of these words whose gematria is 613, could be to show association; Moses was showing that the altar is associated with the 613 Mitzvoth, and all turns made on the altar had to be toward the right: a much more valuable message for the Children of Israel, than for Sihon king of Heshbon. Moses was also emphasizing to the Children of Israel, that although all turns on the altar had to be toward the right, he had assured Sihon that the Children of Israel would not turn off the road. Both aspects of the altar, the association with the 613 Mitzvoth, and all turns made on the altar having to be to the right, have been inferred from the pasuk first quoted. The Torah use the word נלך, "we will go," when the actual request was recorded, for then Moses was assuring Sihon king of Heshbon that the Children of Israel would not go off the road. But when Moses recounted his request, the word אלך, "I will go," was used, for then he was emphasizing to the Children of Israel that he always made all turns on the altar toward the right. The repeating of the word בדרך, "on the way," has been explained, and the changing of the word נלך, "we will go," to אלך, "I will go," has been explained, with the application of a gematria.

The turning toward the right extends far beyond the meaning of what Moses emphasized to the Children of Israel. When the Children of Israel accept Shabbath, and when the priests bless the people, they turn toward the right. The Book of Piskei Teshuvoth writes, ועל פי הכלל ד׳יכל פינות שאתה פונה פונה פנה לימיני (יומא נח:) יש להסתובב דרך צד ימינו, דהיינו דרך צד דרום למערב, וכשאומר בואי כלה יטה עצמו לצד ימינו ולצד שמאלו, ופעם שלישית ללפניו ויאמר בואי כלה שבת מלכתא בלחש, וחוזר דרך צד צפון למזרח (ספר פסקי תשובות מאת הרב שמחה ב״ץ א. רבינוביץ, סימן רסז, תפילת קבלת שבת, דף רנט, הערה 46), "And based on the rule that 'All turns which you turn, turn to the right' (Yoma 58b), one should rotate via his right side. That is, via the south side to the west; and when he says, Enter, O bride, he should lean himself to his right side, and then to his left side, and thirdly in front of himself, and say Enter O bride, Shabbath Queen, quietly. And then return via the north side to the east" (Book of Piskei Teshuvoth by Rabbi Simhah B"Z A. Rabinovits, Siman 267, Kabbath Shabbath Prayer, page 259, note 46). In the sefer he bases the rotations of Children of Israel when accepting Shabbath, and the rotations of the priests when blessing the people, both of which are to the right, on the right turns done on the altar.

Parashath Devarim is always read on Shabbath Hazon, the Shabbath preceding the of Ninth of Av. The Ninth of Av commemorates the destruction of the First and the Second Temples, including the loss of the altars. Certainly, Shabbath Hazon is an auspicious time to remember that Moses emphasized that all turns on the altar had to be toward the right, and that the altar atones for violation of the 613 Mitzvoth.

Parashath Vaethchanan   פרשת ואתחנן

ואתחנן אל ה׳ בעת ההוא לאמר (דברים ג,כג).
And I besought G-d at that time saying (Deuteronomy 3,23).

Moses prayed 515 payers to G-d to allow him to enter
the land of Israel, as stated, והתפלל משה תקט״ו תפלות כמנין
ואתחנן (דעת זקנים מבעלי התוספות, דברים ג,כג וילקוט מעם לועז מאת
דברים ג,כג ,(רבי יעקב כולי) "Moses prayed 515 prayers, like the
number of word Vaethchanan" (Daat Zekenim Mibaale
Hatosafoth, Deuteronomy 3,23, and Yalkut Me'am Lo'ez by
Rabbi Yaakov Culi, Deuteronomy 3,23). Thus, the number
515 is connected with prayers which were not answered.

If Moses had prayed an additional prayer he would
have been answered, as stated, ואותה תפלה לא היתה שבה ריקם
בלי ספק ועל אותה תפלה נאמר לו אל תוסף דבר אלי (דברים ג,כו) שלא
הורשה להתפלל אותה כלל כי אלו הי׳ מתפלל אותה התפלה היתה מנצחת
(ספר חתם סופר דרשות מאת הרב משה סופר, דרוש לז׳ אב תקע״ג, ד״ה
בפי׳ השבוע ואתחנן) "And that prayer without doubt, would not
have returned empty. And about that prayer, it was said to
him, 'do not speak to Me more' (Deuteronomy 3,26). He did
not allow him to pray for it at all, for if he had prayed, that
prayer would have triumphed" (Book of Hatham Sofer,
Derashoth, by Rabbi Moses Schreiber, Drush for the Seventh
of Av, 5673, header words: For Parashath the week of
Vaethchannan). Thus, the number 516 is to some degree
connected with prayers which are answered.

אליהו הנביא, "Elijah the Prophet," Eliyahu Hanavi, who
lived during the reign of Ahab, king of Israel, was a native of
Toshav, but he relocated to Gilad; he is referred to as Tishbi
as well as Giladi. The Jewish People have prayed for him to
come as the precursor of the Messiah. On the night following
Shabbath, Eliyahu records the merits of the Children of Israel
who have kept the Shabbath; likewise the Children of Israel

sing a song whose refrain is a prayer for his coming, as stated, אליהו הנביא, אליהו התשבי, אליהו הגלעדי. במהרה יבוא אלינו עם משיח בן דוד (סידור בית יעקב מאת הרב יעקב מעמדין בן הרב צבי, אשכנזי, דף רג.) "Elijah the Prophet, Elijah the Tishbi, Elijah the Giladi. Speedily may he come to us with Messiah, the son of David" (Siddur Beth Yaakov by Rabbi Yaakov from Emden ben Rabbi Zvi, Ashkenazi, page 203a).

When the Gemara can not resolve an issue or a question, the concluding word is often תיקו, teku, "Let it stand." It means "Eliyahu will answer questions and inquiries," as stated, ונראה לי דמהכא רגילין לומר דתיק"ו שאמרו בגמרא היא נוטריקון תשבי יתרץ קושיות ואבעיות (תוספת יו"ט, עדיות פרק ח משנה ז ד"ה והשיב לב אבות על בנים וגו'), "And it appears to me, that it is from here that it has become customary to say teku. It is an acrostic of 'Tishbi will answer questions and inquiries'" (Tosafoth Yom Tov, Eduyyoth, Chapter 8, Mishnah 7, header words: And he will return the hearts of fathers to sons, etc.). The gematria of תיקו, teku, "Let it stand," is 516.

$$516 \qquad תיקו$$

Since תיקו, teku, expresses the belief that Eliyahu will answer questions and inquires, and the number 516 is connected with prayers which are answered, it is very fitting that תיקו, teku, has a gematria of 516.

Parashath Vaethchannan
or Parashath Vayyeshev

פרשת ואתחנן
או פרשת וישב

והפיץ ה׳ אתכם בעמים ונשארתם מתי מספר בגוים אשר
ינהג ה׳ אתכם שמה (דברים ד,כז).
And G-d will scatter you among the peoples, and you shall be left few in number among the nations, whither G-d shall lead you there (Deuteronomy 4,27).

G-d told the Children of Israel that they would be left few in number among the nations. The gematria of ונשארתם, "and you shall be left," is 997.

997 ונשארתם

Thus, 997 represents the condition in which the Children of Israel will be left among the nations.

The popular expression מעשי אבות סימן לבנים, "The deeds of the forefathers are an omen for the children," can be deduced from the Gemara Sotah 34b; a similar thought is in the Ramban, Genesis 12,10, which is based on the Midrash Rabbah, Sidra Lech Lecha, Parashah 40, Letter 6. The Ramban writes straightforwardly, והוא ענין גדול, הזכירוהו רבותינו בדרך קצרה, ואמרו "כל מה שאירע לאבות סימן לבנים" (רמב"ן, בראשית יב,ו), "And it is an important subject which our Rabbis have mentioned briefly, 'All that happened to to the forefathers is an omen for the sons'" (Ramban, Genesis 12,6). One of the מעשי אבות, "the deeds of the forefathers," which can be a סימן לבנים, "an omen for the children," in exile are the occurrences which happened to Joseph. Joseph began his exile when he was sold to a caravan of Ishmaelites carrying spicery, balm, and ladanum, as stated, וישבו לאכל לחם וישאו עיניהם ויראו והנה ארחת ישמעאלים באה מגלעד וגמליהם נשאים נכאת וצרי ולט הולכים להוריד מצרימה (בראשית לז,כה), "And they [Joseph's brothers] sat down to eat bread, and they lifted up their eyes, and they saw, and behold a caravan of Ishmaelites came from Gilead, and their camels bearing spicery, and balm, and ladanum, going to bring it down to Egypt" (Genesis 37,25). The gematria of נכאת וצרי ולט, "spicery, balm, and ladanum," is 822.

נכאת	471
וצרי	306
ולט	45
	822

     It is pointed out by Rashi that the Torah specifies that this caravan transported this particular merchandise which had a favorable smell for the benefit of Joseph, a righteous man (רש״י, בראשית לז,כה, Rashi, Genesis 37,25). Thus, 822 represents the benefits provided to a Jew in exile.

     However, one must merit to receive such benefits. Rashi makes it clear that the fact that this caravan of Ishmaelites carrying spicery, balm, and ladanum, as opposed to their usual malodorous cargo, was attributed to the benefit and merit of the righteous man, Joseph. The benefits of exile are given, מדה כנגד מדה, "measure for measure." In fact, exile is a punishment, but the severity of the punishment can depend on the person; the benefits received, or the degree to which the severity of the punishment is restrained, is מדה כנגד מדה, "measure for measure." This principle is found in the תלמוד ירושלמי, סוטה, פרק א, הלכה ז, Yerushalmi Gemara, Sotah, Chapter 1, Halakhah 7. The Gemara Shabbath derives the principle of מדה כנגד מדה, "measure for measure," as stated, א״ר חייא בר אבא א״ר יוחנן כל המתעצל בהספדו של חכם אינו מאריך ימים מדה כנגד מדה שנאמר בסאסאה בשלחה תריבנה (ישעי׳ כז,ח) (שבת קה:), "R. Hiyya bar Abba said in R. Johanan's name, Anyone who is indolent with the eulogy of a wise person, his days will not be prolonged. It is measure for measure, as it says, 'In full measure, when you send her away, you will contend with her (Isaiah 37,8)'" (Shabbath 105b). The gematria of מדה כנגד מדה, "measure for measure," is 175.

מדה	49
כנגד	77
מדה	49
	175

Thus, 175 represents how the benefits of exile are provided, or to what degree the severity of punishment is restrained. The gematria representing the benefits provided to a Jew in exile, plus the gematria representing how the benefits of exile are provided to a Jew, total 997.

$$822$$
$$175$$
$$997$$

It has already been shown that the gematria of ונשארתם, "and you shall be left," is 997. The message seems clear. What will the conditions of the Children of Israel in exile be? The Children of Israel in exile can receive benefits just as Joseph did, since מעשי אבות סימן לבנים, "The deeds of the forefathers are an omen for the children." But how are the benefits of exile provided, or to what degree is the severity of punishment is restrained? That depends on the Children of Israel, since G-d punishes מדה כנגד מדה, "measure for measure." This explanation fits together especially well with the Gemara Sanhedrin 100a-b which implies that G-d distributes both good and bad to the Children of Israel on a מדה כנגד מדה, "measure for measure," basis.

אי"ה, all the Children of Israel will behave as Hashem desires and soon He will end the current, seemingly endless, exile, בב"א.

והפיץ ה' אתכם בעמים ונשארתם מתי מספר בגוים אשר ינהג ה' אתכם שמה (דברים ד,כז).

And G-d will scatter you among the peoples, and you shall be left few in number among the nations, whither G-d shall lead you there (Deuteronomy 4,27).

Moses told the Children of Israel that after G-d scattered them, they would be left מתי מספר, "few in number," among the nations. The gematria of מתי מספר, "few in number," is 830.

מתי	450
מספר	<u>380</u>
	830

Even though the Children of Israel will be left few in number, when they seek G-d, He will not forsake them, nor will He forget the ברית אבות, "covenant of the forefathers," (דברים ד,לא, Deuteronomy 4,31). Thus, 830 represents the few remaining of the Children of Israel who will seek Hashem, and who will not be forsaken because of the merit of the forefathers (in this case the covenant with them, as opposed to the forefathers' other merits).

In this same sidrah, Moses tells the Children of Israel that G-d is giving them the land of Israel because of His love of the forefathers, as stated, ותחת כי אהב את אבתיך ויבחר בזרעו אחריו ויוצאך בפניו בכחו הגדל ממצרים. להוריש גוים גדלים ועצמים ממך מפניך להביאך לתת לך את ארצם נחלה כיום הזה (דברים ד,לז-לח), "And because He loved your forefathers, and He chose their seed after them, and with great strength brought you out of Egypt in front of Him. To drive out nations greater and mightier than you from before you, to bring you to give to you their land for an inheritance, as it is today" (דברים ד,לז-לח, Deuteronomy 4,37-38). The gematria of לתת, "to give," is 830.

לתת	830

Thus, 830 represents the giving of the land of Israel to the Children of Israel by G-d because of the merit of the forefathers, in this case the love of the forefathers. In other places in the sidrah the word לתת, "to give," is also used in reference to giving the land of Israel because of the merit of the forefathers (דברים ו,י; ו,כג, Deuteronomy 6,10; 6,23). The giving of the land of Israel mentioned in Deuteronomy 4,38 will be to the few in number mentioned in Deuteronomy 4,27. Moreover, the לתת, "to give," mentioned in Deuteronomy 4, 38 and the מתי מספר, "few in number," mentioned in Deuteronomy 4,27 are both linked to the merit of the forefathers. The connection between these words is reinforced by the fact that their gematrioth are identical.

והפיץ ה' אתכם בעמים ונשארתם מתי מספר בגוים אשר ינהג ה' אתכם שמה (דברים ד,כז).

And G-d will scatter you among the peoples, and you shall be left few in number among the nations, whither G-d shall lead you there (Deuteronomy 4,27).

The Torah says that the Children of Israel will remain few in מספר, "number," when scattered among the nations. The gematria of מספר, "number," is 380.

מספר   380

It is the same מספר, "number," who will seek Hashem משם, "from there," as stated, ובקשתם משם את ה' אלקיך ומצאת כי תדרשנו בכל לבבך ובכל נפשך (דברים ד,כט). "And you shall seek from there G-d your G-d; and you will find Him, if you search after Him with all your heart and with all your soul" (Deuteronomy 4, 29). The gematria of משם, "from there," is 380.

משם   380

Since the gematria of מספר, "number," equals the gematria of משם, "from there," it is an indication that the same few in מספר, "number," will seek Hashem משם, "from there."

שמע ישראל ה' אלקינו ה' אחד (דברים ו,ד).

Hear O Israel, Hashem, our G-d, Hashem is one (Deuteronomy 6,4).

The Gemara Hullin quotes the aforementioned pasuk from Parashath Vaethchannan to show how beloved the Children of Israel are, as stated, חביבין ישראל לפני הקב"ה יותר ממלאכי השרת... וישראל מזכירין את השם אחר שתי תיבות שנאמר שמע ישראל ה' וגו' ומלאכי השרת אין מזכירין את השם אלא לאחר ג' תיבות (חולין צא:), "Israel is beloved before the Holy One, Blessed be He, more than the ministering angels ... and Israel mentions G-d's name after two words, as it says [Shema Yisroel, Hashem], Hear O Israel, Hashem, etc. And the ministering angels do not mention G-d's name except after three words, as it says [Kodosh, Kodosh, Kodosh, Hashem], Holy, holy, holy is the G-d of hosts" (Hullin 91b). Rashi mentions that this Gemara only refers to שירה, "song." When the Children of Israel begin their song, after two words they mention the name of Hashem; while when the ministering angels begin their song, only after three words do they mention the name of Hashem.

The comparison between the Children of Israel and the ministering angels can be further enhanced by a gematria. The first word that the Children of Israel mention in their song is שמע, "Hear," as stated, שמע ישראל ה' אלקינו ה' אחד (דברים ו,ד), "Hear O Israel, Hashem, our G-d, Hashem is one" (Deuteronomy 6,4). The gematria of שמע, "Hear," is 410.

שמע   410

The first word that the ministering angels mention in their song is קדוש, "Holy," as stated, וקרא זה אל זה ואמר קדוש קדוש קדוש ה' צבקות מלא כל הארץ כבודו (ישעי' ו,ג), "And one called to another and said, 'Holy, holy, holy, is the G-d of hosts, the whole earth is full of His glory'" (Isaiah 6,3). The gematria of קדוש, "holy," is 410.

קדוש   410

Since the Gemara compares the expression that begins with שמע, "Hear," to the expression that begins with

קדוש, "Holy," it is very appropriate that the gematria of שמע, "Hear," is equal to the gematria of קדוש, "Holy." The first word of the song of the Children of Israel has the same gematria as the first word of the song of the ministering angels; both approach Hashem via song. The Gemara Hullin says, ואין "The, מה"ש אומרים שירה למעלה עד שיאמרו ישראל למטה (חולין צא:) ministering angels do not say song above until Israel has sung below" (Hullin 91b). This gematria could also be indicative of that attachment between the Children of Israel and the ministering angels.

וכתבתם על מזזות ביתך ובשעריך (דברים ו,ט).
And you shall write them upon the doorposts of your house and upon your gates (Deuteronomy 6,9).

The commandment to have a mezuzah (on one's doorposts and gates) is mentioned twice in the Torah (דברים ו,ט, ויא,כ, Deuteronomy 6,9 and 11,20), but here is the only time it is spelled with just one ו, "vav." The gematria of מזזות, mezuzoth, is 460.

460   מזזות

On the outer side of the mezuzah's parchment the name of G-d, שקי, Shakkai, "All Sufficient," is written. The first time this same name of G-d is mentioned in the Torah is when G-d told Abram התהלך, "walk," before Me and be perfect, as stated, ויהי אברם בן תשעים שנה ותשע שנים וירא ה' אל אברם fect, as stated, "And, ויאמר אליו אני קל שקי התהלך לפני והיה תמים (בראשית יז,א) when Abram was ninety years and nine years old, and G-d appeared to Abram and said to him, I am All Sufficient G-d, walk before Me, and be perfect" (Genesis 17,1). The gematria of התהלך, "to walk," is 460.

460   התהלך

Since מזוזת, "mezuzoth," and התהלך, "to walk," have the same gematria, the word מזוזת, mezuzoth, can insinuate the word התהלך, "to walk," in the pasuk from Genesis. The latter part of the pasuk could now be read as: אני קל שקי מזוזת לפני והיה תמים (בראשית יז,א) "I am All Sufficient G-d, have mezuzoth in your home before Me, and it will be perfect, or complete, that is protected" (Genesis 17,1).

With this reading of the pasuk, it is easy to understand why G-d's name שקי, Shakkai, "All Sufficient," is written on the outside of the mezuzah. Since the name of G-d, שקי, Shakkai, "All Sufficient," is found in the Torah for the first time in a pasuk which through a gematria can insinuate the protection of the mezuzah, it is appropriate that G-d's name שקי, Shakkai, "All Sufficient," is written on the outside of the mezuzah.

נחמו נחמו עמי יאמר אלקיכם (ישעי׳ מ,א).
Be comforted, be comforted, My people, your
G-d has said (Isaiah 40,1).

The Haftarah for פרשת ואתחנן, Parashath Vaethchannan, begins with the words נחמו נחמו, "Be comforted, be comforted." The gematria of נחמו נחמו, "Be comforted, be comforted," is 208.

נחמו	104
נחמו	<u>104</u>
	208

The Midrash and various commentators have given reasons why the word נחמו, "Be comforted," is repeated. The Midrash Eicha Rabbati explains the repetition of the word נחמו, "Be comforted," to relate to the pesukim איכה א,ח, Lamentations 1,8, and ישעי׳ מ,ב, Isaiah 40,2, as stated, חטאו בכפלים דכתיב חטא חטאה ירושלים (איכה א,ח) ולקו בכפלים דכתיב כי לקחה מיד ה׳ כפלים בכל חטאתיה (ישעי׳ מ,ב). ומתנחמים בכפלים דכתיב

נחמו נחמו עמי יאמר אלקיכם (ישעי׳ מ,ב) (מדרש איכה רבתי, פרשה א, אות סה), "They have sinned doubly, as it is written, 'Jerusalem has sinned a sin,' (Lamentations 1,8) and they were be smitten doubly, as it is written, 'For she has received from G-d's hand doubly for all her sins' (Isaiah 40,2). And the comfort will be double, as it is written, 'Be comforted, be comforted, My people, your G-d shall say' (Isaiah 40,1)" (Midrash Eicha Rabbati, Section 1, Letter 65).

The מצודת דוד, Metsudath David, explains the repetition of the word נחמו, "Be comforted," to indicate a strong comfort, as stated, אלקיכם יאמר אל הנביאים נחמו את עמי וכפל המלה יורה על החוזק (מצודת דוד, ישעי׳ מ,א, ד״ה נחמו נחמו), "Your G-d will say to the prophets, comfort My people; and the doubling of the word instructs about its strength" (Metsudath David, Isaiah 40,1, header words: Be comforted, be comforted).

The Malbim explains the repetition of the word נחמו, "Be comforted," to refer to two different ways the redemption can come, as stated, ויען שהגאולה תבוא או קודם הזמן מצד הזכות, או אם יקבלו עונשם, או עכ״פ אם לא יזכו, יגאלנו בזמן הקבוע לכן אמר נחמה כפולה (באור העניין, מאת הרב מאיר ליבש מלביי״ם, ישעי׳ מ,א) "And since the redemption will come, either prior to its time, owing to the merits, or if they will receive their punishment; or in any case if they do not merit, they will be redeemed at the appointed time, therefore he said Be comforted twice" (Be'ur Ha'inyan by Rabbi Meir Lebush Malbim, Isaiah 40,1).

Another possible answer why the word נחמו, "Be comforted," is repeated can be given based on a Rashi in the Gemara, and a gematria. In the Gemara Baba Mezia, Rashi quotes an opinion that: דאליהו הוא פינחס (רש״י, בבא מציעא קיד,: ד״ה לאו כהן מר), "That Elijah is Pinchas" (Rashi, Baba Mezia 114b, header words: Is the master not a Kohen?). In the future G-d will send Elijah to the Children of Israel (Malachi 3,23). His coming will be a comfort for the Children of Israel, for he will bring peace to the world (רש״י, מלאכי ג,כד, Rashi,

Malachi 3,24). Since Elijah is Pinchas, it means that in the future G-d will send Pinchas to the Children of Israel.

The second pasuk in Parashath Pinchas states, פינחס בן אלעזר בן אהרן הכהן השיב את חמתי מעל בני ישראל בקנאו את קנאתי בתוכם ולא כליתי את בני ישראל בקנאתי (במדבר כה,יא), "Pinchas the son of Eleazar, the son of Aaron the priest, has turned My anger away from the Children of Israel, in that he was jealous for My sake among them, and I did not consume the Children of Israel in My jealousy" (Numbers 25, 11). The gematria of פינחס, "Pinchas," is 208.

פינחס   208

Since in the future G-d will send Pinchas to the Children of Israel, and he will bring peace to the world, which will be a comfort for the Children of Israel, therefore it is logical that the word נחמו, "Be comforted," is written twice; its double gematria is equal to the gematria of Pinchas.

ואתה דניאל סתם הדברים וחתם הספר עד עת קץ ישטטו רבים ותרבה הדעת (דניאל יב,ד).
And you, Daniel, close away the words and seal the book, until the time of the end, many will roam about, and knowledge will be increased (Daniel 12,4).

The sidrah for this week, פרשת ואתחנן, Parashath Vaethchannan, is always read on שבת נחמו, Shabbath Nachamu. The Haftarah for פרשת ואתחנן, Parashath Vaethchannan, is one of comfort and hope; it foretells the end of the exile. Interest in the end of the exile can cause one to focus on ספר דניאל, the Book of Daniel, where the time of the redemption is hinted to in the text, but is hidden, as stated, ואתה דניאל סתם הדברים וחתם הספר עד עת קץ ישטטו רבים ותרבה הדעת (דניאל יב,ד), "And you Daniel, close up the words, and seal the book, until the time of the end; many will roam about, and knowledge will be increased" (Daniel 12,4). The מצודת דוד, Metsudath David, explains the end of this pasuk as referring to the people who will search the Book of Daniel to try to calculate the time of the redemption, but will not succeed; however, when the redemption does comes, the sources will be crystal clear, as stated, עד בא עת קץ הגאולה הנה רבים ישוטטו בתנועת המחשבה להשכיל אמתת הקץ ויתרבה הדעת לחקור ביותר וכאמור הנה יחקורו עד עת הקץ ולא ידעו מאומה אבל בבוא העת אז יפקחו עיני כל להבין רמזי זמן הגאולה (מצודת דוד, דניאל יב,ד, ד"ה עד עת קץ ישוטטו וגו'), "Until the time of the end of the exile comes, behold many will roam with thoughtful activity to prudently decide the time of the end, and knowledge will increase to search more, as it says, behold they will examine until the time of the end; and they will know nothing. But, when the time comes, then everyone's eyes will be opened, to understand the hints of the time of the redemption" (Metsudath David, Daniel 12,4, header words: Until the time of the end, they will roam about, etc.). According to this explanation, the phrase ישוטטו רבים, "many will roam about," and the phrase ותרבה הדעת, "and knowledge will be increased," are fundamentally saying the same thing. Perhaps some light can be shed on the phrase ותרבה הדעת, "and knowledge will be increased," which will give a different explanation.

A Gemara based on a pasuk in this week's sidrah can help elucidate the pasuk in the Book of Daniel. In פרשת ואתחנן, Parashath Vaethchanan, the Torah states, לנס שמה רוצח אשר ירצח את רעהו בבלי דעת והוא לא שנא לו מתמל שלשם ונס אל אחת מן הערים האל וחי (דברים ד,מב), "To flee there a manslayer who slew his fellow without knowledge, and he did not hate him in times past, and he might flee to one of these cities and live" (Deuteronomy 4,42). The Gemara Sotah applies this pasuk to two תלמידי חכמים, "disciples of the wise," who are antagonistic toward each other, are not agreeable with each other in Jewish law, as stated, וא"ר אילעא בר יברכיה שני ת"ח הדרין בעיר

אחת ואין נוחין זה לזה בהלכה אחד מת ואחד גולה שנאמר לנוס שמה רוצח אשר ירצח את רעהו בבלי דעת (דברים ד,מב) ואין דעת אלא תורה שנאמר (סוטה מט.) (הושע ד,ו) נדמו עמי מבלי הדעת, "R. Elai b. Jebarekya said, two disciples of the wise who live in the same city and are not agreeable with each other in Jewish law, one dies and one goes into exile, as it says, 'To flee there a manslayer who slew his neighbor without knowledge (Deuteronomy 4,42),' and there is no knowledge except Torah, as it says, 'My people are destroyed for lack of knowledge'" (Hosea 4,6) (Sotah 49a). The תורה תמימה, Torah Temimah, quotes the Gemara Sotah and comments that the תלמידי חכמים, "disciples of the wise," who are antagonistic toward each other in Jewish law are learning Torah for ulterior motives, שלא לשמה, "not for its own sake," (תורה תמימה, דברים ד,מב, אות ע) Torah Temimah, Deuteronomy 4,42, Letter 70).

Since the Gemara Sotah is based on the concept of ואין דעת אלא תורה, "and there is no knowledge except Torah," and בבלי דעת, "without knowledge," refers to learning Torah שלא לשמה, "not for its own sake," it can be concluded that דעת, "knowledge," refers to learning Torah לשמה, "for its own sake." The learning of Torah לשמה, "for its own sake," has treasured consequences, two of which will be mentioned.

The first treasured consequence of learning of Torah לשמה, "for its own sake," is recorded in a Mishnah. The Mishnah in Avoth says, רבי ישמעאל בנו אומר הלומד על מנת ללמד מספיקין בידו ללמוד וללמד והלומד על מנת לעשות מספיקין בידו ללמוד וללמד לשמור ולעשות (אבות, פרק ד, משנה ה) "Rabbi Ishmael his son said, 'He who learns in order to teach, to him the means will be vouchsafed to learn and to teach. And he who learns in order to practice, to him the means will be vouchsafed to learn, and to teach, to observe, and to practice'" (Avoth, Chapter 4, Mishnah 5). The תוספת יום טוב, Tosafoth Yom Tov, explains the Mishnah as follows: הלומד על מנת ללמד, "He who learns in order to teach," refers to one who learns Torah שלא לשמה,

"not for its own sake." והלומד על מנת לעשות, "And he who learns in order to practice," refers to one who learns Torah לשמה, "for its own sake." He further explains that לעשות, "to practice," refers to observance of the Torah (תוספת יום טוב, אבות, פרד ד, משנה ה, Tosafoth Yom Tov, Avoth, Chapter 4, Mishnah 5). Thus, one who learns Torah לשמה, "for its own sake," will be privileged to observe the Torah, that is the 613 Commandments. This point is made even more forcibly by the עיקר דודאי תוספת יום טוב, Ikar Tosafoth Yom Tov, when he states, לעשות היינו לקיים כל התורה, "That certainly 'to practice,' that is to observe the entire Torah" (עיקר תוספת יום טוב, אבות, פרק ד, משנה ה, Ikar Tosafoth Yom Tov, Avoth, Chapter 4, Mishnah 5).

Perhaps the Tosafoth Yom Tov can be elucidated based on a Gemara in Menachoth which says that he who learns the laws of a חטאת, "sin offering," it is as if he offered a חטאת, "sin offering" (מנחות קי., Menachoth 110a). So too, it can be said that the Tosafoth Yom Tov means that one who learns Torah לשמה, "for its own sake," it is as if he observed the entire Torah, that is the 613 Mitzvoth. Hence, one of the treasured consequences for one who learns Torah לשמה, "for its own sake," is that it is as if he observed the entire Torah, that is the 613 Mitzvoth.

The second treasured consequence of learning Torah לשמה, "for its own sake," is recorded in a Gemara. The Gemara Sanhedrin asserts a treasured consequence of the learning of Torah לשמה, "for its own sake," is that it causes the redemption to come sooner. This assertion is based on a pasuk from Isaiah 51,16, as stated, א"ר אלכסנדרי כל העוסק בתורה לשמה... ולוי אמר אף מקרב את הגאולה שנאמר ולאמר לציון עמי אתה (סנהדרין צט:), "Rabbi Alexandri says, Anyone who is involved in the learning of Torah לשמה, 'for its own sake,' ... and Levi said, He causes the redemption to come sooner, as it says, 'And say to Zion, you are My people'" (Sanhedrin 99b). Hence, the second treasured consequences for one who earns Torah לשמה, "for its own sake," is that it causes the redemption to come sooner.

Keeping the above sources in mind, some light can be shed on the phrase ותרבה הדעת, "and knowledge will be increased," from the Book of Daniel. Since אין דעת אלא תורה, "there is no knowledge except Torah," therefore, the phrase ותרבה הדעת, "and knowledge will be increased," can be interpreted as ותרבה התורה, "and Torah learning will be increased." However, דעת, "knowledge," refers to learning Torah לשמה, "for its own sake," as was seen from the Torah Temimah based on the Gemara Sotah. Thus, the phrase ותרבה הדעת, "and knowledge will be increased," can be interpreted as ותרבה תורה לשמה, "and learning Torah for its own sake will be increased." Inasmuch as the subject matter of the pasuk from the Book of Daniel is about the redemption, one would expect this pasuk to refer to learning Torah לשמה, "for its own sake," which causes the redemption to come sooner, as the Gemara Sanhedrin asserts. One of the treasured consequences for one who learns Torah לשמה, "for its own sake," is that it is as if he observed the entire Torah, that is the 613 Mitzvoth, as was elucidated from Tosafoth Yom Tov.

The pasuk from the Book of Daniel states, ואתה דניאל סתם הדברים וחתם הספר עד עת קץ ישטטו רבים ותרבה הדעת (דניאל יב,ד), "And you, Daniel, shut up the words and seal the book, until the time of the end, many will roam about, and knowledge will be increased" (Daniel 12,4). The gematria of ותרבה, "will be increased," is 613.

ותרבה　　　613

It can be deduced that ותרבה, "will be increased," refers to increased observance of the 613 Mitzvoth due to learning Torah לשמה, "for its own sake."

Now, the phrase ישטטו רבים, "many will roam about," and the phrase ותרבה הדעת, "and knowledge will be increased," would have two different meanings. The former refers to the people who will search the Book of Daniel to try to calculate the time of the redemption, but will not succeed; the latter refers to the constructive efforts of people who learn Torah לשמה, "for its own sake," which causes the redemption to come sooner. Those people who learn Torah לשמה, "for its own sake," cause the redemption to come sooner and their learning is as if they observed the entire Torah, that is the 613 Mitzvoth.

Parashath Ekev

פרשת עקב

כי תאמר בלבבך רבים הגוים האלה ממני איכה אוכל להורישם (דברים ז,יז).

If you shall say in your heart, 'These nations are more than I, how shall I be able to dispossess them?' (Deuteronomy 7,17).

The Torah tells that if the Children of Israel have doubts in their heart, as to how they will be able to conquer nations more numerous than themselves, they should dispel such doubts, by remembering what Hashem did to Pharaoh and Egypt. Besides Hashem doing similarly to these feared nations, Hashem will also send הצרעה, "the hornet," against those nations. This interaction can be seen in the gematrioth of two expressions and a word.

The Torah pinpoints doubts in the heart. The gematria of כי תאמר בלבבך רבים הגוים האלה ממני, "If you shall say in your heart, 'These nations are more than I,'" is 1224.

כי תאמרך בלבבך	727
רבים	252
הגוים האלה	105
ממני	140
	1224

To dispel these doubts of the heart, the Torah says to remember what G-d did to Pharaoh and to Egypt, as stated, לא תירא מהם זכר תזכר את אשר עשה ה' אלקיך לפרעה ולכל מצרים (דברים ז,יח), "Do not be afraid of them, remember well what Hashem, your G-d, did to Pharaoh and to all of Egypt" (Deutronomy 7,18). The gematria of זכר תזכר, "remember well," 854.

זכר	227
תזכר	627
	854

Since one expression is telling how to dispel, or eliminate, the fear told by the other expression, their difference could have latent meaning; this difference can be computed. The difference in gematrioth between these two expressions is 370.

$$1224$$
$$-854$$
$$\overline{}$$
$$370$$

The Torah very clearly asserts that G-d will send הצרעה, "the hornet," against those nations, as stated, וגם את הצרעה, "And ישלח ה׳ אלקיך בם עד אבד הנשארים והנסתרים מפניך (דברים ז,כ), also the hornet, Hashem, your G-d, will will send among them until the remaining ones and the hidden ones, perish before you" (Deuteronomy 7,20). The gematria of הצרעה, "the hornet," is 370.

הצרעה   370

The difference in gematrioth between the expressions of having doubts, and the expression of doing what the Torah prescribes to dispel those doubts, is equal to the gematria of הצרעה, "the hornet." Thus, the interaction which the Torah tells, when one has doubts in his heart as to how the Children of Israel will conquer nations more numerous than themselves, how to dispel such doubts, and the sending of the hornet can be seen in gematrioth. After one dispels the doubts of the heart, associated with the gematria of 1224, by remembering well what Hashem did, associated with the gematria of 854, then Hashem will send the hornet, associated with the gematria of the remainder of 1224-854, or 370.

כי תאמר בלבבך רבים הגוים האלה ממני איכה אוכל
להורישם (דברים ז,יז).

If you shall say in your heart, 'These nations are more than I, how shall I be able to I dispossess them?' (Deuteronomy 7,17).

The Torah was aware that there might be fear of certain Canaanite nations in the hearts of some of the Children of Israel. The gematria of כי תאמר בלבבך, "If you shall say in your heart," is 727.

כי	30
תאמר	641
בלבבך	56
	727

The next pasuk tells that the way to counteract these fears of the heart, is simply not to be afraid, as stated, לא תירא מהם זכר תזכר את אשר עשה ה׳ אלקיך לפרעה ולכל מצרים (דברים ז,יח), "Do not be afraid of them, remember well what Hashem, your G-d, did to Pharaoh and to all of Egypt" (Deuteronomy 7,18). The gematria of לא תירא מהם, "Do not be afraid of them," is 727.

לא	31
תירא	611
מהם	85
	727

Since the gematria of כי תאמר בלבבך, "when you shall say in your heart," is equal to the gematria of לא תירא מהם, "do not be afraid of them," this equality reinforces what the Torah says: The way to counteract the fears of the heart, is simply not to be afraid, remembering what Hashem, your G-d, did to Pharaoh and to all of Egypt.

כי תאמר בלבבך רבים הגוים האלה ממני איכה אוכל להורישם (דברים ז,יז).

If you shall say in your heart, "These nations are more than I, how shall I be able to dispossess them?" (Deuteronomy 7,17).

The Torah says that when one has doubts בלבבך, "in

your heart," he should remember what Hashem did to Pharaoh and to all of Egypt. The gematria of בלבבך, "in your heart," is 56.

בלבבך   56

To combat these doubts of the heart, the Torah says to remember what G-d did to Pharaoh and to Egypt, as stated, לא תירא מהם זכר תזכר את אשר עשה ה' אלקיך לפרעה ולכל מצרים (דברים ז,יח), "Do not be afraid of them, remember well what Hashem, your G-d, did to Pharaoh and to all Egypt" (Deuteronomy 7,18). The gematria of זכר תזכר, "remember well," is 854.

זכר	227
תזכר	627
	854

The next pasuk proceeds to list exactly what one should remember, as stated, המסת הגדלת אשר ראו עיניך והאתת והמפתים והיד החזקה והזרע הנטויה אשר הוצאך ה' אלקיך כן יעשה ה' אלקיך לכל העמים אשר אתה ירא מפניהם (דברים ז,יט), "The great trials which your eyes saw, and the signs, and the wonders, and the strong hand, and the outstretched arm whereby Hashem, your G-d, brought you out, thus, Hashem, your G-d, shall do to all the nations of whom you are afraid" (Deuteronomy 7,19). The gematria of המסת הגדלת... והאתת והמפתים והיד החזקה והזרע הנטויה, "the great trials ... and the signs, and the wonders, and the strong hand, and the outstretched arm," is 2863.

המסת הגדלת	947
והאתת והמפתים	1393
והיד החזקה	150
והזרע הנטויה	373
	2863

Therefore, 2863 represents the list of what one is to remember, that is, what one is not to forget.

The Gemara defines precisely the meaning of not forgetting. In Megillath Esther, it is recorded that there is an obligation to remember the days of Purim, as stated, והימים האלה נזכרים ונעשים בכל דור ודור משפחה ומשפחה מדינה ומדינה ועיר ועיר וימי הפורים האלה לא יעברו מתוך היהודים וזכרם לא יסוף מזרעם (אסתר ט,כח), "And these days should be remembered and celebrated by every generation, every family, every province, and every city; these days of Purim shall not cease from among the Jews, and their remembrance shall not perish from their seed" (Esther 9,28). After deriving that the remembering inscribed in Megillath Esther must be read from a book, the Gemara Megillah queries if merely scanning is adequate, or recitation is necessary. The Gemara Megillah says that not forgetting is in the heart, but remembering is done verbally with the mouth, as stated, וממאי דהאי זכירה (אסתר ט,כח) קריאה היא דלמא עיון בעלמא לא סלקא דעתך דכתיב זכור (דברים כה,יז) יכול בלב כשהוא אומר לא תשכח (דברים כה,יט) הרי שכחת הלב אמור הא מה אני מקיים זכור בפה (מגילה יח.). "And how is it known that this remembering (Esther 9,28) means recitation? Perhaps it merely means reading with the eyes. It should not enter your mind, for it is written, 'Remember' (Deuteronomy 25,17). Could it mean with the heart? When it says, 'Do not forget,' (Deuteronomy 25,19) behold forgetting of the heart has been said. How do I fulfill 'remember'? With the mouth (verbally)" (Megillah 18a). Remembering can also be in the heart, but in the particular pasuk with which the Gemara is dealing, remembering is with the mouth. Nonetheless, this Gemara demonstrates that not forgetting is in the heart.

If one remembers what one is suppose to remember, he will not forget the list represented by the gematria of 2863. Thus, בלבבך, "in your heart," represented by the gematria of 56, will be the list represented by the gematria of 2863. The sum of these gematrioth is 2919.

56
2863
———
2919

Thus, 2919 represents having in one's heart what is supposed to be there.

In the same manner that one fulfills זכר תזכר, "remember well," which will cause one to have in his heart what is supposed to be there, so too Hashem will take actions against all the nations which the Children of Israel fear. When the Children of Israel remember what they are supposed to remember, to that degree, Hashem will take action against the feared nations. This quid pro quo relationship can be the meaning of the word כן, "thus," in the pasuk, as stated, המסת הגדלת אשר ראי עיניך והאתת והמפתים והיד החזקה והזרע הנטויה אשר הוצאך ה׳ אלקיך כן יעשה ה׳ אלקיך לכל העמים אשר אתה ירא מפניהם (דברים ז,יט), "The great trials which your eyes saw, and the signs, and the wonders, and the strong hand, and the outstretched arm whereby Hashem, your G-d, brought you out, thus, Hashem, your G-d, shall do to all the nations of whom you are afraid" (Deuteronomy 7,19). The gematria of יעשה ה׳ אלקיך לכל העמים אשר אתה ירא מפניהם, "Hashem, your G-d, shall do to all the nations of whom you are afraid," is 2065.

יעשה ה׳ אלקיך	477
לכל העמים אשר	746
אתה ירא	617
מפניהם	225
	2065

Thus, 2065, represents what G-d will do to the nations which the Children of Israel fear, in the same manner in which the Children of Israel fulfill זכר תזכר, "remember well." The פשוט פשט, "simple meaning," of the word כן, "thus," in the pasuk, refers back to המסת הגדלת וגו׳, "the great trials, etc." Note, that according to this exposition, the word כן, "thus," in the pasuk has been explained to refer to זכר תזכר, "remember well," which the Children of Israel are to do, and not to what Hashem did to Egypt, as the first part of the pasuk could lead one to believe.

The sum of 854, the gematria of זכר תזכר, "remember well," plus 2065, the gematria of יעשה ה׳ אלקיך לכל העמים אשר אתה ירא מפניהם, "Hashem, your G-d, shall do to all the nations of whom you are afraid," is 2919.

$$854$$
$$\underline{2065}$$
$$2919$$

Thus, 2019 represents what Hashem will do to the feared nations in the same manner that the Children of Israel fulfill זכר תזכר, "remember well." As was seen previously, 2919 also represents having in one's heart what is supposed to be there. It is very meaningful that the sum of the two mentioned gematrioth is 2919, for their represented ideas are the same. When the Children of Israel have in their hearts what is supposed to be there, then G-d will take action against the nations which the Children of Israel fear, in the same manner in which the Children of Israel fulfill זכר תזכר, "remember well."

לא תירא מהם זכר תזכר את אשר־עשה ה׳ אלקיך לפרעה ולכל־מצרים (דברים ז,יח).

"Do not be afraid of them, remember well what Hashem, your G-d, did to Pharaoh and to all of Egypt" (Deutronomy 7,18).

The Children of Israel were in Egypt 210 years, and not the 400 years as foretold to Abram. Thus, in a sense, they left Egypt 190 years early (רש״י, בראשית טו,יג, Rashi, Genesis 15,13). In פרשת עקב, Parashath Ekev, the Torah says that when one has doubts in his heart, that is, he fears the Canaanite nations, he should remember what Hashem did to Pharaoh and to all of Egypt, as stated, לא תירא מהם זכר תזכר את אשר עשה ה' אלקיך לפרעה ולכל מצרים (דברים ז,יח), "Do not be afraid of them, remember well what Hashem, your G-d, did to Pharaoh and to all of Egypt" (Deutronomy 7,18). The gematria of זכר תזכר, "remember well," 854.

זכר	227
תזכר	627
	854

The gematria of אשר עשה ה' אלקיך לפרעה ולכל מצרים, "what Hashem, your G-d, did to Pharaoh and to all of Egypt," 1819.

אשר עשה	876
ה' אלקיך לפרעה	477
ולכל מצרים	466
	1819

The sum of the gematria of זכר תזכר, "remember well," plus the gematria of אשר עשה ה' אלקיך לפרעה ולכל מצרים, "what Hashem, your G-d, did to Pharaoh and to all of Egypt," is 2673.

854
1819
2673

Therefore, the gematria of 2673 can be associated with remembering what G-d did to Pharaoh and to all of Egypt. The next pasuk lists the miracles that Hashem wrought to take the Children of Israel out of Egypt, as stated, המסת הגדלת אשר ראו עיניך והאתת והמפתים והיד החזקה והזרע הנטויה אשר הוצאך ה' אלקיך כן יעשה ה' אלקיך לכל העמים אשר אתה ירא מפניהם (דברים ז,יט), "The great trials which your eyes saw, and the signs, and the wonders, and the strong hand, and the outstretched arm whereby Hashem, your G-d, brought you out, thus, Hashem, your G-d, shall do to all the nations of whom you are afraid" (Deuteronomy 7,19). The gematria of המסת הגדלת והאתת והמפתים והיד החזקה והזרע הנטויה, "the great trials, and the signs, and the wonders, and the strong hand, and the outstretched arm," is 2863.

המסת הגדלת	947
והאתת והמפתים	1393
והיד החזקה	150
והזרע הנטויה	373
	2863

Therefore, 2863 can be associated with the miracles that Hashem wrought to take the Children of Israel out of Egypt.

The difference between the gematria of the miracles that Hashem wrought to take the Children of Israel out of Egypt, represented be the minuend of 2863, and the gematria of remembering what Hashem did to Pharaoh and to all Egypt, represented by the subtrahend of 2673, is a remainder of 190.

$$2863 - 2673 = 190$$

This remainder of 190 between the two gematrioth could be an allusion to the 190 years that the Children of Israel left Egypt early. Besides what Hashem did overtly to Egypt, He wrought miracles which can additionally include the early departure from Egypt. This allusion fits nicely into the meaning of the pasuk: When one has fears in his heart, he should remember what Hashem did to Egypt and the miracles He wrought, among which was the shortening of the suffering of the Children of Israel by 190 years. Thus, the will of Hashem was to to limit the suffering of the Children of Israel, and one should remember this limiting, to dispel fears in his heart.

וגם את הצרעה ישלח ה' אלקיך בם עד אבד הנשארי
והנסתרים מפניך (דברים ז,כ).
And also, Hashem, your G-d, will send the hornet among them until the remaining ones and
the hidden ones perish before you (Deuteronomy 7,20).

The first pasuk of פרשת עקב, Parashath Ekev, utilizes
the word עקב, "as a consequence," as stated, והיה עקב תשמעון
את המשפטים האלה ושמרתם ועשיתם אתם ושמר ה' אלקיך לך את הברית
(דברים ז,יב) ,ואת החסד אשר נשבע לאבתיך, "And it will come to pass,
as a consequence of your hearkening to these judgments,
and you will keep them and you will do them, that G-d, your
G-d, will keep with you the covenant and the kindness which
He swore to your fathers," (Deuteronomy 7,12). Ekev has the
additional meaning of heel. Rashi explains the first pasuk of
this sidrah, as referring to מצות קלות, "light commandments,"
as stated, אם המצות קלות שאדם דש בעקביו תשמעון (רש"י, דברים
יב,ז,), "If unto the light commandments which a man treads
with his heel, 'you will hearken'" (Rashi, Deuteronomy 7,12).
However, the Vilna Goan in his ספר אדרת אליהו, Book of
Adereth Eliyahu, renders a novel explanation which can refer
to all of the commandments, as it says, והיה עקב תשמעון וגו' כי
פן יאמר בלבבו מה לי לשמור את המצות הלא אבי שמר דרך ה' והי ישלם
לבניו עד אלף דור אבל כבר פי' הקדמונים שמר הברית והחסד כמו ואביו
שמר את הדבר אם בנו אינו הולך בדרכי אביו, הקב"ה שומר לקיים בריתו
לנכדו ואם גם נכדו אינו זכאי שומר לדור רביעי וכן עד אלף דור. וזהו אומרו
והיה עקב תשמעון וגו' ושמרתם ועשיתם וגו' (ספר אדרת אליהו מאת הרב
אליהו מווילנא, פרשת עקב, דברים ז,יב), "And it will come to pass as
a consequence of your hearkening, etc. For lest it will be that
one will say in his heart: Why should I observe the Commandments? Has not my father observed the ways of G-d,
and G-d will recompense his sons until a thousand generations. But already the early scholars have explained, 'He will
be vigilant about the covenant and the kindness,' as 'and his

father was vigilant about the matter.' If the son is not going in the ways of his father, the Holy One, Blessed be He is vigilant to fulfill His covenant to his grandson. And if also his grandson is not worthy, He is vigilant to the fourth generation, and so until the thousandth generation. And this is what it says, 'And it will come to pass, as a consequence of your hearkening, etc., and you will observe and you will do, etc.'" (Book of Adereth Eliyahu by Rabbi Eliyahu from Vilna, Parashath Ekev, Deuteronomy 7,12). Thus, according to Book of Adereth Eliyahu it is evident that the first pasuk of this sidrah can refer to all the commandments.

There is a total of 613 Mitzvoth, divided between 248 positive Mitzvoth and 365 negative Mitzvoth, as stated, דרש רבי שמלאי שש מאות ושלש עשרה מצות נאמרו לו למשה שלש מאות וששים וחמש לאוין כמנין ימות החמה ומאתים וארבעים ושמונה עשה כנגד איבריו של אדם (מכות כג:), "Rabbi Simlai expounded, 613 Commandments were said to Moses, three hundred and sixty-five negative Commandments corresponding to the number of days in a solar year, and two hundred and forty-eight positive Commandments corresponding to the limbs of a person" (Makkoth 23b). After the first pasuk of this sidrah, which can be explained as referring to all the commandments, the Torah says that as an ensuing result of your hearkening, G-d will send the hornet among the nations whom you fear, as stated, וגם את הצרעה ישלח ה' אלקיך בם עד אבד הנשארים והנסתרים מפניך (דברים ז,כ), "And also, Hashem, your G-d, will send the hornet among them until the remaining ones and the hidden ones, perish before you" (Deuteronomy 7,20). [Note that Rashi (רש"י, דברים ז,כב, Rashi, Deuteronomy 7,22), says that the Children of Israel will sin, but that revelation does not negate the potential ensuing result for observing the commandments.] The gematria of אבד הנשארים, "those remaining ones, perish," is 613.

אבד	7
הנשארים	<u>606</u>
	613

Since the ensuing result for observing the 613 Commandments is that אבד הנשארים, "those who are left, perish," it is very suitable that the gematria of these two words is 613.

המוליכך במדבר הגדל והנורא נחש שרף ועקרב וצמאון אשר אין מים המוציא לך מים מצור החלמיש (דברים ח,טו).

Who led you through the great and terrible desert, fiery serpents, and scorpions, and drought, where there was no water; and who brought forth water for you from a flinty rock (Deuteronomy 8,15).

The Torah describes the desert through which the Children of Israel were led as lacking water. The gematria of מים, "water," is 90.

מים   90

Note that water is the only thing listed in the pasuk that is described as lacking, in the negative.

The Gemara Baba Kamma equates water with Torah, as stated, ואין מים אלא תורה שנאמר הוי כל צמא לכו למים (ישעי׳ נה,א), (בבא קמא יז.), "And there is never a mention of water which can not be explained to refer to Torah, as it says, 'Ho, let all those who are thirsty come to water'" (Isaiah 55,1) (Baba Kamma 17a). Since water is equated with Torah, and the pasuk in Parashath Ekev says there was no water in the desert, thus, על פי דרש, "in the way of a homily," it can be said that to some extent, Torah was lacking in the desert. The Gemara Sotah equates knowledge with Torah, as stated, ואין דעת אלא תורה שנאמר נדמו עמי מבלי הדעת (הושע ד,ו) (סוטה מה.), "And there is no knowledge, except Torah, as it says, 'My people are destroyed because of lack of the knowledge'" (Hosea 4,6) (Sotah 49a). Thus, water may be equated with Torah, and knowledge may be equated with Torah. In the desert where there was no water, there was to some extent a lack of Torah;

and since there was a lack of Torah, there was a lack of knowledge. Consequently, the desert was somewhat void of Torah and knowledge.

The בעל הטורים, Baal Haturim, in Parashath Ekev paraphrases a pasuk from Nehemiah to assert that one of the novel aspects of the manna was that it bestowed knowledge. He writes, מלמד שבאכילת המן ניתן להם דעת וכן בעזרא הוא אומר ומנך נתת להם להשכילם (נחמיה ט,כ) וזהו לא ניתנה תורה אלא לאוכלי המן (בעל הטורים, דברים ח,ג), "It teaches that by eating the manna, knowledge was given to them, and thus in the Book of Ezra it says, and Your manna You gave to them to make them prudent (Nehemiah 9,20). And this is what it means that 'the Torah was only given to those who ate the manna'" (Baal Haturim, Deuteronomy 8,3). [The Book of Ezra originally included the Book of Nehemiah, see גליון הש״ס מאת רבי עקיבא איגר, סוכה יב., Gilyon Hashas by Rabbi Akiva Eiger, Sukkah 12a. The Gemara Baba Bathra 14b lists Ezra as one of the books of Tanakh, but has no mention of Nehemiah] The desert was somewhat void of Torah and knowledge, so Hashem provided manna which bestowed knowledge; the remedy matched the deficiency. The reference to מים, "water," and its gematria of 90, is found in Deuteronomy 8,15 as was previously quoted. The reference to manna is found in the very next pasuk, as stated, המאכלך מן במדבר אשר לא ידעון אבתיך למען ענתך ולמען נסתך להיטבך באחריתך (דברים ח,טז). "Who fed you manna in the desert, which was unknown to your fathers, in order to afflict you, and in order to test you to do good at your latter end" (Deuteronomy 8,16). The gematria of מן, "manna," is 90.

מן   90

In the desert there was a deficiency of מים, "water," and to some extent knowledge was also lacking. To alleviate the lack of knowledge, Hashem provided an antidote, מן, "manna." The deficiency and the antidote each has a gematria of 90.

Additional significance to the gematria of מן, "manna," can be found in פרשת בשלח, Parashath Beshallach, section of this sefer.

זכר לעבדיך לאברהם ליצחק וליעקב אל תפן אל קשי העם הזה ואל רשעו ואל חטאתו (דברים ט,כז).

Remember Your servants, Abraham, Isaac, and Jacob; do not turn toward the stubbornness of this people, nor toward its wickedness, nor toward their sin (Deuteronomy 9,27).

Moses prayed that G-d should not turn toward the wickedness of of the people. The gematria of ואל רשעו, "nor toward its wickedness," is 613.

$$
\begin{array}{rr}
\text{ואל} & 37 \\
\text{רשעו} & \underline{576} \\
& 613
\end{array}
$$

The אלשיך, Alshech, restricts the wickedness written in this pasuk to refer to intentional idol worship, as he writes, אמר ואל רשעו, שהוא אשר עבדו עבודה זרה במזיד (תורת משה, מאת הרב משה אלשיך, ספר דברים, (פרשת עקב, דברים ט,כז ד"ה זכר לעבדיך וגו', "It says, nor toward its wickedness, it is that they intentionally served idol worship" (Torath Moses by Rabbi Moses Alshech, Book of Deuteronomy, Parashath Ekev, Deuteronomy 9,27, header words: Remember Your servants, etc.).

The Gemara considers one who is an apostate for idol worship, as if he were an apostate for the entire Torah, as stated, מומר לעבודת כוכבים הוא מומר לכל התורה כולה (חולין ה.), "He who is an apostate for idol worship, he is an apostate for the entire Torah" (Hullin 5a). There is a total of 613 Commandments in the Torah (מכות כג:, Makkoth 23b). Since ואל רשעו, "nor toward its wickedness," can refer solely to intentional idol worship, and the Gemara considers a person who engages in such worship as if he were an apostate for the entire

Torah, in which there is a total of 613 Commandments, therefore the fact that ואל רשעו, "nor toward its wickedness," has a gematria of 613 is meaningful.

ועתה ישראל מה ה' אלקיך שאל מעמך כי אם ליראה את ה' אלקיך ללכת בכל דרכיו ולאהבה אתו ולעבד את ה' אלקיך בכל לבבך ובכל נפשך (דברים י,יב).

And now Israel what does G-d, your G-d ask from you, only to fear G-d, your G-d, to walk in all His ways and to love Him and to serve G-d, your G-d, with all your heart and all your soul (Deuteronomy 10,12).

In פרשת עקב, Parashath Ekev, the pasuk quoted above proclaims Israel's obligation to fear and serve G-d; that pasuk uses the interrogative מה, "what." The gematria of מה, "what," is 45.

מה   45

The Gemara concentrates on the significance of the word מה, "what," as stated, רבי מאיר אומר חייב אדם לברך מאה ברכות בכל יום שנאמר ואתה ישראל מה ה' אלקיך שואל מעמך (דברים י,יב) (מנחות מג:), "Rabbi Meir says, A person is obligated to say one hundred blessings every day, as it says, And now Israel what does G-d, your G-d ask from you" (Deuteronomy 10,12), (Menahoth 43b).

The Tosafoth besides giving other explanations, elucidates Rashi, as it says, ובקונטרס פירש אל תקרי מה אלא מאה (תוס' ד"ה שואל מעמך), "And in the pamphlet [Rashi's commentary] explains do not read מה, 'what,' but, מאה, 'a hundred'" (Tosafoth header words: Ask from you). If one reads מה, "what," as, מאה, "a hundred," in essence he adds 55 to the gematria of מה, "what," to arrive at the meaning of, מאה, "a hundred."

The query is, how does saying a hundred blessings

every day help one to fear and serve G-d? A possible answer could be that by adding 55 to the gematria of מה, "what," one will recall another pasuk, recorded just two pesukim after this one, whose first word has a gematria is 55, as stated, הן לה׳ אלקיך השמים ושמי השמים הארץ וכל אשר בה (דברים י,יד), "Behold to G-d, your G-d, are the heavens and the heaven of heavens, the earth and all that is therein" (Deuteronomy 10,14). The gematria of הן, "behold," is 55.

הן   55

When one recalls this pasuk, one can start to realize the omnipresence of G-d. Such a realization can help one to fear and serve G-d.

Parashath Reeh   פרשת ראה

הלא המה בעבר הירדן אחרי דרך מבוא השמש בארץ הכנעני הישב בערבה מול הגלגל אצל אלוני מרה (דברים יא,ל).

Behold they are on the other side of the Jordan, after the way of the setting of the sun, in the land of the Canaanites, who dwell in the plain opposite the Gilgal next to the Plains of Moreh (Deuteronomy 11,30).

In reference to Mount Gerizim and Mount Ebal, the Torah says, הלא המה בעבר הירדן, "Behold they are on the other side of the Jordan." The gematria of הלא המה, "Behold they are," is 86.

הלא	36
המה	50
	86

The words הלא המה, "Behold they are," seem superfluous, for these two words could have been replaced by the single word הם, "They are." Rashi comments on these seemingly superfluous words, that they indicate a sign, as he states, נתן בהם סימן (רש״י, דברים יא,ל), "He gave a sign about them," (Rashi, Deuteronomy 11,30). Perhaps another explanation can be given for these words, which might also elucidate this Rashi.

The word אלקים, "G-d," is employed to refer to G-d's attribute of strict justice, as Rashi says ויזכר אלקים. זה השם אלקים. מדת הדין הוא (רש״י, בראשית ח,א), "And G-d remembered. This name of G-d refers to His attribute of strict justice," (Rashi, Genesis 8,1). The gematria of אלקים, "G-d," is 86.

אלקים	86

Since the gematria of הלא המה, "Behold they are," is

identical to the gematria of אלקים, "G-d," the seemingly su-perfluous words הלא המה, "Behold they are," could be read as words of admonishment and caution. The words הלא המה, "Behold they are," would then warn the Children of Israel that G-d can be characterized by מדת הדין, "His attribute of strict justice"; G-d can do as He has threatened and enforce the curses. This warning could be seen as the sign to which Rashi referred.

This explanation is particularly appealing when one realizes that from the beginning of the sidrah until the words הלא המה, "Behold they are," G-d's name is mentioned three times; each time as a form of (דברים יא, כז, כח, וכט) ה׳ אלקים, "Hashem G-d," (Deuteronomy 11, 27,28,and 29). When G-d's attribute of mercy and the attribute of strict justice are jointly alluded to, He is referred to as ה׳ אלקים, "Hashem G-d,"(,רש״י בראשית א,א, Rashi, Genesis 1,1). Therefore, the words הלא המה, "Behold they are," admonish the Children of Israel, G-d can be personified by מדת הדין, "His attribute of strict justice," alone, independent of His attribute of mercy.

ולא ידבק בידך מאומה מן החרם למען ישוב ה׳ מחרון אפו ונתן לך רחמים ורחמך והרבך כאשר נשבע לאבתיך (דברים יג,יח).

And in your hand there should not cleave aught from the consecrated thing, in order that G-d will turn from the fierceness of His anger, and give you mercy, and have mercy upon you, and multiply you as He swore to your fathers (Deu-teronomy 13,18).

The Torah says that in your hand there should not cleave מאומה, "aught," from the consecrated thing from עיר הנדחת, "a city that has been led astray." The gematria of מאומה," aught," is 92.

מאומה   92

Hashem will show the Children of Israel mercy if they do not cleave unto aught from the consecrated thing of a city that has been led astray, because by abstaining they will have listened to the voice of Hashem, as stated, כי תשמע בקול ה׳ אלקיך לשמר את כל מצותיו אשר אנכי מצוך היום לעשות הישר בעיני ה׳ אלקיך (דברים יג,יט), "When you shall hearken to the voice of Hashem, your G-d, to keep all of His commandments which I command you today, to do that which is right in the eyes of Hashem your G-d," (Deuteronomy 13,19). The gematria of ה׳ אלקיך, "Hashem your G-d," is 92.

ה׳	26
אלקיך	66
	92

Since the two mentioned gematrioth are equal, it could mean to convey that the voice of ה׳ אלקיך, "Hashem your G-d," is commanding that you should not cleave onto מאומה, "aught," from the consecrated thing of a city that has been led astray.

כל צפור טהרה תאכלו. וזה אשר לא תאכלו מהם הנשר והפרס והעזניה (דברים יד,יא-יב).
Every bird which is ritually fit [kosher] you may eat. And these are they from which you may not eat: the eagle, and the ossifrage, and the osprey (Deuteronomy 14,11-12).

When referring to the birds which one is permitted to eat (kosher, suitable), the Torah does not proceed to reveal these. Instead it specifies which individual birds may not be eaten. Rashi learns that both of these pesukim instruct in reference to the two birds of a מצורע, "metzora," as he writes להתיר משלחת שבמצורע, "to permit that [bird] which the metzora sends away," and השחוטה את לאסור, "to prohibit that [bird] which is slaughtered," (כל :המתחיל דבור ,יד-יא,יד דברים ,רש״י, Rashi, מהם תאכלו לא אשר וזה :המתחיל דבור ,וגם ,תאכלו טהרה צפור, Deuteronomy 14,11-12, header words: Every bird which is kosher, you may eat, and also, header words: And these are they which you can not eat from them).

One of the principal reasons a person is afflicted with צרעת, "tzoraas," is that he spoke הרע לשון, "malignant speech," as Rashi writes, (ויקרא ,רש״י) הרע לשון על באין שהנגעים (יד,ד, "For the plagues come on account of of malignant speech" (Rashi, Leviticus 14,4). The speaking of הרע לשון, "malignant speech," is considered a grave sin.

The Gemara Arakin says that one who speaks הרע לשון, "malignant speech," enlarges his sin until the level of idolatry, immorality, and murder, as stated, כל ישמעאל רבי דבי תנא וגילוי כוכבים עבודת עבירות שלש כנגד עונות מגדיל הרע לשון המספר (:טו ערכין) דמים ושפיכות עריות, "It was taught in the school of Rabbi Ishmael, Anyone who speaks malignart speech, his sins will be enlarged up to the level of the three cardinal sins: idol worship, immorality, and murder" (Arakin 15b). The Gemara Horayoth individualizes idolatry as the commandment which is equated to all 613 Commandments, as stated, כוכבים עבודת זו אומר הוי המצות ככל שקולה שהיא מצוה היא איזו (ח. הוריות), "Which commandment is one which is equivalent to all the commandments? Say it is idol worship" (Horayoth 8a).

Things equal to the same thing are equal to each other. Since speaking malignant speech is equated to idolatry, and since idolatry is equated to all 613 Commandments, therefore speaking malignant speech can be equated to all 613 Commandments.

Some indication of the gravity of speaking הרע לשון, "malignant speech," can be ascertained by examining the gematria of certain words from the two pesukim initially quoted. The gematria of צפור טהרה וזה, "bird which is kosher, and these" is 613.

$$
\begin{array}{rr}
\text{צפור} & 376 \\
\text{טהרה} & 219 \\
\text{וזה} & \underline{18} \\
& 613
\end{array}
$$

Since speaking לשון הרע, "malignant speech," can be equated to all 613 Commandments; and since Rashi learns that both of the pesukim initially quoted refer to a metzora; and since one of the principal reasons a person is afflicted with צרעת, "tzoraas," is that he spoke malignant speech, therefore the gematria of 613 from these pesukim is an indication that speaking malignant speech can be equated to all 613 Commandments.

כי לא יחדל אביון מקרב הארץ על כן אנכי מצוך לאמר פתח תפתח את ידך לאחיך לעניך ולאבינך בארצך (דברים טו,יא).

For the needy will not cease from the midst of the land; therefore I command you, saying: Surely open your hand to your brother, to your poor, and your needy in your land (Deuteronomy 15,11).

The Torah commands to give charity because אביון, "the needy," will not cease in the land. The gematria of אביון, "needy," is 69.

$$
\begin{array}{rr}
\text{אביון} & 69
\end{array}
$$

The gematria of לאחיך, "your brother," is 69.

$$
\begin{array}{rr}
\text{לאחיך} & 69
\end{array}
$$

The אברבנאל, Abarbanel, says that although one may be living in times of peace and prosperity, he should still give charity. He explains that the word לאחיך, "to your brother," can refer back to אביון, "the needy," for the one in need of charity could be your son, your grandson, even yourself, or whoever it will be, as stated, כי גלגל הוא החוזר בעולם ואם שלום ואמת יהיה בימיך אולי בניך או בני בניך יצטרכו לזה כי לא יחדל אביון מקרב הארץ יהיה מי שיהיה ואפשר שתהיה אתה או בניך. ע"כ אנכי מצוך פתוח תפתח את ידך לאחיך לענייך ולאביונך בארצך (פירוש על התורה מאת הרב יצחק אברבנאל, פרשת ראה, דברים טו,ז, ד"ה כי יהיה בך אביון), "For there is the cycle of time which comes full circle in the world, and if there is peace and truth in your lifetime, perhaps your son, or your grandson, will need this, for the needy will not cease from the midst of the land. It will be whoever it will be; and it is possible that it will be you or your son. Therefore, I command you, surely open your hand to your brother, to your poor, and your needy in your land," (Commentary on the Torah by Rabbi Yitzchak Abarbanel, Parashath Reeh, Deuteronomy 15,7, header words: If there be among you a needy person).

The fact that the word לאחיך, "to your brother," and the word אביון, "the needy," have the same gematria enhances the explanation of the Abarbanel.

חג הסכת תעשה לך שבעת ימים באספך מגרנך ומיקבך. ושמחת בחגך אתה ובנך ובתך ועבדך ואמתך והלוי והגר והיתום והאלמנה אשר בשעריך (דברים טז, יג-יד).
The holiday of Tabernacles, you shall observe for yourself for seven days, when you have gathered in from your threshing floor and from your winepress. And you shall rejoice in your holiday, you and your son, and your daughter, and your male servant, and your female servant, and the Levite, and the stranger, and the orphan, and the widow, who are in your gates (Deuteronomy 16, 13-14).

For the seven-days-long holiday of Tabernacles, Sukkoth, the Torah clearly ordains the mitzvah of rejoicing. The gematria of ימים, "days," is 100.

ימים   100

Since there are seven days of Sukkoth, the gematria of ימים, "days," can be considered a multiplicand and seven a multiplier; their product is 700.

100
x7
———
700

This product may then be considered, על פי דרש, "in the way of a homily," to represent the seven days of the holiday of Tabernacles.

In reference to the holiday of Tabernacles the Torah also says one should be altogether joyful, as stated, שבעת ימים תחג לה׳ אלקיך במקום אשר יבחר ה׳ כי יברכך ה׳ אלקיך בכל תבואתך ובכל מעשה ידיך והיית אך שמח (דברים טז,טו), "Seven days you shall celebrate with Hashem, your G-d, in the place which Hashem will choose; for Hashem, your G-d, shall bless you with all your produce, and all the work of your hands, and you shall be altogether joyful" (Deuteronomy 16,15). The gematria of והיית אך שמח, "and you shall be altogether joyful," is 800.

והיית	431
אך	21
שמח	348
	800

Based on a Gemara, Rashi says that the phrase והיית אך שמח, "and you shall be altogether joyful," is to include the eve of the last [additional] day of the holiday, as stated, לרבות לילי יום טוב האחרון לשמחה (רש״י, דברים טז,טו, וסוכה מח.), "It comes to include the eve of the last day of the holiday for joy" (Rashi, Deuteronomy 16,15 and Sukkah 48a).

The numerical relation between the gematria of ימים, "days," times seven, to the gematria of the phrase והיית אך שמח, "and you shall be altogether joyful," is a ratio of seven to eight, which is the same ratio as the seven-days long holiday of Tabernacles to the eighth day. Therefore, through gematrioth there is further indication that the phrase והיית אך שמח, "and you shall be altogether joyful," comes to include the eve of the last (additional) day of the holiday for joy.

איש כמתנת ידו כברכת ה׳ אלקיך אשר נתן לך (דברים טז,יז).

Every man according to the giving of his hand, according to the blessing of Hashem, your G-d, which He has given to you (Deuteronomy 16,17).

The last pasuk of פרשת ראה, Parashath Reeh, refers to the festival sacrifices, saying that a man offers כמתנת ידו, "according to the giving of his hand." יונתן בן עוזיאל, Jonathan ben Uzziel, translates כמתנת ידו, "according to the giving of his hand," as כמיסת מוהבות ידיה, "commensurate with the degree of his generosity," (תרגום יונתן בן עוזיאל, דברים טז,יז, Targum Jonathan ben Uzziel, Deuteronomy 16,17). A form of the word מיסת, "commensurate," is found in the Torah seven pesukim earlier; also there יונתן בן עוזיאל, Jonathan ben Uzziel, translates the Torah's use of the word as כמסת, "commensurate" (תרגום יונתן בן עוזיאל, דברים טז,י, Targum Jonathan ben Uzziel, Deuteronomy 16,10). Just as in the earlier source it means commensurate, so too in the later source it means commensurate. The Gemara applies the pasuk from Deuteronomy 16,17 to one who has many persons who eat with him, and many possessions (חגיגה ח:, Hagigah 8b).

There is an alternate explanation which is corroborated by a gematria. A person can work on his character to improve his good deeds (מסלת ישרים מאת הרב משה חיים לוצאטו,

פרק ג; ותורת חובות הלבבות מאת הרב בחיי ב״ר יוסף אבן פקודה, הקדמת פתחי לב לשער היחוד מאת פנחס יהודה ליברמן, Mesillath Yesharim by Rabbi Moshe Chaim Luzzatto, Chapter 3; and Torath Chovoth Levavoth by Rabbi Bachya ben Rav Yosef Ibn Pakuda, Introduction Pithchei Lev to Shaar HaYichud by Pinchas Yehuda Liberman).

The second pasuk in Parashath Reeh says that G-d's blessing depends on observance of the commandments, as stated, את הברכה אשר תשמעו אל מצות ה׳ אלקיכם אשר אנכי מצוה אתכם היום (דברים יא,כז), "And the blessing if you will hearken to the commandments of G-d, your G-d, which I command you today" (Deuteronomy 11,27). There is a total of 613 Commandments in the Torah (מכות כג:, Makkoth 23b). The gematria of ידו ה׳ אלקיך אשר, "his hand, Hashem your G-d which," is 613.

ידו	20
ה׳ אלקיך	92
אשר	501
	613

Alternatively, the word ידו, "His hand," in this pasuk can be interpreted as G-d's hand, similar to the explanation of the Keli Yakar (כלי יקר, דברים טז,יז, Keli Yakar, Deuteronomy 16,17). The pasuk would mean, a man according to how generous G-d has been with him, as the blessing of Hashem your G-d, which depends on observance of the commandments, which He gave you. This explanation is in accordance with the Gemara's application of the pasuk (to one who has many persons who eat with him, and many possessions), and allows for the desirability for one to work on his character to improve even his good deeds. Since this pasuk contains the gematria of 613, and G-d's blessings depend on observance of the commandments, therefore the gematria may be seen to corroborate this explanation.

Parashath Shofetim

פרשת שפטים

על פי שנים עדים או שלשה עדים יומת המת לא יומת על
פי עד אחד (דברים יז,ו).

Upon the mouth [testimony] of two witnesses or three witnesses shall he who is to die, be put to death; he shall not be put to death upon the mouth [testimony] of one witness (Deuteronomy 17,6).

The Torah professes that the testimony of two or three witnesses is required for imposing capital punishment; the Torah adds that capital punishment can not be imposed if there is only one עד, "witness." The gematria of עד, "witness," 74.

עד   74

The Gemara discusses the acceptability of unconnected testimony. Ideally, two or three witnesses should be together, that is, they should see each other, when observing an event, or crime. When there is עדות מיוחדת, "unconnected testimony," one witness views an event, and another witness views the same event, but the two witnesses do not see each other. In court cases involving capital punishment, unconnected testimony is not acceptable; however, in court cases involving monetary matters, unconnected testimony is acceptable. The Gemara Makkoth derives these rules from the aforementioned pasuk, Deuteronomy 17,6, as stated, אמר רב נחמן עדות מיוחדת כשירה בדיני ממונות דכתיב לא יומת על פי עד אחד (דברים יז,ו) בדיני נפשות הוא דאין כשירה אבל בדיני ממונות כשירה (מכות ו:), "Rav Nahman said, unconnected testimony is valid for monetary matters as it is written, 'he shall not be put to death at the mouth of one witness' (Deuteronomy 17,6). In cases involving capital punishment it is not valid; but in cases involving monetary settlements it is valid," (Makkoth 6b).

Although the non-application of unconnected testimony is stated in reference to cases involving capital punishment, and the application of unconnected testimony in reference to cases involving monetary settlements is derived by the Gemara, the application of unconnected testimony to cases involving laws of matrimony is the subject of controversy (תורה תמימה, דברים יז,ו, אות כה, Torah Teminah, Deuteronomy 17,6, Letter 25). Thus, unconnected testimony has three strata:

דיני נפשות,	"cases involving capital punishment," — not valid
דיני אישות,	"cases involving matrimony," — controversy
דיני ממונות,	"cases involving monetary matters" — valid

These three concepts are derived from what the Torah expresses about a single עד, "witness," as the Gemara Makkoth says. Two pesukim after that which the Torah expresses about a single עד, "witness," there is a pasuk which mentions דם, "blood," as stated, כי יפלא ממך דבר למשפט בין דם לדם בין דין לדין ובין נגע לנגע דברי ריבת בשעריך וקמת ועלית אל־המקום אשר יבחר ה' אלקיך בו (דברים יז,ח), "When there will be a matter concealed from you in judgment, between blood and blood, between law and law, between plague and plague, matters of controversy within your gates, and you shall arise and go up to the place which Hashem your G-d shall choose" (Deuteronomy 17,8). The standard explanation of בין דם לדם, "between blood and blood," is: between ritually defiled blood and ritually not defiled blood (רש"י דברים יז,ח, ד"ה בין דם לדם, Rashi, Deuteronomy 17,8, header words: Between blood and blood).

However, another possible explanation which can be suggested is that בין דם לדם, "between blood and blood," refers to a case between a man and his wife. When the Torah says על כן יעזב איש את אביו ואת אמו ודבק באשתו והיו לבשר אחד (בראשית ב,כד), "Therefore a man will leave his father and his mother and cleave unto his wife, and they will become one flesh," (Genesis 2,24), the reference is to living flesh. Living flesh must have blood, as the Torah states, כי נפש כל בשר דמו בנפשו הוא ואמר לבני ישראל דם כל בשר לא תאכלו כי נפש כל בשר דמו הוא כל אכליו יכרת (ויקרא יז,יד), "For the soul of all flesh, its blood is its soul, and I said to the Children of Israel, the blood of all flesh you shall not eat, for the soul of all flesh is its blood, whosoever eats it shall be cut off," (Leviticus 17,14). Thus, when the Torah said, "and they will become one flesh," it meant living flesh with blood; thus, בין דם לדם, "between blood and blood," could conceivably refer to a case between flesh and flesh, that is, a case between a man and his wife.

A further indication that blood could conceivably be construed to refer to marital relationships, can be seen from the Gemara Temurah which states, בשר ודם חדא מילתא היא (תמורה כא:), "Flesh and blood are one thing" (Temurah 21b). The Gemara is indicating that the flesh and blood of a first born animal sacrifice are considered two parts of one sacrifice. Although the Gemara is stated in a different context, an inference can be drawn: Flesh and blood are the same and thus can be substituted for each other. When the Torah states, בין דם לדם, "between blood and blood," the word flesh could be substituted for blood, so the pasuk would read, בין בשר לבשר, "between flesh and flesh," that is, a case between a man and his wife.

The pasuk quoted from Genesis 2,24 uses the expression "one flesh," to refer to a circumstance when a man and wife are together, a matrimonial relationship. Thus, בין דם לדם, "between blood and blood," which was shown to possibly be read, בין בשר לבשר, "between flesh and flesh," could refer to relationships between a man and a woman. Since the word blood can refer to matrimonial relationships, when the Torah says, כי יפלא ממך דבר למשפט בין דם לדם, "When there will be matter concealed from you in judgment, between blood and blood," it could well refer to the controversial aspect of cases involving matrimony; that is, the application of unconnected testimony to cases involving laws of matrimony which is controversial. Since the application of unconnected testimony to cases involving matrimony is controversial, and the source of unconnected testimony is mentioned just two pesukim prior to the pasuk which mentions בין דם לדם, "between blood and blood," the expression כי יפלא ממך דבר למשפט בין דם לדם, "When there will be matter concealed from you in judgment, between blood and blood," can refer to the controversy of unconnected testimony to cases involving matrimony. The gematria of לדם, "and blood," is 74.

לדם   74

The gematria of לדם, "and blood," is the same as the gematria of עד, "witness." The rendering of בין דם לדם, "between blood and blood," to refer to relationships between a man and a woman is enhanced by the equality of these gematrioth. Since it is from the word עד, "witness," that the controversy of unconnected testimony developed, and since בין דם לדם, "between blood and blood," can be rendered as referring to the subject of the controversy concerning unconnected testimony, it is very appropriate that both עד, "witness," and לדם, "and blood," should have the same gematria.

רק לא ירבה לו סוסים ולא ישיב את העם מצרימה למען הרבות סוס וה' אמר לכם לא תספון לשוב בדרך הזה עוד (דברים יז,טז).

Only he should not increase horses for himself, that he should not cause the people to return to Egypt in order to increase horses, and G-d has said to you, you shall not return on this way anymore (Deuteronomy 17,16).

The Torah says that a king should not cause the people to return to Egypt למען הרבות סוס, "in order to increase horses." The gematria of הרבות, "increase," is 613.

הרבות 613

In ספר תהלים, Book of Psalms, there is a different expression about horses, as stated, לא בגבורת הסוס יחפץ לא בשוקי האיש ירצה (תהלים קמז,י), "He does not desire in the strength of the horse; He does not take pleasure in the legs of man" (Psalms 147,10). The gematria of בגבורת, "strength," is 613.

בגבורת 613

Why are these two gematrioth of 613 associated with horses? An answer to this question can be based on what the Gemara says about horses. The Gemara Pesahim says, ששה דברים נאמרים בסוס אוהב את הזנות ואוהב את המלחמה ורוחו גסה ומואס את השינה ואוכל הרבה ומוציא קמעה (פסחים קיג:), "Six things were said about a horse: It loves promiscuity, and it loves combat, and its spirit is haughty, and it detests sleep, and it eats much, and excretes little" (Pesahim 113b). Particular consideration can be given toward the third aspect, "its spirit is haughty," for the Gemara foretold what may happen to a man who has a haughty spirit. The Gemara Sotah says, אמר רבי חייא בר אבא א״ר יוחנן כל אדם שיש בו גסות הרוח לבסוף נכשל באשת איש שנא׳ וכו׳... אמרי דבי רבי שילא אפילו קיבל תורה כמשה רבינו דכתיב ביה מימינו אש דת למו (דברים לג,ב) לא ינקה מדינה של גיהנם (סוטה ד:), "Rabbi Hiyya b. Abba said in the name of Rabbi Yohanan, every man who possesses a haughty spirit, in the end he will stumble in the sin of a married woman, as it says, etc., ... They of the School of Shila said, though he received the Torah as did Moses our teacher, of whom it is written, 'At his right hand was a fiery law for them' (Deuteronomy 33,2), he will not be clean from the judgment of Gehinnom" (Sotah 4b). Thus, one possessing a haughty spirit will eventually sin with a married woman, and he who sins with a married woman will not be saved from the judgment of Gehinnom, even if he received Torah as did Moses.

The Gemara Makkoth says that when Moses was given the Torah, he received 613 Mitzvoth, divided between 248 positive Mitzvoth and 365 negative Mitzvoth, as stated, דרש רבי שמלאי שש מאות ושלש עשרה מצות נאמרו לו למשה שלש מאות וששים וחמש לאוין כמנין ימות החמה ומאתים וארבעים ושמונה עשה כנגד איבריו של אדם (מכות כג:), "Rabbi Simlai expounded, 613 Commandments were said to Moses, three hundred and sixty-five negative Commandments corresponding to the number of days in a solar year, and two hundred and forty-eight positive Commandments corresponding to the limbs of a person" (Makkoth 23b).

Combining these sources, there is a train of reasoning: Horses are associated with a haughty spirit; every man who possesses a haughty spirit will eventually sin with a married woman; he who sins with a married woman will not be saved from the judgment of Gehinnom, even if he received Torah as did Moses; and when Moses received the Torah he got 613 Mitzvoth. In short, one possessing a haughty spirit as a horse will be punished in Gehinnom even if he accepted 613 Mitzvoth as did Moses.

Now it can easily be explained why the two gematrioth of 613, one from Deuteronomy 17,16, and one from Psalms 147,10 are associated with horses. One should not possess a haughty spirit as a horse does, for even though he received 613 Mitzvoth, he will not escape punishment.

In reference to a king, the Gemara Kethuboth states, מלך שמחל על כבודו אין כבודו מחול דאמר מר שום תשים עליך מלך שתהא אימתו עליך (כתובות יז.), "A king who forgoes his honor, his honor is not foregone, as a Master said, 'You shall surely place a king upon you,' that his dread shall be upon you" (Kethuboth 17a). The pasuk quoted by the Gemara is from Deuteronomy 17,15. But the next pasuk wherein למען הרבות סוס, "in order to increase horses," is written, has been explained as a warning that one should not possess a haughty spirit as a horse. The directive seems to be that even a king, who can not forgive his honor, should not possess a haughty spirit as a horse does, for even though he received 613 Mitzvoth, he will not escape punishment.

In reference to the Children of Israel, the pasuk from Psalms states that G-d does not delight in one who possesses a haughty spirit as a horse does, for even though he received 613 Mitzvoth, he will not escape punishment. This train of reasoning has explained why the two gematricth of 613 are associated with horses.

וענו ואמרו ידינו לא שפכו את הדם הזה ועינינו לא ראו
(דברים כא,ז).
And they shall raise their voices and say, Our hands have not shed this blood, nor have our eyes seen it (Deuteronomy 21,7).

Near the end of Parashath Shofetim the עגלה ערופה, "a heifer whose neck is broken," is discussed. After the heifer's neck is broken, the elders of the city which was closest to the corpse, say that their hands have not שפכו, "shed," this blood nor have their eyes ראו, "seen," it. Why did the Torah dictate precisely these two verbs be vocalized? One answer is given by the חתם סופר, Hatham Sofer, as he writes, כיון שנמצא ההורג סמוך לעירם שיי'מ יש שום חטא בעיר שאילולא כן לא אירע זה סמוך לעירם והיינו כיון שידינו לא שפכו פי' הרוצח איננו מבני עירנו ואי''כ איך אירע שנרצח פה דוקא ע''כ עינינו לא ראו לא השגיחו על חטאי בני עירנו ועיי'ז חטאו ונתגלגל שנהרג סמוך לכאן (ספר תורת משה מאת הרב משה סופר, פרשת שופטים, ד''ה ידינו לא שפכו וגו'), "Since the one slain was found near their city, from this it may be inferred that there is some vestige of sin in the city. For were it not so, this would not have happened near their city. And this is, since 'our hands have not shed,' its explanation is, the murderer is not among the people of our city, and if so how did a murder happen precisely here? Therefore, 'our eyes did not see,' we did not monitor the sins of the people of our city, and on account of this they sinned. And it evolved that one was slain near to here" (Book of Torath Moshe by Rabbi Moshe Sofer, Parashath Shofetim, header words: Our hands have not shed, etc.).

Thus, according to the Hatham Sofer, the Torah inscrolled precisely the two verbs שפכו, "shed," and ראו, "seen," for they infer some vestige of sin which brought about that one was slain near the city. The Gemara Makkoth says that there is a total of 613 Commandments given to Moses, as stated, דרש רבי שמלאי שש מאות ושלש עשרה מצות נאמרו לו למשה שלש מאות וששים וחמש לאוין כמנין ימות החמה ומאתים וארבעים ושמונה עשה כנגד איבריו של אדם (מכות כג:), "Rabbi Simlai expounded, 613 Commandments were said to Moses, three hundred and sixty-five negative Commandments corresponding to the number of days in a solar year, and two hundred and forty-eight positive Commandments corresponding to the limbs of a person" (Makkoth 23b). Since the murder occurred because of some vestige of sin, therefore there must have been some violation of the 613 Commandments. The sum of the gematria of שפכו, "shed," and ראו, "seen," is 613.

שפכו	406
ראו	207
	613

This gematria adds authentication to the explanation of the חתם סופר, Hatham Sofer. Note that the word שפכו, "shed," is a קרי וכתיב, "ke're and kethiv." Its gematria was calculated according to the ke're.

This gematria and explanation of the עגלה ערופה, "a heifer whose neck is broken," can give meaning to another pasuk. Rashi says, וכל מה שאירע ליעקב אירע ליוסף (רש"י, בראשית לז,ב וגם מדרש רבה, סדר וישב יעקב, פרשה פד, אות ו), "And everything which occurred to Jacob occurred to Joseph" (Rashi, Genesis 37,2, and also Midrash Rabbah, Sidrah Vayyeshev Yaakov, Parashah 84, Letter 6). Jacob sent messengers to tell Esau (בראשית לב,ה) עם לבן גרתי, "I have sojourned with Laban" (Genesis 32,5), which according to Rashi means, "I have kept the 613 Commandments" (רש״י, בראשית לב,ה, Rashi, Genesis 32,5). Where does Joseph send a similar message? Rashi comments that when Joseph sent to Jacob, עגלות, "wagons," it refers to פרשת עגלה ערופה, "the Parashah of a heifer whose neck is broken," (רש״י, בראשית מה,כז, Rashi, Genesis 45,27). Since the murder occurred because of some violation of the 613 Commandments, it could be that the message Joseph sent to Jacob was that he remembered the lesson of the עגלה ערופה, "a heifer whose neck is broken." That lesson was the importance of observing all 613 Commandments, for if there is even a vestige of sin, it could lead to the occurrence of a murder. Note that Rashi's explanation, that Jacob's message to Esau was that he had kept the 613 Commandments, is based on a gematria (גרתי, "I have dwelt," has a gematria of 3+200+400+10=613: the תרי״ג מצות, "613 Commandments"). Likewise, Joseph's message to Jacob of the importance of observing all 613 Commandments, via the heifer whose neck is broken, is also based on a gematria of the same value. Thus, the message Joseph sent to Jacob bears a similarity to the message Jacob sent to Esau.

Parashath Ki Thetze   פרשת כי תצא

כי תהיין לאיש שתי נשים האחת אהובה והאחת שנואה
וילדו לו בנים האהובה והשנואה והיה הבן הבכר לשניאה.
(דברים כא,טו)

When a man will have two wives, one beloved and one hated, and they have borne to him sons, the beloved one and the hated one, and the firstborn son be hers that is hated (Deuteronomy 21,15).

In the Torah discussion of a man who has two wives, one beloved and one hated, the word הבן, "the son" (which is only mentioned once), refers to the firstborn son of the hated wife. The gematria of הבן, "the son," is 57.

הבן   57

This son whom the Torah refers to as הבן, "the son," is the husband's first strength, as stated, כי את הבכר בן השנואה יכיר לתת לו פי שנים בכל אשר ימצא לו כי הוא ראשית אנו לו משפט הבכרה (דברים כא,יז), "For the firstborn, son of the hated one, he shall acknowledge to give him a double portion, in all that is found with him, for he is his first strength, to him is the judgment of the firstborn" (Deuteronomy 21,17). The gematria of אנו, "his strength," is 57.

אנו   57

Since the gematria of אנו, "his strength," equals the gematria of הבן, "the son," and both words allude to the same person, this equality could be a suggestion that הבן, "the son," refers to the husband's אנו, "his strength."

כי יקרא קן צפור לפניך בדרך בכל עץ או על הארץ אפרחים
או ביצים והאם רבצת על האפרחים או על הביצים לא
תקח האם על הבנים (דברים כב,ו).

When a bird's nest chances to be before you in the way, in any tree, or on the ground, young ones or eggs, and the dam is sitting on the young ones or on the eggs, you shall not take the dam with the young (Deuteronomy 22,6).

The Torah says that the commandment of sending away the mother bird from her nest can be performed with any nest, in any tree, or on the ground. The gematria of בכל עץ או על הארץ, "in any tree, or on the ground," is 615.

בכל עץ	212
או על הארץ	403
	615

Thus, 615 represents anywhere the commandment can be performed.

The next pasuk says that one can take the young birds, as stated, שלח תשלח את האם ואת הבנים תקח לך למען ייטב לך והארכת ימים (דברים כב,ז), "You shall surely send away the dam, and the young you may take for yourself, in order that it should be good for you, and you may prolong your days" (Deuteronomy 22,7). The gematria of הבנים תקח, "the young you may take," is 615.

הבנים	107
תקח	508
	615

Thus, 615 represents the taking of the young birds.

One of the rewards for fulfilling this commandment is to beget children. This reward is derived from the words הבנים תקח, "the young you may take," which can be translated, "You shall take the sons." The ספר החינוך, "Book of Hachinuch," writes, אמרו זכרונם לברכה במדרש, שהאדם זוכה לבנים בשכר מצוה זו ... מאמרו "שלח תשלח את האם ואת הבנים תקח לך" כלומר בנים תקח לנפשך (ספר החינוך מאת הרב אהרן הלוי, מצוה תקמה)

"Those [Sages] of blessed memory have said in the Midrash, that a man will merit to beget sons as reward for this commandment... [This reward is learned from the Torah] saying, 'You shall surely send away the dam, and the young you may take for yourself,' that is to say, the children you shall take for yourself" (Book of Hachinuch by Rabbi Aaron Halevi, Mitzvah 545).

It stands to reason that the reward for the completion of the commandment is received when one fulfills the commandment anywhere that it can be performed. This reasoning can be supported by the fact that the gematria of the words representing one of the rewards for fulfilling this commandment equals the gematria of the words representing anywhere the commandment can be performed.

ושם לה עלילת דברים והוצא עליה שם רע ואמר את האשה הזאת לקחתי ואקרב אליה ולא מצאתי לה בתולים (דברים כב,יד).

And he lay wanton charges against her, and bring out upon her an evil name, and say, "This woman I took, and I came nigh to her, and I did not find in her the tokens of virginity" (Deuteronomy 22,14).

A man can lay wanton charges against his wife, claiming she was not a virgin. The אור החיים, Or Hachayyim, explains this claim as an allegory to those of the Children of Israel who turn away from the Torah. In the pasuk "the man" refers to those of the Children of Israel who are so busy with their livelihood, that they neglect the Torah. "The wife" refers to the Torah which the Children of Israel accepted on Mt. Sinai. "The wanton charges and evil name" refers to the claim that those who do learn Torah and are involved with it, do not have a good livelihood, while those who distance themselves from the Torah, have homes filled with abundance. The Or

Hachayyim writes, באומרו את האשה הזאת לקחתי פי' שאינו כופר בליקוחיה אלא שאומר ואקרב אליה ולא מצאתי לה בתולים פי' לשון חוזק כי עוסקיה סביב יחנו לדפוק על דלתי אחריי למצוא טרף (אור החיים, דברים כב,יג), "When he says I took this wife, its explanation is, he does not deny taking her. But when he says, I came near to her and did not find her virginity, its explanation is, an expression of strength. For those who are involved with it, camp around, to knock on the doors of others to find food" (Or Hachayyim, Deuteronomy 22,13). The gematria of ולא מצאתי לה, "and I did not find in her," is 613.

ולא	37
מצאתי	541
לה	35
	613

The Or Hachayyim explains these disparaging words as referring to those who are involved with the Torah, people who often "are not found to have" a good livelihood. The people involved with the Torah are the ones who observe its commandments. Since there is a total of 613 Commandments (מכות כג:, Makkoth 23b), it is significant that the gematria of ולא מצאתי לה, "and I did not find in her," is 613.

A further indication that those who are involved with the Torah observe its commandments is found in the אור בהיר, Or Bahir, a commentary on the Or Hachayyim. Continuing the allegory, the Or Hachayyim writes that G-d claims He gave his daughter [to one who is expected] להתנהג עמה במנהג אשה "to comport לבל יגרע שארה כסותה ועונתה (אור החיים, דברים כב,יג), himself with her in such a behavior as is due a wife, that her food, her raiment, and her conjugal rights will not be diminished" (Or Hachayyim, Deuteronomy 22,13). The אור בהיר, Or Bahir, comments, עונה זה המחשבה לידבק בה' ב"ה, כסות, זה הדיבור בתורה, שאר, זה מעשה המצות (אור בהיר מאת ישעיי הלוי וייס, דברים כב,יג), "conjugal rights, this is the thought to cling to G-d Blessed be He; raiment, this is the speaking in Torah; food, this is the doing of the commandments" (Or Bahir by Yeshayah Halevi Weiss, Deuteronomy 22,13). Thus, the Or Bahir gives a further indication that those who are involved with the Torah are the ones who observe its commandments.

מוצא שפתיך תשמר ועשית כאשר נדרת לה׳ אלקיך נדבה אשר דברת בפיך (דברים כג,כד)

You shall observe that which is gone out of your lips, and do as you vowed to Hashem, your G-d, a freewill offering which you spoke with your mouth (Deuteronomy 23,24).

The pasuk in Parashath Ki Thetze quoted above can be expounded to refer to charity. The gematria of אשר בפיך, "with your mouth," is 613.

אשר	501
בפיך	112
	613

The ספרי, Sifrei, clearly identifies the word בפיך, "with your mouth," with the commandment of charity, as the Malbim more fully explains,

בפיך. בספרי דריש זו צדקה ופי׳ שתיבת בפיך יורה על הדבור ששגור בפה כמו למען תהיה תורת ה׳ בפיך (שמות יג) שימה בפיהם (דברים לא) לזאת דריש שהוא צדקה ששגור בפה (התורה והמצוה, מאת הרב מאיר ליבוש מלביי״ם, דברים כג,כד)

"With your mouth. In the Sifrei it expounds that this is charity. And the explanation is that the word 'with your mouth,' instructs about 'the speech which is fluent in the mouth' as 'in order that the Torah of G-d should be in your mouth' (Exodus 13), 'put it in their mouths' (Deuteronomy 31). Like this it expounds that it is charity which is fluent in the mouth" (The Torah and the Mitzvah by Rabbi Meir Lebush Malbim, Deuteronomy 23,24).

The Gemara says that the commandment of charity is commensurate to all of the commandments, as it says, ואמר

(בבא בתרא ט.) רב אסי שקולה צדקה כנגד כל המצות, "And Rav Assi said: Charity is equated to all the commandments," (Baba Bathra 9a). The Gemara Makkoth says that a total of 613 Commandments were given to Moses, as stated, דרש רבי שמלאי שש מאות ושלש עשרה מצות נאמרו לו למשה שלש מאות וששים וחמש לאוין כמנין ימות החמה ומאתים וארבעים ושמונה עשה כנגד איבריו של אדם (מכות כג:), "Rabbi Simlai expounded, 613 Commandments were said to Moses, three hundred and sixty-five negative Commandments corresponding to the number of days in a solar year, and two hundred and forty-eight positive Commandments corresponding to the limbs of a person" (Makkoth 23b). Since the ספרי, Sifrei, clearly identifies the word בפיך, "with your mouth," with the commandment of charity; and since the Gemara says that the commandment of charity is commensurate to all of the commandments; and since there is a total of 613 Commandments, therefore it is concordant that the gematria of אשר בפיך, "with your mouth," is 613.

ארבעיך יכנו לא יסיף פן־יסיף להכתו על אלה מכה רבה
ונקלה אחיך לעיניך (דברים כה,ג).

Forty stripes he may give him; he may not exceed, lest, if he should exceed to hit him above these with many stripes, then your brother will be slighted in your eyes (Deuteronomy 25,3).

The Torah warns that a guilty man should not be flogged with more than 39 stripes. Although the Torah says forty stripes, Rashi explains that in reality a maximum of thirty-nine is meant, as he says, ולא ארבעים שלמים, אלא מנין שהוא סוכב ומשלים לארבעים והם ארבעים חסר אחת (רש"י, דברים כה,ב), "And it is not the complete number forty, but the number which adds up to and completes to forty, meaning forty less one" (Rashi, Deuteronomy 25,2).

Once the convicted man has suffered the punishment

for his wrongdoing, the other members of the Children of Israel are enjoined to accept him as a brother. After receiving these stripes the Jew who was flogged is called אחיך, "your brother," as the pasuk quoted above says. The gematria of אחיך, "your brother," is 39.

אחיך   39

Rashi on this pasuk emphasizes the significance of the word אחיך, "your brother." Previously, this man was called a wicked man, but after being flogged he is designated your brother, as stated, כל היום קוראו רשע ומשלקה קראו אחיך (רש"י, דברים כה,ג), "The entire day he is called a wicked man, and once he is flogged he is called your brother" (Rashi, Deuteronomy 25,3). This designation of the pasuk is reinforced by the gematria of אחיך, "your brother," being equal to the number of stripes this Jew received before he was designated אחיך, "your brother."

Parashath Ki Thavo

פרשת כי תבוא

ונצעק אל ה' אלקי אבתינו וישמע ה' את קלנו וירא את
עניינו ואת עמלנו ואת לחצנו (דברים כו,ז).

And we cried to Hashem, the G-d of our fathers, and Hashem heard our voice, and He saw our affliction, and our toil, and our oppression (Deuteronomy 26,7).

When one brought his בכורים, "first fruits," to the בית המקדש, "Temple," he was to say a declaration which included the word קלנו, "our voice"; the word is spelled deficiently. (The full spelling includes an additional letter ו, "vav": קולנו, "our voice." The plural rendering, "our voices," features a letter י, "yud": קולינו, "our voices.") The omission of the letter י makes the word singular. The omission of the letter ו makes it חסר, "a deficient word," and changes its gematria. Two questions: 1. Why was the word spelled as חסר, "a deficient word"? 2. To which singular voice does the word refer?

The ספרי, Sifrei, in Parashath Ki Thavo says that the voice refers to the groaning mentioned in Parashath Shemoth in the pasuk of וישמע אלקים את נאקתם וגו' (שמות ב,כד), "And G-d heard their groaning, etc." (Exodus 2,24) (ספרי דברים כו,ז, Sifrei, Deuteronomy 26,7). But this Sifrei is difficult to understand, for if the voice in the pasuk from Parashath Ki Thavo was referring to the groaning in Parashath Shemoth, rather than saying קלנו, "our voice," the Torah should have said נאקתנו, "our groaning."

Possibly קלנו, "our voice," in Parashath Ki Thavo is referring to the voice mentioned in Parashath Mishpatim, as stated, ויבא משה ויספר לעם את כל דברי ה' ואת כל המשפטים ויען כל העם קול אחד ויאמרו כל הדברים אשר דבר ה' נעשה (שמות כד,ג), "And Moses came and told the people all the words of G-d, and all the judgments, and all the people answered with one voice, and they said, All the words which G-d spoke we will do"

(Exodus 24,3). Note that here the word קול, "voice," is refer-ring to a singular voice. The Yalkut Me'am Lo'ez comments on this pasuk that the word נעשה, "we will do," includes the commitment towards both positive and negative command-ments, as stated, והדיבור נעשה כולל הן מצות עשה והן מצות לא תעשה (ילקוט מעם לועז מאת רבי יעקב כולי, שמות כד,ג), "And the word 'We will do,' encompasses the positive commandments and the negative commandments" (Yalkut Me'am Lo'ez by Rabbi Yaakov Culi, Exodus 24,3). Thus, acceptance of all 613 Com-mandments is what the people did with their voice.

While the Children of Israel were in Egypt, G-d was aware that they would later accept the 613 Commandments. The pasuk in Parashath Ki Thavo records the declaration of the one who brought his בכורים, "first fruits." When the pasuk says that while in Egypt, וישמע ה' את קלנו, "and Hashem heard our voice," it could refer to the later voice in Parashath Mishpatim, where there was acceptance of all 613 Command-ments. A strong indication of this referral is that the gematria of ה' את קלנו, "Hashem our voice," is 613.

ה'	26
את	401
קלנו	186
	613

Another indication of this referral is that both the pasuk in Parashath Ki Thavo and the pasuk in Parashath Mishpatim use the word קול, "voice," so it can easily be explained that the former refers to the latter. In Parashath Mishpatim the pasuk says that the people answered with "one voice." It is tempting to wonder if a possible reason why קלנו, "our voice," is חסר, "a deficient word," is to underscore that it, via its gematria, is referring to the "one voice," in Parashath Mishpatim. At this point both questions which were asked have been answered. It has been explained why the word קלנו, "our voice," is חסר, "a deficient word," and it has been explained to which singular voice it refers.

These answers can explain a pasuk in Parashath Shemoth. G-d gave Moses a sign that the people would serve Him on the mountain where Moses stood (שמות ג,יב, Exodus 3,12). That service can be explained to refer to the pasuk in Parashath Mishpatim where all the people answered with one voice. It has been shown that the acceptance of all 613 Commandments is what the people did with their voice, making it a very significant service.

אלה יעמדו לברך את העם על הר גרזים בעברכם את הירדן שמעון ילוי ויהודה ויששכר ויוסף ובנימן. ואלה יעמדו על הקללה בהר עיבל ראובן גד ואשר וזבולן דן ונפתלי (דברים כז,יב-יג).

These shall stand to bless the people on Mount Gerizim when you have passed over the Jordan: Simeon, and Levi, and Judah, and Issachar, and Joseph, and Benjamin. And these shall stand for the curse upon Mount Ebal: Reuben, Gad, and Asher, and Zebulun, Dan, and Naphtali (Deuteronomy 27,12-13).

The Children of Israel were divided into two groups of six tribes; one for the blessings and one for the curses. The six tribes who stood on Mount Gerizim to bless were Simeon, Levi, Judah, Issachar, Joseph, and Benjamin. The gematria of שמעון, "Simeon," ולוי, "and Levi," ויהודה, "and Judah," ויששכר, "and Issachar," ויוסף, "and Joseph," and ובנימן, "and Benjamin," is 1710.

שמעון ולוי	518
ויהודה ויששכר	872
ויוסף ובנימן	320
	1710

The six tribes who stood on Mount Ebal for the curses were Reuben, Gad, Asher, Zebulun, Dan, and Naphtali. The gematria of ראובן, "Reuben," גד, "Gad," ואשר, "and Asher," וזבולן, "and Zebulun," דן, "Dan," ונפתלי, "and Naphtali," is 1504.

266	ראובן גד
608	ואשר וזבולן
630	דן ונפתלי
1504	

The difference in gematrioth between the six tribes who stood on Mount Gerizim and the six tribes who stood on Mount Ebal is 206.

$$1710$$
$$-1504$$
$$206$$

Thus, 206 represents the difference between the two groups of tribes. After each blessing or curse, all the people said, Amen, as stated, ארור אשר לא יקים את דברי התורה הזאת לעשות אותם ואמר כל העם אמן (דברים כז,כו), "Cursed be he who does not uphold the words of this Torah to do them; and all the people shall say, Amen," (Deuteronomy 27,26). The gematria of העם אמן, "the people, Amen," is 206.

115	העם
91	אמן
206	

The Amen of the people is mentioned several times, (Deuteronomy 27,15-26); it was very important, for it represented the acceptance of a vow, as the Gemara Shevuoth states, אמר רבי יוסי ברבי חנינא אמן בו שבועה בו קבלת דברים... בו קבלת דברים דכתיב ארור אשר לא יקים את דברי התורה הזאת לעשות אותם ואמר כל העם אמן (שבועות לו.), "Rabbi Jose the son of Rabbi Hanina said, Amen implies oath, implies acceptance of words... It implies acceptance of words, as it is written, 'Cursed be he who does not confirm the words of this Torah to do them; and all the people shall say, Amen'" (Shevuoth 36a). The Amen of the people was said by everyone, after the blessings and after the curses, regardless if they stood on Mount Gerizim or if they stood on Mount Ebal (תלמוד ירושלמי, סוטה פרק ז, הלכה ד Yerushalmi Gemara, Sotah, Chapter 7, Halakhah 4).

The Amen of the people was the response to the blessings and the curses said by the Levites, who were between the two groups of six tribes. Thus the Amen of the people arose from the two sets of tribes. The Amen response is further explained by the Abarbanel, as stated, מה קללה בלויים, אף ברכה בלויים. מה קללה בקול רם, אף ברכה בקול רם. מה קללה בל' הקדש, אף ברכה בל' הקדש. מה קללה בכלל ופרט, אף ברכה בכלל ופרט. ומה קללה אלו ואלו עונין אמן, אף ברכה אלו ואלו עונין אמן (פירוש על התורה מאת רבינו יצחק אברבנאל, פרשת כי תבוא, דברים כז,יב, ד"ה והנה פרט לברך את העם). "Just as the curses were said by the Levites, also the blessings were said by the Levites. Just as the curses were said in a stentorian voice, also the blessings were said in a stentorian voice. Just as the curses were said in the Holy Language, also the blessings were said in the Holy Language. Just as the curses were said as a general proposition followed by a specifying particular, also the blessings were said as a general proposition followed by a specifying particular. Just as in response to the curses these and those answered Amen, also in response to the blessings these and those answered Amen" (Commentary on the Torah by Rabbeinu Yitzchak Abarbanel, Parashath Ki Thavo, Deuteronomy 27,12, header words: And behold it specified whom to bless the people).

The Levites turned to Mount Gerizim to curse, and turned to Mount Ebal to bless; the Amen of the people arose from the two sets of tribes (סוטה לז:, Sotah 37a). This response of the two groups of six tribes is confirmed by the gematria of 206, which represents the difference between the two groups of six tribes, being exactly equal to the gematria of העם אמן, "the people, Amen."

Note that the Gemara says that the Children of Israel did not actually stand on Mount Gerezim or Mount Ebal, but near them; the same meaning is intended by "stood on," used here.

בשליתה היוצת מבין רגליה ובבניה אשר תלד כי תאכלם בחסר כל בסתר במצור ובמצוק אשר יציק לך איבך בשעריך (דברים כח,נז).

And against her infant which comes out be-tween her feet, and against her children whom she shall bear, because she will eat them for want of everything, secretly in the siege and in the straitness, wherewith your enemy shall dis-tress you in your gates (Deuteronomy 28,57).

Among the curses listed in Parashath Ki Thavo is that the tender woman will turn against her young child which comes out between her feet; Rashi is straightforward in his definition of the word ובשליתה, as stated, בנים הקטנים (דברים כח,נז), "young children," (Rashi, Deuteronomy 28,57). The gematria of היוצת מבין "that comes out between," is 613.

$$\begin{array}{rr} \text{היוצת} & 511 \\ \text{מבין} & \underline{102} \\ & 613 \end{array}$$

Note that the significance of this gematria is enhanced by the spelling of היוצת, "that comes out," which is ortho-graphically defective, spelled without an א, "aleph." Since Rashi clarifies the pasuk as referring to young children, thus, the gematria of 613 is associated with young children. Why is there this association?

There is a total of 613 Commandments in the Torah (מכות כג:, Makkoth 23b). This concept is expressed in the לשם יחוד, "In the name of the union," prayer said before putting on the tallith; it is written, הריני מתעטף גופי בציצת כן תתעטף נשמתי

ורמ״ח אברי ושס״ה גידי באור הציצת העולה תרי״ג וכו׳ (סידור בית יעקב מאת הרב יעקב מעמדין בן הרב צבי, אשכנזי, דף כז. "Behold I am enwrapping my body in tsitsith, fringes, thus, may my soul and my 248 limbs and my 365 sinews be enwrapped with the light of the tsitsith, which adds up to 613, etc." (Siddur Beth Yaakov by Rabbi Yaakov from Emden ben Rabbi Zvi, Ashkenazi, page 27a). Ergo, a person is comprised of 613 body parts. The source of this concept is the Zohar, as it says, בגין דאית בבר נש רמ״ח שייפין לקבל רמ״ח פקודין דאורייתא... ואית בבר נש שס״ה גידין, ולקבלהון שס״ה פקדין דלאו אינון (ספר הזוהר מאת התנא רבי שמעון בן יוחאי, פרשת וישלח, דף קע: "A man has 248 limbs corresponding to the 248 positive Commandments of the Torah... And a man has 365 sinews, and they are corresponding to the 365 negative Commandments" (The Book of the Zohar by the Tanna Rabbi Shimon ben Yochai, Parashath Vayyishlach, Page 170b).

The sum of 613 obviously corresponds to the total number of commandments. If one has never sinned, then he has never violated any of the 613 Commandments, the composition of his 248 limbs and his 365 sinews will be better than those of a sinner. The Gemara Shabbath describes the breath of school children as (שבת קיט:) הבל שאין בו חטא, "Breath which does not have any sin," (Shabbath 119b). The composition of the 248 limbs and the 365 sinews, of school children, as well as those of young children who also have not sinned, would surpass that of others, who have sinned. Since complete young children who have not sinned, are composed of 248 limbs and the 365 sinews, whose composition would surpass that of others who have sinned, it is appropriate that the gematria of 613 is associated with young children. It has be explicated why the gematria of 613 is associated with young children.

והשיב בך את כל מדוה מצרים אשר יגרת מפניהם ודבקו
בך (דברים כח,ס).
And He will return upon you all the diseases of
Egypt, which you dreaded, and they will cleave
to you (Deuteronomy 28,60).

One of the curses listed in Parashath Ki Thavo is that
G-d tells the Children of Israel that the diseases which יגרת,
"you dreaded," will be returned upon you. The gematria of
יגרת, "you dreaded," is 613.

יגרת   613

The Gemara Makkoth says that when Moses received
the Torah, with its 613 Mitzvoth, these were divided between
248 positive Mitzvoth and 365 negative Mitzvoth, as stated,
דרש רבי שמלאי שש מאות ושלש עשרה מצות נאמרו לו למשה שלש מאות
וששים וחמש לאוין כמנין ימות החמה ומאתים וארבעים ושמונה עשה כנגד
איבריו של אדם (מכות כג:), "Rabbi Simlai expounded, 613 Commandments were said to Moses, three hundred and sixty-five
negative Commandments corresponding to the number of
days in a solar year, and two hundred and forty-eight positive
Commandments corresponding to the limbs of a person"
(Makkoth 23b).

Rashi quotes a pasuk from Exodus to show that the
Children of Israel could avoid the diseases of Egypt (רש"י,
דברים כח,ס, Rashi, Deuteronomy 28,60). The complete pasuk
which Rashi quoted states, ויאמר אם שמוע תשמע לקול ה' אלקיך
והישר בעיניו תעשה והאזנת למצותיו ושמרת כל חקיו כל המחלה אשר
שמתי במצרים לא אשים עליך כי אני ה' רפאך (שמות טו,כו), "And he
said: If you will surely listen to the voice of Hashem, your
G-d, and do what is upright in His eyes, and give ear to His
commandments, and keep all His statutes, all the diseases
which I put upon Egypt, I will not put upon you, for I am G-d
who heals you" (Exodus 15,26). From this pasuk it is clear
that observing G-d's commandments is protection from the
diseases of Egypt. Therefore, the dread of the diseases of

Egypt is due to not observing G-d's commandments. This dread is indicated by the gematria of יגרת, "you dreaded," being equal to the number of the commandments.

ולא נתן ה' לכם לב לדעת ועינים לראות ואזנים לשמע עד היום הזה (דברים כט,ג).
And G-d has not given you a heart to know, and eyes to see, and ears to hear, until this day (Deuteronomy 29,3).

The sixth pasuk from the end of Parashath Ki Thavo says that G-d has not given you a heart to know, and eyes to see, and ears to hear, until this day. Rashi offers two explanations; the second one is, ד"א ולא נתן ה' לכם לב לדעת שאין אדם עומד על סוף דעתו של רבו וחכמת משנתו עד ארבעים שנה (רש"י, דברים ו,כט), "Another explanation: And G-d has not given you a heart to know, that a man does obtain the final knowledge of his teacher and the wisdom of his teaching until forty years" (Rashi, Deuteronomy 29,6). The שערי אהרן, Shaarei Aaron, explicates this second explanation of Rashi as a reference to the commandments, as he writes, ולשון השני הכוונה "להשיג חכמת רבו" ויהיה פירושו, אחר שבאת אל המדרגה הזאת להשיג חכמתו יתברך, מעתה הוא מדקדק עמכם בשמירת המצוות, וגו' (ספר שערי אהרן על התורה מאת אהרן ישעי' רוטר, פרשת תבא, פרק כט, פסוק ג, ד"ה היוצא רש"י) (מדברי, "And according to the second interpretation, the intention of 'to attain the wisdom of his teacher,' is explained as follows: After you have come to this level of attaining His wisdom, Blessed be He, He will henceforth be exacting with you regarding observance of the commandments, etc." (Book of Shaarei Aaron on the Torah by Aaron Yeshayah Roter, Parashath Thavo, Chapter 29, pasuk 3, header words: It emerges from the words of Rashi).

There is a total of 613 Commandments in the Torah (מכות כג:, Makkoth 23b). There is an intimation that the sixth pasuk from the end of Parashath Ki Thavo refers to the 613

Commandments. When the gematria of the last word of the seventh pasuk from the end of Parashath Ki Thavo is joined with the gematria of the first three words of the sixth pasuk from the end of Parashath Ki Thavo their total is 613. The gematria of ההם, "those," plus the gematria of ולא נתן ה׳, "and G-d has not given," is 613.

ההם	50
ולא נתן ה׳	<u>563</u>
	613

This explanation and gematria communicate a valuable lesson: G-d has given the Bnei Yisroel a heart to know, eyes to see, and ears to hear, with the intention that they should observe His 613 Commandments with them. Let us hope the Bnei Yisroel can attain that expected intention.

ושמרתם את דברי הברית הזאת ועשיתם אתם למען תשכילו את כל אשר תעשון (דברים כט,ח).

And you shall observe the words of this covenant and do them in order that you will succeed in all that you do (Deuteronomy 29,8).

The last pasuk in Parashath Ki Thavo tells the Children of Israel that they are to observe the words of the covenant. The gematria of את דברי, "the words of," is 617.

את דברי   617

The gematria of הברית, "the covenant," is 617.

הברית   617

It is notable that the pasuk does not tell the Children of Israel simply to observe the covenant, but to observe the words of the covenant. The Gemara focuses on the significance of "the words of the covenant," in relation to one who teaches Torah to the son of his friend, as it states, אמר ריש

לקיש כל המלמד את בן חבירו תורה מעלה עליו הכתוב כאילו עשאו שנאמר ואת הנפש אשר עשו בחרן (בראשית יב,ה). ר' אלעזר אומר כאילו עשאן לדברי תורה שנאמר ושמרתם את דברי הברית הזאת ועשיתם אותם (דברים כט,ח), (סנהדרין צט:) "Resh Lakish said, Anyone who teaches Torah to the son of his friend, the verse considers it as if he had made him, as it says, and the souls that they had made in Haran (Genesis 12,5). Rabbi Eleazar says, it is as if he made the words of Torah, as it says, And you shall keep the words of this covenant, and make them" (Deuteronomy 29,8), (Sanhedrin 99b). The Maharsha explains this passage. If one observes the words of the covenant, that the words of Torah are fluent in his mouth to teach the son of one's friend, then through this teaching, it is considered as if one creates words of Torah, as he states, שעי"י משא ומתן בלימוד עם בן חברו נתחדשו לו דברי' והרי הם כאילו עשאם וחדשם בעולם וז"ש ושמרתם את דברי הברית שיהיה שמור בפיך ד"ת לבן חברך וע"י כך ועשיתם אותם (מהרש"א, סנהדרין דף צט:, ד"ה ושאמר כאלו עשה לדברי תורה כו') "Through give and take discussion in learning with the son of one's friend, new things will emerge. And behold they are as if he made them and created them in the world. And this is what it means to say with, 'And you shall observe the words of this covenant': that words of Torah are retained in your mouth for [the benefit of] the son of your friend, and through this [it will be], 'and you made them'" (Maharsha, Sanhedrin 99b, header words: And it says, as if he made those words of Torah, etc.). Thus, the covenant has the potency to cause those who observe it to create words of Torah. This significance of "the words of the covenant" is reinforced by the fact that את דברי, "the words of," and הברית, "the covenant," have the same gematria.

Interestingly, a gematria can be revealed in the same Gemara, where Rava gives a different significance to the quoted pasuk, as stated, רבא אמר כאילו עשאו לעצמו שנאמר ועשיתם אותם אל תקרי אותם אלא אתם (סנהדרין צט:) "Raba said, it is as though he had made himself, as it says, 'and do them,' do not read 'them' but 'you'" (Sanhedrin 99b). The gematria of עשאו לעצמו, "he had made himself," is 613.

עשאו	377
לעצמו	236
	613

Targum Jonathan ben Uzziel states, man is created with 248 limbs and 365 sinews, together totaling 613 body parts, (תרגום יונתן בן עוזיאל, בראשית א,כז), Targum Jonathan ben Uzziel, Genesis 1,27). It is fitting that the words עשאו לעצמו, "he had made himself," should have a gematria of 613, since man was created with 613 body parts.

Parashath Nitzavim   פרשת נצבים

ותראו את שקוציהם ואת גלליהם עץ ואבן כסף וזהב אשר
עמהם (דברים כט,טז).

And you saw their abominations, and their idols, wood and stone, silver and gold, which were among them (Deuteronomy 29,16).

Moses told the Children of Israel that ותראו, "and you saw," the abominations of various nations. The gematria of ותראו, "and you saw," is 613.

ותראו   613

There is a total of 613 Commandments. These 613 Commandments aid one in seeing, as stated, פקודי ה׳ ישרים משמחי לב מצות ה׳ ברה מאירת עינים (תהלים יט,ט), "The precepts of G-d are upright, rejoicing the heart; the commandment of G-d is crystalline, enlightening the eyes" (Psalms 19,9). Since the 613 Commandments help one in seeing, it is easily understood why ותראו, "and you saw," has a gematria of 613. That which Moses told the Children of Israel that they saw, could be accomplished with the aid of the 613 Commandments, which help one to see and thus to eschew idol worship.

פן יש בכם איש או אשה או משפחה או שבט אשר לבבו פנה
היום מעם ה׳ אלקינו ללכת לעבד את אלהי הגוים ההם פן
יש בכם שרש פרה ראש ולענה (דברים כט,יז).

Lest there be among you a man or a woman or a family or a tribe, whose heart turns away today from Hashem, our G-d, to go to serve the gods of those nations; lest there be among you a root that bears gall and wormwood (Deuteronomy 29,17).

In Parashath Nitzavim the Children of Israel are

warned about turning away from G-d to serve the gods of other nations. When the Torah enumerates the classes of people warned, the first class is איש, "a man"; the last and the largest class is שבט, a tribe." The gematria of איש, "a man," is 311.

איש   311

The gematria of שבט, "a tribe," is 311.

שבט   311

How does an entire tribe turn from G-d? It starts with one man turning from G-d. What are the consequences of one man turning from G-d? It could lead to an entire tribe turning from G-d.

The שערי אהרן, Shaarei Aaron, explains the Sforno on this pasuk, as he says, וספורנו פירש "שרש פרה ראש ולענה" חושב להדיח רבים אל דעותיו הנפסדות ע"כ. כלומר לפי"ד אין כאן הכוונה בדור ראשון שממנו יצמחו דורות רעים. אלא הוא בעצמו מפרה את דעותיו הנפסדים לרבים (ספר שערי אהרן על התורה מאת אהרן ישעי' רוטר, פרשת נצבים, פרק כ"ט, פסוק טו,טז, יז, ד"ה והספורנו פירש) "And the Sforno explains 'a root that bears gall and wormwood,' one thinks to lead astray many to his malignant opinions, until here he is quoted. It means to say, according to his opinion, it does not mean the first generation from which will sprout evil generations. However, he himself produces his malignant opinions for the many." (Book of Shaarei Aaron on the Torah by Aaron Yeshayah Roter, Parashath Nitzavim, Chapter 29, pasuk 15, 16, 17, header words: And the Sforono).

Correspondingly, one person, a מדיח, "an instigator," can subvert the majority of a city to turn from G-d. This subversion is similar to an עיר הנדחת, "a condemned city," in that a group is subverted; however, whereas two corrupt instigators are required to qualify a city as condemned, even one single corrupt instigator qualifies a person to be an instigator. The Yalkut Me'am Lo'ez clarifies this distinction, as

ואילו האנשים שהדיח אינם נחשבים כאנשי עיר הנדחת שדינם, stated,
יתבאר להלן בפרשה, כיון שרק אדם אחד הדיח אותם, והדין הוא שאין דין
עיר הנדחת אלא אם כן המדיחים היו שנים (ילקוט מעם לועז, מאת הרב
יעקב כולי, דברים יג,ט). "And, if the men who were instigated are
not considered as 'the population of a condemned city,'
whose judgment will be explained later in the section, since
only one man enticed them, and the law is that the regula-
tions of a condemned city only apply if the instigators were
two people" (Yalkut Me'am Lo'ez by Rabbi Yaakov Culi, Deuteronomy 13,9).

The possibility that an איש, "man," turning from G-d
could lead an entire שבט, "a tribe," to turn from G-d, might
well be the reason why איש, "a man"; and שבט, "a tribe," have
the same gematria.

ואמרו כל הגוים על מה עשה ה' ככה לארץ הזאת מה חרי
האף הגדול הזה (דברים כט,כג).
And all the nations shall say, for what did G-d
do so to this land; what is the meaning of the
heat of this great anger? (Deuteronomy 29,23).

The nations will wonder about האף, "this anger," of
G-d. The gematria of האף, "this anger," is 86,

האף   86

When Hashem's character of strict justice and judgment is
alluded to, He is referred to as אלקים, "G-d," as Rashi says,
ויזכור אלקים. זה השם מדת הדין (רש"י, בראשית ח,א) ,"And G-d
remembered. This name refers to His attribute of strict justice" (Rashi, Genesis 8,1). The gematria of אלקים, "G-d," is
86.

אלקים   86

G-d's anger is associated with His attribute of strict
justice and judgment. Thus, it is very appropriate that the

gematria of האף "this anger," and the gematria of אלקים, "G-d," are identical.

והיה כי יבאו עליך כל הדברים האלה הברכה והקללה אשר נתתי לפניך והשבת אל לבבך בכל הגוים אשר הדיחך ה' אלקיך שמה. ושבת עד ה' אלקיך ושמעת בקלו ככל אשר אנכי מצוך היום אתה ובניך בכל לבבך ובכל נפשך (דברים ל, א-ב)

And it will be when all these things will come upon you, the blessing and the curse, which I set before you, and you shall reflect upon them in your heart, among all the nations whither Hashem, your G-d, has driven you there. And you shall return unto Hashem, your G-d, and you shall hearken to His voice, according to all that I command you this day, you and your children, with all your heart and with all your soul (Deuteronomy 30,1-2).

The Rambam in הלכות תשובה, "Laws of Repentance," presents two principles which can aid in the understanding of some of the pesukim in Parashath Nitzavim. The first principle is the meaning of תשובה גמורה, "complete repentance." If after one initially sinned, he finds himself in the identical circumstance, but on the second occasion, he resists temptation and does not sin, this resistance is called תשובה גמורה, "complete repentance." The Rambam says, אי זו היא תשובה גמורה, זה שבא לידו דבר שעבר בו ואפשר לעשותו ופירש ולא עשה מפני התשובה, לא מיראה ולא מכשלון כח (משנה תורה, ספר המדע, הלכות תשובה, פרק ב, הלכה א), "What is complete repentance? This is one to whom came the opportunity of the very thing which he transgressed, and he has the opportunity to do it, and he separates himself from the deed, and does not do it because he repented, not because of fear, and not because of weakening strength" (Mishnah Torah, Book of Hamadda, Laws of Repentance, Chapter 2, Law 1).

The second principle is that when one comes and tries to do repentance, G-d helps him. The Rambam says, והוא מה שאמרו רז״ל בא לטהר מסייעין אותו כלומר ימצא עצמו נעזר על הדבר (משנה תורה,ספר המדע, הלכות תשובה, פרק ו, הלכה ה), "And it is what our rabbis, who should be remembered for a blessing, have said, if one comes to purify himself, he receives divine help. That means to say, he finds himself aided in the matter" (Mishnah Torah, Book of Hamadda, Laws of Repentance, Chapter 6, Law 5).

In Parashath Nitzavim there are several pesukim that are seemingly repetitious (דברים ל,א-י, Deuteronomy 30, 1-10). The חתם סופר, "Hatham Sofer," presents a sagacious explanation of these pesukim as depicting four events in the repentance process. Firstly, the Children of Israel initially sinned in the land of Israel and were condemned to exile. Secondly, the Children of Israel do repentance in exile. Although G-d helps them to be in a somewhat similar situation as when they sinned, nonetheless this repentance was not yet a complete repentance, as they were not in the identical circumstances as when they sinned, that is, they were not in the land of Israel. Thirdly, G-d returns them to the land of Israel, where He helps them procreate and be in the identical circumstances as when they sinned.

Fourthly, the Children of Israel will do a complete repentance. The Hatham Sofer writes, שעיקור התשובה המעולה הוא תשובת המשקל דהיינו באותו מקום ובאותו כח וגדולה ותאות הגוף ואי״כ לכאורה יש׳אל שחטאו ע״י גדולת הארץ... ואם אח״כ ישובו בגלות לא אפשר שתשובה ההיא תהי׳ תשובה גמורה בארץ הגלות. אך מצד גודל חסדו ב״ה אם אדם ממציא עצמו לתשובה אז נותן לו הקב״ה כח ועשירו וכל טוב שהי׳ לו בשעת החטא אף שלא ראוי׳ לו מצד הדין כדי להעמיד האדם לנסיון אם ישוב אח״כ תשובת מעולה. וזהו כוונת הפרשה ושבת עד ה׳ אלקי׳ בארץ הגלות ואח״כ ושב ה׳ את שבותך ורחמיך ושב יקבצך מכל העמים והביאך אל ארץ אבותיך והטיבך והרבך.... ואם אח״כ תשוב ושמעת בקול ה׳ ועשית כל מצוותיו (ספר תורת משה מאת הרב משה סופר, פרשת

(נצבים, ד״ה בפרשת התשובה) "That the essence of the highest level of repentance is equivalent repentance, that is, it should be done in the same place, and with the same strength and development, and bodily desires. And if so, it would seem that Israel who sinned through the greatness of the Land ... and if afterwards they will repent when in exile, it will not be possible that the repentance will be a complete repentance when in the land of the exile. However, from the aspect of His great kindness, Blessed be He, if a person put himself forth to repent, then the Holy One, Blessed be He, gives him the same measure of strength and wealth and all good, that he possessed as at the time he sinned, even though he is not deserving from the aspect of judgment, in order to position the person to be tested whether afterward he will achieve the highest level of repentance. And this is the intention of the section, 'And you shall return unto Hashem, your G-d, in the land of exile.' And afterwards G-d will return your captivity and have mercy upon you and He will again gather you from amongst all the nations and bring you to the land of your forefathers and He will do good to you and multiply you ... and if afterwards you will repent and listen to the voice of G-d and observe all of His commandments" (Book of Torath Moses by Rabbi Moses Schreiber, Parashath Nitzavim, header words: In the section of repentance).

This sagacious explanation fits nicely with how the Ramban understands the words, ומל ה׳ אלקיך את לבבך, "And Hashem, your G-d will circumcise your heart," as a direct reference to help from G-d. The Ramban quotes the same expression that the Rambam quotes in his Laws of Repentance, משנה תורה, ספר המדע, הלכות תשובה, פרק ו, הלכה ה, Mishnah Torah, Book of Hamadda, Laws of Repentance, Chapter 6, Law 5). The Ramban says, זהו שאמרו הבא לטהר מסייעין אותו, מבטיחך שתשוב אליו בכל לבבך והוא יעזור אותך (רמב״ן, דברים ל,ו) "And this is what they said, if one comes to purify himself, he receives divine help. He [G-d] assures you, that if you return to Him with all your heart, He will aid you" (Ramban, Deuteronomy 30,6,).

It can be comprehended from these sources that even when repentance is not done in the identical circumstances as the sin, still such repentance can be a necessary and sufficient condition for G-d to help restore the identical circumstances so that תשובה גמורה, "complete repentance," can be done. This comprehension can be attested to by a gematria.

According to the Hatham Sofer, the words ושבת עד ה' אלקיי, "And you shall return unto Hashem, your G-d," refer to the repentance the Children of Israel will do when in exile. According to the Ramban the words ומל ה' אלקיך את לבבך, "And Hashem, your G-d, will circumcise your heart," refers to Hashem helping those who did repentance. The Torah says the Children of Israel will do repentance when in exile, as stated, והיה כי יבאו עליך כל הדברים האלה הברכה והקללה אשר נתתי לפניך והשבת אל לבבך בכל הגוים אשר הדיחך ה' אלקיך שמה. ושבת עד ה' אלקיך ושמעת בקלו ככל אשר אנכי מצוך היום אתה ובניך בכל לבבך ובכל נפשך (דברים ל, א-ב), "And it will be when all these things will come upon you, the blessing and the curse, which I set before you, and you shall reflect upon them in your heart, among all the nations whither Hashem, your G-d, has driven you there. And you shall return unto Hashem, your G-d, and you shall hearken to His voice, according to all that I command you this day, you and your children, with all your heart and with all your soul" (Deuteronomy 30, 1-2). The gematria of ושבת עד ה' אלקיך, "And you shall return unto Hashem, your G-d," is 874.

ושבת	708
עד ה'	100
אלקיך	66
	874

The Torah further says that once the Children of Israel have been returned to the land of Israel, G-d will help them procreate and be in the identical circumstances as when they sinned so they will do complete repentance, as stated, והביאך ה׳ אלקיך אל הארץ אשר ירשו אבתיך וירשתה והיטבך והרבך מאבתיך. ומל ה׳ אלקיך את לבבך ואת לבב זרעך לאהבה את ה׳ אלקיך בכל לבבך ובכל נפשך למען חייך (דברים ל,ה-ו), "And Hashem, your G-d, will bring you to the land which your forefathers possessed, and you shall possess it; and He will do good to you, and multiply you more than your forefathers. And Hashem, your G-d, will circumcise your heart and the heart of your seed, to love Hashem, your G-d, with all your heart and with all your soul, in order that you may live" (Deuteronomy 30,5-6). The gematria of והרבך מאבתיך ומל ה׳ אלקיך, "and multiply you more than your forefathers. And Hashem, your G-d, will circumcise," is 874.

והרבך מאבתיך	706
ומל ה׳	102
אלקיך	66
	874

The words ושבת עד ה׳ אלקיך, "And you shall return unto Hashem, your G-d," conveys that the Children of Israel will do repentance in exile, which can be a necessary and sufficient condition to fulfill the words והרבך מאבתיך. ומל ה׳ אלקיך, "and multiply you more than your forefathers. And Hashem, your G-d, will circumcise," which conveys that He will help them procreate and be in the identical circumstances as when they sinned so they can do complete repentance. This condition is underscored by the fact that both groups of words have the same gematria.

לא בשמים הוא לאמר מי יעלה לנו השמימה ויקחה לנו וישמענו אתה ונעשנה (דברים ל,יב).

It is not in the heaven that you should say, "Who will go up to the heaven for us and take it for us and cause us to hear it that we may do it" (Deuteronomy 30,12)?

Rashi clearly identifies the subject of this pasuk and the next two pesukim as the Torah, as stated, התורה נתנה לכם בכתב ובעל פה (רש״י, דברים ל,יד), "The Torah was given to you in written and oral form" (Rashi, Deuteronomy 30,14). Among the hypothetical justifications for not observing the Torah, is that the Torah is בשמים, "in heaven." The gematria of בשמים, "in heaven," is 392.

בשמים   392

In the very next pasuk, another of the hypothetical justifications for not observing the Torah, is that the Torah is מעבר לים, "beyond the sea," as stated, ולא מעבר לים הוא לאמר מי יעבר לנו אל עבר הים ויקחה לנו וישמענו אתה ונעשנה (דברים ל,יג), "And neither is it beyond the sea, that you should say, 'Who will pass over to the other side of the sea for us and and take it for us and cause us to hear it that we may do it'" (Deuteronomy 30,13)? The gematria of מעבר לים, "beyond the sea," is 392.

מעבר	312
לים	80
	392

Why is the gematria of בשמים, "in heaven," equal to the gematria of מעבר לים, "beyond the sea"? It is rare that one would claim that he can not learn Torah because it is not here on earth, but is in the heaven; this claim is obviously a very poor excuse. However, it is more common that one would claim that he can not learn Torah because it is not here, but elsewhere, as with his rebbi in Europe, in a yeshiva in Israel, or across the sea; this claim seems more legitimate. This second type of claim is more frequently heard, and sounds more plausible. Nonetheless, the Torah is telling that both excuses are equally faulty and defective; both supposed justifications are equally illegitimate. This equal illegitimacy could be the reason why the gematria of בשמים, "in heaven," equals the gematria of מעבר לים, "beyond the sea."

כי יבעל בחור בתולה יבעלוך בניך ומשוש חתן על כלה ישיש
עליך אלהיך (ישעי׳ סב,ה).

For as a young man espouses a virgin, so will your sons espouse you; and as a bridegroom rejoices over the bride, so will your G-d rejoice over you (Isaiah 62,5).

The Haftarah of Parashath Nitzavim, as well as לכה דודי, Lechah Dodi, the "Come my friend" prayer (which welcomes the Sabbath as the bride of the Jewish People) by the sixteenth century Kabbalist, Rabbi Shlelomoh Alkabetz (סידור בית יעקב מאת הרב יעקב מעמדין בן הרב צבי, אשכנזי, דף קמו., Siddur Beth Yaakov by Rabbi Yaakov from Emden ben Rabbi Zvi, Ashkenazi, page 146a) contain the expression חתן על כלה, "a bridegroom over the bride." In contrast, the sixth and seventh blessings of שבע ברכות, "Seven Benedictions" (part of the Jewish wedding ceremony), end with חתן וכלה, "a bridegroom and a bride," and חתן עם הכלה, "a bridegroom with the bride" respectively (סידור בית יעקב מאת הרב יעקב מעמדין בן הרב צבי, אשכנזי, דף קכד:-קכה., Siddur Beth Yaakov by Rabbi Yaakov from Emden ben Rabbi Zvi, Ashkenazi, page 124b-125a). The expression חתן על כלה, "a bridegroom over the bride," comes from the aforementioned pasuk in Isaiah, which refers to G-d rejoicing over the Children of Israel like a bridegroom rejoicing over a bride. The Malbim explains that G-d will take back the Children of Israel as a bridegroom takes a bride. But, in truth, the Children of Israel were perfidious, forsaking G-d and His holy commandments; G-d should take back the Children of Israel as a husband takes back his divorcee, not as a bridegroom takes a bride. A bridegroom rejoices over a bride with far greater enthusiasm than a husband who takes back his divorcee; the latter had a previous separation, a previous bitter relationship; the former had none. However, G-d will overlook the previous separation of the Children of

Israel from Him, and He will accept back the Children of Israel as a bridegroom takes a bride, (באור הענין, מאת הרב מאיר ליבש מלביי״ם, ישעיי סב,ה, Be'ur Ha'inyan by Rabbi Meir Lebush Malbim, Isaiah 62,5).

The Children of Israel separated themselves from G-d by forsaking His 613 Mitzvoth. When G-d takes back the Children of Israel it will be as if they had always observed all 613 Mitzvoth. This concept is reinforced by a gematria. The gematria of חתן על כלה, "a bridegroom over the bride," is 613.

חתן	458
על	100
כלה	55
	613

As was mentioned, the expression חתן על כלה, "a bridegroom over the bride," refers to G-d taking back the Children of Israel as if they had observed His 613 Mitzvoth. Thus, it is particularly appropriate that this expression should have a gematria of 613, achieved by the use of the word על, "over," rather than עם, "with," or ו, "and," between the words חתן, "a bridegroom," and כלה, "the bride."

Parashath Vayyelech   פרשת וילך

בבוא כל ישראל לראות את פני ה׳ אלקיך במקום אשר יבחר תקרא את התורה הזאת נגד כל ישראל באזניהם (דברים, לא,יא).

When all of Israel comes to appear before Hashem, your G-d, in the place He shall choose, you shall read this law, opposite all of Israel in their ears (Deuteronomy 31,11).

Once every seven years, the king was required to read parts of the Book of Deuteronomy publicly. The Torah says that בבוא כל ישראל לראות, "When all of Israel comes to appear," the reading should be done נגד כל ישראל, "facing all of Israel." Since the former expression precedes the latter one, it is a condition for the latter one: When all of Israel comes to appear, that is when the reading from the Book of Deuteronomy should be facing all of Israel. This relationship can be seen with the aid of gematrioth. The gematria of בבוא לראות, "when he comes to appear," is 648.

בבוא	11
לראות	637
	648

The gematria of נגד כל ישראל, "opposite all Israel," is 648.

נגד	57
כל	50
ישראל	541
	648

The equality of these expressions echoes the condition for Israel that בבוא לראות, "when he comes to appear," that is when the reading from the Book of Deuteronomy should be נגד כל ישראל, "facing all Israel."

בבוא כל ישראל לראות את פני ה׳ אלקיך במקום אשר
יבחר תקרא את התורה הזאת נגד כל ישראל באזניהם
(דברים לא,יא).

When all of Israel comes to appear before Hashem, your G-d, in the place He shall choose, you shall read this law, opposite all of Israel in their ears (Deuteronomy 31,11).

The reading of parts of the Book of Deuteronomy was to be נגד, "opposite," all of Israel. The gematria of נגד, "opposite," is 57.

57   נגד

On the pasuk just quoted, Rashi comments that a בימה, "platform," was erected for the reading, as stated, המלך היה קורא מתחלת אלה הדברים (דברים א,א), כדאיתא במס׳ סוטה, על בימה של עץ שהיו עושין בעזרה (רש״י, דברים לא,יא), "The king would read from the beginning of 'These are the words' (Deuteronomy 1,1), as it is stated in Tractate Sotah, on a wooden platform which was erected in the Court" (Rashi, Deuteronomy 31,11). The gematria of בימה, "platform," is 57.

57   בימה

Rabbi Pinchas Kehati writes that a Mishnah in Tractate Sotah indicates that the purpose of the platform was to fulfill the Torah's command that the reading of the Book of Deuteronomy was to be opposite all Israel. He writes, והמלך יושב על הבימה, כדי לקרוא את התורה "נגד כל ישראל באזניהם" (משניות מבוארות מאת רב פינחס קהתי, מסכת סוטה, פרק ז, משנה ח), "And the king would sit upon the platform, in order to read the Torah 'opposite all Israel' in their ears" (Mishnayoth Clarified by Rabbi Pinchas Kehati, Tractate Sotah, Chapter 7, Mishnah 8).

The gematria of נגד, "opposite," equals the gematria of בימה, "platform." Perhaps they are equal because the בימה, "platform," was used in a reading that was to be נגד, "opposite," all of Israel.

בבוא כל ישראל לראות את פני ה׳ אלקיך במקום אשר יבחר
תקרא את התורה הזאת נגד כל ישראל באזניהם (דברים
לא,יא).

When all of Israel comes to appear before Hashem, your G-d, in the place He shall choose, you shall read this law, opposite all of Israel, in their ears (Deuteronomy 31,11).

The Torah tells that when the king was required to read from the Book of Deuteronomy publicly, it was to be באזניהם, "in their ears." The gematria of באזניהם, "in their ears," is 115.

באזניהם   115

The very next pasuk says that the reading was to be heard by העם, "the people," as stated, הקהל את העם האנשים והנשים והטף וגרך אשר בשעריך למען ישמעו ולמען ילמדו ויראו את ה׳ אלקיכם ושמרו לעשות את כל דברי התורה הזאת (דברים לא,יב), "Assemble the people, the men, the women, and the children, and the stranger who is within your gates, in order that they may hear, and in order that they may learn, and fear Hashem, your G-d, and observe to do all the words of this law" (Deuteronomy 31,12). The gematria of העם, "the people," is 115.

העם   115

The gematria of באזניהם, "in their ears," is equal to the gematria of העם, "the people," conceivably emphasizing that the reading was to be in the ears of the people.

הקהל את העם האנשים והנשים והטף וגרך אשר בשעריך
למען ישמעו ולמען ילמדו ויראו את ה׳ אלקיכם ושמרו
לעשות את כל דברי התורה הזאת (דברים לא,יב).

Assemble the people, the men, the women, and the children, and the stranger who is within your gates, in order that they may hear, and in order that they may learn, and fear Hashem, your G-d, and observe to do all the words of this law (Deuteronomy 31,12).

The Torah records that Moses commanded that when

the Children of Israel come to the place that G-d shall choose, they should assemble in order that they may learn to fear and observe. The gematria of ילמדו, "that they may learn," is 90.

90   ילמדו

According to the Ramban, the word ילמדו, "that they may learn," only refers to the men and women (but not the children) (רמב"ן, דברים לא,יב, Ramban, Deuteronomy 31,12).

One of the purposes of assembling the people was for the children who do not know. The next pasuk after the quoted one, states, ובניהם אשר לא ידעו ישמעו ולמדו ליראה את ה' אלקיכם כל הימים אשר אתם חיים על האדמה אשר אתם עברים את הירדן שמה לרשתה (דברים לא,יג), "And their children, who have not known, may hear and learn to fear Hashem, your G-d, all the days that you are living on the land whither you pass over the Jordan there to possess it," (Deuteronomy 31,13). The gematria of ידעו, "know[n]," is 90.

90   ידעו

According to the Ramban the word ידעו, "know[n]" refers to the children, for they will ask others who will teach them (רמב"ן, דברים לא,יג, Ramban, Deuteronomy 31,13). Those others ostensibly are the ones described in the previous pasuk as ילמדו, "that they may learn." It is very fitting that ילמדו, "that they may learn," and ידעו, "know[n]," should have the same gematria, for those referred to in the category of ילמדו, "that they may learn," will teach those referred to in the category of לא ידעו, "not know[n]."

ובניהם אשר לא ידעו ישמעו ולמדו ליראה את ה' אלקיכם כל הימים אשר אתם חיים על האדמה אשר אתם עברים את הירדן שמה לרשתה (דברים לא,יג).

"And their children, who have not known, may hear and learn to fear Hashem, your G-d, all the days that you are living on the land whither you pass over the Jordan there to possess it," (Deuteronomy 31,13).

This pasuk concerning the mitzvah of הקהל, "Assemble," relates that the children, who do not know, will hear and learn to be G-d fearing, all the days that they are on the land which they will possess. The gematria of כל הימים, "all the days," is 155.

כל	50
הימים	105
	155

The gematria of על האדמה, "on the land," is 155.

על	100
האדמה	55
	155

Two questions are apparent. One, why are the gematrioth of כל הימים, "all the days," and על האדמה, "on the land," equal? Two, why is the land of Israel even mentioned here at all? The clue to resolving these questions can be found in a pasuk in Psalms which states, אתהלך לפני ה' בארצות החיים (תהלים קטז,ט), "I shall walk before G-d in the lands of the living," (Psalms 116,9). On this pasuk several commentators define the land of the living as the land of Israel (רש"י, רד"ק, מצודת דוד תהלים קטז,ט, Rashi, Radak, Metsudath David, Psalms 116,9). This definition can be easily understood. There is a Midrash which states, וזהב הארץ ההיא טוב (בראשית ב,יב). מלמד שאין תורה כתורת א"י (מדרש רבה, סדר בראשית, פרשה טז, אות ג), "And the gold of that land is good (Genesis 2,12). It teaches that there is no Torah like the Torah of the land of Israel" (Midrash Rabbah, Sidrah Bereshith, Parashah 16, Letter 3). Thus, the Torah of the land of Israel is exceptional. The Torah in general is called life, as stated, תורה נקראת חיים שנא' עץ חיים היא למחזיקים בה ותומכיה מאושר (משלי ג,יח) (אבות דרבי נתן פרק לד, אות י), "Torah is called life, as it says, 'It is a tree of life to those who take hold of it, and happy are those who firmly grasp it (Proverbs 3,18),'" (Avoth d'Rabbi Nathan Chapter

34, Letter 10). Since Torah is called life, and the Torah of the land of Israel is exceptional, therefore the life in the land of Israel is exceptional. Perhaps, it is because the life in the land of Israel is exceptional, that several commentators define the land of the living as the land of Israel.

Now the two questions asked earlier can be answered. One, why are the gematrioth of כל הימים, "all the days," and על האדמה, "on the land," equal? Since life in the land of Israel is an exceptional life, complete days, כל הימים, "all the days," can only be obtained על האדמה, "on the land," that is, on the land of Israel. This obtainment may well be why the two gematrioth are equal. Two, why is the land of Israel mentioned here at all? Since here the Torah mentions the life of those who may hear and learn to fear Hashem, your G-d, it describes a life where one can perform at his utmost. Such a life can only be in the land of Israel. Both questions have been resolved.

לקח את ספר התורה הזה ושמתם אתו מצד ארון ברית ה'
אלקיכם והיה שם בך לעד (דברים לא,כו).

Take this Book of the Law and put it by the side of the Ark of the Covenant of Hashem, your G-d, and it will be there for a witness against you (Deuteronomy 31, 26).

Prior to the termination of Parashath Vayyelech, Moses commands the Levites to place the ספר, "book," of the law by the side of the Ark of the Covenant, where it was to remain שם, "there." The gematria of ספר, "book," is 340.

$$ספר \qquad 340$$

The gematria of שם, "there," is 340.

$$שם \qquad 340$$

The Torah is described as a ספר, "book," and the place

where it is to remain is described as שם, "there." This association is alluded to by the fact that both words have the same gematria.

הקהילו אלי את כל זקני שבטיכם ושטריכם ואדברה
באזניהם את הדברים האלה ואעידה בם את השמים ואת
הארץ (דברים לא,כח).

Assemble to me all the elders of your tribes, and your officers, and I will speak in their ears these words, and I will call to witness against them the heaven and the earth (Deuteronomy 31,28).

Before Moses gave his final speech and rebuke to the Children of Israel, he directed them to הקהילו, "Assemble." The gematria of הקהילו, "Assemble," is 156.

$$\text{156} \qquad \text{הקהילו}$$

When Joseph revealed himself to his brothers, they could not bear the implicit rebuke, scolding, even though he was younger than those who received this implicit rebuke. The Midrash Rabbah states, יוסף קטנן של שבטים היה ולא היו יכולים לעמוד בתוכחתו הדא הוא דכתיב ולא יכלו אחיו לענות אותו כי נבהלו מפניו, לכשיבא הקב״ה ויוכיח וכו׳ (מדרש רבה, סדר ויגש, פרשה צג, אות י,) "Joseph was the youngest of the tribes, and they could not withstand his rebuke, as is written, 'And his brothers could not answer him for they were stunned from his presence.' When the Holy One, Blessed be He, will come and rebuke, etc." (Midrash Rabbah, Sidrah Vayyiggash, Parashah 93, Letter 10).

It is well known that the Children of Israel were warned to group together and fulfill the Torah, rather than to act as individuals who separately fulfill the Torah. The ספר החינוך, Book of Hachinuch, writes, שלא יהו שני בתי דינין בעיר אחת זה נוהג במנהג אחד וזה נוהג במנהג אחר, שדבר זה גורם למחלקת. ולשון

"לא תתגודדו" כלומר לא תעשו אגדות אגדות (ספר החינוך מאת הרב אהרן הלוי, מצוה תסז), "There should not be two courts in one city, this one follows one custom, and this one follows another custom, for this matter causes dissension. And this is implied in the terminology, 'Do not separate into caucuses,' that is, do not form disparate groups," (Book of Hachinuch by Rabbi Aaron Halevi, Mitzvah 467). Thus, it is clear that G-d does not want the Children of Israel to be divided.

The ספרא, "Sifra," comments on the pasuk, ורדפו מכם חמשה מאה ומאה מכם רבבה ירדפו ונפלו איביכם לפניכם לחרב (ויקרא כו,ח), "And five of you shall pursue a hundred, and a hundred of you shall pursue ten thousand, and your enemies shall fall before you by the sword" (Leviticus 26,8), that increased numbers of the Children of Israel doing the will of G-d are more than proportionally better. The Sifra writes, אין דומה המרובים העושים את התורה למעוטים העושים את התורה (ספרא פרשת בחוקותי, פרק ב, אות ד), "The many who fulfill the Torah can not be compared to the few who fulfill the Torah" (Sifra, Parashath Bechukosai, Chapter 2, Letter 4). Other sources רש"י, בראשית יא,ט ; רש"י, ויקרא כו,ח ; ותפארת ישראל, עוקצים פרק ג, משנה יב, אות צז), Rashi Genesis 11,9; Rashi Leviticus 26,8; and Tifereth Yisroel, Ukzin, Chapter 3, Mishnah 12, Letter 97) express a similar idea and the importance of peace.

Since there is more strength in a united Children of Israel, it is plausible that Moses, before giving rebuke, advised them to assemble and unite. Implicit here might be a reminder that when Joseph revealed himself to his brothers, they could not bear the implied rebuke. Moses could have been subtly conveying to the Children of Israel that, as an assembled group, they would be more able to bear his own implicit and explicit rebuke. The Children of Israel could learn from what happened with Joseph, as stated, ויאמר יוסף אל אחיו אני יוסף העוד אבי חי ולא יכלו אחיו לענות אתו כי נבהלו מפניו (בראשית מה,ג), "And Joseph said to his brothers, 'I am Joseph; is my father still alive?' And his brothers could not answer him, for they were frightened from his presence" (Genesis 45,3). The gematria of יוסף," Joseph," is 156.

יוסף   156

The gematria of יוסף, "Joseph," is equal to the gematria of הקהילו, "Assemble." Since the two gematrioth are the same, it can be said, that what happened with Joseph might encourage the Children of Israel to obey Moses' directive to Assemble.

Parashath Haazinu   פרשת האזינו

האזינו השמים ואדברה ותשמע הארץ אמרי פי (דברים
לב,א).

Give ear, O heavens, and I will speak; and let the earth hear the words of my mouth (Deuteronomy 32,1).

Moses called on the heavens and earth tc be witnesses on the Children of Israel. The gematria of השמים, "the heavens," is 395.

השמים   395

The gematria of הארץ, "the earth," is 296.

הארץ   296

The difference between השמים, "the heavens," and הארץ, "the earth," in gematrioth is 99.

$$395$$
$$-296$$
$$99$$

Rashi mentions two reasons why Moses called on the heavens and earth to be witnesses. One is that they exist forever; two is that they will pay, or withhold payment, from the Children of Israel. Rashi further mentions that the payment of the heavens is טלם, "their dew," and מטר, "rain"; the payment of the earth is יבולה, "its produce"; Rashi writes, העיד בהם שמים וארץ עדים שהן קימים לעולם. ועוד שאם יזכו יבואו העדים ויתנו שכרכ הגפן תתן פריה, והארץ תתן יבולה, והשמים יתנו טלם. ואם יתחיבו תהיה בהם יד העדים תחלה ועצר את השמים ולא יהיה מטר והאדמה לא תתן את יבולה וכו'' (רש"י, דברים לב,א), "He had heaven and earth witness against them, witnesses who endure forever. And additionally, if they [the Children of Israel] merit, the witnesses will come give their remuneration; the vine will give its fruit, and the earth will give its produce, and the heavens will give their dew. And if they will be guilty, then the hand of the witnesses will be first against them: And He will restrain the heavens and there will be no rain, and the earth will not give its produce, etc." (Rashi, Deuteronomy 32,1). The gematria of לעולם, "forever," is 176.

לעולם   176

The gematria of טלם, "their dew," מטר, "rain," and יבולה, "its produce," is 79, 249, and 53 respectively.

טלם   79

מטר   249

יבולה   53

It follows from Rashi, that the difference between the heavens and the earth, both of which are forever, is that the former gives dew and rain, while the latter gives produce. This difference can be seen in gematrioth. Note that this difference can be seen by combining the two explanations of Rashi which are closely connected.

As was shown above, the difference between השמים, "the heavens," and the הארץ, "the earth," in gematrioth is 99. Since this difference is לעולם, "forever," which has a gematria of 176, ergo the sum of 176 and 99 signify that their difference is forever.

176
99
———
275

Thus, 275 represents the לעולם, "forever," difference between השמים, "the heavens," and הארץ, "the earth." The difference between (on the one hand) טלם, "their dew," plus מטר, "rain," and (on the other hand) יבולה, "its produce," can be equated to the difference between השמים, "the heavens,"

and הארץ, "the earth," which is לעולם, "forever." The difference between (on the one hand) טלם, "their dew," plus מטר,
"rain," and (on the other hand) יבולה, "its produce," in
gematrioth is 275.

טלם	79
מטר	249
	328
	328
יבולה	-53
	275

Therefore, this difference, 275, can be equated in gematrioth
to the difference between השמים, "the heavens," and הארץ,
"the earth," which is לעולם, "forever."

Parashath Haazinu is read just before the Children of
Israel leave their homes and move into their sukkoth. One
reason for the timing of this move might be to serve as a
reminder to obey the will of G-d; for the reward or the
punishment will be paid or administered by the heavens and
the earth. People who live in sturdy, solid homes might feel
secure and protected from the effects of nature, but when
they move from their homes into a sukkah, they are very
much affected by השמים, "the heavens," and הארץ, "the
earth." Thus, it is fitting that Parashath Haazinu should precede the holiday of Sukkoth.

ה' בדד ינחנו ואין עמו קל נכר. ירכבהו על במותי ארץ
ויאכל תנובת שדי וינקהו דבש מסלע ושמן מחלמיש צור
(דברים לב,יב-יג)

G-d alone did lead him, and there was no
strange god with Him. He shall make him ride
on the high places of the earth; and he will eat
the fruitage of the field; and He shall make him
to suck honey from a stone, and oil from a flinty
rock (Deuteronomy 32, 12-13).

In Parashath Haazinu there are two sequential pesukim which might seem unrelated. The first pasuk refers to G-d as being alone without any strange deity. The gematria of נכר, "strange," is 270.

$$270 \qquad נכר$$

The second pasuk refers to G-d causing the Children of Israel to ride on the high places of the earth. The gematria of ירכבהו על, "He shall make him ride on," is 343.

$$243 \qquad ירכבהו$$
$$\underline{100} \qquad על$$
$$343$$

What is the connection between these two sequential, but seemingly unrelated pesukim? By combining the thoughts of two different commentators a connection can be substantiated.

The תורה אור, Torah Or, interprets the end of the first pasuk as Moses warning the Children of Israel not to sin, as the Torah Or writes, ועייי תפלתו ותשובתם שעשו חזר ה' לנחותם לבדו. והזהיר להם שלא יוסיפו לחטוא (תורה אור, מאת הרב מאיר ליבוש מלבייים, דברים לב,יב), "And through his prayer and their repentance which they did, G-d returned to guide them by Himself. And He warned them that they should not continue to sin" (Torah Or by Rabbi Meir Lebush Malbim, Deuteronomy 32,12).

The העמק דבר, Haamek Davar, interprets the beginning of the second pasuk as G-d preventing the Children of Israel from sinning, as he writes, שמשמעו שכונן את ישראל ביחוד באופן שלא יבאו לידי חטא... והקבייה ראה טוב לישראל ויתן להם ארץ שהעסק בה מרובה עד שנדרש לבלות ימיהם בעבודת הארץ (העמק דבר מאת הרב נפתלי צבי יהודה ברלין מאוואלאזין, דברים לב,יג), "The implication is that He supports Israel, particularly in a manner that they should not come to sin... And the Holy One, Blessed be He, saw it was good for Israel to give them land whose occupation is great to the point that it requires [them] to consume their days with working the land" (Haamek Davar by Rabbi Naphtali Zevi Judah Berlin from Volozhin, Deuteronomy 32,13).

Since the end of the first pasuk can be interpreted as G-d warning the Children of Israel not to sin, and the beginning of the second pasuk can be interpreted as G-d preventing the Children of Israel from sinning, it seems plausible that not sinning could be the common theme connecting these pesukim. An underscoring of this connection can be seen by inspecting the gematria of the last word of the first pasuk, and the gematria of the first two words of the second pasuk. The sum of the gematria of נכר, "strange," and the gematria of ירכבהו על, "He made him ride on," is 613.

$$
\begin{array}{r}
270 \\
343 \\
\hline
613
\end{array}
$$

Certainly not sinning can be defined as observing the 613 Commandments; so the sum of these gematrioth emphasizes the connection which was substantiated.

כי אש קדחה באפי ותיקד עד שאול תחתית ותאכל ארץ ויבלה ותלהט מוסדי הרים (דברים לב,כב).

For a fire has been kindled in My nostril, and it has burned unto the depths of the netherworld, and it will consume land and its produce, and it will set ablaze the foundations of mountains (Deuteronomy 32,22).

The pasuk preceding the one quoted above reveals that what has aroused G-d's consuming anger was idolatry. The gematria of באפי ותיקד, "in My nostril, and it has burned," is 613.

$$
\begin{array}{rr}
\text{באפי} & 93 \\
\text{ותיקד} & \underline{520} \\
& 613
\end{array}
$$

There is a total of 613 Commandments in the Torah (מכות כג:, Makkoth 23b). The Gemara Horayoth says that worshiping idols is equated to violating all of the commandments, as stated, איזו היא מצוה שהיא שקולה ככל המצות, הוי אומר זו עבודת כוכבים (הוריות ח.), "Which mitzvah is equated to all the mitzvoth? Say it is idol worship" (Horayoth 8a). Since the transgression of idol worship is equal to all the other commandments, therefore it is logical that the pasuk telling of G-d's anger at the Children of Israel because they had committed idol worship, should contain the gematria of 613.

כי גוי אבד עצות המה ואין בהם תבונה (דברים לב,כח).
For they are a nation void of counsel, and there is no understanding in them (Deuteronomy 32,28).

In Parashath Haazinu a nation is described as אבד עצות המה, "they are void of counsel." To which nation does the pasuk refer, and what is the counsel it lacks? According to one opinion in the Sifrei on this pasuk, the nation is the Children of Israel, and the counsel is the Torah, as stated, ר' יהודה דורשו כלפי ישראל אבדו ישראל עצה טובה שנתנה להם ואין עצה אלא תורה (ספרי, דברים לב,כח), "Rabbi Yehuda expounded it vis-à-vis Israel. Israel lost the good counsel that was given to them; and there is no counsel except Torah" (Sifrei, Deuteronomy 32,8).

Later in Parashath Haazinu Moses tells the Children of Israel to command their children to observe the Torah, as stated, ויאמר אלהם שימו לבבכם לכל הדברים אשר אנכי מעיד בכם היום אשר תצום את בניכם לשמר לעשות את כל דברי התורה הזאת (דברים לב,מו), "And he said to them, Set you heart to all the words which I testify among you today, that you shall command them to your children to observe to do all the words of this Torah" (Deuteronomy 32,46). The gematria of התורה, "the Torah," is 616.

התורה   616

Previously in Parashath Haazinu, according to one opinion in the Sifrei, the Children of Israel lacking Torah are described as "a nation lacking counsel are they." The gematria of עצות המה, "counsel, are they," is 616.

עצות   566
המה   50
―――――
616

Since התורה, "the Torah," and עצות המה, "counsel, are they," both have the same gematria (also they both are in Parashath Haazinu), they reflect the opinion in the Sifrei, that the Children of Israel lacking Torah are described as a nation lacking עצות המה, "counsel, are they."

―――――

לו חכמו ישכילו זאת יבינו לאחריתם (דברים לב,כט).
If they were wise they would reason this, they would understand their end (Deuteronomy 32,29).

The Torah says conditionally, לו, "if" they were wise. The gematria of לו, "if," is 36.

לו   36

The next pasuk tells what they would understand, as stated, איכה ירדף אחד אלף ושנים יניסו רבבה אם לא כי צורם מכרם וה' הסגירם (דברים לב,ל), "How did one chase a thousand, and two put ten thousand to flight, if not that their Rock had sold them, and G-d had delivered them up?" (Deuteronomy 32,30). The gematria of איכה, "how," is 36.

איכה   36

The word איכה, "how," is a interrogative word; the pasuk is telling what should have been understood if they were wise. The conditional word לו, "if," relates to the interrogative word איכה, "how"; "if" they were wise they would understand "how." This relationship could be the reason why the words have the same gematria.

כי ידין ה׳ עמו ועל עבדיו יתנחם כי יראה כי אזלת יד ואפס עצור ועזוב (דברים לב,לו).

When G-d will judge His people and upon His servants He will reconsider; when He sees that their power is gone, and there is nothing shut up or fortified (Deuteronomy 32,36).

According to Daat Zekenim Mibaale Hatosafoth, the pasuk quoted above refers to G-d reconsidering about the Children of Israel, whom the Torah refers to as עבדיו, "His servants." He writes, ועל ישראל יתנחם במה שהרגיזו לפניו (דעת זקנים מבעלי התוספות, דברים לב,לו, ד״ה ועל עבדיו יתנחם), "And upon Israel He will reconsider, in the manner in which He was angry with them," (Daat Zekenim Mibaale Hatosafoth, Deuteronomy 32,36, header words: And and upon His servants He will reconsider). The gematria of עבדיו, "His servants," is 92.

עבדיו   92

The next pasuk states, ואמר אי אלקימו צור חסיו בו (דברים לב,לז), "And he will say, Where is their G-d, the Rock in Whom they trusted" (Deuteronomy 32,37). According to the Ramban this pasuk refers to the enemy saying where is the G-d of the Children of Israel, whom the Torah refers to as אלקימו, "their G-d." He writes, האויב יאמר איה אלקי ישראל כענין (תהלים קטו,ב) למה יאמרו הגוים איה נא אלקיהם (רמב״ן, דברים לב,לז), "The enemy will say, where is the G-d of Israel? Similar to the subject of the pasuk (Psalms 115,2), Why should the nations say, Where now is their G-d?" (Ramban, Deuteronomy 32,37).

The Torah in the pasuk quoted refers to the G-d of the Children of Israel as אלקימו, "their G-d." The gematria of אלקימו, "their G-d," is 92.

אלקימו   92

Thus, 92 can represent the Children of Israel as עבדיו, "His servants," and 92 can represent the G-d of the Children of Israel as אלקימו, "their G-d". Since עבדיו, "His servants," and אלקימו, "their G-d," are associated with each other, it is appropriate that their gematrioth are the same.

ויכל משה לדבר את כל הדברים האלה אל כל ישראל (דברים לב,מה).
And Moses finished speaking all these words to all the Children of Israel (Deuteronomy 32,45).

According to the רמב״ם, "Rambam," the last mitzvah of the 613 Mitzvoth prescribed by the Torah is found in Parashath Haazinu. This last mitzvah is the warning not to drink יין נסך, "heathen wine," and it is based on the pasuk that states, אשר חלב זבחימו יאכלו ישתו יין נסיכם יקומו ויעזרכם יהי עליכם סתרה (דברים לב,לח), "Who did eat the fat of their sacrifices, and drank the wine of their drink offerings? Let them get up and help you; let him be a protection for you" (Deuteronomy 32,38). Thus, according to the Rambam, Moses completed giving the 613 Mitzvoth to the Children of Israel when he concluded saying Haazinu, (ספר המצוות מאת רבינו משה בן מימון, Book of מצוות לא תעשה קצד, ומפתח לסדר המצוות לפי סדר הפרשיות HaMitzvoth by Rabbeinu Moses ben Maimon, Negative Commandment 194, and Index to the Order of the Mitzvoth According to the Order of the Parashiyyoth). A gematria alludes to this completion.

The Torah records Moses' conclusion of Haazinu, as stated, ויכל משה לדבר את כל הדברים האלה אל כל ישראל (דברים לב,מה), "And Moses finished speaking all these words to all

Israel" (Deuteronomy 32,45). The sum of the gematrioth of האלה, "these," אל, "to," and ישראל, "Israel," is 613.

האלה	41
אל	31
ישראל	541
	613

Thus, this pasuk which records Moses conclusion of Haazinu, contains an inference to the 613 Mitzvoth which Moses completed giving to the Children of Israel when he finished saying Haazinu.

עלה אל הר העברים הזה הר נבו אשר בארץ מואב אשר על פני ירחו וראה את ארץ כנען אשר אני נתן לבני ישראל לאחזה (דברים לב,מט).

Go up to this Mount Abarim, Mount Nebo, which is in the land of Moab, which is over against Jericho, and see the land of Canaan which I give to the Children of Israel for an inheritance (Deuteronomy 32,49).

Before Moses died, G-d told him to see the land of Israel. The gematria of וראה את, "and see," is 613.

וראה	212
את	401
	613

The Gemara Makkoth says that when Moses received the Torah he got 613 Mitzvoth, as stated, דרש רבי שמלאי שש מאות ושלש עשרה מצות נאמרו לו למשה שלש מאות וששים וחמש לאוין כמנין ימות החמה ומאתים וארבעים ושמונה עשה כנגד איבריו של אדם (מכות כג:), "Rabbi Simlai expounded, 613 Commandments were said to Moses, three hundred and sixty-five negative Commandments corresponding to the number of days in a solar year, and two hundred and forty-eight positive Commandments corresponding to the limbs of a person" (Makkoth 23b). Since there is a total of 613 Mitzvoth, it can be understood, that G-d told Moses that he should see the land of Israel through the 613 Commandments. That is, G-d told Moses that the land of Canaan would be given to the Children of Israel for an inheritance, contingent on the Children of Israel observing all 613 Mitzvoth.

The necessity for the Children of Israel to observe the mitzvoth in order to remain in the land of Israel is mentioned by Rashi, as stated, ארץ ישראל אינה מקימת עוברי עבירה (רש״י, ויקרא יח, כח), "The land of Israel does not maintain those who commit a transgression" (Rashi, Leviticus 18,28). Note that Rashi uses the singular עוברי עבירה, "those who commit a transgression"; if some individuals do not observe even one of the 613 Mitzvoth, the land can not tolerate those persons. The reason that the gematria of וראה את, "and see," is 613 could conceivably be that G-d told Moses that the land of Canaan will be given to the Children of Israel for an inheritance, contingent on the Children of Israel observing all 613 Mitzvoth. A slightly different interpretation of these words is given in the פרשת פינחס, Parashath Pinchas, section of this sefer.

ומת בהר אשר אתה עלה שמה והאסף אל עמיך כאשר מת אהרן אחיך בהר ההר ויאסף אל עמיו (דברים לב,נ).
And die on the mountain upon which you go up there, and be gathered to your people, as Aaron your brother died on mount Hor, and was gathered to his people (Deuteronomy 32,50).

In this week's sidrah G-d tells Moses to go up to mount Nebo where he will die, as Aaron, his brother, died. Rashi says that Moses desired that sort of death, as stated, אשרי מי שמת במיתה זו (רש״י, דברים לב,נ), "Fortunate he who dies this death" (Rashi, Deuteronomy 32,50). What made Aaron's death so desirable? One reason is that he died with a kiss (התורה והמצוה, מאת הרב מאיר ליבוש מלביי״ם, במדבר כ,כו), The Torah and the Mitzvah by Rabbi Meir Lebush Malbim, Numbers 20,26). Rashi says that Moses died with a kiss from G-d (רש״י, דברים לד,ה, Rashi, Deuteronomy 34,5).

Perhaps a different answer could be suggested. The Gemara says, תנו רבנן שבעה לא שלט בהן רמה ותולעה ואלו הן אברהם, "Our יצחק ויעקב משה ואהרן ומרים ובנימין בן יעקב (בבא בתרא יז.) Rabbis taught, there were seven over whom maggots and worms did not have dominion, and these are they: Abraham, Isaac, and Jacob, Moses, and Aaron, and Miriam, and Benjamin the son of Jacob" (Baba Bathra 17a). Aaron's being one of the people over whose body worms and maggots would never have dominion, could well be what Moses perceived as the special status in Aaron's death, leading to Moses' desiring a similar death.

Worms and maggots never having dominion over Aaron's body made his death desirable. Man was created with 248 limbs and 365 sinews, together totaling 613 body parts (תרגום יונתן בן עוזיאל, בראשית א,כז), Targum Jonathan ben Uzziel, Genesis 1,27). In the pasuk from which it was learned that Moses desired the sort of death that Aaron had, it states, כאשר מת אהרן אחיך בהר ההר ויאסף, "as Aaron your brother died on the mount Hor, and was gathered." The gematria of אחיך בהר ההר ויאסף, "your brother on the mount Hor, and was gathered," is 613.

אחיך	39
בהר ההר	417
ויאסף	157
	613

This gematria suggests that it could be that Moses perceived in Aaron's death that worms and maggots would never have dominion over Aaron's 613 body parts; this perception could well have played a role Moses' desiring a similar death.

ומת בהר אשר אתה עלה שמה והאסף אל עמיך כאשר מת
אהרן אחיך בהר ההר ויאסף אל עמיו (דברים לב,נ).
And die on the mountain upon which you go up
there and be gathered to your people, as Aaron
your brother died on mount Hor, and was gathered to his people (Deuteronomy 32,50).

Three pesukim before the end of Parashath Haazinu,
G-d tells Moses that "you," will die on the mountain which you
will ascend. The combined gematria of בהר, "on the mount,"
and אתה, "you," is 613.

בהר	207
אתה	406
	613

Why did the Torah see fit to write the words בהר אשר אתה עלה,
"on the mountain upon which you go up"? The meaning would
be clear if just ומת שמה, "and die there," were written; the
previous pasuk already said that Moses was to ascend mount
Nebo (דברים לב,מט, Deuteronomy 32,49).

It could be that the words בהר אשר אתה עלה, "on the
mountain upon which you go up" communicate an additional
idea. Targum Jonathan ben Uzziel states, that man is created
with 248 limbs and 365 sinews, together totaling 613 body
parts, (תרגום יונתן בן עוזיאל, בראשית א,כז, Targum Jonathan ben
Uzziel, Genesis 1,27). As men grow older some of their limbs
or sinews start to deteriorate, sometimes they even cease to
function. However, Moses was unique; his strength did not
wane; his limbs and sinews were fully functional until his
death, as stated, ומשה בן מאה ועשרים שנה במתו לא כהתה עינו ולא
נס לחה (דברים לד,ז), "And Moses was one hundred and twenty
years old at the time of his death, his eye had not dimmed
and his vigor had not abated" (Deuteronomy 34,7) (העמק דבר,
דברים לד,ז, Haamek Davar, Deuteronomy 34,7). The 613 body
parts of Moses were fully functional at the time of his death.

These 613 functional body parts could be what the Torah alluded to when it writes בהר אשר אתה עלה, "on the mountain which you go up," containing the words בהר, "on the mount," and אתה, "you," whose combined gematria is 613.

על אשר מעלתם בי בתוך בני ישראל במי מריבת קדש מדבר צן על אשר לא קדשתם אותי בתוך בני ישראל (דברים לב,נא).

Because you trespassed against Me in the midst of the Children of Israel at the waters of Meribath-Kadesh, in the desert of Zin; because you did not sanctify Me in the midst of the Children of Israel (Deuteronomy 32,51).

In the sidrah of Haazinu, G-d tells Moses that he may not go into the land of Israel because Moses had transgressed against G-d. The sum of the gematrioth of על אשר, "because," and בי, "Me," is 613.

על אשר	601
בי	12
	613

There is a total of 613 Commandments (מכות כג:, Makkoth 23b). Since the gematrioth of על אשר, "because," and בי, "Me," is 613, it can be explained that the way one transgresses against G-d is by not observing His 613 Commandments. The opposite can also be inferred, mainly that the only way one leads a life as G-d so designated is by observing His 613 Commandments.

Parashath Vezoth Haberachah   פרשת וזאת הברכה

> תורה צוה לנו משה מורשה קהלת יעקב (דברים לג,ד).
> Torah was commanded us by Moses, an inher-
> itance of the congregation of Jacob (Deuteron-
> omy 33,4).

The fourth pasuk in this sidrah is considered very special by the שלחן ערוך, Shulhan Arukh, for it pinpoints this pasuk as the first one a father should teach his son; the Shulhan Arukh, based on a Gemara (.סוכה מב, Sukkah 42a), writes, מאימתי מתחיל ללמד לבנו משיתחיל לדבר מתחיל ללמדו תורה "From when צוה לנו וגו' (שלחן ערוך, יורה דעה, סימן רמה, סעיף ה) does one begin to teach his son? From when he begins to speak, one begins to teach him 'Torah commanded us, etc.'" (Shulhan Arukh, Yoreh Deah, Siman 245, Seif 5). There are many very pedagogically important pesukim in the Torah; why does the Shulhan Arukh pinpoint this pasuk as the first one a father should teach his son?

Two supplementary questions can be asked. One, why does the pasuk say, "the congregation of Jacob," as opposed to the congregation of Abraham, or the congregation of Isaac? Two, the ספרי, Sifre, writes, אל תקרי מורשה אלא מאורסה מורשה, "Do not read שהתורה מאורסה היא לישראל (ספרי דברים לג,ד) 'inheritance,' but מאורסה, 'betrothed,' for the Torah is be-trothed to Israel" (Sifre, Deuteronomy 33,4). By changing the ש, "shin," to a ס, "samech," and adding an א "aleph," after the מ, "mem," a change is made in how the word מורשה, 'inheritance,' is read. The question is, why did the Sifre feel compelled to transform the letters to have an alternate read-ing of the pasuk?

This last question has been addressed by Rabbi Moses Pollack. He explains that in order to successfully imbue chil-dren with Torah and mitzvoth, the parents must show by example that they love Torah and mitzvoth, analogous to the love a fiance shows the woman to whom he is betrothed. Rabbi Moses Pollock writes, כמו שמכבד אשתו יותר מגופו ומקשט אותה בקישוטין ואץ וזריז לעשות רצונה כן תהיה התורה והמצות ואז היא ירושה לעולם לבניו אחריו. וזה שכתוב אל תקרי מורשה אי"א לך לקרוא התורה ירושה אלא כשהיא מאורסה חביבה על בעלה כאשה.... וכמה שכתוב תהלים קי"ב אשרי איש ירא ה' במצותיו חפץ מאד אז גם זרעו אחריו יהיו דור ישרים יבורך (ספר וידבר משה מאת הרב משה הלוי פאללאק, פרשת וזאת הברכה, ד"ה תורה צוה לנו משה), "Just like one honors his wife more than himself, and adorns her with ornaments, and hurries and is quick to do her will, so too should it with be with the Torah and mitzvoth. And then it will be an inheritance forever, for his sons after him. And this is what is written, Do not read מורשה, 'inheritance'; it is impossible for you to call the Torah an inheritance, unless it is betrothed, beloved by her husband as his wife... And this is like it is written in Psalms 112, 'Happy is the man who fears G-d, who is very delighted with His commandments,' then also his seed after him will be 'a blessed, upright generation'" (Book of Vayedaber Mosheh by Rabbi Moses Halevi Pollak, Parashah Vezoth Haberachah, header words: Torah was commanded us by Moses). Now all the questions can be answered.

The first question, why does the Shulhan Arukh pinpoint this pasuk as the first one a father should teach his son, is easily resolved. This pasuk contains a vital message for parents; in order to successfully imbue children with Torah and mitzvoth, the parents must show by example that they love the Torah and mitzvoth. This vital message could be the reason why this pasuk was pinpointed.

The two supplementary questions can also can also be easily resolved. One, why does the pasuk say, "the congregation of Jacob," as opposed to the congregation of Abraham, or the congregation of Isaac? The answer is that parents want their children to be like the children of Jacob, that is, all their children live adhering to Torah values. Since Abraham had a son, Ishmael (who was not righteous), and Isaac had a son, Esau (who was not righteous), the pasuk does not mention Abraham or Isaac. Since all of Jacob's children were righteous, the pasuk says the congregation of Jacob. Two, why did the Sifre feel compelled to transform the letters to have an alternate reading of the pasuk? The answer is that the alternate reading of the pasuk tells that parents must show by example that they love Torah and mitzvoth analogous to the love a fiance shows his betrothed. This analogous relationship could be the reason why there is an alternate reading of the pasuk.

Note that to demonstrate the validity of this explanation, Rabbi Moses Pollock quotes from Psalm 112 where it says that a man who takes delight in G-d's commandments will be blessed with an upright generation. There is a total of 613 Commandments which the Children of Israel are to observe (מכות כג:, Makkoth 23b). Therefore, the fourth pasuk in this sidrah can be explained as relating to the 613 Commandments. There are three people cited in the pasuk: משה, "Moses," לנו, "us," and יעקב, "Jacob." The gematria of משה, "Moses," לנו, "us," and יעקב, "Jacob," is 613.

לנו	86
משה	345
יעקב	182
	613

This gematria helps to verify the explanation of Rabbi Moses Pollock.

Parashath Vezoth Haberachah or Hanukkah

פרשת וזאת הברכה או חנוכה

ברך ה' חילו ופעל ידיו תרצה מחץ מתנים קמיו ומשנאיו מן יקומון (דברים לג,יא).

G-d bless his substance, and accept the work of his hands; smash the loins of those who rise up against him, and do not let rise those who hate him (Deuteronomy 33,11).

When Moses blessed Levi, the tribe from whom the kohanim descend, part of the blessing was that ברך ה' חילו, "G-d bless his substance." The gematria of ברך, "Bless," is 222.

222   ברך

Rashi as a דבר אחר, "Another meaning," on this pasuk explains that ברך ה' חילו, "G-d bless his substance," refers to the Hasmonean and his sons (רש"י, דברים לג,יא, Rashi, Deuteronomy 33,11). The Hasmonean is Mattisyahu, the kohen gadol and his sons at the time of the Hanukkah events. Thus, the gematria of 222 can represent the Hasmonean and his sons, according to this דבר אחר, "Another meaning," in Rashi.

The Ramban in the beginning of פרשת בהעלתך, Parashath Behaalosecha, at the commandment to light the Menorah, quotes a Midrash which states that this commandment refers to the future lighting by the Hasmonean and his sons (רמב"ן במדבר ח,ב, Ramban, Numbers 8,2). Thus, the lighting of the Menorah can be explained to refer to the Hasmonean and his sons.

The first time the Torah mentions the lighting of the Menorah is in פרשת תרומה, Parashath Terumah, as stated, ועשית את נרתיה שבעה והעלה את נרתיה והאיר על עבר פניה (שמות כה,לז), "And you shall make its lamps seven, and he shall light its lamps, so as to give light toward its face" (Exodus

25,37). The gematria of והאיר, "that they should give light,"
is 222.

והאיר   222

Although the pasuk from Parashath Terumah refers to
the Menorah in the משכן, "Tabernacle," and not directly to the
Menorah of the Hasmoneans, based on the Midrash quoted
by the Ramban, it can be said בדרך דרוש, "by the route of a
homily," that, "that they should give light," with a gematria
of 222 refers to the lighting of the Hasmonean and his sons.

It is striking to note that Blessing and Light are already
conjoined (with the word יברכך, "May [G-d] bless you," and
with the word יאר, "May [G-d] illuminate"), in the the blessing
of the kohanim, which they bestow on the Children of Israel
in every generation. It is also striking that blessing and light
share the same gematria; moreover in two places in the
Torah, words with a gematria of 222 can refer to the the
Hasmonean and his sons.

לכל האתת והמופתים אשר שלחו ה' לעשות בארץ מצרים
לפרעה ולכל עבדיו ולכל ארצו (דברים לד,יא).

For all the signs and wonders which G-d sent
him to do in the land of Egypt to Pharaoh and to
all his servants and for all his land (Deuteronomy 34,11).

The penultimate pasuk in the Torah tells of the signs
and wonders which G-d did in Egypt. The gematria of האתת,
"the signs," is 806.

האתת   806

The gematria of לעשות "to do," is 806.

לעשות   806

Since the האתת, "the signs," were לעשות "to do," it is
fitting that both words should have the same gematria.

ולכל היד החזקה ולכל המורא הגדול אשר עשה משה לעיני
כל שראל (דברים לד,יב).

And for all the mighty hand, and in the great terror which Moses wrought in the eyes of all Israel (Deuteronomy 34,12).

The last pasuk in the Torah refers to all the mighty hand which Moses wrought. The gematria of ולכל, "and in all," is 86.

ולכל   86

The Ramban writes that the mighty hand refers to G-d's character of strict justice. G-d's attribute of justice is identified with His name of אלקים, "G-d," as stated, זה. ויזכר אלקים. השם מדת הדין הוא (רשי, בראשית ח,א), "And G-d remembered. This name is identified with His attribute of strict justice," (Rashi, Genesis 8,1). The gematria of אלקים, "G-d," is 86.

אלקים   86

It can easily be hypothesized why ולכל, "and for all," was placed directly before היד החזקה, "the mighty hand." Since the latter term refers to G-d's attribute of strict justice, it is particularly appropriate that the term was preceded by ולכל, "and for all," which has the same gematria as אלקים, "G-d," with its allusion to G-d's character of strict justice. Thus, ולכל, "and for all," and אלקים, "G-d," have the same theme and the same gematria.

Holidays — חגים

Month of Elul   חדש אלול

לדוד ה׳ אורי וישעי ממי אירא ה׳ מעוז חיי ממי אפחד
(תהלים כז,א).

By David: G-d is my light and my salvation;
from whom should I fear? G-d is the fortress of
my life; from whom should I dread (Psalms
27,1)?

The month of Elul is the sixth in the Jewish calendar;
being immediately prior to Rosh Hashanah and Yom Kippur,
it is a time to intensify one's repentance. It is the custom in
many congregations to say the 27th Chapter of Psalms from
the beginning of Elul until Shemini Atsereth (משנה ברורה, סימן
תקפ״א ס״ק ב, Mishnah Berurah, Siman 581, Seif Katon 2).
This chapter has been explained as referring to Torah and
mitzvoth, as stated, אבל ענינו שאין הצלחת התורה והמצות כהצלחת
כסף וזהב, אשר במותו ישאר ריק מהם לא ירד אחריו עשרו וטובו, אבל
הצלחת התורה היא שלימות בעצמו של אדם, לא יתפרד ממנו כלל (פירוש
לספר תהלים מאת הרב יוסף יעבץ, פרק כז, פסוק א), "But its subject
is that success with the Torah and the mitzvoth is not like
success with silver and gold. When a person dies, he is left
empty of them, his wealth and its worth do not go down after
him. But success with the Torah is the completion of the
essence of man; it will not be separated from him at all"
(Commentary to the Book of Psalms by Rabbi Joseph Yavetz,
Chapter 27, verse 1). The first pasuk of this chapter says,
that G-d is אורי וישעי, "my light and my salvation." The
gematria of אורי וישעי, "my light and my salvation," is 613.

אורי	217
וישעי	396
	613

Since there is a total of 613 Mitzvoth, this gematria in
the chapter's first pasuk, enhances the explanation that this
chapter refers to the Torah and its mitzvoth.

Rosh Hashanah   ראש השנה

כי חק לישראל הוא משפט לאלקי יעקב (תהלים פא,ה).
For it is a statute for Israel, an ordinance of the
G-d of Jacob (Psalms 81,5).

One of the most famous pesukim associated with Rosh Hashanah refers to the blowing of the shofar as a statute, as stated, כי חק לישראל הוא, "For it is a statute for Israel." This pasuk is said on Rosh Hashanah in תפלת ערבית, "Evening Service," before שמנה עשרה, "Shemoneh Esreh," in the קדוש, Kiddush said during the day, and in the אתה נגלית, "You did reveal Yourself," paragraph of the תפלת מוסף, "Additional Service," (סידור בית יעקב מאת רב יעקב מעמדין בן הרב צבי, אשכנזי, דף קכט: ודף של:, Siddur Beth Yaakov by Rabbi Yaakov from Emden ben Rabbi Zvi, Ashkenazi, page 129b and page 330b).

Why is the blowing of the shofar referred to as a statute? The ספורנו, Sforno, explains that the חק, "statute," is that the blowing of the shofar is to be accomplished in order to fulfill the mitzvah of the Torah. It should be engraved upon the Children of Israel as another mitzvah of the Torah, as the Sforno writes, כי חק לישראל הוא, ותהי תקיעת השופר לקיים מצות התורה על ישראל (כתבי רבי עובדיה ספורנו, תהלים פא,ה) "For it is a statute for Israel, And the blowing of the shofar should be to fulfill the commandment of the Torah upon Israel" (The Writings of Rabbi Ovadiah Sforno, Psalms 81,5).

There is a gematria which coincides with the explanation of the Sforno. The gematria of כי לישראל הוא, "For it is for Israel," is 613.

כי	30
לישראל	571
הוא	12
	613

G-d has commanded the Children of Israel to observe 613 Mitzvoth, divided between 248 positive Mitzvoth and 365 negative Mitzvoth, as stated, דרש רבי שמלאי שש מאות ושלש עשרה מצות נאמרו לו למשה שלש מאות וששים וחמש לאוין כמנין ימות החמה ומאתים וארבעים ושמונה עשה כנגד איבריו של אדם (מכות כג:), "Rabbi Simlai expounded, 613 Commandments were said to Moses, three hundred and sixty-five negative Commandments corresponding to the number of days in a solar year, and two hundred and forty-eight positive Commandments corresponding to the limbs of a person" (Makkoth 23b). The blowing of the shofar should be a statute, engraved upon the Children of Israel as another commandment of the Torah, of which there is a total of 613. The חק, "statute," is that the blowing of the shofar is כי לישראל הוא, "For it is for Israel," as another commandment of the Torah, of which there are 613. Thus, the gematria coincides with the explanation of the Sforno. A different meaning which the חק, "statute," conveys is that the shofar reminds us to observe the commandments of G-d, of which there are 613 (משנה תורה, ספר המדע, הלכות תשובה, פרק ג, הלכה ד, Mishnah Torah, Book of Hamadda, Laws of Repentance, Chapter 3, Law 4).

Yom Kippur   יום כפור

Toward the end of חזרת הש״ץ, "the reader's repetition of the Amidah," for שחרית, "Shaharith," מוסף, "Musaf," and מנחה, "Minhah," on Yom Kippur, the order of the על חטא, "Al Het," is said. The one phrase which is repeated four times within it is ועל כלם אלוק סליחות סלח לנו מחל לנו כפר לנו, "And for all of these, G-d of forgiveness, forgive us, pardon us, grant us remission." The gematria of לנו, "us," is 86.

לנו   86

When Hashem's character of strict justice and judgment is alluded to, He is referred to as אלקים, "G-d," as Rashi says, ויזכור אלקים. זה השם מדת הדין (רש״י, בראשית ח,א), "And G-d remembered. This name refers to His attribute of strict justice" (Rashi, Genesis 8,1). The gematria of אלקים, "G-d," is 86.

אלקים   86

Since the gematria of לנו, "us," is the same as the gematria of אלקים, "G-d," the phrase ועל כלם אלוק סליחות סלח לנו מחל לנו כפר לנו, "And for all of these, G-d of forgiveness, forgive us, pardon us, grant us remission," can be interpreted as praying that G-d forgive, pardon, and grant remission, from His character of strict justice. His character of strict justice is associated with divine punishment, from which Bnei Yisroel plead for G-d to save us.

The Sukkoth Holiday   חג הסכות

טובים השנים מן האחד אשר יש להם שכר טוב בעמלם
(קהלת ד,ט).
"Two are better than one, because they have a
good reward for their toil" (Ecclesiastes 4,9).

There is an oft quoted pasuk from קהלת, "Ecclesiastes," which states, טובים השנים מן האחד אשר יש להם שכר טוב בעמלם (קהלת ד,ט), "Two are better than one, because they have a good reward for their toil" (Ecclesiastes 4,9). Many interpretations have been given for this pasuk, but a novel one can be explored based on a Gemara. The Gemara Avodah Zarah states, מכאן א״ר פנחס בן יאיר תורה מביאה לידי זהירות זהירות מביאה לידי זריזות זריזות מביאה לידי נקיות נקיות מביאה לידי פרישות פרישות מביאה לידי טהרה טהרה מביאה לידי קדושה קדושה מביאה לידי ענוה ענוה מביאה לידי יראת חטא יראת חטא מביאה לידי חסידות חסידות מביאה לידי רוח הקודש רוח הקודש מביאה לידי תחיית המתים (עבודה זרה כ:), "From here R. Pinchas B. Jair said, Torah leads to vigilance, vigilance leads to zeal, zeal leads to cleanliness, cleanliness leads to separation, separation leads to purity, purity leads to holiness, holiness leads to humility, humility leads to fear of sin, fear of sin leads to saintliness, saintliness leads to the holy spirit, and the holy spirit leads to revival of the dead" (Avodah Zarah 20b). The gematria of זהירות, "vigilance," is 628.

זהירות   628

The gematria of זריזות, "zeal," is 630.

זריזות   630

The gematria of יראת חטא, "fear of sin," is 629.

יראת   611
חטא   __18__
629

When the Gemara Avodah Zarah is applied to the pasuk in Ecclesiastes, the pasuk might be explained as follows: טובים השנים, "Two are better than one," it is better to go from זהירות, "vigilance," to זריזות, "zeal," which is a move of two, from 628 to 630 in gematrioth; מן האחד, "than one," than to go from זהירות, "vigilance," to יראת חטא, "fear of sin," which is a move of one, from 628 to 629 in gematrioth.

Why is זהירות, "vigilance," seen as a preferable to יראת חטא, "fear of sin?" The Gemara Avodah Zarah previously quoted is explained by Rabbi Moshe Chayim Luzzatto in his sefer, Mesillath Yesharim. He defines זהירות," vigilance," as referring to the negative commandments, and זריזות, "zeal," as referring to the positive commandments, as he writes, כי הזהירות סובב על ה"לא תעשה" והזריזות על ה"עשה" (מסלת ישרים מאת הרב משה חיים לוצאטו, פרק ו), "For vigilance revolves around the negative commandments and zeal around the positive commandments" (Mesillath Yesharim by Rabbi Moshe Chaim Luzzatto, Chapter 6).

Thus, when one goes from זהירות, "vigilance," to זריזות, "zeal," he goes from scrupulousness in observing the negative commandments to scrupulousness in performing the positive commandments. It is better to perform a positive commandment rather than to observe a negative commandment, as the Gemara states, אתי עשה ודחי לא תעשה (יבמות ג:), "a positive commandment comes and pushes aside a negative commandment" (Yebamoth 3b). The Ramban explains the reason why "when a positive commandment occurs it pushes aside a negative commandment." He writes, כי מדת זכור רמזו במצות עשה והוא היוצא ממדת האהבה והוא למדת הרחמים, כי העושה מצות אדוניו אהוב לו ואדוניו מרחם עליו, ומדת שמור במצות לא תעשה, והוא למדת הדין ויוצא ממדת היראה, כי הנשמר מעשות דבר הרע בעיני אדוניו ירא אותו, ולכן מצות עשה גדולה ממצות לא תעשה, כמו שהאהבה גדולה מהיראה, כי המקיים ועושה בגופו ובממונו רצון אדוניו הוא גדול מהנשמר מעשות הרע בעיניו, ולכך אמרו דאתי עשה ודחי לא תעשה

(רמב״ן, שמות כ,ח), "For the attribute of remembering is intimated through the positive commandments, and it emerges
from the attribute of love, and it is associated with the attribute of mercy. For one who performs the commandments of
his master, is beloved by him, and his master will have mercy
on him. And the attribute of watching is through the negative
commandments and it is associated with the attribute of
judgment, and it emerges from the attribute of fear. For one
who watches not to do anything bad in the eyes of his master,
fears him. And therefore the positive commandments are
greater than the negative commandments, just as love is
greater than fear. For one who maintains and performs with
his body and his money the will of his master is greater than
one who watches from doing the bad in his eyes. And therefore, they have said, when a positive commandment occurs
it pushes aside a negative commandment" (Ramban, Exodus
20, 8).

The fear about which the Ramban writes is one of the
types of יראת חטא, "fear of sin." The Mesillath Yesharim identifies two types of fear of sin: They are יראת העונש, "fear of
punishment," and יראת הרוממות, "fear of His Majesty." The
first type of fear is the more basic type which most anyone
can attain, as he writes, יראת העונש כפשוטה, שאדם יירא מעבור את
פי ה' אלקיו, מפני העונשים אשר לעברות, אם לגוף ואם לנפש. והנה זאת
קלה ודאי, כי כל אדם אוהב את עצמו וירא לנפשו. ואין דבר שירחיק אותו
מעשות דבר אחד יותר מן היראה, שלא תבואהו בו איזה רעה. ואין יראה זו
ראויה אלא לעמי הארץ ולנשים אשר דעתן קלה, אך אינה יראת החכמים
ואנשי הדעת (מסלת ישרים מאת הרב משה חיים לוצאטו, פרק כד), "Fear
of punishment, according to its simple meaning, is that a man
fears to transgress the word of Hashem, his G-d, because of
the punishment for such transgression, whether it be to the
body or to the soul. And surely this [fear] is easily [achieved],
for every man loves himself and fears for his soul. And there
is nothing which will keep him further from doing something,

more than the fear, that something bad should befall him. However, this type of fear is only fit for the ignorant and women, who are fickle minded, but it is not the fear of the wise men and the sagacious" (Mesillath Yesharim by Rabbi Moshe Chaim Luzzatto, Chapter 24).

This basic type of fear can be associated with the fear to which the Ramban refers: a fear which corresponds to the observance of the negative commandments. The term יראת חטא, "fear of sin," can be defined as this basic type of fear.

It is also the intention of Pinchas B. Jair to portray יראת חטא, "fear of sin," as a higher spiritual plateau than both זהירות, "vigilance," and זריזות, "zeal." However, that fear of sin is for the wise and the sagacious; it is the second type of fear of sin. The Mesillath Yesharim writes, המין השני הוא יראת הרוממות, והוא שהאדם ירחק מן החטאים ולא יעשם מפני כבודו הגדול יתברך שמו.... זאת היראה שאנחנו בבאורה עתה, דהיינו יראת החטא, היא כמו חלק מיראת הרוממות זכרנו, וכמו מין בפני עצמו (מסלת ישרים מאת הרב משה חיים לוצאטו, פרק כד), "The second type is fear of His Majesty, and it brings about that a man will keep far from sins, and not do them, because of the great honor of the Blessed One's Name... This fear which we are clarifying now, that is fear of sin, it is part of fear of His Majesty which we mentioned, and it is like a category in itself" (Mesillath Yesharim by Rabbi Moshe Chaim Luzzatto, Chapter 24). But fear of sin can also be defined as the basic fear which was quoted from the Mesillath Yesharim; this fear of sin is not on a higher spiritual plateau than זריזות, "zeal."

Now it can be understood why זריזות, "zeal," is seen as preferable to יראת חטא, "fear of sin." The former refers to the positive commandments, and the latter to the fear which corresponds to the observance of the negative command-ments. Since אתי עשה ודחי לא תעשה, "when a positive com-mandment occurs it pushes aside a negative command-ment," therefore, זריזות, "zeal," is preferable to יראת חטא, "fear of sin."

There is an additional point that can be derived from the Gemara Yebamoth. Kilayim refers to certain diverse kinds that are together; shaatnez refers specifically to clothing that has wool and linen intermingled together. The Gemara learns אתי עשה ודחי לא תעשה, "a positive commandment comes and pushes aside a negative commandment," from the juxtaposition of the mitzvoth of שעטנז, "shaatnez," and ציצית, "tsitsith," in the Torah. Rashi in the Gemara states, לא תלבש שעטנז. וסמיך ליה גדילים תעשה לך ודרשינן סמוכין ושרינן כלאים בציצית אלמא אתי עשה ודחי לא תעשה (רש"י, יבמות ד., ד"יה לא תלבש שעטנז), "You shall not wear shaatnez. And adjacent to it is stated, 'Fringes you shall make for yourself.' And we expound the adjacency, and allow tsitsith made from kilayim. Thus, a positive commandment comes and pushes aside a negative commandment" (Rashi, Yebamoth 4a, header words: You shall not wear shaatnez). Thus, the Gemara learns that when a positive commandment occurs it usually pushes aside a negative commandment, as one is allowed to wear tsitsith made from kilayim: meaning the mitzvah of shaatnez is pushed aside for the mitzvah of tsitsith.

The Gemara Menahoth says that the mitzvah of tsitsith is equivalent to all the mitzvoth, as stated, תניא אידך וראיתם אותו וזכרתם את כל מצות ה' שקולה מצוה זו כנגד כל המצות כולם (מנחות מג:), "And another Baraitha taught, 'And you shall see it and remember all of the commandments of G-d.' This commandment is equivalent to all the mitzvoth entirely" (Menahoth 43b). However, if one wears tsitsith made from kilayim, the mitzvah of shaatnez is pushed aside, then the mitzvah of tsitsith is equivalent to 612 mitzvoth; the sum of all the commandments, 613, minus the mitzvah of shaatnez, equals 612 (מכות כג:, Makkoth 23b).

What is the reward for doing a mitzvah? One of the rewards for doing a mitzvah is another mitzvah, as stated, ששכר מצוה מצוה (אבות, פרק ד משנה ב), "That the reward for a mitzvah is a mitzvah" (Avoth, Chapter 4, Mishnah 2). There-fore, it follows, that if one wears tsitsith made from kilayim, which is equal to 612 mitzvoth, he has the reward of gaining 612 mitzvoth. Recall the initially quoted pasuk from קהלת, "Ecclesiastes," which states, טובים השנים מן האחד אשר יש להם שכר טוב בעמלם (קהלת ד,ט), "Two are better than one, because they have a good reward for their toil" (Ecclesiastes 4,9). The gematria of להם שכר טוב, "they have a good reward," is 612.

להם	75
שכר	520
טוב	17
	612

What is the reward in the preceding case, of one who wears tsitsith made from kilayim, that is, for doing a positive commandment which pushes aside a negative command-ment? The reward is 612 mitzvoth, as was shown. This re-ward could be what the pasuk means in saying, להם שכר טוב, "they have a good reward," whose gematria is 612; the reward is the gaining of 612 other mitzvoth; as in the case of one who wears tsitsith made from kilayim, there is a good reward of gaining 612 mitzvoth. If one had observed the negative commandment he would only have the reward of one mitzvah.

Please note that the pasuk ends יש להם שכר טוב בעמלם, "they have a good reward for their toil." The word toil indi-cates doing, as performing a positive commandment, a very befitting closing for a pasuk that communicates the idea, when appropriate, to perform a positive mitzvah rather than observe a negative mitzvah.

Now when the Gemara Avodah Zarah is applied to the pasuk in Ecclesiastes, the pasuk can be explained as follows:

טובים השנים, "Two are better than one," it is better to go from זהירות," vigilance," to זריזות "zeal," which is a move of two, from 628 to 630 in gematrioth; מן האחד, "than one," than to go from זהירות, "vigilance," to יראת חטא," fear of sin," which is a move of one, from 628 to 629 in gematrioth; for the former represents the positive mitzvoth and the latter to the fear which corresponds to the observing the negative mitzvoth.

אשר יש להם שכר טוב בעמלם, "because they have a good reward for their toil"; the performing of a positive mitzvah and the pushing aside a negative mitzvah, which is derived from the case of one who wears tsitsith made from kilayim, has a reward of 612 mitzvoth. The gematria of להם שכר טוב, "they have a good reward," is 612; בעמלם, "in their toil," when one performs a positive mitzvah.

Additional significance to the difference between זהירות, "vigilance," and זריזות, "zeal," can be found in the חג הפסח, The Passover Holiday, section of this sefer.

The Passover Holiday   חג הפסח

הא לחמא עניא די אכלו אבהתנא בארעא דמצרים (הגדה
של פסח).
This is the bread of affliction which our fathers
ate in the land of Egypt (Passover Haggadah).

There are various reasons offered for the mitzvah of eating matzoth on Passover. The Torah says that when the Children of Israel left Egypt their dough did not have time to leaven (שמות יב,לט, Exodus 12,39). But in addition to that reason, the Passover Haggadah says that our forefathers ate matzoth while in Egypt. Rashi calculates that the Children of Israel were in Egypt for a total of 210 years (רש״י, בראשית טו,יג, Rashi, Genesis 15,13). Although the matzoth were given as food to slaves, and slavery did not begin immediately, still the Children of Israel in Egypt could have eaten matzoth during the entire 210 years.

The מגיד, "Recitation," section of the Haggadah begins with an Aramaic expression pertaining to matzoth, as stated, הא לחמא עניא, "This is the bread of affliction." The gematria of לחמא עניא, "bread of affliction," is 210.

לחמא	79
עניא	<u>131</u>
	210

Although the paragraph ends in Hebrew, why is this expression written in Aramaic and not in Hebrew? Possibly, the Haggadah chose to use the Aramaic expression for matzoth since its gematria equals the number of years the Children of Israel could have eaten matzoth in Egypt.

אמר רבי אלעזר בן עזריה, הרי אני כבן שבעים שנה, ולא
זכיתי שתאמר יציאת מצרים בלילות (ברכות, פרק א,
משנה ה).

Rabbi Eleazar ben Azariah said, "Behold I am
like a seventy-year-old, and I have not merited
that the departure out of Egypt ought to be said
at nights" (Berakoth, Chapter 1, Mishnah 5).

In the third paragraph after the four questions, the
הגדה של פסח, the Passover Haggadah, quotes the Mishnah in
מסכת ברכות, Tractate Berakoth, where Rabbi Eleazar ben Azariah says, "Behold I am like a seventy-year-old." Why did
Rabbi Eleazar ben Azariah say, "I am like a seventy-year-
old"? He could have just said, "I am seventy years old," or "I
am not seventy years old," but rather I am some other age.

The last Mishnah in the third chapter of מסכת ידים,
Tractate Yadayim, and the first four Mishnayoth of the fourth
chapter list five rulings which were decided on the day Rabbi
Eleazar ben Azariah was appointed the head of the yeshiva in
Yavneh. But in all five Mishnayoth, Rabbi Eleazar ben Azariah
only once gives his own opinion. That Mishnah, the third
Mishnah of the fourth chapter, discusses if there is an obligation to give מעשר עני, "poor man's tithe," or מעשר שני, "second
tithe," in the lands of עמון ומואב, Ammon and Moab, during the
שמיטה, "Shemittah," the Sabbatical year. Rabbi Tarfon says
that the obligation is to give מעשר עני, "poor man's tithe";
Rabbi Eleazar ben Azariah says that the obligation is to give
מעשר שני, "second tithe." Rabbi Joshua presents a convincing
argument for Rabbi Tarfon's view, as stated, מצרים מעשה חדש,
ובבל מעשה ישן. והנדון שלפנינו מעשה חדש, ידון מעשה חדש ממעשה חדש,
ואל ידון מעשה חדש ממעשה ישן. מצרים מעשה זקנים, ובבל מעשה נביאים,
והנדון שלפנינו מעשה זקנים, ידון מעשה זקנים ממעשה זקנים, ואל ידון
מעשה זקנים ממעשה נביאים. נמנו וגמרו עמון ומואב מעשרים מעשר עני
בשביעית. וכשבא רבי יוסי בן דורמסקית אצל רבי אליעזר בלד... אמר לו,
נמנו וגמרו, עמון ומואב מעשרים מעשר עני בשביעית. בכה רבי אליעזר

ואמר, סוד ה' ליראיו ובריתו להודיעם (תהלים כה,יד) (ידים פרק ד משנה ג), "The obligation of tithes in Egypt is a new institution, and the obligation in Babylon is an old institution. And the subject under discussion is a new institution; a new institution should be decided from a new institution, and let not a new institution be decided from an old institution. The obligation of tithes in Egypt is an institution of elders, and the obligation in Babylon is an institution of prophets. And the subject under discussion is an institution of elders; an institution of elders should be decided from an institution of elders, and let not an institution of elders be decided from an institution of prophets. They took a count and concluded that those in Ammon and Moab are obligated to tithe a poor man's tithe in the Seventh year, the Sabbatical year. And when Rabbi Jose ben Durmaskith came to Rabbi Eliezer in Lod ... he said to him, 'They took a count and concluded that those in Ammon and Moab are obligated to tithe a poor man's tithe in the Seventh year, the Sabbatical year.' Rabbi Eliezer wept and said, 'G-d's secret is for those who fear Him, and His covenant to make them know it'" (Psalms 25,14) (Yadayim, Chapter 4, Mishnah 3). The gematria of ידון, "should be decided," is 70.

ידון   70

The gematria of סוד, "secret," is 70.

סוד   70

     Since Rabbi Joshua said that the instituting of tithes ידון, "should be decided," from a new institution, it was decided that those in Ammon and Moab are obligated to tithe the poor man's tithe in the Shemittah, the Sabbatical year. This decision was referred to as a סוד, "secret,"

     Now Rabbi Eleazar ben Azariah's statement from the Passover Haggadah can be explained. While the word שנה can mean year, it can also be read as the third person past tense of the verb לשנות, to learn. Thus, the word שנה in the Passover

Haggadah, can mean "learned," as opposed to "year." Rabbi Eleazar ben Azariah said that behold it is as if he could have learned seventy; for the words ידון, "should be decided," and סוד, "secret," each has a gematria of seventy. One word refers to how it was concluded (by vote), and the other word refers to the conclusion itself, that there is an obligation to give the poor man's tithe in the Shemittah, for those in the lands of Ammon and Moab. The decision was according to the opinion of Rabbi Tarfon. So Rabbi Eleazar ben Azariah said that it is as if he could have learned seventy; for although the decision was not according to his view, it was decided on the day he was appointed ריש מתיבתא, "head of the yeshiva." It was as if he learned seventy.

Of the five Mishnayoth mentioned in מסכת ידים, Tractate Yadayim, this one is the only one in which Rabbi Eleazar ben Azariah gives his opinion. It is possible that he agreed or disagreed with the opinions mentioned in the other four Mishnayoth. Nevertheless, it is indisputable that he disagreed with Rabbi Tarfon's view, since he himself argues against that view. Therefore, in this particular Mishnah, he says that it is as if he learned seventy.

Since it was concluded, that there is an obligation to give the poor man's tithe in the Shemittah, for those in the lands of Ammon and Moab, the conclusion was not according to the view of Rabbi Eleazar ben Azariah. So when Rabbi Eleazar ben Azariah said, "I have not merited that the departure out of Egypt ought to be said at nights," the reason could be because the decision about the lands of Ammon and Moab was not according to his opinion. Although these are different issues, since one הלכה, halakhah, "decided law," was decided against him, people could have suspected that the decisions about saying the departure from Egypt at night would also be decided not according to his opinion.

אמר רבי אלעזר בן עזריה, הרי אני כבן שבעים שנה, ולא זכיתי שתאמר יציאת מצרים בלילות (ברכות, פרק א, משנה ה).

Rabbi Eleazar ben Azariah said, "Behold I am like a seventy-year-old, and I have not merited that the departure out of Egypt ought to be said at nights" (Berakoth, Chapter 1, Mishnah 5).

In the third paragraph after the four questions, the הגדה של פסח, the Passover Haggadah, quotes the Mishnah in מסכת ברכות, Tractate Berakoth, where Rabbi Eleazar ben Azariah says, "Behold I am like a seventy-year-old." Why did Rabbi Eleazar ben Azariah say "I am like a seventy-year-old?" Just say, "I am seventy-years-old," or I am not seventy years old, but some other age. Of course the answer given in Gemara Berakoth is that he was really only eighteen years old, but when he was appointed ריש מתיבתא, "head of the yeshiva," his hair turned white so he would be accorded due respect (ברכות כח., Berakoth 28a). Note that Rashi says that he was appointed נשיא, "Nasi," (רש״י, ברכות יב:, ד״ה כבן שבעים שנה, Rashi, Berakoth 12b, header words: Like a seventy year old). However, that answer does not explain why here Rabbi Eleazar ben Azariah mentions his age, and not in other places where he is quoted.

A second question is why was Rabbi Eleazar ben Azariah's view not accepted? If he said that the departure out of Egypt ought to be said at nights, then he should have merited to have it said in his name.

The answer to both questions can be given from a Gemara in מסכת מגילה, Tractate Megillah. The Gemara asks, why does the Mishnah say, דבר שמצותו בלילה כשר כל הלילה, "That which is a commandment to be observed at night, it is valid throughout the night"? The Gemara answers that this phrase was inserted to exclude the opinion of Rabbi Eleazar ben Azariah, who said the korban pesach should only be eaten until midnight. The Tosafoth while coming to a determination about the הלכה, "decided law," the Halakhah, phrases Rabbi Eleazar ben Azariah's opinion about the korban pesach as an obligation to eat it קודם חצות, "before midnight," (תוספות, מגילה כא., ד״ה לאתויי אכילת פסחים ודלא כרבי) אלעזר ב״ע, Tosafoth, Megillah 21a, header words: To include the eating of the pesachim and not like Rabbi Eleazar ben Azariah). The gematria of קודם, "before," is 150.

קודם   150

The phrase from the Mishnah which is quoted by the Gemara says דבר שמצותו בלילה כשר כל הלילה, "That which is a commandment to be observed at night, it is valid throughout the night." The gematria of הלילה, "the night," is 80.

הלילה   80

This word הלילה, "the night," refers to the entire night. The difference between the gematria of קודם, "before," and the gematria of הלילה, "the night," is 70.

150
-80
___
70

Rabbi Eleazar ben Azariah's use of the word שנה, shanah, most often meaning "year," in fact has a second meaning. While the word שנה can mean year, it can also be read as the third person past tense of the verb לשנות, "to learn." Thus, the word שנה in the Passover Haggadah, can mean "learned," as opposed to "year."

Now the two questions which were posed can be answered. The first question was, why did Rabbi Eleazar ben Azariah say, "Behold I am like one seventy years old?" Since he learns that the korban pesach should be eaten קודם, "before," midnight, but the Mishnah uses the word הלילה, "the night," to refer to eating the entire night, therefore he said it is as if I learned seventy, for the difference in the gematria of קודם, "before," and the gematria of הלילה, "the night," is seventy.

Rabbi Eleazar ben Azariah never said the number seventy, but it is as if he learned it, for the difference in the two gematrioth is equal to seventy. He only mentioned seventy here, because in Gemara Berakoth he is referring to the commandment to mention the going forth from Egypt, which relates to the korban pesach, and in Gemara Megillah he is also referring to the korban pesach. Thus, when referring to the korban pesach in Gemara Berakoth he mentions the "seventy" difference in gematrioth from Gemara Megillah where the korban pesach was referenced. The first question has been answered.

The second question was, why was Rabbi Eleazar ben Azariah's view not accepted? The answer may be that the Gemara in Tractate Megillah says that the Mishnah inserted a phrase to exclude the opinion of Rabbi Eleazar ben Azariah. It could be that since the Mishnah went to such exertion to exclude his opinion, therefore he said he had not merited to have said in his name that the departure out of Egypt should be said at night. The second question has been answered.

אמר רבי אלעזר בן עזריה, הרי אני כבן שבעים שנה, ולא זכיתי שתאמר יציאת מצרים בלילות (ברכות, פרק א, משנה ה).

Rabbi Eleazar ben Azariah said, "Behold I am like a seventy-year-old, and I have not merited that the departure out of Egypt ought to be said at nights" (Berakoth, Chapter 1, Mishnah 5).

The הגדה של פסח, Passover Haggadah, in the third paragraph after the four questions, quotes the Mishnah in מסכת ברכות, Tractate Berakoth, where Rabbi Eleazar ben Azariah says, "Behold I am like a seventy-year-old." Two questions can be asked. One, why did Rabbi Eleazar ben Azariah say, "I am like a seventy-year-old?" He could have just said his age; what is the significance of the word "like"? Two, when he said, "I have not merited, that the departure out of Egypt ought to be said at nights," why did he feel his opinion was not accepted?

A possible answer to these questions can be based on the Gemara which says, ואף הוא פתח ודרש דברי חכמים כדרבונות וכמסמרות נטועים בעלי אסופות נתנו מרועה אחד (קהלת יב,יא). למה נמשלו דברי תורה לדרבן לומר לך מה דרבן זה מכוין את הפרה לתלמיה להוציא חיים לעולם אף דברי תורה מכוונין את לומדיהן מדרכי מיתה לדרכי חיים (חגיגה ג:), "And he [Rabbi Eleazar ben Azariah or Rabbi Joshua] also commenced and elucidated, 'The words of the sages are like goads, and like nails well secured, are the words of the masters of assemblies; they are given from one shepherd' (Ecclesiastes 12,11). Why are words of Torah compared to a goad? To teach you, just as this goad guides the cow to its furrows to bring out life to the world, also words of Torah guide those who learn them, from the ways of death to the ways of life" (Hagigah 3b). The gematria of כדרבונות, "like goads," is 688.

כדרבונות   688

The gematria of לדרבן, "to a goad," is 286.

לדרבן   286

The gematria of לדרכי חיים, "to the ways of life," is 332.

לדרכי   264
חיים   68
          332

The combined gematria of לדרבן, "to a goad," and לדרכי חיים, "to the ways of life," is 618.

286
332
618

The word כדרבונות, "like goads," is quoted from a source in כתובים, "Writings," (קהלת יב,יא, Ecclesiastes 12,11); it is from this word that the Gemara elucidates that the words of Torah are compared לדרבן, "to a goad," which guides those who learn them לדרכי חיים, "to the ways of life." The difference between the gematria of the source word כדרבונות, "like goads," and the gematrioth of the words which the Gemara uses to compare words of Torah, לדרבן, "to a goad," and לדרכי חיים, "to the ways of life," is 70.

$$\begin{array}{r} 688 \\ -618 \\ \hline 70 \end{array}$$

Who did say this Gemara? Usually the Gemara is very meticulous to record who said every piece; however here the Gemara only says ואף הוא פתח ודרש, "And he also commenced and elucidated." According to Rashi the speaker is Rabbi Eleazar ben Azariah. Now the first question can be answered. While the word שנה can mean "year," it can also be read as the third person past tense of the verb לשנות, "to learn." Thus, the word שנה in the Passover Haggadah, could mean learned, as opposed to year. In which case Rabbi Eleazar ben Azariah would have been saying, "It is as if I learned seventy [For I learned from the source word כדרבונות, 'like goads,' that words of Torah are compared לדרבן, 'to a goad,' which guide those who learn them לדרכי חיים, 'to the ways of life.' The difference between the gematria of the source word כדרבונות, 'like goads,' and the gematrioth of the three other words used to elucidate the guiding power of words of Torah is 70]." Albeit Rabbi Eleazar ben Azariah never actually expressed the number 70 in this Gemara, it is as if, like, he learned 70, for the difference between the words mentioned in gematrioth is 70. This difference could be the reason for the significance of the word "like." The first question has been answered.

As mentioned, the Gemara is very meticulous to record who said every piece, but here in Gemara Hagigah the speaker is not mentioned. In the Mishnah Berakoth, Rabbi Eleazar ben Azariah said, "I have not merited that the exodus from Egypt should be said at night." It is conceivable, since the Gemara Hagigah did not mention Rabbi Eleazar ben Azariah by name, therefore in the Mishnah Berakoth he said, I have not merited that the exodus from Egypt should be said at night. The second question has been answered.

There is a connection between the Gemara Hagigah and the exodus from Egypt. Rabbi Eleazar ben Azariah says that words of Torah guide those who learn them לדרכי חיים, "to the ways of life." In משלי, Proverbs, there is a pasuk which defines דרכי חיים, "the ways of life,"as stated, כי נר מצוה ותורה אור ודרך חיים תוכחות מוסר (משלי ו,כג), "For the commandment is a lamp, and the Torah is light, and instructional rebukes are the way of life" (Proverbs 6,23). The Malbim on this pasuk explains that the instruction which leads to the ways of life is יראת ה', "fear of G-d," as stated, אולם המוסר שבסי' זה הוא יראת ה' כמ"ש יראת ה' מוסר חכמה וכמ"ש למעלה (א,ז) וע"י יראת ה' יתוכח אח"כ בראיות השכל ויקבל חקי החכמה מצד השכל וילך בדרך חיים (מוסר חכמה, באור המלות, מאת הרב מאיר ליבוש מלבים, משלי ו,כג) "However, the instruction in this book is fear of G-d, just as it is stated, fear of G-d is instructional wisdom. And just as it is stated above (1,7), And through fear of G-d he will be rebuked. Afterwards the intellect perceives and he will accept the statutes of wisdom intellectually and will go on the way of life" (Musar Chochmah, Be'ur Hamiloth by Rabbi Meir Lebush Malbim, Proverbs 6,23).

From the Malbim just quoted, it is clear that the instruction which leads to the way of life, is fear of G-d. One of the principal consequences of the exodus from Egypt was fear of G-d, as stated, וירא ישראל את היד הגדלה אשר עשה ה' במצרים וייראו העם את ה' ויאמינו בה' ובמשה עבדו (שמות יד,לא), "And

Israel saw the great hand which G-d used against the Egyptians, and the people feared G-d, and they believed in G-d and in Moses His servant" (Exodus 14,31). A similar thought is found in Parashath Vaethchannan (דברים ו,כא-כד, Deuteronomy 6,21-24).

In the Mishnah Berakoth, Rabbi Eleazar ben Azariah said, "I am like a seventy-year-old, and I have not merited that the exodus from Egypt should be said at night." In the Gemara Hagigah, Rabbi Eleazar ben Azariah is quoted (by Rashi) to have said said, that words of Torah guide those who learn them, to the way of life. From this latter Gemara, there is a gematria of seventy. From the Malbim on the pasuk from Proverbs, it is clear that the instruction which leads to the way of life is fear of G-d. One of the principal consequences of the exodus from Egypt was fear of G-d. It is tempting to speculate why Rabbi Eleazar ben Azariah remarked, "I have not merited that the exodus from Egypt should be said at night." For he said that words of Torah guide those who learn them to the way of life, and the instruction which leads to the way of life is fear of G-d. This fear was one of the principal consequences of the exodus from Egypt. What Rabbi Eleazar ben Azariah said in the Gemara Hagigah, would have the same consequence as the exodus from Egypt, that is: fear of G-d. Consequently what he said is very suitable to be said on the night of the seder.

אמר רבי אלעזר בן עזריה, הרי אני כבן שבעים שנה, ולא זכיתי שתאמר יציאת מצרים בלילות (ברכות, פרק א, משנה ה).

Rabbi Eleazar ben Azariah said, "Behold I am like a seventy-year-old, and I have not merited that the departure out of Egypt ought to be said at nights" (Berakoth, Chapter 1, Mishnah 5).

The הגדה של פסח, Passover Haggadah, in the third

paragraph after the four questions, quotes the Mishnah in מסכת ברכות, Tractate Berakoth, where Rabbi Eleazar ben Azariah says, "Behold I am like a seventy-year-old." Why did Rabbi Eleazar ben Azariah say, "I am like a seventy-year-old?" Just say, "I am seventy years old," or I am not seventy years old, but some other age. There are many answers; an additional one could give a different perspective.

Rabbi Eleazar ben Azariah's use of the word שנה, shanah, most often meaning "year," in fact has a second meaning. It can also be read as the third person past tense of the verb לשנות, "to learn." Thus, the word שנה in the Passover Haggadah, can mean "learned," as opposed to "year." Rabbi Eleazar ben Azariah in a Mishnah in Tractate Kelim says that if one plugged a wooden or an earthen funnel with pitch, it is טמא, "ritually defiled" (capable of contracting defilement); Rabbi Akiva says it is only ritually defiled if the funnel is made of wood. The Mishnah states, משפך של עץ ושל חרס שפקקו בזפת רבי אליעזר בן עזריה מטמא, רבי עקיבא מטמא בשל עץ ומטהר בשל חרס (כלים פרק ג משנה ח), "A funnel of wood or earthenware which was plugged with pitch, Rabbi Eleazar ben Azariah declares it ritually defiled. Rabbi Akiva declares it ritually defiled if it is made of wood, but declares it undefined if it is made of earthenware," (Kelim, Chapter 3, Mishnah 8). The gematria of מטמא, "ritually defiled," is 90.

מטמא   90

The gematria of עץ, "wood," is 160.

עץ   160

The difference between the gematria of מטמא, "ritually defiled," and the gematria of עץ, "wood," is 70.

160
-90
——
70

So, Rabbi Eleazar ben Azariah said, I could have

learned seventy, for I declared מטמא, "ritually defiled," with a gematria of 90, but Rabbi Akiva only declared it מטמא, "ritually defiled," if the funnel is made of עץ, "wood," with a gematria of 160. Since the difference in gematrioth is 70, Rabbi Eleazar ben Azariah could be saying that he could have learned like seventy, for the difference in gematrioth is seventy. That is, he is not saying that he could have learned the actual number 70, but he could have learned like seventy, for the difference between his opinion and that of Rabbi Akiva is 70 in gematrioth.

Please be aware that this explanation does not mean to imply that Rabbi Eleazar ben Azariah wanted to change his opinion. He is merely commenting about his opinion relative to that of Rabbi Akiva. In the above case, the הלכה, "decided law," the Halakhah, follows the opinion of Rabbi Akiva (ר״ע מברטנורה, כלים פרק ג משנה ח, ד״ה רבי יוסי מטהר בשניהם, Rabbi Ovadiah Bertinoro, Kelim, Chapter 3, Mishnah 8, header words: Rabbi Jose declares both unsusceptible to defilement). It is reasonable, that since the Halakhah is not like Rabbi Eleazar ben Azariah in the Mishnah in Tractate Kelim, in the Mishnah in מסכת ברכות, Tractate Berakoth, he says, "I have not merited to have convinced the sages that the exodus from Egypt should be said at night." Now it is easy to appreciate why Rabbi Eleazar ben Azariah said, "Behold I am like a seventy," and why he immediately said afterwards, "I have not merited that the Exodus ought to be said at nights."

אמר רבי אלעזר בן עזריה, הרי אני כבן שבעים שנה, ולא זכיתי שתאמר יציאת מצרים בלילות (ברכות, פרק א, משנה ה).

Rabbi Eleazar ben Azariah said, "Behold I am like a seventy-year-old, and I have not merited that the departure out of Egypt ought to be said at nights" (Berakoth, Chapter 1, Mishnah 5).

The הגדה של פסח, Passover Haggadah, in the third

paragraph after the four questions, quotes the Mishnah in מסכת ברכות, Tracate Berakoth, where Rabbi Eleazar ben Aza-riah says, "Behold I am like a seventy-year-old." A first question is, why did Rabbi Eleazar ben Azariah say that he is like a seventy-year-old, rather than simply saying he is seventy years old? A second question is, why did Rabbi Eleazar ben Azariah seem to mention his age at all, saying that he is like a seventy-year-old? The Gemara says that he was really only eighteen years old, but a miracle occurred and his beard turned white (ברכות כח., Berakoth 28a). Note that Rashi says that he was appointed נשיא, "Nasi," (ד"ה כבן, רש"י, ברכות יב:, שבעים שנה, Rashi, Berakoth 12b, header words: Like a seventy year old). But why does Rabbi Eleazar ben Azariah seem to allude to this miracle; he surely was not bragging? A third and last question is, in numerous other places Rabbi Eleazar ben Azariah is quoted in the Mishnah, but only in this one Mishnah (which the Passover Haggadah quotes), does he say, he is like a seventy-year-old. Why is this quote about his age associated with the seder night?

There are many answers to these questions, but with the understanding of a gematria a fresh interpretation can be suggested. The last Mishnah in the fifth chapter of מסכת שבת, Tractate Shabbath, says פרתו של רבי אלעזר בן עזריה היתה יוצאה "The cow ברצועה שבין קרניה שלא ברצון חכמים (שבת, פרק ה, משנה ד) of Rabbi Eleazar ben Azariah would go out [on Shabbath] with a thong between her horns, without the approval of the sages" (Shabbath, Chapter 5, Mishnah 4). The Gemara elab-orating on this Mishnah says, לא שלו היתה אלא של שכינתו היתה it was his neighbor's, and because he did not protest about it, ומתוך שלא מיחה בה נקראת על שמו (שבת נד:) "It was not his, but it is called with his name" (Shabbath 54b). The gematria of מיחה בה, "protest about it," is 70.

מיחה	63
בה	7
	70

Normally, if one has a neighbor who did something wrong, the blame would be placed on the wrongdoer, not on the wrongdoer's neighbor. The obligation of הוכח תוכיח, "You shall surely rebuke," (depending on the situation) is upon every Jew, regardless of his spiritual level. However, great people are held to a higher standard than others. When one is of the high spiritual status of Rabbi Eleazar ben Azariah, then he is blamed if his neighbor did something wrong but he did not protest. Such a person would be called, על פי הדרש, "in the way of a homily," a בן מיחה בה, "one who is expected to protest."

The word בן, in Hebrew does not necessarily mean son of, or age; it can also designate one who possesses a particular trait. There are several examples which prove the point. A free man is called בן חורין, "a son of freedom" (אבות, פרק ו, משנה ב, Avoth, Chapter 6, Mishnah 2). A sensible person is called בן דעת, "a son of wisdom" (בבא מציעא ח., Baba Mezia 8a). One who is privileged to a portion in the world to come is called בן העולם הבא, "son of the world to come" (שבת קנג., Shabbath 153a). One who has knowledge of Torah is called בן תורה, "son of Torah" (תלמוד ירושלמי, תענית פרק ד, הלכה א, וילקוט שמעוני, חבקוק סימן תקס"ב, אות ב, Yerushalmi Gemara, Taanith, Chapter 4, Halakhah 1, and Yalkut Shimoni, Habakkuk, Siman 562, Letter 2). Similarly, when one is on such a high spiritual status that he is expected to protest, he would be called בן מיחה בה, "one who is expected to protest." Which could be the meaning of, "Behold I am like a seventy-year-old."

In Hebrew the word שנה, "year," does not have to mean year; when used as a verb it can also mean taught (יבמות קח:, Yebamoth 108b). So in the Passover Haggadah when Rabbi Eleazar ben Azariah says, "Behold I am like a seventy year old," it could be translated that he said, "It was taught I am like one of seventy." He said that it was taught that he is like one מיחה בה, "who is expected to protest," since the gematria of מיחה בה, "expected to protest," is 70. He was saying that it was taught that he is like one on such a high spiritual status that he was expected to protest the wrongdoing of his neighbor.

Even though Rabbi Eleazar ben Azariah conceded that he was worthy of being blamed for the wrongdoing of his neighbor, he did not merit the credit for saying that the narration of the going out of Egypt should be said at night. It is possible that he reasoned that since it was taught that he was on a spiritual level of one who is מיחה בה, "one who is expected to protest," but did not, thus he did not merit the credit for saying that the narration of the going out of Egypt should be said at night. It is also possible that he did not believe that he was on a spiritual level of one who is מיחה בה, "one who is expected to protest." Thus, he said that he is only like one of 70; he is only like one who is expected to מיחה בה, "to protest."

The three questions asked earlier have now been answered. It has been explained why specifically here does Rabbi Eleazar ben Azariah say, "Behold I am like a seventy-year-old." It has also been explained why he seems to mention his age, saying, "I am like a seventy-year-old." It has also been explained why this quote about his age is associated with the seder night. Thus, with the understanding of a gematria, the three questions have been answered.

אמר רבי אלעזר בן עזריה, הרי אני כבן שבעים שנה, ולא זכיתי שתאמר יציאת מצרים בלילות (ברכות, פרק א, משנה ה).

Rabbi Eleazar ben Azariah said, "Behold I am like a seventy-year-old, and I have not merited that the departure out of Egypt ought to be said at nights" (Berakoth, Chapter 1, Mishnah 5).

The הגדה של פסח, Passover Haggadah, in the third paragraph after the four questions, quotes the Mishnah in מסכת ברכות, Tractate Berakoth, where Rabbi Eleazar ben Azariah says, "Behold I am like a seventy-year-old." Two questions can be asked. Why did Rabbi Eleazar ben Azariah say, "I am like a seventy-year-old," just say, "I am seventy years old," or I am not seventy years old, but a different age? Another question is, why in this particular Mishnah in Tractate Berakoth did Rabbi Eleazar ben Azariah say, "I am like a seventy-year-old"? He is mentioned in many places in the Mishnayoth, but only in this particular Mishnah did he say, "I am like a seventy-year-old." Although there are several answers, the approach to be presented is novel.

Both questions can be answered with an understanding of a Gemara in מסכת בבא מציעא, Tractate Baba Mezia. A proper Jewish marriage consists of two parts: the betrothal, know as erusin, and the actual marriage, known as nesuin; after the latter, the bride enters her husband's home. The Gemara says, א״יל מר קשישא בריה דרב חסדא לרב אשי ואלמנה מן האירוסין דאית לה כתובה מנא לן אילימא מהא דתנן נתארמלה או נתגרשה בין מן האירוסין ובין מן הנישואין גובה את הכל דלמא היכא דכתב לה וכי תימא מאי למימרא לאפוקי מדברי אלעזר בן עזריה דאמר שלא כתב לה אלא על מנת לכונסה אצטריכא ליה (בבא מציעא יז:), "Mar Kashisha, the son of Rav Hisda said to Rav Ashi, And from where do we know that a widow from the erusin receives her [even if unwritten] kethubah? If I were to say [it is known] from that which we have learned [in a mishnah]: A woman who became a widow or a divorcee, whether from the erusin or from the nesuin collects everything (כתובות פרק ה משנה א, Kethuboth Chapter 5, Mishnah 1). Maybe the Mishnah refers to a case where the husband wrote [a kethubah] for her. And if you will say why was it necessary to say? It is necessary to exclude the opinion of Rabbi Eleazar ben Azariah, for he said a man only wrote [a kethubah] for her on the condition to have her enter nesuin; [thus] it is necessary [to say]" (Baba Mezia 17b). The gematria of הנישואין, "the nesuin," is 432.

הנישואין   432

The gematria of לכונסה אצטריכא, "to have her enter; it is necessary," is 502.

לכונסה   171
אצטריכא   <u>331</u>
         502

The difference between the gematria of הנישואין, "the nesuin," and the gematria of לכונסה אצטריכא, "to have her enter; it is necessary," is 70.

$$502$$
$$-432$$
$$\overline{70}$$

In Hebrew the word שנה, does not have to be translated as year; as a verb, it can be translated as taught or learn (יבמות קח:, Yebamoth 108b). Note that Rabbi Eleazar ben Azariah taught לכונסה, "to have her enter"; the Gemara said, regarding this opinion: אצטריכא, "it is necessary." This difference in who said which word, could be the reason Rabbi Eleazar ben Azariah said, אני כבן שבעים שנה "I am like one who taught seventy"; for he only taught one of the two words whose difference from the word הנישואין, "the nesuin," is 70.

So when Rabbi Eleazar ben Azariah said, "Behold I am like a seventy-year-old," it could mean, "Behold it is like I learned 70." I said that a man would only write a kethubah on the condition to have the woman enter nesuin (and the Mishnah felt it necessary to exclude my opinion). When the numerical value of הנישואין, "the nesuin," is subtracted from the numerical value of לכונסה אצטריכא, "to have her enter; it is necessary," the remainder is equal to the gematria of seventy (representing my opinion which the Mishnah felt it necessary to exclude). This interpretation could explain why Rabbi Eleazar ben Azariah said, הרי אני כבן שבעים, "Behold I am like a seventy-year-old."

This interpretation also answers the other question, namely why in this particular Mishnah did Rabbi Eleazar ben Azariah say, "I am like a one who taught seventy?" Rabbi Eleazar ben Azariah, as if anticipating the Gemara in Baba Mezia which excludes his opinion, notes that the Mishnah also rejected his opinion about when to narrate the exodus from Egypt. Therefore, only in this particular Mishnah in Tractate Berakoth where his opinion is rejected does he allude to the Gemara in Baba Mezia.

אמר רבי אלעזר בן עזריה, הרי אני כבן שבעים שנה, ולא זכיתי שתאמר יציאת מצרים בלילות (ברכות, פרק א, משנה ה).

Rabbi Eleazar ben Azariah said, "Behold I am like a seventy-year-old, and I have not merited that the departure out of Egypt ought to be said at nights" (Berakoth, Chapter 1, Mishnah 5).

The הגדה של פסח, Passover Haggadah, in the third paragraph after the four questions, quotes the Mishnah in מסכת ברכות, Tractate Berakoth, where Rabbi Eleazar ben Azariah says, "Behold I am like a seventy-year-old." Questions: 1. Why did Rabbi Eleazar ben Azariah say, "I am like a seventy-year-old," rather than simply saying I am seventy years old? 2. Why did Rabbi Eleazar ben Azariah mention his age at all? The Gemara says that he was really only eighteen years old, but a miracle occurred and his beard turned white (ברכות כח.), Berakoth 28a). But why did Rabbi Eleazar ben Azariah seem to mention this miracle; he surely was not bragging? 3. Lastly, why is this story associated with the seder night? In numerous other Mishnayoth Rabbi Eleazar ben Azariah is quoted, but only in one Mishnah, which the Passover Haggadah quotes, does he say, "I am like a seventy-year-old."

A possible answer can be given based on a Mishnah and a gematria. In the תלמוד ירושלמי, "Talmud Yerushalmi," there is Mishnah in which Rabbi Eleazar ben Azariah expresses his opinion concerning whether a baby can be washed with hot water on a Sabbath which occurs on the third day after circumcision. The פני משה, Penei Moshe, spells out that opinion, as stated, ור״יא בן עזריה פליג ואמר מרחיצין אותו כדרכו במקום שדרכן להרחיץ את הקטן ואפי׳ ביום השלישי שחל להיות בשבת וכו׳ והלכה כר״יא בן עזריה (פני משה מאת הרב משה מרגלית בן הרב ר׳ שמעון, תלמוד ירושלמי, שבת, פרק יט, הלכה ג), "And Rabbi Eleazar ben Azariah disputes, and said, one may wash him in the usual way, in a place where it is usual to wash the small child, and even on the third day which occurs on Sabbath, etc., and the Halakahah, 'decided law,' is according to Rabbi Eleazar ben Azariah" (Penei Moshe by Rabbi Moshe Margoliot son of Rabbi Shimon, Yerushalmi Gemara, Shabbath, Chapter 19, Halakah 3). The gematria of מרחיצין, "one may wash," is 408.

מרחיצין   408

The gematria of שחל, "which occurs," is 338.

שחל   338

Note that these two words quoted from the Penei Moshe also appear in the Mishnah with the exact same spelling, so obviously they have the same gematrioth. The Penei Moshe was quoted because of its language; it designates the special nature of the third day even שחל, "which occurs," on Sabbath.

Also note that the כסף משנה, Kesef Mishnah, explaining the Rambam, also writes concerning whether a baby can be washed with hot water on a Sabbath which occurs on the third day after circumcision, but with a different implication. He writes, דאוקי הא בחמין שהוחמו בשבת למילה דוקא ולא אמר דקאי נמי אלאחר המילה (כסף משנה, משנה תורה, ספר אהבה, הלכות מילה, פרק ב, הלכה ח). "It is established that (the allowance) for hot water which has been heated up on Shabbath, refers particularly to the third day following circumcision, and it is not saying that it is also referring to [any other day] after the circumcision" (Kesef Mishnah, Mishnah Torah, Book of Ahavah, Laws of Circumcision, Chapter 2, Law 8).

When the gematria of שחל, "which occurs," is subtracted from the gematria of מרחיצין, "one may wash," the remainder is seventy.

$$408$$
$$-338$$
$$70$$

The Bertinoro comments, similarly to the Penei Moshe, that the Halakhah is according to the opinion of Rabbi Eleazar ben Azariah (פירוש ר״ע מברטנורה, שבת, פרק יט, משנה ג, ד״ה רבי) אליעזר בן עזריה, Rabbi Ovadiah Bertinoro, Shabbath, Chapter 19, Mishnah 3, header words: Rabbi Eleazar ben Azariah). Rabbi Eleazar ben Azariah's use of the word שנה, shanah, many times means "year," in fact has a second meaning. While the word שנה can mean year, it can also be read as the third person past tense of the verb לשנות, "to learn." Thus, the word שנה in the Passover Haggadah, can mean learned, or should have learned.

Now support can be given for what Rabbi Eleazar ben Azariah said in the Mishnah of מסכת ברכות, Tractate Berakoth, and answers can be given for the questions posed. When Rabbi Eleazar ben Azariah said, "I am like seventy years old," it could mean, it is as if I learned seventy, for the difference between the gematria of שחל, "which occurs," and the gematria of מרחיצין, "you can wash," is seventy. He never mentioned the number seventy in the Mishnah in Shabbath, but the number seventy is insinuated in the gematrioth of his opinion in that Mishnah. The first question of why Rabbi Eleazar ben Azariah said, "I am like a seventy-year-old," has been answered.

When Rabbi Eleazar ben Azariah mentioned the number seventy, he may have been alluding in gematrioth to his opinion in the Mishnah in Shabbath, for there the Halakhah is according to his opinion. He surely was not bragging; on the contrary, he was saying in a modest way, that even though the Halakhah was according to his opinion in that Mishnah, still he has not merited to have convinced the sages that the exodus from Egypt should be said at night. The second question of why did Rabbi Eleazar ben Azariah said that he is like seventy years old (he was not mentioning any miracle), has been answered.

When Rabbi Eleazar ben Azariah said that he is like seventy years old, he might have been referencing the number seventy in gematrioth from the Mishnah in which the Halakhah is according to his opinion. This opinion has direct association to the seder night, for even though the Halakhah is according to his opinion in that Mishnah, still he has not merited to have convinced the sages that the exodus should be said at night. The last question of why Rabbi Eleazar ben Azariah is quoted on the seder night has been answered.

Of course, the Mishnah in מסכת שבת, "Tractate Shabbath," and the Mishnah in מסכת ברכות, "Tractate Berakoth," deal with two entirely separate laws; neither is dependent on the other. The decided law could be according to Rabbi Eleazar ben Azariah's opinion in one instance and not the other. All that is being said here is that conceivably Rabbi Eleazar ben Azariah might have been referencing the number seventy in gematrioth, where the decided law followed his opinion in Tractate Shabbath; still he was not able to convince the sages of his opinion in Tractate Berakoth.

There is a compelling lesson from this Torah thought, for all those who are seder participants. The participants may have strong and valid opinions about what and how a seder should be conducted. They should remember that Rabbi Eleazar ben Azariah also had a strong and valid opinion; he could even have cited this Mishnah in Shabbath where the Halakhah was decided according to his opinion. Instead, he chose to express himself in a modest way, by alluding to his opinion via gematrioth. All those who participate in a seder can learn the compelling lesson, to express their opinion in a modest way, whether at a seder or in any life circumstance.

אמר רבי אלעזר בן עזריה, הרי אני כבן שבעים שנה, ולא זכיתי שתאמר יציאת מצרים בלילות (ברכות, פרק א, משנה ה).

Rabbi Eleazar ben Azariah said, "Behold I am like a seventy-year-old, and I have not merited that the departure out of Egypt ought to be said at nights" (Berakoth, Chapter 1, Mishnah 5).

In the third paragraph after the four questions, the הגדה של פסח, Passover Haggadah, quotes from a Mishnah in מסכת ברכות, Tractate Berakoth, where Rabbi Eleazar ben Azariah says, "Behold I am like a seventy-year-old." Why did Rabbi Eleazar ben Azariah say I am like a seventy year old? Just say, "I am seventy years old," or I am not seventy years old, but some other age. Although there are several answers, the following proposed answer is innovative.

While the word שנה can mean year, it can also be read as the third person past tense of the verb לשנות, to learn. Thus, the word שנה in the Passover Haggadah, can mean "learned," as opposed to "year." An indication of the number 70 comes from what Rabbi Eleazar ben Azariah said about an admonition in פרשת משפטים "Parashath Mishpatim." In that parashah there is a warning not to accept לשון הרע, "malignant speech," as stated, לא תשא שמע שוא אל תשת ידך עם רשע להיות עד חמס (שמות כג,א), "Thou shall not take up a false report, do not put your hand with the wicked to be an unrighteous witness" (Exodus 23,1). Note that Rashi defines לא תשא, "Thou shall not take up," as a warning not to accept לשון הרע,

"malignant speech," as stated, לא תקבל שמַע דִשקר, אזהרה למקבל
לשון הרע ולדיין שלא ישמַע דברי בעל דין עד שיבא בעל דין חברו (רש״י,
שמות כג,א), "Do not accept a false report. It is an admonition
against one who accepts malignant speech, and to a judge
that he should not hear the words of one litigant until the
other litigant arrives" (Rashi, Exodus 23,1).

The Gemara Pesahim quotes Rabbi Eleazar ben Azariah who elucidates this pasuk, as stated, ואמר רב ששת משום
ר״א בן עזריה כל המספר לשון הרע וכל המקבל לשון הרע וכל המעיד עדות
שקר בחבירו ראוי להשליכו לכלבים שנאמר לכלב תשליכון אותו (שמות
כב,ל) וכתיב בתריה לא תשא שמע שוא וקרי ביה לא תשיא (פסחים קיח.)
"And Rav Shesheth said in the name of Rabbi Eleazar ben
Azariah, Anyone who speaks malignant speech, and anyone
who accepts malignant speech, and anyone who testifies false
testimony against his friend, it is fitting that they throw him to
the dogs; as it says, To the dog you shall throw it (Exodus
22,30), and it is written afterwards, You shall not take up a
false report, and read it as, You shall not cause it to be taken"
(Pesahim 118a).

Rabbi Eleazar ben Azariah derives from the quoted
pesukim that both the speaking and the accepting of malignant speech are prohibited. The gematria of לשון הרע, "malignant speech," is 661.

לשון	386
הרע	275
	661

The gematria of שנאמר, "as it says," is 591.

שנאמר	591

The difference between the gematria of לשון הרע, "malignant speech," and the gematria of שנאמר, "as it says," is 70.

661
-591
70

So when Rabbi Eleazar ben Azariah said, "Behold I am like a seventy-year-old," it could mean, "It is as if I learned seventy"; for the difference in gematrioth between the words לשון הרע, "malignant speech," and the word שנאמר, "as it says," which is used to quote the provenience pesukim, is 70.

A second indication of the number 70 can be derived from what Rabbi Eleazar ben Azariah said. He quotes the words of the Torah לכלב תשליכון אותו, "to the dog you shall throw it." The word תשליכון, "you shall throw," could be understood as subtract (cast away), that is, subtract the gematria of לכלב, "to the dog," from the gematria of אותו, "it." When such a subtraction is performed, the minuend is 413, the subtrahend is 82, and the remainder is 331.

$$
\begin{array}{rr}
\text{אותו} & 413 \\
\text{לכלב} & -82 \\
\hline
& 331
\end{array}
$$

When 70 is added to 331, the sum is 401.

$$
\begin{array}{r}
331 \\
70 \\
\hline
401
\end{array}
$$

The gematria of להשליכו, "to throw him," is 401.

$$
\text{להשליכו} \quad 401
$$

Since להשליכו, "to throw him," is the word which Rabbi Eleazar ben Azariah used to describe what is fit to do to someone who speaks or accepts לשון הרע, "malignant speech," or who bears false witness, so when Rabbi Eleazar ben Azariah said, "Behold I am like a seventy-year-old," it could mean, "It is as if I learned seventy"; for the difference between the subtraction of the gematria of לכלב, "to the dogs," from the gematria of אותו, "it" (331), and the gematria of להשליכו, "to throw him" (401), is 70.

A third and final indication of the number 70 can be

found in how the רשב"ם, "Rashbam," comprehends the Gemara Pesahim which quotes Rabbi Eleazar ben Azariah. It is evident that the Rashbam had a different version of the text, for he explains that even the prohibition of false witnesses which is mentioned in the Gemara is derived from the word שמע, "report," as he writes, נראה בעיני דלא גרסינן ליה דכולהו משתמע מלא תשא שכשמספר או מעיד הרי נושא בפיו שמע שוא (רשב"ם ד"ה וקרי ביה לא תשיא, פסחים קיח.), "It appears to me that the words [וקרי ביה לא תשיא] are not read, for everything is apparent from the term 'You shall not carry.' For when one speaks or testifies, behold he carries in his mouth a false report" (Rashbam, Pesahim 118a, header words: And read it, you shall not cause it to be carried). The gematria of עדות, "testimony," is 480.

עדות   480

The gematria of שמע, "report," is 410.

שמע   410

The difference between the gematria of עדות, "testimony," and the gematria of שמע, "report," is 70.

$$\begin{array}{r} 480 \\ -410 \\ \hline 70 \end{array}$$

So when Rabbi Eleazar ben Azariah said, "Behold I am like a seventy-year-old," it could mean, "Behold it is as if I learned seventy"; for the difference in gematrioth between עדות, "testimony," the word mentioned in the Gemara, and שמע, "report," the word from which the Rashbam derives the prohibition of false testimony, is 70.

Observe, that in each of the three approaches the number 70 was implicit, conveyed indirectly via gematrioth. This implicit referral to the number 70 could be the reason that Rabbi Eleazar ben Azariah said that it is as if he learnt 70, since he never learned 70 explicitly.

אמר רבי אלעזר בן עזריה, הרי אני כבן שבעים שנה, ולא
זכיתי שתאמר יציאת מצרים בלילות (ברכות, פרק א,
משנה ה).

Rabbi Eleazar ben Azariah said, "Behold I am
like a seventy-year-old, and I have not merited
that the departure out of Egypt ought to be said
at nights" (Berakoth, Chapter 1, Mishnah 5).

The הגדה של פסח, Passover Haggadah, in the third paragraph after the four questions, quotes the Mishnah in מסכת
ברכות, Tractate Berakoth, where Rabbi Eleazar ben Azariah
says, "Behold I am like a seventy-year-old." First, why did
Rabbi Eleazar ben Azariah say that he is like a seventy-year-
old, rather than simply saying he is seventy years old? Second, why did he feel he had not merited to have his opinion
accepted? There are many answers, but an uncommon one
can be suggested from מסכת בבא מציעא, Tractate Baba Mezia.

The Gemara discusses the liability of a person who is
paid to assume responsibility for the safekeeping of another
person's property: does his liability extend to both theft and
loss of property? The Gemara Baba Mezia asks: Inasmuch as
according to the מאן דאמר, "the one who says," the Torah
speaks in commonly employed terminology, how is it known
that a paid custodian is liable for a loss? There is a divergent
opinion; a different מאן דאמר, "the one who says," who does
not accept that the Torah speaks in commonly employed
terminology. Since the Torah uses the double expression, גנוב
יגנב (שמות כב,יא), "it is surely stolen," (Exodus 22,11) that
divergent opinion maintains that from this double expression
it can be derived that a paid custodian is liable for a lost
object (in addition to a stolen object). But according to the
opinion that the Torah speaks in commonly employed terminology, then, this double expression may just be a commonly
employed term from which nothing more is to be derived.

The Gemara does not say who this מאן דאמר, "the one who says," is. However, both Rashi and Tosafoth identify him as the one who is named on דף לא:, page 31b, of the tractate (רש״י, בבא מציעא צד:, ד״ה הניחא למאן דאמר כו׳, ותוסות, ד״ה אלא למאן דאמר דברה תורה כלשון בני אדם כו׳, Rashi, Baba Mezia 94b, header words: This is good according to the one who says etc., and Tosafoth header words: But according to the one who says that the Torah speaks in human terms etc.). This מאן דאמר, "the one who says," is none other than Rabbi Eleazar ben Azariah who is named on דף לא:, page 31b. In general Rabbi Eleazar ben Azariah does derive implications from double expressions in the Torah, but from the expression גנוב יגנב, "it is surely stolen," he does not derive that a paid custodian is liable for a lost object. Since the Torah writes "stolen," he feels that the pasuk confines its meaning to stealing rather than a loss.

The Tosafoth writes למ״ד דברה תורה כלשון בני אדם מאי איכא למימר התם נמי איכא הוכחה דגניבה משמע דוקא גניבה ולא אבידה (תוסי ד״ה דברה תורה כלשון בני אדם, בבא מציעא לא:), "According to the one who says the Torah speaks in commonly employed terminology, what is there to say? Also there, there is proof that stealing is implied—exclusively stealing and not a loss" (Tosafoth header words: The Torah spoke in commonly employed terminology Baba Mezia 31b). The gematria of גניבה, "stealing," is 70.

גניבה   70

Thus, the unnamed מאן דאמר, "the one who says," on Baba Mezia 94b is Rabbi Eleazar ben Azariah, who learns that the double expression גנוב יגנב, "it is surely stolen," means exclusively גניבה, "stealing." Now both questions initially asked can be answered.

First, why did Rabbi Eleazar ben Azariah say that he is like a seventy-year-old? Rabbi Eleazar ben Azariah's use of the word שנה, shanah, often meaning "year," in fact has a second meaning. While the word שנה can mean year, it can also be read as the third person past tense of the verb לשנות, "to learn." Thus, the word שנה in the Passover Haggadah can mean "learned," as opposed to year. So, it could be that Rabbi Eleazar ben Azariah was saying, "It is as if I learned seventy," for I learned exclusively גניבה "stealing," which has a gematria of seventy. It is as if he was saying, "I never learned 70, but it is as if I learned 70," since גניבה, "stealing," has a gematria of seventy.

Second, why did Rabbi Eleazar ben Azariah feel he had not merited to have his opinion accepted? The Gemara on Baba Mezia 94b quotes his opinion as a מאן דאמר, "the one who says," without any mention of his name. It is easy to understand that Rabbi Eleazar ben Azariah might have concluded that since the Gemara on page 94b did not mention his name, so too his opinion would not be accepted that the departure from Egypt should be said at night. Both questions have been answered.

אמר רבי אלעזר בן עזריה, הרי אני כבן שבעים שנה, ולא זכיתי שתאמר יציאת מצרים בלילות (ברכות, פרק א, משנה ה).

Rabbi Eleazar ben Azariah said, "Behold I am like a seventy-year-old, and I have not merited that the departure out of Egypt ought to be said at nights" (Berakoth, Chapter 1, Mishnah 5).

In the third paragraph after the four questions, the הגדה של פסח, the Passover Haggadah, quotes the Mishnah in מסכת ברכות, Tractate Berakoth, where Rabbi Eleazar ben Azariah says, "Behold I am like a seventy-year-old." Why did Rabbi Eleazar ben Azariah say, "I am like a seventy-year-old?" Just say, "I am seventy years old," or I am not seventy years old. There are many answers, but perhaps an unconventional one can be introduced.

In the course of a discussion (of Aggadah versus Hala-khah), the Gemara Hagigah records what Rabbi Eleazar ben Azariah said to Rabbi Akiva, as stated, אמר לו ר"א בן עזריה עקיבא מה לך אצל הגדה כלך מדברותיך (חגיגה יד.), "Rabbi Eleazar ben Azariah said to him, Akiva, what are you doing with Aggadah? Cease from your words" (Hagigah 14a). The gematria of כלך, "Cease," is 70.

70   כלך

The word שנה can mean year; it can also be read as the third person past tense of the verb לשנות, to learn. Thus, the word שנה in the Passover Haggadah, can mean "learned," as opposed to "year." So when Rabbi Eleazar ben Azariah said, "Behold I am like a seventy-year-old," it could be explained, "Behold it is as if I learned 70," for I said, כלך, "Cease," whose gematria is 70. He never learned seventy explicitly, just simply said a word whose gematria is seventy. In addition, it could be explained, that Rabbi Eleazar ben Azariah said that it is as if he learned, and not that he actually learned, because the word כלך, "Cease," is not teaching a new Torah jurispru-dence thought; rather it is the word used to retort to Rabbi Akiva. Therefore, Rabbi Eleazar ben Azariah said that it is as as if he learned 70, for the word כלך, "Cease," does not present a new Torah jurisprudence thought, just a retort.

אמר רבי אלעזר בן עזריה, הרי אני כבן שבעים שנה, ולא זכיתי שתאמר יציאת מצרים בלילות (ברכות, פרק א, משנה ה).

Rabbi Eleazar ben Azariah said, "Behold I am like a seventy-year-old, and I have not merited that the departure out of Egypt ought to be said at nights" (Berakoth, Chapter 1, Mishnah 5).

In the third paragraph after the four questions, the הגדה של פסח, the Passover Haggadah, quotes the Mishnah in

מסכת ברכות, Tractate Berakoth, where Rabbi Eleazar ben Azariah says, "Behold I am like a seventy-year-old." Why did Rabbi Eleazar ben Azariah say, "I am like a seventy-year-old?" The answer given in Gemara Berakoth is that he was really only eighteen years old, but when he was appointed ריש מתיבתא, "head of the yeshiva," his hair turned white so he would be accorded due respect (ברכות כח., Berakoth 28a).

  There are several problems with this explanation. First, Rabbi Eleazar ben Azariah is quoted many times in the Mishnah and Gemara, but why was the miracle of his beard turning white only mentioned here? Second, Rashi says that he was appointed נשיא, "Nasi," (ד"ה כבן שבעים, רש"י, ברכות יב:, שנה, Rashi, Berakoth 12b, header words: Like a seventy year old). Rabbi Eleazar ben Azariah was obviously a super genius to be appointed ריש מתיבתא, "head of the yeshiva," at the age of eighteen. בן זומא, Ben Zoma, whose opinion (to say the departure from Egypt at nights) is mentioned and is the accepted opinion, although a great man, never got סמיכה, "ordination," (ד"ה בן עזאי ובן זומא, רש"י, קידושין מט:, Rashi, Kiddushin 49b, header words: Ben Azzai and Ben Zoma). Certainly, Rabbi Eleazar ben Azariah knew the interpretation of Ben Zoma; why did Rabbi Eleazar ben Azariah say, "I have not merited that the departure out of Egypt ought to be said at nights"? Third, and lastly, immediately prior to Rabbi Eleazar ben Azariah's statement, the Passover Haggadah conveys a story that several of the great sages of Israel, amongst them Rabbi Eleazar ben Azariah, stayed up all night expounding upon the exodus from Egypt. The night of the seder is the one night of the year when there is a special mitzvah to narrate the exodus from Egypt. The Rabbis mentioned were all great men; one would almost expect that they should stay up all night, that night. There are countless stories of other Rabbis who would stay up and learn Torah all night. Although a beautiful story, why was it incorporated here into the Passover Haggadah?

These questions can be answered with an understanding of a Gemara in מסכת בבא מציעא, Tractate Baba Mezia. The Gemara deals with a a debtor who "sold" his field to a creditor, with the understanding that if the debtor did not pay, the creditor would keep the field. If the debtor managed to pay, the field would be returned. The question raised is: if the creditor does enjoy the fruits of the field, and the debtor pays back the loan, then does the enjoyment of the fruits appear to be prohibited interest? Rabbi Judah relates a story that seems to allow the creditor to enjoy the fruits, as stated, איל רבי יהודה מעשה בביתום בן זונין שעשה שדהו מכר על פי ר' אלעזר בן עזריה ולוקח אוכל פירות היה (בבא מציעא סג.), "Rabbi Judah said to them, an event occurred with Boethus ben Zunin who sold his field with the affirmation of Rabbi Eleazar ben Azariah, and the buyer consumed the fruits" (Baba Mezia 63a). The gematria of מכר, "sold," is 260.

260   מכר

The gematria of על פי, "with the affirmation," is 190.

190   על פי

The difference between 260 and 190 is 70.

260
-190
———
70

While the word שנה can mean year, it can also be translated as the third person past tense of the verb לשנות, "to learn." Now all three questions can be answered. When Rabbi Eleazar ben Azariah said, "Behold I am like a seventy-year-old," it can be translated as, "Behold it is as if I learned 70." The expression, "as if I learned 70," is very precise, for he never learned seventy. However, the story which Rabbi Judah related, was reported on Rabbi Eleazar ben Azariah's authority, contains the gematria of seventy; that is why he said, "it is as if I learned seventy."

The Gemara says the story was distorted. Since the story reported on Rabbi Eleazar ben Azariah's authority was misconstrued, his authority was questioned to some degree. It could be because his authority was questioned that he said ולא זכיתי, "and I have not merited." In other situations where Rabbi Eleazar ben Azariah gave his opinion, it was accepted or rejected, but here he said he has not merited to have his opinion accepted because of the story with a gematria of seventy. The first question is answered.

Of course Rabbi Eleazar ben Azariah knew the interpretation of Ben Zoma. But since to some degree Rabbi Eleazar ben Azariah's authority was questioned, he said, "I have not merited that the departure out of Egypt ought to be said at nights." The second question is answered.

The story of the great sages of Israel staying up all night telling the exodus from Egypt, includes Rabbi Eleazar ben Azariah. The fact that he was appointed Nasi over such other great sages, emphasizes that Rabbi Eleazar ben Azariah was the super genius that he was. Even though he said, "I have not merited that the departure out of Egypt ought to be said at nights," he surely knew what Ben Zoma said. The third and last question has been answered.

לא תאכל עליו חמץ שבעת ימים תאכל עליו מצות לחם עני כי בחפזון יצאת מארץ מצרים למען תזכר את יום צאתך מארץ מצרים כל ימי חייך (דברים טז,ג).

You shall not eat leavened bread with it; for seven days you shall eat unleavened bread with it, the bread of affliction; for in haste you went out of the land of Egypt; in order that you shall remember the day you went out of the land of Egypt all the days of your life (Deuteronomy 16,3).

The הגדה של פסח, Passover Haggadah, before the mentioning of the four sons, quotes the pasuk which ends למען

תזכר את יום צאתך מארץ מצרים כל ימי חייך, "in order that you shall remember the day you went out of the land of Egypt all the days of your life." The gematria of למען, "in order that," is 190.

למען   190

The purpose of leaving Egypt was to observe the commandments of G-d, many of which, such as the eating of the Passover korban, unleavened bread, and bitter herbs, help one remember the departure from Egypt (רש״י, שמות יג,ח, Rashi, Exodus 13,8). This same concept is also conveyed in the pasuk which ends למען תזכר את יום צאתך מארץ מצרים כל ימי חייך (רש״י, דברים טז,ג), "in order that you shall remember the day you went out of the land of Egypt all the days of your life" (Rashi, Deuteronomy 16,3).

The Bnei Yisroel were in Egypt 210 years (רש״י, בראשית טו,יג, Rashi, Genesis 15,13). Although G-d had foretold Abraham that his seed would be in a strange land for 400 years, the Bnei Yisroel actually were in Egypt only 210 years. Thus, in a sense, they departed from Egypt 190 years early. Had the Children of Israel remained longer in Egypt, they would have been totally assimilated. The Sefer Sifthei Cohen says, ואם היו יושבים במצרים אפילו יום אחד לא היו יכולין לצאת שהיתה מתגברת עליהם מדת הדין כמו שהיה אחר כך, ולזה היה המכוון קודם שיסתם שער חמישים של שערי טומאה, כי לזה נזכר ארבעים ותשע פעמים בתורה יציאת מצרים (ספר שפתי כהן על חמשה חמשי תורה מאת הרב מרדכי הכהן, שמות יב,ז), "And if they had dwelt in Egypt, even for one more day, they would not have been able to go out. For His attribute of strict justice would have overcome them, as it did later; and this was the intention, before the fiftieth gate of ritual defilement would seal shut. Because of this forty-nine times the going out of Egypt is mentioned in the Torah" (Sefer Sifthei Cohen on Chomishah Chumshei Torah by Rabbi Mordechai Cohen, Exodus 12,7). There is a commensurate explanation in the Or Hachayyim (אור החיים שמות ג,ז, Or Hachayyim, Exodus 3,7). The purpose of leaving Egypt was in order to observe the commandments of Hashem, notably including such commandments as the eating of the Passover korban, unleavened bread, and bitter herbs, whose expressed purpose is to help one remember the departure from Egypt. Thus, it is fitting that למען, "in order that," should have a gematria of 190: the number which, in itself, refers to the Children of Israel's accelerated departure from Egypt.

והיא שעמדה לאבותינו ולנו. שלא אחד בלבד עמד עלינו לכלותינו אלא שבכל דור ודור עומדים עלינו לכלותינו והקדוש ברוך הא מצילנו מידם (הגדה של פסח).

And it is this that has stood for our fathers and for us. For not one alone has risen against us to annihilate us, but in every generation and generation, they rise against us to to annihilate us, and the Holy One, Blessed be He, saves us from their hand (Passover Haggadah).

In the הגדה של פסח, Passover Haggadah, after the mentioning of the four sons, it says that in every generation עומדים עלינו לכלותינו והקדוש ברוך הא מצילנו מידם, "they rise against us to to annihilate us, and the Holy One, Blessed be He, saves us from their hand." The gematria of עומדים, "they rise," is 170.

עומדים   170

The gematria of מצילנו, "He saves us," is 226.

מצילנו   226

The difference in gematrioth between those who are עומדים, "they rise," against the Bnei Yisroel, and G-d, Who is מצילנו, "He saves us," is 56.

$$\begin{array}{r} 226 \\ -170 \\ \hline 56 \end{array}$$

The gematria of 56 is found in the Torah, in connection with G-d redeeming the Bnei Yisroel from Egypt. There the pasuk uses the word להי, "to G-d," as stated, ליל שמרים הוא להי להוציאם מארץ מצרים הוא הלילה הזה להי שמרים לכל בני ישראל לדרתם (שמות יב,מב), "It is a night of watching to G-d to take them out of the land of Egypt; it is this night a watching to G-d for all the Children of Israel throughout their generations" (Exodus 12,42). The gematria of להי, "to G-d," is 56.

56   להי

Rashi comments on this pasuk, שהיה הקב״ה שומר ומצפה לו, לקיים הבטחתו להוציאם מארץ מצרים (רש״י, שמות יב,מב), "For the Holy One, Blessed be He, had been watching and awaiting eagerly for it, to fulfill His promise to take them out of the land of Egypt" (Rashi, Exodus 12,42). Thus, the gematria of 56 is associated with G-d's promise to redeem the Children of Israel from Egypt.

There is a pasuk in Psalms which also uses the word להי, "to G-d," as stated, כי להי המלוכה ומשל בגוים (תהלים כב,כט), "For to G-d is the Kingship, and He rules over the nations" (Psalms 22,29). The gematria of להי, "to G-d," is 56.

56   להי

Thus, the gematria of 56 is associated with G-d's rulership over the nations of the world. It is this rulership over the nations of the world which assures that those who stand against the Children of Israel will not succeed, because G-d is מצילנו, "saves us," from their hands.

The gematria of 56 is associated with G-d's redeeming the Children of Israel from Egypt and with G-d's rulership over the nations of the world which ensures that G-d will save the Children of Israel in every generation. These associations help account for why the difference in gematrioth between those who are עומדים, "they who rise," against the Bnei Yisroel, and G-d, Who is מצילנו, "He who saves us," is 56.

These associations might shed light on the expression in the הגדה של פסח, Passover Haggadah, which states, והיא שעמדה לאבותינו ולנו, "And it is this that has stood for our fathers and for us." Conceivably, the explanation could be: והיא, "And it is this," the gematria of 56 (which is equal to לה׳, "to G-d"), which is the promise that 56 stands between those who are עומדים, "they rise," against the Bnei Yisroel, and G-d, Who is מצילנו, "He saves us," from their hand. The gematria of 56, then, is distinctly associated with G-d's keeping His promise to redeem לאבותינו ולנו, "our fathers and ourselves"; this promise is associated with G-d's absolute rulership over the nations of the world, assuring that He will save us in every generation.

בכל דור ודור חיב אדם לראות את עצמו כאלו הוא יצא ממצרים וכו׳ (הגדה של פסח).

In every generation and generation a person is obligated to see himself as if he went out of Egypt, etc. (Passover Haggadah).

In the הגדה של פסח, Passover Haggadah, just before the first half of Hallel, it says that בכל דור ודור, "In every generation and generation," a person is obligated to see himself as if he personally went forth from Egypt. The gematria of דור, "generation," is 210.

$$\text{דור} \qquad 210$$

This gematria gives rise to the following observation. The Children of Israel were enslaved in Egypt for 210 years (רש״י, בראשית טו,יג, Rashi, Genesis 15,13). Since the gematria of דור, "generation," is equal to the number of years that the Children of Israel were enslaved in Egypt, this gematria underscores that each and every generation should feel as if it were enslaved in Egypt for 210 years.

לא את אבותינו בלבד גאל הקדוש ברוך הוא, אלא אף
אותנו גאל עמהם, שנאמר ואותנו הוציא משם למען הביא
אתנו לתת לנו את הארץ אשר נשבע לאבתינו (דברים ו,כג)
(הגדה של פסח).

It was not our fathers alone whom the Holy
One, Blessed be He, redeemed, but also us He
redeemed with them, as it says, "And He took
us out from there in order to bring us in to give
us the land which He swore to our fathers"
(Deuteronomy 6,23) (Passover Haggadah).

In the הגדה של פסח, Passover Haggadah, just before the
first half of Hallel, it says that אותנו הוציא משם, "And He took
us out from there." The gematria of משם, "from there," is 380.

משם   380

The word משם, "from there," in the quoted pasuk refers to מצרים, "Egypt," as can be seen from the context of the
Haggadah preceding this quoted pasuk. The gematria of
מצרים, "Egypt," is 380.

מצרים   380

Since the gematrioth of משם, "from there," and מצרים,
"Egypt," are identical, it is very appropriate that the pasuk
uses משם, "from there," to refer to מצרים, "Egypt."

לפיכך אנחנו חיבים להודות להלל לשבח לפאר לרומם
להדר לברך לעלה ולקלס למי שעשה לאבותינו ולנו את כל
הנסים האלו (הגדה של פסח).

Therefore, we are obligated to thank, to praise,
to laud, to glorify, to exalt, to adore, to bless, to
extol, and to acclaim Him Who performed all
these miracles for our fathers and for us (Passover Haggadah).

In the הגדה של פסח, Passover Haggadah, just before the

first half of Hallel, it says that לפיכך אנחנו חיבים להודות להלל וכו׳ "Therefore, we are obligated to thank, to praise, etc." When expressing the obligation to thank and praise G-d for all He has done for us, we refer to ourselves as אנחנו, "we." The gematria of אנחנו, "we" is 115.

115   אנחנו

When Moses commanded the Children of Israel to remember the departure from Egypt, he addressed them as העם, "the people," as stated, ויאמר משה אל העם זכור את היום הזה אשר יצאתם ממצרים מבית עבדים כי בחזק יד הוציא ה׳ אתכם מזה ולא יאכל חמץ (שמות יג,ג), "And Moses said to the people, Remember this day on which you went out from Egypt, from the house of bondage, for with a strong hand G-d took you out from here, and you shall not eat leavened bread" (Exodus 13,3). The gematria of העם, "the people," is 115.

115   העם

The word העם, "the people," which is from the Torah, and the word אנחנו, "we," which is from the Haggadah, both refer to the Children of Israel and the departure from Egypt. Both words also refer to the Children of Israel shouldering an obligation. Since both העם, "the people," and אנחנו, "we," have such strong similarities, it is appropriate that both words should have the same gematria.

לקחתי אתכם לי לעם והייתי לכם לאלקים וידעתם כי אני ה׳ אלקיכם המוציא אתכם מתחת סבלות מצרים (שמות ו,ז).

And I will take you to Me for a people, and I will be to you for a G-d, and you shall know that I am Hashem, your G-d, Who takes you out from under the burdens of Egypt (Exodus 6,7).

The Torah reading for the last day of Passover (outside

the land of Israel) includes the following pasuk, שמור את חדש האביב ועשית פסח לה' אלקיך כי בחדש האביב הוציאך ה' אלקיך ממצרים לילה (דברים טז,א), "Observe the month of spring and keep the Passover to Hashem, your G-d, for in the month of spring Hashem, your G-d, took you out of Egypt at night" (Deuteronomy 16,1). From this pasuk the Gemara learns that Nisan, the month in which the Passover holiday falls, must occur in the spring; therefore, Jewish leap years are declared so that the vernal equinox should occur on or before the fifteenth of the month of Nisan, according to Tosafoth and the Rambam. According to Rashi the vernal equinox should occur before the fifteenth of the month of Nisan (סנהדרין יג:, ושערי זמנים מאת הרב דוד הלוי העבער, סימן א, אות ה, Sanhedrin 13b, and Shaarei Zemanim by Rabbi Dovid Halevi Heber, Siman 1, Letter 5). Consequently, the Jewish lunar calendar is made to calibrate with the solar calendar so that the Passover holiday will occur in the spring (ראש השנה כא., Rosh Hashanah 21a).

Two questions arise about the quoted Torah reading. First, why was this Torah portion chosen to be read on the last day of Passover, as opposed to any other day of the holiday? Second, why is the Passover holiday and its season designated as the criterion for the establishment of when a leap year is to be declared? Why not designate the Shavuoth holiday to occur in the beginning of the summer, or the Sukkoth holiday to occur in the autumn, etc.?

A second pair of questions comes from the הגדה של פסח, Passover Haggadah. Just before the first half of Hallel, it says that בכל דור ודור, "In every generation and generation," a person is obligated to see himself as if he went forth from Egypt. Again, two questions arise. One, why is it an obligation on the Passover holiday, as opposed to any other holiday, for one to see himself as if he went forth from Egypt? On the Sukkoth holiday the Children of Israel live in a sukkah, but this living is to remember either the clouds of glory, or the huts which G-d provided the Children of Israel when they went forth from Egypt (ספר החנוך מאת הרב אהרן הלוי, פרשת אמור, מצוה שכה, Book of Hachinuch by Rabbi Aaron Halevi, Parashath Emor, Mitzvah 325). Yet, there is no obligation on the Sukkoth holiday for one to see himself as if G-d provided him with a sukkah, as He did when the Bnei Yisroel went forth from Egypt. Why is it an obligation on the Passover holiday for one to see himself as if he went forth from Egypt? Two, since there is an obligation on the Passover holiday for one to see himself as if he went forth from Egypt, why is there no obligation to totally re-enact the going forth from Egypt? Although there is a seder with many mitzvoth, the actual re-enactment is not done. On the first night of Passover one should be obligated to don ancient Jewish garments, wear ancient sandals, leave his home, etc. Why is there no such obligation?

A first step to begin to answer these questions is to understand the difference between זהירות, "vigilance," and זריזות, "zeal," which are defined by the מסלת ישרים, Mesillath Yesharim. The term זהירות, "vigilance," as the name implies, means being watchful and careful, not to deteriorate, tergiversate, or retrogress to a worse or bad state. Those lacking זהירות, "vigilance," can fall into a bad state, as stated, ונמצא שהם נופלים ברעה בלי ראות אותה (מסלת ישרים מאת הרב משה ב פרק ,לוצאטו חיים), "And it ends up that they fall into evil, without being aware of it" (Mesillath Yesharim by Rabbi Moshe Chaim Luzzatto, Chapter 2). The essential method of obtaining זהירות, "vigilance," is by Torah learning, as stated, על כן נצטוינו לקבע עתים לתורה, וכבר זכרנו שהיא המצטרכת יותר לאדם לשיגיע אל הזהירות, וכמאמר רב פינחס: "תורה מביאה לידי זהירות" (מסלת ישרים מאת הרב משה חיים לוצאטו, פרק ה), "Therefore we are commanded to establish times to learn Torah, and we have already mentioned that it is the greatest necessity for man to reach vigilance, as the saying of R. Pinchas, 'Torah leads to vigilance'" (Mesillath Yesharim by Rabbi Moshe Chaim Luzzatto, Chapter 5). The gematria of תורה, "Torah," is 611.

611   תורה

Thus, זהירות, "vigilance," which is acquired through learning Torah, whose gematria is 611, keeps one from falling into bad ways.

The next higher level after זהירות, "vigilance," is זריזות, "zeal," which, as the name implies, means being zealous and eager, to observe the commandments. This level of observance includes the 365 negative Mitzvoth being kept because one is זהיר, "vigilant," and the additional 248 positive Mitzvoth being kept because one is זריז, "zealous." Those who achieve זריזות, "zeal," observe all the mitzvoth. This observing of the mitzvoth is referred to as טוב, "good," as stated, אחר הזהירות יבוא הזריזות, כי הזהירות סובב על ה"לא תעשה" והזריזות על ה"עשה" והינו, "סור מרע ועשה טוב" (תהלים לד,טו). וענינו של הזריזות מבאר, שהוא ההקדמה למצות ולהשלמת ענינם. וכלשון הזה אמרו ז"ל: "זריזים מקדימים למצות" (מסלת ישרים מאת הרב משה חיים לוצאטו, פרק ו), "After vigilance comes zeal. For vigilance revolves around the negative commandments, and zeal around the positive commandments, and this is, 'Turn away from evil and do good' (Psalms 34,15). And the meaning of zeal has been elucidated; it is the precursor to perform commandments and to complete them. According to this terminology, have of our Rabbis of blessed memory said, 'the zealous are eager to perform commandments.'" (Mesillath Yesharim by Rabbi Moshe Chaim Luzzatto, Chapter 6). It is reiterated that זריזות, "zeal," is defined as observing the commandments, as stated, כללו של דבר, חזוק גדול צריך האדם להתחזק ולהתגבר בזריזות לעשות המצות וכו' (מסלת ישרים מאת הרב משה חיים לוצאטו, פרק ו), "To sum up, a man needs great strength to be strong and to invigorate himself with zeal to perform the commandments, etc.," (Mesillath Yesharim by Rabbi Moshe Chaim Luzzatto, Chapter 6). It is also reiterated that זריזות, "zeal," is referred to as doing good, as stated, אלא על זה נאמר "בטח בה' ועשה טוב שכן ארץ ורעה אמונה" (תהלים לז,ג) (מסלת ישרים מאת הרב משה חיים לוצאטו, פרק ט), "But about this it is said, 'Trust in G-d and do good, dwell in the land and let your sustenance be faithfulness'" (Psalms 37,3) (Mesillath Yesharim by Rabbi Moshe Chaim Luzzatto, Chapter 9). Therefore, זריזות, "zeal," which is defined as observing the commandments, is referred to as doing good.

The difference between זהירות, "vigilance," and זריזות, "zeal," as defined by the מסלת ישרים, Mesillath Yesharim, parallels the difference between המעלה אתכם, "Who raises you up," and המוציא אתכם, "Who takes you out," in the Torah as defined by the אור החיים, "Or Hachayyim," and the קדושת לוי על התורה, "Kedushath Levi on the Torah," by Rav Levi Yitzchak Berdichev. The third pasuk from the end of פרשת שמיני, Parashath Shemini, is the only time that the Torah uses the expression המעלה אתכם, "Who raises you up," as stated, כי אני ה' המעלה אתכם מארץ מצרים להית לכם לאלקים והייתם קדשים כי קדוש אני (ויקרא יא,מה), "For I am G-d, Who raises you up out from the land of Egypt, to be your G-d, and you shall be holy, for I am holy" (Leviticus 11,45). The gematria of המעלה אתכם, "Who raises you up," is 611.

המעלה	150
אתכם	<u>461</u>
	611

On this pasuk the Or Hachayyim states, ואם לא ישמרו עצמם מהתיעוב הנה הנם חוזרים להיות כמות שהיו קודם עלותם מא"ים וייהו מושללים מבחינה זו (אור החיים, ויקרא יא,מה), "And if they do not guard themselves from the abominable, then they will return to be like they were before their elevation up out from the land of Egypt, and they will be negated from this elevated aspect" (Or Hachayyim, Leviticus 11,45). Thus, the expression המעלה אתכם, "Who raises you up," as used by the Torah implies being watchful and careful not to deteriorate,

tergiversate, or retrogress to a worse or bad state. The implication of the expression המעלה אתכם, "Who raises you up," in
the Torah is the same as the implication of the term זהירות,
"vigilance," as defined by the מסלת ישרים, Mesillath Yesharim,
which is obtained by the learning of Torah. The gematria of
תורה, "Torah," is 611.

The gematria of המעלה אתכם "Who raises you up," is
the same as the gematria of תורה, "Torah," for the implication
of the expression המעלה אתכם, "who raises you up," in the
Torah is the same as the implication of the term זהירות,
"vigilance," for learning Torah is the sine qua non with which
the Children of Israel can achieve זהירות, "vigilance."

The sixth pasuk of פרשת וארא, Parashath Vaayra, is the
first of three times that the Torah uses the exact expression
המוציא אתכם, "Who takes you out," as stated, ולקחתי אתכם כי
לעם והייתי לכם לאלקים וידעתם כי אני ה' אלקיכם המוציא אתכם מתחת
סבלות מצרים (שמות ו,ז), "And I will take you to Me for a people,
and I will be to you for a G-d, and you shall know that I am
G-d, your G-d, who takes you out from under the burdens of
Egypt" (Exodus 6,7). The gematria of המוציא אתכם, "Who
takes you out," is 613.

המוציא	152
אתכם	461
	613

There are two other instances where the Torah uses
the expression המוציא אתכם, "Who takes you out," (ויקרא כב,לג
ודברים יג,ו, Leviticus 22,33 and Deuteronomy 13,6). This explanation will apply to the first instance only.

Rav Levi Yitzchak Berdichev explains that Torah and
mitzvoth are the wherewithal with which the Children of
Israel can achieve וידעתם כי אני ה' אלקיכם, "and you shall know
that I am G-d, your G-d," as he says, אנחנו עמו ב"י משיגים אור
השכינה ע"י התורה והמצות וכו' (קדושת לוי על התורה מאת רב לוי יצחק
(ברדיטשוב, פרשת וארא ד"ה ולקחתי אתכם לי לעם וכו', "We, His

people, the Children of Israel, can attain the light of the divine Presence by means of the Torah and the mitzvoth, etc." (Kedushath Levi on the Torah by Rav Levi Yitzchak Berdichev, Parashath Vaayra, header words: And I will take you to Me for a people, etc.). Thus, the expression המוציא אתכם, "Who takes you out," as used by the Torah, implies observing the mitzvoth, for the observing of the mitzvoth is the sine qua non with which the Children of Israel can achieve knowing G-d Who took them out. But the Children of Israel must be zealous and eager to observe the mitzvoth, so that this observance will continually progress.

A person must always strive to improve his performance of the commandments, as man's goal is to continually progress to higher and higher spiritual levels.This sempiternal striving for higher levels of spiritual elevation is based on pesukim, as רב אהרן קטלר, Rav Aaron Kotler, expressed so assertively, אורח חיים למעלה למשכיל למען סור משאול מטה (משלי טו,כד) האדם צריך להיות עולה תמיד, וניתן כך בכוחו שיהא עולה תמיד, כדכתיב (זכריה ג,ז) : ונתתי לך מהלכים בין העומדים האלה, האדם הוא בגדר מהלך, שתמיד הוא מהלך מדרגה לדרגה וכו' (משנת רבי אהרן מאת רב אהרן The", (קטלר, חלק ראשון, שער שמיני, פרק ח, וארח צדיקים־הולך ואור, ב way of life of the intelligent is to rise, in order to turn from the grave beneath' (Proverbs 15,24). A person needs to be constantly ascending, and thus he was given this strength so that he can be constantly ascending, as it is written (Zechariah 3,7): 'And I will give you [the strength] to proceed among these who are standing.' A person is in the category of one who proceeds, always proceeding from echelon to echelon, etc." (Mishnath Rabbi Aaron by Rabbi Aaron Kotler, first volume, Section 8, Chapter 8, and the way of the righteous-proceed and light, b).

The implication of the expression המוציא אתכם, "Who takes you out," in the Torah is the same as the implication of the term זריזות, "zeal," as defined by the מסלת ישרים, Mesillath

Yesharim, which is the observance of the mitzvoth. There is a total of 613 Mitzvoth. The gematria of המוציא אתכם, "Who takes you out," is the same as the total number of mitzvoth, in keeping with the implication of the expression המוציא אתכם, "Who takes you out," being the same as the implication of the term זריזות, "zeal," which is defined as the observance of the mitzvoth.

The difference between זהירות, "vigilance," and זריזות, "zeal," as defined by the מסלת ישרים, Mesillath Yesharim, which parallels the difference between המעלה אתכם, "Who raises you up," and המוציא אתכם, "Who takes you out," in the Torah with their respective gematrioth can give a fascinating explanation to a pasuk in Ecclesiastes. That pasuk says, טובים השנים מן האחד אשר יש להם שכר טוב בעמלם (קהלת ד,ט), "Two are better than one; for they have a good reward in their toil" (Ecclesiastes 4,9). The pasuk might be explained as follows:

טובים השנים, "Two are better": It is better to achieve a spiritual level associated the expression המוציא אתכם, "Who takes you out," whose implication is the same as the implication of the term זריזות, "zeal"; than the spiritual level associated with the expression המעלה אתכם, "who raises you up," whose implication is the same as the implication of the term זהירות, "vigilance." Those who achieve the level of being a זריז, "zealous," have already achieved being a זהיר, "vigilant"; thus they observe 613 Commandments. The gematria of המוציא אתכם, "Who takes you out," is numerically two greater than the gematria of המעלה אתכם, "Who raises you up."

מן האחד, "Than one": Than to achieve the spiritual level associated with the expression המעלה אתכם, "Who raises you up," which the Torah uses only once.

אשר יש להם שכר טוב בעמלם, "for they have a good reward in their toil": The two, the spiritual level associated with the words which are numerically two greater, have שכר טוב בעמלם, "a good reward in their toil."

The spiritual level associated with the expression המוציא אתכם, "Who takes you out" (that is numerically two greater), is זריזות, "zeal."

$$
\begin{array}{r}
613 \\
-611 \\
\hline
2
\end{array}
$$

Zealousness means being eager to observe the commandments. The Mishnah says that the reward for performing a mitzvah is another mitzvah. This Mishnah has been explained to mean that each mitzvah observed, divinely induces one to observe an additional mitzvah, as stated, שמן השמים מסייעין ומזמינים ביד מי שעשה מצוה אחת שיעשה אחרת וכו' (רבינו עובדיה מברטנורה, אבות פרק ד, משנה ב) "From Heaven he is helped and it is facilitated in the hand of him who performs one mitzvah, that he should perform another, etc." (Rabbeinu Ovadiah Bertinoro, Avoth, Chapter 4, Mishnah 2). Also note that the תפארת ישראל, Tifereth Yisroel, too, uses the word זריז, "zealous," to explain this Mishnah (תפארת ישראל, אבות פרק ד, משנה ב, אות יד, Tifereth Yisroel, Avoth, Chapter 4, Mishnah 2, Letter 2). The cumulative result of each additional mitzvah inducing another mitzvah to be observed or studied is that all 613 Mitzvoth will be observed at some level. Consequently, each mitzvah has the potential reward of inducing a person to observe all 613 Mitzvoth. The observing of the mitzvoth is referred to as good by the Mesillath Yesharim, as was said previously. Thus, there is a good reward in the toil of the spiritual level associated with this expression המוציא אתכם, "Who takes you out." That reward is the observing of the mitzvoth which is referred to as good.

Now that the pasuk from Ecclesiastes has been given a fascinating explanation, the two pairs of questions which were mentioned earlier can be answered. First, why was the Torah portion which includes the pasuk from Deuteronomy

16,1, chosen to be read on the last day of the Passover holiday? Second, why does the Torah choose to designate the Passover holiday and its season, to establish when a leap year is declared?

The answer is that the spring mentioned in Deuteronomy 16,1 is the time of budding and sprouting, of verdant new beginnings, corresponding to the implication of the term זריזות, "zeal." The Children of Israel should be zealous and eager to observe the commandments, so that this observance will continually progress. The Jewish lunar calendar will intercalate with the solar calendar, and the Passover holiday will occur in the spring, for each year is to continually progress, as a year to sprout, a year of zealousness in observing the commandments. Indeed the Torah counts the months of the year from the month of the spring, as stated, החדש הזה לכם ראש חדשים הוא לכם לחדשי השנה (שמות יב,ב), "This month [the Passover month] shall be to you the beginning of months; it shall be to you the first of the months of the year" (Exodus 12,2).

The outlook for each year should be one of zealousness. It is with this message that the Passover holiday is concluded. On the last day of Passover when the holiday is soon to depart, the Torah reading tells that the coming year should be a year when the Children of Israel should be zealous and eager to observe the commandments. This message could be the reason why the Torah portion for the last day of the Passover holiday (outside the land of Israel) includes the pasuk from Deuteronomy 16,1, a pasuk which mentions both the month of Spring and Passover. The first question has been answered.

Thus, it is valid that one might venture to say that the Passover holiday and its season, are the time to establish when a leap year is declared, because the expression המוציא אתכם, "Who takes you out," which has the same implication as זריזות, "zeal," refers to the time of year of the Passover holiday; that is, the year should be a time to progress in observance of the commandments. The second question has been answered.

The second pair of questions came from the הגדה של פסח, Passover Haggadah. One, why is it an obligation on the Passover holiday, as opposed to any other holiday, for one to see himself as if he went forth from Egypt? Two, since there is an obligation on the Passover holiday for one to see himself as if he went forth from Egypt, why is there no obligation to re-enact the going forth from Egypt?

The answer might be that the obligation on the Passover holiday for one to see himself as if he went forth from Egypt, is an obligation to feel zealous and eager to observe the commandments so that this observance will continually progress. This progress is what the expression המוציא אתכם, "Who takes you out," can imply. The expression המוציא אתכם, "Who takes you out," is written with regard to the going forth from Egypt, which the Passover holiday specifically commemorates. Thus, there is an obligation on the Passover holiday, as opposed to any other holiday, for one to see himself as if he went forth from Egypt. Question number one has been answered. One is not obligated to totally re-enact the going forth from Egypt, because the obligation to feel as if he went forth from Egypt (that is, to achieve progress in his observing the commandments), is an obligation to feel the implications of the expression המוציא אתכם, "Who brings you out." Question number two has been answered.

The learning of Torah is a dynamic, continually growing process. The parallel between the expression המעלה אתכם, "Who raises you up," and the term זהירות, "vigilance," is valid. The essential method of obtaining זהירות, "vigilance," is Torah learning.

Additional significance to the difference between the

gematrioth of זהירות, "vigilance," and זריזות, "zeal, can be found in the חג הסכות, The Sukkoth Holiday, section of this sefer.

ויאמר אלי בן אדם העצמות האלה כל בית ישראל המה הנה אמרים יבשו עצמותינו ואבדה תקותנו נגזרנו לנו (יחזקאל לז,יא).

And He said to me, "Son of man, these bones are the entire house of Israel; behold they say: Our bones are dried up, and our hope is lost, and we are cut off" (Ezekiel 37,11).

The הפטרה, Haftarah, for שבת חול המועד פסח, Passover Shabbath Chol Hamoed, contains a puzzling phrase: G-d's proclamation that העצמות, "the bones," are the entire house of Israel. The gematria of העצמות, "the bones," is 611.

העצמות   611

How could the entire house of Israel be compared to some bones? One answer is based on the writings of רב סעדיה גאון, Rav Saadia Gaon. He writes, וכן... שאמרה התורה, תורה צוה לנו משה מורשה (דברים לג,ד), ועוד... לפי שאומתינו, בני ישראל, אינו אומה אלא בתורותיה (ספר הנבחר באמונות ובדעות, מאת הרב סעדיה בן יוסף פיומי, תרגם לעברית באר והכין בכה"ר דוד קאפח, המאמר השלישי, פרק ז), "And also ... that the Torah says, 'Moses commanded us the Torah an inheritance' (Deuteronomy 33,4), and further ... our nation, the Children of Israel, is only a nation by virtue of its Torah," (Book of Hanivchar in Emunoth Vedaioth, Beliefs and Opinions by Rav Saadia ben Joseph Fiyumi, translated to Hebrew, explained and prepared by Joseph son of the honored Rabbi David Kapach, Essay three, Chapter 7). The gematria of תורה, "Torah," is 611.

תורה   611

The writings of Rav Saadia Gaon affirm that the Children of Israel are a nation solely on account of the Torah. Thus, G-d's proclamation that העצמות, "the bones," are the entire house of Israel, could imply that the Children of Israel are a nation solely on account of the Torah, meaningfully underscored by העצמות, "the bones," having a gematria equal to the gematria of תורה, "Torah."

The Holiday of Shavuoth חג השבעות

ישלם ה׳ פעלך ותהי משכרתך שלמה מעם ה׳ אלקי ישראל
אשר באת לחסות תחת כנפיו (רות ב,יב).
Hashem will remunerate your work, and your recompense will be full from Hashem, the G-d of Israel, under Whose wings that you have come to take refuge (Ruth 2,12).

מגלת רות, Megillath Ruth, is read on חג השבעות, the holiday of Shavuoth. At his first encounter with Ruth, Boaz speaks of G-d's methods of compensation, as he says, ישלם ה׳ פעלך, "G-d will remunerate your work." In that pasuk, Boaz uses two different expressions to refer to G-d: one is ה׳, "Hashem," the other is ה׳ אלקי ישראל, "Hashem, the G-d of Israel." Boaz also uses two different nouns to refer to the motives of G-d's remuneration: one is פעלך, "your work," and the other is משכרתך, "your recompense." The Malbim explains the divergence between these nouns. The difference between a פועל, "a worker" (from the same root as פעלך, "your work"), and a שכיר, "a hireling" (from the same root as משכרתך, "your recompense"), is that the former gets paid only for the work completed, but the latter gets paid for the time he works, regardless of how much he accomplishes. Thus, what Boaz is telling Ruth is: When any person performs a good deed, G-d, referred to as Hashem, pays him for his accomplishment. But when one has committed to convert to Judaism, to accept to fulfill all of the Torah's 613 Commandments, then he is paid as a hireling, that is, even if in fact he did not perform every commandment; and G-d is referred to as Hashem the G-d of Israel, as the pasuk goes on to say, ...ותהי משכרתך שלמה מעם, "... and your recompense will be full from Hashem, the G-d of Israel, as he says, ה׳ אלקי ישראל אשר באת לחסות תחת כנפיו ,"... and your recompense will be full from Hashem, the G-d of Israel, under Whose wings you have come to take refuge." The Malbim writes, שהפועל או אומן יקבל שכר בעד המלאכה אשר עשה... אבל השכיר

מושכר לזמן קצוב... בין יעשה איזה מלאכה בין לא יעשה... על מה שבאה להתגייר שאז קבלה עליה לעבוד עבודת ה׳ ולקיים כל מצותיו... ומאז מגיע לה שכר שכיר שישלם לה שכר תמידי בין תעשה בין לא תעשה (גזע ישי, רות ב,יב, מאת הרב מאיר ליבש מלביי״ם), "For the worker or artisan will receive recompense for the work which he did ... But the hireling is hired for a set time ... whether he will do any work or not do ... Regarding that she came to convert, since then she accepted upon herself to serve the service of G-d and fulfill all His commandments ... as of that time, she is worthy for the recompense of a hireling, who is paid a constant recompense whether she will do, or she will not do" (Geza Yishai by Rabbi Meir Lebush Malbim, Ruth 2,12).

Perhaps now a reason can be given for the difference in expressions which refer to G-d. When referring to the pay of a פועל, "a worker," who is paid for that which he produces, G-d is referred to as ה׳, "Hashem." However, when referring to the pay of a שכיר "a hireling," who even if he did not perform all of the commandments is still recompensed, G-d is referred to as ה׳ אלקי ישראל, "G-d, the G-d of Israel." The gematria of ה׳ אלקי ישראל, "G-d, the G-d of Israel," is 613.

ה׳	26
אלקי	46
ישראל	<u>541</u>
	613

The Gemara Makkoth says that there is a total of 613 Mitzvoth given to Moses, as stated, דרש רבי שמלאי שש מאות ושלש עשרה מצות נאמרו לו למשה שלש מאות וששים וחמש לאוין כמנין ימות החמה ומאתים וארבעים ושמונה עשה כנגד איבריו של אדם (מכות כג:), "Rabbi Simlai expounded, six hundred and thirteen Commandments were said to Moses. Three hundred and sixty-five negative Commandments corresponding to the number of days in a solar year, and two hundred and forty-eight positive Commandments corresponding to the number of limbs of a man" (Makkoth 23b).

Since a שכיר "a hireling," is paid for all 613 Commandments, and the gematria of הי אלקי ישראל, "G-d, the G-d of Israel," is 613, therefore it is appropriate that G-d is referred to here with this expression. Thus, utilizing a gematria can help explain the two different expressions used to refer to G-d. How pertinent for the holiday of Shavuoth to read how abundantly G-d remunerates for the commitment to observe the 613 Commandments, for this very day commemorates the Children of Israel receiving the Torah with its 613 Mitzvoth.

Hanukkah   חנוכה

There are various reasons why the חשמונאים, Hasmoneans, adopted the name מכבי, "Maccabi." Perhaps, through the use of gematrioth, another aspect of the name can be gained. The gematria of מכבי, "Maccabi," is 72.

מכבי   72

The Hasmoneans tried to return the Children of Israel (many of whom had abandoned G-d's Torah, in favor of the ways of their Greek-Syrian rulers) to the Torah and to observing G-d's 613 Mitzvoth. The gematria of ישראל, "Israel," is 541.

ישראל   541

When the gematria of מכבי, "Maccabi," is added to the gematria of ישראל, "Israel," the sum is 613.

72
<u>541</u>
613

Since the Hasmoneans tried to return the Children of Israel to the Torah and observing G-d's 613 Mitzvoth, it is fitting that the gematria of the name they adopted, when added to the gematria of ישראל, "Israel," should have the sum of 613.

There are various reasons why the חשמונאים, Hasmoneans, adopted the name מכבי, "Maccabi." One reason for the name, is that מכבי, "Maccabi," is an acronym for מי כמוך באלים הי (שמות טו,יא), "Who is like You among the mighty, O G-d?" (Exodus 15,11). Through the use of gematrioth, a further insight into this name can be revealed. The gematria of מכבי, "Maccabi," is 72.

מכבי   72

There is a Mishnah which states, בן עשרים לרדוף (אבות, פרק ה, משנה כא), "The age of twenty is for pursuing," (Avoth, Chapter 5, Mishnah 21). The תפארת ישראל, Tifereth Yisroel, explains this phrase as referring תפארת ישראל) לצאת למלחמת ישראל (ישראל, אבות, פרק ה, משנה כא, אות קסד), "To go out for a war of Israel," (Tifereth Yisroel, Avoth, Chapter 5, Mishnah 21, Letter 164). Thus, the age of twenty is when one was considered eligible to enter the army. The age of twenty is when one was considered able to fight in a war. The age of twenty can be written as בן כי, "twenty years old." The gematria of בן כי, "twenty years old," is 72.

בן	52
כי	20
	72

Thus, a possible reason why the חשמונאים, Hasmoneans, adopted the name מכבי, "Maccabi," might be that מכבי, "Maccabi," has the same gematria as בן כי, "twenty years old." Maccabi represented the age when one was considered able to fight in a war, which is what the Hasmoneans did for the sake of G-d's people, Israel. Thus it is appropriate that they adopted the name מכבי, "Maccabi."

Hanukkah or Parashath Vayyeshev   חנוכה או פרשת וישב

Hanukkah usually occurs during the days following Parashath Vayyeshev. There are various reasons why the חשמונאים, Hasmoneans, adopted the name מכבי, "Maccabi." Through the use of gematrioth, the name can be linked to Parashath Vayyeshev. The gematria of מכבי, "Maccabi," is 72.

מכבי   72

During the time of the חשמונאים, Hasmoneans, when Israel was under the rule of the Greek-Syrians, many Jews had forsaken Judaism and embraced Hellenism. The Hasmoneans wanted these Jews to return to their faith and recognize their Jewishness. The banner, symbol, used by the Hasmoneans was the name מכבי, "Maccabi."

In Parashath Vayyeshev, the brothers of Joseph took his coat and presented it to Jacob asking him to recognize it, as stated, וישלחו את כתנת הפסים ויביאו אל אביהם ויאמרו זאת מצאנו הכר נא הכתנת בנך הוא אם לא (בראשית לז,לב), "And they sent the coat of many colors and they brought it to their father and they said: 'This we found, please recognize, is it the coat of your son or not'" (Genesis 37,32). The gematria of אם לא, "or not," is 72.

אם   41
לא   31
        72

Thus, a possible reason why the Hasmoneans adopted the name מכבי, "Maccabi," is that מכבי, "Maccabi," has the same gematria as אם לא, "or not." מכבי, "Maccabi," could represent recognizing. Just as Jacob was asked to recognize the coat which was the representation of Joseph, so too were the Jews in the time of the Hasmoneans asked to return to their faith and recognize their Jewishness, the banner and representation of which was מכבי, "Maccabi."

Thus, the name, מכבי, "Maccabi," can represent an analogous question of identification: You are Jewish, are you not? This interrogation is precisely what the Hasmoneans were asking. Therefore it is fitting that they adopted the name מכבי, "Maccabi."

Also from פרשת וישב, Parashath Vayyeshev, another possible motive why the חשמונאים, Hasmoneans, adopted the name מכבי, "Maccabi," might be derived. When Joseph was in prison, the Torah says, ויהי ה' את יוסף ויט אליו חסד ויתן חנו בעיני שר בית הסהר (בראשית לט,כא), "And G-d was with Joseph and He extended upon him kindness, and He gave him favor in the eyes of the officer in charge of the prison" (Genesis 39,21). The gematria of חסד, "kindness," is 72.

חסד   72

Thus, another motive why the חשמונאים, Hasmoneans, adopted the name מכבי, "Maccabi," could be that it has the same gematria as חסד, "kindness." Just as G-d extended kindness to Joseph when he was under foreign rule, so too the Hasmoneans hoped that G-d would extend kindness to them while they were fighting a foreign rule, bent on destroying the Children of Israel's allegiance to G-d. Therefore it is fitting that they adopted the name מכבי, "Maccabi."

Ethics of the Fathers — פרקי אבות
and Siyyumim — וסיומים

Ethics of the Fathers

רבי אלעזר בן חסמא אומר קנין ופתחי נדה הן הן גופי הלכות, תקופות וגימטריאות פרפראות לחכמה (אבות, פרק ג, משנה יח).

Rabbi Elazar ben Chisma said, "The laws concerning the sacrifices of birds and the onset of a menstrual impurity are legal constitutions, while calculations of the seasons and gematrioth are condiments to wisdom" (Avoth, Chapter 3, Mishnah 18).

The Mishnah states that gematrioth are condiments to wisdom. The gematria of פרפראות לחכמה, "condiments to wisdom," is 1070.

פרפראות	967	
לחכמה	103	
	1070	

The Mishnah in Avoth gives precedence to deeds over wisdom, as stated, כל שמעשיו מרבים מחכמתו חכמתו מתקיימת וכל שחכמתו מרבה ממעשיו אין חכמתו מתקיימת (אבות, פרק ג, משנה ט), "Anyone whose deeds exceed his wisdom, his wisdom shall endure, but anyone whose wisdom exceeds his deeds, his wisdom shall not endure" (Avoth, Chapter 3, Mishnah 9). The תוספת יום טוב, Tosafoth Yom Tov, explains this Mishnah in the name of Rabbeinu Yona, and also refers to Avoth d'Rabbi Nathan regarding this explanation. Acceptance of doing Hashem's will has precedence over wisdom, since once Hashem's will is accepted, it is considered as if it is done; so acceptance is counted as greater than wisdom. He says, במה שמקבל על עצמו לעשות כל הדברים אשר יגידו לו החכמים ולא יסור ימין ושמאל, הרי זה מעשיו מרובין מחכמתו. כי מעתה מעלה עליו כאילו קיים כל התורה כולה... תנן מרובין שכיון להשמיענו זאת שהקדימה היא הקבלה, והקבלה היא במרובה מהחכמה (תוספת יום טוב, אבות פרק ג, משנה ט,

(ד"ה כל שמעשיו מרובין), "Pertaining to someone who accepts upon oneself to do everything which the [Torah oriented] wise men tell him, and he does not veer to right or left, behold this is one [to whom applies the expression]: his deeds exceed his wisdom. For now it is considered as if he observed all the Torah in its entirety... It was taught, 'exceed,' for it intended to let us hear that precedence is given to acceptance, and the acceptance exceeds wisdom" (Tosafoth Yom Tov, Avoth Chapter 3, Mishnah 9, header words: Anyone whose deeds exceed). According to the Tosafoth Yom Tov, this Mishnah is saying that acceptance to do Hashem's will must precede wisdom, if the wisdom is to endure.

One of the phrases that the Torah uses (three times) to express acceptance to do Hashem's will is כי תשמע בקול ה' אלקיך, "when you will listen to the voice of Hashem your G-d," (דברים יג,יט ; כח,ב ; ול,י), Deuteronomy 13,19; 28,2; and 30,10). Note that in each of these three places, Targum Onkelos translates תשמע, "you will listen," with the word תקבל, "you will accept." Although in other places (דברים יג,יג, וכח,מט, Deuteronomy 13,13, and 28,49) Targum Onkelos translates the word תשמע, "you will listen," with the same word תשמע, "you will listen." Therefore, כי תשמע בקול ה' אלקיך, "when you will listen to the voice of Hashem your G-d," can be specifically an expression of acceptance to do Hashem's will.

From the Tosafoth Yom Tov, it is known that acceptance must precede wisdom if the wisdom is to endure. From the Targum Onkelos it is known that כי תשמע בקול ה' אלקיך, "when you will listen to the voice of Hashem your G-d," is an expression of acceptance. It can be deduced that one must first be on the level of כי תשמע בקול ה' אלקיך, "when you will listen to the voice of Hashem your G-d," before engaging in wisdom, or condiments to wisdom. The gematria of כי תשמע בקול ה' אלקיך, "when you will listen to the voice of Hashem your G-d," is 1070.

כי	30
תשמע	810
בקול	138
ה׳	26
אלקיך	66
	1070

The gematria of פרפראות לחכמה, "condiments to wisdom," is equal to the gematria of כי תשמע בקול ה׳ אלקיך, "when you will listen to the voice of Hashem your G-d." One must first be on the level of 1070 before engaging in wisdom or the condiments to wisdom. This thought is further appealing since the תוספת יום טוב, Tosafoth Yom Tov, explains פרפראות, "condiments," as something eaten before the meal, as stated, אלא נראה ודאי דלדבריו פירוש פרפראות הדברים הרגילים לבא קודם הסעודה להמשיך האכילה (תוספת יום טוב, אבות פרק ג, משנה יח, ד״ה פרפראות לחכמה), "But it appears certain, that according to his words, the meaning of condiments is those thing which are usually brought before the meal to evoke the eating" (Tosafoth Yom Tov, Avoth Chapter 3, Mishnah 18, header words: Condiments to wisdom). The message is clear; only when one has accepted to do the will of Hashem, can he engage in gematrioth.

רבי יהודה אומר, הוה זהיר בתלמוד ששגגת תלמוד עולה זדון (אבות, פרק ד, משנה יג).

Rabbi Yehuda said, "Be cautious in study, for an error of study may amount to intentional sin" (Avoth, Chapter 4, Mishnah 13).

The Mishnah says that an error in study may amount to זדון, "intentional sin." The gematria of זדון, "intentional sin," is 67.

זדון	67

The word עולה, "may amount to," can be translated as,

"sums up," or "totals." Thus, the expression עולה זדון, "may amount to intentional sin," can be translated as, "sums up," or "totals," זדון, "intentional sin," which has a gematria of 67. The Bertinoro comments on this Mishnah, הקב״ה מעלה על ידך כאילו עשית מזיד (רב עובדיה מברטנורה, ד״ה תלמוד עולה זדון), "The Holy One, Blessed be He, considers it for you as if you did it intentionally," (Rabbi Ovadiah Bertinoro, header words: Study may amount to intentional sin). The gematria of כאילו, "as if," is 67.

כאילו   67

How interesting, then, that the gematrioth of זדון, "intentional sin," and כאילו, "as if," are one in the same; for the gematria parity reinforces the Bertinoro's comments.

Siyyum on Seder
Mishnayoth Zeraim

סיום סדר
משניות זרעים

Upon the completion of the learning of a seder (order) or a mesechta (tractate), it is a long-standing practice to connect the the end with the beginning of that same tractate or seder. One reason for this connection is that after having learned a tractate once, one can learn it a second time with clearer understanding. Consequently, when one has concluded a tractate, it is customary to start the same tractate anew (מעין בית השואבה מאת הרב שמעון בן יהודה שוואב, וזאת הברכה, דברים לד,יב, Maayan Beth Hashoevah by Rabbi Shimon ben Yehuda Schwab, Vezoth Haberachah, Deuteronomy 34,12).

Seder Zeraim ends with a discussion of an אנדרוגינוס, "hermaphrodite," and begins with a discussion of when Shema is to be read. What possible connection could there be between these two seemingly unrelated topics? Perhaps by utilizing a gematria, a link can be found.

The תלמוד ירושלמי, "Talmud Yerushalmi," says, one reason why the Shema should be said every day is that it alludes to the Ten Commandments (תלמוד ירושלמי, ברכות, פרק א, הלכה ה, Yerushalmi Gemara, Berakoth, Chapter 1, Halakhah 5). Rashi remarks that the Ten Commandments encompass all 613 Commandments, as stated, כל שש מאות ושלש עשרה מצות בכלל עשרת הדברות הן (רש״י שמות כד,יב), "All 613 Commandments are included in the Ten Commandments" (Rashi, Exodus 24,12). Since the Shema includes the Ten Commandments, and the Ten Commandments encompass all 613 Commandments, thus, the Shema also includes all 613 Commandments.

The first two paragraphs of the Shema refer, respectively, to the acceptance of the yoke of heaven, and to the acceptance of the yoke of the commandments (which include all 613 Commandments) (ברכות יג., Berakoth 13a). The acceptance of these two yokes is how the Malbim explains a repetition in the Torah. Four pesukim from the end of Parashath Kedoshim, Hashem says that He will separate them, referring to the Children of Israel, from the nations (ויקרא כ,כד, Leviticus 20,24). Two pesukim later Hashem says again that He will separate them from the nations (ויקרא כ,כו, Leviticus 20,26). The Malbim explains that the separation in the earlier pasuk stems from the acceptance of the yoke of heaven; the separation in the later pasuk stems from the acceptance of yoke of the commandments (התורה והמצוה, מאת הרב מאיר ליבוש מלביי״ם, ויקרא כ,כו, The Torah and the Mitzvah by Rabbi Meir Lebush Malbim, Leviticus 20,26).

From the explanation of the Malbim it is clear that the acceptance of the yoke of heaven and the acceptance of yoke of the commandments cause the Children of Israel to be unique, single, solitary, and different from the other nations.

The last Mishnah in Seder Zeraim characterizes an אדרוגינוס, "hermaphrodite," as unique, as stated (in some of the editions of the Mishnah), רבי יוסי אומר אנדרוגינוס בריה בפני עצמה הוא ולא יכלו חכמים להכריע עליו אם איש או אשה (בכורים, פרק ד, משנה ה), "Rabbi Jose says, An hermaphrodite is a unique creature, and the sages were not able to make a determination whether it is a man or a woman" (Bikkurim, Chapter 4, Mishnah 5). The gematria of בריה בפני עצמה הוא ולא, "a unique creature, and were not," is 613.

בריה	217
בפני	142
עצמה	205
הוא	12
ולא	37
	613

The last Mishnah in Seder Zeraim characterizes an אדרוגינוס, "hermaphrodite," as unique, and it contains the gematria of 613. The first Mishnah in Seder Zeraim begins with a discussion of when Shema is to be read; the Shema contains acceptance of the yoke of all 613 Commandments. The reading of the Shema properly, causes the Children of Israel to be unique from the other nations. Hence, by utilizing a gematria a link can connect the end with the beginning of Seder Zeraim.

Siyyum on Seder Mishnayoth Tahoroth   סיום סדר
משניות טהרות

The last Mishnah at the end of Seder Tahoroth says that in the future every צדיק, "righteous man," will inherit 310 worlds, as stated, אמר רבי יהושע בן לוי עתיד הקדוש ברוך הוא להנחיל לכל צדיק וצדיק שלש מאות ועשרים עולמות (עוקצים, פרק ג, משנה יב), "Rabbi Joshua ben Levi said, In the future the Holy One, Blessed be He, will cause each righteous man to inherit three hundred and ten worlds" (Ukzin Chapter 3, Mishnah 12). The gematria of צדיק, "righteous man," is 204.

$$\text{צדיק} \qquad 204$$

What is the significance of these 310 worlds? הרב פינחס קהתי, Rabbi Pinkas Kehati, refers to the תפארת ישראל, "Tifereth Yisroel," who cites his father, who says that the number 310 is half the sum of 613 מצות דאורייתא, "commandments from the Torah," plus seven מצות דרבן, "commandments from the rabbis." The seven מצות דרבן, "commandments from the rabbis," are:

1. To say a blessing before and after enjoyments, excluding grace after meals (which is of Biblical origin)
2. To make any of the three types of עירובין, "eruvin"
3. To wash the hands
4. To light candles on the eve of Shabbath and the eve of Yom Tov
5. To say הלל, "Hallel"
6. To observe Hanukkah
7. To read מגלת אסתר, "Megillath Esther," on Purim

When these seven מצות דרבן, "commandments from the rabbis," are added to the 613 מצות דאורייתא, "commandments from the Torah," the total is 620 (באור משנה מאת הרב) Commentary, פינס קהתי, עוקצים פרק ג, משנה יב, ד"ה בעניין מאמרו on the Mishnah by Rabbi Pinkas Kehati, Ukzin, Chapter 3, Mishnah 12, header words: In the subject of the saying). Hence, a צדיק, "righteous man," is one who observes the commandments.

The ספר טעמי המנהגים ומקורי הדינים, Book of Jewish Customs and Traditions, gives a reason why on Simhath Torah, בראשית, Genesis, is read right after the end of the Torah is read, as stated, טעם שבשמחת תורה אחר שמסיימין בו את התורה קורין מיד בראשית עד סוף ויכולו, כדי שלא יהא פתחון פה לשטן לקטרג ולומר רבש"ע כבר סיימו אותה ואינם רוצים לקרות עוד (ספר טעמי המנהגים ומקורי הדינים מאת הרב אברהם יצחק שפרלינג, עניני שמחת תורה, אות תתכט), "The reason why on Simhath Torah immediately after the conclusion of the Torah, 'Genesis,' until the end of 'And they were finished,' is read, is in order that there should not be a pretext for the Satan to accuse and say, 'Master of the world, They have already finished it, and they do not want to read anymore'" (Book of Jewish Customs and Traditions by Rabbi Abraham Yitzchak Sperling, Simhath Torah Subjects, Letter 829). A similar reason is given the the Mishnah Berurah (משנה ברורה, סימן תרסח, ס"ק י, Mishnah Berurah, Siman 668, Small Seif 10).

This same reasoning can be extended to include the custom to connect the end of a סדר משניות, seder of Mishnayoth with the beginning of that seder. In the case of Seder Tahoroth the end of the seder can be connected to the beginning of the seder with the assistance of a gematria. From the Commentary on the Mishnah by Rabbi Pinkas Kehati at the end of Seder Tahoroth, a צדיק, "righteous one," was identified as one who observes the commandments. This same identification is avouched by יחזקאל, Ezekiel, as stated, בחקותי יהלך ומשפטי שמר לעשות אמת צדיק הוא חיה יחיה נאם ה' אלקים (יחזקאל יח,ט), "He who will walk in My statutes, and will keep My ordinances, to do truth, he is a righteous man, he shall surely live, said G-d, Hashem" (Ezekiel 18,9).

Besides observing the commandments, a צדיק, "righteous man," has the character trait of giving profusely, as opposed to the slothful, as stated, כל היום התאוה תאוה וצדיק יתן ולא יחשך (משלי כא,כו), "He coveted greedily the entire day, whereas a righteous man gives and does not spare"(Proverbs 21,26). Thus, there are two character traits identified with a righteous man: one, he observes the commandments, and two, he gives profusely.

The first Mishnah of Seder Tahoroth begins, אבות הטומאות השרץ ושכבת זרע וטמא מת והמצורע בימי ספרו וכוי (כלים פרק א, משנה א), "The primary transmitters of ritual defilement are the creeping thing [referring to the eight creeping creatures listed in the Torah, when dead], and semen, and one who was impure from a corpse, and the metzora in his days of counting, etc." (Kelim, Chapter 1, Mishnah 1). The gematria of אבות, "primary transmitters," is 409.

אבות   409

Just like a righteous man gives profusely, so too the אבות הטומאות, "the primary transmitters of impurity," transmit or give ritual defilement. The last Mishnah at the end of Seder Tahoroth alludes to the observing of the 613 Commandments, which a righteous man does. The beginning of Seder Tahoroth alludes to transmitting or giving ritual defilement. It has been demonstrated that the gematria of צדיק, a righteous man," is 204 and the gematria of אבות, "primary transmitters," is 409. Their combined gematria is 613.

204
409
———
613

There is a total of 613 Commandments which the Children of Israel are to observe (מכות כג:, Makkoth 23b).

Therefore, the combined gematria of צדיק, "a righteous man," and the gematria of אבות, "primary transmitters," is the important value of 613, relating to a righteous man. Thus, the end of Seder Tahoroth has been connected to the beginning of Seder Tahoroth with the assistance of a gematria.

Appendix   נספח

The Torah was written in לשון הקדש, "the Holy Tongue," (Hebrew). Every sentence, every word, and even every letter has holiness to it. The Torah is perfect, written by the perfect G-d. Each and every time the Torah expresses a thought, every letter of every word that makes up that thought is highly significant. The gematria of every letter and the way G-d wrote it has special meaning. Throughout this sefer, the gematrioth are invariably based on the spelling of words exactly as they appear in the text, since the way they appear in the text is highly significant.

Those gematrioth calculated on an altered spelling of the text, as the omission of וו החבור, "conjunction vav," have been placed in this Appendix.

Parashath Yisro   פרשת יתרו

ויסעו מרפידים ויבאו מדבר סיני ויחנו במדבר ויחן שם
ישראל נגד ההר (שמות יט,ב).

And they traveled from Rephidim and they
came to the desert of Sinai, and they encamped
in the desert; and there Israel encamped opposite the mountain (Exodus 19,2).

Regarding the Children of Israel's camping in the desert of Sinai, Rashi comments that they were united כאיש אחד
בלב אחד, "Like one man with one heart," (רש"י, שמות יט,ב,
Rashi, Exodus 19,2). The gematria of לב, "heart," is 32.

32   לב

Note that the ב, "beth," of בלב, "with heart," has been
excluded from the calculation of this gematria; it only serves
as a preposition (with). This unity is a unique trait that only
the Children of Israel possess, as stated, שבעצם בני ישראל הם
כאיש אחד משורשם, וחסר רק שיהיה להם גם רצון אחד ולב אחד, לעומת
זה אומות העולם הן מפוצלות משורשן וכו' (מעינה של תורה מאת הרב
אלכסנדר זושא פרידמן, שמות יד,י), "That in essence the Children
of Israel are like one man from their origin; and the only thing
lacking is for them to also have unity of desire and heart. As
opposed to this, the nations of the world are fragmented from
their origin, etc." (Wellsprings of Torah by Alexander Zusia
Friedman, Exodus 14,10). This unique character of the Children of Israel is recorded in the Book of Samuel, as stated, ומי
כעמך כישראל גוי אחד בארץ אשר הלכו אלקים לפדות לו לעם ולשום לו
שם ולעשות לכם הגדולה ונראות לארצך מפני עמך אשר פדית לך ממצרים
גוים ואלהיו (שמואל ב ז,כג), "And who is like Your people, like
Israel, a unique nation in the earth, whom G-d went to
redeem as a people to Himself, and to make Him a name, and
to do for you great and fearful things for your land, from

before Your people whom You redeemed for Yourself from Egypt, from nations and their gods?" (II Samuel 7,23). The gematria of גוי אחד, "a unique nation," is 32.

$$
\begin{array}{rr}
\text{גוי} & 19 \\
\text{אחד} & \underline{13} \\
& 32
\end{array}
$$

Since the unity of one heart is a unique trait of the Children of Israel, and this character of the Children of Israel is recorded in the Book of Samuel as גוי אחד, "a unique nation," it is fitting that לב, "heart," and גוי אחד, "a unique nation," should have the same gematria. The unity of one heart is one of the reasons the Children of Israel are a unique nation.

Parashath Bechukosai   פרשת בחקתי

ואם משדה אחזתו יקדיש איש לה׳ והיה ערכך לפי זרעו זרע
חמר שערים בחמשים שקל כסף (ויקרא כז,טז).
And if from a field of his inheritance, a man will
sanctify to G-d, then your evaluation shall be in
proportion to its sowing, the sowing of a homer
of barley, for fifty shekels of silver (Leviticus
27,16).

When one sanctifies from his field of his inheritance or
from his bought field, the evaluation is to be with shekels that
are קדש לה׳, "holy to G-d." When one sanctifies from a field of
his inheritance, for example, the evaluation is to be with a
holy silver shekel. The gematria of שקל, "shekel," is 430.

שקל   430

When one sanctifies from his bought field, the evaluation is to be קדש לה׳, "holy to G-d," as stated, וחשב לו הכהן את
מכסת הערכך עד שנת היבל ונתן את הערכך ביום ההוא קדש לה׳ (ויקרא
כז,כג), "And the priest shall reckon to him the worth of your
evaluation until the jubilee year, and he shall give your evaluation on that day as a holy thing to G-d" (Leviticus 27,23).
The gematria of קדש, "a holy thing," is 404.

קדש   404

The gematria of ה׳, "G-d," is 26.

ה׳   26

Note that the ל, "lamed," of לה׳, "to G-d," has been
excluded from the calculation of this gematria; it only serves
as a preposition (to). The Torah tells that the shekel is to be
holy to G-d. The gematria of שקל, "shekel," is equal to the
gematria of קדש, "a holy thing," plus the gematria of ה׳, "G-d."

קדש   404
ה׳   26
_____
430

This gematria hints to what the Torah says, that the shekel is to be קדש לה׳, "holy to G-d." The mathematical difference between the shekel money, and holiness, is G-d's name. A shekel used in G-d's name is holy; if it is used for any other purpose, it is only a shekel.

This difference is further indicated by the Ramban who compares the holy shekel to the holy language. The holy language is the language of G-d, as stated, וכן שקלי המשכן וכן כל כסף קצוב האמור בתורה יקרא לו הכתוב [השקל] שקל הקדש וכן הטעם אצלי במה שרבותינו קורין לשון התורה לשון הקודש... והנה הוא הלשון שהקדוש ברוך הוא יתעלה שמו מדבר בו עם נביאיו ועם עדתו וכו׳ (רמב״ן שמות ל,יג), "And just like the shekels of the Tabernacle, and just like all fixed amounts of money which are said in the Torah, the verse calls it [the shekel] the holy shekel. And this is also what I hold to be the reason why our Rabbis call the language of the Torah the holy language... And behold it is the language with which the Holy One, Blessed be He, may His name be exalted, speaks with His prophets and His congregation, etc." (Ramban, Exodus 30,13).

Another indication that G-d's name differentiates between שקל, "shekel," and קדש, "a holy thing," is in the pasuk previously quoted, as stated, וחשב לו הכהן את מכסת הערכך עד שנת היבל ונתן את הערכך ביום ההוא קדש לה׳ (ויקרא כז,כג), "And the priest shall reckon to him the worth of the evaluation until the jubilee year, and he shall give the evaluation on that day as a holy thing to G-d" (Leviticus 27,23). When is the shekel considered holy? When it is לה׳, "to G-d."

Parashath Naso

פרשת נשא

יברכך ה' וישמרך. יאר ה' פניו אליך ויחנך. ישא ה' פניו
אליך וישם לך שלום (במדבר ו,כד־כו).
May G-d bless you and keep you. May G-d illuminate His countenance towards you and be
gracious to you. May G-d lift up His countenance towards you, and grant you peace (Numbers 6, 24-26).

There are six verbs in the three pesukim of ברכת כהנים,
"the priestly blessing"; they are: יברכך, "May He bless you,"
וישמרך, "and may He keep you," יאר, "May He illuminate,"
ויחנך, "and may He be gracious to you," ישא, "May he lift up,"
and וישם, "and grant." The sum of the gematrioth of יברכך,
"May He bless you," וישמרך, "and may He keep you," יאר,
"May He illuminate," ויחנך, "and may He be gracious to you,"
ישא, "May he lift up," and וישם, "and grant" is 1800.

יברכך וישמרך	828
יאר ויחנך	305
ישא וישם	667
	1800

Immediately after the three pesukim of ברכת כהנים,
"the priestly blessing," the Torah talks about placing G-d's
name on the Children of Israel, as stated, ושמו את שמי על בני
ישראל ואני אברכם (במדבר ו,כז), "And they shall put My name
upon the Children of Israel, and I will bless them" (Numbers
6,27). The gematria of שמו את שמי על בני ישראל, "they shall put
My name upon the Children of Israel," is 1800.

שמו את	747
שמי על	450
בני ישראל	603
	1800

Note that the first ו, "vav," of ושמו, "And they shall put," has been excluded from the calculation of this gematria; it only serves as as וו החבור, "conjunction vav" (and). The Gemara Sotah says, ותניא אידך כה תברכו את בני ישראל (במדבר ו,כג) בשם המפורש אתה אומר בשם המפורש או אינו אלא בכינוי תלמוד לומר ושמו את שמי שמי המיוחד לי (סוטה לח.), "And it was taught in another Baraitha, [When the Torah states,] In this wise shall you bless the Children of Israel (Numbers 6,23), [it means the the priests shall pronounce the blessing] with the explicit Name [of G-d]. You say [that they pronounce the blessing] with the explicit Name, but maybe it is only with the alternative pronunciation [of the Name]. The Torah says, And they shall put My name, My Name which is unique to Me" (Sotah 38a).

Thus, 1800 is associated with the verbs of ברכת כהנים, "the priestly blessing," and is also associated with the placing of G-d's name upon the Children of Israel. After the priests bless the people with G-d's name, then G-d will bless the Children of Israel (רש״י, במדבר ו,כז, Rashi, Numbers 6,27). The equality of these gematrioth shows that when the priests bless the people, it is by placing G-d's name on the Children of Israel. G-d must be seen as the source of blessing.

Parashath Mattos   פרשת מטות

ונכבשה הארץ לפני ה' ואחר תשבו והייתם נקים מה'
ומישראל והיתה הארץ הזאת לכם לאחזה לפני ה' (במדבר
לב,כב).

And the land shall be subdued before G-d and afterwards you shall return, and you shall be guiltless before G-d and Israel, and this land shall be for you for an inheritance before G-d (Numbers 32,22).

Moses told the members of the tribe of Gad and the tribe of Reuben, that if they did as he instructed, they would be guiltless מה' ומישראל, "before G-d and Israel." The gematria of ה' ומישראל, "G-d and before Israel," is 613.

ה'	26
ומישראל	587
	613

Note that the מ, "mem," of מה', "before G-d," has been excluded from the calculation of this gematria; it only serves as a preposition (before). Since there is a total of 613 Comments, (מכות כג:, Makkoth 23b), the pasuk could be read as, והייתם נקים מתריג מצות, "and you shall be guiltless from transgressing any of the 613 Commandments." Indeed, it is from this pasuk that the Mishnah learns that one should always appear בנקיות, "clean" (שקלים, פרק ג, משנה ב) Shekalim, Chapter 3, Mishnah 2).

This gematria is further validated by a Rashi in the Talmud where נקיות, "cleanliness," is defined as נקי באין חטא, "guiltless without a sin" (רש"י, עבודה זרה כ:, ד"ה נקיות) (Rashi, Avodah Zarah 20b, header words: Cleanliness). One who has never committed a sin is one who has not transgressed any of the 613 Commandments. The meaning of נקיות, "guiltless-ness," that Moses told the members of the tribe of Gad and

the tribe of Reuben, and the meaning of נקיות, "guiltlessness,"
that Rashi in the Talmud defines, are identical, which adds to
the validation of this gematria.

Parashath Shofetim   פרשת שפטים

שפטים ושטרים תתן לך בכל שעריך אשר ה׳ אלקיך נתן לך
לשבטיך ושפטו את העם משפט צדק (דברים טז,יח).
Judges and officers you shall appoint for yourself in all your gates which G-d, your G-d, gives you according to your tribes, and they shall judge the people a righteous judgment (Deuteronomy 16,18).

The first pasuk in this week's sidrah mentions שפטים ושטרים, "judges and officers." The gematria of שפטים, "judges," is 439.

שפטים   439

The gematria of שטרים, "officers," is 559.

שטרים   559

Note that the ו, "vav," of ושטרים "and officers," has been excluded from the calculation of this gematria; it only serves as וו החבור, "conjunction vav" (and). The difference between שפטים, "judges," and שטרים, "officers," in gematrioth is 120.

559
-439
―――
120

On this first pasuk of the sidrah, Rashi defines the שטרים, "officers," as those who do the מכין, "hitting," as ושטרים הרודים את העם אחר מצותם שמכין וכופתין במקל וברצועה עד שיקבל עליו את דין השופט (רש״י, דברים טז,יח) "And officers who subjugate the people after their judgmental command, who beat and force with a stick or a whip until he [the individual] accepts upon himself the law of the judge" (Rashi, Deuteronomy 16,18). The gematria of מכין, "hitting," is 120.

120   מכין

Note that the ש, "shin," of שמכין "who beat," has been excluded from the calculation of this gematria; it only serves as a pronoun (who). Thus, the difference between the שפטים, "judges," and שטרים, "officers," is that the latter group does the מכין, "hitting." The gematria of מכין, "hitting," equals the difference between שפטים, "judges," and שטרים, "officers," in gematrioth.

Parashath Ki Thetze

פרשת כי תצא

ארבעים יכנו לא יסיף פן יסיף להכתו על אלה מכה רבה
ונקלה אחיך לעיניך (דברים כה,ג).

Forty stripes he may give him; he may not exceed, lest, if he should exceed to hit him above these with many stripes, then your brother will be slighted in your eyes (Deuteronomy 25,3).

Rashi clarifies that the number forty in this instance really means thirty-nine, as stated, ולא ארבעים שלמים אלא מנין שהוא סוכם ומשלים לארבעים והן ארבעים חסר אחת (רש״י, דברים כה,ב), "And not with a total of forty, but with the number which sums up until and completes to forty; it is thirty-nine" (Rashi, Deuteronomy 25,2). The gematria of יכנו, "he may be beaten," is 86.

יכנו   86

When the lashes were sentenced, it was by a judge in the name of judgment, as stated, כי יהיה ריב בין אנשים ונגשו אל המשפט ושפטום והצדיקו את הצדיק והרשיעו את הרשע. והיה אם בן הכות הרשע והפילו השפט והכהו לפניו כדי רשעתו במספר (דברים כה,א-ב), "If there will be a dispute between men, and they have recourse to judgment, and they judge them, and they vindicate the righteous one, and condemn the wicked one. And it shall be if the wicked one is liable to be beaten, then the judge shall cause him to lie down and have him flogged before him, according to his wickedness by number" (Deuteronomy 25,1-2). The Torah also tells that the judgment is G-d's, as stated, לא תכירו פנים במשפט כקטן כגדל תשמעון לא תגורו מפני איש כי המשפט לאלקים הוא והדבר אשר יקשה מכם תקרבון אלי ושמעתיו (דברים א,יז), "You shall not respect persons in judgment; you shall hear the small and the great alike; you shall not be intimidated by any man, for the judgment is G-d's, and the cause which is too hard for you, bring it to me, and I will hear it" (Deuteronomy 1,17). The gematria of אלקים, "G-d," is 86.

אלקים   86

Note that the ל, "lamed," of לאלקים, "G-d's," (belonging to G-d) has been excluded from the calculation of this gematria; it only serves as a preposition ([belonging] to). When G-d's character of strict justice is alluded to, He is referred to as אלקים, "G-d" (א,א וח,א בראשית ,רש״י, Rashi, Genesis 1,1 and 8,1). From the pesukim quoted above, it is perspicuous that המשפט, "the judgment," is G-d's, and G-d is alluded to as אלקים, "G-d of strict justice." It is significant that both יכנו, "he may be beaten," and אלקים, "G-d of strict justice" have the same gematria; for when יכנו, "he may be beaten," is done, it was done in the name of המשפט, "the judgment," which is G-d's; He being personified as אלקים, "G-d of strict justice."

Parashath Ki Thavo   פרשת כי תבוא

אלה יעמדו לברך את העם על הר גרזים בעברכם את הירדן שמעון ולוי ויהודה ויששכר ויוסף ובנימן. ואלה יעמדו על הקללה בהר עיבל ראובן גד ואשר וזבולן דן ונפתלי (דברים כז,יב-יג).

These shall stand to bless the people on Mount Gerizim, when you pass over the Jordan: Simeon, and Levi, and Judah, and Issachar, and Joseph and Benjamin. And these shall stand for the curse on Mount Ebal: Reuben, Gad, and Asher, and Zebulun, Dan, and Naphtali (Deuteronomy 27, 12-13).

Parashath Ki Thavo tells how the tribes of the Children of Israel were to be divided into two groups of six tribes; the tribe of Levi (comprising the Levites and priests) stood between them (רש״י, דברים כז,יב, Rashi, Deuteronomy 27,12). The Gemara Sotah says how the tribe of Levi was divided; according to one opinion the division was based on their ability to serve, as stated, רבי יאשיא אומר כל הראוי לשרת למטה והשאר למעלה (סוטה לז.), "Rabbi Joshiyah says, All those who were fit to serve [as bearers of the ark] were below [between the mountains] and the remainder [of the tribe stood] above [on Mount Gerizim]" (Sotah 37a). The six tribes who stood on Mount Gerizim were Simeon, and Levi, and Judah, and Issachar, and Joseph and Benjamin. The gematria of הר גרזים, "Mount Gerizim," is 465.

הר	205
גרזים	<u>260</u>
	465

The gematria of שמעון, לוי, יהודה, יששכר, יוסף, בנימן, "Simeon, Levi, Judah, Issachar, Joseph, and Benjamin," is 1680.

שמעון לוי	512
יהודה יששכר	860
יוסף בנימן	308
	1680

Note that the first ווים, "vavs," of ולוי ויהודה ויששכר ויוסף "and Levi, and Judah, and Issachar, and Joseph and Benjamin," ובנימן have been excluded from the calculation of this gematria; they only serve as וו החבור, "conjunction vav" (and). When the gematria of הר גרזים, "Mount Gerizim," is removed from the gematria of the six tribes who stood on Mount Gerizim, the remainder is 1215.

$$1680$$
$$-465$$
$$\overline{1215}$$

Thus, 1215 can be said to represent the six tribes who stood on Mount Gerizim; for 1215 is the remainder, when the gematria of the tribes is the minuend, and the gematria of the mountain is the subtrahend.

The six tribes who stood בהר עיבל, "on Mount Ebal," were ראובן גד ואשר וזבולן דן ונפתלי, "Reuben, Gad, and Asher, and Zebulum, Dan, and Naphtali." The gematria of הר עיבל, "Mount Ebal," is 317.

הר	205
עיבל	112
	317

Note that the ב, "beth," of בהר "on Mount," has been excluded from the calculation of this gematria; it only serves as a preposition (on). The gematria of ראובן גד אשר זבולן דן נפתלי, "Reuben, Gad, Asher, Zebulun, Dan, and Naphtali," is 1486.

ראובן גד	266
אשר זבולן	596
דן נפתלי	624
	1486

Note that the first וויים, "vavs," of ואשר וזבולן ונפתלי, "and Asher, and Zebulun, and Naphtali," have been excluded from the calculation of this gematria; they only serve as וו החבור, "conjunction vav" (and). When the gematria of הר עיבל, "Mount Ebal," is removed from the gematria of the six tribes who stood on Mount Ebal, the remainder is 1169.

$$1486$$
$$-317$$
$$1169$$

Thus, 1169 can be said to represent the six tribes who stood on Mount Ebal; for 1169 is the remainder, when the gematria of the tribes is the minuend, and the gematria of the mountain is the subtrahend.

The difference between the two groups of six tribes when they are separated from their respective mountains is 46.

$$1215$$
$$-1169$$
$$46$$

As was previously mentioned, the tribe of לוי, "Levi," stood between the two groups of six tribes. The gematria of לוי, "Levi," is 46.

לוי   46

Thus, the gematria of לוי, "Levi," who stood between the two groups of six tribes, is equal to the gematria of the difference between the two groups of six tribes.

Parashath Vayyelech   פרשת וילך

הקהל את העם האנשים והנשים והטף וגרך אשר בשעריך
למען ישמעו ולמען ילמדו ויראו את ה׳ אלקיכם ושמרו
לעשות את כל דברי התורה הזאת (דברים לא,יב).
Gather the people together, the men, the
women, and the little ones, and your stranger
who is within your gates, in order that they may
hear, and in order that they may learn, and fear
G-d, your G-d, and observe to do all the words
of this Torah (Deuteronomy 31,12).

The Torah says that one of the purposes of the public
reading of the Book of Deuteronomy, commanded in
Parashath Vayyelech, is in order that ילמדו, "they may learn."
The gematria of ילמדו, "they may learn," is 90.

90   ילמדו

Rashi comments on the previous pasuk, that the reading was done by the מלך, "king," as stated, המלך היה קורא
(The", מתחלת אלה הדברים כדאיתא במסכת סוטה (רש״י, דברים לא,יב
king would read from the beginning of 'These are the words'
[at the start of the Book of Deuteronomy], as stated in
Tractate Sotah" (Rashi, Deuteronomy 31,11). The gematria
of מלך, "king," is 90.

90   מלך

Note that the ה, "hey," of המלך "the king," has been
excluded from the calculation of this gematria; it only serves
as the definite article (the).

Since the gematria of ילמדו, "they may learn," and מלך,
"king," are the same, it underscores that one of the purposes
of the king's reading the Book of Deuteronomy, commanded
in Parashath Vayyelech, was in order that ילמדו, "they may
learn." This emphasis is further enhanced by virtue of a קל
וחומר, "an inference drawn from a minor premise to a major

one." The Children of Israel were to realize from the king's reading that they should learn. If the king must obey the Torah, all the more so the common man, as stated, וני״ל דמה שהמלך קורא זהו מדרבנן כדי ליתן כבוד לתורה וגם כדי שיזהרו טפי במצות התורה בשיראו שגם המלך חייב לשמור מצותיה, כל שכן כל יחיד (תפארת ישראל, סוטה, פרק ז, משנה ח, אות נב), "And it appears to me, that the fact that it is the king who reads, is a Rabbinic law, in order to give honor to the Torah, and also, in order that people should be more careful in observing the commandments of the Torah. They will see that just as the king is obligated to observe its commandments, all the more so every individual" (Tifereth Yisroel, Sotah, Chapter 7, Mishnah 8, Letter 52).

Yom Kippur   יום כפור

The Gemara Sukkah denotes the amount that the Torah forbids one to eat on Yom Kippur is a very specific minimum, ככותבת הגסה, "that of a large date," as stated, שרוב "The, שיעוריה כזיתים דבש ככותבת הגסה ביום הכפורים (סוכה ו.) majority of minima [for the consumption of forbidden foods] is the volume of an olive. In the case of Yom Kippur, the word honey is a euphemism for the minimum volume, which is that of a large date" (Sukkah 6a). This minimum is associated by the Gemara with the pasuk in which the word honey is mentioned, meaning that of dates, as stated, ארץ חטה ושערה וגפן ותאנה ורמון ארץ זית שמן ודבש (דברים ח,ח), "A land of wheat and barley, and vine[s] and fig tree[s] and pomegranate[s]; a land of olive oil and [date] honey" (Deuteronomy 8,8). The gematria of דבש, "[date] honey," is 306.

דבש   306

Note that the ו, "vav," of ודבש, "and [date] honey," has been excluded from the calculation of this gematria; it only serves as וו החבור, "conjunction vav" (and). Thus, 306 represents the amount that is designated as the minimum prohibited on the day of Yom Kippur. The gematria of כפור, "kippur," is 306.

כפור   306

Thus, one can refer to Yom Kippur as the day of 306. This referral is befitting, for 306 represents the amount that is designated as applicable for the day of Yom Kippur.

The Passover Holiday   חג הפסח

והגדת לבנך ביום ההוא לאמר בעבור זה עשה ה׳ לי בצאתי
ממצרים (שמות יג,ח).

And you shall tell your son on that day saying,
It is because of that which G-d did for me when
I went out from Egypt (Exodus 13,8).

Rashi says clearly that what Hashem did for our ancestors when they were redeemed from Egypt was done in order that they should fulfill the mitzvoth, as stated, בעבור שאקיים מצותיו וכו׳ (רש״י, שמות יג,ח), "In order that I shall fulfill His commandments, etc." (Rashi, Exodus 13,8). The Gemara Sotah says that mitzvoth have a protective power, as stated, א״ר יוסף מצוה בעידנא דעסיק בה מגנא ומצלא בעידנא דלא עסיק בה אגוני מגנא אצולי לא מצלא ... אמר רבא ... מצוה בין בעידנא דעסיק בה בין בעידנא דלא עסיק בה אגוני מגנא אצולי לא מצלא (סוטה כא.), "Rabbi Joseph said, At the time one is performing a commandment it protects and saves; at the time one is not performing it, it surely protects, but it surely does not save ... Raba said ... a commandment whether at the time one is performing it or whether at the time one is not performing it, it surely protects, but surely does not save" (Sotah 21a). Thus, the commandments were the reason our ancestors were redeemed; and the commandments are the reason the Jewish people have been protected. This redemption and protection can be seen in a gematria.

In the הגדה של פסח, Passover Haggadah, just before the paragraph beginning צא ולמד, "Go forth and learn," it says, והיא שעמדה לאבותינו ולנו. שלא אחד בלבד עמד עלינו לכלותינו אלא שבכל דור ודור עומדים עלינו לכלותינו והקדוש ברוך הא מצילנו מידים (הגדה של פסח). "And it is this that has stood for our fathers and for us. For not one alone has risen against us to annihilate us; rather in every generation and generation, they have risen against us to annihilate us, and the Holy One, Blessed be He, saved

us from their hands" (Passover Haggadah). The gematria of
היא לאבותינו ולנו, "It is this for our fathers and for us," is 613.

היא	16
לאבותינו	505
ולנו	92
	613

Note that the ו, "vav," of והיא, "And it is this," has been
excluded from the calculation of this gematria; it only serves
as as וו החבור, "conjunction vav" (and). The gematria of 613
is symbolic of the commandments, since there are 613 Commandments (מכות כג:, Makkoth 23b). It has been shown from
the Rashi on Exodus 13,8, that what Hashem did for our
ancestors when He redeemed them from Egypt was done in
order that they should fulfill the mitzvoth. It has also been
shown that the commandments are the reason the Jewish
people have been protected. Therefore, when the Passover
Haggadah says היא... לאבותינו ולנו, "It is this ... for our fathers
and for us," it has an apt gematria, for it could well refer to
the 613 Mitzvoth which stood by our fathers and us.

כי אתה תאיר נרי ה' אלקי יגיה חשכי (תהלים יח,כט).
For You will illuminate my lamp; G-d, my G-d,
will lighten my darkness (Psalms 18,29).

There is a custom to say the eighteenth chapter of
Psalms on the seventh day of Passover (סידור בית יעקב מאת הרב
יעקב מעמדין בן הרב צבי, אשכנזי, מפתחות, דף תו:, Siddur Beth
Yaakov by Rabbi Yaakov from Emden ben Rabbi Zvi, Ashkenazi, Maftechoth, page 406b; סדר עבודת ישראל מאת הרב זליגמן
בער, הדף האחרון, וגם מעשה רב על מנהגי הגר״א מווילנא, מאת הרב
יששכר בער, דף רכה, Seder Avodat Yisroel by Rabbi Seligmann
Baer, the last page; and also, Ma'aseh Rav about the Customs the Gra from Vilna by Rabbi Yissachar Ber, page 225).
In this chapter of Psalms it says כי אתה תאיר נרי, "For

You will illuminate my lamp." The gematria of תאיר, "will illuminate," is 611.

611   תאיר

On this pasuk the Midrash says, כי אתה תאיר נרי. בתורה ובמצות, כדכתיב כי נר מצוה ותורה אור (משלי ו,כג) (מדרש תהלים, מזמור כג אות כג, יח), "'For You will illuminate my lamp': with Torah and commandments, as it is written, 'For the commandment is a lamp, and the Torah is light'" (Proverbs 6,23) (Midrash Psalms 6,23). The gematria of תורה, "Torah," is 611.

611   תורה

Note that the ו, "vav," of ותורה, "and Torah," has been excluded from the calculation of this gematria; it only serves as וו החבור, "conjunction vav" (and). The Midrash distinctly defines תאיר, "will illuminate," as referring to Torah; this definition is further indicated by the fact that the gematria of תאיר, "will illuminate," is equal to the gematria of תורה, "Torah."

Ethics of the Fathers   פרקי אבות

רבי אלעזר בן חסמא אומר קנין ופתחי נדה הן הן גופי הלכות, תקופות וגימטריאות פרפראות לחכמה (אבות, פרק ג, משנה יח).

Rabbi Eliezer ben Chisma says, "The laws concerning the sacrifices of birds and the beginnings of a woman's menstrual impurity are legal constitutions, but astronomy and gematrioth are condiments to wisdom" (Avoth, Chapter 3 Mishnah 18).

The Mishnah states that gematrioth are condiments to wisdom. The Bertinoro explains that, החכמות הללו מכבדות את בעליהם בעיני הבריות (ר"ע מברטנורה, אבות, פרק ג, משנה יח, ד"ה פרפראות לחכמה), "Such wisdom makes its masters honored in the eyes of people," (Rabbi Ovadiah Bertinoro, Avoth, Chapter 3, Mishnah 18, header words: Condiments to wisdom). The gematria of כבוד, "honor," is 32.

כבוד   32

Note that the מ, "mem," and ת, "tov," have been excluded from the calculation of this gematria, for the gematria arises from the noun form, כבוד, "honor." In reference to the aforementioned Mishnah, the Tosafoth Yom Tov explains that, gematrioth are פרפראות הממשיכים לב האדם לחכמה (תוספת יום טוב, אבות, פרק ג, משנה יח, ד"ה פרפראות לחכמה), "condiments that draw the heart of man to wisdom" (Tosafoth Yom Tov, Avoth, Chapter 3, Mishnah 18). The gematria of לב, "heart," is 32.

לב   32

From the Bertinoro and the Tosafoth Yom Tov's explanations, it is clear that gematrioth affect the honor and the heart of a person. This idea is further reinforced by the fact that כבוד, "honor," and לב, "heart," have the same gematria."

Additional significance to the gematrioth of לב, "heart," and כבוד, "honor," can be found in the פרשת בשלח, Parashath Beshallach, section of this sefer.

רשימת מלים — Glossary

GLOSSARY · רשימת מלים

(This Glossary is only a partial list of Jewish concepts and of the prominent rabbinical sources quoted in this sefer.)

Bertinoro — רבי עובדיה ירא מברטנורא Rabbi Ovadiah Yarei of Bertinoro was born in Bertinoro, Italy c. 1445-1450, and died in Jerusalem c. 1500-1510. The name Yarei is an acrostic of (דברים לג,כד) יהי רצוי אחיו, "He shall be favored by his brothers" (Deuteronomy 33,24). He was a student of Rabbi Joseph ben Solomon Colon, and became the rabbi of Bertinoro, located in the province of Flori. From Oct. 29, 1486 until March 25, 1488 he traveled to Jerusalem, but had sojourns in Naples, Salerno, Messina, and Egypt. The Mohammedan government had placed heavy taxes on the Jewish population of Jerusalem which Rabbi Bertinoro managed to have repealed and replaced. In 1492 the Jews were expelled from Spain; some found refuge in Jerusalem, and accepted him as their leader; he established a yeshiva there. His most famous work is his commentary on the Mishnah. Parts of the Mishnah were written cryptically; the Bertinoro Commentary in a lucid style explains difficult and obscure passages extensively drawing on the Gemara, Rashi, and the Rambam. His commentary has been so widely accepted that Rabbi Ovadiah Yarei of Bertinoro is commonly referred to as the Rav.

Bnei Yisroel — בני ישראל The Children of Israel.

Derash — דרש A homiletical interpretation or exegesis.

Gemara — גמרא The word Gemara (also called Talmud) is Aramaic for "learning." It refers to the oral amplifications of the Mishnah (q.v.) by the Amoraim in Palestine and Babylonia, crystallized as the תלמוד ירושלמי and תלמוד בבלי, Yerushalmi Gemara and the Bavli Gemara. The Bavli Gemara originated in the third, fourth, and fifth centuries, postdating the Yerushalmi Gemara of the third and fourth centuries. The Bavli Gemara is more extensive, more authoritative, and more widely studied than the Yerushalmi Gemara. The term Gemara is used loosely to refer to the Bavli Gemara. The Vilna edition, first published in 1859, has been widely accepted; it consists of 2725 folio pages of rabbinic amplifications on the Mishnayoth of 37 tractates; the remaining 26 tractates have no Gemara amplifications; usually the commentary of Rashi is on one side of the text, and the commentary of Tosafoth is on the other side. The 2725 figure is inflated, since it is calculated by totalling the last page number of the various tractates, although the talmudic pagination begins with page two. The Talmud includes both the Mishnah and the Gemara. In addition to the 63 tractates, there are several smaller tractates, which date from geonic times, such as Derekh Eretz Rabbah.

Gematria — גימטריא The numerical value of a Hebrew letter, word, or expression. Each letter of the Hebrew alphabet has a numerical value; these values, or their sum, are known as the gematria of the letter, word, or expression being analyzed. The Hebrew letters and their numerical values are listed in the following table:

Letter	Value
א	1
ב	2
ג	3
ד	4
ה	5
ו	6
ז	7
ח	8
ט	9
י	10

כ	20
ל	30
מ	40
נ	50
ס	60
ע	70
פ	80
צ	90
ק	100
ר	200
ש	300
ת	400

Gematrioth — גימטריאות The plural of gematria.

Haggadah of Passover — הגדה של פסח The book read on the first night of Passover in the land of Israel and on the first two nights of Passover in countries outside the land of Israel. It includes the narrative of the exodus from Egypt and the obligations one is to fulfill for this night or nights.

Hashem — השם (literally "the Name") According to Jewish law, the letters of G-d's name (י, "yud," ה, "hey," and ו, "vav," and ה, "hey"), are not spelled out, unless in a holy context, as in books of the Bible and the Siddur (the Prayer Book). Therefore, in this sefer, He is referred to as ה׳, "hey," (the abbreviation for Hashem, the Name). Thus, the gematria calculation is done with the value of the original י, "yud," and ה, "hey," and ו, "vav," and ה, "hey," not the value of the printed replacement-ה׳. Also, when the specific name of אלקים ("G-d of strict justice") a ק, "kuf," has replaced the ה, "hey," of the actual Name. Thus, the gematria calculation is done with the value of the original ה, not the value of the printed replacement-ק. Also, when the specific name of שקי ("G-d the All Sufficient,") is used, a ק, "kuf," has replaced the

ד, "dalid," of the actual Name. Thus, the gematria calculation is done with the the value of the original ד, not the value of the printed replacement-ק.

Ibn Ezra — רבי אברהם אבן עזרא Rabbi Abraham Ibn Ezra was born in Toledo, Spain in either 1089 or 1090; he died in 1164. His life was one of poverty and displacement; he moved between Cordova, London and other places in Europe and North Africa. In 1135 he was forced to flee to Rome where he wrote his commentary, which tries to explain the straightforward meaning of pesukim, often by examining the Hebrew grammar. He wrote tersely and sometimes it is difficult for the inerudite to grasp his intentions. He stressed the meaning of words, for without that meaning the true meaning of the text could be lost.

Mikveh — מקוה A body of water for ritual purification, containing at least 40 se'ah of water, approximately 88 gallons. The water must be running, as opposed to being drawn, when the mikveh is initially established, and come from a natural source as rainwater, spring, stream, river, lake, bay, or ocean. The water used to initially establish a mikveh should not be contained in a vessel.

Mishnah — משנה The word Mishnah is Aramaic for teaching. It refers to the six-volume authoritative text of Jewish law, which, known as the Oral Law, or Oral Torah, accompanied the Written Law, or Written Torah, when both were given to Moses and the the Children of Israel at Mount Sinai. Both were transmitted from generation to generation in their respective oral and written forms. The Oral Law was redacted, as the Mishnah, in the early part of the third century C.E. by Rabbi Judah the Prince, who was born (c. 135) and died (c.220) in the land of Israel. He was the leader of the Yerushalmi community; he became the nasi, head of the Sanhederin. In the Talmud (q.v.), Rabbi Judah the Prince has the distinction of being referred to as simply "Rabbi." He was the son of Rabbi Shimon ben Gamliel and the great grandson of Gamliel the Elder, or Hazaken. The teachers mentioned in the Mishnah are called "Tannaim." This authoritative text is divided into six sedarim, or orders; they are: (1) "Zeraim," or seeds, (2) "Moed," or holiday, (3) "Nashim," or women, (4) "Nezikin," or damages, (5) "Kadashim," or holy objects and animals, and (6) "Taharoth," or ritual purity. These sedarim are further subdivided into sixty-three tractates, which are further subdivided into five hundred twenty-three chapters. Generally, the tractates are arranged in their respective sedarim in decreasing order of the number of chapters they contain. The Mishnah is the basis of the Gemara.

Pasuk — פסוק A verse from the Bible.

Pesukim — פסוקים The plural of pasuk.

Rambam — רבי משה בן מיימון Rabbi Moshe ben Maimon was born in Cordova, Spain in 1135, and died in Cairo, Egypt 1204. The Rambam studied under his father; but when he was just 13 years old, Cordova was invaded by the Almohads, who conquered Moorish Spain and then Algeria and Tunis. The family was forced to flee; after wandering they settled in Fez, Morocco. In 1165 the Rambam found asylum in Cairo. He also studied medicine and was appointed to be the doctor of the Sultan Saladin. It is believed he began to write his Mishneh Torah in approximately 1170; it was completed in 1180. It is written in extremely clear Hebrew. It covers in detail not only laws which apply to his own time right though today, but also rulings about sacrifices, purification, the Holy Temple, etc., making it the most well organized and complete work of Jewish Law. The Mishnah Torah is composed of 14 books which are subdivided into 83 sections of Halakhah, "decided law," as given in the table below.

No.	ספרים	Books	Sect.
1	ספר המדע	Book of Knowledge	5
2	ספר אהבה	Book of Love	6
3	ספר זמנים	Book of Times	10
4	ספר נשים	Book of Women	5
5	ספר קדושה	Book of Holiness	3
6	ספר הפלאה	Book of Articulations	4
7	ספר זרעים	Book of Seeds	7
8	ספר עבודה	Book of Service	9
9	ספר קרבנות	Book of Sacrifices	6
10	ספר טהרה	Book of Purification	8
11	ספר נזיקים	Book of Damages	5
12	ספר קנין	Book of Acquisitions	5
13	ספר משפטים	Book of Judgments	5
14	ספר שופטים	Book of Judges	5

Ramban — רבי משה בן נחמן Rabbi Moshe ben Nachman was born in Gerona, Calabri, Spain in 1195, and died in the land of Israel in 1270. He learned Torah from Rabbi Yehuda ben Yakar and Rabbi Nassan ben Meir. The former was a talmudist and kabbalist who studied under Isaac ben Abraham, the tosafist; the latter was a French talmudist and Bible commentator who wrote "Sefer Haterumot." The Ramban also studied and practiced medicine. His love of the land of Israel is well known; in 1267 he moved there where he tried to rebuild Jewish life. He wrote a letter describing the conditions in Jerusalem which reveal the destruction the Crusaders had wrought. The small synagogue which he established in Jerusalem was reopened after the Six Day War in 1967. His extensive commentary on the Torah deals with theological issues, analysis of other commentaries, grammar and Kabbalah. He explains his points in detail.

Rashi — רב שלמה יצחק — רש״י Rabbi Shelomoh Yitzchaki-Rabbi Shlomo ben Yitzchok was born in Troyes, France in 1040; he died there in 1105. Rashi studied with his father, Rabbi Yitzchak and later went to Worms, Germany where he studied under Rabbi Yaakov ben Yakar. Rabbi Yakar was in Worms, later headed a yeshiva in Mainz, and returned to Worms. Rashi refers to him as "my teacher in Scripture." At approximately age 30 Rashi returned to Troyes and earned a living as a wine merchant. Rashi's commentary is written in a clear Hebrew revealing his comprehensive knowledge of the Mishnah, Talmud, and Midrash. Difficult words are clarified by cross reference to other examples where the meaning is more explicit. Besides his indispensable commentary on all of Tanach, Rashi's commentary on the Talmud is considered indispensable as well, for grasping the meaning of the text. He is considered the commentator par excellence.

Shulhan Arukh — שלחן ערוך — רבי יוסף קארו Rabbi Yosef Caro was born in Toledo, Spain in 1488 and died in Safed, Eretz Yisroel in 1575. When Yosef was only four years old his family was forced to leave Spain and settled in Constantinople, Turkey. He studied under Rabbi Shelomoh Molcho, and followed the ascetic life style of his teacher. In 1530 he moved to Safed where he established a yeshiva. Rabbi Caro finished writing the Beit Yosef in 1542, and then the Shulhan Arukh in 1565, the latter work to be a synopsis of the former work. Generally the Shulhan Arukh decided the Halakhah, "decided law," based on three authoritative sources; the Rif, the Rambam, and the Rosh, siding with the opinion of the two against the one. The Shulhan Arukh has become the authoritative law for Jews worldwide. Rabbi Moses Isserles (1525-1572), the

Rema, wrote a complementary commentary to adjust for Ashkenazi laws and customs. Rabbi Moses Isserles was a rabbi in Cracow, Poland where he established a yeshiva. The name Shulhan Arukh means a set table; the glosses which Rabbi Isserles wrote, he called Mapah; the name Mapah means a tablecloth.

The Shulhan Arukh is divided into four volumes, as given in the table below.

Number	כרך	Volume	Sample Topics
1	אורח חיים	Orach Chayyim	Laws dealing with Daily Conduct, Shabbath, and Holidays
2	יורה דעה	Yoreh Deah	Laws dealing with Kashruth and Vows
3	אבן העזר	Even Haezer	Laws dealing with Women, Marriage, and Divorce
4	חושן משפט	Choshen Mishpat	Laws dealing with Civil and Judical Issues

Sidrah — סדרה One of the fifty-four sections into which the first five books of the Bible are divided. These sections are read on the Sabbath consecutively until all fifty-four are read annually. They are also referred to as Parashiyoth.

Sidroth — סדרות The plural of sidrah.

Seif — סעיף Its practical meaning is a paragraph. Its literal translation is a subdivision.

Siddur Beth Yaakov — סידור בית יעקב The text of the prayer book, Ashkenazi, with commentary by Rabbi Yaakov from Emden ben Zvi, who was born in 1697 in Altona, Germany, and died in the same city in 1776. He was rabbi in Emden from 1728 to 1733. Although he was a very prolific writer, this might well be his most famous work, published in 1745-48. His knowledge of grammar and kabbalah is evinced in this commentary. Rabbi Emden also founded a private printing press in Altona. In addition, he was also a renowned, uncompromising campaigner against the Shabbateans (promoters of the false messiah, Shabbatai Zvi).

Siman — סימן Its practical meaning is a chapter. Its literal translation is a sign.

Talmud — תלמוד See Gemara — גמרא

Tifereth Yisroel — תפארת ישראל A commentary on the Mishnah by Rabbi Yisroel Lipschitz, who was born in 1782 and died in 1860 in Danzig, Germany (today Poland), where he had served as rabbi. This commentary is divided into two sections; יכין Yachin, a short definition of concepts, and בועז Boaz, an analysis of the subject under discussion. He explains the words of the Mishnah, difficult passages, and identifies decisions of Halakhah.

Torah — תורה The word Torah is Hebrew for teaching. In its narrower meaning it refers to the first five books of the Bible, or the Pentateuch, the Written Torah. In its broader meaning it includes as well, the entire breadth and scope of the Oral Torah, both of which were given to Moses and the Children of Israel at Mount Sinai, and subsequent religious knowledge.

Numerical Index — מפתח מספרי

Gematria	Page
263	410
266	128
275	579
277	331
306	703
311	130
311	368
311	557
313	206
314	315
316	301
316	303
330	250
330	385
340	575
350	338
350	406
365	285
370	506
380	116
380	189
380	495
380	649
385	307
390	358
391	281
392	566
400	105
400	156
400	179
400	372
409	175
410	137
410	495
430	688